Analogy in Grammar

Analogy in Grammar: Form and Acquisition

EDITED BY
JAMES P. BLEVINS AND JULIETTE BLEVINS

OXFORD
UNIVERSITY PRESS

Great Clarendon Street, Oxford OX2 6DP

Oxford University Press is a department of the University of Oxford.
It furthers the University's objective of excellence in research, scholarship,
and education by publishing worldwide in

Oxford New York

Auckland Cape Town Dar es Salaam Hong Kong Karachi
Kuala Lumpur Madrid Melbourne Mexico City Nairobi
New Delhi Shanghai Taipei Toronto

With offices in

Argentina Austria Brazil Chile Czech Republic France Greece
Guatemala Hungary Italy Japan Poland Portugal Singapore
South Korea Switzerland Thailand Turkey Ukraine Vietnam

Oxford is a registered trade mark of Oxford University Press
in the UK and in certain other countries

Published in the United States
by Oxford University Press Inc., New York

© 2009 organization and editorial matter James P. Blevins and Juliette Blevins

The moral rights of the author have been asserted
Database right Oxford University Press (maker)

© 2009 the chapters their various authors

British Library Cataloguing in Publication Data

Data available

Library of Congress Cataloging in Publication Data

Data available

Typeset by SPI Publisher Services, Pondicherry, India
Printed in Great Britain
on acid-free paper by
the MPG Books Group, Bodmin and King's Lynn

ISBN 978–0–19–954754–8

1 3 5 7 9 10 8 6 4 2

Contents

Notes on Contributors

Farrell Ackerman works on a range of syntactic and morphological issues viewed from the perspective of lexicalism and construction-theoretic approaches, with a focus on Uralic languages. He has worked on complex predicates (Ackerman and Webelhuth, *A Theory of Predicates*, 1998), argument-encoding and mapping theories (Ackerman and Moore, *Proto-properties and grammatical encoding*, 2001), and the typology of relative clauses (Ackerman, Nikolaeva, and Malouf, *Descriptive Typology and Grammatical Theory*, forthcoming). Over the past few years he has been exploring word-based implicative models of morphology. He is Professor of Linguistics and Director of the Interdisciplinary Graduate Program in Human Development at the University of California, San Diego.

Adam Albright received his BA in linguistics from Cornell University in 1996 and his Ph.D. in linguistics from UCLA in 2002. He was a Faculty Fellow at UC Santa Cruz from 2002–4, and since then has been an Assistant Professor at the Massachusetts Institute of Technology. His research interests include phonology, morphology, and learnability, with an emphasis on using computational modeling and experimental techniques to investigate issues in phonological and morphological theory.

Harald Baayen is Professor of Linguistics at the University of Alberta, Edmonton. His research interests include lexical statistics in literary and linguistic corpus-based computing, general linguistics, morphological theory, and the psycholinguistics of morphological processing. He has published in, e.g., *Language, Linguistics, Folia Linguistica, Computational Linguistics, Yearbook of Morphology, Computers and the Humanities, Literary and Linguistic Computing, Journal of Quantitative Linguistics, Journal of Memory and Language, Journal of Experimental Psychology, Language and Cognitive Processes, Cognition, Brain and Language*, and the *Philosophical Transactions of the Royal Society* (Series A: Mathematical, Physical and Engineering Sciences) and has a new book, *Analyzing Linguistic Data: A Practical Introduction to Statistics using R* (Cambridge University Press, 2008).

James P. Blevins is Assistant Director of Research at the Research Centre for English and Applied Linguistics in the University of Cambridge. He received his Ph.D. in linguistics from the University of Massachusetts, Amherst, in

1990, and has taught at the University of Western Australia, the University of Texas, the University of Alberta, and the University of California, Berkeley. His research deals mainly with the description and analysis of morphological systems and syntactic constructions, with a particular emphasis on paradigm structure and discontinuous dependencies. Areal interests include Germanic, Balto-Finnic, Balto-Slavic, and Kartvelian.

Juliette Blevins is a Senior Scientist in the Department of Linguistics, Max Planck Institute for Evolutionary Anthropology, Leipzig. She received her doctorate in linguistics from MIT in 1985, and then joined the Department of Linguistics at the University of Texas at Austin. Her research interests range from historical, descriptive, and typological studies, to theoretical analysis with a synthesis in her recent book *Evolutionary Phonology* (Cambridge University Press). Other interests include Oceanic languages, Australian Aboriginal languages, and Native American languages.

Raphael Finkel received a Ph.D. from Stanford University in 1976 in robotics and has been a professor of computer science at the University of Kentucky in Lexington since 1987. His research involves operating system administration, computational morphology, reliable data backup, and web-based organic chemistry homework. He was associated with the first work on quad trees, k-d trees, quotient networks, and the Roscoe/Arachne, Charlotte, and Unify operating systems. He helped develop DIB, has published over eighty articles, and has written two textbooks: *An Operating Systems Vade Mecum* (Prentice-Hall, 1988), and *Advanced Programming Language Design* (Benjamin-Cummings, 1996). He is also a co-author of *The Hacker's Dictionary* (Harper and Row, 1983).

LouAnn Gerken received her Ph.D. in experimental psychology from Columbia University in 1987. She is currently Professor of Psychology and Linguistics and Director of Cognitive Science at the University of Arizona. The focus of her research is behavioral indicators of the computational mechanism by which human infants and young children learn the structure of their native language. In addition, she works on issues of social justice in the academy.

John Goldsmith is a professor in the departments of Linguistics and Computer Science at the University of Chicago. His research interests include phonological theory, especially autosegmental phonology and harmonic phonology, implementations of linguistic theory using current tools of machine learning, and the history of linguistics and the other mind sciences. His work on automatic grammar induction has focused on the problems of inferring morphological structure from raw data, and is available at <http://linguistica. uchicago.edu/>.

Rebecca Gómez obtained her Ph.D. in experimental psychology at New Mexico State University in 1995. She completed a postdoctoral position at the University of Arizona before taking her first faculty position at Johns Hopkins University in 1999. She returned to the University of Arizona in 2001 where she is presently an Associate Professor. She is known for her work on learning in cognitive development and child language acquisition.

Andrea Krott is a lecturer in the School of Psychology at the University of Birmingham. She holds an M.A. from the University of Trier, Germany, and a Ph.D. from the Radboud University Nijmegen, The Netherlands. Her research focuses on the processing and acquisition of word morphology. In particular, she investigates the role of analogy in the production and comprehension of noun-noun compound words in adult speakers across different languages and its role in preschool children's understanding of compound words. Her interests also include electrophysiological measures of language processing in adults.

Victor Kuperman is a Ph.D. candidate at Radboud University Nijmegen and a researcher at the Max Planck Institute for Psycholinguistics in Nijmegen. He is engaged in information-theoretical research of production and comprehension of morphologically complex words. His interests include morphological and sentence processing in visual and auditory domains; interaction of phonological and orthographic encodings in silent reading; sex differences in the uptake and processing of visual information, as revealed in eye movements; and statistical methods in language research.

Robert Malouf received his Ph.D. in linguistics from Stanford University in 1998. He has held positions at Stanford University, UC Berkeley, and the University of Groningen, and is currently an assistant professor in the computational linguistics program of the Department of Linguistics and Asian/Middle Eastern Languages at San Diego State University. His research focuses on constructional approaches to morphology and syntax, statistical natural language processing, and the application of text-mining techniques to research in theoretical linguistics.

Petar Milin is an assistant professor of research methodology and cognitive psychology at the Department of Psychology, University of Novi Sad, and holds a research position at the Laboratory for Experimental Psychology, University of Belgrade. He received his Ph.D. in psychology from the University of

Belgrade in 2004. His research interests include the psycholinguistics of morphological processing, probabilistic models of language processing, and lexical statistics. Together with **Aleksandar Kostić**, he has started a publishing project devoted to frequency dictionaries and electronic corpora of famous Serbian writers.

After being awarded a Ph.D. in Psychology from Yale University in 2006, **Erika Nurmsoo** worked as a postdoctoral research fellow at the University of Warwick in England. She is currently a research fellow at Bristol University, UK, studying children's cognitive development.

Royal Skousen is Professor of Linguistics and English Language at Brigham Young University. He has also taught at the University of Illinois, the University of Texas, the University of California at San Diego, and the University of Tampere in Finland. He is the author of *Analogical Modeling of Language* (1989) and *Analogy and Structure* (1992). More recently, he has developed a quantum mechanical approach to Analogical Modeling that uses quantum computing to avoid the exponential processing time inherent in sequential models of Analogical Modeling. Since 1988 he has been the editor of the critical text of the Book of Mormon.

Gregory Stump is Professor of Linguistics at the University of Kentucky. He is the author of *Inflectional Morphology* (Cambridge, 2001) and of numerous articles on morphological theory and typology. In recent years, his research has focused on the theoretical and typological significance of inflectional paradigms; he has asserted the need for an inferential-realizational theory of inflectional exponence and has demonstrated that the implicative relations among the parts of inflectional paradigms are an important domain of typological variation.

Andy Wedel began his academic life in molecular biology with a Ph.D. dissertation on bacterial control circuits, followed by postdoctoral work in in-vitro evolution of RNA enzymes. After discovering linguistics, he turned his experience in complex systems and evolution toward attempting to illuminate the ways in which feedback at lexical and community levels interacts with biases in variation to create and modify language patterns. His hobbies include Turkish and tall-grass prairie restoration.

After finishing her Ph.D. in 2002, **Rachel Wilson** went on to become a lawyer. She currently works at a non-profit organization representing victims of torture and persecution.

Preface

This volume grew out of a workshop, entitled "Analogy in Grammar: Form and Acquisition," which took place on September 22 and 23, 2006 at the Max Planck Institute for Evolutionary Anthropology in Leipzig, Germany. This was the first workshop on analogy at the Institute, and quite possibly the first meeting in Leipzig dedicated to this topic since the late nineteenth century. At that time, analogy was a prominent concern of the *Junggrammatiker* (or Neogrammarians) at the University of Leipzig, who met often to discuss not only sound laws and their regularity, but exceptions to the regularity principle, most of which were explained with direct reference to analogy.

As organizers of the workshop, our goal was to gather researchers from a wide range of disciplines, in order to compare approaches to central questions about the form and acquisition of analogical generalizations in language, and to share results that have been obtained so far. The discussion was framed by a number of basic questions. What kinds of patterns do speakers select as the basis for analogical extension? What types of items are susceptible or resistant to analogical pressures? At what levels do analogical processes operate, and how do processes interact? What formal mechanisms are appropriate for modeling analogy? How does analogical modeling in cognitive psychology carry over to studies of language acquisition, language change, and language processing? The participants who addressed these questions included cognitive psychologists, developmental psychologists, psycholinguists, historical linguistics, descriptive linguists, phoneticians, phonologists, morphologists, syntacticians, computational linguists, and neurolinguists.

The bulk of the workshop was devoted to the presentation of original research. Papers and their authors were: "Paradigmatic heterogeneity" by Andrew Garrett; "Multi-level selection and the tension between phonological and morphological regularity" by Andrew Wedel; "Principal parts and degrees of paradigmatic transparency" by Rafael Finkel and Gregory Stump; "Analogy as exemplar resonance: Extension of a view of sensory memory to higher linguistic categories" by Keith Johnson; "Learning morphological patterns in language" by John Goldsmith; "The sound of syntax: Probabilities and structure in pronunciation variation" by Susanne Gahl; "Patterns of relatedness in complex morphological systems" by Farrell Ackerman and Robert Malouf; "Linguistic generalization by human infants" by LouAnn Gerken; "Banana shoes and bear tables: Children's processing and interpretation of noun-noun compounds" by Andrea Krott; "Analogy in the acquisition of constructions" by Mike Tomasello; "Acquisition of syntax by analogy: Computation of new utterances out of previous utterances" by Rens Bod; "Expanding analogical modeling into a general theory of language prediction" by Royal Skousen; "Analogical processes in learning grammar" by Dedre Gentner; "Modeling analogy as probabilistic grammar" by Adam Albright; and "Bits and pieces of an information-theoretical approach to inflectional paradigms" by Harald Baayen and Fermín Moscoso del Prado Martín. Formal commentary was provided by Colin Bannard on analogical modeling and computation, by Elena Lieven on analogy in language acquisition, and by Jim Blevins on modeling approaches. Not all of these authors were able to contribute to this volume directly, but the stimulating discussions which followed each talk, and continued over coffee and beer, can be felt throughout. We thank all the participants in the workshop for their enthusiastic participation, thought-provoking papers, and gracious handling of comments and questions.

The Analogy Workshop would not have been possible without the financial support of the Max Planck Society. We are grateful to Bernard Comrie, Head of the Department of Linguistics at the Max Planck Institute for Evolutionary Anthropology, for generously agreeing to host this workshop, and for hosting Jim as a visiting scholar at the Institute. Additional thanks are due to Mike Tomasello, Head of the Department of Developmental and Comparative Psychology, to administrative assistants Claudia Büchel, Julia Cissewski, Eike Lauterbach, Martin Müller, Claudia Schmidt, and Henriette Zeidler, for ensuring that everything ran smoothly, and to Claudio Tennie, for the memorable zoo tour.

Thanks to the support and enthusiasm of John Davey and Julia Steer at Oxford University Press, the workshop led seamlessly to this book project. As chapters were submitted, a small group of dedicated referees offered useful commentary. We are grateful for their assistance, and respectful of their wishes to remain anonymous. The contributors, in addition to offering original research, made great efforts to write with a general linguistics audience in mind, and to relate their work to that of others. For all of this, we are greatly appreciative. Finally, we would like to take this opportunity to thank each other for all that went into the preparation of this volume.

Abbreviations

1	1st person
2	2nd person
3	3rd person
abl	ablative
acc	accusative
AM	Analogical Modeling
AML	Analogical Modeling of Language
avg	average
CARIN	Competition Among Relations in Nominals
CE	cross entropy
conj	conjugation class
dat	dative
D	disyllabic verb stem diacritic
du	dual
ERP	event-related potential
exp	experiment
F	falling tone
feat	feature
FSA	finite state automaton
GCM	Generalized Context Model
gen	genitive
H	high tone
indic	indicative
iness	inessive
inf	infinitive
ins	instrumental
IPA	International Phonetic Alphabet
L	low tone
lexdec	lexical decision
loc	locative

LSA	Latent Semantic Analysis
M	mid tone
MDL	Minimum Description Length
MGL	Minimum Generalization Learner
N	noun
nom	nominative
part	partitive
PCFC	Paradigm Cell Filling Problem
perf	perfect
pl	plural
pres	present
pro	prolative
pros	prosecutive
QAM	Quantum Analogical Modeling
QM	Quantum Mechanics
RE	Relative Entropy
rel	relative
RT	reaction time
seg	segment
sg	singular
SPE	*The Sound Pattern of English*
subj	subjunctive
TiMBL	Tilburg Memory-Based Learner
V	verb
WP	Word and Paradigm
WPM	Word and Paradigm morphology

1

Introduction: Analogy in grammar

James P. Blevins and Juliette Blevins

1.1 Analogy: The core of human cognition

The human mind is an inveterate pattern-seeker. Once found, patterns are classified, related to other patterns, and used to predict yet further patterns and correlations. Although these tasks are performed automatically, they are far from trivial. The analogical reasoning that underlies them requires the discovery of structural similarities between perceptually dissimilar elements. Similarities may be highly abstract, involving functional and causal relationships. And while the recognition of analogical relations may seem like a passive process, it is in fact an aggressive process, driven by a search for predictability. A systematic structural similarity independent of perceptual similarity can be extended to yield novel inferences about the world.

There is mounting evidence from work in cognitive psychology that the talent for analogical reasoning constitutes the core of human cognition (Penn, Holyoak, and Povinelli 2008, and references cited therein), and that analogy may be a highly domain-independent cognitive process (Halford and Andrews 2007). Analogy is part of what allows humans to evaluate cause and effect, to come up with new solutions to old problems, to imagine the world other than the way it is, and to use words evocatively (Gentner, Holyoak, and Kokinov 2001). Other creatures create and use complex tools (Hunt and Gray 2004) and meta-tools (Taylor *et al.* 2007), recognize perceptual similarity and, after training, can perform better than chance on tests in which two objects must be judged as "same" or "different" (Premack 1983; Pepperberg 1987; Katz and Wright 2006). However, only humans, the symbolic species (Deacon 1997), effortlessly go beyond perceptual similarities, to recognize structural similarities that are independent of surface difference (Penn, Holyoak, and Povinelli 2008). Children as young as 1 or 2 years of age show evidence of perceptual analogies, and by the age of 4 or 5, they can understand that *bird* is to *nest*, as *dog* is to *doghouse*, using functional analogies based on real-world knowledge (Goswami and Brown 1989, 1990; Goswami 2001).

As a central and pervasive property of human cognitive function and categorization, it is not surprising that analogy has been identified as a core component of linguistic competence from the earliest times to the present. In ancient Rome, Varro (116–127 BC) saw *analogia* as a central grammatical process (Law 2003), while ancient Arabic grammarians used the term *qiyaas* 'measuring' in a similar way: constructing a *qiyaas* involved "exploring an unknown configuration of data and trying to recognize in it a patterning already met and which, in other situations, lent itself to analysis" (Bohas, Guillaume, and Kouloughli 1990: 23). A thousand years later, analogy was central to one of the most important discoveries in linguistic history: the Neogrammarian insight that sound change was regular (Paul 1880/1920). Regular sound change, in contrast to analogy, was the foundation of the comparative method by which the world's major language families were firmly established (Campbell and Poser 2008). To this day, regular sound change and analogy are introduced together to students of historical linguistics as the primary internal mechanisms of change (Hock 1991; Campbell 1998; Deutscher 2005), as research on the nature of analogical change continues (e.g. Lahiri 2000; Garrett 2008; Albright 2008). From its central role in historical linguistics, analogy became a cornerstone of analysis in the twentieth-century American descriptivist tradition (Whitney 1875/1979; Bloomfield 1933: 275; Sturtevant 1947: 96–109; Hockett 1966: 94) and, despite generative neglect, remains central to our understanding of synchronic grammars to this day (Anttila and Brewer 1977; Skousen 1989, 1992; Skousen, Lonsdale, and Parkinson 2002; Itkonen 2005; Kraska-Szlenk 2007).

The notion of analogy discussed above refers to a general cognitive process that transfers specific information or knowledge from one instance or domain (the analogue, base, or source) to another (the target). Sets of percepts, whether visual images, auditory signals, experiences, or dreams, are compared, and higher-order generalizations are extracted and carried over to new sets. This knowledge transfer is often schematized in terms of classical "proportional" or "four-part" analogies. In a proportional analogy, the relationship R between a pair of items A:B provides a basis for identifying an unknown item, given an item that matches A or B. Knowing R and knowing that C is similar to A permits one to identify D as the counterpart of B. The analogical deduction that "C is to D" as "A is to B" is standardly represented as in (1). The initial recognition of similarity and difference between percepts is the basis of analogy, but this is only the first step. Humans show great creativity in classifying different ways objects can be similar and different, and in organizing these similarities and differences into complex schemata, which can then be extended to classify and understand new stimuli (Penn, Holyoak, and Povinelli 2008, and references cited therein).

(1)   Four-part analogy: A is to B as C is to D

	A	:	B	==	C	:	D
a.	◐	:	◑	==	◧	:	◨
b.	+ * +	:	* + *	==	XOX	:	OXO
c.	BIRD	:	NEST	==	DOG	:	DOGHOUSE

In (1a), one can look at the two circles ◐ : ◑ and establish a structural relationship between the two which is more general than the concrete circle and black and white shadings of its halves. The relationship could be extremely general: one figure is the reflection of the other. This structural relationship can then be recognized in other pairs, like the two squares, ◧: ◨, and, in this general form, could be further extended to images without shading, like d:b, or Xxx:xxX. In (1b), there is a recognizable pattern ABA: BAB, where "A" and "B" can be replaced by any symbols, and where a more general statement of the pattern would allow reference to tones, melodies, or even conversational turn-taking. In (1c), where words in small capitals refer to concepts, the abstract structural relationship is a functional one relating an animal to its home or sleeping place. Again, the human mind is creative and flexible, and we can imagine the analogy extending to inanimate objects (CONTACT LENS : LENS CASE), musical traditions (JAZZ : NEW ORLEANS), or human emotions (ANGER : SPLEEN).

Before turning to the particular role that analogy plays in grammar, it is worth highlighting some general aspects of these relational patterns. First, although the analogues in (1) constitute paired objects, strings, and concepts, there is, in principle, no limit to how internally complex the analogue or base can be. We recognize human families, as well as language families, with mother tongues, daughter languages, and sister dialects. In language too, words can come in families, with complex kinship relations. These word families, often called **paradigms**, are a central locus of analogy in grammar. Inflectional paradigms can be extremely small, as in English {*dog, dogs*} or too large to list here, as in the approximately 1,000 inflected forms of a common Yupik (Eskimo) verb. The size of word families can also be highly item-specific within a language, as illustrated by the variation in the size of derivational paradigms in many languages, variation that is reflected in morphological family size effects (Bertram, Schreuder, and Baayen 2000; de Jong, Schreuder, and Baayen 2000). Although word-based analogies are often expressed as four-part analogies like those in (1), when large word-families are involved, analogy may be much more complex. The nature of these complex analogical patterns is explored in several papers in this volume (Finkel and Stump; Ackerman, Blevins, and Malouf; and Milin *et al.*).

1.2 Analogy in grammar

In the domain of grammar, analogy is most strongly associated with language change (Anttila 1977; Hock 1991, 2003). Analogy is typically viewed as a process where one form of a language becomes more like another form due to an indirect association that is mediated by some higher-order generalization or pattern. While patterns can be observed across many linguistic categories, it is patterns between related words or word families that lead most often to analogical change. The short list of English singular and plural nouns in (2) exhibits a pattern that holds of the great majority of nouns in the language. Discounting compounds and derived forms, the families of these nouns are very small, consisting only of the two forms in (2).

(2) Some English singular and plural nouns

i. Singular	Plural	ii. Singular	Plural	iii. Singular	Plural
duck	ducks	kiss	kisses	baby	babies
cup	cups	dish	dishes	sister	sisters
sock	socks	fox	foxes	spoon	spoons
pot	pots	match	matches	apple	apples
chip	chips	lunch	lunches	bed	beds

Once a child has heard even a small set of nouns in the singular and plural, a pattern will start to emerge. The pattern relates a singular noun to a plural noun, where the plural noun is typically identical to the singular, except that it includes a predictable ending: /s/ after voiceless nonstrident sounds {p, t, k, f, θ} (2i); /əz/ after strident sounds {s, z, ʃ, ʒ, tʃ, dʒ} (2ii), and /z/ elsewhere (2iii). A proportional analogy like *sister:sisters = brother:X*, allows a child acquiring English to aggressively predict plurals not yet encountered on the basis of the singular form. Analogy yields *brothers*, the modern English plural, though similar analogical reasoning presumably led earlier to the replacement of *brethren* by *brothers*. Child language is full of analogical formations of this kind (*oxes, fishes, sheeps*, etc.) as well as others based on less robust patterns (e.g. *goose:geese = mongoose: mongeese*). The most salient examples are those that differ from adult forms, resulting in the strong association between analogy and language change.

However, there is a growing body of empirical evidence that linguistic change is continuous throughout the lifetime of an individual (Harrington, Palethorpe, and Watson 2000; Sankoff and Blondeau 2007, and references cited therein). Patterns of change suggest that linguistic knowledge is acquired incrementally, and that there is a feeding relationship between the production and perception of speech, which results in an ongoing process of grammar development (Pierrehumbert 2006; Wedel 2006, 2007). If this perspective is broadly correct, it suggests that the modern dichotomy between synchrony and diachrony is misconceived and that analogy is panchronic, and integral to the constantly evolving linguistic system of the individual. Recent simulations that use production/perception feedback loops have shown considerable promise in modeling the evolution of syntactic, morphological, phonological, and phonetic aspects of linguistic systems, and the success of these models is often enhanced by the introduction of analogy (see, e.g. Sproat 2008; Wedel this volume, and references cited therein.)

As suggested above, many of the most robust analogies in language involve word families as in (2), and can be referred to as **word-based analogy** or **morphological analogy**. In these cases, a recurrent **sound pattern and meaning** runs through a set of words, and forms the basis of the abstract pattern that newly heard words are associated with. In many cases, these can be stated as four-part analogies, but, as recognized as early as Paul (1880/1920), and further supported by Finkel and Stump (this volume), and Ackerman, Blevins, and Malouf (this volume), larger word sets may be necessary to discover patterns of predictability within complex inflectional systems. Furthermore, word families need not be limited to those defined by inflection or derivation. As shown by Krott (this volume), compounds define word families within which analogical formation is robust, and indeed the only explanation available for certain patterns.

There is evidence of word-based analogy in every language where analogical patterns have been investigated. The attraction of analogical patterns may be due in part to the fact that they impose a measure of order on the typically arbitrary sound–meaning correspondences in a language. But why should words play a distinguished role? In the cognitive psychology literature, it has been argued that the validity or strength of an analogy is partly determined by the number of distinct points at which one domain or entity can be aligned with another (Gentner 1983; Holyoak and Thagard 1989; Gentner and Markman 1997). This structural alignment will be very strong in word families, like the singulars and plurals in (2), since words can be aligned at phonetic, phonological, categorial, and inflectional feature points. In linguistic terms, the more shared features of different types a set of words has, the more likely the set will be used as the basis of analogical modeling (Skousen 1989). Evidence for a minimal degree of structural alignment in word-based analogy is presented in Gerken *et al.* (this volume).

Because it is so widespread, word-based analogy has given rise to the greatest number of descriptive generalizations and theoretical proposals. At the descriptive level, the bulk of analogical changes are analyzed as instances of *extension* or *leveling*. Extension is the case where an alternating pattern is introduced to a historically nonalternating paradigm: e.g. English irregular *drive-drove* is extended in some dialects to *dive*, so that *dive-dived > dive-dove*. Under leveling, paradigmatic alternations are eliminated, as in the regularization of any historically strong verb, such as *cleave-cleaved* replacing the older *cleave-clove* in some varieties of English. More theoretical proposals attempt to define the most common directions of analogical change, taking into account phonological, morphological, syntactic, and semantic information. The best known of these are Kuryłowicz's laws of analogy (Kuryłowicz, 1945–9/1995) and Mańczak's tendencies in analogical change (Mańczak 1958). Both authors summarize recurrent aspects of word-based analogical change, from tendencies for transparent inflection to extend and replace synthetic forms, to generalizations governing which meanings are associated with old and new forms once analogy has taken place. However, as more morphological systems have been explored, few, if any, of these generalizations have survived. In their place, we see more general proposals. Deutscher (2001) divides internal word-based analogical change into "extension" and "reanalysis," in parallel with the typology of internal syntactic change (Harris and Campbell 1995). In a similar vein, Garrett (2008) suggests that pure leveling, in the sense outlined above, does not exist: instead, all cases of leveling are analyzed as extensions of an existing uniform paradigm on a nonuniform paradigm. Baayen *et al.* (2003*b*) demonstrates the importance of probabilistic knowledge in modeling morphological productivity, while Albright (2008) emphasizes an association between analogues and general informativeness.

Word-based analogies are by far the most widely recognized and carefully studied type, and their effects on language change are most salient. Nevertheless, analogy in grammar need not be limited to word-based comparisons, and cases involving phonetic, phonological, syntactic, and semantic alignment have also been proposed. In the domain of sound patterns, **phonetic analogy** is the case where a phonetically based variant of a particular segment is extended to another segment type or another context on the basis of phonetic similarity between segments or contexts (Bloomfield 1933: 366; Vennemann 1972; Steriade 2000; Yu 2007; Mielke 2008: 88–95). For example, in Tigrinya, velar stops /k/ and /g/ undergo spirantization to [x] and [ɣ] respectively between vowels. In one dialect, spirantization has been extended to /b/ and /p/ as well, but not to /t/ or /d/. One analysis of this pattern is that the original velar spirantization is extended to labials, but not coronals, on the basis of analogy: labials and velars are phonetically similar, both being grave, with greater acoustic energy in the lower frequencies (Mielke 2008: 89–90). Though in some cases, alternative, purely phonetic, analyses are possible, and well supported (e.g. Barnes and Kavitskaya 2002, on French schwa deletion), it remains to be seen whether all cases can be dealt with in similar ways.

Direct sound–meaning or phonology–semantics alignments that are not mediated by the lexicon are usually characterized as systems of **sound symbolism** (Hinton, Nichols, and Ohala 1994). Conventional sound symbolism, where sound–meaning correspondences are highly language-specific, and to some extent arbitrary, provide the best examples of **phonological analogy**, especially where **phonaesthemes** are involved. Phonaesthemes are recurring sound–meaning pairs that cannot be construed as words or as morphemes, like English word-initial *gl-* in *glitter, glisten, glow, gleam, glint* which evokes light or vision (Firth 1930; Bloomfield 1933; Bergen 2004). Though they may arise by accidental convergence, the statistically significant distribution of sound–meaning pairs are interesting, in that they, like other patterns, are seized upon by language learners, forming the basis of productive analogies. As Bloomfield (1895: 409) observed colourfully: "Every word, in so far as it is semantically expressive, may establish, by hap-hazard favoritism, a union between its meaning and any of its sounds, and then send forth this sound (or sounds) upon predatory expeditions into domains where the sound is at first a stranger and parasite…." In the case of English phonaesthemes, the psychological reality of the sound–meaning correspondence is evident in priming experiments (Bergen 2004), as well as in neologisms, where the correspondence is extended analogically (Magnus 2000). Looking for a new dishwashing powder? "Everything glistens with *Glist.*" or so an advertising slogan would have us believe. Direct sound meaning alignments need not be mediated by discrete phonological units. Words may have their own "gestalts," or holistic patterns, and these may also be the basis of productive analogies (Hockett 1987).

Semantic analogies are usually classified as **metaphors**. In semantic analogies, relations between aspects of meaning of the analogue are mapped to those of the target (Gentner *et al.* 2001b). Though words are used to express semantic analogies, it is clear that, in some cases, words are merely vehicles for deeper conceptual alignments. The use of space to talk about time is a clear example: *a long illness; a short recovery; two weeks in advance; one month behind schedule,* etc. Cross-linguistically the metaphorical relationship between space and time is asymmetrical: people talk about time in terms of space more often than they talk about space in terms of time (Lakoff and Johnson 1980; Alverson 1994). A range of psychophysical experiments supports a conceptual, nonlinguistic basis for this asymmetry: subjects take irrelevant spacial information into account when judging duration, but do not take special notice of irrelevant temporal information when judging space, providing evidence that semantic representations of time and space are inherently asymmetrical (Casasanto and Boroditsky 2007). Semantic analogies may also play a significant role in semantic change across time and space, and determine, in many cases, specific directions of grammaticalization, e.g. verbs > auxiliaries; verbs > adpositions; adpositions > case markers; ONE > indefinite markers; spacial adverbs > temporal adverbs (Traugott and Heine 1991; Heine 1993; Hopper and Traugott 2003).

Although highly intricate proposals have been advanced to account for syntactic knowledge, there is little counter-evidence to a very simple proposal. This classic model, which dominated language science until the rise of generative grammar, posits two basic mechanisms of human sentence production and comprehension (see, e.g. Sturtevant 1947:104–7). The first mechanism is memorization: people memorize utterances they have heard. These can range from very short phrases and simple sentences, to complex sentences, whole songs, poems or stories (Jackendoff 2002:152–4; 167–82). The second way in which people produce and understand phrases and sentences is by analogy with those they have memorized. In order to make use of **syntactic analogy**, a language learner must perform some segmentation of the utterance into smaller chunks (phrases or words) on the basis of sound/meaning correspondences. Based on this parsing, analogous bits or chunks of sentences can replace each other in different sentence frames (Tomasello 2003: 163–9). Two models that incorporate syntactic analogy have proved highly successful in accounting for syntactic acquisition and form. In language acquisition research, the "traceback" method analyzes dense corpora of child language in its natural context (Lieven *et al.* 2003; Dąbrowska and Lieven 2005). In the earliest stages of acquisition, one third of all children's utterances are exact imitations of adult speech, while over 80 per cent of their speech is made up of exact copies of earlier utterances with only one analogically based operation (substitution, addition, deletion, insertion, or reordering). From utterances like *more milk, more juice,* the child is able to identify a frame "more N," and extend it: *more jelly, more popsicle, more swimming,* etc. A similar perspective emerges from some of the models of construction grammar (Kay and Fillmore 1999; Croft 2001; Goldberg and Jackendoff 2005; Goldberg 2006), where syntactic productivity is viewed as the extension of learned constructions.

Constructions are the syntactic analogue of words: they typically embody arbitrary relations between form and meaning. The internal complexity of a construction, whose form may include phonological, morphological, syntactic, and pragmatic components, results in multiple anchor points for analogical extension.

A number of factors have contributed to the diminished role that analogy plays in generative accounts. The marginalization of morphology in general, and the neglect of complex inflectional systems in particular, shifted attention away from many of the patterns that traditional accounts had regarded in analogical terms. A primary focus on synchronic description likewise eliminated much of the traditional evidence for the influence of analogical pressures on the development of grammatical systems. A model of grammar that conceives of the mental lexicon as a largely redundancy-free collection of minimal units also lacks the word stock that provided the traditional base for analogical extensions of word-based patterns. In addition, the use of symbolic "rules" to provide a discrete description of a linguistic system imposes a strict separation between "data" and "program". This departs from the more exemplar-based conception of approaches that treat analogy as the principal creative mechanism in language and recognize the probabilistic nature of linguisitic generalizations (Bod, Hay, and Jannedy 2003; Gahl and Yu 2006). Hence, while Chomsky's early remarks on grammar discovery echo some aspects of the descriptivist tradition (which retained a role for analogy), they also assume the notion of a "structural pattern" that corresponds to item-independent rules, not individual constructions or instances of any type of expression:

A primary motivation for this study is the remarkable ability of any speaker of a language to produce utterances which are new both to him and to other speakers, but which are immediately recognizable as sentences of the language. We would like to reconstruct this ability within linguistic theory by developing a method of analysis that will enable us to abstract from a corpus of sentences a certain structural pattern, and to construct, from the old materials, new sentences conforming to this pattern, just as the speaker does. (Chomsky 1955/1975: 131)

In later writings, Chomsky is dismissive of analogy on the few occasions that he mentions it at all (Itkonen 2005: 67–76), and his general position seems to be that "analogy is simply an inappropriate concept in the first place" (Chomsky 1986: 32). Work within the generative tradition has tended likewise to think of rules as the basis of broad generalizations, reserving analogy for local, lexically restricted patterns. A particularly clear and accessible exposition of this perspective is *Words and Rules* (Pinker 1999). However, from a traditional perspective, a rule can be understood as a highly general analogy. There is no need for any qualitative difference between general and restricted analogies, and it is entirely plausible to assume that their differences reside solely in the specificity of the pattern that must be matched to sanction an analogical deduction. A number of psycholinguistic studies provide a measure of support for this more uniform view of grammatical devices by showing that there is no stable behavioral correlate of posited differences between irregular items (stored "words") and productive formations (outputs of "rules"). Instead, different types of frequency information appear to be of central importance in conditioning variation in speakers' responses in the lexical access and recognition tasks that are used to probe the structure of the mental lexicon (Stemberger and MacWhinney 1986; Hay and Baayen 2002, 2005; Baayen *et al.* 2003*b*). One further virtue of a unified notion of analogy that subsumes general and restricted cases is that it can account for the competition between candidate analogies in terms of the natural trade-off between the specificity of an analogical pattern and the number of encountered instances that match the pattern. It may even be possible to model or measure the attraction exerted by competing analogies given the advances in psycholinguistic methods for probing the structure of the mental lexicon (Milin *et al.*, this volume) and advances in techniques for modeling the effects of lexical neighborhoods (Wedel, this volume).

At this particular point in the development of the field of linguistics, it is useful to be reminded of the pivotal role that analogy has played in earlier grammatical models and to appreciate its renewed importance in the emerging quantitative and data-driven methodologies that feature in many of the papers in this volume. Nearly all grammatical traditions have regarded analogy as a central determinant of the form and evolution of linguistic subsystems, though it is only with the advent of better modeling techniques that it has become possible to investigate the psycholinguistic reality of analogical patterns and to represent and even measure the analogical pressures on a system. From this standpoint, it is perhaps the generative attitudes toward analogy that appear anomalous, a point that adds a further dimension to the reappraisal of generative approaches that is currently underway in phonology (Bybee 2001; J. Blevins 2004, 2006*b*; Mielke 2008), morphology (Anderson 2004; Deutscher 2005; J. P. Blevins 2006*b*); and syntax (Goldberg 2006; Matthews 2007; J. P. Blevins 2008). However one reconciles generative scepticism about analogy with more traditional perspectives, it would seem that this is an auspicious time to reconsider the role of analogy in grammar. In the chapters that follow, authors seek to understand better the ways in which analogical reasoning, the core of human cognition, shapes the form and acquisition of linguistic knowledge.

1.3 Organization of this volume

The papers in this volume are organized thematically into three parts. The papers in each part address a group of related or overlapping issues, usually from slightly different or complementary perspectives.

The papers in Part 1 consider aspects of the organization of linguistic systems and the levels at which analogy operates in these systems. The central role attributed to analogy in morphological analysis is clear in the practice of matching principal parts against cells of exemplary paradigms to deduce unencountered forms. Yet although the deductions themselves can be represented by proportional analogies, many other aspects of this analysis remain imprecise, notably the criteria that guide the selection of principal parts. In Chapter 2, Finkel and Stump address this issue by proposing a typology of principal part systems, and by developing a notion of "paradigmatic transparency" that measures the degree of predictability between principal parts and paradigm cells. The information-theoretic approach outlined by Ackerman, Blevins, and Malouf in Chapter 3 offers a complementary perspective on this issue by representing implicational structure in terms of uncertainty reduction. In Chapter 4, Wedel sets out some of the ways that the organization of linguistic systems can evolve, reflecting different initial biases in a system or different ways of resolving conflicts between analogical pressures that operate at phonological and morphological levels.

The papers in Part 2 turn to the role that analogy plays in language learning, by humans but also by machines. In Chapter 5, Gerken *et al.* suggest that analogical reasoning about "secondary cues" accounts for the facilitatory effect that these cues apparently exert in the learning of lexical categories on the basis of paradigm-completion tasks. In Chapter 6, Krott reviews the pervasive influence of analogy on the form of compound structures in a range of languages. In Chapter 7, Goldsmith summarizes a body of research that has been devoted to building a general model of automatic morphological analysis and examines the contribution that analogy can make to the learning algorithm of this model.

Goldsmith's paper provides a natural transition to the papers in Part 3, which take up the challenge of modeling analogy formally. In Chapter 8, Skousen offers a concise synopsis of the theory of Analogical Modeling, and presents analyses that motivate particular extensions of this theory.

In Chapter 9, Albright considers three restrictions on analogical inference that he argues can be attributed to limitations of context-sensitive rules. In the final chapter, Milin *et al.* return to issues concerning the organization of linguistic systems and present a range of studies that indicate the predictive value of information-theoretic measures, and also suggest the psychological relevance of traditional notions of paradigms and inflection classes.

Taken together, these papers reflect a resurgence of interest in traditional approaches to the representation and extension of grammatical patterns. It is hoped that collecting these papers together in the present volume will help to highlight significant points of contact across different domains and encourage further investigation of the role of analogy in language structure and use.

2

Principal parts and degrees of paradigmatic transparency

Raphael Finkel and Gregory Stump

2.1 Principal parts and inflectional paradigms

It is natural to suppose that in the case of many lexemes, language users store some of the forms in an inflectional paradigm and use these stored forms as a basis for deducing the other forms in that paradigm. Given that hypothesis, how much storage should one assume? At the maximal extreme, there could be full storage; this conclusion is not implausible for highly irregular paradigms or for paradigms whose forms are exceptionally frequent. At the minimal extreme, by contrast, there could be storage of only the minimum number of forms in a paradigm that are necessary for deducing all of the paradigm's remaining forms. Principal parts embody this notion of a minimal extreme. Postulating principal parts does not, of course, commit one to the assumption that speakers store a lexeme's principal parts and nothing more, only to the assumption that they are the minimum that could be stored if unstored forms are to be deduced from stored ones.

Principal parts have a long history of use in language pedagogy; generations of Latin students have learned that by memorizing a verb's four principal parts (those exemplified in Table 2.1), one can deduce all remaining forms in that verb's paradigm. But because principal parts are a distillation of the implicative relations that exist among the members of a lexeme's paradigm, they also reveal an important domain of typological variation in morphology.

In this paper, we use principal parts to identify a crucial dimension of this typological variation: that of PARADIGMATIC TRANSPARENCY—intuitively, the ease with which some cells in a paradigm can be deduced from other cells in that paradigm. We begin by distinguishing two types of principal-part analyses: static and dynamic (§2.2). Drawing upon principal-part analyses of the latter type, we develop a detailed account of paradigmatic transparency. For

TABLE 2.1 Principal parts of five Latin verbs

Conjugation	1st person singular present indicative active	Infinitive	1st person singular perfect indicative active	Perfect passive participle (neuter nominative singular)	Gloss
1st	laudō	laudāre	laudāvī	laudātum	'praise'
2nd	moneō	monēre	monuī	monitum	'advise'
3rd	dūcō	dūcere	dūxī	dūctum	'lead'
3rd (-iō)	capiō	capere	cēpī	captum	'take'
4th	audiō	audīre	audīvī	audītum	'hear'

concreteness, we exemplify our account by reference to the conjugational system of the Comaltepec Chinantec language (§2.3). Some of the conjugation classes in Comaltepec Chinantec give rise to maximally transparent paradigms; most others, however, deviate from maximal transparency in one or more ways (§2.4). We propose a formal measure of paradigm predictability to elucidate the degrees of such deviation (§2.5). The observable degrees of deviation from maximal transparency in both Comaltepec Chinantec and Fur turn out to be irreconcilable with the No-Blur Principle (Cameron-Faulkner and Carstairs-McCarthy 2000), according to which the affixes competing for the realization of a particular paradigmatic cell either uniquely identify a particular inflection class or serve as the default affixal realization of that cell (§2.6). At the same time, the proposed measure of paradigm predictability affords a precise account of cross-linguistic differences in paradigmatic transparency, as we demonstrate in a comparison of the conjugational systems of Comaltepec Chinantec and Fur (§2.7). We summarize our conclusions in §2.8.[1]

Our work here contributes to the (by now quite vast) body of work demonstrating the typological and theoretical significance of inflectional paradigms in the structure of natural languages. Much of the research in this area has focused on the importance of paradigms for defining relations of inflectional exponence (e.g. Matthews 1972; Zwicky 1985; Anderson 1992; Stump 2001); other research, however, has drawn particular attention to the

---

[1] An earlier version of this paper was presented at the workshop on Analogy in Grammar: Form and Acquisition, September 22–3, 2006, at the Max Planck Institute for Evolutionary Anthropology, Leipzig. We thank several members of the audience at that event for their helpful comments; thanks, too, to two anonymous referees for several useful suggestions. Thanks finally to Eric Rowland for the dodecagon in Fig. 2.1.

significance of implicative relations among the cells in a paradigm (e.g. Wurzel 1989, J. P. Blevins 2006*b*, Finkel and Stump 2007). Our concerns here relate most directly to the latter sphere of interest.

2.2 Two conceptions of principal parts

Before proceeding, we must distinguish two importantly different conceptions of principal parts in natural language. (See Finkel and Stump 2007 for additional discussion of this distinction.)

2.2.1 *The static conception*

According to the STATIC conception of principal parts, the same sets of morphosyntactic properties identify the principal parts for every inflection class for lexemes in a given syntactic category. To illustrate, consider the hypothetical inflection-class system depicted in Table 2.2. In this table, there are four morphosyntactic property sets, represented as W, X, Y, and Z; there are six inflection classes, represented as Roman numerals I through VI; for each realization of a morphosyntactic property set within an inflection class, there is a particular exponent, and these exponents are represented as the letters **a** through **o**. We might represent this system of inflection classes with static principal parts as in Table 2.3. In this table, the shaded exponents represent the principal parts for each of the six inflection classes: The three shaded principal parts in each inflection class suffice to distinguish it from the other five inflection classes. A static system of principal parts for the set of inflection classes in Table 2.2 gives each lexeme belonging to the relevant syntactic category three principal parts: its realizations for the property sets W, X, and Y.

This static conception of principal parts is in fact the traditional one: The principal parts for Latin verbs in Table 2.1 are static, because they represent the same four morphosyntactic property sets from one inflection class to another.

TABLE 2.2 A hypothetical inflection-class system

	W	X	Y	Z
I	a	e	i	m
II	b	e	i	m
III	c	f	j	n
IV	c	g	j	n
V	d	h	k	o
VI	d	h	l	o

TABLE 2.3 Static principal parts for the hypothetical system

	W	X	Y	Z
I	a	e	i	m
II	b	e	i	m
III	c	f	j	n
IV	c	g	j	n
V	d	h	k	o
VI	d	h	l	o

(1)   Sample static principal-part specifications:
         Lexeme L belonging to inflection class I : L_a, L_e, L_i
         Lexeme M belonging to inflection class IV : M_c, M_g, M_j
         Lexeme N belonging to inflection class VI : N_d, N_h, N_l

2.2.2 *The dynamic conception*

According to the DYNAMIC conception of principal parts, principal parts are
not necessarily parallel from one inflection class to another. The hypothetical
inflection-class system in Table 2.2 admits the dynamic system of principal
parts in Table 2.4. Each inflection class has only one shaded cell. If we observe
that a lexeme has the exponent **a** in the form expressing the morphosyntactic
property set W, we can deduce that it belongs to inflection class I; if we instead
find that it has the exponent **b** in the realization of the property set W, we
deduce that it belongs to inflection class II; if it exhibits the exponent **f** in the
realization of property set X, we know that it belongs to inflection class III;
and so forth. In a way, the dynamic conception of principal parts is more
economical than the static because it allows each inflection class in this
hypothetical example to have only a single principal part.

   It's important to note, though, that under the dynamic conception of
principal parts, the lexical specification of a lexeme's principal part must
specify the morphosyntactic property set which that principal part realizes.
Consider the slightly more complicated hypothetical system of inflection
classes in Table 2.5. Here, the exponent **g** realizes the property set X in
inflection class IV, but this same exponent **g** realizes the morphosyntactic
property set Z in inflection class VII. In representing lexemes for this hypothetical system, it does not suffice simply to specify that a lexeme has a
realization involving the exponent **g** as its principal part, because this fact
fails to indicate whether that lexeme belongs to inflection class IV or inflection
class VII. So lexical specifications of principal parts under the dynamic

TABLE 2.4 Dynamic principal parts for the hypothetical system

	W	X	Y	Z
I	a	e	i	m
II	b	e	i	m
III	c	f	j	n
IV	c	g	j	n
V	d	h	k	o
VI	d	h	l	o

TABLE 2.5 Dynamic principal parts for a slightly larger system

	W	X	Y	Z
I	a	e	i	m
II	b	e	i	m
III	c	f	j	n
IV	c	g	j	n
V	d	h	k	o
VI	d	h	l	o
VII	c	e	j	g

conception are pairings of morphosyntactic property sets with realizations, as in (2). We refer to such pairings as CELLS.

(2) Sample dynamic principal-part specifications:
     Lexeme L belonging to inflection class I : $W:L_a$
     Lexeme M belonging to inflection class IV : $X:M_g$
     Lexeme N belonging to inflection class VI : $Y:N_l$
     Lexeme O belonging to inflection class VII : $Z:O_g$

The static and dynamic conceptions of principal parts differ in the answer they give to the question "What are a lexeme's principal parts?" In the static approach, a lexeme's principal parts are a list of words realizing a corresponding list of morphosyntactic property sets invariant across inflection classes; but under the dynamic approach, a lexeme's principal parts are an unordered set of cells (pairings of realizations with morphosyntactic property sets).

For both the static and the dynamic conception of principal parts, the relation between a lexeme's principal parts and its nonprincipal parts is fundamentally analogical in nature: if the principal parts of $Lexeme_1$ and

Lexeme$_2$ express the same morphosyntactic properties and are alike in form, then the nonprincipal parts of Lexeme$_1$ are analogous in form and content to those of Lexeme$_2$. For instance, given that the static principal parts of the Latin verb *amāre* 'love' (*amō, amāre, amāvī, amātum*) are parallel in form and content to those of *laudāre* 'praise' (cf. Table 2.1), their nonprincipal parts are entirely analogous; the same is true under a dynamic analysis, in which *amāre* and *laudāre* each have only a single principal part (the perfect passive participle).

Analogical relations have a range of implications for language acquisition and processing, not all of which are directly relevant to our discussion here. The principal-part analyses that we develop in this paper are based on a language's complete system of inflection classes. Accordingly, our analyses are meant to account for fluent, adult speakers' inference of analogical certainties:

(3)   If lexeme L has a particular set of principal parts, then it is a certainty that it has the associated set of nonprincipal parts.

Our central interest is in showing that the conditions licensing inferences of this sort vary in their complexity, both across a language's paradigms and across languages. At the same time, we regard this work as providing the theoretical underpinnings necessary for a broader range of future investigations into the role of analogy in language. It is plausible to assume that language learners also make inferences such as (3) but that their inferences are defeasible by counter-evidence (which then necessitates a reconception of the implicative relations among paradigmatic cells). It is likewise plausible that inferences such as (3) have a role in online language processing, though we suspect that the extent to which this is true depends critically on a lexeme's degree of paradigmatic transparency; for instance, a lexeme whose paradigm only requires a single dynamic principal part may give rise to such online inferences much more reliably than one whose paradigm requires five principal parts. We also suppose that inferences such as (3) could be successfully pressed into service in machine learning algorithms.

In this paper, we restrict our attention to dynamic principal parts as the basis for our account of paradigmatic transparency. Moreover, we generally restrict our attention to optimal sets of dynamic principal parts, where a set S of dynamic principal parts is OPTIMAL for inflection class J iff there is no valid set of dynamic principal parts for J whose cardinality is less than that of S. For example, although the set of dynamic principal parts specified in (4) is perfectly valid for deducing the exponence of the four lexemes listed, it is not optimal, since the smaller set of dynamic principal parts in (2) is also valid for deducing this exponence.

(4)   Sample dynamic principal-part specifications:
      Lexeme L belonging to inflection class I :   W:L$_a$, X:L$_e$
      Lexeme M belonging to inflection class IV :   X:M$_g$
      Lexeme N belonging to inflection class VI :   Y:N$_l$
      Lexeme O belonging to inflection class VII :   Z:O$_g$

For concreteness, we develop this account with reference to the system of dynamic principal parts embodied by the system of conjugations in Comaltepec Chinantec (Oto-Manguean; Mexico).

2.3 Conjugation classes in Comaltepec Chinantec

We begin with an overview of the system of conjugation classes in Comaltepec Chinantec. Verbs in Comaltepec Chinantec inflect in two ways: through stem modulation and through the addition of affixes. The affixes include (i) aspectual prefixes expressing the progressive, the intentive, and the completive aspects and (ii) pronominal suffixes expressing the first-person singular, the first-person plural, the second-person singular, and the third person. (Verbs with a second-person plural subject lack any pronominal suffix.) The forms in Table 2.6 exemplify these affixes, whose use is essentially constant across all of the language's sixty-seven conjugations.

Patterns of stem modulation also serve to distinguish the three aspects as well as four person/number combinations (first-person singular, first-person plural, second person, and third person). In accordance with these patterns, a stem's final syllable may vary in tone (the seven possibilities being low [L], mid [M], high [H], and the combinations [LM], [MH], [LH], and [HL]); in stress (we leave controlled stress unmarked and mark ballistic stress with [']); in length (we leave short syllables unmarked and mark long syllables with [:]); in its capacity to trigger tone sandhi (we leave nontriggers unmarked and mark triggers as [$]); and in the presence or absence of final glottality ("open"

TABLE 2.6 Inflectional paradigm of the verb 'play' (Conjugation P2B) in Comaltepec Chinantec

Aspect	1SG	1PL	2SG	3
Progressive	kó:^{L}-R	ko:^{M}-R?	ko:^{L}-?	kó:^{L}-r
Intentive	ni^L-kó:^{LH}-R	ni^L-kó^H-R?	ni^L-kó:^{H}-?	ni^L-kó^M-r
Completive	ka^L-kó^M-R	ka^L-kó^H-R?	ka^L-ko:^{M}-?	ka^L-kó:^{L}-r

R represents reduplication of a syllable-final segment; for details, see Pace 1990, Anderson *et al.* 1990.

(*Source*: Pace 1990: 42)

syllables–those lacking final glottality–we leave unmarked, and checked syllables–those exhibiting final glottality–we mark with [ʔ]).

A verb's membership in a particular conjugation class depends on (i) the particular pattern of stem modulation that its stem exhibits and (ii) the number of syllables in its stem. Stems are either monosyllabic or disyllabic; in the tables below, we represent disyllabic verb stems with the diacritic "ᴅ."

Given these syllabic and prosodic differences among the conjugation classes, one can discern three broadly different groups of conjugations. In her description of Comaltepec Chinantec verb inflection, Pace (1990) calls these three groups Class A, Class B, and Class C verbs. Class A verbs, the largest such class, are represented in Table 2.7. Pace (1990: 43f.) distinguishes Class A verbs from verbs in the other classes by the following criteria:

In Class A verbs, first vs. nonfirst persons are distinguished in progressive aspect. Third person may also be distinguished. The three aspects have different inflectional patterns.

Within this broad characterization of Class A verbs, there is a range of variants; thus, there are thirty-five different conjugation classes represented among the Class A verbs in Table 2.7.[2]

Pace (1990: 46) uses the following criteria to distinguish the Class B verbs:

In Class B verbs, only third person is distinguished in noncompletive aspects. Like Class A verbs, the three aspects have different inflectional patterns.

As Table 2.8 shows, this broad characterization of Class B verbs subsumes nineteen different conjugations.

Finally, Pace (1990: 48) distinguishes Class C verbs by the following criteria.

In Class C verbs, third person is distinguished from nonthird. Aspect has different inflectional patterns in third person only.

---

[2] Here and further on, we represent an inflection class as a set of pairings of a particular morphosyntactic property set with an associated exponence; in any such pairing, the exponence may include affixes, prosodic markings, and phonological properties characteristic of the stems belonging to the inflection class at hand. This mode of representation reveals patterns that recur across two or more inflection classes (e.g. a pattern in which whatever exponence is associated with property set A is also associated with property set B); distinct inflection classes participating in patterns of this sort can then be grouped into superclasses, which can in turn be useful for expressing complex implicative relationships in the most general possible way. Here, we are not concerned with the task of superclassing, since a superclass does not, in itself, afford any economy in the number of principal parts required by the inflection classes that it subsumes.

Note that Conjugations P2A through P2G deviate from Pace's general description of Class A verbs insofar as their first-person singular stems are like their third-person stems in the progressive aspect. Note, too, that certain verbs (e.g. *tánʔ*[LM] 'put into') inflect as members of more than one conjugation; compare English verb forms such as *dreamed/dreamt*.

TABLE 2.7 Class A conjugations in Comaltepec Chinantec

Conj	Progressive				Intentive				Completive				Sample lexemes (cited by their 2nd person completive stem)
	1sg	1pl	2	3	1sg	1pl	2	3	1sg	1pl	2	3	
P1A	M	M	L	LM	MH	H?	H?	M?	M?	H?	L?	M?	ká?^{L} 'charge'
P1B	M	M	L	LM	MH	H?	H?	M?	M?	H?	H?	L?	tá?^{H} 'prune'
P1C	M	M	L	LM	MH	H?	H?	M?	M?	H?	L?	L?	?ɨ:^{L} 'read'
P1D	M	M	L	LM	MH	H?	H?	M?	M?	H?	H?	LM	ŋí:^{H} 'walk', ná:^{H} 'open'
P1E	M	M	L	LM	MH	H?	H?	M?	M?	H?	LM?	LM	ná^{LM} 'open'
P2A	L?	M:	L:	L:?	LH:?	H?	H:?	M?	M?	H?	M	L:?	kiṵ^{M} 'hit with fist'
P2B	L?	M:	L:	L:?	LH:?	H?	H:?	M?	M?	H?	M:	L:?	?ê:^{M} 'kick'
P2C	L?	M:	L:	L:?	LH:?	H?	H:?	M?	M?	H?	M:?	L:?	gí:^{M} 'tear'
P2D	L?	M:	L:	L:?	LH:?	H?	H:?	M?	M?	H?	L:	L:?	ke:^{L} 'place'
P2E	L?	M:	L:	L:?	LH:?	H?	H:?	M?	M?	H?	LH:?	L:?	?ɨ:^{LH} 'sell'
P2F	L?	M:	L:	L:?	LH:?	H?	H:?	M?	M?	H?	M:?	M?	tó:^{M} 'bake'
P2G	L?	M:	L:	L:?	LH:?	H?	H:?	M?	M?	H?	LH:?	M?	tṵ:^{LH} 'pour out'
P3A	M$?'	M$?'	L?'	L?'	H?'	H?'	H?'	L?	M?'	H?	L?	L?'	to?^{L} 'apply'
P3B	M$?'	M$?'	L?'	L?'	H?'	H?'	H?'	L?	M?'	H?	L?	L?'	hú?^{L} 'cough'
P3C	M$?'	M$?'	L?'	L?'	H?'	H?'	H?'	L?	M?'	H?	LH?	L?'	gen?^{LH} 'swing', ko?^{LH} 'play with', huên?^{LH} 'speak to'
P3D	M$?'	M$?'	L?'	L?'	H?'	H?'	H?'	L?	M?'	H?	LM?	L?'	hŋan?^{LM} 'kill'
P3E	M$?'	M$?'	L?'	L?'	H?'	H?'	H?'	L?	M?'	H?	LM?	L?'	sén?^{LM} 'hold', ?nó?^{LM} 'look for', tán?^{LM} 'put into'

(Continued)

TABLE 2.7 (Continued)

Conj	Progressive				Intentive				Completive				Sample lexemes (cited by their 2nd person completive stem)
	1sg	1pl	2	3	1sg	1pl	2	3	1sg	1pl	2	3	
P3F	M$ʔ	M$ʔ	Lʔ	Lʔ	Hʔ	Hʔ	Hʔ	Lʔ	Mʔ	Hʔ	LMʔ	Mʔ	laʔ^{LM} 'bathe'
P3G	M$ʔ	M$ʔ	Lʔ	Lʔ	Hʔ	Hʔ	Hʔ	Lʔ	Mʔ	Hʔ	LMʔ	Mʔ	ʔnóʔ^{LM} 'look for'
P3H	M$ʔ	M$ʔ	Lʔ	Lʔ	Hʔ	Hʔ	Hʔ	Lʔ	M$ʔ	Hʔ	Lʔ	Lʔ	béʔ^{L} 'roll up'
P3I	M$ʔ	M$ʔ	Lʔ	Lʔ	Hʔ	Hʔ	Hʔ	Lʔ	M$ʔ	Hʔ	LMʔ	Lʔ	koʔ^{LM} 'play with'
P3J	M$ʔ	M$ʔ	Lʔ	Lʔ	Hʔ	Hʔ	Hʔ	Lʔ	M$ʔ	Hʔ	LMʔ	Lʔ	hǐʔ^{LM} 'smell'
P3K	M$ʔ	M$ʔ	Lʔ	Lʔ	Hʔ	Hʔ	Hʔ	Lʔ	Mʔ	LHʔ	LMʔ	Lʔ	huénʔ^{LM} 'speak to'
P3L	M$ʔ	M$ʔ	Lʔ	Lʔ	Hʔ	Hʔ	Hʔ	Lʔ	Mʔ	LHʔ	LMʔ	Mʔ	tánʔ^{LM} 'put into'
P4A	M$ʔ	M$ʔ	LMʔ	LMʔ	Hʔ	Hʔ	Hʔ	Mʔ	Mʔ	Hʔ	Lʔ	LMʔ	ʔíen^{L} 'spray, wave'
P4B	M$ʔ	M$ʔ	LMʔ	LMʔ	Hʔ	Hʔ	Hʔ	Mʔ	Mʔ	Hʔ	LHʔ	LMʔ	ténʔ^{LH} 'drop'
P4C	M$ʔ	M$ʔ	LMʔ	LMʔ	Hʔ	Hʔ	Hʔ	Mʔ	Mʔ	Hʔ	LMʔ	LMʔ	ciuʔ^{LM} 'kiss', ʔienʔ^{LM} 'spray, wave'
P12A	M:	M:	L:	L:	Lʔ	Lʔ	Lʔ	Lʔ	Mʔ	Mʔ	Mʔ	L:	kuán^{M} 'grow'
P12B	M:	M:	L:	L:	Lʔ	Lʔ	Lʔ	Lʔ	Mʔ	Mʔ	M:ʔ	Mʔ	kó:^{M} 'burn'
P12C	M:	M:	L:	L:	Lʔ	Lʔ	Lʔ	Lʔ	Mʔ	Mʔ	L:	M:ʔ	iẹ:^{L} 'swell'
P13A	M$ʔ	M$ʔ	Lʔ	Lʔ	Mʔ	Mʔ	Lʔ	Lʔ	Mʔ	Mʔ	Mʔ	Mʔ	rǫ́ʔ^{M} 'bear weight of'
P13B	M$ʔ	M$ʔ	Lʔ	Lʔ	Mʔ	Mʔ	Lʔ	Lʔ	Mʔ	Mʔ	Lʔ	Lʔ	hínʔ^{L} 'hiccough'
P16A	DMʔ	DMʔ	DLʔ	DLʔ	DM$ʔ	DMʔ	DLʔ	DLʔ	DM$ʔ	DMʔ	DLʔ	DLʔ	hmǐ:^{H}ʔèʔ^{L} 'defend'
P16B	DM:	DM:	DHL:	DL'	DM:	DM:	DHL:	DL'	DM:	DM:	DHL:	DL'	hmǐ:^{HL}kiu:^{HL} 'toast, dry'
P16C	DM$ʔ	DM$ʔ	DHLʔ	DLʔ	DM$ʔ	DM$ʔ	DHLʔ	DLʔ	DM$ʔ	DM$ʔ	DHLʔ	DLʔ	hmǐ:^{L}uiʔ^{HL} 'smooth, plane'

(*Source:* Pace 1990: 43–6; 49–51)

TABLE 2.8 Class B conjugations in Comaltepec Chinantec

Conj	Progressive				Intentive				Completive				Examples
	1sg	1pl	2	3	1sg	1pl	2	3	1sg	1pl	2	3	
P5A	$^{L}ʔ$	$^{L}ʔ$	$^{L}ʔ$	$^{L}ʔ$	$^{H}ʔ$	$^{H}ʔ$	$^{H}ʔ$	$^{L}ʔ$	$^{L}ʔ$	$^{H}ʔ$	$^{L}ʔ$	$^{L}ʔ$	bá^{L} 'hit'
P5B	$^{L}ʔ$	$^{L}ʔ$	$^{L}ʔ$	$^{L}ʔ$	$^{H}ʔ$	$^{H}ʔ$	$^{H}ʔ$	$^{L}ʔ$	$^{L}ʔ$	$^{H}ʔ$	$^{LM}ʔ$	$^{L}ʔ$	ʔa^{LM} 'wade across'
P6A	$^{Mː}ʔ$	$^{Mː}ʔ$	$^{Mː}ʔ$	$^{Mː}ʔ$	$^{H}ʔ$	$^{H}ʔ$	$^{H}ʔ$	$^{Mː}ʔ$	$^{Mː}ʔ$	$^{Mː}ʔ$	$^{M}ʔ$	$^{Mː}ʔ$	hlí^{M} 'cover'
P6B	$^{Mː}ʔ$	$^{Mː}ʔ$	$^{Mː}ʔ$	$^{Mː}ʔ$	$^{H}ʔ$	$^{H}ʔ$	$^{H}ʔ$	$^{Mː}ʔ$	$^{Mː}ʔ$	$^{Mː}ʔ$	$^{Mː}ʔ$	$^{Mː}ʔ$	hnú^{M} 'rub against'
P6C	$^{Mː}ʔ$	$^{Mː}ʔ$	$^{Mː}ʔ$	$^{Mː}ʔ$	$^{H}ʔ$	$^{H}ʔ$	$^{H}ʔ$	$^{Mː}ʔ$	$^{Mː}ʔ$	$^{Mː}ʔ$	$^{LM}ʔ$	$^{Mː}ʔ$	hín^{LM} 'scold'
P7A	$^{LM}ʔ$	$^{LM}ʔ$	$^{LM}ʔ$	$^{LM}ʔ$	$^{LH}ʔ$	$^{LH}ʔ$	$^{LH}ʔ$	$^{M}ʔ$	$^{M}ʔ$	$^{LH}ʔ$	^{Mː}	$^{LM}ʔ$	kuë:n^{M} 'give'
P7B	$^{LM}ʔ$	$^{LM}ʔ$	$^{LM}ʔ$	$^{LM}ʔ$	$^{LH}ʔ$	$^{LH}ʔ$	$^{LH}ʔ$	$^{M}ʔ$	$^{M}ʔ$	$^{LH}ʔ$	$^{Mː}ʔ$	$^{LM}ʔ$	ʔi:n^{M} 'pardon, hnió:n^{M} 'drag'
P7C	$^{LM}ʔ$	$^{LM}ʔ$	$^{LM}ʔ$	$^{LM}ʔ$	$^{LH}ʔ$	$^{LH}ʔ$	$^{LH}ʔ$	$^{M}ʔ$	$^{M}ʔ$	$^{LH}ʔ$	^{Lː}	$^{LM}ʔ$	kuë:n^{L} 'give'
P7D	$^{LM}ʔ$	$^{LM}ʔ$	$^{LM}ʔ$	$^{LM}ʔ$	$^{LH}ʔ$	$^{LH}ʔ$	$^{LH}ʔ$	$^{M}ʔ$	$^{M}ʔ$	$^{LH}ʔ$	$^{Lː}ʔ$	$^{LM}ʔ$	hnió:n^{L} 'drag'
P7E	$^{LM}ʔ$	$^{LM}ʔ$	$^{LM}ʔ$	$^{LM}ʔ$	$^{LH}ʔ$	$^{LH}ʔ$	$^{LH}ʔ$	$^{M}ʔ$	$^{M}ʔ$	$^{LH}ʔ$	$^{LHː}ʔ$	$^{LM}ʔ$	ʔŋi^{LH} 'blow nose, spit'
P7F	$^{LM}ʔ$	$^{LM}ʔ$	$^{LM}ʔ$	$^{LM}ʔ$	$^{LH}ʔ$	$^{LH}ʔ$	$^{LH}ʔ$	$^{M}ʔ$	$^{M}ʔ$	$^{LH}ʔ$	$^{LM}ʔ$	$^{LM}ʔ$	ʔin^{LM} 'pardon'
P14A	$^{L}ʔ$	$^{L}ʔ$	$^{L}ʔ$	$^{L}ʔ$	$^{L}ʔ$	$^{L}ʔ$	$^{L}ʔ$	$^{L}ʔ$	$^{L}ʔ$	$^{L}ʔ$	$^{L}ʔ$	$^{L}ʔ$	tá^{L} 'drop'
P14B	$^{L}ʔ$	$^{L}ʔ$	$^{L}ʔ$	$^{L}ʔ$	$^{L}ʔ$	$^{L}ʔ$	$^{L}ʔ$	$^{L}ʔ$	$^{M}ʔ$	$^{M}ʔ$	$^{M}ʔ$	$^{M}ʔ$	ʔi^{M} 'enter'
P15A	$^{M}ʔ$	$^{M}ʔ$	$^{M}ʔ$	$^{M}ʔ$	$^{M}ʔ$	$^{M}ʔ$	$^{M}ʔ$	$^{M}ʔ$	$^{M}ʔ$	$^{M}ʔ$	$^{M}ʔ$	$^{M}ʔ$	ze^{M} 'go'
P15B	$^{M}ʔ'$	$^{M}ʔ'$	$^{M}ʔ'$	$^{M}ʔ'$	$^{M}ʔ'$	$^{M}ʔ'$	$^{M}ʔ'$	$^{M}ʔ'$	$^{M}ʔ'$	$^{M}ʔ'$	$^{M}ʔ'$	$^{M}ʔ'$	huín^{M} 'lazy'
PDBA	$^{DH}ʔ$	$^{DH}ʔ$	$^{DH}ʔ$	$^{DH}ʔ$	$^{DH}ʔ$	$^{DH}ʔ$	$^{DH}ʔ$	$^{DH}ʔ$	$^{DH}ʔ$	$^{DH}ʔ$	$^{DH}ʔ$	$^{DH}ʔ$	hmí^{L}ʔí^{H} 'count'
PDBB	$^{DHLː}ʔ$	$^{DHLː}ʔ$	$^{DHLː}ʔ$	$^{DLː}ʔ$	$^{DHLː}ʔ$	$^{DHLː}ʔ$	$^{DHLː}ʔ$	$^{DLː}ʔ$	$^{DHLː}ʔ$	$^{DHLː}ʔ$	$^{DHLː}ʔ$	$^{DLː}ʔ$	hmí^{L}go:^{HL} 'deceive'
PDBC	$^{DH}ʔ$	$^{DH}ʔ$	$^{DH}ʔ$	$^{DM}ʔ$	$^{DH}ʔ$	$^{DH}ʔ$	$^{DH}ʔ$	$^{DM}ʔ$	$^{DH}ʔ$	$^{DH}ʔ$	$^{DH}ʔ$	$^{DM}ʔ$	hmí^{L}ʔme^{H} 'sharpen'
PDBD	$^{DMH}ʔ$	$^{DMH}ʔ$	$^{DMH}ʔ$	$^{DLH}ʔ$	$^{DMH}ʔ$	$^{DMH}ʔ$	$^{DMH}ʔ$	$^{DLH}ʔ$	$^{DMH}ʔ$	$^{DMH}ʔ$	$^{DMH}ʔ$	$^{DLH}ʔ$	hmí^{L}koʔ^{MH} 'help'

(*Source:* Pace 1990: 46–8; 50–1)

TABLE 2.9 Class C conjugations in Comaltepec Chinantec

Conj	Progressive				Intentive				Completive				Examples
	1sg	1pl	2	3	1sg	1pl	2	3	1sg	1pl	2	3	
P8A	M:	M:	M:	L:ʔ	M:	M:	M:	Mʔ	M:	M:	M:	L:ʔ	ʔmeːnʔ^M 'hide', naːnʔ^M 'begin'
P8B	M:	M:	M:	L:ʔ	M:	M:	M:	Mʔ	M:	M:	L:	L:ʔ	naːn^L 'begin'
P9A	LHʔ	LHʔ	LHʔ	LMʔ	LHʔ	LHʔ	LHʔ	Mʔ	LHʔ	LHʔ	M:ʔ	LMʔ	kiáːn^M 'sweep'
P9B	LHʔ	LHʔ	LHʔ	LMʔ	LHʔ	LHʔ	LHʔ	Mʔ	LHʔ	LHʔ	L:ʔ	LMʔ	híːn^L 'argue'
P9C	LHʔ	LHʔ	LHʔ	LMʔ	LHʔ	LHʔ	LHʔ	Mʔ	LHʔ	LHʔ	LH:ʔ	LMʔ	huːˊ^{LH} 'lie', kiáːn^{LH} 'sweep', híːn^{LH} 'argue'
P10	LHʔ	LHʔ	LHʔ	LMʔ	LHʔ	LHʔ	LHʔ	Mʔ	LHʔ	LHʔ	LHʔ	LMʔ	hunʔ^{LH} 'squat down'
P11	LMʔꞌ	LMʔꞌ	LMʔꞌ	LMʔꞌ	LMʔꞌ	LMʔꞌ	LMʔꞌ	LMʔꞌ	LMʔꞌ	LMʔꞌ	LMʔꞌ	LMʔꞌ	huˊnʔ^{LM} 'tire'
PCMA	M	M	M	M	M	M	M	M	M	M	M	M	ʔiuːn^M 'inside'
PCMB	LHʔ	LHʔ	LHʔ	LHʔ	LHʔ	LHʔ	LHʔ	LHʔ	LHʔ	LHʔ	LHʔ	LHʔ	niʔ^{LH} 'open out'
PCMC	LHʔ	LHʔ	LHʔ	LHʔ	LHʔ	LHʔ	LHʔ	LHʔ	LHʔ	LHʔ	LHʔ	LHʔ	ʔíːn^{LH} 'want'
PDCA	DM:	DM:	DM:	DM:	DM:	DM:	DM:	DM:	DM:	DM:	DM:	DM:	hmiːˋʔaːn^M 'hungry'
PDCB	DLMʔꞌ	DLMʔꞌ	DLMʔꞌ	DLMʔꞌ	DLMʔꞌ	DLMʔꞌ	DLMʔꞌ	DLMʔꞌ	DLMʔꞌ	DLMʔꞌ	DLMʔꞌ	DLMʔꞌ	hmiːˋʔínʔ^{LM} 'rest'
PDCC	DHʔ	DHʔ	DHʔ	DHʔ	DHʔ	DHʔ	DHʔ	DHʔ	DHʔ	DHʔ	DHʔ	DHʔ	hmiːˋguänʔ^H 'bless'

(*Source:* Pace 1990: 48–51)

The different variant possibilities within Class C are represented in Table 2.9, with thirteen different conjugations.

We say that the paradigm P of a member of conjugation J is MAXIMALLY TRANSPARENT if each pairing of a property set with an exponent in P is unique across all conjugations to the paradigms of members of J. If lexeme L has a maximally transparent paradigm P, any cell in P can serve as L's sole dynamic principal part.

Fig. 2.1 represents a maximally transparent paradigm having twelve cells. The numbers 1 through 12 in this diagram represent twelve different morphosyntactic property sets; the letters *a* through *l* represent the realizations of those twelve different property sets (so that each vertex in Fig. 2.1 is labeled as a cell); and each of the lines in this diagram represents a relation of bidirectional implication between two cells. In other words, the pairing of a realization with a morphosyntactic property set in every cell implies the pairing of a realization with a morphosyntactic property set in every other cell. If a language user has learned the implicative relations in which a maximally transparent paradigm P_1 participates, then upon learning that the paradigm P_2 of a newly encountered verbal lexeme has a cell analogous to a cell in P_1, the language user can deduce every other cell in P_2. Thus, transparency is associated with the ease with which some of the cells in a paradigm can be deduced from other cells in the same paradigm.

In the inflection of Comaltepec Chinantec verbs, there are (as in Fig. 2.1) twelve different morphosyntactic property sets. In the remainder of the paper,

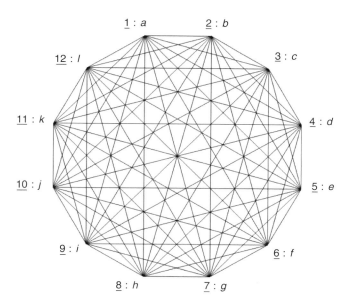

FIGURE 2.1 A maximally transparent paradigm with twelve cells

TABLE 2.10 Abbreviations for the twelve property sets realized by Comaltepec Chinantec verb forms

Abbreviation	Property set	
1	1sg	
2	1pl	Progressive
3	2	
4	3	
5	1sg	
6	1pl	Intentive
7	2	
8	3	
9	1sg	
10	1pl	Completive
11	2	
12	3	

we number these 1 through 12; the significance of these twelve numerals is given in Table 2.10.

The question now arises whether there are any maximally transparent paradigms in Comaltepec Chinantec. That is, are there conjugation classes whose paradigms could be represented as in Fig. 2.1? The answer is yes; in fact there are four such conjugations. One of these is Conjugation PDBB in Table 2.8, whose twelve alternative principal-part analyses are given in Table 2.11.

In Table 2.11, the cells in a lexeme's paradigm are given on the horizontal axis (where 1 through 12 represent the twelve morphosyntactic property sets corresponding to a verbal paradigm's twelve cells), and the different possible principal-part analyses are given on the vertical axis. Thus, each row represents a distinct principal-part analysis, and within a given row, the numeral n (any of the numerals *1* through *12*) represents the morphosyntactic property set of the sole principal part in the principal-part analysis represented by that row. If a principal part P is listed in the column headed by a property set $\underline{M}$ in a given analysis, the realization of $\underline{M}$ is deducible from P in that analysis.

In Conjugation PDBB, any one of the cells in a lexeme's paradigm can be used as that lexeme's sole principal part–can be used, in other words, to deduce the realization of every one of the remaining eleven cells in the paradigm. This fact arises because each of the exponents of property sets 1 through 12 in Conjugation PDBB is unique to that conjugation. Table 2.12 lists the exponents of cells 1 through 12 in Conjugation PDBB; a comparison of these exponents with those given earlier in Tables 2.7-9 reveals that in each one of the twelve cells in the paradigm of a lexeme belonging to this conjugation, the exponence is absolutely distinctive of this conjugation.

TABLE 2.11 The twelve alternative optimal principal-part analyses for Conjugation PDBB in Comaltepec Chinantec

Alternative principal-part analyses	Morphosyntactic property sets											
	1	2	3	4	5	6	7	8	9	10	11	12
1	1	1	1	1	1	1	1	1	1	1	1	1
2	2	2	2	2	2	2	2	2	2	2	2	2
3	3	3	3	3	3	3	3	3	3	3	3	3
4	4	4	4	4	4	4	4	4	4	4	4	4
5	5	5	5	5	5	5	5	5	5	5	5	5
6	6	6	6	6	6	6	6	6	6	6	6	6
7	7	7	7	7	7	7	7	7	7	7	7	7
8	8	8	8	8	8	8	8	8	8	8	8	8
9	9	9	9	9	9	9	9	9	9	9	9	9
10	10	10	10	10	10	10	10	10	10	10	10	10
11	11	11	11	11	11	11	11	11	11	11	11	11
12	12	12	12	12	12	12	12	12	12	12	12	12

TABLE 2.12 The exponence of property sets 1–12 in Conjugation PDBB in Comaltepec Chinantec

Morphosyntactic property sets												
1	2	3	4	5	6	7	8	9	10	11	12	Example
DHL:ˊ	DHL:ˊ	DHL:ˊ	DL:ˊ	DHL:ˊ	DHL:ˊ	DHL:ˊ	DL:ˊ	DHL:ˊ	DHL:ˊ	DHL:ˊ	DL:ˊ	hmïˡ·góːᴴᴸ 'deceive'

Only four conjugations have this property of maximal transparency in Comaltepec Chinantec; that is, most conjugations in this language deviate from maximal transparency. We now consider the consequences of this deviation.

2.4 Deviations from maximal transparency in Comaltepec Chinantec verb paradigms

Although every cell is fully informative in the paradigm of a verb belonging to Conjugation PDBB (and can therefore potentially serve as that verb's sole principal part), this full informativeness is comparatively rare. In the paradigms of most verbs, many cells are to some extent uninformative; that is, they have either a limited capacity or no capacity to serve as optimal principal parts. The system of conjugations in Comaltepec Chinantec exhibits various means of compensating for this less-than-full informativeness of certain cells.

Consider first a case in which a particular cell in a verb's paradigm uniquely determines only one other cell. In the paradigm of a verb belonging to Conjugation P1A, the cell containing the realization of property set 1 (whose exponence is tone M with controlled stress) uniquely determines the cell containing the realization of property set 2 (which has the same exponence), since no matter what the conjugation, the implicative relation in (5) holds true in Comaltepec Chinantec.

(5)

Even so, the cell containing the realization of property set 1 doesn't uniquely determine any of the remaining ten cells in the paradigm of a verb belonging to Conjugation P1A. In order to deduce the latter cells, the cell associated with property set 12 must be appealed to—either by itself or in addition to the cell associated with property set 1, as in Table 2.13. (In this table and those below, if a pair *P, Q* of principal parts is listed in the column headed by a property set M, the realization of M can only be deduced by simultaneous reference to *P* and *Q*.)

As Table 2.13 shows, the uninformativeness of the cell containing the realization of property set 1 in Conjugation P1A makes it necessary to deduce certain cells by simultaneous reference to two principal parts. The cells containing the realizations of property sets 1 and 12 are not, however, the only viable set of principal parts for a verb of this conjugation; another possibility is the set of cells containing the realizations of property sets 3 and 12, as in Table 2.14. Like the analysis in Table 2.13, the analysis in Table 2.14 requires two principal parts for this conjugation; although both analyses are optimal, the latter analysis might be preferred on the grounds that it makes lesser use of simultaneous reference to both principal parts in deducing the various nonprincipal parts.

As Table 2.14 shows, the number of nonprincipal parts that must be deduced by simultaneous reference to both principal parts can be minimized to one in Conjugation P1A. This sort of minimization isn't always possible, however. For

TABLE 2.13 A representative optimal principal-part analysis for Conjugation P1A in Comaltepec Chinantec

Principal parts	Morphosyntactic property sets											
	1	2	3	4	5	6	7	8	9	10	11	12
1,12	*1*	*1*	*1,12*	*1,12*	*1,12*	*1,12*	*1,12*	*1,12*	*12*	*1,12*	*1,12*	*12*

TABLE 2.14 A representative optimal principal-part analysis for Conjugation P1A in Comaltepec Chinantec

Principal parts	Morphosyntactic property sets											
	1	2	3	4	5	6	7	8	9	10	11	12
3,12	3	3	3	3	3	3	3	3	3	3	3,12	12

TABLE 2.15 The sole optimal principal-part analysis for Conjugation P2C in Comaltepec Chinantec

Principal parts	Morphosyntactic property sets											
	1	2	3	4	5	6	7	8	9	10	11	12
11,12	11,12	12	11,12	12	11,12	11,12	11,12	12	11,12	11,12	11	12

TABLE 2.16 The sole optimal principal-part analysis for Conjugation P1B in Comaltepec Chinantec

Principal parts	Morphosyntactic property sets											
	1	2	3	4	5	6	7	8	9	10	11	12
11,12	11	11	11	11	11	11	11	11	11	11	11	12

instance, in the only optimal principal-part analysis for Conjugation P2C, seven of ten nonprincipal parts are deducible only by simultaneous reference to both principal parts; this analysis is given in Table 2.15.

Even so, the need to postulate two principal parts doesn't always entail a need for simultaneous reference to both of the principal parts in deducing one or another nonprincipal part. Consider, for example, Conjugation P1B, whose sole optimal principal-part analysis is given in Table 2.16. In the paradigm of a verb belonging to this conjugation, two principal-part specifications are necessary in order to deduce all of the remaining cells in the paradigm. In the only optimal analysis, the exponents of property sets 1 through 10 can all be deduced from the exponence of property set 11; the cell containing the realization of property set 11 is therefore one of the two principal parts of a verb belonging to this conjugation. The exponence of property set 12, however, cannot be deduced from that of property set 11, nor from that of any of the other property sets, and so must be independently specified. So here we have a conjugation that must have two principal parts, but no cell of which must be deduced by simultaneous reference to both principal parts.

TABLE 2.17 A representative optimal principal-part analysis for Conjugation P2F in Comaltepec Chinantec

Principal parts	Morphosyntactic property sets											
	1	2	3	4	5	6	7	8	9	10	11	12
1,11,12	1	1	1	1	1	1	1	1	1	1	11	12

TABLE 2.18 The sole optimal principal-part analysis for Conjugation P3E in Comaltepec Chinantec

Principal parts	Morphosyntactic property sets											
	1	2	3	4	5	6	7	8	9	10	11	12
9,10,11,12	10	10	12	12	10	10	10	12	9	10	11	12

Another example of the same type is Conjugation P2F, which involves three principal parts. In the representative principal-part analysis proposed in Table 2.17, the principal parts of a verb belonging to Conjugation P2F are the realizations associated with property sets 1, 11, and 12.

In Conjugation P3E, four principal parts are necessary. Table 2.18 represents the sole optimal principal-part analysis for this conjugation: The principal parts are the realizations of property sets 9, 10, 11, and 12.

In the deviations from maximal transparency that we have considered so far, the uninformativeness of certain realizations has forced us to postulate two or more principal parts; some but not all of these analyses involve deducing certain nonprincipal parts by simultaneous reference to more than one principal part. But uninformativeness needn't always lead to the postulation of more than one principal part. In some instances, it simply imposes limits on the range of alternative analyses.

For instance, a single principal part can be postulated for a verb belonging to Conjugation P16B, but there are only six cells in the paradigm of such a verb that can possibly serve as this sole principal part, namely the cells associated with property sets 3, 4, 7, 8, 11, and 12. The realizations in such a verb's paradigm can be deduced from any one of these cells but not from any other. Thus, a verb belonging to Conjugation P16B has the six alternative principal-part analyses represented in Table 2.19, but the realizations of property sets 1, 2, 5, 6, 9, and 10 in its paradigm are uninformative in any optimal principal-part analysis.

Conjugation P12A exhibits an even more severe restriction on the range of alternative analyses. In the paradigm of a verb belonging to this conjugation,

TABLE 2.19 The six optimal principal-part analyses for Conjugation P16B in Comaltepec Chinantec

Alternative principal-part analyses	Morphosyntactic property sets											
	1	2	3	4	5	6	7	8	9	10	11	12
3	3	3	3	3	3	3	3	3	3	3	3	3
4	4	4	4	4	4	4	4	4	4	4	4	4
7	7	7	7	7	7	7	7	7	7	7	7	7
8	8	8	8	8	8	8	8	8	8	8	8	8
11	11	11	11	11	11	11	11	11	11	11	11	11
12	12	12	12	12	12	12	12	12	12	12	12	12

TABLE 2.20 The sole optimal principal-part analysis for Conjugation P12A in Comaltepec Chinantec

Principal part	Morphosyntactic property sets											
	1	2	3	4	5	6	7	8	9	10	11	12
12	12	12	12	12	12	12	12	12	12	12	12	12

only one cell (namely the cell associated with property set 12) can serve as the verb's sole principal part; the other eleven cannot. That is, the remaining realizations in such a verb's paradigm can be deduced from the cell containing the realization of property set 12 but not from any other cell. Thus, Conjugation P12A has the sole optimal principal-part analysis in Table 2.20; in this respect, it contrasts starkly with Conjugation PDBB (Table 2.11), any one of whose twelve cells may serve as its sole principal part.

The examples presented here show that the uninformativeness of one or more cells in a lexeme's paradigm may have either or both of two effects on the principal-part analysis of that lexeme: (i) it may necessitate the postulation of more than one principal part for that lexeme; and (ii) it may limit the number of alternative optimal principal-part analyses to which that lexeme is subject. These effects therefore imply two practical criteria for paradigmatic transparency:

(6) Two practical criteria for paradigmatic transparency
    All else being equal,
    a. fewer dynamic principal parts needed to deduce a lexeme's paradigm in an optimal analysis implies greater transparency of that paradigm;

    b.   more alternative optimal principal-part analyses of a lexeme's para-
        digm implies greater transparency of that paradigm.

The transparency of Comaltepec Chinantec paradigms varies widely according to both of the criteria in (6), as we now show. Consider first Table 2.21,
which relates to criterion (6a). As Table 2.21 shows, many of the conjugations
involve paradigms that can be deduced from a single dynamic principal part;
even more, however, have paradigms requiring two dynamic principal parts,
and some require as many as three or even four dynamic principal parts. Thus,
the successive rows in Table 2.21 represent decreasing levels of transparency
according to criterion (6a).

Conjugations whose optimal analysis requires the same number of principal parts may nevertheless vary in the extent to which they require simultaneous reference to more than one principal part in deducing a cell's realization.
Table 2.22 shows the average number of principal parts needed to deduce a
cell's realization in each conjugation in Comaltepec Chinantec. The conjugation classes in rows A through D house verbs each of whose realizations can
always be deduced by reference to a single principal part; those in the
succeeding rows house verbs whose realizations must–to a progressively
greater degree–be deduced through simultaneous reference to more than
one principal part.

Table 2.23 relates to criterion (6b). Here the different conjugations are
arranged according to the number of optimal principal-part analyses that

TABLE 2.21 Numbers of dynamic principal parts for Comaltepec Chinantec
conjugation classes

Comaltepec Chinantec conjugation classes	Number of dynamic principal parts needed to identify a particular inflection class
P3A, P10, P11, P12A, P14A, P15A, P15B, P16A, P16B, P16C, PCMA, PCMB, PCMC, PDBA, PDBB, PDBC, PDBD, PDCA, PDCB, PDCC	1
P1A, P1B, P1D, P1E, P2A, P2B, P2C, P2D, P2E, P2G, P3C, P3F, P3H, P3I, P3J, P3K, P3L, P4A, P4B, P4C, P5A, P5B, P6A, P6B, P6C, P7A, P7B, P7C, P7D, P7E, P7F, P8A, P8B, P9A, P9B, P12B, P12C, P13A, P13B, P14B	2
P1C, P2F, P3D, P3G, P9C	3
P3B, P3E	4

TABLE 2.22 Average number of principal parts needed to identify a cell in Comaltepec Chinantec

Comaltepec Chinantec conjugation classes		Number of dynamic principal parts needed to deduce a lexeme's paradigm	Average number of principal parts needed to deduce a cell in a lexeme's paradigm
A.	P3A, P10, P11, P12A, P14A, P15A, P15B, P16A, P16B, P16C, PCMA, PCMB, PCMC, PDBA, PDBB, PDBC, PDBD, PDCA, PDCB, PDCC	1	1.00
B.	P1B, P1D, P1E, P3H, P3I, P3J, P3K, P3L, P4A, P4B, P4C, P6A, P6B, P6C, P7A, P7B, P7C, P7D, P7E, P7F, P8A, P8B, P9B, P13A	2	1.00
C.	P1C, P2F, P3D, P9C	3	1.00
D.	P3B, P3E	4	1.00
E.	P1A, P2A, P2B, P2D, P12B, P12C, P13B	2	1.08
F.	P3F, P9A	2	1.25
G.	P3G	3	1.25
H.	P5B	2	1.33
I.	P3C, P14B	2	1.42
J.	P2C, P2E	2	1.58
K.	P5A	2	1.67
L.	P2G	2	1.75

they afford. The conjugation allowing the largest number of optimal principal-part analyses is P9C, which allows twenty optimal analyses; but succeeding rows show conjugations allowing fewer analyses, with the bottom rows showing conjugations allowing only a single optimal principal-part analysis. Thus, by criterion (6b), Table 2.23 lists conjugation classes in decreasing order of paradigmatic transparency.

The application of criterion (6b) is complicated, however, by the fact that a paradigm is open to more alternative principal-part analyses the more principal parts it has. Thus, (6b) should be interpreted as meaning that the larger the number of principal-part analyses a conjugation has, the more transparent its paradigms are in comparison with those of other conjugations having the same number of principal parts. Where lexeme L has k principal parts and n is the number of morphosyntactic property sets for

TABLE 2.23 Numbers of optimal principal-part analyses for Comaltepec Chinantec conjugations

Conjugation	Number of principal parts	Number of optimal principal-part analyses
P9C	3	20
P12C	2	17
P14B	2	16
P3B	4	16
PDBB, PDBD, PDCB, PDCC	1	12
P11	1	11
P2A, P6A	2	11
P6B	2	10
PCMA	1	9
P7A, P7C, P7F, P12B	2	9
P6C, P13B	2	8
P15A	1	7
P1A, P5B, P7D, P8A, P9B, P13A	2	7
P1C, P2F	3	7
P16A, P16B, P16C, PDCA	1	6
P1E, P2B, P7B, P7E, P8B, P9A	2	6
P15B	1	5
P2D	2	5
P3C, P4A, P4C	2	4
PCMB, PCMC, PDBA, PDBC	1	3
P4B	2	2
P3A, P10, P12A, P14A	1	1
P1B, P1D, P2C, P2E, P2G, P3F, P3H, P3I, P3J, P3K, P3L, P5A	2	1
P3D, P3G	3	1
P3E	4	1

which L inflects, the largest possible number of optimal principal-part analyses for L is the binomial coefficient of n and k, i.e. $n!/(k!(n-k)!)$. The maximum possible number of optimal principal-part analyses for a Comaltepec Chinantec verb varies according to the number of principal parts it has, as in Table 2.24. Although the paradigm of a lexeme belonging to Conjugation P9C has the twenty alternative optimal principal-part analyses in Table 2.25, this paradigm is not all that transparent, since it has three principal parts, and is therefore far below the ceiling of 220 optimal analyses that a lexeme with three principal parts could imaginably have.

TABLE 2.24 Maximum possible number of optimal principal-part analyses for Comaltepec Chinantec verbs

Number (k) of principal parts	Maximum possible number $12!/(k!(12-k)!)$ of optimal principal-part analyses
1	12
2	66
3	220
4	495

TABLE 2.25 The twenty alternative optimal principal-part analyses for Conjugation P9C in Comaltepec Chinantec

Alternative principal-part analyses	Morphosyntactic property sets											
	1	2	3	4	5	6	7	8	9	10	11	12
1,4,11	1	1	1	4	1	1	1	4	1	1	11	4
1,8,11	1	1	1	1,8	1	1	1	8	1	1	11	1,8
1,11,12	1	1	1	12	1	1	1	12	1	1	11	12
2,4,11	2	2	2	4	2	2	2	4	2	2	11	4
2,8,11	2	2	2	2,8	2	2	2	8	2	2	11	2,8
2,11,12	2	2	2	12	2	2	2	12	2	2	11	12
3,4,11	3	3	3	4	3	3	3	4	3	3	11	4
3,8,11	3	3	3	3,8	3	3	3	8	3	3	11	3,8
3,11,12	3	3	3	12	3	3	3	12	3	3	11	12
4,5,11	4,5	4,5	4,5	4	5	4,5	4,5	4	4,5	4	11	4
4,6,11	6	6	6	4	6	6	6	4	6	4	11	4
4,7,11	7	7	7	4	7	7	7	4	7	4	11	4
4,9,11	9	9	9	4	9	9	9	4	9	4	11	4
5,11,12	5,12	5,12	5,12	12	5	5,12	5,12	12	5,12	12	11	12
6,8,11	6	6	6	6,8	6	6	6	8	6	6	11	6,8
6,11,12	6	6	6	12	6	6	6	12	6	6	11	12
7,8,11	7	7	7	7,8	7	7	7	8	7	7	11	7,8
7,11,12	7	7	7	12	7	7	7	12	7	7	11	12
8,9,11	9	9	9	8,9	9	9	9	8	9	9	11	8,9
9,11,12	9	9	9	12	9	9	9	12	9	9	11	12

By the criteria in (6), Comaltepec Chinantec verb conjugations exhibit widely varying degrees of paradigmatic transparency. At the high extreme, that of total paradigmatic transparency, are the conjugations in (7a): lexemes in these conjugations exhibit only a single principal part and allow the maximum number of alternative optimal principal-part analyses. At the opposite extreme is the conjugation in (7b): lexemes in Conjugation P3E have four principal parts and allow only a single optimal principal-part analysis. Between these extremes, other lexemes exhibit a range of intermediate degrees of paradigmatic transparency.

(7)   Extreme degrees of paradigmatic transparency in Comaltepec Chinantec
      a.   High: PDBB, PDBD, PDCB, PDCC   b.   Low: P3E

2.5 A measure of paradigmatic transparency

Although the practical criteria in (6) are useful for distinguishing degrees of paradigmatic transparency, we would like to give more explicit content to the notion of paradigmatic transparency than these criteria allow. We therefore propose a precise measure of paradigmatic transparency; we call this measure PARADIGM PREDICTABILITY. The fundamental idea underlying this proposed measure is that where (i) M is the set of morphosyntactic property sets associated with the cells in the paradigm P_L of some lexeme L and (ii) M' is the set $\{N: N \subseteq M$ and the exponence in P_L of the morphosyntactic property sets belonging to N suffices to determine the exponence in P_L of every morphosyntactic property set belonging to $M\}$, L's paradigm predictability PP_L is calculated as in (8). In effect, this measure calculates the fraction of the members of M's power set $\mathscr{P}(M)$ that are viable (though not necessarily optimal) sets of dynamic principal parts for L.

(8) $\text{PP}_L = \dfrac{|M'|}{|\mathscr{P}(M)|}$

We refine this measure of paradigm predictability in two ways. First, the set M sometimes contains multiple morphosyntactic property sets whose exponence is the same across all inflection classes. We propose to eliminate all but one of these sets from M for purposes of calculating paradigm predictability. To understand why, consider the two hypothetical inflection-class systems in (9), in which I through IV represent inflection classes; s_1 through s_3 represent morphosyntactic property sets; and **a** through **c** represent inflectional exponents.

(9) System (9a)   System (9b)

	s_1	s_2	s_3			s_1	s_2
I	a	b	b		I	a	b
II	a	c	c		II	a	c
III	b	b	b		III	b	b
IV	c	c	c		IV	c	c

If paradigm predictability is calculated as in (8), then lexemes belonging to inflection class I in system (9a) have greater paradigm predictability than lexemes belonging to inflection class I in system (9b): the former have a predictability of 3/8 ($M = \{s_1, s_2, s_3\}$, M' has three members $\{s_1, s_2\}$, $\{s_1, s_3\}$, $\{s_1, s_2, s_3\}$, and $\mathcal{P}(M)$ has eight), while the latter have a predictability of 1/4 ($M = \{s_1, s_2\}$, M' has one member $\{s_1, s_2\}$, and $\mathcal{P}(M)$ has four). We prefer to think of lexemes in these systems as having the same predictability, namely 1/4. To accommodate this preference, we let M_- be a maximal subset of M such that no two of members of M_- are identical in their exponence across all conjugations. (If the property sets in M are ordered, M_- is the result of removing from M every property set s_n such that for some s_m in M, (a) $s_m < s_n$ and (b) s_m and s_n have the same exponence across all conjugations.) Accordingly, M'_- is the set $\{N: N \subseteq M_-$ and the exponence in P_L of the morphosyntactic property sets belonging to N suffices to determine the exponence in P_L of every morphosyntactic property set belonging to $M_-\}$, and L's paradigm predictability PP_L is calculated as in (10) rather than as in (8).

$$(10) \quad PP_L = \frac{|M'_-|}{|\mathcal{P}(M_-)|}$$

The second refinement in the calculation of paradigm predictability stems from the fact that where N is a large subset of M_-, the exponence in P_L of the morphosyntactic property sets belonging to N is generally very likely to determine the exponence in P_L of every morphosyntactic property set belonging to M_-. That is, the subsets of M_- that are best for distinguishing degrees of paradigm predictability tend to be the smaller subsets of M_-. We have therefore chosen–somewhat arbitrarily–to base our calculation of paradigm predictability on subsets of M_- having no more than seven members. For any set S of sets, we use $\leq_7 S$ to represent the largest subset of S such that for every $s \in \leq_7 S$, $|s| \leq 7$. We accordingly calculate L's paradigm predictability PP_L as in (11) rather than as in (10).

(11) $\mathrm{PP}_L = \dfrac{|_{\leq 7} M'_-|}{|_{\leq 7}\mathscr{P}(M_-)|}$

This measure of paradigm predictability accounts for both of the practical criteria in (6). Consider first criterion (6a), which associates a smaller number of dynamic principal parts with greater paradigmatic transparency. By this criterion, Conjugation P3A exhibits greater paradigmatic transparency than Conjugation P3J, since the only optimal analysis of Conjugation P3A involves a single principal part (Table 2.26), while the only optimal analysis for Conjugation P3J involves two principal parts (Table 2.27). This difference reflects a measurable contrast in the paradigm predictability of the two conjugations: the predictability of a member of Conjugation P3A is 0.450, while that of a member of P3J is merely 0.193.

Consider now criterion (6b), which associates greater paradigmatic transparency with a greater number of alternative inflection-class analyses. By this criterion, Conjugation PDBB exhibits greater paradigmatic transparency than Conjugation P3A, since the former allows the twelve optimal principal-part analyses in Table 2.11, while the latter only allows the single optimal principal-part analysis in Table 2.26. This difference reflects a measurable contrast in the paradigm predictability of these two conjugations: the predictability of a member of Conjugation PDBB is 1.000, while the predictability of a member of P3A is merely 0.450.

Applying the measure of paradigm predictability to all of the conjugations in Comaltepec Chinantec yields the results in Table 2.28 (represented

TABLE 2.26 The sole optimal principal-part analysis for Conjugation P3A in Comaltepec Chinantec

Principal part	Morphosyntactic property sets											
	1	2	3	4	5	6	7	8	9	10	11	12
11	*11*	*11*	*11*	*11*	*11*	*11*	*11*	*11*	*11*	*11*	*11*	*11*

TABLE 2.27 The sole optimal principal-part analysis for Conjugation P3J in Comaltepec Chinantec

Principal part	Morphosyntactic property sets											
	1	2	3	4	5	6	7	8	9	10	11	12
9,11	*9*	*9*	*9*	*9*	*9*	*9*	*9*	*9*	*9*	*9*	*11*	*9*

TABLE 2.28 Paradigm predictability across conjugations in Comaltepec Chinantec

Conjugations	Paradigm predictability
A. PDBB, PDBD, PDCB, PDCC	1.000
P11	0.999
PCMA	0.998
P15A	0.994
P16A, P16B, P16C, PDCA	0.981
P15B	0.980
P14B	0.868
P14A	0.855
PDBA, PDBC, PCMB, PCMC	0.848
P10	0.846
P12C	0.704
P12A	0.687
P12B	0.681
P13A	0.674
P13B	0.649
B. P2A, P3A, P6A	0.450
P6B, P7A, P7C, P7F	0.449
P6C	0.448
P1E	0.447
P5B	0.446
P1A, P2B, P7B, P7D, P7E, P8A, P8B, P9A, P9B	0.445
P2D	0.443
P3C, P4A, P4C	0.412
P4B	0.411
P5A	0.407
P9C	0.371
C. P1B, P1D, P2C, P2E, P2G, P3F, P3H, P3I, P3J, P3K, P3L	0.193
P1C, P2F	0.191
P3B	0.156
D. P3D, P3G	0.078
E. P3E	0.028

graphically in Table 2.28a). Close inspection reveals four points at which the gradient of paradigm predictability in Table 2.28 breaks sharply; these breaks are the boundaries between parts A through E of the table. We believe that these breaks are best understood with respect to a second measure pertinent to paradigmatic transparency. CELL PREDICTABILITY measures the predictability of a cell's realization from the realization of the other cells in its paradigm (whether or not these are optimal principal parts).

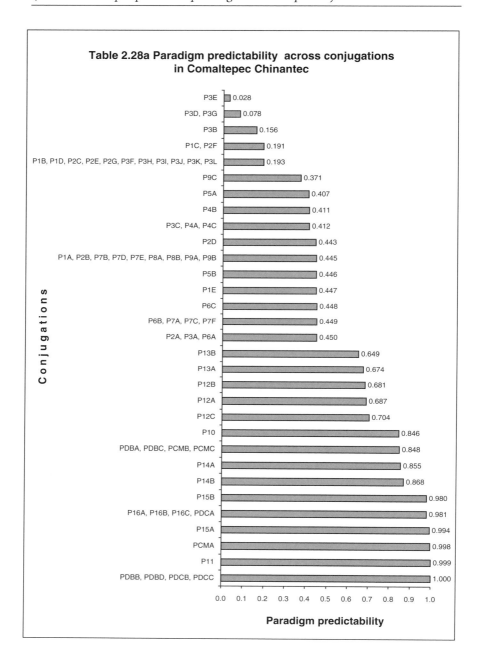

Table 2.28a Paradigm predictability across conjugations in Comaltepec Chinantec

The fundamental idea underlying our proposed measure of cell predictability is that where (i) M is the set of morphosyntactic property sets associated with the cells in the paradigm P_L of some lexeme L and (ii) M_s is the set $\{N: N \subseteq M_-$ and the exponence in P_L of the morphosyntactic property sets belonging to N suffices to determine the exponence in P_L of the property set $s\}$, the cell predictability $\text{CP}_{s,L}$ of s in P_L is calculated as in (12).

$$(12) \quad \text{CP}_{s,L} = \frac{|\leq_7 M_s|}{|\leq_7 \mathcal{P}(M_-)|}$$

Here, too, a refinement must be made. Because the exponence of property set s always suffices to determine itself, the inclusion of s in M_s invariably enhances cell predictability, thereby diminishing distinctions in cell predictability. We therefore exclude s from M_s in calculating cell predictability. For any collection C of sets, we use $C_{[s]}$ to represent the largest subset of C such that no member of $C_{[s]}$ contains s. Cell predictability is then calculated as in (13).

$$(13) \quad \text{CP}_{s,L} = \frac{|\leq_7 M_{s[s]}|}{\left|\leq_7 \mathcal{P}(M_-)_{[s]}\right|}$$

By this measure, the cells in the paradigms of Comaltepec Chinantec verbs have the cell predictability in Table 2.29; average cell predictability and paradigm predictability are listed in the table's rightmost two columns. The measure of cell predictability shows that the major breaks in the gradient of paradigm predictability correspond to the appearance of an unpredictable cell (i.e. one whose cell predictability is 0). The conjugations in part A of Table 2.28 have no unpredictable cells; those in part B have one unpredictable cell; those in part C have two unpredictable cells; and so on. (The cell predictability measures of unpredictable cells are shaded in Table 2.29.) Thus, the cell predictability measure reveals an important fact about paradigmatic transparency: Cell unpredictability degrades paradigm predictability. Inevitably, an unpredictable cell must be a principal part. (Table 2.29 is represented graphically in Fig. 2.2, in which morphosyntactic property sets are listed on the horizontal axis, conjugations are listed on the vertical axis (in order of decreasing paradigm predictability), and the lightness of a cell's shading represents its degree of cell predictability.)

2.6 Paradigmatic transparency and the No-Blur Principle

There can be no doubt that paradigmatic transparency helps the language user, both in the domain of language learning and in that of lexical storage.

TABLE 2.29 Cell predictability in all conjugations in Comaltepec Chinantec

Conj	1	2	3	4	5	6	7	8	9	10	11	12	Avg cell predictability	Paradigm predictability
PDBB, PDBD, PDCB, PDCC	0.999	0.999	0.999	0.999	0.999	0.999	0.999	0.999	0.999	0.999	0.999	0.999	0.999	1.000
P11	0.999	0.999	0.999	0.999	0.999	0.999	0.999	0.999	0.999	0.999	0.999	0.999	0.999	0.999
PCMA	0.999	0.999	0.997	0.997	0.997	0.997	0.997	0.997	0.997	0.997	0.998	0.999	0.998	0.998
P15A	0.989	0.989	0.989	0.989	0.989	0.989	0.989	0.991	0.998	0.997	0.998	0.997	0.991	0.994
P16A, P16C	0.999	0.965	0.965	0.999	0.999	0.965	0.965	0.999	0.999	0.965	0.965	0.965	0.982	0.981
P16B, PDCA	0.999	0.999	0.965	0.965	0.999	0.999	0.965	0.965	0.999	0.999	0.965	0.999	0.982	0.981
P15B	0.964	0.964	0.964	0.964	0.997	0.997	0.964	0.965	0.999	0.997	0.989	0.990	0.979	0.980
P14B	0.892	0.892	0.892	0.892	0.974	0.974	0.974	0.991	0.859	0.857	0.798	0.798	0.900	0.868
P14A	0.990	0.990	0.990	0.990	0.860	0.860	0.860	0.998	0.858	0.737	0.807	0.859	0.900	0.855
PDBA, PDBC, PCMB	0.999	0.999	0.999	0.724	0.999	0.999	0.999	0.724	0.999	0.999	0.999	0.724	0.930	0.848
PCMC	0.997	0.997	0.997	0.724	0.998	0.997	0.997	0.724	0.997	0.998	0.860	0.724	0.917	0.848
P10	0.996	0.996	0.996	0.724	0.996	0.996	0.996	0.720	0.996	0.996	0.998	0.724	0.927	0.846
P12C	0.956	0.963	0.960	0.954	0.987	0.987	0.987	0.987	0.987	0.980	0.466	0.461	0.890	0.704
P12A	0.926	0.930	0.928	0.925	0.991	0.991	0.991	0.991	0.989	0.986	0.467	0.432	0.879	0.687
P12B	0.914	0.928	0.927	0.913	0.979	0.979	0.979	0.979	0.989	0.973	0.428	0.463	0.871	0.681
P13A	0.965	0.965	0.961	0.961	0.930	0.930	0.896	0.961	0.982	0.930	0.432	0.467	0.865	0.674
P13B	0.991	0.991	0.983	0.983	0.860	0.860	0.852	0.983	0.930	0.860	0.432	0.463	0.849	0.649
P2A	0.979	0.990	0.982	0.986	0.980	0.986	0.979	0.993	0.988	0.985	0.000	0.466	0.859	0.450
P3A	0.999	0.999	0.930	0.930	0.930	0.930	0.930	0.930	0.467	0.467	0.000	0.467	0.748	0.450
P6A	0.994	0.994	0.994	0.994	0.997	0.998	0.998	0.994	0.994	0.994	0.000	0.995	0.912	0.450
P6B	0.994	0.994	0.994	0.994	0.996	0.998	0.997	0.994	0.994	0.994	0.000	0.994	0.912	0.449
P7A	0.988	0.988	0.988	0.995	0.988	0.988	0.988	0.998	0.990	0.996	0.000	0.995	0.908	0.449
P7C	0.988	0.988	0.988	0.995	0.988	0.988	0.988	0.997	0.990	0.996	0.000	0.995	0.908	0.449
P7F	0.988	0.988	0.988	0.995	0.988	0.988	0.988	0.998	0.991	0.996	0.000	0.995	0.908	0.449
P6C	0.991	0.991	0.991	0.991	0.995	0.998	0.998	0.991	0.991	0.991	0.000	0.991	0.910	0.448
P1E	0.983	0.983	0.981	0.981	0.981	0.994	0.987	0.989	0.989	0.991	0.000	0.461	0.860	0.447
P5B	0.982	0.982	0.982	0.982	0.917	0.929	0.927	0.982	0.965	0.921	0.000	0.970	0.878	0.446
P1A	0.976	0.976	0.974	0.974	0.974	0.993	0.980	0.988	0.989	0.992	0.458	0.000	0.856	0.445

P2B	0.970	0.988	0.972	0.985	0.971	0.976	0.970	0.993	0.980	0.976	0.000	0.465	0.854	0.445
P7B	0.980	0.980	0.980	0.995	0.980	0.980	0.980	0.997	0.982	0.996	0.000	0.995	0.904	0.445
P7D	0.981	0.981	0.981	0.997	0.981	0.981	0.981	0.998	0.982	0.998	0.000	0.997	0.905	0.445
P7E	0.980	0.980	0.980	0.994	0.980	0.980	0.980	0.997	0.982	0.996	0.000	0.994	0.904	0.445
P8A	0.982	0.998	0.981	0.996	0.981	0.981	0.981	0.998	0.981	0.981	0.000	0.993	0.905	0.445
P8B	0.982	0.998	0.980	0.994	0.980	0.980	0.980	0.996	0.980	0.980	0.000	0.992	0.904	0.445
P9A	0.980	0.980	0.980	0.856	0.982	0.980	0.980	0.859	0.980	0.996	0.000	0.856	0.869	0.445
P9B	0.981	0.981	0.981	0.858	0.982	0.981	0.981	0.860	0.981	0.998	0.000	0.858	0.870	0.445
P2D	0.967	0.988	0.972	0.981	0.968	0.974	0.967	0.989	0.980	0.973	0.000	0.461	0.852	0.443
P3C	0.998	0.998	0.860	0.860	0.929	0.929	0.929	0.860	0.466	0.466	0.000	0.397	0.724	0.412
P4A	0.996	0.996	0.857	0.858	0.988	0.988	0.988	0.858	0.928	0.958	0.000	0.858	0.856	0.412
P4C	0.996	0.996	0.857	0.858	0.993	0.993	0.993	0.858	0.928	0.962	0.000	0.858	0.858	0.412
P4B	0.994	0.994	0.855	0.858	0.991	0.991	0.991	0.856	0.961	0.960	0.000	0.858	0.859	0.411
P5A	0.980	0.980	0.980	0.980	0.844	0.860	0.858	0.980	0.963	0.856	0.000	0.972	0.854	0.407
P9C	0.980	0.980	0.980	0.721	0.982	0.980	0.980	0.724	0.980	0.996	0.000	0.721	0.835	0.371
P1B	0.985	0.985	0.983	0.983	0.983	0.996	0.989	0.989	0.989	0.994	0.000	0.000	0.823	0.193
P1D	0.989	0.989	0.987	0.987	0.987	0.996	0.990	0.993	0.993	0.994	0.000	0.000	0.826	0.193
P2C	0.972	0.986	0.979	0.980	0.975	0.980	0.972	0.988	0.986	0.979	0.000	0.000	0.816	0.193
P2E	0.976	0.987	0.979	0.983	0.979	0.983	0.976	0.992	0.986	0.982	0.000	0.000	0.819	0.193
P2G	0.969	0.978	0.975	0.971	0.971	0.982	0.969	0.988	0.991	0.981	0.000	0.000	0.814	0.193
P3F	0.998	0.998	0.858	0.858	0.930	0.930	0.930	0.858	0.467	0.467	0.000	0.688	0.691	0.193
P3H	0.999	0.999	0.930	0.930	0.930	0.930	0.930	0.930	0.000	0.688	0.000	0.467	0.746	0.193
P3I	0.999	0.999	0.930	0.930	0.965	0.965	0.965	0.930	0.000	0.724	0.000	0.467	0.739	0.193
P3J	0.999	0.999	0.964	0.964	0.964	0.964	0.964	0.964	0.467	0.467	0.000	0.000	0.726	0.193
P3K	0.998	0.998	0.964	0.964	0.929	0.929	0.929	0.964	0.724	0.000	0.467	0.000	0.718	0.193
P3L	0.997	0.997	0.963	0.963	0.929	0.929	0.929	0.963	0.980	0.000	0.467	0.000	0.738	0.193
P1C	0.976	0.976	0.974	0.974	0.974	0.994	0.988	0.980	0.990	0.993	0.000	0.000	0.817	0.191
P2F	0.960	0.977	0.974	0.963	0.963	0.974	0.960	0.980	0.000	0.973	0.000	0.000	0.810	0.191
P3B	0.999	0.999	0.860	0.860	0.860	0.860	0.860	0.860	0.000	0.397	0.000	0.397	0.662	0.156
P3D	0.999	0.999	0.860	0.860	0.930	0.930	0.930	0.860	0.467	0.467	0.000	0.000	0.653	0.078
P3G	0.997	0.997	0.928	0.928	0.929	0.929	0.929	0.928	0.000	0.000	0.000	0.000	0.669	0.078
P3E	0.998	0.998	0.929	0.929	0.929	0.929	0.929	0.929	0.000	0.000	0.000	0.000	0.631	0.028

Figure 2.2 Cell predictability in all conjugations in Comaltepec Chinantec

Nevertheless, the facts presented above raise doubts about the extent to which paradigmatic transparency is necessary in human language. In particular, they cast doubt on the No-Blur Principle, a hypothesis which portrays the avoidance of paradigmatic opacity as a structural principle of natural language.

Cameron-Faulkner and Carstairs-McCarthy (2000: 816) formulate the No-Blur Principle as in (14).

(14)   The No-Blur Principle

Among the rival affixes for any inflectional cell, at most one affix may fail to be a class-identifier, in which case that one affix is the class-default for that cell.

This principle entails that all of the affixal exponents for the inflection of lexemes belonging to a particular category fall into two classes: class-identifiers and class-defaults.

(15)   a.   A CLASS-IDENTIFYING affix is one that is peculiar to one inflection class, so that it can be taken as diagnostic of membership in that class.

      b.   A CLASS-DEFAULT affix is one that is shared by more than one inflection class, and all of whose rivals (if any) are class-identifiers.

(Cameron-Faulkner and Carstairs-McCarthy 2000: 815)

If all affixes have to be either class-identifiers or class-defaults (as the No-Blur Principle assumes), then any lexeme that ever inflects by means of a class-identifier needs only one principal part: the word containing that class-identifier suffices to indicate which inflection class the lexeme belongs to. The only situation in which this won't hold true is one in which none of the words in a lexeme's paradigm contains a class-identifier; in that case, the lexeme's words must inflect entirely by means of class-default affixes. But if at most one affix per cell may fail to be a class-identifier, then there can only be one inflection class whose inflection is based entirely on class-default affixes. This, therefore, is the only inflection class whose members could have more than one principal part. That is, the No-Blur Principle has the entailment in (16):

(16)   Of all the inflection classes for lexemes of a given syntactic category, at most one requires more than one principal part.

The No-Blur Principle is apparently disconfirmed by Comaltepec Chinantec; but Cameron-Faulkner and Carstairs-McCarthy assume that the No-Blur Principle only relates to affixal exponence, and in Comaltepec Chinantec,

TABLE 2.30 Affixal and nonaffixal exponents of Fur conjugations

Conj	Examples[1]	Nonthird person — Subj	Perf	Pres	Singular — Subj	Perf	Pres	Plural Nonhuman — Subj	Perf	Pres	Plural Human — Subj	Perf	Pres
I,1a	buuN 'descend'	LH-o	LH-ò	LH-èl	HH-o	HH-ò	HH-èl	HH-òl	HH-ùl	HH-èl-à/-ì	LH-òl	LH-ùl	LH-èl-à/-ì
I,1b	jaan 'wait'	LH-o	LH-ò	LF-Ø	HH-o	HH-ò	HF-Ø	HH-òl	HH-ùl	HH-è	LH-òl	LH-ùl	LH-è
I,1c	irt 'shake'	LH-o	LH-ò	LH-ì	HH-o	HH-ò	HH-ì	HH-òl	HH-ùl	HH-è	LH-òl	LH-ùl	LH-è
I,2a	tall 'chew'	HH-ò	HH-o	HH-èl	LL-o	LL-ò	LL-èl	LL-òl	LL-ùl	LL-èl-à/-ì	HH-òl	HH-ùl	HH-èl-à/-ì
I,2b	fuul 'spin'	HH-ò	HH-o	HF-Ø	LL-o	LL-ò	LL-Ø	LL-òl	LL-ùl	LL-è	HH-òl	HH-ùl	HH-è
I,2c	kir 'cook'	HH-ò	HH-o	HH-ì	LL-o	LL-ò	LL-ì	LL-òl	LL-ùl	LL-è	HH-òl	HH-ùl	HH-è
II,1a	rii 'snatch'	LH-i	LH-i	LH-iti	HH-i	HH-i	HH-iti	HH-i-A(l)	HH-i-è	HH-iti-A(l)	LH-i-A(l)	LH-i-è	LH-iti-A(l)
II,1b	tiir 'meet'	LH-i	LH-i	LF-Ø	HH-i	HH-i	HF-Ø	HH-i-A(l)	HH-i-è	HH-è	LH-i-A(l)	LH-i-è	LH-è
II,2a	*faul 'open'	HH-ì	HH-ì	HH-iti	LL-i	LL-i	LL-iti	LL-i-A(l)	LL-i-è	LL-iti-A(l)	HH-i-A(l)	HH-i-è	HH-iti-A(l)
II,2b	*kaun 'grind'	HH-ì	HH-ì	HF-Ø	LL-i	LL-i	LF-Ø	LL-i-A(l)	LL-i-è	LL-è	HH-i-A(l)	HH-i-è	HH-è
IIIa	arr 'measure'	HH-ì	HH-à	HH-èl	LH-ì	LH-à	LH-èl	LH-è	LH-e	LH-èl-à	HH-è	HH-e	HH-èl-à
IIIb	awi 'pound'	HH-ò	HH-ò	HH-èl	LH-ò	LH-ò	LH-èl	LH-è	LH-e	LH-èl-à	HH-è	HH-e	HH-èl-à
IIIc	dus 'tear' (tr)	HH-Ø	HH-ò	HH-èl	LF-Ø	LH-ò	LH-èl	LH-è	LH-e	LH-èl-à	HH-è	HH-e	HH-èl-à
IIId	*kair 'stop' (itr)	HF-Ø	HH-à	HH-èl	LF-Ø	LH-à	LH-èl	LH-è	LH-e	LH-èl-à	HH-è	HH-e	HH-èl-à
IIIe	*tai 'hold, seize'	HF-Ø	HH-à	HH-èl	LF-Ø	LH-ò	LH-èl	LH-è	LH-e	LH-èl-à	HH-è	HH-e	HH-èl-à
IVa	jum 'cover'	HF-Ø	HH-ò	HH-èl	LF-Ø	LH-ò	LH-èl	LH-Al	LH-e	LH-èl-à	HH-Al	HH-e	HH-èl-à
IVb	bul 'find'	HH-ò	HH-ò	HH-èl	LH-ò	LH-ò	LH-èl	LH-Al	LH-e	LH-èl-à	HH-Al	HH-e	HH-èl-à
IVc	juuN 'terrify'	HF-Ø	HH-à	HH-èl	LF-Ø	LH-à	LH-èl	LH-Al	LH-e	LH-èl-à	HH-Al	HH-e	HH-èl-à
IVd	kur 'touch'	HH-à	HH-à	HH-èl	LH-à	LH-à	LH-èl	LH-Al	LH-e	LH-èl-à	HH-Al	HH-e	HH-èl-à

Shaded cells represent dynamic principal parts in one optimal principal-part analysis.

1. The root forms in this column exclude tone markings.

(Source: Jakobi 1990: 103–13)

TABLE 2.31 Affixal exponents of Fur conjugations

Conj	Examples[1]	Nonthird person			Third person									
					Singular			Plural						
								Nonhuman			Human			
		Subj	Perf	Pres	Subj	Perf	Pres	Subj	Perf	Pres	Subj	Perf	Pres
I,1a	buuN 'descend'	-o	-ô	-èl	-o	-ô	-èl	-òl	-ùl	-èl-à/-ì	-òl	-ùl	-èl-à/-ì
I,1b	jaan 'wait'	-o	-ô	-Ø	-o	-ô	-Ø	-òl	-ùl	-è	-òl	-ùl	-è
I,1c	irt 'shake'	-o	-ô	-î	-o	-ô	-î	-òl	-ùl	-è	-òl	-ùl	-è
I,2a	tall 'chew'	-ô	-ô	-èl	-o	-ô	-èl	-òl	-ùl	-èl-à/-ì	-òl	-ùl	-èl-à/-ì
I,2b	fuul 'spin'	-ô	-ô	-Ø	-o	-ô	-Ø	-òl	-ùl	-è	-òl	-ùl	-è
I,2c	kir 'cook'	-ô	-ô	-î	-o	-ô	-î	-òl	-ùl	-è	-òl	-ùl	-è
II,1a	rii 'snatch'	-i	-i	-iti	-i	-i	-iti	-i-A(l)	-i-è	-iti-A(l)	-i-A(l)	-i-è	-iti-A(l)
II,1b	tiir 'meet'	-i	-i	-Ø	-i	-i	-Ø	-i-A(l)	-i-è	-è	-i-A(l)	-i-è	-è
II,2a	*faul 'open'	-î	-î	-iti	-i	-i	-iti	-i-A(l)	-i-è	-iti-A(l)	-i-A(l)	-i-è	-iti-A(l)
II,2b	*kaun 'grind'	-î	-î	-Ø	-i	-i	-Ø	-i-A(l)	-i-è	-è	-i-A(l)	-i-è	-è
IIIa	arr 'measure'	-î	-à	-èl	-î	-à	-èl	-è	-e	-èl-à	-è	-e	-èl-à
IIIb	awi 'pound'	-ô	-ô	-èl	-o	-ô	-èl	-è	-e	-èl-à	-è	-e	-èl-à
IIIc	dus 'tear' (tr)	-ô	-ô	-èl	-Ø	-ô	-èl	-è	-e	-èl-à	-è	-e	-èl-à
IIId	*kair 'stop' (itr)	-Ø	-à	-èl	-Ø	-à	-èl	-è	-e	-èl-à	-è	-e	-èl-à
IIIe	*tai 'hold, seize'	-Ø	-à	-èl	-Ø	-ô	-èl	-è	-e	-èl-à	-è	-e	-èl-à
IVa	jum 'cover'	-Ø	-ô	-èl	-Ø	-ô	-èl	-Al	-e	-èl-à	-Al	-e	-èl-à
IVb	bul 'find'	-ô	-ô	-èl	-o	-ô	-èl	-Al	-e	-èl-à	-Al	-e	-èl-à
IVc	juuN 'terrify'	-Ø	-à	-èl	-Ø	-à	-èl	-Al	-e	-èl-à	-Al	-e	-èl-à
IVd	kur 'touch'	-à	-à	-èl	-à	-à	-èl	-Al	-e	-èl-à	-Al	-e	-èl-à

Only the two affixal exponents in heavy boxes are class-identifiers.

Shaded cells represent dynamic principal parts in one optimal principal-part analysis.

1. The root forms in this column exclude tone markings.

(*Source*: Jakobi 1990: 103–13)

TABLE 2.32 Number of dynamic principal parts needed to identify each Fur conjugation

Conjugation	Number of dynamic principal parts	
	With only affixes taken into account	With tonality and affixes both taken into account
IIIa; IVd	1 (class-identifier)	1
I,1a; I,1c; I,2a; I,2b; I,2c; II,1a; II,2a; II,2b	2	1
I,1b; II,1b; IIIb; IIIc; IIIe; IVa; IVb	2	2
IIId; IVc	3	3

conjugation classes are distinguished by non-affixal morphology. What about affixal exponence?

The affixal inflection of Fur (Nilo-Saharan; Sudan) decisively disconfirms the No-Blur Principle. In Fur, different conjugations are distinguished by the tonality of the verb root and by suffixation, as in Table 2.30.

Whether one takes account of the tonality of the root (as in Table 2.30) or not–that is, even if one restricts one's attention purely to the affixes used in conjugation (as in Table 2.31)–there are nineteen conjugations in Fur.

The number of dynamic principal parts for a Fur conjugation class depends on whether one takes account of tonality. The two possibilities are given in Table 2.32. In this table, the lefthand column of numbers indicates the number of dynamic principal parts needed to identify each conjugation if only affixes are taken into account; the righthand column indicates the number required if root tonality as well as affixes are taken into account.

As the first column of Table 2.32 shows, only two of the nineteen conjugations have a class-identifier among their affixal exponents. By the assumptions of the No-Blur Principle, all of the other affixes in each column of Table 2.31 should be the class-default for that column; but this means that every one of the columns (= every morphosyntactic property set) in Table 2.31 has more than one class-default–contrary to the assumptions of the No-Blur Principle.

Cameron-Faulkner and Carstairs-McCarthy (2000) discuss an apparently similar instance from Polish in which a particular morphosyntactic property set (locative singular) seemingly has more than one class-default, namely the suffixes -*e* and -*u*. They argue, however, that these two suffixes actually constitute a single default, since they are in complementary distribution: -*e* only appears in combination with a lexeme's special "minority" stem alternant, and -*u* appears elsewhere. In this way, they claim, the Polish evidence can be reconciled with the No-Blur Principle.

This same strategy won't work for Fur, however. Notice, for example, that in the nonthird-person perfect, some conjugations exhibit a low-toned -*à* suffix and others exhibit a low-toned -*ò* suffix. Yet, the paradigms of conjugations exhibiting the -*à* suffix may exhibit exactly the same pattern of stem tonality as those of conjugations exhibiting the -*ò* suffix. For instance, Conjugations IIIe and IVa differ in that the first shows the -*à* suffix and the second shows the -*ò* suffix; yet, these two conjugations exhibit precisely the same pattern of stem tonality, and the two suffixes are therefore in contrastive rather than complementary distribution. More generally, for each of the six sets of conjugations listed in (17), the only differences in exponence between the conjugations are affixal, and none of the distinguishing affixes is a class-identifier. These facts lead inevitably to the conclusion that the No-Blur Principle cannot be maintained.

(17) a.   I-1a, I-1c and II-1a
      b.   I-1b and II-1b
      c.   I-2a, I-2c and II-2a
      d.   I-2b and II-2b
      e.   IIIb and IVb
      f.   IIId, IIIe, IVa and IVc

The theoretical antecedent of the No-Blur Principle is the Paradigm Economy Principle (Carstairs 1987), which Carstairs-McCarthy (1991: 222) formulates as in (18):

(18) Paradigm Economy Principle
      There can be no more inflectional paradigms for any word-class in any language than there are distinct "rival" inflectional realizations available for that morphosyntactic property-combination where the largest number of rivals compete.

As with the No-Blur Principle, it is intended that this principle be interpreted as relating specifically to affixal inflection; thus, it entails that the maximum number of conjugations in Fur should be no larger than the maximum number of affixes that compete to realize the same property set in Fur verbal inflection. Just as the Fur evidence fails to confirm the predictions of the No-Blur Principle, it likewise fails to confirm the predictions of principle (18): in Fur, the largest number of "rival" suffixes for the inflection of a particular morphosyntactic property set is six (in both the nonthird-person subjunctive and the third-person singular subjunctive; cf. Table 2.31)–far fewer than the total number of conjugations (of which there are nineteen). While the benefits of paradigm economy for language learning cannot be doubted, these facts show that paradigm economy is not clearly enforced by any grammatical constraint.

Accordingly, evidence from languages such as Fur and Comaltepec Chinantec raises similar doubts about Albright's (2002*a*: 11) single surface base hypothesis:

[T]he single base hypothesis means that for one form in the paradigm (the base), there are no rules that can be used to synthesize it, and memorization is the only option. Other forms in the paradigm may be memorized or may be synthesized, but synthesis must be done via operations on the base form. Since we are assuming here a word-based model of morphology, the base is a fully formed surface member of the paradigm, and for this reason, I will call this the *single surface base* hypothesis.

Albright acknowledges that in order to synthesize forms in a complex inflectional paradigm, it is sometimes necessary to refer to multiple, local bases; this might be taken to suggest that the paradigms of a richly inflected language can be subdivided into sectors such that each sector S has a base

TABLE 2.33 Degrees of transparency exhibited by Fur conjugations (with tonality as well as affixes taken into account)

Conjugation	Number of dynamic principal parts	Average number of principal parts needed to deduce a particular cell in a lexeme's paradigm	Number of optimal analyses	Paradigm predictability
I,1a ; II,1a ; II,2a	1	1.00	4	0.923
I,2a	1	1.00	3	0.922
II,2b	1	1.00	1	0.921
II,1b	2	1.00	32	0.918
I,1c ; I,2c ; IVd	1	1.00	2	0.707
IIIa	1	1.00	1	0.707
I,2b	1	1.00	1	0.706
I,1b	2	1.00	16	0.703.
IVb	2	1.00	4	0.491
IVa	2	1.17	1	0.399
IVc	3	1.00	8	0.333
IIIb	2	1.00	2	0.309
IIIc ; IIIe	2	1.33	1	0.273
IIId	3	1.00	4	0.206

by which the single surface base hypothesis is satisfied within S. But it's not clear that the single surface base hypothesis can be maintained even in this weakened form, since as we have seen, some of the forms in a paradigm are only deducible by simultaneous reference to two or more implicative forms within that paradigm. (See Finkel and Stump 2007 for additional relevant discussion.)

2.7　Paradigmatic transparency as a dimension of typological variation

Like the Comaltepec Chinantec facts, the Fur facts demonstrate that languages tolerate considerable variation in the amount of paradigmatic transparency that they exhibit. The relevant Fur facts are summarized in Table 2.33, where conjugations are distinguished according to four criteria: according to the number of dynamic principal parts required to characterize them, according to the average number of principal parts needed to deduce an individual cell in a lexeme's paradigm, according to the number of alternative optimal principal-part analyses available to them, and according to their paradigm predictability.

The measure of paradigm predictability reveals some significant typological contrasts between Comaltepec Chinantec and Fur. By this measure, Comaltepec Chinantec tolerates a lower degree of paradigmatic transparency than Fur does: more than a fourth of the conjugations in Comaltepec Chinantec have a paradigm predictability below 0.2, while none of the Fur conjugations has a paradigm predictability this low. This difference in tolerance is reflected in a number of ways. First, Comaltepec Chinantec has optimal analyses involving as many as four principal parts, in comparison with a maximum of three in Fur. Second, seventeen of the sixty-seven conjugations in Comaltepec Chinantec involve paradigms at least some of whose words have to be deduced by simultaneous reference to more than one principal part; in Fur, by contrast, only three of the nineteen conjugations involve paradigms some of whose words have to be deduced through simultaneous reference to more than one principal part. Third, Comaltepec Chinantec provides an example of a conjugation (namely P3E) requiring four principal parts but allowing only one analysis out of a logically possible 495; Fur presents no conjugation class with a comparably constrained number of analyses. And fourth, well over half of the conjugations in Comaltepec Chinantec include one or more cells having a cell predictability of 0; by contrast, only four of the nineteen conjugations in Fur (namely IIIb, IIIc, IIId, and IIIe) have unpredictable cells, and none has more than one unpredictable cell. Notwithstanding the fact that Comaltepec Chinantec clearly tolerates a lower degree of paradigmatic transparency than Fur, it does, at the same time, achieve maximal transparency in four conjugations, which no conjugation does in Fur.

2.8 Conclusions and projections for future research

Much past research on morphological typology has tended to focus on the structure of individual word forms, invoking such criteria as the average number of morphemes per word form and the degree of morpheme fusion within a word form. The criteria proposed here extend the focus of typological classification from the structure of individual word forms to that of whole paradigms and to the implicative relations that paradigms embody.

The principal-part analysis undertaken here dovetails with current probability-based research on the structure of inflectional paradigms (e.g. that of Ackerman, Blevins, and Malouf and Milin *et al.* in this volume). The latter work focuses on the probability that a given cell C in the paradigm of a given lexeme L of category G will have a given realization, where the factors affecting this probability include the number and relative frequency of the inflection classes to which members of G belong, the number and frequency of exponents competing for the realization of C across members of G, the realization of other cells in L's paradigm, and so on. The central measure of this probability is the information-theoretic notion of entropy: the higher a cell's ENTROPY, the less predictable (the more informative) its realization.

The notion of CONDITIONAL ENTROPY discussed by Ackerman, Blevins, and Malouf is particularly relevant to the notion of principal parts. If we already know the realization of cell A in some paradigm, that information may serve to diminish the entropy of cell B (i.e. to make its realization more predictable); this diminished entropy is the conditional entropy of B with respect to A. Where cell B belongs to a paradigm having $A_1, \ldots, A_n$ as its principal parts, $A_1, \ldots, A_n$ effectively reduce the entropy of cell B to zero (i.e. they make it fully predictable).

This, then, is the point of contact between principal-part analysis and probability-based research on paradigmatic structure: the former focuses on the number and identity of conditions that must be present in a paradigm in order to reduce the entropy of each of its cells to zero; in other words, it focuses not on the probability that a given cell has a given realization, but on the circumstances in which a cell's realization becomes a certainty. Thus, while the probability-based research of Ackerman, Blevins, and Malouf and Milin *et al.* is concerned with varying degrees of entropy in a language's paradigms, our principal-part analyses are concerned with its varying degrees of paradigmatic transparency, i.e. the varying degrees of ease with which cells' realizations can be deduced with certainty from those of other cells in the same paradigm.

As we have shown, languages differ considerably in the extent to which they exhibit paradigmatic transparency. In view of the prima facie benefits of paradigmatic transparency for language learning and lexical storage, it is initially somewhat unexpected that languages should differ in this way. But paradigmatic transparency is by no means the only property of inflectional systems that may confer benefits on the language user. Transparadigmatic transparency–the ease with which a cell in one paradigm can be deduced from the corresponding cell in another paradigm – surely confers benefits of this sort; for instance, knowing that 1pl present indicative forms are alike across all conjugations makes the 1pl present indicative form of a newly learned verbal lexeme immediately deducible from those of existing lexemes. Yet the grammatical patterns that constitute paradigmatic transparency may be essentially the opposite of those constituting transparadigmatic transparency: a language all of whose conjugations possess maximal paradigmatic transparency (cf. again Fig. 2.1) possesses minimal transparadigmatic transparency; by the same token, a language in which distinct conjugation classes participated in a high degree of transparadigmatic transparency would inevitably exhibit low paradigmatic transparency. Thus, to understand the cross-linguistic variability of paradigmatic transparency, it will ultimately be necessary to understand the ways in which this property interacts with, counterbalances, or compensates for other, different grammatical properties.

3

Parts and wholes: Implicative patterns in inflectional paradigms

Farrell Ackerman, James P. Blevins, and Robert Malouf

> The whole has value only through its parts, and the parts have value only by virtue of their place in the whole. (Saussure 1916: 128)
>
> ... we cannot but conclude that linguistic form may and should be studied as types of patterning, apart from the associated functions. (Sapir 1921: 60)

3.1 Introduction

This chapter addresses an issue in morphological theory – and, ultimately, morphological learning – that we feel has received far less attention than it deserves. We will refer to this issue as the **Paradigm Cell Filling Problem** (PCFP):

Paradigm Cell Filling Problem: What licenses reliable inferences about the inflected (and derived) surface forms of a lexical item?

The problem does not arise in an isolating language, in which each lexical item (or "lexeme") is realized by a single form. English, for all intents and purposes, approaches an isolating ideal, so that the PCFP has not been prominent in analyses of English (or, for that matter, in the post-Bloomfieldian morphological models that have been developed mainly within the English-speaking world).[1]

However, the PCFP arises in an acute form in languages with complex inflectional systems, especially those which contain large inflectional paradigms

---

[1] Though a concern with form and structure of paradigms has remained a central focus of other morphological traditions, as represented by Seiler (1965), Wurzel (1970), and Carstairs (1983).

and intricate inflection-class systems. For example, a typical Estonian noun paradigm contains 30-odd forms, which exhibit patterns of variation that place the noun within anywhere between a half-dozen and a dozen major declension classes (Viks 1992; Erelt *et al.* 1995; Blevins 2005). It is implausible to assume that a speaker of Estonian will have encountered each form of every noun, so that native command of the language must involve the ability to generalize beyond direct experience. Moreover, Estonian is far from an extreme case. A typical transitive verb in Georgian has upwards of 200 forms, whose inflectional patterns identify the verb as belonging to one of four major conjugation classes (Tschenkéli 1958). Even Georgian is relatively conservative in comparison with descriptions of verb paradigms in Archi, which, according to one estimate (Kibrik 1998: 467), may contain "more than one and a half million" members.

The basic challenge that a speaker faces in each of these cases is the same, irrespective of the size of the form inventory. Given prior exposure to at most a subset of forms, how does a speaker produce or interpret a novel form of an item? One superficially attractive intuition is that knowing **what** one wants to say suffices in general to determine **how** one says it. The idea that variation in form reflects differences in "grammatical meaning" is encapsulated in the post-Bloomfieldian "morpheme," and underlies morphemic models from Harris (1942) and Hockett (1947) through Lieber (1992) and Halle and Marantz (1993). Yet, if one thing has been established about morphological systems in the half-century since Hockett (1954), it is that complex systems exhibit genuinely morphological variation, which is not conditioned by differences in grammatical meaning (or, for that matter, solely by phonological factors). Purely morphological variation (or what Aronoff 1994 terms "morphology by itself") may seem enigmatic in the context of simple systems. But in larger and more complex systems, variation that identifies the class of an item contributes information of vital importance because it allows a speaker to predict other forms of the item.

In a language with inflection classes, a speaker must be able to identify the class of an item in order to solve the PCFP. That is, to produce or interpret a novel form of an item, it is not enough for the speaker to know just that the grammatical meaning "motion into" is expressed by the illative case. The speaker must also know how the illative is realized for the item in question. In an inflection-class language, the choice of stem choice or exponent is precisely what is not in general determinable from the semantic or grammatical properties of an item. Instead, a speaker must know, or be able to deduce, one of the diagnostic forms of an item. For example, no known grammatical properties explain why the Estonian noun LUKK 'lock' has the short illative singular form *lukku* alongside the long form *lukusse*, whereas KIRIK 'church' has just the long form *kirikusse*. However, this contrast follows immediately if one knows that the partitive singular of LUKK is *lukku* and that the partitive singular of KIRIK is *kirikut*. There is likewise no morphosyntactic motivation for the variation in the form of the illative singulars in the Saami paradigms in Table 3.3 below. It is a morphological fact that the illative singular *bihttái* is based on the strong stem of BIHTTÁ 'piece' whereas the illative singular *bastii* is based on the weak stem of BASTE 'spoon.' This contrast is again predictable from the grade of the nominative singular forms of each noun (or, indeed, from the grade of any other form, as shown in Section 3.1).

In short, morphological systems exhibit interdependencies of precisely the kind that facilitate the deduction of new forms, based on knowledge of other forms. In some cases, it may be possible to mediate these deductions through a level of analysis in which recurrent units of form are associated with discrete grammatical meanings. However, this type of analysis tends to be most applicable to simple or recently grammaticalized patterns, and most morphological systems are not organized in a way that facilitates the identification of "minimal meaningful units". In many cases, the interdependencies that hold between word forms do not hold between subword units, so that further analysis disrupts the implicational structure. For example, the partitive singular *lukku* implies the homophonous short illative singular *lukku*, even though neither *lukk* nor -*u* can be associated with the grammatical meaning "partitive" or "illative" (Blevins 2005).

To develop this perspective, Section 3.2 outlines the word and paradigm assumptions that underlie our analysis, together with the basic information theoretic measures we use to test these assumptions. In Section 3.3, we apply these measures to portions of the morphological systems of Saami and Finnish and argue that – even in the absence of accurate frequency information – these measures bring out an implicational structure that offers a solution to the PCFP. We then show how the same measures apply to a description of Tundra Nenets nouns that supplies information about type frequency.[2] Taken together, these case studies suggest how information theory can be used to measure the implicational relations that underlie **symmetrical** approaches to word relatedness. By measuring the information that multiple surface forms provide about other forms, these approaches capture patterns of interdependency that cannot always be expressed in terms of an **asymmetrical** relation between surface forms and a single underlying or surface base.[3] We illustrate a symmetrical approach by examining Tundra Nenets nominal

    [2] The fieldwork on Tundra Nenets was supported by a Hans Rausing Endangered Language Major Documentation Project Grant 2003–6, in which the first author was a co-PI with Irina Nikolaeva and Tapani Salminen. This support is gratefully acknowledged.
    [3] See Albright (2002*a*, this volume) for a single base approach that addresses language change.

declension classes for absolute paradigms, and offer some provisional results about paradigm organization in this language. Section 3.4 then closes with some general conclusions and speculates about their ramifications for theoretical approaches to morphological analysis.

3.2 Analytical assumptions

Processes of analogical pattern matching and pattern extension play a central role in traditional analyses of interdependencies within and across paradigms. In classical word and paradigm (WP) models, a morphological system is factored into two components: a set of exemplary paradigms that exhibit the inflectional patterns of a language, and sets of diagnostic principal parts for nonexemplary items. Matching diagnostic forms of an item against the corresponding cells in an exemplary paradigm provides an analogical base for the deduction of novel forms of the item. This process of matching and deduction tends to be expressed symbolically in terms of proportional analogies (discussed in more detail in Albright (this volume) and Milin *et al.* (this volume)). The same process is invoked in grammars of inflectionally complex languages, as illustrated by the "rules of analogy" in Viks (1992: 46), which identify those forms of an Estonian noun that are predictable from the genitive singular and from the genitive plural.

3.2.1 *Morphological assumptions*

Traditional WP models offer a general solution to the PCFP that exploits the implicational structure of inflectional systems. Strategies that use exemplary patterns to extend principal part inventories are strikingly effective, as Matthews (1991: 187) notes in connection with their pedagogical relevance. They are also remarkably economical. In general, a small set of principal parts is sufficient to identify the class of an item and predict other forms of the item. Yet traditional solutions to the PCFP also raise some basic questions, including those in (1):

(1)   a.   What is the structure of units that license implicative relations?
         b.   How are units organized into larger structures within a system?
         c.   How can one measure implicative relations between these units?
         d.   How might the implicative organization of a system contribute to licensing inferences that solve the paradigm cell filling problem?
         e.   How does this organization, and the surface inferences it licenses, contribute to the robustness and learnability of complex systems?

Questions (1a) and (1b) centrally concern the relation of parts to wholes along two independent dimensions of analysis. Question (1a) concerns the internal complexity of word forms. Within post-Bloomfieldian models, words are treated as aggregates of smaller meaningful elements. These parts combine to produce a whole whose meaning is just the sum of the meaning its parts. Within the WP approach adopted here, words are regarded as complex configurations of recurrent elements whose specific **patterns of combination** may be meaningful irrespective of whether any particular piece bears a discrete meaning.

From this perspective, a surface word form is a whole in which the patterns exhibited by parts – whether affixes, tones, ablaut, or other "features of arrangement" (Bloomfield 1933: 163) – merely signal morphosyntactic, lexical, or morphological properties.[4] For example, in Tundra Nenets, the same members of a suffix set can be used with different lexical categories, sometimes serving essentially the same function, and sometimes serving different functions.[5]

As shown in Table 3.1, markers from Suffix Set I can appear both on nouns and verbs, and the inflected word functions as the predicate of the clause. In either case, the set I markers reflect person and number properties of the clausal subject. While markers from Suffix Set II also occur either with with nouns or with verbs, their function differs within each class: they reflect person/number properties of the possessor when they appear with nouns, but number properties of clausal objects when they appear with (transitive) verbs. Hence, there is a configurational dynamic whereby the same elements in different combinations are associated with different meanings. These patterns show why words are best construed as **recombinant gestalts**, rather

---

[4] This perspective does not preclude the possibility of associating grammatical meaning with subword units (morphemes) in constructions and/or languages where they would be motivated. In contrast, a morphemic model is less flexible, as it uniformly associates grammatical meaning with minimal elements and ignores configurational (emergent) properties of patterns.

[5] This discussion follows the presentation in Salminen (1997: 96, 103, 126), though elsewhere we have simplified his transcriptions for a general audience. In section 3.3.3 we have largely rendered the traditional Cyrillic written conventions into an IPA-based system where digraphs such as ny indicate palatalized consonants, `refers to a glottal stop with nasalizing or voicing effects in sandhi contexts, and ¨ refers to a glottal stop without nasalizing effects in sandhi contexts. (For a detailed discussion of motivations for the specific orthographic symbols employed in exemplary word forms see Salminen (1993).) Also, while predicate nominals and adjectives in Tundra Nenets host markers from Suffix Set I, they differ from the verbal predicates that host these suffixes in exhibiting nominal stem formation rather than verbal stem formation, in the inability to host future markers, and in their manner of clausal negation. All of these differences suggest that two different lexical categories host markers from Suffix Set I, and that there is no N-to-V conversion operation.

TABLE 3.1 Suffix homonymy in Tundra Nenets

	N	V
Suffix Set I	Predicative	Subjective
Suffix Set II	Possessive	Objective

than simple (or even complex) combinations of bi-unique content-form mappings (i.e., morphemes).[6]

This perspective on complex words is intimated in Saussure (1916: 128) in his discussion of **associative** (= paradigmatic) relations:

A unit like **painful** decomposes into two subunits (**pain-ful**), both these units are not two independent parts that are simply lumped together (**pain + ful**), The unit is a product, a combination of two interdependent elements that acquire value only through their reciprocal action in a higher unit (**pain × ful**). The suffix is non-existent when considered independently; what gives it a place in the language is series of common terms like **delight-ful, fright-ful**, etc. . . . The whole has value only through its parts, and the parts have value by virtue of their place in the whole.

Accordingly, while we are often able to isolate pieces of complex form, it is the configurations in which these pieces occur and the relation of these configuration to other similar configurations that are the loci of the meanings that are relevant in morphology. This property becomes even more evident if one considers the structure of Tundra Nenets verbs as insightfully discussed and schematized in Salminen (1997).

Table 3.2 exhibits little in the way of a one-to-one correspondence between cells across columns. Consider first the general finite stem, whose use is exemplified in (2). This stem serves as the base for the subjective conjugation,

TABLE 3.2 More suffix homonomy in Tundra Nenets (Salminen 1997:96)

Conjugation	Number of Object	Morphological Substem	Suffix Set
subjective		general finite stem (modal substem)	I
	sg		II
objective	du	dual object (modal) substem	III
	pl	special finite stem	
reflexive		special modal stem	IV

---

[6] See Gurevich (2006) for an constructional analysis of Georgian along these lines.

as shown in (2a), the objective conjugation, as shown in (2b), and may also encode singular object agreement for verbs marked by Suffix Set II. The dual object (modal) substem hosts members of Suffix Set III, as exemplified in (3), but the same suffix set also serves to mark plural objects with the special finite stem in (4a). Finally, as (4b) shows, the special finite stem is not restricted to the plural object conjugation, given that it is also associated with the reflexive conjugation and the distinguishing characteristic of this conjugation is the use of suffix set IV.

(2)   General finite stem:
    a.   Subjective:
        tontaød^{0}m
        cover.I   (= 1sg)
        'I cover (something)'

    b.   Objective Singular:
        tontaøw^0
        cover.II (= 1sg/sg)
        'I cover it'

(3)   Dual Object Stem:
    tontangax^0 yun^0
    cover.dual.III   (= 1sg/du)
    'I cover them (two)'

(4)   Special finite stem:
    a.   Objective Plural
        tonteyøn^0
        cover.III   (= 1sg/pl)
        'I cover them (plural)'

    b.   Reflexive
        tonteyøw^{0}q
        cover.IV (= 1sg)
        'I got covered'

In sum, it is the pattern of arrangements of individual elements that realize the relevant lexical and morphosyntactic content associated with words that is important in these examples, rather than the sum of uniquely meaningful pieces.

A word-based perspective on these aspects of the **internal** organization of lexical units is highly compatible with a traditional conception of the second part-whole dimension, namely the **external** organization of words. In what Matthews (1991) below terms the "ancient model", individual words function

as minimal elements in networks of elements, including inflectional paradigms, and paradigms are organized into larger networks, which include
inflection classes.

> In the ancient model the primary insight is not that words can be split into formatives,
> but they can be located in paradigms. They are not wholes composes of simple parts,
> but are themselves the parts within a complex whole. (Matthews 1991: 204)

The notions of internal and external structure are not exclusive – as they are
sometimes thought to be – but, instead, represent complementary perspectives on a morphological system. Indeed, these two dimensions give rise to a
paradigmatic variant of "duality of patterning" (Hockett 1960), in that they
show how combinations of individually meaningless elements, whether
morphs or other "features of arrangement", compose words whose meaning
depends in part on the place they occupy within larger paradigmatic structures. These complementary notions also permit an exploration of the intuitions evident in the twin themes of the epigrams above. In order to address
these issues, the following sections explore how several Uralic languages
(Saami, Finnish, and particularly Tundra Nenets) provide fertile ground for
identifying the nature of the challenges posed by the PCFP, as well as the type
of analysis best suited to address them.

Traditional WP approaches suggest answers to the other questions in (1),
though in addressing these questions, it is important to separate the substantive claims and hypotheses of a WP model from any idealizations or simplifying assumptions introduced in the use of these models in reference or
pedagogical grammars. For practical purposes, it is usually convenient in
written grammars to represent lexical items by a single principal part wherever possible. Yet there is no reason to attribute any linguistic or psychological
relevance to this extreme level of lexical economy. There are many well-
described systems in which class can only be identified on the basis of
multiple principle parts. Estonian conjugations provide a fairly straightforward illustration (Blevins 2007) as do the systems described in Finkel and
Stump (this volume).[7] From a psycholinguistic perspective, there is considerable evidence that frequency is, in fact, the primary determinant of whether
a given form is stored in the mental lexicon of a speaker (Stemberger and
MacWhinney 1986; Baayen *et al.* 2003*b*). Similarly, grammars tend to take the
smallest diagnostic forms of an item as principal parts, even though any form

---

[7] It may be significant that models incorporating something like the "single base hypothesis"
(Albright 2002*a*, this volume) tend to be developed on the basis of comparatively simple systems.

(or set of forms) that identifies class is equally useful, and the choice of memorized forms is again likely to reflect frequency or other distributional properties rather than morphosyntactic or morphotactic properties.

Other issues that are implicit in traditional analogical models have been addressed in recent work. Methods for identifying and classifying principal part inventories are set out in Finkel and Stump (2007, this volume). The psychological status of proportional analogies is likewise addressed in Milin *et al.* (this volume). But traditional solutions to the PCFP remain fundamentally incomplete to the extent that they lack a means of gauging the diagnostic value of principal parts or of measuring the implicational structure of networks of forms.

The approach outlined in this paper proceeds from the observation that implicational structure involves a type of **information**, specifically information that forms within a set convey about other forms in that set. Information in this sense corresponds to reduction in **uncertainty**. The more informative a given form is about a set of forms, the less uncertainty there is about the other forms in the set. The PCFP just reflects the fact that a speaker who has not encountered all of the forms of a given item is faced with some amount of uncertainty in determining the unencountered forms. If the choice of each form were completely independent, the PCFP would reduce to the problem of learning the lexicon of an isolating language. However, in nearly all inflectional systems, there are at least some forms of an item that reduce uncertainty about the other forms of the item. It is the reduction in uncertainty due to the knowledge of these forms that defines the implicational structure of the system. The diagnostic value of a given form likewise correlates with the reduction in uncertainty that is attributable to the knowledge of this particular form. Once these notions are construed in terms of uncertainty reduction, the task of measuring implicational structure and diagnostic value is susceptible to well-established techniques of analysis.

3.2.2 *Information theoretic assumptions*

The uncertainty associated with the realization of a paradigm cell correlates with its **entropy** (Shannon 1948) and the entropy of a paradigm is the sum of the entropies of its cells. The implicational relation between a paradigm cell and a set of cells is modeled by **conditional entropy**, the amount of uncertainty about the realization of the set that remains once the realization of the cell is known. Finally, the diagnostic value of a paradigm cell correlates with the **expected conditional entropy** of the cell, the average uncertainty that remains in the other cells once the realization of the cell is known.

A straightforward application of these information-theoretic notions provides a natural means of measuring the implicational structure of inflectional systems. In particular, we use the notion of **information entropy** to quantify the uncertainty in the realization of a particular cell of a paradigm. As in Moscoso del Prado Martín *et al.* (2004), Milin *et al.* (2009) and Milin *et al.* (this volume), an information-theoretic perspective permits us to reconsider basic linguistic questions, in this case questions about the synchronic structure of inflectional systems.

In order to quantify the interrelations between forms in a paradigm, we use the information theoretic notion **entropy** as the measure of predictability. This permits us to quantify "prediction" as a change in uncertainty, or information entropy (Shannon 1948). The idea behind information entropy is deceptively simple: Suppose we are given a random variable X which can take on one of a set of alternative values $x_1, x_2, \ldots, x_n$ with probability $P(x_1), P(x_2), \ldots, P(x_n)$. Then, the amount of uncertainty in X, or, alternatively, the degree of surprise we experience on learning the true value of X, is given by the entropy $H(X)$:

$$H(X) = -\sum_{x \in X} P(X) \log_2 P(X)$$

The entropy $H(X)$ is the weighted average of the **surprisal** – $\log_2 P(x_i)$ for each possible outcome x_i. The surprisal is a measure of the amount of information expressed by a particular outcome, measured in bits, where 1 bit is the information in a choice between two equally probable outcomes. Outcomes which are less probable (and therefore less predictable) have higher surprisal. Surprisal is 0 bits for outcomes which always occur ($P(x) = 1$) and approaches ∞ for very unlikely events (as $P(x)$ approaches 0). The more choices there are in a given domain and the more evenly distributed the probability of each particular occurrence, the greater the uncertainty or surprise there is (on average) that a particular choice will be made among competitors and, hence, the greater the entropy. Conversely, choices with only a few possible outcomes or with one or two highly probable outcomes and lots of rare exceptions have a low entropy.

For example, the entropy of a coin flip as resulting in either heads or tails is 1 bit; there is equal probability for an outcome of either heads or tails:

$$\begin{aligned}
H(X) &= -\sum_{x \in X} P(x) \log_2 P(x) \\
&= -(P(h) \times \log_2 P(h) + P(t) \times \log_2 P(t)) \\
&= -(0.5 \times \log_2 0.5 + 0.5 \times \log_2 0.5) \\
&= 1
\end{aligned}$$

The entropy of a coin rigged to always come up heads, on the other hand, is
0 bits: there is no uncertainty in the outcome:

$$H(X) = -\sum_{x \in X} P(x) \log_2 P(x)$$
$$= -(P(h) \times \log_2 P(h) + P(t) \times \log_2 P(t))$$
$$= -(1.0 \times \log_2 1.0 + 0.0 \times \log_2 0.0)$$
$$= 0$$

For other possible unfair coins, the entropy will fall somewhere between these
extremes, with more biased coins having a lower entropy. We can extend this
to find the **joint entropy** of more than one random variable. In general,
the joint entropy of independent events is the sum of the entropies of the
individual events. Suppose X is the outcome of one flip of a fair coin and Y is
the outcome of a second flip. If the two flips are independent, then the
probability of getting, say, heads on the first flip and tails on the second is
the probability of getting heads on first times the probability of getting tails
on the second, or $\frac{1}{2} \times \frac{1}{2} = \frac{1}{4}$. So, then, the joint entropy $H(X, Y)$ is:

$$H(X,Y) = -\sum_{x \in X, y \in Y} P(x,y) \log_2 P(x,y)$$
$$= -(P(h,h) \times \log_2 P(h,h) + P(h,t) \times \log_2 P(h,t)$$
$$+ P(t,h) \times \log_2 P(t,h) + P(t,t) \times \log_2 P(t,t))$$
$$= -4 \times (0.25 \times \log_2 0.25)$$
$$= 2$$

3.3 Modeling implicational structure

With the previous section as background we can now measure the entropy of
the inflectional systems mentioned earlier. In order to exhibit the general
character of the PCFP and demonstrate how an information-theoretic approach calculates the relative diagnosticity of words, the following subsections
present several morphological patterns with ascending levels of complexity.
We first describe the basic patterns, restricting attention to instructive aspects
of the organization of these systems, and then develop entropy-based analyses
that reveal their implicational structure. The inflectional paradigms of Uralic
languages are particularly instructive because of the way that they realize
inflectional properties by distinctive combinations of stem alternations and
affixal exponence. Hence these systems are not amenable to a standard

head-thorax-abdomen analysis in which lexical properties are expressed by the root, morphological class properties by stem formatives, and inflectional properties by inflectional affixes. For expositional convenience, we will initially assume, contrary to fact, that each cell in the paradigms below are equiprobable, so that speakers are just as likely to encounter one specific cell as any other.[8] As will be shown in the following sections, an appealing property of an entropy-based measure of word relatedness is that they can be easily scaled up to data sets of increasing veridicality.

3.3.1 *Northern Saami*

Noun declensions in Northern Saami (Bartens 1989; Nickel 1990) offer a straightforward illustration of the PCFP. First-declension nouns, i.e., nouns whose stems have an even number of syllables, may inflect according to either of the patterns in Table 3.3. In nouns of the "weakening" type, the nominative and illative singular and the essive are all based on the strong stem of a noun, and the remaining forms are based on the weak stem. Nouns of the "strengthening" variety exhibit a mirror-image pattern, in which the nominative and illative singular and essive are based on the weak stem, and other forms are based on the strong stem. Strong forms, which are set in bold in Table 3.3, contain a geminate consonant which corresponds to a nongeminate in the corresponding weak forms.

On standard descriptions that recognize a single, number-neutral essive form, there are eleven cells in a first-declension paradigm. Hence, to solve the PCFP, a speaker must deduce at most ten forms. This task is greatly facilitated

TABLE 3.3 Gradation in first declension nouns in Saami (Bartens 1989: 511)

	'Weakening'		'Strengthening'	
	Sing	Plu	Sing	Plu
Nominative	**bihttá**	bihtát	baste	**basttet**
Gen/Acc	bihtá	bihtáid	**bastte**	**basttiid**
Illative	**bihttái**	bihtáide	bastii	**basttiide**
Locative	bihtás	bihtáin	**basttes**	**basttiin**
Comitative	bihtáin	bihtáiguin	**basttiin**	**basttiiguin**
Essive		**bihttán**		basten
		'piece'		'spoon'

---

[8] Assuming equiprobable realizations also gives us an upper bound on the uncertainty in a paradigm. Since it is unlikely that all realizations are in fact equally likely, the actual entropy will almost always be lower than this.

TABLE 3.4 Invariant case endings in Saami
(*e* assimilates to *i* before *i*)

	Sing	Plu
Nominative	—	-t
Gen/Acc	—	-id
Illative	-i	-ide
Locative	-s	-in
Comitative	-in	-iguin
Essive		-n

by three general patterns. First, case endings are invariant, as illustrated in Table 3.4, so the endings can be memorized and need not be determined for individual first-declension nouns. Second, the comitative singular and locative plural are always identical, so a speaker must encounter at most one of these two forms. The third and most fundamental pattern relates to stem alternations. Given that endings are invariant, solving the PCFP for an item reduces to the problem of determining the distribution of strong and weak stems. This task is made much easier by the fact that the cells of a first-declension paradigm divide into the same two "cohort sets" in the weakening and strengthening patterns. Set A contains the nominative and illative singular and essive, and Set B contains the remaining cells. In nouns of the weakening type, Set A is strong and Set B is weak; in nouns of the strengthening type, Set A is weak and Set B is strong.

A striking consequence of this symmetry is that **every** form of a first-declension noun is diagnostic. A strong form from Set A identifies a noun as belonging to the weakening type, and licenses the deduction that the remaining Set A forms are strong and the Set B forms are weak. Conversely, a weak form from Set A identifies a noun as belonging to the strengthening type, and licenses the deduction that the remaining Set A forms are weak and the Set B forms are strong. Any Set B form, whether strong or weak, is equally diagnostic. In sum, knowing the form of any one paradigm cell eliminates nearly all uncertainty about the forms that fill the other cells in a first declension paradigm. This implicational structure is completely symmetrical. Each form of a paradigm is equally informative, and the nominative and accusative singular forms that realize noun stems play no privileged role in distinguishing noun types.

A straightforward application of information-theoretic notions provides a natural means of measuring the implicational structure of the Saami system. To measure the uncertainty of forms in an inflectional paradigm P, we let P be a matrix whose dimensions are defined by features, and a paradigm cell C be a variable which takes as values the different realizations of the features associated with C. If the entropy of each cell of the Saami paradigm is 1 bit, and there are eleven cells in the paradigm, then if all cells were independent we would expect the overall entropy of the paradigm (that is, the joint entropy of all the cells) to be 11 bits. However, there are only two subdeclensions in Table 3.3, and if we again assume that each is equally likely, then the overall entropy of the paradigm is also 1 bit. This shows that there is a significant amount of shared information in the Saami paradigm. In fact, once you know the realization of one cell, you know the realization of every other cell: any one cell completely predicts the others. One can quantify the degree of prediction between these cells using entropy. The average uncertainty in one variable given the value another is the **conditional entropy** $H(Y|X)$. If $P(y|x)$ is the conditional probability that $Y = y$ given that $X = x$, then the conditional entropy $H(Y|X)$ is:

$$H(Y|X) = -\sum_{x \in X} P(x) \sum_{y \in Y} P(y|x) \log_2 P(y|x)$$

Conditional entropy can also be defined in terms of joint entropy:

$$H(Y|X) = H(X,Y) - H(X)$$

The smaller that $H(Y|X)$ is, the more predictable Y becomes on the basis of X, i.e., the less surprised one is that Y is selected. In the case where X completely determines Y, the conditional entropy $H(Y|X)$ is 0 bits: given the value of X, there is no question remaining as to what the value of Y is. On the other hand, if X gives us no information about Y at all, the conditional entropy $H(Y|X)$ is equal to $H(Y)$: given the value of X, we are just as uncertain about the value of Y as we would be without knowing X.

Given the paradigm in Table 3.3, we can calculate the conditional entropy of any one cell given any other cell. Let us take the nominative singular and the locative plural, which happen to belong to different cohort sets. Each cell has two possible realizations, and the entropy of each is 1 bit. To find the joint entropy, we look at the four possible combinations of realizations:

Nom Sg	Loc Pl	*P*
strong	strong	0.0
strong	weak	0.5
weak	strong	0.5
weak	weak	0.0

Once again, we have two equally likely possible outcomes, and the joint entropy is 1 bit. So, the conditional entropy is:

$$H(\text{loc.pl}|\text{nom.sg}) = H(\text{nom.sg, loc.pl}) - H(\text{nom.sg})$$
$$= 1.0 - 1.0$$
$$= 0.0$$

That is, knowing the nominative singular realization for a particular noun completely determines the realization of the locative plural. One could repeat this calculation for any pair of cells in the paradigm and we would get the same result, as the Saami nominal inflection is a completely symmetric system.

In contrast, merely knowing one or both of the stem forms of a noun does not reduce uncertainty about whether a noun is of the weakening or strengthening type, because one must still know whether **which cell** the stem realizes. Knowing that the noun BIHTTÁ in Table 3.3 has the strong stem *bihttá* and the weak stem *bihtá* does not identify the subtype of this noun unless one knows which stem underlies which cohort set. Knowing that BASTE has the strong stem *bastte* and the weak stem *baste* is similarly uninformative. Hence, the type of these nouns cannot be determined from their stem inventories but only from the distribution of stems in the inflectional paradigms of the nouns.

3.3.2 *Finnish*

The Finnish subparadigm in Table 3.5 illustrates a more typical pattern, in which different **combinations** of cells are diagnostic of declension class membership.[9] Although individual forms may be indeterminate with respect to class membership, particular combinations of forms in Table 3.5, varying from class to class, reduce the uncertainly of class assignment. Consider forms *laseissa, nalleissa* and *kirjeissa*, which realize the inessive plural in the paradigms of the nouns of LASI, NALLE, and KIRJE. None of these forms alone reliably predicts the corresponding nominative singular forms. But collectively

---

[9] The numbers in Table 3.5 refer to the declension classes in Pihel and Pikamäe (1999).

TABLE 3.5 Finnish *i*-stem and *e*-stem nouns (Buchholz 2004)

Nom Sg	Gen Sg	Part Sg	Part Pl	Iness Pl	
ovi	oven	ovea	ovia	ovissa	'door' (8)
kieli	kielen	kieltä	kieliä	kielissä	'language' (32)
vesi	veden	vettä	vesiä	vesissä	'water' (10)
lasi	lasin	lasia	laseja	laseissa	'glass' (4)
nalle	nallen	nallea	nalleja	nalleissa	'teddy' (9)
kirje	kirjeen	kirjettä	kirjeitä	kirjeissä	'letter' (78)

they provide information that the appropriate class is restricted to 4, 9, or 78, but not 8, given that the inessive plural in class 8 is *ovissa*, not *oveissa*. Certain cells among these classes resolve class assignment more reliably than others. For example, *kirjeitä*, the partitive plural of KIRJE, appears unique among the forms in the partitive plural column and, therefore, is serviceable as a diagnostic cell for membership in class 78. This becomes particularly clear when we compare this form with the partitive plural forms *laseja* and *nalleja*: even in conjunction with the previously mentioned inessive plurals, these forms do not resolve class assignment between 4 and 9. This is accomplished, however, by comparing the partitive singular forms, *lasia* and *nallea*, or several other contrasts that would serve just as well.

These class-specific sets are reminiscent of the notion of **dynamic** principal parts, which Finkel and Stump (this volume) contrast with what they term "static" and "adaptive" inventories. In fact, there are many equally good alternative sets of principal parts for Finnish, and many more solutions that are almost as good. We speculate that this is a recurrent feature of complex morphological systems (reminiscent of resilience in biological systems). Even though there may be a few very hard cases or true irregulars, in general most cells in the paradigm of most words are of value in predicting the form of most other cells.

As the traditional principal part inventories in Table 3.5 show, the information that facilitates paradigm cell filling in Finnish is not localized in a single form or even in a class-independent set of forms. Instead, forms of an item are partitioned into cohort sets or "subparadigms" that share "recurrent partials." One pair of subparadigms in Finnish declensions are distinguished by what are conventionally termed the "basic form" and the "inflectional stem" of an item. A typical pattern is illustrated by the paradigm of OVI 'door', in which the basic form *ovi* realizes the nominative singular and underlies the partitive and inessive plurals, and the inflectional stem *ove* underlies the genitive and partitive singular forms. As in Saami, the organization of cells into subparadigms identifies the form of other declensional cohorts, while variation in the structure of subparadigms across items facilitates the identification of declension classes.

Given this overview of the patterns in Table 3.5, we now outline how to calculate the joint and conditional entropy of the corresponding paradigm cells. Let us first consider how many distinct realizations of the genitive singular are exhibited in Table 3.5. From a traditional perspective, there is exactly one affixal realization, given that "[t]he genitive singular ending is always -*n*, which is added to the inflectional stem" (Karlsson 1999: 91). However, this description already presupposes knowledge of the inflectional stem, which is precisely the type of information that a speaker may need to deduce in order to solve the PCFP. To avoid presupposing information about the organization of Finnish declensions, it is useful to adopt more structurally agnostic descriptions in terms of a "base", which underlies the basic form (and, usually, the inflectional stem), and an "ending" (which may include the theme vowel of the inflectional stem).[10] On this type of description, the six inflectional classes in Table 3.5 exhibit four distinct realizations. In classes 8, 32, and 9, the genitive singular ends in -*en*. In class 10, it ends in -*en* and the base exhibits a change in the stem consonant. In class 9, it ends in -*in*, and in class 78 it ends in -*een*. If we assume that each of the six declensions has a probability of $\frac{1}{6}$, then the entropy $H(\text{GEN.SG})$ is:

$$H(\text{gen.sg}) = -\left(\frac{3}{6}\log_2\frac{3}{6} + \frac{1}{6}\log_2\frac{1}{6} + \frac{1}{6}\log_2\frac{1}{6} + \frac{1}{6}\log_2\frac{1}{6}\right)$$
$$= 1.792$$

Repeating this calculation for each of the cells in the paradigm, we get: The **expected** entropy $E[H]$ is the average across all cells. Producing a randomly

	Nom Sg	Gen Sg	Part Sg	Part Pl	Ines Pl	$E[H]$
H	0.918	1.792	2.252	1.459	1.000	1.484

chosen cell of the paradigm of a randomly chosen lexeme (assuming that the declensions are equally likely) requires on average 1.484 bits of information.

Given the paradigms in Table 3.5, we can also calculate the pairwise conditional entropy. Suppose we know that the NOM.SG of a particular lexeme ends in -*i*. What is the genitive singular? Our information about the NOM.SG rules out classes 9 and 78, so we are left choosing among the remaining four classes with three different GEN.SG realizations. Given this information, the uncertainty in the GEN.SG becomes:

---

[10] This type of pretheoretical description is found particularly in pedagogical grammars and descriptions. For example, noun classes 16–22 in Oinas (2008: 57f.) distinguish *i*- and *e*-stem nouns in terms of the surface variation in their genitive singular forms.

$$H(\text{GEN.SG}|\text{NOM.SG} = -i) = -\left(\frac{2}{4}\log_2\frac{2}{4} + \frac{1}{4}\log_2\frac{1}{4} + \frac{1}{4}\log_2\frac{1}{4}\right)$$

$$= 1.5$$

In other words, knowing that the NOM.SG ends in -*i* gives us $1.793 - 1.5 = 0.292$ bits of information about the form of the GEN.SG. And, if instead we know that the NOM.SG of a particular lexeme ends in -*e*, then we must choose between two declensions with two GEN.SG realizations, and the entropy is:

$$H(\text{GEN.SG}|\text{NOM.SG} = -e) = -\left(\frac{1}{2}\log_2\frac{1}{2} + \frac{1}{2}\log_2\frac{1}{2}\right)$$

$$= 1$$

Assuming again that all declensions are equally likely, the probability that the NOM.SG of a particular lexeme actually ends in -*i* is $\frac{4}{6}$, and the probability that it ends in -*e* is $\frac{2}{6}$. So, on average, the uncertainty in the GEN.SG realization of a lexeme given we know that lexeme's NOM.SG realization will be:

$$H(\text{GEN.SG}|\text{NOM.SG}) = \frac{4}{6} \times 1.5 + \frac{2}{6} \times 1.0$$

$$= 1.333$$

In other words, the NOM.SG gives us, on average, $1.793 - 1.333 = 0.46$ bits of information about the GEN.SG. Table 3.6 gives the pairwise conditional entropy of a column given a row. That is, e.g., $H(\text{NOM.SG}|\text{INESS.PL})$ is 0.541 bits.

The row expectation $E[\text{row}]$ is the average conditional entropy of a column given a particular row. This is a measure of the **predictiveness** of a form. By this measure, the partitive singular is the most predictive form: if we know the partitive singular realization for a lexeme and want to produce on other paradigm cells chosen at random, we will require only 0.250 bits of additional information on average. In contrast, given the nominative singular, we would

TABLE 3.6 Conditional entropy $H(\text{col}|\text{row})$ of Finnish *i*-stem and *e*-stem nouns

	Nom Sg	Gen Sg	Part Sg	Part Pl	Ines Pl	$E[\text{row}]$
Nom Sg	—	1.333	1.667	0.874	0.541	1.104
Gen Sg	0.459	—	0.459	0.459	0.459	0.459
Part Sg	0.333	0.000	—	0.333	0.333	0.250
Part Pl	0.333	0.792	1.126	—	0.000	0.563
Ines Pl	0.459	1.252	1.585	0.459	—	0.939
$E[\text{col}]$	0.396	0.844	1.209	0.531	0.333	0.663

need an addition 1.104 bits of information on average. The column expectation $E[\text{col}]$ is the average uncertainty given a row remaining in a particular column.

In contrast to the row expectations, this is a measure of the **predictedness** of a form. By this measure, the inessive plural is the most predicted form: if we want to produce the inessive plural for a lexeme and know some randomly selected other form, we will require on average another 0.333 bits of information.

One cannot of course draw any general conclusions about the implicational structure of Finnish declensions from the calculations in Table 3.6, given that they are based on a small subset of patterns, and that they assume that all classes and variants are equiprobable. Nevertheless, it should be clear that the method applied to this restricted data set scales up, as the description becomes more comprehensive through the addition of further patterns and as it becomes more accurate through the addition of information about type and token frequency.

3.3.3 *Tundra Nenets*

The present section now extends the approach outlined above in order to provide a preliminary case study of nominal inflection in Tundra Nenets (Samoyed branch of Uralic). The basic question is this: Given any Tundra Nenets inflected nominal word form, what are the remaining 209 forms of this lexeme for the allowable morphosyntactic feature property combinations CASE: {nom, acc, gen, dat, loc, abl, pro}, NUMBER: {singular, dual, plural}, POSSESSOR: {3 persons × 3 numbers}? The problem can be schematized as in (5a) and (5b). Specifically, given exposure to a stimulus such as that in (5a), the nominal *nganu″mana* 'boat (plural prosecutive)', what leads to the inference that its nominative singular form is the target *ngano*? In contrast, if confronted with the plural prosecutive of the nominal *wíngo″ mana* 'tundra (plural prosecutive)', what leads to the inference that its nominative singular is the target *wí*?

(5)   a.   Stimulus: Target   vs b.   Stimulus   Target
           nganu″mana *ngano*   *wíngo″mana*   *wí*
           boat.PL.PROS   boat.SG.NOM   tundra.PL.PROS tundra.SG.NOM

In line with the hypotheses set out in the previous section, we must identify the patterns of interpredictability for a subset of Tundra Nenets nominal declensions within and across subparadigms. This entails stating the principles of arrangement within and across stem types. For the absolute declension (i.e., nonpossessive, nonpredicative nominals), lexical categories are divisible into the gross stem-type classification in Table 3.7 (again ignoring the role of syllabicity;

TABLE 3.7 Tundra Nenets nominal types (Salminen 1997, 1998)

Type 1 (T1):	stem ends in C (other than a glottal stop) or V;
Type 2 (T2):	subtype 1: stem ends in nasalizing/voicing glottal (')
	subtype 2: stem ends in non-nasalizing/devoicing glottal (")

see Salminen (1997, 1998) for a detailed exposition of types.[11] For simplicity, we demonstrate the basic pattern with an example of Type I in Table 3.8.

Examination of Table 3.8 yields a basic observation: the nominal paradigms for all stem classes are partitioned into subparadigms, each of which is defined by the presence of a characteristic and recurring stem (*ngano, nganu,* or *nganoxo*). In what follows we will refer to these forms as recurrent partials and the sets in which they recur as coalitions or alliances (or cohorts) of forms. This brings out the following generalization about Tundra Nenets absolute nominal paradigms:

Subparadigms are domains of interpredictability among alliances of word forms, rather than sets of forms derived from a single base.[12]

An approach based on recurrent partials, and patterns of relatedness among forms, develops the approach in Bochner (1993), in which no form need serve as a privileged base form among different surface expression of a lexeme.

TABLE 3.8 Type I: Polysyllabic vowel stem: *ngano* 'boat'

	Singular	Plural	Dual
Nominative	*ngano*	*ngano"*	*nganoxo'*
Accusative	*nganom'*	*nganu*	*nganoxo'*
Genitive	*ngano'*	*nganu"*	*nganoxo'*
Dative-Directional	*nganon'*	*nganoxo"*	*nganoxo' nya'*
Locative-Instrumental	*nganoxona*	*nganoxo" na*	*nganoxo' nyana*
Ablative	*nganoxod*	*nganoxot*	*nganoxo' nyad*
Prolative	*nganowna*	*nganu" mana*	*nganoxo' nyamna*

[11] There are phonological properties associated with particular glottal-final stems (as in Saami and Finnish) that decrease the uncertainty of predicting class assignment and related forms of words within the class. For example, the occurrence of a specific allomorph, e.g., *wingana* (where -*gana* is part of a family allomorphs such as -*xana* and -*kana*) leads to the inference that this word belongs to the class of stem-final nasalizing glottals. In this way, surface allomorphy can be used as a diagnostic clue for guiding paradigm-based inferences.

[12] As expected from positing that patterns of inflected forms exist, there is a need to access certain of them for purposes of derivational relatedness in Tundra Nenets. In particular, there are at least two verbal derivation operations built upon the form used to express genitive plural nominals. See Kupryanova (1985: 139).

Regardless of whether a stem exists as an independent word, all these systems share the property that they have clusters of related forms where it is at least somewhat arbitrary to take any one form as basic. This is what I take to be defining characteristic of a paradigm. Thus, we need a way to relate to the various members of paradigm directly to each other without singling out any one of them as a base for the others. (Bochner 1993: 122)

On this type of analysis, alliances of word forms share recurrent partials, but the elements in such alliances need not be thought of as bearing derivational or "constructive" relations (in the sense of J. P. Blevins 2006*b*) to one another, let alone to a single isolable base form. The relations among members of subparadigms are symmetrical, since there is no one form that serves as the base from which the others are derived.[13] This organization is depicted in Figure 3.1, which partitions the Tundra Nenets nominal declension into three alliances of forms. Each form in a subparadigm provides information about other forms in the same subparadigm. The members of a subparadigm share partials, thereby making an alliance a system of interpredictability among related word forms.[14]

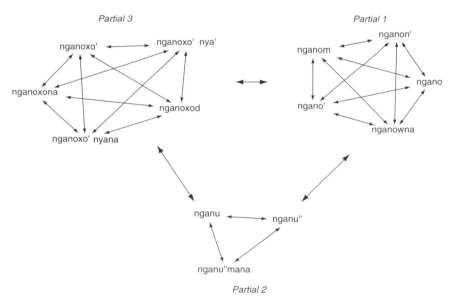

FIGURE 3.1 Symmetric paradigm organization

[13] However, the lack of a single privileged base does not entail that there cannot be multiple subparadigms in which a particular recurring form (a partial) serves a pivotal role.

[14] This is compatible with Albright's observation that "when we look at larger paradigms ... it often appears that we need local bases for each sub-paradigm (something like the traditional idea of principal parts, or multiple stems)" (Albright 2002*a*: 118).

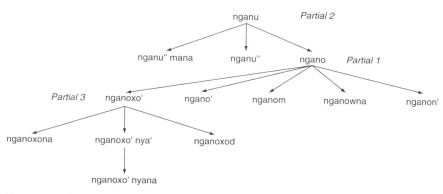

FIGURE 3.2 Asymmetric paradigm organization

In contrast, derivational or constructive relations based on a single form are asymmetric in assuming that some specific form is predictive of the other forms. An asymmetric structure, organized in in terms of local bases, is depicted in Figure 3.2. In contrast to Figure 3.1, each subparadigm contains a base from which the rest of the forms in it are derived. There is no notion of interpredictability of the sort manifest in Figure 3.1: the base gives information about derived forms, but the derived forms need not give information about a base.

3.3.3.1 *Implications across subparadigms* The strategy we have chosen to demonstrate the utility of symmetric organization is to focus on the most challenging and problematic instance of relatedness between two word forms within Tundra Nenets nominal paradigms, specifically the NOM.SG and ACC.PL. The logic of this task is straightforward: if we can identify a direction with reliably low conditional entropy, i.e., most predictive, between the two least transparently related word forms, then there is reason to believe that asymmetric derivation may be viable. In other words, one could hypothesize that knowing e.g., NOM.SG, would suffice to predict the ACC.PL across all classes, either directly, or by identifying a common base that underlies both forms. In contrast, the symmetric proposal is compatible with a situation in which there is no single reliably predictive form, but that classes are organized into patterns of interpredictability within alliances of forms.

Consider the pairs of NOM.SG and ACC.PL forms in Table 3.9. A comparison of the forms in the columns reveals that there is indeterminacy or uncertainty with respect to predictability in both directions. For example, while the ACC.PL of 'boat' and 'harnessed deer' both end in the vowel -*u*, their NOM.SG forms

TABLE 3.9 Tundra Nenets inflected nominals

Nom Sg	Acc Pl	
ngano	nganu	'boat'
lyabtu	lyabtu	'harnessed deer'
ngum	nguwo	'grass'
xa	xawo	'ear'
nyum	nyubye	'name'
yí	yíbye	'wit'
myir	myirye	'ware'
wí´	wíngo	'tundra'
we´	weno	'dog'
nguda	ngudyi	'hand'
xoba	xob	'fur'
sawənye	sawənyi	'magpie'
tyírtya	tyírtya	'bird'

end in -*o* and -*u* respectively. Likewise, while the NOM.SG of 'boat' ends in -*o*, the ACC.PL of 'grass' ends in -*o* and its NOM.SG ends in the consonant -*m*.

The basic question is, given exposure to one form, how well can one predict the other? This is just the PCEP relativized to Tundra Nenets. In the following preliminary study, we use data from a corpus of 4,334 nominals. These are extracted from Salminen's compilation of 16,403 entries, which is based on Tereshchenko's Nenets-Russian dictionary (1965/2003). The compilation specifies meaning, frequency, as well as the stem-class assignment. We explore the relative predictiveness of NOM.SG and ACC.PL, with the following query in mind: which of these forms, if either, is more useful for predicting the other? The first calculation maintains the idealization adopted in the analyses of Saami and Finnish and assumes that all declension classes are equally likely. We start by identifying 24 different types of nominative singulars. The entropy of this distribution is $H(\text{NOM.SG}) = 4.173$ bits. There are likewise 29 different types of accusative plurals, and their entropy is $H(\text{ACC.PL}) = 4.693$ bits. Taken together, there are 43 nominal 'declensions' represented in the compilation (each declension being a combination of a NOM.SG realization and an ACC.PL realization), and the joint entropy of the two forms is $\log_2 43 = 5.426$ bits.

These calculations assume (as in the case of Saami and Finnish) that all declensions are equally likely. However, it is clear from the compilation that all declensions are **not** equally likely. In fact, the distribution of type frequencies across declensions is highly skewed: the five most frequent declensions account for more than half of the noun lexemes (see Figure 3.3 for the complete distribution). Taking the type frequencies of declensions into account, we now find that the entropy associated with each individual form is $H(\text{NOM.SG}) = 3.224$ bits and $H(\textit{acc.pl}) = 3.375$ bits. The true joint entropy $H(\text{NOM.SG}, \text{ACC.PL})$ is 3.905 bits, a level of uncertainty equivalent to 15 equiprobable declensions.

Having quantified the degree of uncertainty in the choice of NOM.SG and ACC.PL types individually, we can now calculate predictability of one realization given the other, using conditional entropy $H(Y|X)$. Consider first the task of predicting the ACC.PL form from the NOM.SG. We can evaluate the difficulty of this prediction using the conditional entropy $H(\text{ACC.PL}|\text{NOM.SG})$, the uncertainty in the ACC.PL given the NOM.SG. Out of the $24 \times 29 = 696$ possible pairings of NOM.SG and ACC.PL types, 43 are actually attested in the lexicon. In some cases, knowing the NOM.SG of a word uniquely identifies its ACC.PL, e.g. a word ending in *-ye* in the NOM.SG always has an ACC.PL in *-yi*. For such words, once we know the NOM.SG there is no uncertainty in the ACC. PL and the conditional entropy $H(\text{ACC.PL}|-ye) = 0$ bits. In other cases, however, knowing the NOM.SG narrows down the choices for the ACC.PL but does not uniquely identify it. For example, polysyllabic words whose NOM.SG ends in *-ya* might have an accusative plural in *-∅*, *-yi*, or *-e*. Furthermore, of the 289 polysyllabic lexemes with a NOM.SG in *-ya*, 268 have an ACC.PL in *-yi*, 19 in *-∅*, and only 2 in *-e*. So, the entropy is:

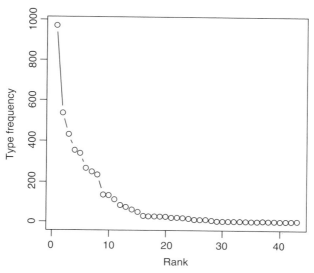

FIGURE 3.3 Type frequencies of Tundra Nenets nominal declensions, by rank

$$H(\text{ACC.PL}|\text{NOM.SG} = \text{-}ya) = -\left(\frac{268}{289}\log_2\frac{268}{289} + \frac{19}{289}\log_2\frac{19}{289} + \frac{2}{289}\log_2\frac{2}{289}\right)$$
$$= 0.410 \text{ bits}$$

Averaging across the whole (sample) lexicon, the uncertainty in the ACC.PL given the NOM.SG is $H(\text{ACC.PL}|\text{NOM.SG}) = 0.681$ bits. In other words, the NOM.SG "predicts" all but 0.681 of the 3.375 bits of uncertainty previously calculated for the ACC.PL. Now, if we switch directions, going from ACC.PL to NOM.SG, it turns out that the conditional entropy $H(\text{NOM.SG}|\text{ACC.PL}) = 0.530$. In other words, the ACC.PL "predicts" all but 0.530 of the 3.224 bits in the NOM. SG. Since the conditional entropy is closer to 0 in the latter than in the former, the ACC.PL appears to be more helpful for predicting the NOM.SG than vice versa, but only by a slim margin. More importantly, neither conditional entropy is 0 bits or close to it, meaning neither form is especially useful for predicting the other.

Hence, there is no principled grounds for hypothesizing that one form or the other serves as (or even identifies) a single privileged base. Either choice would still leave a large inventory of irregular pairings to be memorized by the language learner. This arbitrary choice is avoided on a symmetric account, where there is no need to suppose that some forms are reliably predictable from others. Instead, a symmetrical proposal posits alliances which cohere into coalitions of interpredictable forms and which together partition the entire paradigm. We do not expect forms that take part in different alliances to be mutually predictive, so the fact that knowledge of a member of one alliance does not reliably reduce uncertainty about a member of another is not surprising.

More positively, the utility of alliances becomes clearer if one considers the distribution of Tundra Nenets forms. Although the NOM.SG and ACC.PL are equally unsuitable as single bases, the NOM.SG will still make a more prominent contribution to defining the implicational structure of a paradigm, given that speakers are far more likely to encounter the NOM.SG form of a noun than the ACC.PL form. The distributional difference between these forms is reflected in the frequency counts in Table 3.10, representing the 12,152 noun tokens in Salminen's sample sentence corpus. The NOM.SG represents 33.8 percent of the tokens, while the ACC.PL represents only 2.7 percent. Speakers cannot just assume that the most frequent form is the most useful for solving the PCFP, given that the NOM.SG is not even a reliable predictor of the ACC.PL. The ACC. PL itself is an even less suitable candidate. Even if the predictive value of the ACC.PL made it potentially useful as a base, the attested frequencies suggest that speakers would have a low likelihood of encountering this form for any

TABLE 3.10 Word-form frequencies in Tundra Nenets

	Singular	Plural	Dual
Nominative	4,117	770	7
Accusative	1,077	355	6
Genitive	3,002	376	5
Dative-Directional	762	89	0
Locative-Instrumental	724	108	0
Ablative	291	50	0
Prolative	372	41	0

given item. The situation is worse yet for forms such as the direct case dual forms, which account for 0.1 percent of the tokens. In fact, no individual word form (other than the NOM.SG and the GEN.SG) occurs with high enough frequency to be a reliable source of information about a word's inflectional class. This makes Tundra Nenets a challenging language from a "single base" point of view, as speakers cannot be sure of encountering the diagnostic forms necessary to identify a word's inflection class.

However, the issue takes on a different complexion when we look at forms in terms of alliances, organized around the Partials 1, 2 and 3 in Figure 3.1. Although the ACC.PL is a relatively low-frequency form, it is predictable from other forms that it is transparently related to. For example, the GEN.PL adds a final glottal stop to the ACC.PL, as illustrated by the relation between *nganu*, the ACC.PL form of 'boat', and the corresponding GEN.PL *nganu''*. Hence, while there is a low likelihood of encountering the ACC.PL, there is a much higher likelihood of encountering the **partial** associated with ACC.PL (from which the ACC.PL can be defined), if paradigms are organized into alliances of interpredictable forms that "pool" the frequency of individual forms. The effect of this structure is shown by the contrast between the form frequencies in Figure 3.1 and the totals in Table 3.11, which sum the token frequencies of all absolute and possessive forms.

The organization of forms into subparadigms thus serves two related functions. On the one hand, high-frequency forms such as the NOM.SG or GEN.SG identify the shape of lower-frequency members of the same alliance, such as the prolative singular. On the other hand, "pooling" the frequencies of the members of each alliance allows Partial 2, and the forms based on this partial, to be identified either by the ACC.PL and the GEN.PL, while Partial 3, and forms based on it, can be identified by the locative-instrumental forms or by the ablative singular. By relying on alliances of related forms within subparadigms, speakers may gain reliable cues about the shape of even very low-frequency word forms.

Significantly, accounts that assume an asymmetrical relation between a privileged base and derived forms have no obvious analogue to alliances of mutually reinforcing forms. On such asymmetrical approaches, the patterns within subparadigms appear epiphenomenal, not, as suggested here, as central to the organization of the declensional system and critical to the solution of the PCFP.

3.3.3.2 *Summary*   The preceding sections suggest that neither the NOM.SG nor ACC.PL form can serve reliably as the single base from which the other is predicted. Yet the fact that neither form is fully predictive does not mean that they are uninformative. Instead, the association of forms with subparadigms allows speakers to exploit the fact that partials appear with much higher frequency than any given word-form. Hence, there is no need to encounter a privileged member of an alliance in order to predict allied forms. What is important is just that each alliance contain at least some high-frequency forms and that the the aggregate frequency of partials within the alliance is high enough to be useful. In this way, the organization of the Nenets declensional system makes available many of the basic ingredients for a solution to the paradigm cell filling problem.

3.4 Conclusions

We conclude by returning to the questions in (6), repeated from (1), which concern issues raised by traditional solutions to the Paradigm Cell Filling Problem.

(6)   a.   What is the structure of units that license implicative relations?
      b.   How are units organized into larger structures within a system?
      c.   How can one measure implicative relations between these units?
      d.   How might the implicative organization of a system contribute to licensing inferences that solve the paradigm cell filling problem?
      e.   How does this organization, and the surface inferences it licenses, contribute to the robustness and learnability of complex systems?

This chapter has focused primarily on questions (6a), (6b), and (6c). The central hypothesis has been that words are organized into paradigms and that information-theoretic measures provide an insightful measure of relatedness among members of declension classes. In fact, distinctive patterns of relatedness clearly enter into what it means to be a declension class, with some forms or combinations of forms being more diagnostic of class membership than others. Once conditional entropies for families of forms are identified, they can be used, along the lines we have suggested, to solve the Paradigm Cell

Filling Problem. Individual forms or alliances of forms serve as cues for simplifying the assignment of class membership for novel words on the basis of the analogies provided by the patterns of known words. It is worth emphasizing that the answers to questions (6a), (6b), and (6c) presuppose access to (patterns of) surface word forms. There are, accordingly, several theoretical consequences associated with our results.

First, there must be more to morphological analysis and morphological theory than the distillation of rules or patterns for the composition of individual word forms. In focusing exclusively interest on the syntagmatic dimension of morphological analysis, the post-Bloomfieldian tradition has been led to adopt questionable claims about the nature of the grammatical system and the mental lexicon. Work within this tradition has assumed that morphological analysis consists of identifying morphemes and stating rules for describe morpheme combinations. Larger structures such as words and paradigms tend to be treated as derivative or even as epiphenomenal. The emphasis on identifying minimal units has also fostered the *a priori* belief that the lexicon consists entirely of minimal elements, and, in particular, that productive and regular word forms are not part of the mental lexicon of a speaker, on the grounds that such forms would be "redundant" if they could be constructed from available morphemes and combinatoric rules. Yet a range of psycholinguistic studies has shown that the processing of a given word may be influenced (whether facilitated or inhibited) by other related forms in a way that suggests that the related words are available as elements of a speaker's mental lexicon (Baayen *et al.* 1997; Schreuder & Baayen 1997; Hay 2001; de Jong 2002; Moscoso del Prado Martín 2003). Another group of studies provide evidence for various types of paradigm-based organization (Baayen & Moscoso del Prado Martín 2005; Milin *et al.* 2009).

The traditional word and paradigm assumptions adopted here appear to be more compatible with these results than the post-Bloomfieldian assumptions that still guide modern generative accounts. In order to unify these perspectives, one might take them to adopt have complementary foci, with WP approaches focusing on whole words and their organization into paradigms, and morphemic accounts focusing on the internal structure and construction of word forms. We suggest that this is misleading. For the languages discussed above and others of comparable complexity, the answer to question (6a) must appeal to the whole words and larger paradigmatic structures recognized in WP approaches. There is little evidence that syntagmatic approaches have any means of characterizing the role that whole words play in morphology, let alone the place of larger paradigmatic structures. In contrast, a WP approach is largely agnostic about the internal structure of complex words. A WP approach is compatible with an agglutinative **morphotactic** analysis, in cases where such an analysis is motivated. But a WP account is also able to characterize the extraordinary variety of strategies for the creation of complex word forms attested cross-linguistically, without reducing them to an underlying basic structure. In order to arrive at a general answer to question (6a), we suggested that complex words are recombinant gestalts. On this pattern-based view, agglutination is just a particularly simple pattern. Finally, with respect to question (6e), we suggest that it is the very pattern-based nature of morphology – both at the level of individual (types of words) and in their organization into paradigms – that makes even highly complex morphological systems learnable and, by hypothesis, guides the development, maintenance, and change of these systems.

4

Resolving pattern conflict: Variation and selection in phonology and morphology

Andrew Wedel

4.1 Introduction

Every language system comprises many intersecting levels of organization, each with its own structures and patterns. When these levels overlap, patterns at different levels can come into conflict. For example, phonological regularity may entail morphological irregularity, as when addition of an affix requires a change in a stem. In Catalan, for example, some verbal suffixes are underlyingly stressed such that they may induce a shift in stress in the stem. This interacts with phonological vowel reduction processes in Catalan to result in differences in stem vowel realizations between members of a verbal paradigm, as exemplified below (Wheeler 2005).

(1)   a. /don/   [dónu]   [dunɛ́m]   'give'
      b. /pas/   [pásu]   [pəsɛ́m]   'pass'

Morphological regularity in turn can entail phonological irregularity, as when a stem fails to undergo an otherwise regular phonological change upon affixation resulting in the maintenance of consistency across the paradigm. A classic example of such a "paradigm uniformity effect" was noted by Chomsky and Halle (1968) in the occasional absence of an otherwise expected vowel reduction to schwa in English. For example, the words 'comp[ə]nsation' and 'cond[ɛ]nsation' have very similar prosody, but the latter maintains a full vowel pronunciation of [ɛ] rather than the expected reduction to schwa that we see in 'comp[ə]nsation'. On the basis of this and a number of other similar cases, Chomsky and Halle argue that the phonological irregularity of cond[ɛ]nsation arises because it is constrained to remain similar to its base of affixation: compare the associated bases 'comp[ə]nsate' and 'cond[ɛ]nse'.

Another example involving stress can be found in Polish (Rubach and Booij 1985). Polish has primary stress on the penultimate syllable, while preceding syllables are organized into left-headed feet aligned to the beginning of the prosodic word (compare example 2a and b). When prefixed with an enclitic, initial stress shifts such that the prosodic word begins with a foot. However the remainder of the foot structure of the stem remains parallel to the form without the enclitic in violation of the default stress pattern (compare Figures 2c and d).

(2) a. kònstantỳnopòlitánczyk   (ὸσ)(ὸσ)(ὸσ)(όσ)   'Inhabitant of
                                                          Constantinople-NOM'
      b. kònstantỳnopòlitanczýka (ὸσ)(ὸσ)(ὸσ)σ(όσ) 'Inhabitant of
                                                          Constantinople-GEN'
      c. àmerỳkanína   (ὸσ)(ὸσ)(όσ)   'American-GEN'
      d. dò amerỳkanína   (ὸσ)σ(ὸσ)(όσ)   'to an American-GEN'

Analogy, in the sense of pattern extension, is a significant route for change in systems of categories (Itkonen 2005). This chapter is an exploration of the ways that conflicting patterns at different levels of organization may mutually influence one another to produce change. Working within an evolutionary framework (see, e.g., Blevins 2004; Pierrehumbert 2006; Croft 2008), I have argued that similarity-biased variation can contribute to the entrenchment and extension of regular patterns over many cycles of language use and transmission (Wedel 2007). An evolutionary approach to pattern development and change is supported by the great deal of evidence that lexical memory is richly detailed at a number of levels, rather than limited to storage of symbolic, contrastive features as proposed in many classical models (reviewed in Pierrehumbert 2003). Within a model incorporating this evidence for rich memory, biases in production and perception toward previously experienced forms create a positive feedback loop promoting pattern entrenchment (Wedel 2006, 2007, reviewed in Pierrehumbert 2006). Given that a given system can potentially evolve toward many different meta-stable states, a task for anyone working within this evolutionary model of language pattern development is to understand what factors encourage or inhibit the transition from a given pattern into another. Recent examples of work in this area can be found in Blevins (2004), Mielke (2004), Chitoran and Hualde (2007), J. Blevins (2008), and many others. In this chapter I argue that pattern conflict across distinct levels of organization can be understood in a feedback-driven model of change as an instance of multilevel selection, and that this can help us think productively about the role of within-category variance in promoting or inhibiting change throughout the language system.

In the following section I review the role of noise in creating similarity biases in category processing. In Section 4.3 I go over some of the kinds of language change in which similarity-biased error may plausibly play a role. In Section 4.4 I review how variation introduced by error influences the development of patterns within a rich memory model, as well as the use of evolutionary theory to model this process. Section 4.5 discusses possible mechanisms for similarity biases in production and perception that can feed language change. Section 4.6 introduces multilevel selection as a potentially useful way to think about conflicts between different levels of generalization. Finally, Section 4.7 presents an illustrative simulation of a multilevel selection at work in a model lexical system evolving under competing attractors formed by distinct phonological and morphological regularities.

4.2 Error and similarity bias in categorization

Information processing is always errorful to some degree due to noise. The simplest error pattern arises in processing of individual bits of information in which there are just two possible states, e.g., 0 and 1. In this case, noise can only result in the transformation of one bit value into the other.

(3)　$\{\ldots, 1, 1, 1, \ldots\} \rightarrow \text{noise} \rightarrow \{\ldots, 1, 0, 1, \ldots\}$

Much of the processing in language, however, involves processing compositional signals in which the unit of interest is above the level of an indivisible bit. For example, a word is composed of subsidiary units of information, such as segments. Successful transmission of a higher-order category such as this requires that both the information source and target have access to a common lower-level information pattern identifying the category, e.g., a segment sequence. In this case, there are two possible outcomes of noise in processing. If noise results in a pattern that is not successfully matched to any existing category, processing fails altogether at that level. However, noise can also result in a match to a different category, as when an American English speaker utters *can't* but I understand *can*.

In a system in which categories can overlap to varying degrees, that is, can share variable amounts of lower-level information, noise will always favor mismatches between more similar over less similar categories. As an example, consider four categories each comprising two bits of information: $\{[1, 1], [1, 0], [0, 1], [0, 0]\}$. At any level of noise below that producing complete randomization, the odds that [1, 1] will be mismatched to [0, 1] or [1, 0] is always greater than the probability of matching to [0, 0]. As an illustration, (4) shows the rate of matching [1, 1] to [0, 1], and to [0, 0] respectively, at varying noise levels, where a noise level of 1 represents complete randomization of original information. Numerically predicted rates are shown as well as simulated rates averaged over 1000 trials at each noise level.

(4)   Pattern-matching error to similar versus less similar categories under noise.

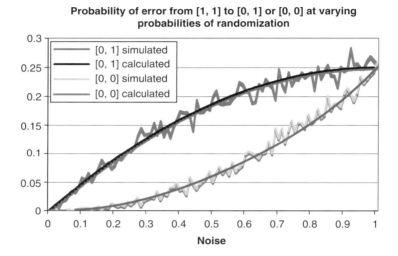

Given that language involves the processing of compositional categories that vary in their similarity along various dimensions, noise-driven mismatch errors will always be biased toward similar categories. In previous work I have argued that similarity-biased, "analogical" error can serve as a seed for phonological change and entrenchment of patterns within a rich-memory model of language production and perception (Wedel 2004, 2006, 2007). Here, I will explore some consequences of the hypothesis that a general similarity-biased error also contributes to analogical change at the morphological level. Because dimensions of phonological and morphological similarity can cut across one another, similarity-biased error and variation should set up conflicts between these distinct kinds of regularity. My goal in the next sections is to show that considering analogical change of all kinds to be initiated by similarity-biased error has the potential to shed light on the outcomes of conflict between and among phonological and morphological regularities (Sturtevant 1947).

4.3 Pattern extension in phonology and morphology

Many sound changes are "unnatural" in the sense that they do not appear to originate in common articulatory or perceptual tendencies. Some of these appear instead to originate in pattern extension. For example, in phonology, sound patterns can be extended from an original, "natural" context into contexts in which the change is not clearly phonetically motivated (for examples, see Mielke 2004: 102–14; J. Blevins 2006a).

In morphology, both *leveling* and *extension* changes can be considered instances of pattern extension (discussed in Deutscher 2001; Hock 2003). In leveling, members *within* a paradigm become more alike in some way. For example, the historical stem-final [f ~ v] alternation in the singular-plural pair *dwarf ~ dwarves* has leveled for many speakers of American English to *dwarf ~ dwarfs*. Paradigmatic extension occurs when a change creates a relationship within one paradigm that is parallel in some way to a relationship holding in another. For example, the originally regular present-past paradigm of *dive ~ dived* has shifted for many speakers to *dive ~ dove*, presumably by extension on the model of the group containing *drive ~ drove, ride ~ rode*, etc.

None of these phonological or morphological patterns can be fully understood without making reference to the existing language system. Given that learners and adult users alike have some knowledge of the ambient linguistic system, there are two conceptually distinct pathways by which patterns in the existing system can influence change: (i) by influencing the range of variants presented by adults to learners as input, and (ii) by influencing the ways that learners organize this input as they bootstrap between input and their current system toward the adult system (Pierrehumbert 2003; cf. CHANCE and CHOICE in the framework of Evolutionary Phonology, Blevins 2004[1]). In both cases, similarity biases can accentuate asymmetries within the experience of an individual. Within a rich-memory model of language production and processing (e.g., Pierrehumbert 2001; Bybee 2002; Wedel 2004, 2007), this asymmetry in experience is recorded in a corresponding asymmetry in the language system at some level. What dimensions of similarity are most salient in a particular system is an empirical question, dependent on both relatively universal as well as system-specific details (see e.g., Albright (this volume) and Pierrehumbert (2006) for discussion of these issues).

---

[1] In Evolutionary Phonology (Blevins 2004, 2006b) CHANCE is a pathway of change by which features of a percept are intrinsically ambiguous, allowing different learners to impose different underlying structure on a common surface form. CHOICE is an abstractly similar pathway for differential development of underlying structure, where given a range of variant productions a single category one learner chooses a different prototypical form than another.

4.4 Rich memory, feedback, and evolution

There is abundant evidence that the mental lexicon stores a great deal of information about perceived variants of lexical forms. In turn, there is evidence that new experiences continually contribute to this store of information, and that this information biases both subsequent perception (e.g., Johnson 1997; Guenther *et al.* 2004; Eisner and McQueen 2005) and production (Goldinger 2000; Harrington *et al.* 2000). As a result, processing a particular instance of a form increases the probability that a similar form will be processed in the same way in the future, and that corresponding forms will be produced in a similar way in the future. This creates positive feedback that promotes the entrenchment of patterns over many cycles of production and perception in acquisition, and to some degree in adult usage as well (Wedel 2006, 2007, reviewed in Pierrehumbert 2006).

In a clever demonstration of feedback between perception and production Goldinger (2000) had a group of subjects produce a baseline recording of a set of words. The next day they *heard* the same words spoken some number of times in a particular voice. They returned five days later and were recorded again reading the same list of words. For each word recorded by each subject, an AXB test stimulus was made from (i) the subject baseline recording of the word, (ii) the word as heard by the subject the second day, and (iii) the final subject test recording of that word (where the order of the baseline and test recording was random). These recordings were played for a separate group of listeners who were given the task of rating which of the two subject recordings of the word was more like the middle reference recording in the other voice. The listeners identified the second test recording as more similar to the reference recording at significantly above chance, indicating that for the subjects, phonetic details of a pronunciation heard five days earlier had a significant influence on their own current pronunciation of that word.

Within a model of language in which variation within and across categories can be stored in some form, reproduced, and transmitted, the system as a whole can change through evolutionary processes (e.g., Wedel 2006; Kirby 2007; Croft 2008). The most well-known mechanism for a reproducing population to evolve over time is through selection, in which some variant elements in the population reproduce more than others via some interaction within the system. As long as there is some mechanism for variation to arise and persist, selection can favor some variants over others in some way, thereby altering the distribution of characteristics within the population over time. Although some rich-memory models assume that the only content of categories is in the form of fully detailed exemplars (reviewed in Tenpenny 1995), there is evidence that behavior also proceeds through use of independent, more abstract generalizations about input data (e.g., Kuehne *et al.* 2000; Albright this volume). For the purposes of the argument here, provided that within-category variation can persist in the system at some level – whether at the level of exemplars or of generalizations about some form – selection among these variants can result in change in the system.

When patterns conflict within systems including positive feedback, the most stable outcome is dominance of one pattern over the other. Examples from familiar life include the direction that a ball rolls down a symmetrical hill starting from the top. At the top all directions may be equally likely, but once the ball begins moving in a particular direction, other directions become increasingly unlikely. A more complex example comes from economics, where in many cases the larger a company is, the better it can compete. All else being equal, in this situation the most stable state may be a monopoly (Sharkey 1982).

In previous work, I have argued that similarity-biased errors in production and perception may serve as an underlying cause of the development of regular phonological patterns in language through positive feedback, despite the ability of the language system to store and use otherwise predictable information (Wedel 2007). The development of consistent patterns in morphology has also been argued to arise through positive feedback over many cycles of errorful learning (e.g., Hare and Elman 1995; Kirby 2001). Hare and Elman, for example, showed that sequential errorful learning and production by connectionist networks could reproduce the general trajectory of pattern changes that occurred in present-past verb paradigms between two stages of Old English. They first trained a connectionist network to reproduce a large set of Old English present-past verb-form pairs, and then used the output of this network as the learning input to a subsequent naïve network, the output of which served as input to the next, and so on. Because errors in network outputs tend to favor robust generalizations at the expense of less well-attested patterns, the result over many transfers was a gently accelerating consolidation as, for example, the incipient "regular" past-tense pattern became increasingly robust within the data.

4.5 Similarity biases in production and perception

In any process that distinguishes between categories, the rate of error in element identification or manipulation due to noise will be greater between more similar categories relative to less similar categories. Processes in language use that provide opportunities for these kinds of similarity-biased errors include (i) motor entrenchment in production, (ii) the magnet effect in perception, and

(iii) the application of relational categories to compose related forms. Motor entrenchment is a general property of motor systems in which practiced motor routines bias future motor execution in some relation to similarity (Zanone and Kelso 1997). This sets up a positive feedback loop in which, *ceteris paribus*, less frequent production variants should be steadily deformed toward more frequent production variants over time (Bybee 2002, discussed in Wedel 2006, 2007). On the perceptual side, the perceptual magnet effect (Kuhl 1991, 1995) provides another potential source of positive feedback which can act to enhance the similarity of forms over time. The perceptual magnet effect refers to the finding that percepts tend to be biased systematically toward the centers of categories relative to the stimuli that gave rise to them. This systematic warping should pull similar pronunciations closer together over time through feedback between perception and production (Wedel 2007).

Both motor gestures and linguistically relevant sound categories often have a relational internal structure, meaning that they cannot be fully characterized by a simple list of properties. Instead, these categories must include some higher-order relational information. Phonological examples with concrete internal relational structure include sound-categories with temporally ordered gestures such as diphthongs, affricates, and contour tones. The central importance for language of such "relational categories" has been discussed at length by Dedre Gentner and colleagues in the context of semantics (Gentner and Kurtz 2005). Morphophonological patterns are also relational, in that they describe some mapping between forms (Bybee 1985). These patterns are often described in terms of rules, but they may be described as well in terms of relational categories, identified with, for example, the large number of possible patterns in the relationship between present and past forms of English verbs (Albright and Hayes 2002). Generalizations (whether expressed as rules or relational categories) play a role in production or identification of linguistic forms whenever some form is reconstructed through reference to some other form or pattern. This is analogy. The parade example of this use is in the production of a novel form fitting a pattern. In this case, a large body of research indicates that the applicability of a generalization to a novel form is gradient and dependent on similarity to other forms that are covered under that generalization (e.g., Long and Almor 2000; Albright 2002a; Krott *et al.* 2002; Ernestus and Baayen 2003). For example, the novel present-past verb form pair 'spling $\sim$ splung' is highly similar to members of a significant subpattern in English verb forms including 'sing $\sim$ sung', 'spring $\sim$ sprung', etc. Despite the fact that 'spling' is a novel form, 'splung' is rated as a very good possible past-tense form for this verb (Albright 2002a), contrary to models that assume that all novel forms will be produced via a default pattern (e.g., Pinker 1991).

It has been noted that production of previously learned, morphologically complex forms within a paradigm might proceed by direct retrieval from memory, or through reconstruction from a base or related word-form using an associated generalization (e.g., Baayen 1992; Schreuder and Baayen 1995; Alegre and Gordon 1999). Error in application of a generalization in this process can result in an extended or leveled output pattern depending on the source of the generalization (Hock 2003). Extension of a compositional pattern results in a leveled output, as when speakers of English occasionally produce the past tense of an irregular verb regularly, e.g., 'teached' rather than 'taught'. Conversely, extension of irregular patterns also occur, and have been shown to be more likely in bases that share phonological features with the set of forms exhibiting that irregular pattern (Bybee and Modor 1983; Long and Almor 2000; Albright and Hayes 2002), as for example when the past tense of 'bring' is produced as 'brang' by analogy to the 'sing ~ sang' group of verbs.

There are a wide variety of generalizations that are potentially involved in production and perception of any linguistic form, from lower-level phonotactic generalizations about feature groupings and segment sequences, to higher-level relational, morphological generalizations about possible paradigmatic relationships. Because the sequences referred to by these generalizations can overlap to any degree, there is the possibility of conflict between distinct kinds of generalizations. The following section discusses the possible outcomes of this conflict in terms of competition between levels of selection.

4.6 Similarity biases and selection

In biological evolution, errors in the replication of a gene are thought to be random, at least with respect to the phenotype conferred by the gene. Selection on the basis of the interaction of a variant gene product with its environment influences the likelihood of reproduction of some unit containing the gene (such as a cell, a multicellular organism, or a kin group). As a consequence, the production of variants and the filter on what variants survive to reproduce are mechanistically distinct. On the other hand, within a model of language in which errors can be biased by similarity to other existing forms and patterns, variation in what is produced and what is perceived is nonrandom with regard to the "phenotype" of the system (cf. CHANCE and CHOICE in the framework of Evolutionary Phonology; Blevins 2004). In this regard, similarity-biased error acts in production as a selective filter acting on the pool of *potential* variants, influencing which variants actually emerge to become part of the exemplar set of the larger system. In perception, similarity-biased error acts as a selective filter by biasing identification and storage into categories.

In biological systems, genes exist within a Russian doll of nested units that are potentially the objects of selection, ranging from the gene itself, through the chromosome, the cell, the multicellular individual organism, the kin group and potentially beyond (Mayr 1997). Selection can potentially act at each of these levels, often mediated by distinct mechanisms and on different time scales.[2] For example, selection at the level of the cell strongly favors cells that are unconstrained in their growth, which promotes the development of cancer within an individual's lifetime. Selection at the level of the individual on the other hand strongly favors strong control over cell division. In concert, these two selective pressures lead both to selection for cancer within the population of cells within a single individual, and to selection against early development of cancer over a timescale of many lifetimes within the population of individuals (Merlo *et al.* 2006).

Within a single level of selection, the net selection pressure deriving from multiple independent loci of selection can often be approximated as a simple sum. For example, if a trait increases fitness in some way to a given degree, but decreases it by the same degree through an independent pathway, the net selection pressure on that trait may be near zero. In contrast, when selection pressures on a given trait operate at different levels of selection, say the cell versus the individual, these pressures can interact in a more complex way. Selection against a trait at one level can often proceed through creating a systemic change that makes selection *for* that trait at another level less efficient. One way to influence the efficiency of selection is through modifying the amount of variation present at a given level of selection; greater variance provides more opportunities for a fitter variant to be selected (e.g.,Taylor *et al.* 2002).

Within the model presented here, the competition between selection for regularity at distinct levels of linguistic organization is similar to biological multilevel selection in that change at one level can influence the opportunities for change at another. Within the present model, a pattern serves as a self-reinforcing attractor by biasing variation/error toward itself. Because linguistic categories can overlap with or contain one another (as, for example, when a sound category is a component of a sound–meaning category such as a word), a change that increases the regularity of a pattern at one categorial level can decrease it at another. A decrease in regularity of a pattern (i.e., an increase in variance) therefore has two interacting effects on further change: (i) as variance increases at that level, the range of future variation increases,

---

[2] The well-known phenomenon of kin selection is a particular case of selection beyond the individual. In kin selection, selection at the level of the kin group favors the evolution of behavior detrimental to the self when it supports the greater reproductive success of a close relative.

potentiating change; (ii) as variance increases, similiarity-driven selection pressure toward the mean is weakened. Both of these effects should independently potentiate a shift further away from regularity in the contents of a category through evolutionary change. This is illustrated in the next section.

4.7 Illustrating multilevel, selection-driven pattern development by simulation

In Wedel (2007) I illustrated the evolution of regular stress patterns through similarity-based positive feedback within a simulated lexicon over many cycles of production and perception. In these simulations, the only relationships encoded between lexical items were on the basis of shared segmental properties in temporal order. Segmental properties that were provided to the system included stress value, segmental category features and word-edge status. An example of a three-syllable lexical entry is

(5)   [1, a, I] [−1, b] [1, c, F]

where square brackets enclose syllables. Each syllable is characterized by a stress value and one or more additional features: "1" and "−1" represent stress and stresslessness, respectively, lower-case letters represent segmental features, and "I" and "F" correspond to "word-initial" and "word-final".

Lexical production in each round of the simulation proceeded by copying the information stored in the lexical entry into an output form with a low probability of error in the stress value, and then restoring it in the lexical entry, replacing the original. Directional change could intervene in this process through the action of two kinds of error-bias in output production, one external, and the other system-dependent. The external error bias was a constant, lexicon-independent bias favoring alternating stress, such that each word would eventually tend to exhibit alternating stress regardless of the initial state. The second kind of error consisted of a similarity-bias in which output stress values had a slight probability of deviating from the stored value toward the values of other forms, in relation to similarity and type-frequency. The simulation detected pattern trends within the lexicon by identifying every existing combination of features and stress values in the lexicon, and looking for robust generalizations. When an existing robust feature-set $\sim$ stress-value generalization conflicted with the stored version of a word, the output based on that word had a greater than chance probability of shifting stress values to match the larger generalization. As a result, the system showed a strong tendency to create broad associations between stress values and features over many cycles of production and restorage.

Within the lexicon, there were many possible segmental features, but only two edge features (initial vs final). Many words therefore failed to share any segmental features at all, while every word had both an initial- and final-edge feature associated with the initial and final syllables, respectively. As a consequence, the most robust generalization that the lexicon could possibly evolve was one in which a given stress value was consistently associated with the initial and/or final word edge, rather than to some other segmental feature(s). When both even- and odd-syllable words were included in the lexicon, the dominant pattern was the evolution of an alternating stress pattern consistently aligned *either* to the initial *or* the final syllable.

To illustrate multilevel selection within this model, I modified the simulation architecture to include two optional suffix syllables for a subset of the words in the lexicon, identified with the abstract features [y] and [z] respectively. A portion of a sample lexicon is shown in Figure (3). The final syllable of every word contains a final-edge feature (F). The lexicon consists of 80 words. Half of the words in the lexicon do not have a related suffixed form, illustrated in (6a). The other half, as illustrated in (6b), appear in addition in a suffixed form. An [F] feature appears on the final syllable in all forms.[3]

(6)   Example of a statically regular lexicon
    (a)   Stem-only paradigms
            Stem
        $\overbrace{\hspace{4cm}}$
        [-1, a] [1, b, F]
        [-1, c] [1, d, F]

    (b)   Stem and Stem+Suffix paradigms
            Stem   Stem   Suffix
        $\overbrace{\hspace{3.5cm}}$ $\overbrace{\hspace{3cm}}$ $\overbrace{\hspace{2.5cm}}$

        [-1, e] [1, f, F]   ∼ [1, e] [-1, f]   [1, y, F]
                            ∼ [1, e] [-1, f]   [1, z, F]
        [-1, g] [1, h, F]   ∼ [1, g] [-1, h]   [1, y, F]
                            ∼ [1, g] [-1, h]   [1, z, F]

The lexicon in (6) is "statically regular" with regard to stress, because all entries show alternating stress aligned to the final syllable. In this example, the stress pattern of every word can be written as [(+), −, +]. It is "relationally irregular" with regard to stress, because stems in bare and suffixed forms show

---

[3] In order to focus the simulation on conflict between emergent phonological and morphological patterns, the development of stress associations at the final word-edge was encouraged by eliminating the initial-edge feature. Within over fifty independent trial simulations, the system always rapidly developed a stress pattern in stem-only paradigms in which stress was aligned to the final edge.

opposite stress patterns: the stress patterns of the stems in (b) are $[-, +]$ when unsuffixed and $[+, -]$ when suffixed.

The system retains the ability to detect robust static generalizations across all words in each cycle. In addition, the system has been equipped with the ability to identify the global stress-pattern relationship between suffixed and unsuffixed forms and discover any robust associations between this relationship and any existing combination of features, using a parallel computational mechanism to that used for the discovery of static generalizations (described in Wedel 2004, 2007). This latter ability allows the emergence of relational generalizations of varying specificity. For example, a maximally specific generalization would match the stress pattern of a particular unsuffixed form to its related suffixed form, whereas a less specific generalization could emerge if a number of different unsuffixed forms shared the same stress-pattern relationship with their suffixed forms. Although implemented in a computationally distinct way, this is conceptually parallel to the mechanism of relational generalization discovery in Albright and Hayes's Minimal Generalization Algorithm (2002).[4] As before, the process of encoding an output corresponding to a stored form was subject to error biased toward existing patterns in the lexicon in proportion to similarity and type frequency. As in the single-level simulations in Wedel (2007), low-level noise was also included, in the form of a very small probability of context-free error in correctly reproducing the stored stress value in any syllable.

The result is a system that has two distinct levels of system-dependent generalization that can influence error: static generalizations at the level of features, and relational generalizations between related words, where the targets of relational generalizations contain the targets of static generalizations. Pattern competition within and between these two levels of generalization resulted in three common classes of patterns. In one class of patterns, alternating stress developed with a given stress value consistently associated with the final edge of all words, with no reference to word identity or morphological category. This is the type of pattern that emerges in the absence of any possible relational generalization linking related words. This pattern represents full regularity with regard to phonological categories, and full irregularity within each morphologically related pair, as the stress pattern for the stem in the unsuffixed form is opposite that found in the corresponding suffixed form, as in (6) above.

In a second common pattern, all two-syllable forms in the lexicon had the same stress value associated with the final edge, while each suffixed form had the opposite stress value at its final edge, thereby preserving the stress pattern

---

[4] Previous work compared the mechanism of pattern discovery used here to several computational mechanisms including Analogical Language Modeling (Skousen 1989), and showed that they all produced qualitatively similar regular patterns (Wedel 2004).

of the stem. This represents full morphological, or relational regularity with regard to stem stress pattern, and full phonological, or static irregularity with regard to final-edge stress alignment. The lexicon in (7) below exhibits this pattern: stems maintain the same stress pattern whether suffixed or not (compare to (6) above). A third pattern occasionally arose in which the paradigm associated with one suffix showed phonological regularity, and the other showed morphological regularity (see cycle 990 in (9) below).

(7)   Example of a relationally regular lexicon
    (a)   Stem-only paradigms

$$\overbrace{\phantom{\text{Stem}}}^{\text{Stem}}$$

          [-1, a] [1, b, F]
          [-1, c] [1, d, F]

    (b)   Stem and Stem+Suffix paradigms

$\overbrace{\phantom{\text{Stem}}}^{\text{Stem}}$	$\overbrace{\phantom{\text{Stem}}}^{\text{Stem}}$	$\overbrace{\phantom{\text{Suffix}}}^{\text{Suffix}}$
[-1, e] [1, f, F]	~ [-1, e] [1, f]	[-1, y, F]
	~ [-1, e] [1, f]	[-1, z, F]
[-1, g] [1, h, F]	~ [-1, g] [1, h]	[-1, y, F]
	~ [-1, g] [1, h]	[-1, z, F]

In this model, both leveling and extension occur in the same way: through errorful application of a different generalization true of some other part of the system, just as has been argued to be the case for language by, e.g., Deutscher (2001) and Hock (2003). In the event that there is only one primary relational generalization that fits all the data, then the only available mechanism for change in stress pattern lies in the low-level noise factor which provides a continual, small input of stress-pattern variants into the system. This occasionally leads to the fortuitous emergence of a different generalization, which can then spread through similarity-based error. As expected, it first spreads through the most similar subset of words within the lexicon, after which it may spread further. This is illustrated in the graph in (8) below, where a value of "1" represents full relational regularity in the stress of stems in related suffixed and unsuffixed forms, and "-1" represents full static identity in the stress patterns of all words in the lexicon with respect to the final word edge. The simulation is seeded with a lexicon exhibiting full relational regularity in both the "y" and "z" suffix paradigms, like that shown above in (4). This pattern remains stable for 1000 cycles despite the steady introduction of low-level variation in stress patterns by noise.

(8)   Competition between static and relational regularities

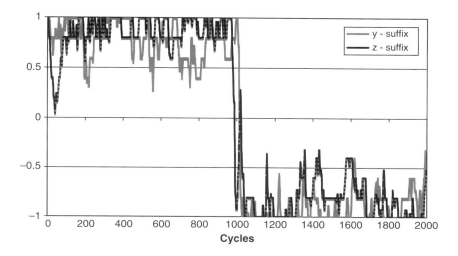

Shortly after the z-suffix paradigm switches to a pattern in which all forms have the same stress with regard to the final word edge, the y-suffix forms are able to follow suit. This change is potentiated because the z-suffix paradigm presents a similar group of words governed by a distinct generalization which can itself be errorfully applied to members of the y-suffix paradigm. In other words, as soon as a new generalization emerges, its misapplication provides a new pathway of change. A close-up of this transition is shown in (9) below.

(9)   Competiton between static and relational regularities: cycle 885–1150.

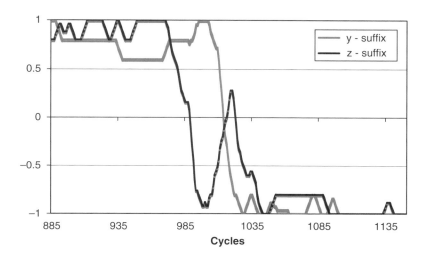

The dependence of a change between a static and relational stress pattern on the pre-existence of a target pattern in the lexicon holds in both the "extension" and "leveling" directions. In 10 simulations in which the seed lexicon was statically regular throughout (that is, where stress was aligned to the final edge of all words), it took an average of ~1400 cycles for a change to a relational pattern within one of the suffix paradigms to emerge. Likewise, in 10 simulations seeded with a lexicon exhibiting relational regularity in all suffixed-unsuffixed word pairs (that is, where the stem in each pair had the same stress), the average time to a change to static regularity was near 1700 cycles. In contrast, if the seed lexicon started with static regularity in one suffix paradigm, and relational regularity in the other, in 10 simulations it took on average less than 300 cycles for a further change to occur in one of the paradigms. The rate of change is greater when there are multiple existing patterns in the lexicon because each pattern represents a template for analogical extension.

The potentiating effect of multiple patterns can also be seen in the rate of error in output stress among the stem-only paradigms within the lexicon. When the stress pattern is statically regular, all stress patterns are edge-aligned across the entire lexicon. Under this condition, random noise is the only source of error in stress output in stem-only paradigms. When the stress pattern is relationally regular, however, some lexical entries have the opposite stress pattern as that in stem-only paradigms. In this case, there is an additional pattern in the lexicon to provide a pathway for variation in stress output beyond random noise. Within the simulation, this can be seen by comparing the number of stem-only paradigm outputs with a variant stress patterns in a statically regular, versus relationally regular lexicon. Figure 10 below shows the error rate in stress within stem-only paradigm outputs over 10 independent runs of 1000 cycles each in the context of either a statically, or relationally regular lexicon. When the stress pattern is consistently aligned to the final word-edge over the entire lexicon (i.e, is statically regular), the error rate in stress in stem-only paradigm outputs is .04. However, when the stress pattern is instead aligned to a stem edge within stem ∼ stem+suffix paradigms (i.e., is relationally regular), the average error rate in stem-only paradigm outputs goes up to .16.

This higher error rate in the relationally regular lexicon comes about through the existence of an additional pattern in the lexicon, which provides an additional pathway to a change in stress. The resulting increased variance in stress patterns within stem-only paradigms has two related effects: (i) the dominant stress pattern of stem-only paradigms is *less* stable, and therefore more likely to change over time, and (ii), the dominant stress pattern of

(10)   Error rate in stem-only paradigm outputs given static versus relational regularity in stem ~ stem+suffix paradigms.

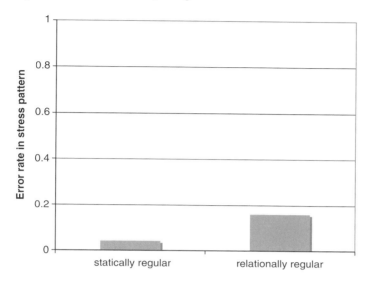

stem ~ stem + suffix paradigms is *more* stable, because any similarity bias promoting static regularity is weakened. This is conceptually parallel to cases in biological evolution in which selection at one level acts by modulating variance at another (e.g., Taylor *et al.* 2002).

4.8 Summary and conclusions

The statistics of error in pattern matching ensure that similar patterns will substitute for each other more often than less similar patterns in production and perception. In any model of language production and perception in which intra-categorical variants can coexist and compete within the system, positive feedback promotes the evolution of regular patterns. Under the assumption that both static and relational generalizations are manipulated during language production and perception, error between similar generalizations should produce a wide range of similarity effects at different levels, from phonotactics to morphology (Itkonen 2005).

When similarity at separate levels of organization cannot be simultaneously maximized, similarity-biased error and feedback promotes the entrenchment of one pattern at the expense of the other. The potentiation of change by similarity-biased error allows this snowball effect to proceed in opposite directions at different levels: as variance decreases at one level, further change to solidify the spreading pattern is potentiated by feedback; at the same time, the more variance increases at the other level, the less similarity bias can work against further change. When we view similarity bias as a form of selection on the range of possible variants that enter the linguistic system over time (Wedel 2006), the interaction between overlapping levels of organization in the lexicon can be understood as a form of multilevel selection. As an illustration, I presented results from a simple simulation showing that in a system in which errorful pattern extension is a primary pathway of change, competition between a static regularity and a relational regularity resulted in the rapid stabilization of one over the other, in part by modulating variance at distinct levels of organization. Further, if a new pattern establishes itself in a subset of the lexicon, the existence of this new generalization potentiates development of a similar pattern in other, similar words. More generally, unresolved conflicts in regularity create a reservoir of instability in the system, maintaining a greater number of pathways for change and therefore a more diverse pool of variants than might otherwise exist. A motto for this model could therefore be phrased as "conflict begets variation begets extension."

This is conceptually consistent with the both the notions that analogical extension tends to result in global simplification of grammar (e.g., Halle 1962), and yet that extension is based on local generalizations (e.g., Joseph and Janda 1988, Venneman 1993). Importantly however, this model does not propose that extension serves a teleological goal of grammar simplification, but only that extension may occur more frequently when there are more grammatical patterns in competition. Multiple competing patterns provide more available pathways for error, and multiplicity itself weakens the relative strength of the behavioral attractor represented by any given pattern. Although any given analogical change may result in a relative simplification or complexification of grammar at some larger scale, any change that happens to reduce global pattern conflict also undermines the properties of the system that potentiate further analogical change. Consequently, within this model global pattern coherence is not an explicit goal of the system, but simply a relatively stable state in a continuing trajectory of change through time.

5

The relation between linguistic analogies and lexical categories*

*LouAnn Gerken, Rachel Wilson,
Rebecca Gómez, and Erika Nurmsoo*

5.1 Introduction

This chapter is an attempt to find points of contact between two normally distinct lines of research. One line is concerned with the psychological mechanisms that allow language learners to discover lexical categories, such as noun, verb, etc., in the linguistic input. The other is concerned with the human ability to see two domains as analogous, such that structural components of one domain align with structural components of the other domain (e.g., Gentner 1983). For example, even children are able to complete the analogies in 1a-b, below.

1a. chick : hen :: calf : _____
1b. dog : dogs :: wug : _____

  There are at least two reasons to explore the role of our human ability to see analogies as a possible mechanism for lexical category learning. The first is that the most frequently used approach to studying lexical category learning in the laboratory employs the completion of an extended analogy, or paradigm. In such studies, experiment participants are presented with an incomplete lexical paradigm, such as the one shown in Table 5.1, below. The cells containing question marks are not presented during the initial learning phase.

  Such a paradigm might reflect a variety of lexical categories. For example, the words in the top two rows might be nouns with different number markings *o* and *a*, while the bottom two rows might be verbs with different tense inflections *of* and *op*. Or, the top two rows might be case-marked

  * This research was supported by NSF grant #9709774 to LAG and NIH grant #R01HD42170 to RLG and LAG. We thank David Eddington, Toben Mintz, and Royal Skousen for helpful comments.

TABLE 5.1 An example of stimuli that might be used in a paradigm completion task. Items that would fill the cells marked by "???" are withheld during training and presented with their ungrammatical counterparts during test.

blicka	snerga	pela	jica	tama	kusa
blicko	snergo	pelo	jico	tamo	???
deegof	votof	rudof	wadimof	meefof	ritof
deegop	votop	rudop	wadimop	meefop	???

feminine nouns and the bottom two rows masculine nouns. That is, without associating the paradigm with any reference field, it simply reflects a situation in which two sets of lexical items co-occur with different markers.

Once participants have been exposed to a subset of the paradigm, they are tested for their willingness to accept paradigm-conforming items that they have not yet heard, such as *kuso* and *ritop*, as well as equally new but nonconforming items, such as *kusop* and *rifo*. Participants' ability to distinguish the conforming vs nonconforming items is taken to mean that they treat the newly learned lexical items as having distinct privileges of co-occurrence, which is viewed by many researchers as the basis for lexical categories (e.g., Braine 1966; Maratsos 1982; but see Grimshaw 1981; Pinker 1982 for the alternate conception of category acquisition). Thus, both in terms of many researchers' construal of the language learners' problem, and in terms of the way in which we test for category learning in the laboratory, lexical category formation is viewed as presenting learners with an extended analogy (in the form of a morphophonological paradigm), in which generalization from the input is viewed as filling in the blank, just as in Table 5.1 above.

The second reason to explore the role of our analogy-making capacity as a possible mechanism for lexical category learning is that, as we will document more fully below, adults and infants are unable to complete paradigms like the one shown in Table 5.1 without some additional cues to category structure. We will review the types of additional cues that have been explored by researchers, including ourselves, in the next two sections. The notion that we will explore in the final section is that the psychological mechanisms by which additional cues promote category learning is one of analogy-making. To foreshadow, the argument that we will entertain is that learners require a sufficient amount of similarity among items in a paradigm to complete the paradigm and to infer lexical categories. Put simply, we suggest that learners are more likely to detect the analogy in examples like (2b) than they are in (2a), and to use that analogical structure to group the stems in (2b) into the same lexical category.

2a.   blicka : blicko :: kusa : _____
2b.   tivorblicka : tivorblicko :: tivorkusa : _____

5.2 Previous explorations into paradigm completion

The earliest studies asking whether adults are able to complete four-part morphological analogies were done several decades ago (Braine 1966; Smith 1966). Smith (1966) asked whether adults could show evidence of learning categories by presenting them with a paradigm-completion task of the sort outlined in conjunction with Table 5.1. Participants were familiarized for one minute with 12 bigrams in which the letters came from four classes that Smith called M, N, P, and Q. Bigrams either had the form MN or PQ. Some of the possible MN and PQ pairings were withheld. At test, participants generated a number of incorrect strings of the MQ or PN type, suggesting that they had not kept the categories separate. That is, participants learned that M and P come first and Q and N second, but not that there are co-occurrence restrictions.

Braine (1987) dubbed the errorful performance of Smith's participants the "MN/PQ problem" and hypothesized that simple co-occurence information alone is insufficient for humans to form categories. In a second class of accounts of how lexical categories are acquired, he hypothesized that, if referential information was included in addition to distributional informa-tion, categories may be learnable. In one study testing this hypothesis, Braine (1987) presented participants with an MN/PQ type language, now with MN and PQ each a phrase comprising two auditory nonsense words. Each phrase was presented with a picture. Half of the N words were accompanied by pictures of women and half of the Q words by pictures of men. The other half of the pictures depicted inanimate objects with no apparent referential regu-larity. Additionally, the M and P words corresponded to cardinality in the pictures. Thus, there were M words for 'one' and 'two', and P words for 'one' and 'two'. As in the work by Smith, some of the possible MN and PQ pairings were withheld.

Participants made grammaticality judgments of the phrases, and unlike the participants in Smith's study, they were correctly able to distinguish unpre-sented paradigm-conforming from nonconforming cases. Generalization was even correct when the phrase corresponded to a picture of an inanimate object, suggesting that participants had formed categories of M, N, P, and Q words and did not need reference to access the categories, once they had been formed. Braine speculated that the mechanism learners used to solve the

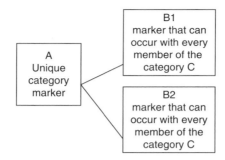

Stage 1, Unique marker A associated with items B1-Bn

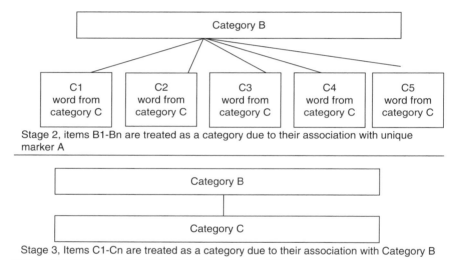

Stage 2, items B1-Bn are treated as a category due to their association with unique marker A

Stage 3, Items C1-Cn are treated as a category due to their association with Category B

FIGURE 5.1 Schematic of Braine's (1987) conception of category formation from morphophonological paradigms. The presence of the A element is critical using the morphophonological markers in B with the lexical category C.

MN/PQ problem was to note first that N and Q words behave as categories, based in this case on referential information. Learners then noted that the referentially based categories co-occur with morphophonological markers (in this case, number words differentially marked for gender), and ultimately used the markers themselves as the basis of categorization. Note that Braine's account holds that learners first discover the existence of categories based on a unique cue to each category (e.g., referring to masculine vs feminine pictures; see Fig. 5.1 for a schematic). Braine also suggested that reference was not necessary for learners to hypothesize the existence of categories and that additional morphological or phonological cues might work as well.

Other researchers began to test Braine's claim that reference might not be necessary for adults to be able to complete a morphophonological paradigm, but rather that phonological or morphological information could be used to first establish the existence of categories. Until recently, the results of these investigations have been equivocal. In one study by Brooks and colleagues, participants were familiarized with one of two artificial languages (Brooks, Braine, Catalano, Brody, and Sudhalter 1993). The languages each comprised 30 words for objects (half in each of two categories), two sets of three locative suffixes (each set went with one of the object categories) and one agent (the subject of all the sentences and not relevant here). Note that the locative suffixes are the marker elements. The difference between the languages was that, in the experimental language, 60 percent (18 of 30) of the object words contained the syllables *oik* or *oo*, depending on their category. In the control language, no common phonetic information occurred on the object words. The question was whether *oik* and *oo* would function like the referential information in Braine's earlier studies. An experimenter acted out each phrase for the participant with props; however, the props and actions did not contain category information. Two results are of interest for the current discussion. First, participants trained on the experimental language recalled significantly more items than those trained on the control language. Second, participants trained on the experimental language generalized more to withheld items, as shown by more generation of these items in the recall task. However, generalization to items that did not contain *oik* or *oo* was equivocal. Therefore conclusions about whether salient nonreferential information can trigger category learning must remain speculative based on these investigations.

Frigo and McDonald (1998) continued to explore correlated cues to category learning. In their experiments, they told the participants that they would be learning two kinds of greetings: two of them were to be used in the evening and two during the day. The participants were also told that there were two groups of people and that one set of greetings was used in front of the ten names of people in one group and the other set of greetings before the ten names of people in the other. Thus, the two greetings for each group were equivalent to the two gendered cardinalities in the study by Braine (1987). The task for the participants was to correctly categorize which greetings went with which names. A subset of the names was distinguished with phonological markers, whereby 60 percent (6 of 10) of the names of members of one group shared a sequence of sounds, making this study similar to Brooks *et al.* (1993). Like the earlier study, Frigo and McDonald found in two experiments that participants were correctly able to generalize to unpresented items when those greeting-name combinations contained the phonological marker. However, when the unpresented greeting-name combinations did not contain the phonological marker, participants performed no better than chance at associating the proper greeting with the person. In a third experiment, Frigo and McDonald placed phonological markers at only the beginnings of names, only the ends, or at both the beginning and end. Participants were not able to generalize to unstudied, unmarked forms unless the markers were salient (at least a syllable in length) and redundant (appeared at the beginning and the end of the word). Even the latter finding was weak, because it was not significant in the analysis by items. What is most striking about these results is that participants knew in advance how many categories there were. They were told that there were two kinds of greetings for two groups of people, and given distributional information that correlated with that number of categories. One might think it would have been easy for participants to form the categories and generalize to new cases, but it was not.

Kempe and Brooks (2001) examined a natural language, Russian, that has gender-based categorization of nouns. They noted in the CHILDES database (MacWhinney 2000) that language directed at children contains diminutive suffixes on 35–40 percent of nouns. This percentage differs from adult-directed speech where it was estimated that 2.7 percent of nouns are diminutives. Kempe and Brooks hypothesized that diminutive suffixes may serve to mark categories in the same way that the suffixes *oik* and *oo* did in the earlier study by Brooks *et al.* (1993). To test this hypothesis, they presented adult participants with two-word phrases of Russian, consisting of a color word (either masculine or feminine) and a noun. Color words served as markers. Half of the participants were familiarized with diminutivized nouns, and half were trained on the same nouns without suffixes. Phrases were presented with pictures, but the pictures added no category information. The group trained on diminutivized nouns outperformed the other group in a recall task. However, as in Brooks *et al.* (1993), generalization to phrases not containing diminutives was weak.

There are at least two explanations of the equivocal results found by Brooks *et al.* (1993), Frigo and McDonald (1998), and Kempe and Brooks (2001). The first is that human adults find it extremely difficult to form categories that are not at least in part referentially cued. However, a second explanation arises when one considers that participants in these three studies were presented with a referential field for each familiarization phrase. Importantly, the referential field did not contain any category information. Therefore, participants may have focused more fully on learning the referents for words in the familiarization phrases than on the structure of the language. The second explanation maintains the viability of Braine's original view that any add-

TABLE 5.2 Critical stimuli from Mintz (2002). The item that would fill the cell marked "???" was presented at test along with a new ungrammatical foil. The empty cell in the lower right was not presented at all during the study.

bool nex jiv	bool kwob jiv	bool zich jiv	bool pren jiv
sook nex runk	sook kwob runk	sook zich runk	???
zim nex noof	zim kwob noof	zim zich noof	zim pren noof
poz nex fen	poz kwob fen	poz zich fen	poz pren fen
choon pux wug	choon yult wug	choon plif wug	

itional pair of cues to the existence of categories might allow paradigm completion. However, tests of the hypothesis must take into account the possibility that the presence of referential information that is not relevant to the categories may disrupt category formation.

Mintz (2002) used a version of paradigm completion with adults and showed a much clearer ability to complete the paradigm based on linguistic (non-referential) cues alone. As in the examples we have been considering, Mintz employed two categories of words – those in rows 1 to 4 of Table 5.2 and those in row 5. As in the examples that we have considered, Mintz asked adults about their acceptance of the cell withheld during the initial exposure (*sook pren runk*) and compared that to their acceptance of another novel sequence (*choon pren wug*). Specifically, he asked participants to say whether or not test items were grammatical and also how confident they were in their ratings. He found that, when grammaticality ratings (1 or -1) were multiplied by confidence ratings (1–7), adults had significantly higher ratings for the paradigm-conforming than the nonconforming stimuli.

One construal of Mintz's findings is that adults used the two simultaneously present cues to categories (e.g., *bool-jiv* vs *choon-wug*) to divide the medial words into two categories. Therefore, the study demonstrates that paradigm completion can be achieved in the absence of referential information. However, Mintz's paradigm is not typical of the other studies using the paradigm-completion approach. Rather than presenting participants with two categories, each with two sets of markers, and testing them on unpresented cells from each category (as in Table 5.1), Mintz presented one category with four fully correlated pairs of markers (rows 1–4 of Table 5.2) and one category with one fully correlated pair of markers (row 5 of Table 5.2). Further, Mintz only tested participants on the unpresented cell of one of the two categories. It is difficult to say how this particular approach to paradigm completion might have yielded different results than the more traditional approach shown in Table 5.1 and used by most other researchers. Nevertheless, it would be helpful to know if learners can show clear evidence of paradigm completion when exposed to the more traditional paradigm-completion task without referential cues. A set of studies from our own laboratory using the traditional task is presented in the next section.

In addition to its unusual use of the paradigm-completion task, Mintz's study does not appear to support Braine's construal of the role of additional cues to category membership. Recall that Braine hypothesized that the presence of a pair of cues to categories (e.g., masculine and feminine referents, the syllables *oo* and *ee*) alerted participants to the existence of two categories, which they then more fully filled in from the paradigm. However, there does not appear to be such a pair of cues in Mintz's paradigm. Rather, as noted above, four fully correlated pairs of syllables mark one category and one pair marks the other.[1] Perhaps participants could have noted a category that always began with *choon* and used that to initially form a *choon* category and an "other" category. However, Mintz's success at finding paradigm completion in a situation at least superficially different from the one characterized by Braine as learnable suggests that the psychological mechanism underlying paradigm completion may be different from the one envisioned by Braine. We will explore analogy-making as the alternate mechanism in the last section of this chapter.

5.3 Work on paradigm completion from our laboratory[2]

This section presents four studies that demonstrate adults' and infants' ability to complete paradigms based on linguistic cues alone, as long as just a subset of the input is marked with an additional pair of cues to category membership.

Adult Experiment 1

The stimuli consisted of 12 words of Russian, six masculine and six feminine, each with two different case endings (see Table 5.3, below). The case endings in this experiment were *oj* and *u* on feminine nouns and *ya* and *yem* on masculine nouns. Three of the feminine nouns shared a common derivational suffix (-k) and three of the masculine nouns shared a common derivational suffix (-tel). These derivational suffixes constituted partially correlated phonological information. Note that phonological information was presented on 50 percent of the words, the same percentage used by Braine (1987) for referential cues, and the same as or lower than the percentages in the other studies reviewed above. The 12

---

[1] Mintz (2002) referred to his stimuli as being composed of three words. They were read with the intonation of the sentence *I see you.*

[2] Experiments 1–3 were part of the Ph.D. dissertation of Rachel Wilson (2002).

TABLE 5.3 Stimuli used in Experiment 1. The items that would fill the cell marked "???" were presented at test along with new ungrammatical foils.

Feminine Words					
polkoj	rubashkoj	ruchkoj	???	knigoj	korovoj
polku	rubashku	ruchku	vannu	knigu	korovu

Masculine Words					
uchitel'ya	stroitel'ya	zhitel'ya	???	korn'ya	pisar'ya
uchitel'yem	stroitel'yem	zhitel'yem	tramvayem	korn'yem	pisar'yem

words each with two case inflections yielded 24 possible stimuli. However, following the typical paradigm-completion design, one feminine and one masculine item were withheld during familiarization to be presented at test, yielding 22 stimulus items presented during familiarization.

Familiarization stimuli consisted of 22 Russian words in four different random orders and presented across four blocks of trials, for a total of 88 stimuli. The stimuli were recorded by a fluent, non-native speaker of Russian (RW). Two seconds of silence was inserted between adjacent items. The familiarization session lasted a total of approximately four minutes. The critical test items were the unprecedented paradigm-conforming items *vannoj* and *tramvaya* and the equally new but unconforming items *vannya* and *tramvayoj*. An ANOVA on the number of "grammatical" responses to these two types of items was significant ($F (1, 15) = 25.90$, $p < .001$; see Fig. 5.2).

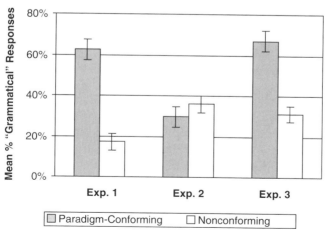

FIGURE 5.2 Mean "grammatical" responses and standard errors in Exps. 1–3. Lexical categories were marked with partially correlated cues in Exps. 1 and 3, but only case-marking cues in Exp. 2.

The data from Exp. 1 suggest that adults are able to successfully complete a linguistic paradigm based on morphological and phonological cues alone. Therefore, they are consistent with the data from Mintz (2002), but demonstrate paradigm completion using a more typical paradigm than the one used by Mintz. This study also raises two questions: First, as the literature review in Section 5.2 revealed, finding evidence of category learning by adults has been extremely difficult, and there has been no evidence at all that adults can learn when categories are marked with a single morphosyntactic cue. Indeed, our research team has failed in every one of our varied attempts to find category learning based on a single cue. Therefore, in order to further support the view that at least a subset of the words in a paradigm, such as the one shown in Table 5.3, must have two simultaneously available cues to lexical categories, we examined category learning in the presence of a single cue in Exp. 2.

The second question raised by Exp. 1 concerns the possibility of an unintended phonological cue to categories. All of the consonants that precede the inflectional ending in the feminine set are nonpalatalized. In contrast, all of the consonants preceding the inflectional ending in the masculine set are palatalized. Palatalization of the last consonant affects the shape of the inflectional ending in Russian, thereby providing additional correlational information for the learner. Put another way, because the masculine words ended in palatalized consonants, the feminine case endings that were added to these words in the ungrammatical test items sounded like *yu* and *yoj*. But in familiarization and in the grammatical test items, these endings sounded like *u* and *oj*. This additional cue might have helped participants discriminate grammatical from ungrammatical test items. This potential confound was eliminated in Exp. 3.

Adult Experiment 2

Exp. 2 presented adults with the same types of Russian words used in Exp. 1. However, in Exp. 2, the only cues to gender categories were morphosyntactic case endings. Based on the existing literature, and unpublished studies from our laboratory (Gerken, Gómez, and Nurmsoo 1999) we predicted no category learning. Because the materials for Exp. 1 had phonological cues that partially correlated with the morphosyntactic markers to gender categories, the same stimuli could not be used in Exp. 2. Therefore, a different set of 12 Russian words, each with two case endings, was used (see Table 5.4, below). These words did not provide a phonological cue to gender categories. In all other respects, Exp. 1 was identical to Exp. 2.

Table 5.4 Stimuli used in Experiment 2.

Feminine Words					
malinoj	rubashkoj	lapoj	vannoj	knigoj	korovoj
malinu	rubashku	lapu	vannu	knigu	???

Masculine Words					
dekana	mal'chika	vora	shkafa	plakata	brata
dekanom	mal'chikom	vorom	shkafom	plakatom	???

An ANOVA on the "grammatical" responses to the unpresented paradigm-conforming vs nonconforming items showed no difference ($F < 1$; see Fig. 5.2). Additionally, a 2 experiment (Exp. 1 vs Exp. 2) × 2 grammaticality ANOVA showed a significant interaction between experiment and grammaticality ($F(1, 30) = 19.77, p < 0.001$), such that only Exp. 1 participants engaged in successful paradigm completion.

Adult Experiment 3

Recall from the discussion of Exp. 1 that the goal of Exp. 3 was to rule out the possible confound of palatalization. The familiarization stimuli and paradigm-conforming test items were identical to those used in Exp. 1. However, paradigm-nonconforming test items were replaced, such that the test items that had been palatalized (e.g., *vannya* and *tramvayoj*) were now unpalatalized. An ANOVA on "grammatical" responses to paradigm-conforming and nonconforming test items was also significant ($F(1, 15) = 17.75, p < .001$; see Fig. 5.2). The fact that the results are the same in Exps. 1 and 3 suggest that the potential confound of palatalization noted with respect to Exp. 1 is not responsible for adults' successful paradigm completion.

The data from Exps. 1–3 reported here clearly show that adults can successfully complete a morphophonological paradigm without reference, but only when the paradigm includes an additional cue that is simultaneously present with the morphological cue on a subset of the items. A remaining question from these studies is whether infants show the same ability.

Infant Experiment

Gerken *et al.* (2005) reported on a series of experiments using the Russian gender paradigm described in Adult Exps. 1–3 above. The final experiment of the published set is the most interesting for the current purposes. In it,

17-month-old infants were exposed to six masculine and six feminine Russian nouns, each with the same two case endings used in the adult studies (*oj, u, ya, yem*). Two groups of infants were tested. One group was familiarized for two minutes with words in which a subset (three feminine and three masculine) included the additional phonological cue to gender (-*k* for feminine words and −*tel*) for masculine words (see Table 5.3). This group received the same stimuli used in Adult Exp. 3, with the palatalization cue removed. The other group of 17-month-olds was familiarized with words in which none of the items had the additional phonological marker for gender. Out of the 24 possible training words (six feminine, six masculine, each with two different case endings), four words were withheld and used as the grammatical test items. Four ungrammatical words were created by putting the incorrect case ending on the four stems used for the grammatical items. Both groups of infants were tested on the paradigm-conforming and nonconforming items. Infants were familiarized and tested using the Headturn Preference Procedure (Kemler Nelson *et al.* 1995). The results mirror the findings in the adult studies – infants who were familiarized with the words with partially correlated cues to gender discriminated grammatical vs ungrammatical items at test. In contrast, infants familiarized with words exhibiting only the case-ending cue to gender failed to discriminate the test items. Further, the drop-out rate among the latter group was significantly higher, suggesting that even during familiarization, they found it difficult to discern any pattern in the stimuli.

Although 12-month-olds were not successful at learning the Russian gender paradigm that 17-month-olds so readily learned, Gómez and Lakusta (2004) reported on an apparent precursor to the category learning by 12-month-olds. They asked if these infants could learn the relationship between specific a- and b-words and features defining X- and Y-categories. During training infants heard one of two training languages. One language consisted of aX and bY pairings, the other of aY and bX pairs. Xs were two-syllable words and Ys were one syllable so that infants could use syllable number as a feature for distin-guishing X- and Y-categories (e.g. *erd-kicey, alt-jic*). At test, infants trained on aX and bY pairings had to discriminate these from aY and bX pairs. However, in order to assess generalization, all X- and Y-words were novel. The infants successfully discriminated the legal from illegal pairs, suggesting that they had learned the relationships between the a- and b-elements and the abstract feature characterizing X- and Y-words (syllable number).

The difference between 12-month-olds and 17-month-olds appears to be that the latter group is able to create a cross-utterance association among "a" items and among "b" items. In terms of the Russian gender paradigm,

17-month-olds must have formed an association between *oj* and *u* and between *ya* and *yem*. This association is what allows them, upon hearing *pisarya* to know that *pisaryem* is likely. Twelve-month-olds do not yet appear capable of this cross-utterance association.

5.4 A role for analogy in lexical category learning

Let us begin with a quick summary of three main points made in the preceding sections: First, many of the studies in the literature that have examined lexical category learning by adults, children, and infants, have employed a paradigm-completion task. Many researchers, including us, view the completion of morphophonological paradigms as an important component of lexical category learning in natural language. That is, the paradigm-completion task reflects, for many researchers, not just a useful experimental task, but a task that is close to the one faced by real language learners.

Second, a growing number of studies suggest that adults, children, and infants are unable to successfully complete morphophonological paradigms of the sort illustrated in Table 5.1 unless there are additional cues to category membership presented on at least a subset of the items. In the study by Braine (1987), the additional cue came from referential categories (masculine and feminine people) that were associated with a subset of the lexical items. In Mintz (2002), the additional cue appears to be the presence of correlated syllables flanking the syllable that is crucial at test. In the Russian gender studies conducted in our laboratory, the additional cue is a phonological marker presented on a subset of the to-be-categorized word stems.

Third, Braine (1987) proposed that the function of the additional cue is to provide initial evidence of two (or more) categories, which learners then come to associate with morphophonological markers, which ultimately become the basis of the categories. Braine's own work is consistent with this view, as are the data from our Russian gender studies. In the latter studies, the phonological markers –*k* and –*tel* could, on Braine's account, serve to inform learners that there are two categories, which they then more fully discover via the case endings, finally extending the categories to items not containing –*k* or –*tel*. However, as we noted in discussing the Mintz (2002) research, that study does not lend itself as easily to Braine's account of the basis of paradigm completion or lexical category learning.

In the remainder of this section, we explore the possibility that the role of additional cues to lexical categories is in analogy-making. The presence of two simultaneous cues to category membership might be related to at least two approaches to analogy-making. One approach concerns the observation by several analogy researchers, who suggest that the "goodness" of analogy is determined by the number of points at which one domain can be aligned with another ("structural alignment", e.g., Gentner 1983; Gentner and Markman 1997; Holyoak and Thagard, 1997). In the Introduction, we used examples (2a) and (2b), repeated below as (3a) and (3b), to foreshadow this point. We suggested that we might feel more confident in our response to the analogy in (3b) than (3a), perhaps because (3b) has more alignable elements and therefore constitutes a better analogy than (3a). On the analogical alignment view, categories might arise as clusters of items that participate in the same high-quality structural analogies.[3]

3a.   blicka : blicko :: kusa : _____
3b.   tivorblicka : tivorblicko :: tivorkusa : _____

Another, more specifically linguistic approach can be found in the work of Skousen (1989; this volume) and other researchers using his models (e.g., Eddington 2002; Elzinga 2006). Within the model, a database is searched for items similar to a given form based on a set of potentially shared features. Items sharing particular subsets of features are grouped into sets called "supracontexts". A subset of the supracontexts that meet a test for homogeneity (Skousen 1989) provides potential analogical models. One of the properties determining whether a supracontext will serve as the basis of analogy-making is "proximity", in which items from the database that share more features with the given form will appear in more supracontexts and will therefore have a greater chance of being used as an analogical model (Skousen 1989). In (3a-b) above, *tivorblick* and *trivorkus* should appear in more supracontexts than *blick and kus*.

Applying this model of analogy-making to the question of lexical category formation, a lexical category is a set of lexical items that shares a large number of supracontexts (e.g., phonological, morphological, syntactic, semantic). Discovering lexical categories in paradigms such as the ones we have been discussing is facilitated when some cells in the paradigm share a large number of supracontexts, such as Russian feminine nouns that end in −k plus *oj*. Essentially, the strength of proximity effects can be determined by looking

---

[3] An alternative to the structural alignment view of analogy-making comes from work on similarity-based or Bayesian category induction (e.g., Hahn and Chater 1998; Tenenbaum and Griffiths 2001). Here, the greater number of overlapping syllables (and possible morphemes) in 3b than 3a make it more likely that 'tivorblick' and 'tivorsnick' belong to the same lexical category and therefore are able to participate in the same morphological paradigm. Thus, on this view, category membership is determined separately and contributes to the evaluation of similarity.

for the degree of similarity across rows of paradigms like the one shown in Tables 5.1–4.

Although proximity might explain why paradigms with two or more simultaneous cues to category membership are more likely to allow paradigm completion, this principle by itself does not appear to explain how items sharing fewer supracontexts (e.g., feminine nouns without the *−k* marker but with *oj*) come to be included in the category. "Gang effects" might be invoked here, which is a property by which, if a group of similar examples behaves alike, the probability of selecting one of these examples as an analogical model is increased (Skousen 1989). An example of similar behavior from the Russian gender-category-learning studies might be that words ending in *oj* also end in *u*, and words ending in *ya* also end in *yem*. Thus, morphological paradigms are essentially "gangs". The strength of gang effects can be determined by looking down the column of a paradigm like the ones shown in Tables 5.1–4; the more rows there are in the column, the greater the gang effects.

So far, our attempt to view the Russian gender data in terms of analogical modeling does not seem conceptually very different from the view proposed by Braine (1987; see Fig. 5.1). The important observation we are making here, though, is that both proximity and gang effects contribute to the process by which a learner is able to demonstrate category learning by completing a paradigm. That is, unlike in Braine's proposal, there is no need for category discovery via a unique marker (such as the *−k* ending on a subset of Russian feminine nouns). Rather, this marker can contribute to proximity effects, but its uniqueness to the category may not be necessary. This observation raises the interesting possibility that paradigms with relatively strong proximity and gang effects properties are discoverable even when no unique marker is present. Perhaps what we are seeing in the paradigms are the kinds of effects discussed by Mintz (2002, see Fig. 5.3). Note in Table 5.2 above, which shows the paradigm used by Mintz, that proximity effects are very strong: each of the four items in a row contains exactly three syllables and, importantly, begins and ends in the same syllables. In contrast, the words used on the Russian gender paradigm shown in Table 5.3 range from two to four syllables, and syllables in a row share either one or two morphophonological markers (e.g., *-oj* and *−k* on some items). Mintz's stimuli also show strong gang effects: each column of the tested category contains four rows, in contrast with the two rows used in the Russian gender paradigm work and most other paradigm-completion studies. The account given here suggests that either reducing the Mintz' frames (rows) to a single marker element, or reducing the number of frames, should yield less successful category learning. This account also suggests that learners might be able to engage in successful paradigm

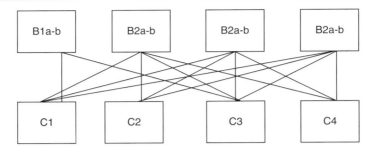

Stage 1, Frequent frames (e.g., *bool-jlv*) are associated with medial elements (e.g., *pren*)

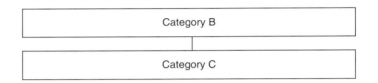

Stage 2, Items B1-Bn are treated as a category due to their association with items C1-Cn, and items C1-Cn are treated as a category due to their association with items B1-Bn.

FIGURE 5.3 Schematic of category formation in the experiment by Mintz (2002).

completion in a Russian gender paradigm with only case-marking cues (e.g., Table 5.4) if they heard each noun with four different case endings. Such a finding would provide strong evidence against Braine's view of category formation. We are currently undertaking the relevant experiment in our laboratories. Interestingly, we might use the notion of proximity and gang effects properties to account for the difference we observed between 17- and 12-month-olds. Recall that, while the older group was able to complete the Russian gender paradigm, the younger group was not. However, the younger group was able to associate a marker element with number of syllables in the adjacent word. Perhaps the younger infants were only able to employ the proximity principle in their creation of protocategories, while older infants, as we suggested above, were able to use both principles under discussion.

Let us end by acknowledging two negative points about the proposal we have sketched here. One point applies specifically to viewing lexical category learning as analogy-making. Skousen's model has been applied to a number of synchronic and diachronic linguistic problems with good success. It appears to offer an interesting way of thinking about lexical category formation that we hope researchers will pursue. However, an analogical approach to category formation would need to utilize a wide range of features in computing supracontexts, including reference (as seen in the Braine's (1987) study with masculine and feminine referents) and words in phrases (Mintz 2006). The latter point suggests that the database from which supracontexts are computed must be something other than the lexicon. In short, the computational problem suggested by our proposal may simply be intractable (see Skousen in this volume).

The second potential negative that we should acknowledge applies to all approaches to lexical category formation that are driven by distributional cues (phonological, morphological, and sentence-structural contexts). The categories formed by such an approach cannot be easily linked to labels such as "noun", "verb", etc. Rather, they are simply groups of words that share similar properties. Insofar as linguistic theories require learners to have innate category knowledge, the category-formation mechanism that we are exploring is problematic (see Gerken *et al.* 2005 for further discussion). Conversely, insofar as a distributional model of category learning can be shown to be successful for accounting for human learning, we may need to abandon notions of innate categories in favor of some form of guided category learning. We hope that viewing category learning within an analogy-making framework can contribute to this important debate.

6

The role of analogy for compound words

Andrea Krott

The aim of many linguistic investigations is to discover productive patterns of a language. If a pattern is very regular, it can be described by means of rules. For example, the rule for the English past tense accounts for a new form such as *wug + ed > wugged*. As in this example, novel formations are often based on patterns that are very regular and therefore can easily be described by rules. But novel formations can also be coined without the existence of a regular pattern. For instance, *ambisextrous* or *chocoholic* are based on the single exemplar *ambidextrous* and the small set of similar exemplars *alcoholic* and *workaholic*. Such seemingly accidental formations are creative and might appear exceptional. The structure or process used to explain them is analogy. Analogy is therefore sometimes viewed as an exceptional and rare process that stands in contrast to the productive formation of novel word-forms using rules (e.g., Marcus *et al.* 1995; Pinker and Ullman 2002). In contrast, some scholars view rules as extreme cases of analogy. In other words, a novel word that appears to be formed using a rule is assumed to be formed in analogy to many exemplars (e.g., Bybee 1995; see also connectionist approaches such as McClelland and Patterson 2002). While this debate predominantly concentrates on formations such as the English past tense that seemingly can be explained by both approaches, this chapter will present a type of word formation that can only be captured by analogical mechanisms, namely noun-noun compounds such as *landlady, airport,* or *boy scout.* I will show how analogy can systematically govern a whole category of words across different languages and how the same analogical basis can play a role in different domains of language processing, from language acquisition to visual word processing. From the presented studies it will become clear that analogy is a very powerful tool that is not rare and exceptional but frequently used and that can explain much more than accidental coinages.

In the literature, different types of noun-noun combinations have been distinguished. For instance, French has a large number of noun-preposition-noun combinations such as *sac à main* 'bag at hand' meaning a handbag or *chef de police* 'chief of police' meaning police chief as well as a small number of noun-noun combinations such as *timbre-poste* > lit. stamp-post + office, 'a postage stamp'. There has been a discussion as to whether French has nominal compounding at all because pure noun-noun combinations are rather rare. Robinson (1979), for example, classifies only some noun-preposition-noun combinations as compounds. In English, some scholars distinguish between noun-noun phrases and noun-noun compounds (e.g., Bloomfield 1933). Stress has been viewed as the distinguishing feature between the two, with noun-noun compounds having compound stress, which is defined as primary stress on the modifier as in *bookshelf,* and noun-noun phrases having phrasal stress as in *apple pie* (e.g., Bloomfield 1933; Giegerich 2004; Lees 1960). Due to this difference it has been argued that noun-noun phrases belong to the syntax of a language, while noun-noun compounds are part of the lexicon (e.g., Giegerich 2004). However, this distinction cannot be sustained, especially because stress in noun-noun constructs is highly variable (Bauer 1998; Di Sciullo and Williams 1987; Giegerich 2004; Levi 1978; Plag 2006). Because there is no generally accepted definition of what constitutes a compound (see Fabb 1998) and because analogy – as will become apparent hereinafter – seems to play the same role for all noun-noun constructs, I will treat noun-noun constructs of different languages as a homogeneous class and refer to them as *compounds.*

The type of analogy that is important for compounds is based on similarities within sets of words rather than isolated single words. These sets are groups of compounds that share a constituent, either the modifier or the head. Sets of compounds that share a modifier are also referred to as modifier families, while sets of compounds that share a head are referred to as head families (see also de Jong *et al.* 2002; Krott, Schreuder, and Baayen 2001; Krott *et al.* 2002c). The following show the modifier and head family of the novel compound *chocolate bread.*

(a)   Modifier family of *chocolate:*
      chocolate cookie, chocolate bar, chocolate cake, chocolate chips, chocolate icing, chocolate mouse, chocolate pudding, chocolate brownie, chocolate muffin, chocolate milk, etc.

(b)   Head family of *bread:*
      banana bread, cheese bread, ginger bread, olive bread, rye bread, sandwich bread, wheat bread, etc.

In what follows, I will present evidence that modifier and head families play a central role in the processing of compounds. They provide an analogical basis for production, comprehension, interpretation, and acquisition of compounds for a variety of languages across different language families. Although compounding is one of the most productive word-formation processes across languages, studies of the role of constituent families to date have focused very much on Indo-European languages such as English, Dutch, German, and French. To show that we are indeed dealing with a more general phenomenon, I will also present evidence from Indonesian, Japanese, and Chinese.

6.1 Production of compounds

Maybe the strongest evidence that modifier families and head families function as analogical bases for compound processing comes from research into the production of novel compounds in Japanese, Dutch, and German, specifically the use of interfixes in these compounds as well as stress assignment in English compounds.

It has been shown that constituent families affect the choice of interfixes[1] in novel Dutch and German noun-noun compounds such as -s- in Dutch *schaap + s + kop > schaapskop* 'sheep's head' or -en- in German *Schwan + en + see > Schwanensee* 'swan lake'. The majority of Dutch noun-noun compounds, i.e., 69 percent of the noun-noun compounds listed in the CELEX database (Baayen, Piepenbrock, and Gullikers 1995), are similar to English compounds, being mere concatenations of two nouns such as *water + druppel > waterdruppel* 'water drop'. However, the remaining compounds contain either -s- (20 percent) such as *visser + s + boot > vissersboot* 'fishing boat', -en- (11 percent) such as *sigaret + en + etui > sigarettenetui* 'cigarette case', or in rare cases -er- such as *ei + er + dopje > eierdopje* 'egg cup'.[2] Van den Toorn (1982*a*, 1982*b*) and Mattens (1984) have attempted to formulate a set of rules that capture the occurrence of interfixes by focusing on the phonological, morphological, and semantic make-up of the constituents. All of these rules, however, turned out to have exceptions. One of the phonological rules says, for instance, that interfixes should not occur after a modifier ending in a vowel as in *thee + bus* 'tea box', which is contradicted by a compound such as *pygmee + en + volk* 'pygmy people'. On a morphological

---

[1] Interfixes are also referred to as linking elements, linking morphemes, connectives, or juncture suffixes.

[2] Note that the interfix -en- is occasionally spelled as -e-, but both variants are pronounced as schwa.

level, some suffixes of modifiers occur mostly with one interfix and occasionally with another. For instance, the abstract nominal suffix *–heid* occurs most frequently with the interfix -s- as in *snelheid + s + controle > snelheidscontrole* 'speed control', sometimes without any interfix as in *oudheid + kunde > oudheidkunde* 'archaeology', and occasionally with -en- as in *minderheid + en + beleid > minderhedenbeleid* 'minority policy'. On a semantic level, modifiers that end in the suffix -er and that are human agents tend to occur with -s-, but see *leraar + en + opleiding > leraarenopleiding* 'teacher training'. Due to the large set of exceptions van den Toorn (1982*a*, 1982*b*) concluded that there are no rules and that the regularities that can be observed are mere tendencies.

Compared to rules, analogy over constituent families has been proven to be a much more successful approach to Dutch interfixes (Krott, Baayen, and Schreuder 2001; Krott, Hagoort, and Baayen 2004; Krott, Schreuder, and Baayen 2002*b*). The usage of interfixes has been shown to be related to their occurrence in modifier families and head families, although the effect of the modifier is stronger (Krott, Schreuder, and Baayen 2001; Krott, Schreuder, and Baayen 2002*b*). In a cloze-task experiment, participants were asked to combine two nouns into a novel compound. Their responses with a particular interfix were well predicted by the support that the interfix received from the modifier family and to a lesser degree from the head family. For instance, the modifier *onderzoek* 'research' of the novel combination *onderzoek + schaal* 'research scale' occurs most frequently with -s- in existing compounds, while the head *schaal* is neutral in terms of occurrence of -s-. The results showed that 95 percent of the participants chose an -s-. Furthermore, constituent families not only predicted the choice of Dutch interfixes very accurately, they also predicted the speed with which they were selected (Krott, Schreuder, and Baayen 2002*b*). The higher the support for a particular interfix was, i.e., the higher the percentage of the interfix in the constituent families, the faster participants selected this interfix for a novel compound.

Other factors that can predict participants' choices of interfixes are the suffix and rime of the modifier and the semantic class of the modifier. In Krott, Schreuder, and Baayen (2002*a*), participants were asked to create compounds from a nonword modifier and a real head as in *lantan + organisatie* 'lantan organization'. The rime of the nonword modifier was chosen to predict the usage of different interfixes. Although participants reported higher uncertainty than for combinations of real words, the rime had a significant effect on participants' responses. Similar results were obtained when participants selected interfixes for combinations of real heads and nonword modifiers that ended in a suffix as in *illuni-teit* + *toename* 'illuniteit increase' (Krott, Baayen, and Schreuder 2001). Nevertheless, constituent families are the most powerful predictors of Dutch interfixes. When modifier families are in competition with the suffix or the rime of the modifier, then it is the modifier family that determines which interfix participants choose (Krott, Schreuder, and Baayen, 2002*a*). Thus, rime or suffix of modifiers are only fallen back on when there is no modifier family available that can provide an analogical basis for the selection. In contrast to rime and suffixes, an experiment testing the effect of semantic features of the modifier, i.e., concreteness and animacy, showed that semantic features contribute to interfix selection in addition to constituent families (Krott, Krebbers, Schreuder, and Baayen 2002).

Additional evidence for the analogical nature of the influence that constituent families have on interfix selection stems from computational simulation studies, using the exemplar-based models TiMBL (Daelemans *et al.* 2000) and AML (Skousen 1989). Constituent family effects in the behavioral experiments were all manifestations of type counts, i.e., they were based on percentages of family members with a particular interfix and not on the family members' frequency of usage. In contrast to other types of models that implement analogical predictions such as connectionist networks, exemplar-based models easily and transparently accommodate the effect of type counts because predictions are based on explicitly stored earlier experiences, i.e., exemplars, and not, e.g., based on modified hidden nodes in a network. For instance, in Skousen's analogical modeling of language (AML), a target word is compared with stored exemplars using a similarity algorithm defined over a series of user-selected features and then classified into a class, for instance, into an inflectional class. Exemplars that are most similar to the target provide the analogical basis for the target's classification. The Tilburg Memory Based Learner (TiMBL) implements a similar mechanism. However, exemplars are not stored as wholes. During its learning phase, TiMBL integrates exemplars into a decision tree, which makes neighborhood searches more efficient than searching through a list of exemplars. One additional advantage of TiMBL is that it provides a measure of relevance for each user-defined feature, by calculating the information gain that the feature contributes to the prediction.

Simulation studies of the selections of interfixes in our experiments with TiMBL have confirmed the prime importance of modifier families. Modeling participants' choices for the combinations in Krott, Baayen, and Schreuder (2001) and Krott, Schreuder, and Baayen (2002*a*) revealed that the modifier was by far the strongest predictor and that adding rime or suffix to the predictive feature set did not improve the prediction accuracy when a modifier family was available. Modeling participants' responses in Krott, Schreuder, and Baayen (2002*a*) with AML led to equally high prediction accuracies as those obtained with TiMBL. Furthermore, comparing the models' choices with participants' choices revealed that the selection is equally difficult for human participants and the models, confirming that exemplar-based models are very good approximations of human behavior. In addition, the prediction accuracies of the models were superior to that of rules.

Similar to interfixes in novel Dutch compounds, constituent families also play an important role for the choice of interfixes in German compounds (Krott, Schreuder, Baayen, and Dressler 2007). Although German and Dutch are etymologically very close, German has a more complex system of interfixes. There are seven non-Latinate interfixes: -s-, -e-, -n-, -ens-, -es-, -er-. In addition, the modifier, i.e., the left constituent, sometimes changes its root vowel via umlaut in combination with an interfix as in *Huhn* + *er* + *ei* > *Hühnerei* 'chicken egg'.[3] Other modifiers are reduced to their root as in *Farbe* + *Fernsehen* > *Farbfernsehen* 'color TV'. Similar to Dutch noun-noun compounds, 65 percent of all compounds in CELEX (Baayen, Piepenbrock, and Gullikers 1995) contain an interfix, the others are pure concatenations of nouns. While previous studies had explored the predictability of German interfixes by rules (Dressler *et al.* 2001; Libben *et al.* 2002), we focused on the prediction by analogy. In behavioral experiments we showed that the modifier family is not only a strong predictor for Dutch interfixes, but also for German interfixes. The smaller effect of the head family, which we had observed for Dutch interfixes, was less important and depended on the compound. We also tested whether we could simulate participants' selections using TiMBL. We compared the predictive power of the modifier family with that of features of the modifier, which had been proposed in a rule-based account (Dressler *et al.* 2001; Libben *et al.* 2002). The simulations confirmed the important role of the modifier family. However, they also showed that it was not the constituent family alone that best predicted the selection of interfixes. Adding properties of the modifier such as gender, inflectional class, and particularly its rime improved the prediction.

---

[3] Compounds such as *Hühnerei* or *Wort* + *er* + *Buch* > *Wörterbuch* word + book > 'dictionary' might also be analyzed as *Hühner* + *Ei* or *Wörter* + *Buch* because the left constituent is identical to the plural form of *Huhn* 'chicken' or *Wort* 'word'. Semantically this might make sense for *Wörterbuch*, which refers to a book that contains lots of words, but not for *Hühnerei* because a chicken egg is an egg laid by one chicken only. Interfixes are therefore represented in this chapter as independent morphemes instead of plural suffixes of modifiers. Note that the effect of the constituent family is not affected by the choice of representation.

These properties did not enhance the prediction for Dutch interfixes. The difference between the languages is probably due to the overall greater importance of inflectional class and gender in German. One might argue that the predictive power of rime, gender, and inflectional class can be taken as evidence for rules and that these rules have an effect that is independent of the analogical effect of the constituent family. It is difficult to explain, however, why the effectiveness of rules and analogy varies for different modifiers (Krott *et al.* 2007). A more parsimonious account is therefore that the properties of the modifier are analogical in nature as well, i.e., their rule-like behavior is rather an extreme and highly consistent form of analogy.

Inspired by TiMBL and AML, we developed a computational psycholin-guistic model of analogy that does not only predict the choices for interfixes in novel compounds, but also the speed with which participants choose (Krott, Schreuder, and Baayen 2002*b*; Krott *et al.* 2007). Like exemplar-based models, our model is a type-based, as opposed to a token-based, model of analogy, having symbolic representations of words. Figure 6.1 illustrates the connectivity between constituents, compounds, and interfixes for the Dutch example *schaap + oog* 'sheep's eye'. Activation initially flows from the lemma nodes of the constituents to the nodes of their constituent families and further to the interfixes that they contain. Activation only flows to the relevant family, i.e., the modifier SHEEP activates the compounds that contain SHEEP as a modifier. Note that the larger effect of the modifier family is modeled by a larger weight of the connections between the modifier and its family compared to the weight between the head and its family. In the case of German compounds, this weight would be zero for most right constituents. Activation flows back and forth between interfix nodes, compound nodes, and constituent nodes. This builds up activation in the interfixes until one of them reaches a predefined activation threshold. The time it takes to reach the threshold simulates the time that human participants take to respond. An analysis of the simulated response times showed the same effects of the modifier family and the predicted lack of an effect of the head family on response times that had been observed in the behavioral studies with human participants (Krott, Schreuder, and Baayen 2002*b*).

Research into Japanese compounds has shown that constituent families also play a role in a language of a very different kind. Japanese rendaku is the voicing of the initial obstruent of the second constituent in compounds or stem-and-affix formations. For example, the compound /ami/ + /to/ 'net + door' becomes /amido/ 'screen door' and /iro/ + /kami/ 'color + paper' becomes /irogami/ 'colored paper'. However, rendaku is not applied in all cases. Lyman's Law states that rendaku does not occur if the second

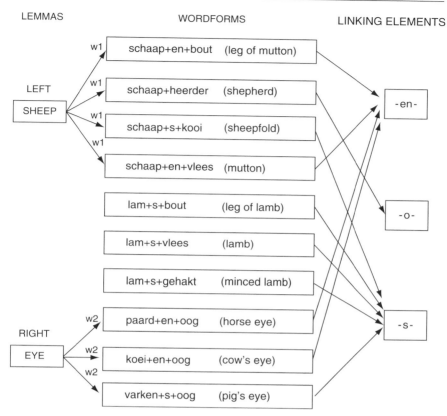

LEMMAS   WORDFORMS   LINKING ELEMENTS

FIGURE 6.1 Connectivity of a simple Dutch compound lexicon: lemmas (left layer), word-form representations (central layer, equivalent to lexemes in Levelt, Roelofs, and Meyer's 1999 model), and interfixes (right layer), as developed by Krott, Schreuder, and Baayen (2002b).

constituent already contains a voiced obstruent (Vance 1980). Vance (1980) tested the psychological status of Lyman's law for novel compounds. He found a correlation between participants' preference for rendaku in a compound and the likelihood of rendaku in the head family of the compound. Importantly, head families had a stronger effect on participants' responses than Lyman's law. The law was only effective if the second constituent was a nonword, i.e., when there was no head family.

An effect of constituent families that is of a slightly different nature is its role for assigning stress in English compound production. As mentioned, stress in English noun-noun constructs is highly variable (Bauer 1998; Plag 2006). Plag (2006) investigated what affects this variability, by focusing on three factors in existing and novel noun-noun combinations. The first factor was compound structure, predicting that complement-head combinations such as *opera-singer*, with *opera* as complement to *singer*, are clearly left-stressed in contrast to modifier-head compounds such as *opera glasses*. The second factor was semantics, predicting that compounds with modifier relations that express authorship such as *Groskinsky symphony* are right-stressed, while compounds with modifier relations that express a title such as *Moonlight Symphony* are left-stressed. The third factor was analogy, more precisely the effect of the head family. For example, compounds with the head *street* are stressed on the modifier such as *Óxford Street, Máin Street*, while compounds with the head *avenue* are stressed on the head such as *Fifth Ávenue, Madison Ávenue*. Measuring pitch differences between modifiers and heads in participants' oral compound productions, Plag found some evidence for all three factors. In terms of analogy, he found that compounds with *symphony* as head such as *Spring Symphony, Hoffman symphony* etc. showed a smaller pitch difference than compounds with *sonata* as heads such as *Twilight Sonata, Winter Sonata* etc., or *opera* such as *Surprise Opera, Groskinsky opera*, etc. In addition, the analogical factor of the head family overruled the effect of the semantic relation of the compounds. For example, all compounds with the head *symphony* behaved equally with regards to stress, which is expected given the head family of *symphony*. The semantic factor predicts, however, that modifier relations that express authorship such as *Hoffman symphony* should have led to right stress and modifier relations that express a title such as *Spring Symphony* should have led to left stress. Plag's results therefore again show that constituent families can overrule other factors.

In sum, we have seen that constituent families provide powerful analogical bases for the production of compounds in a number of languages and across language families. They are highly predictive of participants' behavior, when asked to produce novel compounds. They quite accurately predict participants' decisions as well as the speed with which the participants make those decisions. Simulations with exemplar-based models provide independent support for the conclusion that constituent families are an important basis of analogical generalization in language production.

6.2 Visual processing of existing compounds

Constituent families also affect the comprehension of compounds. De Jong *et al.* (2002) studied the processing of Dutch and English compounds when those were presented visually. They asked native speakers to decide whether or not the words appearing on a computer screen were existing words by pressing a yes or no button as fast and as accurately as possible. English compounds differ from Dutch compounds in terms of orthography. While Dutch compounds are always written as one word, English compounds can be written as one or two words, depending on the individual compound. For instance, while *heartbeat* is written as one word, *heart attack* is written as two, even though these words are very similar, sharing the modifier. De Jong *et al.* (2002) investigated whether the size of constituent families or the summed frequency of constituent family members might have an effect on how quickly speakers decide that a word is a familiar compound. Response times to Dutch compounds as well as to English compounds that were written as single words were driven by summed frequencies of modifier families. This suggests that participants' processing of compounds is sensitive to the probability that a constituent occurs as a modifier in a compound. It is likely that modifiers that occur more often are easier to recognize than modifiers that occur seldom. In case of English compounds that were written as two words, participants' reaction times reflected the size of the modifier family. Participants recognized compounds faster when the family of the modifier was large than when it was small. Head families did not appear to affect responses, which either means that they are not "active" during compound processing or that their effect is masked by an overwhelming effect of the modifier family.

Krott, Hagoort, and Baayen (2004) also investigated the processing of visually presented Dutch compounds, more specifically the support of constituent families on participants' decisions about the well-formedness of novel and existing compounds. The compounds contained interfixes that were or were not in line with the interfix bias within the modifier family. In case of existing compounds, interfixes also differed as to whether they were conventional for the particular compound as in *rat + en + vergif > rattenvergif* 'rat poison' or unconventional as in *rat + s + vergif > *ratsvergif*, with the latter leading to novel compounds that are very similar to existing ones. Similar to the effects on the selection of interfixes in production (Krott, Schreuder, and Baayen 2002b), the bias of the modifier family predicted both acceptance rates and acceptance speed. More support for an interfix in the family led to higher acceptance and faster responses. Remarkably, nonconventional interfixes in existing compounds such as -en- in **kleur + en + bad > kleurenbad* 'color bath', were accepted as correct as often and as fast as conventional interfixes such as -en- in *dier + en + kliniek > dierenkliniek* 'animal hospital', as long as they had the support of the modifier family. This effect was independent of the frequency of the compound. Thus, the modifier family determined yes responses independently of the novelty or familiarity of the compound.

Constituent families have also been shown to affect the recognition of written Chinese compounds. Similar to the paradigm used by De Jong *et al.* (2002) for English, Tsai *et al.* (2006) and Huang *et al.* (2006) investigated the effect of family size on reading Chinese compounds. Tsai *et al.* (2006) examined the effect of family size[4] of first characters on the speed with which isolated compounds are recognized as well as its effect on eye movements when compounds are embedded in sentences. For example, the first character of 糗事 *qiǔshì*[5] 'dry-ration thing', meaning embarrassing thing, occurs in a very small set of words, while the first character of 善事 *shànshì* 'good thing', meaning good deeds, occurs in several other words. Tsai *et al.* found that compounds with first characters that come from large families were recognized more quickly than compounds with first characters that come from small families. Eye movements revealed a higher skipping rate and shorter fixation durations for words with larger families than those with smaller ones. Both findings suggest that a large family facilitates recognition. Huang *et al.* (2006) investigated the effect of family size of both first and second characters on recognition speed, while partly simultaneously recording brain activations, i.e., ERPs (event-related encephalograms). They confirmed Tsai *et al.*'s (2006) finding that large families of first characters facilitate responses. In addition, families of first characters affected response times more strongly than families of second characters and high-frequency competing family members inhibited responses. ERPs suggested that larger families lead to increased lexical activity compared to smaller families and that a high-frequency competing family member leads to greater competition during word recognition than a low-frequency competing family member. These findings show that constituent families play a role in written compound recognition cross-linguistically. They also reveal that constituent families do not simply facilitate word recognition. A high-frequency competitor can slow recognition down.

6.3 Interpretation of compounds

Noun-noun compounds have three semantic components: a head that determines the category, a modifier that determines how the subcategory is different from other subcategories, and a relation between modifier and head. For example, an *apple pie* belongs to the superordinate category pie

---

[4] Both Tsai *et al.* (2006) and Huang *et al.* (2006) used the term 'neighborhood' instead of 'family'.
[5] Examples are in Mandarin Romanization.

and is a pie that has apples in it, in contrast to pies that have cherries, lemons, etc. in them. Although there is in principle no limit to how nouns can be related in compounds, linguists and psycholinguists have suggested ten to twenty very common relation categories (Downing 1977; Gleitman and Gleitman 1970; Kay and Zimmer 1976; Lees 1960; Levi 1978), including the very common FOR as in *juice cup,* a cup FOR juice, HAS as in *banana muffin,* a muffin that HAS bananas in it, and MADE OF as in *carrot sticks,* sticks MADE OF carrots. To understand the meaning of a novel compound, one needs to identify its modifier and head and then to infer an appropriate semantic relation between them. Several approaches have been proposed to account for this inference process (e.g., Costello and Keane 2001; Estes 2003; Gagné and Shoben 1997; Murphy 1990; Wisniewski 1996). Most relevant for this chapter are studies by Ryder (1994), van Jaarsveld, Coolen, and Schreuder (1994), and the Competition-Among-Relations-in-Nominals (CARIN) model by Gagné and Shoben (Gagné 2001; Gagné and Shoben 1997, 2002). Ryder (1994) was the first to systematically investigate the importance of analogy for the interpretation of novel noun-noun compounds. She investigated analogical effects at various levels: specific compounds, constituent families, templates such as whole-part or container-contained, and the very general schema XY, which she defines as "an Y that has some relation to X". She asked participants to define the meaning of novel noun-noun compounds and found that interpretations could indeed be based on all four levels of analogy. It is not clear from this research, however, what drives participants to decide which level to use.

Van Jaarsveld, Coolen, and Schreuder (1994) sought additional evidence for two of the analogy levels identified by Ryder (1994), namely the levels of specific compounds and constituent families. They constructed novel compounds with large and small sizes of constituent families. They asked participants to rate them for interpretability and then tested how fast participants recognized them as real English words in a lexical decision experiment (similar to that by de Jong *et al.* 2002). They found that compounds with larger constituent families were responded to faster than those with smaller constituent families, and the speed was independent of the compounds' interpretability. This indicates that responses were affected by the size of constituent families, similar to the results for visual compound processing above.

Gagné and Shoben (Gagné 2001; Gagné and Shoben 1997, 2002) took a similar approach to that by van Jaarsveld, Coolen, and Schreuder (1994) in their CARIN model. They argue that the selection of a relation for a novel compound is affected by how the compound modifier has been used in previous combinations. Therefore the availability of the relation is argued to affect the ease of interpretation. Availability is, for instance, influenced by a modifier's previous usage with a particular relation, which includes its usage in the modifier family. In contrast to van Jaarsveld *et al.*, Gagné and colleagues focused on modifier families rather than head families, and they used an experimental task that taps directly into the interpretation process. They asked participants to decide whether a visually presented novel compound made sense or not. The most likely modifier-head relation of a novel compound was either supported by a strong bias towards this relation in the modifier family or not. Participants were faster to accept the novel compound as making sense when the modifier family strongly supported its modifier-head relation than when it did not support it (Gagné and Shoben 1997). Head families affected response times only when the novel combination was ambiguous as for *student vote*, which can be a vote for students or by students (Gagné and Shoben 2002). A subsequent study showed that modifier-relation pairs can even prime sense-nonsense decisions to familiar compounds (Gagné and Spalding 2004), suggesting that modifier families are activated not only for novel compounds, but for all compounds. The findings of Gagné and colleagues for English modifier families have since been confirmed by Storms and Wisniewski (2005) for Indonesian, i.e., a language with left-headed compounds (see also a study on French compounds by Turco; as cited in Gagné and Spalding 2006). Modifier and modifier families therefore seem to play an important role in compound interpretations cross-linguistically. The role of the modifier lies in the crucial information that it provides to distinguish a particular compound from others within the same category. Part of this distinguishing information is the relation that holds between modifier and head.

6.4 Acquisition of compounds

The studies reviewed so far all dealt with the role of constituent families in compound processing in adults, i.e., in participants who have mastered the production, recognition, and interpretation of compounds. The question arises when do constituent families become effective during language development? Do children who have a limited vocabulary already make use of constituent families? In order to answer these questions, one needs to study compound processing by young children. To be able to place the emergence of the importance of constituent families into children's development, I will first give a brief description of what we know about compound acquisition. I will then present three studies that show how constituent families are already important for 4- and 5-year-old children.

The literature on compound acquisition presents contradictory findings. On the one hand, compounds and the system of compounding appear to be learned very early. There is evidence that children start to spontaneously coin their first novel compounds such as *nose-beard* or *car-smoke* around the age of 2 (e.g., Becker 1994; Clark 1983). Two-year-olds also seem to understand already the different roles of heads and modifiers (Berman and Clark 1989; Clark 1981, 1983; Clark and Berman 1987; Clark, Gelman, and Lane 1985; Mellenius 1997). Furthermore, 3-year-olds can use compounds to refer to subcategories, suggesting that they understand the subcategorization function of compounds (Clark, Gelman, and Lane 1985).

On the other hand, there is evidence that the development is much slower. Nicoladis (2003) presented results suggesting that children's subcategorization knowledge is not completed at the age of 3. In her experiment, children were presented with novel compounds (e.g., *dragon box*) and a set of pictures and asked to pick the picture that corresponds to the compound. Three-year-olds selected a picture showing a dragon next to a box rather than a box decorated with dragons more often than 4-year-olds. This suggests that 3-year-olds are still developing with regards to compound interpretations. Other studies present evidence that this process is not completed until well into the school years. Berko (1958) found that children between 4 and 7 years still had difficulties explaining the meaning of common compounds such as *birthday*. They often responded with a salient feature or function of the compound instead of an explanation that related modifier and head. In case of *birthday* they said it is called this way because one gets presents or eats cake. Only 2 percent of the children mentioned that it is a day (Berko 1958). While one might argue that a word like *birth* might not be fully understood by all children at this age, the results are in concordance with those by Parault, Schwanenflugel, and Haverback (2005), who compared interpretations of novel noun-noun compounds by 6- and 9-year-olds as well as adults. They found that children's interpretations, although quite adult-like, are nevertheless significantly different from those of adults. Striking were explanations that did not integrate the meanings of the constituents, but left them in an unconnected side-by-side status as in "a big magazine and a little book" as an explanation for *book magazine*.

These findings are in accordance with the assumption that children learn their first compounds as unstructured units and slowly develop knowledge of the roles of heads and modifiers as well as modifier-head relations. The seeming contradictions in the literature might indicate that children's understanding of compounding differs from compound to compound. While they might be able to identify head and modifier of one compound, they might not be able to do the same for another compound. It might also be that children understand from early on that heads and modifiers are somehow related, but they appear to take a long time until their relation inferences become adult-like. These assumptions are in line with a usage-based theory of language acquisition, which assumes that children acquire linguistic constructions such as subject-verb-object or agent-action-patient on an item-by-item basis such as "I love you" and gradually generalize to more abstract patterns such as the subject-verb-object construct (e.g., Akhtar 1999; Goldberg 2006; Tomasello 2000, 2003).

In Krott and Nicoladis (2005) we investigated whether children's understanding of the complex structure of a particular familiar compound is enhanced by the knowledge of constituent families. Are children more likely to parse a compound into head and modifier when they know other compounds with the same head or modifier than when they do not know other compounds? We asked English-speaking children between the ages 3 and 5 to explain to an alien puppet why we say compounds such as *chocolate cake*. We selected compounds that contained heads and modifiers with either large or small constituent families and confirmed the sizes of the constituent families by questionnaires given to the parents of the children. The results showed that the children were more likely to mention a constituent in their responses when they knew several other compounds with this constituent, i.e., when the constituent had a large constituent family (see Figure 6.2), both for modifier and head families. We confirmed this finding in an equivalent study with French noun-noun and noun-preposition-noun combinations (Nicoladis and Krott 2007). Together, these studies support the possibility that children's understanding of specific familiar compounds relies on knowledge of similar compounds. In other words, the more exemplars there are that can form an analogical knowledge basis for the understanding of a compound, the better children understand the compound and the better they are in explaining its meaning.

In a recent study, we addressed the question whether the knowledge of constituent families also guides children's interpretations of novel noun-noun compounds (Krott, Gagné, and Nicoladis, 2009). We asked adults and 4–5-year-olds to explain the meaning of novel compounds such as *dog shoes*. In accordance with previous research by Gagné and colleagues (Gagné 2001; Gagné and Shoben 1997), adults used their knowledge of relations in modifier families to infer modifier-head relations. For *dog shoes* they used their knowledge of other compounds with the modifier *dog* such as *dog house*,

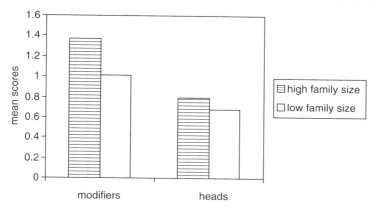

FIGURE 6.2 Children's average scores for modifiers and heads (max. 2) by family size (high versus low) in Krott and Nicoladis (2005).

dog biscuit or *dog leash*. Their interpretations were in line with the relational bias in modifier families, the relation FOR in case of *dog shoes*. Children's responses showed that they also used their knowledge of constituent families. However, they drew on their knowledge of relations in head families, i.e., other shoes such as *ballet shoes, snow shoes, horse shoe*. There was only weak evidence that they also used their knowledge of modifier families. That means that adults were influenced by their knowledge of how a particular modifier is used to create subcategories within different categories, while children were influenced by their knowledge of a particular category and the modifier relations in this category. It is not clear why children and adults should use different knowledge. One reason might be that children do not know much about possible modifications yet due to their limited compound vocabulary. As there is evidence that children at this age might still be developing their understanding of heads and modifiers, children might also focus on heads because identifying the category of the novel compound is the first step in understanding it. The latter might be linked to high task demands and the slow development of executive functions.

Ryder's (1994) research on adults' compound interpretations suggests that adults have access to a repertoire of analogical bases when interpreting compounds. They can choose between their knowledge of specific compounds, compound families, or more abstract schemas. The findings for compound acquisition, namely that children appear to know something about a very abstract level of compounds when they are as young as 2 years, while this knowledge does not appear to be fully developed yet when they are 4 or 5 or even later, might mean that young children develop analogical bases of different levels of abstractness, but that the choice between these levels is not adult-like yet. Alternatively, as mentioned above, children's knowledge of a very abstract level of compounding might be an illusion. What looks like general knowledge about heads and modifiers might be knowledge about particular constituent families. Both explanations are in line with a usage-based theory of language acquisition (e.g., Goldberg 2006; Tomasello 2003).

6.5 Conclusion

We have seen that constituent families play an important role for noun-noun compounds and that this role is not limited to a specific aspect of processing, but appears to affect all types of aspects of compound processing. The analogical nature of this role is especially apparent for phenomena that are highly variable, i.e., that lack the systematicity of a rule-driven pattern. We have seen various types of evidence that constituent families provide an analogical basis for the production of compounds, in particular for the realization of phenomena appearing at constituent boundaries such as Japanese rendaku or German and Dutch interfixes as well as for stress assignment in English compounds. For the interpretation of novel noun-noun combinations, constituent families guide people's selection between various possible modifier-head relations. But even when compound processing is not characterized by choice and variability, constituent families play a role. We have seen their effect on the processing of familiar compounds, namely when familiar compounds are recognized in a lexical decision experiment or when they are judged as to whether or not they make sense. This suggests that the analogical basis of constituent families is not turned on or off depending on the task. When we process compounds, constituent families appear to be "active" regardless of the linguistic aim. They affect us when we create novel compounds as speakers and when we try to make sense of what somebody else says or writes.

It is remarkable that analogical compound processing is already in place in preschool children. Similar to adults, children use constituent families to discover internal structure in familiar compounds and to interpret noun-noun combinations that they have not encountered before. However, children seem to differ from adults in that they tend to focus on head families rather than modifier families. As pointed out, children's knowledge of possible modifications might not be developed yet. Future research will need to investigate whether this is indeed the case.

Throughout this chapter I have been assuming that constituent families are represented in the mental lexicon. We have seen that constituent families play an important role in very different domains of language processing. The question therefore arises whether the observed effects are based on a single lexical system that is involved in all these domains or whether they are based on two or more systems that are domain-specific, but structurally very similar. Morphological family effects that have been found for visual word recognition have been explained by overlapping semantic representations of family members (Bertram, Schreuder, and Baayen 2000; de Jong, Schreuder, and Baayen 2000; Schreuder and Baayen 1997). Thus, these effects are assumed to arise on a level of conceptual representations. The interpretation of novel compounds is likely to arise on the same level because it involves conceptual knowledge. Constituent family effects found for the production of novel compounds, however, are likely to arise on a level of morphophonological representation because these effects are all related to the form of the compounds. In the model of interfix selection in Krott, Schreuder, and Baayen (2002b) constituent family effects arise due to connections between morphophonological representations of compounds and interfixes. The voicing of obstruents in Japanese compounds and stress assignment in English compounds also involve morphophonological representations. The most likely scenario therefore is that constituent family effects, although very similar at first sight, originate from two structurally similar but nevertheless different subsystems of the lexicon, one situated at the level of conceptual representations, the other at the level of morphophonological representations. It is unclear whether constituent family effects at the morphophonological level might differ for written and oral processes because it is not clear yet whether morphophonological representations in the mental lexicon are domain-independent or not, i.e., whether there are different representations for written and oral comprehension and production (e.g., Caramazza 1997; Miozzo and Caramazza 2005). The results for interfixes rather suggest that morphophonological representations are domain-independent because interfixes occur in both oral and written production. Voicing in Japanese compounds and stress in English compounds, on the other hand, both concern only oral word production and therefore suggest domain-dependent analogical effects.

What also remains unclear is why for some phenomena it is the modifier family that plays the important role, while for other phenomena it is the head family. Taking together all findings, modifier effects seem to occur in languages such as German, Dutch, and Indonesian. These languages all have main stress on compound modifiers. However, it is unlikely that stress is the driving factor. First, most of these studies presented compounds visually, i.e., without stress information. Second, for English, children revealed a stronger focus on head families, while adults revealed a stronger focus on modifier families for the exact same compounds. The focus on one or the other constituent is more likely due to distributional patterns in the language. For instance, as had been shown in simulation studies with TiMBL and AML, interfixes in Dutch or German compounds are better predicted by modifiers than heads and Japanese rendaku is better predicted by heads than modifiers. Speakers appear to be sensitive to this information and to make use of it.

In sum, we have seen how an entire class of words across languages and language families can be governed by analogy. It is likely that analogy is not restricted to noun-noun compounds, but that it plays an important role for other areas of morphology as well. It is therefore not at all unlikely that analogy underlies regularities that appear to be governed by rules.

Acknowledgment

The author would like to thank Antje Meyer and two anonymous reviewers for their comments on an earlier version of this chapter and James Myers for bringing the studies on Chinese constituent families to her attention.

7

Morphological analogy:
Only a beginning

John Goldsmith

All reasoning is search and casting about, and requires pains and application.
John Locke, *An Essay Concerning Human Understanding* (1975 [1690])

7.1 Introduction

The perspective that I will describe in this paper is the result of some work over the last ten years or so aimed at building an automatic morphological analyzer—that is, an explicit algorithm that takes natural language text as its input, and produces the morphological structure of the text as its output.[1] The main conclusion, as far as analogy is concerned, is that formal notions that correspond very naturally to the traditional notion of analogy are useful and important as part of a boot-strapping heuristic for the discovery of morphological structure, but it is necessary to develop a refined quantitative model in order to find the kind of articulated linguistic structures that are to be found in natural languages.

I take the perspective that the three principal tasks (we could call them the *first* three tasks) of someone who wishes to develop a theory of morphology that applies to natural languages is to develop an account for (1) the segmentation of words into morphs; (2) the description of a grammar to generate words, on the basis of the morphs, among other things; and (3) the labeling of morphs, in two different ways: (a) a labeling that indicates which morphs are different realizations of the same morpheme, and (b) a labeling that indicates the morphosyntactic feature representation of each morpheme. Of these three, I will focus on the first two, and of the first two, I will emphasize the first. I underscore this because if we were historians of linguistics in the future

[1] I am grateful to Juliette and Jim Blevins, to Susan Rizzo, and to anonymous referees for comments on the original version of this chapter.

looking back at what questions were the focus of discussion in the first decade of the twenty-first century, it would appear that the first question must have been settled, in view of how little discussion there is of it.[2] I mean very simply, how do we justify the statement (for example) that *books* is composed of two morphs, *book* and *s*, while *tax* is not? One of the reasons that the problem of segmentation is interesting is that we cannot call upon the resources within generative grammar that most of us are familiar with, and have grown dependent upon—which is to say, appeal to substance in an innate Universal Grammar. There is no plausible account of how speakers of English learn that *"ing"* is a suffix, while speakers of Swahili learn that *"an"* is a suffix, that appeals to a small list of discrete parameters, each with a small number of settings.[3] In fact, from a certain point of view, this is one of the reasons why the study of morphology so interesting: there is so much that must be learned.

I will begin with a discussion of the computational problem of *word* segmentation—that is, the problem of dividing a long string of symbols into words, with no prior knowledge of the words of the language. This is one of the problems that any child language learner faces. We will see that a large part of the difficulty that we run into when we tackle this problem derives from the importance of having a good model of morphology, without which all of our efforts to learn words would be in severe trouble. Rather than trying to solve both problems at the same time (the problem of word segmentation, and the problem of morphology induction), we will turn

---

[2] There is a perspective on word structure, articulated notably by Rajendra Singh and Sylvain Neuvel (Neuvel and Singh (2001), Neuvel and Fulop (2002)), which denies the existence of morphs and the internal segmentation of words. While I appreciate the force of their arguments, it seems to me that the same arguments against the decomposition of words into morphs holds, with essentially the same degree of conviction, against dividing sentences up into words—there are unclear cases, there is semantic noncompositionality in quite a few cases, and so on. But at the same time, it seems to me that linguists have to agree that concatenation is the preferred formal operation in both morphology and syntax, and the focus on segmentation into words and morphs can be understood as no more and no less than a consequence of that preference.

[3] There is a tradition of no great antiquity in linguistic theory of seeing the adult grammar as a collection of objects selected from a fixed, universal inventory of objects, rather than as an algebraic representation of some sort whose length is in principle unbounded. The first explicit mention of this, as far as I know, is found in David Stampe's work on natural phonology in the early 1970s (see Stampe (1980) [1972]), followed by Daniel Dinnesen's atomic phonology (see Dinnsen (1979)); the strategy was adopted in Chomsky's principles and parameters at the end of the 1970s, and it has never left the charts since then. It gained renewed vigor with the rise of optimality theory in the 1990s. Its appeal is no doubt due to the pious hope it has been known to inspire that the problem of language learning may turn out to be trivial, because the differences between languages will amount to a small number of bits of information. I find this sad, in part because, if we can't count on linguists to tell the world about the richness and variety found across humanity's languages, there is no one else to do it. It's doubly sad, in that even if it *were* the case that learning a language could be modeled as being much like selecting a set of, say, 50 items out of a universal set of 1,000, we would still need to do some heavy lifting to produce an account of learning; since there are some $\frac{1000!}{50!\ 950!}$ ways to do that, the fact that this is a finite number is not much consolation. I will return to this in the conclusion.

specifically to the task of discovering the morphology of a language with no prior knowledge of the morphology, but with prior knowledge of where word boundaries are (as if we had already solved the word segmentation problem), and discuss the role that analogy plays in this latter task. Naturally, we would like to merge these two tasks, and present an algorithm that takes an unsegmented segment stream as input and produces both a word list and a morphology; we are not yet able to accomplish that (though I suspect we have the tools at our disposal now to tackle that problem). I would like to emphasize, however, that the materials on which we base our experiments are not prepared corpora or toy data; they are in every case natural materials from natural languages.

There is a more general point behind my account as well, which deserves at the very least a brief presentation before we settle into a discussion of a specific problem. It is this: the present paper assumes that we can specify a scientific goal for linguistics which is independent of psychology, and which depends only on computational considerations. Being independent of psychology, it does *not* presume to tell psychologists what conclusions they will or should reach in their exploration of the human mind and brain, nor does it depend on those explorations. Its premise is very simple: given a particular corpus from a language (that is, a finite sample, which can be as little as a few thousand words, or as large as the internet as of some moment in time, like today), the goal is to find the best grammar (or set of grammars) that accounts for that data. This suggestion is only as useful as our ability to explicate what it means for a grammar G to account for a set of data, or corpus, C, and we will define this as the probability of the grammar G, given the data C; and we will see below that by this we shall have meant the grammar G such that its probability (based on its form) multiplied by the probability that G assigns to C, is the greatest. How such a view is possible and reasonable will become clearer shortly.[4]

Before proceeding any further, I would like to say what I mean by analogy in morphology. Unless specified otherwise, I will assume that our goal is to analyze the internal structure of words, and also that we actually know where words begin and end in the sound (or letter) stream of the language we happen to be looking at. In fact, I will assume that our problem is to find internal structure when presented with a word list in a language. In traditional terms, *book* : *books* :: *dog* : *dogs* would constitute an analogy; so would *jump* : *jumped* : *jumping* :: *walk* : *walked* : *walking*. A more perspicuous way to look at this sort of analogy is as in (1), which we call a "signature"; a computer

---

[4] This notion is also presented, in greater detail, in Goldsmith (2007).

scientist would prefer to represent the same data as in (2), which he would call a representation of a finite state automaton (FSA).

$$
\left\{ \begin{array}{c} walk \\ jump \end{array} \right\} \left\{ \begin{array}{c} \emptyset \\ ed \\ ing \end{array} \right\} \tag{1}
$$

$$\tag{2}$$

But before we talk about morphological analysis, let us turn first to the problem of word segmentation.

7.2 The problem of word segmentation

In the mid-1990s, Michael Brent and Carl de Marcken (both graduate students in computer science at the time working with Robert Berwick at MIT) developed computational methods for inferring word boundaries in a continuous stream of discrete symbols, relying on Minimum Description Length (or *MDL*) analysis (Brent (1999), de Marcken (1996), Rissanen (1989)). Their projects could be interpreted (as they did interpret them) as representing an idealization of how a child can learn the words of a language when exposed only to a stream of phonemes. This is the *word segmentation problem*: how to find words in a larger stream of symbols. Now, there are two fundamentally different approaches that one could take in dealing with the word segmentation problem (and one could certainly adopt both approaches, since they are not incompatible): one can either focus on finding the *boundaries* between words, or focus on finding words *themselves* in the stream, the sequences of recurring symbol strings, and inferring the boundaries from knowledge of the words. I think that there is a widespread (and natural) tendency to feel that the first of these two methods (finding cues in the signal that show where the boundaries between words are) is the more appealing way to approach the problem, perhaps on the grounds that you cannot take the second approach without engaging in some kind of inappropriate circular reasoning. This intuition is probably encouraged, as well, by the observation that in a good number of European languages, there are relatively straightforward superficial phonological cues to mark the delimitations between words, such as can be found in words in which the initial syllable is regularly stressed (as in Finnish, and as was once the case in German), or in which the penultimate syllable is stressed.[5]

---

[5] As an aside, I would mention my belief that this approach is hopeless as a general solution to the problem of word segmentation. The reason for this pessimistic view is that the difference in

The second approach, as I noted, is to say that we will *first* find the words in the signal, and *then* divide the signal up into words in the most likely way based on that knowledge of the words, along with the assumption that the speech signal can be partitioned without overlap into a succession of words. But how can this kind of learning be done?

I will give a brief summary here of the Brent-de Marcken approach to answering this question, based on MDL modeling. My account leans more heavily on de Marcken's specific approach than on Brent's, but it is a simplification of both, and the reader who would like to learn more is strongly advised to read the original works.

Minimum description length modeling was first developed by the Finnish-American statistician, Jorma Rissanen, notably in a book published in 1989 (Rissanen (1989)). The question he is concerned with is not specifically linguistic at all. It is simply this: given a body of data, how can we be sure to extract all and only the regularities that inhere in the data? We want to fit the model to the data, or the data to a model, and we want neither to overfit nor to underfit. Underfitting would mean failing to extract some significant regularity in the data; overfitting would mean misinterpreting something that was, in some sense, accidentally true of the data which was sampled, but would not be true of a larger sample from the same source.

Rissanen's approach is inherently probabilistic in two ways. To explain what these ways are, I shall discuss the problem of word segmentation in particular, even though Rissanen's approach is very general and was not developed with linguistic problems in mind. The first way in which the MDL approach is probabilistic is that an MDL analysis is a model (or grammar) that assigns a probability to every conceivable string of phonemes (or letters, if we are working with a language sample from a written source). This is a stringent condition: a probabilistic model is by definition one which assigns a non-negative number to every possible input, in such a fashion that the grand total of the probabilities adds up to 1.0—and this must be true even if the set of possible inputs is infinite (which is virtually always the case). Probability is thus *not* a measure of something like uncertainty or randomness; if anything, imposing the condition that the model be probabilistic imposes a very tight

---

probabilities that such approaches can assign to cuts in different places in a sound stream are far too small to allow a successful overall division of the stream to be accomplished in a local way, that is, based only on local information. The problem can only be solved by maximizing the probability of a parse over the longer string, which allows us to take into account the probabilities of the hypothesized words, as well as the conditional probabilities of the hypothesized words. To put this in a slightly different way, in order to segment a stream into words, it is not sufficient to have a model that predicts the phonetics of the word boundaries; one must also have a language model, assigning a probability to the sequence of hypothesized words. The interested reader can find a survey of much of the material on segmentation in Goldsmith (2009). See also Roark and Sproat 2007.

overall constraint on the system as a whole. In the language of probability, we are required to specify ahead of time a sample space and a distribution over that sample space; the distribution is essentially a function that maps a member of the sample space (or a subset of the members of the sample space) to a real number, in such a way that the whole sample space maps to 1.0.

The second way in which an MDL analysis is probabilistic is more abstract. We set a condition that the grammars *themselves* are the subject of a probability distribution; which is to say, every possible grammar is assigned a probability (a non-negative real number), subject to the condition that these probabilities sum to 1.0—and this must be true even if the set of possible grammars is infinite (which is virtually always the case). The reader may note that this condition puts MDL within the broader context of approaches which includes Bayesian approaches to modeling; MDL puts the priority on the quantitative notion of encoding, both regarding the data and the grammar, but there is an overall commonality from a distant enough perspective.

Although it may not sound like it at first, this second condition is very similar in spirit to Chomsky's view of grammar selection in early generative grammar (that is, in classical generative grammar (Chomsky (1975 [1955]), which in the late 1970s many generative grammarians abandoned—after little discussion—in favor of the principles and parameters approach (Chomsky and Lasniik (1977))). According to this perspective, the primary goal of linguistic theory is to make explicit a formalism for grammar writing, but not just *any* formalism. The goal was a formalism with which predictions (or, more modestly, claims) could be made as to which grammar was correct among a set of grammars all consistent with the given data; those predictions would be based purely on the length of the grammar in the some-day-to-be-discovered formalism.

MDL employs a few simple ideas to assign a probability to a (potentially infinite) set of grammars, and we should at least sketch these ideas. Perhaps the most important is what is known as Kraft's inequality. Kraft's inequality holds for uniquely decodable codes, but we will consider (as does most MDL modeling) a special case of that—those codes which are said to respect the prefix condition. The term *coding* here should simply be interpreted as meaning something like *formalized as a grammar*, and in general we want to consider the class of all grammars that are permitted by a certain formalism. The prefix condition sounds innocuous: it says that there are no two grammars (G and H, say) which have the property that H equals all of G plus some additional material (as computer scientists put it: there are no two grammars G and H such that G is a prefix of H—but remember that computer scientists just use "prefix" to mean a substring that starts at the beginning of some other string). Another way to put it is this: when you are reading a grammar, you know when you reach the end of it. (The condition seems innocuous, but its consequences are major, for reasons that we will not go into here.)

Kraft's inequality says that if a set of strings (here, grammars) does indeed respect the prefix condition, then we can assign a probability to each string (grammar) S equal to $2^{-length(S)}$. Why the number 2 here? I have assumed (as computer scientists tend to) that we encode the grammar using strictly binary encodings, the way a computer does, using only 0's and 1's. If we want to use a vocabulary like the Latin alphabet, then the base is going to be 26—or more likely 27, if we include a punctuation symbol, like space,[6] and so below I will replace "2" by "27." If the length of a grammar is 100 0's and 1's, then we assign it a probability of $\frac{1}{2^{100}}$; if it's 100 *letters*, then we assign it a probability of $\frac{1}{27^{100}}$. Unless we're very careful with our assignment of lengths, this quantity (based solely on grammar length) will sum to a finite number less than 1 (call it k); and then, to turn these numbers into true probabilities, we divide each of them by k, so that the sum totals 1.0.

In short, with a very mild condition (the prefix condition) imposed, we can easily specify a natural probability distribution over the infinite class of grammars, according to which a shorter grammar is a more probable grammar. In fact, if grammar G has length g, and grammar H has length h, then the ratio of their probabilities is simply $2^{(g-h)}$ if binary encoding is used, and $27^{(g-h)}$ if the Latin alphabet is employed.

Now we take two further steps. The first involves Bayes' rule, which is nothing more than an algebraic restatement of the definition of conditional probability. The second involves the assumption that there is a single correct answer to our question.

Bayes' rule says that (in the case that we are considering) the probability of a grammar, given our corpus, is closely related to the probability of the grammar, given the corpus, as follows:

$$pr(G|D) = \frac{pr(D|G)pr(G)}{pr(D)} \tag{3}$$

The left-hand side refers to the probability of a grammar G, given the data D at hand (i.e., the corpus), while the right-hand side is the product of the probability of the corpus assigned by the grammar G, times the probability of the grammar, divided by the probability of the data. Since our goal is to find

---

[6] There is a fine line here between clarity of exposition and accuracy of modeling. In general, we *don't* want to use special boundary symbols to demarcate the ends of representations, because this is typically a wasteful and inefficient way of marking boundaries; an encoding which respects the prefix condition is better. But ease of exposition will sometimes trump formal niceties in this chapter.

the grammar whose probability is the greatest (given the data at hand, and what else do we have other than the data at hand?), we can interpret (3) to mean: find the grammar G for which this quantity is the greatest. The denominator, $pr(D)$, is perhaps the hardest to compute, but we do not in fact need to calculate it, because it is a constant. Since we have just finished discussing how to calculate the probability of the grammar G, based on its length, calculating $pr(G)$ is not a problem. And calculating $pr(D|G)$ is not a problem, either, since we have assumed from the start that our model is probabilistic, which is to say, that it assigns a probability to every conceivable corpus. So in the end, our task simply boils down to this: find the probabilistic grammar G such that the probability of the corpus, given the grammar, times the probability of the grammar itself, is the greatest.

Brent's and de Marcken's insight was that the method that we have just described could be applied to the problem of word segmentation and lexicon induction. We need to do three things: first, figure out how a lexicon (with its probability) actually assigns a probability to any corpus; second, figure out how to associate a lexicon with a length, so that we can in turn assign it a probability; and third, figure out how to actually come up with a candidate lexicon, along with probabilities assigned to each word in the lexicon. It turns out that none of these is too difficult, at least as a first approximation.

First, how do we assign a probability to a corpus D, given a probabilistic lexicon? We need to take into consideration the fact that there will, generally speaking, be many ways of parsing a corpus up into words. If all we know about English is its words (and nothing about syntax, meaning, and so on), then a string like: THISMEANSTHAT that can be divided up in many ways. There is THIS-MEANS-THAT, but then (since every individual letter can be used as an individual word in languages, in general), there is also THIS-ME-AN-S-THAT, and T-HIS-ME-AN-S-T-HAT, and many others. So first of all, we make the assumption that only one parse of a given corpus is actually correct,[7] and that the parse that is assigned the highest probability by our corpus is the correct one. And the probability assigned to a given parse is defined as the product of two factors: the first is the probability that the corpus has exactly as many words in it as the parse has pieces, while the second is the product of the probabilities of all of the words in the parse. In

---

[7] That this assumption is a bit too strong is illustrated by the ambiguity of phrases like "cookmea-napplesauce", which has perhaps two reasonable parses: *cook me an apple sauce* and *cook mean apple sauce*. The reader is invited to construct similar examples in other languages.

the case of THIS-MEANS-THAT, the probability of that parse is equal to the probability that a string has three words in it, times the product of the probabilities of each of the three words *this*, *means*, and *that*.[8]

Second, what is a lexicon's length? If we define a lexicon as a concatenation of words, then as long as we separate each of the words by a space, the words satisfy the conditions for Kraft's inequality, and we can assign a (prior) probability to a lexicon equal to 1 divided by 27 raised to the power of the length of the lexicon, in letters: $\frac{1}{27^{length(lexicon)}}$.

Third, how do we *find* a lexicon, given a corpus? We proceed in a bottom-up fashion, assuming initially that the lexicon consists of all the letters of the corpus. Then we iteratively repeat the following process: we look at all "words" that appear next to each other in the corpus, and pick the most frequent such pair. (Initially, this may be T-H in the case of a written corpus of English, since our initial assumption is that the words of the lexicon are the letters of the language). We use our MDL criterion to decide whether to declare that T-H is really a word TH. Our MDL criterion is simply this: does the expression described in (3) increase when we add our candidate to the grammar? Does the probability of the corpus increase enough by the addition of TH (for example) to offset the decrease in probability of the lexicon that comes about from increasing its length (from 26 real members to 27, the alphabet plus TH)? If so, then we include the new member; if not, we leave the grammar as it is and try some different candidates. This process stops when there are no neighboring chunks in the corpus whose addition would increase the overall probability of the corpus.[9]

There is one more step that we need to take to appreciate the beauty of Rissanen's MDL framework. If we take the logarithm of both sides of equation (3) and multiply these two expressions by −1, we obtain the following quantity: $-log\,pr(D|G) - length(G) + log\,pr(D)$. The third term is a constant. However, the first term has a very real significance: it is called the *optimal compressed length of the data*, and the second term also has a real significance: it is, quite simply, the length of the grammar, which we use in order to evaluate how well the grammar succeeds at being a compact formulation. The first term, the optimal compressed length of the data, given the model, is a well-understood quantity expressing how well the model does at extracting generalizations from the data. Thus the task of finding the grammar that *minimizes* this quantity (*minimizes* instead of *maximizes* because we

---

[8] There are several ways to establish a reasonable distribution over number of words in sentence, but they do not bear on our discussion here.

[9] See the Appendix.

multiplied it by -1, and the logarithm function is monotonic increasing) is equivalent to finding the most probable grammar, given the data at hand.

We intend by this to mean what was suggested above: there are no constraints on the forms of possible grammars, above and beyond the condition that they be programs for a Turing machine, and thus are algorithms.[10] This means that the purpose of linguistic theory is to serve as a set of heuristics to help the linguistic scientist come up with a tight, snug grammar, given a set of data. MDL can determine which of a set of grammars is the best one, given the data; no feasible process can search all possible grammars, so there is no guarantee that another linguist will not come along tomorrow with a *better* grammar for the data. But it will be *truly* better, better as far as the length of its Turing machine program is concerned. We know that there is a best analysis (up to the unlikely possibility that two or more grammars have (along with the data) an equal description length), because the minimum description length will be some positive number *less* than the description length provided by the (dumb) grammar consisting of exactly the corpus with no internal structure (along with some reasonable closure conditions).

7.3 Success with word discovery?

How well does this method work? Anyone who has worked with corpora knows that, to some extent, an answer to this question depends heavily on the corpus used for training and for testing. In the case at hand, there is no training corpus as such; the input to the algorithm is a long string that has no indication of word boundaries, and the output is a guess (or prediction) as to where the word boundaries are, or should be. In view of the fact that the system has no prior knowledge of the language, the results are in some respects very impressive, but at the same time, when we look at the results with the eyes of a linguist, we quickly see some linguisticky things that have gone awry.

In Figure 7.1 is the beginning of a passage from the first 100,000 words of the Brown corpus and Figure 7.2 is the beginning of a similar passage from a Portuguese document.

Three things jump out when we look at these results. First, there are many errors caused by the algorithm finding "pieces" that are too small, such as *produc-ed*: it seems as if the system is finding morphemes in this case, while in

---

[10] The point may be purely terminological, but I would argue that the position I am describing clearly falls under the definition of generative grammar, at least as it was considered in Chomsky (1975) [1955]; algorithmic complexity is the simplicity metric utilized.

The Fulton County Grand Ju ry s aid Friday an investi gation of At l anta 's recent prim ary e lection produc ed no e videnc e that any ir regul ar it i e s took place. Thejury further s aid in term - end present ment s thatthe City Ex ecutive Commit t e e, which had over - all charg e ofthe e lection , d e serv e s the pra is e and than k softhe City of At l anta forthe man ner in whichthe e lection was conduc ted.

FIGURE 7.1 The first sentences of the Brown Corpus

De muitosoutros re curso s da fl o r esta ,não apenas folh as, fl ores era íz esma s também de se mente se da cas ca de árvo res re ti ram produto s medi cin a i s comos quai s se habitu aram nas u a s o li dão e nos seu s s o nhos a en fre nta ra s do ença s que hoje coma chega da dos branco s começa ma trata r comos re médi os da indústri a u r ba na–e que muitas vezes não produz em e feito.

FIGURE 7.2 The first sentences of a Portuguese document

other cases it is finding words. Second, in some cases the algorithm finds pieces that are too big: they are "pieces" like *forthe* which occur together often enough in English that the algorithm erroneously decides that the language treats them as a word. Third, there are far too many single letter words: we need a prior probability for word length that makes the probability of one-letter words much lower.

We will focus here on just the first of these points. Why should the system find morphemes rather than words some of the time? The answer is perhaps obvious: the system that we are considering is nothing more than a lexicon, bereft of any ability to find structure in the data other than frequency of appearance of strings of various lengths. There is no ability built into the system to see relationships between words, nor any ability to see that words may enter into relationships with the words around them. We need to add linguistic structure to this approach, then. And that is what we turn to now.

7.4 The *Linguistica* project

I have been working since 1997, along with Colin Sprague, Yu Hu, and Aris Xanthos, on the development of a software package, *Linguistica*, whose primary goal is the automatic inference of morphological structure on the basis of an unmodified sample corpus from a real language, and whose

method is MDL as we have described it in this chapter; see http://linguistica.
uchicago.edu[11]

A big, and I would say controversial, assumption made by the *Linguistica*
project is that meaning can be ignored in the process of inferring or inducing
the morphological structure of a word or a language. The fact is, the proced-
ures we have explored make little or no reference to meaning. Any successes
that we achieve can be interpreted as showing that reference to meaning is not
necessary, but we certainly cannot infer that human language learners do not
use meaning in their search to discover language structure. It is natural to
interpret our project as an effort to figure out, from a linguistic point of view,
exactly *where* a learner, one who has access neither to a rich innate component
nor to the meaning of utterances, will fail.

In some ways, the work that I am describing could be viewed as a neo-
Harrisian program, in the sense that Zellig Harris believed, and argued, that
the goal of linguistic theory was to develop an autonomous linguistic method
of analyzing linguistic data, in which the overall complexity of the grammar
was the character that the linguist would use in order to evaluate competing
analyses, and in which the linguist was, in the final analysis, more interested in
the methods of analysis than in the analysis of any particular language.[12] As
long as we are clear what we mean by the term *discovery procedure*, it would be
fair to say that this work aims at developing a discovery procedure for
morphology. While it does not propose a simple step-by-step process for
this end, it does propose something so close to an algorithm as to be
indistinguishable from a computer program—which is why it has been
relatively easy to encode the proposals as computer code which can be tested
against small and large natural language corpora.

7.5 MDL, grammar simplicity, and analogy

One way to summarize what MDL methods have in common is to say that they
seek to extract redundancy in the data. In the case of word segmentation, the
redundancy is the reappearance of the same substrings on many occasions,
while in the case of morpheme discovery, it is the reappearance of morphemes
under quite particular and restricted conditions. What I will describe here is a
considerable simplification of the model as it actually works, and the reader
can find detailed discussion in Goldsmith (2001, 2006). As we saw above,
the prior probability that is assigned to a grammar is based entirely on its

---

[11] See Goldsmith (2000, 2001, 2006).
[12] See Goldsmith (2005) for a recent discussion.

length, quite literally, and hence any redundancy in the formulation of a grammar leads to a heavy cost paid by the grammar, in terms of the lowering of the probability assigned to it. Conversely, a grammar which has been shortened by the elimination of redundancy is assigned a considerably higher probability. And, as we will see, analogy is one essential way in which redundancy can be discovered by the language learner.

The basic idea is this: when sets of words can be broken up into two pieces in precisely parallel ways (as in the signature shown in (1), repeated here as (4)), we can extract measurable redundancies. Here, we have taken the six words *jump, jumped, jumping, walk, walked,* and *walking,* and observed that there is a pattern consisting of two distinct stems, and three distinct suffixes, and all combinations of stem and suffix appear in our data set.

$$\left\{ \begin{array}{c} walk \\ jump \end{array} \right\} \left\{ \begin{array}{c} \emptyset \\ ed \\ ing \end{array} \right\} \tag{4}$$

Before any such analysis, we were responsible for encoding all the letters of the six words, which comes to forty letters (including a final space or word boundary), while after we extract the regularity, only sixteen letters need to be specified (again, counting a boundary symbol along with each suffix).

In somewhat more useful—that is, generalizable—terminology, we can describe this data with a finite state automaton (FSA), as in (2), repeated here as (5).

$$\tag{5}$$

To encode this, we need a formal method for describing the three states and their transitions, and then we need to label each transition edge; we have already seen a simple (and, as it turns out, overly simple) way of measuring the complexity of the labels, which was by counting the number of symbols. We will ignore the computation of the complexity of the FSA itself; it is very simple from a technical point of view.[13]

---

[13] Each FSA consists of a set of pointers to nodes, along with labels that are themselves pointers to strings. A maximum likelihood model provides probabilities in each of those two domains; the complexity of the overall FSA is the sum of the inverse log probabilities of all of the pointers in the representation.

This overall system can then naturally be regarded as a device capable of expressing morphological analogies of the *book* : *books* :: *dog* : *dogs* sort. How does it operate in practice? Does it work to find real linguistic morphological regularities?

The answer, in a nutshell, is this: we can find patterns, locally and in the small; but a very large proportion of them are spurious (that is to say, linguistically wrong and irrelevant) unless they participate in larger patterns of the language as a whole. An example of a linguistically real discovery is as in (4) or (5), and a spurious example is as in (6), which captures the nongeneralization inherent in the words *change, changed, charge, charged,* or (7), which captures the nongeneralization inherent in the words *class, cotton, glass, gotten* (and I could offer dozens of examples of this sort from any language of which we have a few thousand words in computer-readable form: it was not I, of course, who discovered these patterns, but rather an over-eager analogy-seeking computer program):

$$cha\left\{\begin{matrix} n \\ r \end{matrix}\right\} ge\left\{\begin{matrix} \emptyset \\ d \end{matrix}\right\} \tag{6}$$

$$\left\{\begin{matrix} c \\ g \end{matrix}\right\}\left\{\begin{matrix} lass \\ otten \end{matrix}\right\} \tag{7}$$

What is wrong with the spurious generalizations in (6) and (7) is that the proposed morphemes do not appear outside of this generalization, more generally in the language. Analogy, as we see it here, is an excellent and important source of hypotheses, but it is not more than that. We need to develop means (and, it appears, largely formal means) to evaluate the hypotheses suggested by analogies.

The use of Minimum Description Length analysis provides at least a part of the response to this need, and it sheds some interesting light on the role played by information theory in linguistic description. Embedded within the work cited above by de Marcken is the key insight formalized by the use of information-theoretic formalisms—namely, that reuse of a grammatical object (such as a morpheme, a context, or anything else) is the best kind of evidence we can have of the linguistic reality of the object. What makes the n, r pairing in (6) linguistically irrelevant is the small number of times it is found in the linguistic analysis of English—unlike the $\emptyset$, d pairing, but like the c, g pairing in (7).

But this should not lead us to thinking that we simply need to count occurrences and look for some magic threshold count, because information theory provides a much better method for understanding what is at play. The key point is this: the edges in the finite state automaton in (5) should be understood not as being labeled with strings of phonemes, but rather as being labeled by pointers to morphemes in a separate inventory of morpheme spell-outs. This simple formal decision has two consequences. The first is a consequence that comes from information theory: the complexity (in quantifiable bits) of a pointer to a morpheme is directly controlled by the frequency with which a morpheme is used throughout the grammar. The second is that we arrive at a natural understanding of the view, famously voiced by Meillet, that language is a system in which everything is interconnected.[14]

The decision to label edges of a morphology with pointers rather than phonic substance makes strong predictions: strong enough to build a program that figures out the structure by itself, without human oversight. *Linguistica* discovers affixes by seeking robust clusters of stems and affixes, such as the large set of stems in English that take exactly the suffixes Ø, *ed*, *ing*, *s*. But what of stems that occur with an idiosyncratic set of affixes, a set of affixes shared by no other stem? Consider the examples in (8) and (9).

$$
act \begin{Bmatrix} \emptyset \\ ed \\ s \\ ion \end{Bmatrix} \tag{8}
$$

$$
car \begin{Bmatrix} d \\ e \\ l \\ p \end{Bmatrix} \tag{9}
$$

Each of these signatures is an example of a stem that appears with exactly four suffixes in a pattern shared by no other stem in a particular corpus. But the information-theoretic cost of building a pattern with the suffixes in (8) is much less than that of building the pattern shown in (9)—not because of the number of letters (phonemes) in each case, but rather because /l/ and /p/ are both rare affixes in English (note: *affixes*, not phonemes). An affix that occurs

---

[14] In particular, "Comme pour tout autre langage, les différentes parties du système linguistique indo-européen forment un ensemble où tout se tient et dont il importe avant tout de bien comprendre le rigoureux enchaînement" (Meillet (1915) p. x).

on one word in a lexicon of 20,000 words will "cost" approximately log_2 20,000 bits (about 14 bits), while a suffix that occurs on 1,000 words will cost about 4 bits—a very large difference, in the event; and the cost of positing /l/ and /p/ as affixes outweighs the gain saved by positing /car/ as a stem in (9). The same is not true of the case in (8), where the cost of building a subgeneralization to deal with the words based on the stem /act/ is much cheaper, because all of the observed suffixes are cheap, in an information-theoretic sense: they are independently used enough throughout the grammar that using them additionally in the creation of a new generalization costs the grammar very little. This implicit "thought process" is easy to formalize and to embed within an automatic morphological analyzer.

In Table 7.1, I have given some data from a sequence of steps of learning the morphology of the first 100,016 words of the Brown Corpus.

The first row in Table 7.1 shows the length of the "trivial" morphology at the beginning: it expresses the phonological cost (so to speak) of listing all 13,005 distinct words without any analysis: all words are stems, no stems are analyzed (we speak of "cost" to underscore the fact that we try to minimize this quantity). Row 2 shows the result of a relatively conservative effort to find signatures with several stems and several affixes, and we see that the information stored in the analyzed stems is now 53,835, while the information that we have taken away from the unanalyzed stems is greater: it is the difference between 486,295 and 390,160 (or 96,135). The additional infrastructure (affixes plus signatures) to accomplish this cost 1,220 + 22,793 (=24,013), for a total cost of 53,835 + 24,013 = 77,848. This cost (77,848) is much less than what was saved (96,135); the difference is 96,135 − 82,848 = 18,287. (Against this gain must be reckoned a slight decrease in the probability computed for the corpus.)

In the third, fourth, and fifth rows, we see the result of extending the discovery of signatures, stems, and affixes accomplished on the first pass to

TABLE 7.1 Description Length of morphology evolution during learning

Steps	Total	Unanalyzed stems	Analyzed stems	Affixes	Signatures
1. Before analysis	486,295	486,295	0	0	0
2. Bootstrap heuristic	468,008	390,160	53,835	1,220	22,793
3. Extend known stems and affixes	456,256	377,635	58,835	1,220	23,566
4. Find new signatures	434,179	320,405	74,440	1750	37,584
5. Find singleton signatures	429,225	235,390	128,830	1710	63,295

analyze words that were not initially analyzable. These are words for which the simple analogies of the first step were insufficient to uncover them, which include the discovery of patterns as in (8) and the rejection of those like in (9).

The algorithms explored in Goldsmith (2006) are remarkably good at discovering morphemes and morphological structure in a language with a complexity comparable to that of English. In the next sections, I will focus not so much on what they get right (which is better covered in the papers I have cited) but rather on where the challenges (some of them quite daunting) appear to be.[15]

7.6 The challenging of "collapsing" cases

Consider once more the case of English, where stems can be followed by a rather small set of affixes: verbs by {∅, *ed*, *ing*, *s*}, nouns by {∅, *s*}, adjectives by {∅, *er*, *est*}. In even a modest-sized corpus, we will find a large number of stems that appear with all of their suffixes inside the corpus. But in addition, we will find a good number of stems that only appear with a subset of their possible suffixes. In the simplest case, this is due to the fact that the stem did not appear very often in the corpus. This is illustrated in (10), where each node represents one of the signatures, or small FSAs, that we have considered, and it is labeled with its set of suffixes. Below the label are two numbers: the first indicates the number of distinct stems that occurred in the corpus with this set of suffixes, and the second indicates the total number of words that occurred with these stems and suffixes. The two filled nodes are the "saturated" ones in which, from a linguistic point of view, all the suffixes that could have appeared have appeared. The node on the top row has four suffixes; those on the middle row have three suffixes, each a subset of those of the node on the top row; and the node on the bottom row has two suffixes, a subset of the two nodes from which it hangs on the middle row.

---

[15] A reviewer of this chapter noted that "work on morphological processing (e.g. Baayen and Moscoso del Prado Martín (2005); Hay and Baayen (2005)) and [other work by Ernestus and Baayen]) suggests analogical relations are sensitive to semantic similarity, phonetic similarity, frequency effects, and more". The information-theoretic models of the sort discussed in the present chapter give a firm theoretical foundation for why frequency effects are found; the reason is that information links in a grammar contribute a measurable amount to the complexity of the system, and that amount is equal to the reciprocal of the logarithm of the element being linked to. In the morphological analyses that we have studied in the *Linguistica* project, phonetic similarity has never emerged as a factor which, if integrated, would allow for superior performance. The relevance of semantic information is a difficult question; while I believe that it is relevant and could potentially improve performance in many cases, it is not easy to integrate meaning into a learning algorithm in a way that does not beg the question of learnability by building in too much information and treating that information as if it had been observable.

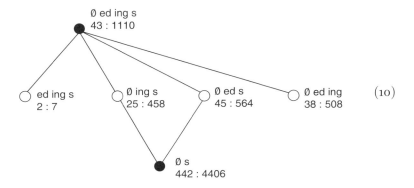

(10)

We need a method that determines that the white nodes in (10) are only partial generalizations, while the filled nodes are complete. To be sure, I have expressed this in categorical terms, when it is clear (or it becomes clear, when we look at more data) that the distinction is a soft one, rather than a hard one—but discussion of this point would lead us afield. I will return below to this question in the context of a language like Swahili, where it becomes even more pressing. To rephrase the problem, we can ask, when we have two signatures that are partially identical and partially different, when is the similarity between them great enough to allow us to generalize the suffixes that are seen in one, but not in the other, to both of them? This remains an unsolved problem.

7.7 From analogy to algorithm

How does one actually *find* analogies along the lines of *book* : *books* :: *dog* : *dogs* in a language? It turns out that questions of this sort are not at all easy to answer, and a large part of the work devoted to the *Linguistica* project has been aimed at providing answers to this question. In this section, I will describe two problems that seem simple enough, and are certainly typical, and try to give a sense of why they are not as simple as one might expect them to be. The first example is the treatment of gender and plural marking of adjectives in French; the treatment of parallel forms in a number of other languages, such as Spanish, would be similar. The second is the treatment of morphological patterns in a rich system like that of the Swahili verb. "Treatment" in this context means the breaking up of the string into substrings corresponding to morphemes and the correct formulation of a finite-state automaton (or its equivalent) to generate the observed patterns. Thus we address both the first and the second question articulated in the first section of this paper.

As I noted above, some pre-generative linguists took such questions very seriously—notably, Zellig Harris (1955, 1967) did (but see Hafer and Weiss 1974). Harris apparently believed that he had solved the problem through the computation of what he called successor frequency (and predecessor frequency) in a large corpus. By successor frequency, Harris meant a characteristic of a specific string, in the context of a specific corpus: given a string S of length n (typically the first n letters of a word), one considers only the subset of words in the corpus that begin with the string S (computer scientists would say: consider the set of words with the prefix S—but then computer scientists use the term *prefix* rather differently than linguists), and then one asks: in this subset, how many different letters are there in the $(n + 1)^{st}$ position (which is the position right after the string S)? That value is the successor frequency of string S, in the corpus.

Harris believed that by calculating the successor frequency and the predecessor frequency at each point in each word of a corpus, he could find the morpheme boundaries (although Hafer and Weiss note that on the basis of their experiments neither choosing a threshold nor looking for a local maximum of successor frequency works very well in English). To make a long story short (see Goldsmith (2001, 2006) for the long version), such a purely local method does not work, and some more global characteristics of the overall grammar need to be taken into consideration, as we have already suggested.

Still, Harris's notion of successor frequency can serve as a useful heuristic for locating potential breaks, as the simple data in (1) suggest: the presence of the words *jump, jumped*, and *jumping* in a corpus leads to a successor frequency of three after the stem *jump*, just as it is after *walk*.

But successor frequency fails to work, even as a heuristic, when we turn to languages with much richer morphologies (that is, where the average number of morphemes per word is considerably higher than it is in English), and as linguists know, the morphological richness of English is on the poor side, as languages go.

The first case we will consider is that of the regular inflectional pattern of written modern French, which represents an earlier form of spoken French (some of this material is discussed in greater detail in Goldsmith and Hu (2004)). In the treatment of a subcorpus like *petit, petits, petite, petites, grand, grands, grande, grandes* (the masc. sg., masc. pl., fem. sg., and fem. pl. forms for *small, large*), the system we have described in Goldsmith (2006) will generate an FSA as in (11), and an algorithm described in Goldsmith and Hu (2004) generates the FSA in (12) rather than (13), which is the correct structure. The FSA in (11) misanalyzes the segmentation of the feminine plural forms, and (12) correctly segments, but does not represent the correct grammar, which is that given in (13). In terms of analogy, all three systems capture the analogy *petit* : *petits* : *petite* : *petites* :: *grand* : *grands* : *grande* : *grandes*, but only (13) expresses the analogy *petit* : *petits* :: *petite* : *petites* and also *petit* : *petite* :: *petits* : *petites*. (In fact, it appears to me easier to understand the nature of the generalization being captured by looking at the FSA than by using the traditional notation associated with analogy expressed with colons.)

$$\begin{array}{c} \text{petit} \\ \text{grand} \end{array} \qquad \begin{array}{c} \varnothing \\ \text{—s—} \\ \text{e} \\ \text{es} \end{array} \tag{11}$$

$$\begin{array}{c} \text{petit} \\ \text{grand} \end{array} \qquad \begin{array}{c} \varnothing \\ \varnothing \\ \text{—e—} \\ \text{s} \\ \text{s} \end{array} \tag{12}$$

$$\begin{array}{c} \text{petit} \\ \text{grand} \end{array} \qquad \begin{array}{c} \varnothing \quad \varnothing \\ \text{e} \quad \text{s} \end{array} \tag{13}$$

The two big questions are: does a natural complexity measure unambiguously choose (13) over (11) and (12), and do we have a good search procedure that finds (13)? A relatively brief summary provides a positive answer to the first question; the second is more difficult to answer, and I will leave it open for now. The complexity of an FSA is almost exactly equal to the sum of the informational complexity associated with each of its nodes plus that of each of its edges plus that associated with the labels on the edges. As noted above, the informational complexity is in each case the inverse log probability of the item in question. In (11), there are three nodes, each of which has roughly the same informational complexity, equal in this case to $\sigma = -\log S$, where S is the frequency of words that is described by this FSA in the corpus (that is, the total count of the words in this FSA divided by the total number of words in the corpus). The information complexity of the labels on each edge are also equal to the inverse log frequency of their usage, and *es* is a relatively rare suffix in French (i.e., there are relatively few feminine plural adjectives), and hence its informational cost is quite large. In addition, one must pay twice for the two pointers to each of the suffixes ø and *s*, and there is one more node in (12) than in (11). Hence (12) turns out to be more costly than (11). By contrast, (13) is less complex than either (11) or (12), despite the fact that it has one more node than (11). By avoiding positing a morpheme *es* (expensive because rare—it costs less than (11)), while by positing *s* only once, it costs less than (12).

I think this example clearly illustrates the basic point of this paper: formal complexity can, in many cases, be used to evaluate and compare alternative analyses, and algorithmic and information-theoretic complexity suffices to define the relevant complexity.

The second example we will look at represents still uncharted waters. It come from Swahili; consider (14), which gives a sample of some of the richness of the Swahili finite verb; I use the traditional Bantu terminology where appropriate. The positions indicated in this diagram illustrate subject markers, tense markers, object markers, verb roots, the passive/active marker, and the final vowel, respectively; there are also other affixes, such as a relative clause marker that can appear after the tense markers, which are not indicated here. There is little question but that the correct solution is formally much simpler than any of the partial solutions; algorithmic complexity will correctly identify an FSA as in (14) as a very simple grammar.

$$(14)$$

In order to even have a chance to discover these morphemes and the structure that lies behind them, we need to implement the notion of analogy in a richer fashion; what follows is taken from Hu *et al.* (2005).

We first look for elementary alignments between pairs of strings, as in (15), where m_1 or m_4 can be null, and m_2 or m_3 can be null. These elementary alignments can be found using the well-known string edit distance algorithm.

$$(15)$$

We expand these structures by finding ways to collapse them, either as suggested by (16), or as in (17) and (18).

$$(16)$$

$$(17)$$

$$(18)$$

But establishing a clear and workable algorithm to correctly collapse these FSAs is no simple task, in the presence of only a realistic amount of data (and it is not clear that increasing the amount of data available would change the difficulty in an essential way). The simple cases illustrated here work fine to collapse small FSAs when the difference between them is small. But the problem becomes harder quite quickly when we try to induce the correct structure, for example, of what is perhaps the structure best represented in the data, that found in the first two "columns" of (14), representing the subject markers and the tense markers. Because each column has a large number of possible morphemes in it, the subgeneralizations that we easily find—typified by the one in (18), which has a single subject marker (*a*) followed by two tense markers (*li* and *na*)—become harder and harder to analogize to.

Let's be a bit more specific, to make concrete what we're talking about. In a corpus of 25,000 Swahili words (4,100 distinct words among them), we find 254 three-state FSAs with the methods we have sketched, and of these, virtually all of them are linguistically reasonable; the place where the strings are cut are, indeed, morpheme boundaries from the linguist's perspective. These three-state FSAs (and I have sketched the top eight in (19–26)) can be ranked with respect to how much information they compress: those that compress a good deal of information are necessarily those that express a large number of words with relatively few edges in the automaton. In theory, that kind of compression can happen in either of two ways: by specifying an FSA with a single stem but a wide range of affixes, or by specifying an FSA with a smaller set of affixes and a wide range of stems. It turns out that the latter is by far the most common kind of generalization obtained.

The task now is to generalize, which is effectively just another way of saying to learn what the morphological pattern of Swahili is. As far as I can see, there is little or nothing that we can posit as a simple innate premise that will help, nor will appealing to analogy help us, because the question now is really: when should two (or more) patterns be treated as analogous? Now, it is very likely true that if these strings of letters were labeled as the morphemes that they are (that is, if the labels told us more than just the phonemes: if they furthermore identified the functional category of the morpheme), our task would be considerably lightened. But taking that information for granted seems to me like question-begging. Swahili, just like most languages, often employs the same sequence of phonemes to realize different morphemes (for example, the subject and object markers for various person and number classes is the same: *tu* marks both subject and object marker for first-person plural, etc.) It is morphological analysis, and the inference of a morphological generator, that is an important step on the way to understanding the morphological identity of strings of letters (or phonemes); we risk circularity if we assume that knowledge of morpheme identity can serve as the basis of our knowledge of the morphological grammar. We would like to understand how a learner would generalize by recognizing the identity of the prefix *a* in patterns (19), (20), (22), (24);[16] but *a* is the most common phoneme and also the most common morpheme in the language, and occurs with several functions; mere phonological identity is simply *not* enough to lead the learner to treat all occurrences of *a* in the same way.

$$
\left\{ \begin{array}{ll} a & \text{Subject} \\ wa & \text{Markers} \end{array} \right\} \left\{ \begin{array}{l} \text{55 stems:} \\ baki \\ ende \\ fanye \\ \ldots \end{array} \right\} \tag{19}
$$

$$
\left\{ \begin{array}{ll} a & \text{Subject} \\ m & \text{Markers} \end{array} \right\} \left\{ \begin{array}{l} \text{17 stems:} \\ cheni \\ kaanguka \\ kapoteza \\ \ldots \end{array} \right\} \tag{20}
$$

$$
\left\{ \begin{array}{l} \text{17 stems:} \\ akaongez \\ alifany \\ ameja \\ \ldots \end{array} \right\} \left\{ \begin{array}{ll} \text{NULL} & \text{active} \\ w & \text{passive} \end{array} \right\} \tag{21}
$$

---

[16] And perhaps (25): the system posits *ana* as a prefix, and it is an inductive leap to treat this as the concatenation of *a* and *na* at this point.

$$\left\{ \begin{matrix} a & \text{Subject} \\ wa & \text{Markers} \end{matrix} \right\} \left\{ \begin{matrix} \text{14 stems:} \\ changa \\ heshimuni \\ lilokataa \\ \ldots \end{matrix} \right\} \qquad (22)$$

$$\left\{ \begin{matrix} \text{12 stems:} \\ akawaachi \\ amewaweke \\ fany \\ \ldots \end{matrix} \right\} \left\{ \begin{matrix} a & \text{default ending} \\ eni & \text{plural imperative} \end{matrix} \right\} \qquad (23)$$

$$\left\{ \begin{matrix} a & \text{Subject} \\ & \text{Marker} \end{matrix} \right\} \left\{ \begin{matrix} li & \text{Tense} \\ na & \text{Markers} \end{matrix} \right\} \left\{ \begin{matrix} \text{11 stems:} \\ batiza \\ chaguliwa \\ kwenda \\ \ldots \end{matrix} \right\} \qquad (24)$$

$$\left\{ \begin{matrix} ana & \text{Subject Marker} \\ & \text{and Tense Marker} \end{matrix} \right\} \left\{ \begin{matrix} NULL & \text{default} \\ ye & \text{Rel Clause marker} \end{matrix} \right\}$$
$$\times \left\{ \begin{matrix} \text{10 stems:} \\ fanana \\ ishi \\ kuja \\ \ldots \end{matrix} \right\} \qquad (25)$$

$$\left\{ \begin{matrix} \text{18 stems:} \\ akili \\ bahari \\ dunia \\ \ldots \end{matrix} \right\} \left\{ \begin{matrix} NULL & \text{default} \\ ni & \text{postposition} \end{matrix} \right\} \qquad (26)$$

We are currently working on a method to link the low-level FSAs illustrated in (19–26) to the larger, simpler, and correct pattern, that of (15), and I will sketch the intuition that lies behind it. These FSAs can be thought of themselves as expressions (for example, by alphabetizing all the elements in a column and concatenating them with a punctuation marker between them), and we can establish a distance measure across pairs of string expressions which we can then use to hypothesize which items should be collapsed to form a larger generalization. When two or more morphemes—especially high-frequency morphemes—appear in the same column (that is, in a paradigmatic morphological relationship), then they may be analyzed as likely alternatives for the same morphological position.

This is easier to explain with a real example. There are several high-frequency FSAs that begin with the subject marker *a*, followed by two alternative tense markers, followed by a set of verbal stems. In the first case, the two tense markers are *li* and *na*; in the second, the two tense markers are *li* and *me*; in the third, they are *ka* and *na*; in the fourth, *ka* and *li* (I have not listed these FSAs here). We can capitalize upon each of these pairings to create a distance metric among these morphemes with this information, increasing the simplicity of assigning them to the same morphological position. We do this in order to overcome the problem of the sparsity of the data: we never find a single stem in a finite corpus appearing in all of its possible forms; what we need to do is use the partial information that the data actually provide, and much of that information is bundled into the observation that various subsets of morphemes appear in the same position of the word—and we can infer that even before we have a clear global understanding of what the overall structure of the word is. In a sense, that's the key to understanding learning: understanding how we can incrementally advance the analysis of the data, through analyzing the data, even though we have not yet achieved a global understanding of how everything fits together. In this case, the appearance of a pair of stems (*keti, mtuma*) appearing with the subject marker *a* and three of the four tense markers (*ki, li, na*, in fact) strongly supports the hypothesis that they are all realizations of the same morphological position. The sense in which this is true can be mathematically formulated and integrated into the search algorithm. But considerable work remains if we are to correctly induce the simple, and globally coherent, morphological structure of forms like the Swahili verb.

7.8 Discussion and conclusion

We have covered—or at least touched on—quite a number of topics, all closely joined by the question of how morphology can be learned. We have focused on the task of learning to segment words into morphs and discovering the grammar which puts them back together. This task is already difficult enough, but I hope it is clear that in a sense this task is a surrogate for the larger and more difficult task of segmenting entire utterances (into the pieces we call words) and discovering the grammar which puts them back together.

In the case of morphology, there is little or no hope that an appeal to a magical slate of innate principles will greatly simplify the task (I refer, of course, to an information-rich Universal Grammar). As far as learning morphology is concerned, Locke was surely right: all the reasoning is search and casting about; it requires pains and application. But we must not lose sight of the fact that even if language learning means searching and casting about on the part of the learner, there still must be an overarching model which describes what it is that is being sought. It seems to me that only a highly mathematical model which comes to grips with the complexity (in the technical sense) of the hypothesis has even a chance of shedding light on the problem of language learning. And if this conjecture is correct, then it seems to me almost a certainty that the same learning mechanisms can be used to induce a syntax as well. While it is not logically impossible that learning morphology requires a rich and powerful learning theory and learning syntax does not, such a state of affairs is highly unlikely at best.

A word, in closing, is perhaps appropriate regarding the relationship between the kind of linguistic work we have sketched and the study of child language acquisition, since it is only natural to ask what connection is being posited between the two. The two answer different questions: the linguist asks how language *can be* learned; the psycholinguist asks how language *is* learned. Each has his work cut out for him. If the linguist had several adequate theories of how language could be learned, the psycholinguist could figure out which was the right one—but the linguist does not. If the psycholinguist could provide an account of how language *is* learned, we would have at least one answer to the question as to how language can be learned—but the psycholinguist does not. We are making progress, I think, regarding the models on the market for morphology learning, and some aspects of phonology learning, and there is a time-honored law according to which once we find *one* way to accomplish something, several more will present themselves virtually overnight.

These questions are reflections of an old and traditional debate between rationalist and empiricist inclinations in the study of mind, but the most familiar versions of how *both* schools have treated language acquisition are, in my view, coarse oversimplifications. Rationalists of the principles-and-parameters sort attempt to account for language learning by denying its existence, and hoping that the variation across the world's languages will simply go away, while empiricists of the old school hope that knowledge can be reduced to memory. Both of these are losing strategies, in my view, and I have tried to offer some specifics with regard to one small, but not insignificant, part of language learning. It is an empiricist account that sets a high bar for formal grammatical accounts of the relevant data.

7.9 Appendix

Let us consider how the probability of a corpus changes when we begin our word discovery process. Originally, the lexicon consists of the observed letters in the corpus. Our first guess will add the string TH to the lexicon. When we add the element TH, the log probability of the corpus is changed in three ways. First, the total number of words in the corpus decreases by the number of THs found in the corpus (that may not be obvious, but it is true, if you think about it). Second, the total number of Ts and Hs also decrease (since a T that is followed by an H is no longer parsed as a T, but rather as part of a TH), and hence the probability of both Ts and Hs decreases, since those probabilities are based on observed frequencies. (Note, by the way, that this illustrates the point that even frequencies are theory-dependent notions!) Third, the probability of the substring TH has gone up considerably, because it had previously been calculated as the product of the probabilities of T and H independently, but now it is calculated on the basis of the observed frequency of the sequence TH. The actual change in log frequency is $-N\Delta N + [t]\Delta[t] + [h]\Delta[h] + [th] \, log \frac{freq_2(th)}{freq_2(t)freq_2(h)}$, where N is the original length of the corpus and thus the number of words on the first analysis, ΔN is the log ratio of the count of words *after* versus *before*, i.e., $log \frac{N - number \; of \; THs}{number \; of \; letters}$, $[t]$ and $[h]$ are the number of Ts and Hs in the original corpus, $\Delta[t]$ is the log ratio of the counts of T after vs before and likewise for $\Delta[h]$, and $[th]$ is the number of substrings TH found in the corpus; $freq_2(x)$ is the frequency of x in the second model, that in which TH is interpreted as a single lexical item. Note that ΔN, $\Delta[t]$, and $\Delta[h]$ are all negative.

8

Expanding Analogical Modeling into a general theory of language prediction

Royal Skousen

8.1 The core theory

Analogical Modeling (AM) is a general theory for predicting behavior. It can also be considered a system of classification or categorization according to a particular set of outcomes. Predictions are directly based on a dataset of exemplars. These exemplars give the outcome for various configurations of variables, which may be structured in different ways (such as strings or trees). A common method in AM is to define the variables so that there is no inherent structure or relationships between the variables (that is, each variable is defined independently of all the other variables). In this case, the variables can be considered a vector of features. In the dataset, each feature vector is assigned an outcome vector. The dataset is used to predict the outcome vector for a test set of various feature vectors for which no outcome vector has been assigned (or if one has been assigned, it is ignored).

In AM we distinguish between the core theory and its application to language. In terms of the theory, the goal is to predict the **outcome** for a set of conditions referred to as the **given context** (sometimes the given context is referred to as the **test item**). From the given context, we construct more general versions of that context, which we refer to as **supracontexts**. Our goal is to predict the behavior (or outcome) of the given context in terms of the behavior of its supracontexts. The source for determining those behaviors comes from a **dataset of exemplars**; for each exemplar in the dataset, the outcome is specified. These exemplars, with their own specifications and associated outcomes of behavior, are assigned to the various supracontexts defined by the given context. Supracontexts that behave uniformly (referred to as **homogeneous** supracontexts) are accepted, with the result that exemplars contained within the homogeneous supracontexts can be analogically used to predict the behavior of the given context. The exemplars found in nonuniformly behaving supracontexts (referred to as **heterogeneous** supracontexts) cannot be used to make the analogical prediction for the given context. The term *nonuniformity* means that a heterogeneous supracontext has a plurality of subcontexts and a plurality of outcomes (that is, exemplars within the supracontext not only have different outcomes but they are also found in different subspaces of the contextual space). Finally, the relative probability of using a homogeneous supracontext is proportional to the square of its frequency, while the probability of using a heterogeneous supracontext is zero. (For a basic introduction to AM and how it works, see Skousen, Lonsdale, and Parkinson 2002: 12–22 or Skousen 2003.)

AM differs considerably from traditional analogical approaches to language. First of all, traditional analogy is not explicit. In the traditional practice of analogy, virtually any item can serve as the exemplar for predicting behavior, although in practice the first attempt is to look to nearest neighbors for the preferred analogical source. But if proximity fails, one can almost always find some item considerably different from the given item that can be used to analogically predict the desired outcome. In other words, if needed, virtually any occurrence with a minimum of similarity can serve as the analogical source. AM, on the other hand, will allow occurrences further away from the given context to be used as the exemplar, but not just any occurrence. Instead, the occurrence must be in a homogeneous supracontext. The analogical source does not have to be a near neighbor. The probability of an occurrence further away acting as the analogical model is usually less than that of a closer occurrence (all other things being equal), but this probability is never zero (providing the occurrence is in a homogeneous supracontext). Proximity is important in AM, but it is not the only factor.

A second important property of AM is that analogy is not used as a stop-gap measure to be used whenever the rules fail to account for the behavior. Instead, everything in AM is analogical. Rule-governed behavior, so called, comes from homogeneous groups of occurrences that behave alike, leading to gang effects that enhance the probability of using occurrences in frequently occurring homogeneous supracontexts. In other words, categorical and regular/exceptional behaviors are accounted for in terms of exemplars, not categorical rules or regular rules with lists of exceptions.

Another important property of AM is that it does not determine in advance which variables are significant and the degree to which these variables determine the outcome (either alone or in various combinations). In addition, AM does not have a training stage except in the sense that one must obtain a database of occurrences. Predictions are made "on the fly", and all variables are considered equal a priori (with certain limitations due to restrictions on short-term memory). The significance of a variable is determined locally – that is, only with regard to the given context. Gang effects are related to the location of the given context and the amount of resulting homogeneity within the surrounding contextual space.

One simplified way to look at AM is in terms of traditional rules, where the term *rule* basically stands for the supracontext and its associated behavior. In trying to predict the behavior of the given context, we consider all the possible rules that could apply. We eliminate those rules that behave nonuniformly (that is, the rules with heterogeneous supracontexts). All uniformly behaving rules (the rules with homogeneous supracontexts) are then applied, with the probability of applying a given homogeneous rule proportional to the square of its frequency. One important aspect of AM is that each rule's homogeneity can be determined independently of every other rule. This property of independent determination of uniformity means that we can examine a rule's uniformity without having to determine whether any subrule (that is, any more specific version of the rule) behaves differently.

AM is computationally intensive. For each variable added to the specification of a given context, both the memory requirements and the running time doubles (so if there are n variables in the given context, the memory and time are of the order 2^n). This problem of exponential explosion has been theoretically solved by redefining AM in terms of Quantum Analogical Modeling (QAM), a quantum mechanical approach to doing AM. The main difference is that everything is done simultaneously in QAM, in distinction to the sequential application that AM is forced to follow. Still, the same basic procedure is followed, only the system of rules (or supracontexts) is now treated as a quantum mechanical one:

(1) all possible rules for a given context exist in a superposition; the initial amplitude for each rule is zero;

(2) the exemplars are individually but simultaneously assigned to every applicable rule; after all the exemplars have been assigned, the resulting amplitude for each rule is proportional to its frequency (that is, to the number of exemplars assigned to that rule);

(3) the system evolves so that the amplitude of every heterogeneous rule becomes zero, while the amplitude of each homogeneous rule remains proportional to its frequency (that is, to the number of exemplars originally assigned to that rule);

(4) measurement or observation reduces the superposition to a single rule where the probability of it being selected is proportional to its amplitude squared.

See Skousen 2002: 319–46 for an introductory essay on treating AM as a quantum mechanical system. For a complete discussion of how QAM works, see Skousen 2005.

One notices here that nothing in the core of AM specifies how AM is to be applied to language. All such language applications have their own linguistic assumptions, and it is an open question not directly related to AM itself concerning what those assumptions should be. But by choosing various assumptions and seeing what kinds of predictions AM makes about the behavior, then by comparing the predicted behavior to the actual behavior, we can assess the empirical validity of those linguistic assumptions.

A similar situation exists in quantum mechanics, which seems appropriate to bring up here since QAM itself is a quantum mechanical system. As explained by Charles Bennett, there is a "set of laws" (like the Ten Commandments, as he puts it) that form the basics of quantum mechanics (QM), but QM has to be applied in order to serve as a theory of physics: "For most of the 20th century, physicists and chemists have used quantum mechanics to build an edifice of quantitative explanation and prediction covering almost all features of our everyday world." The core theory is actually very simple, but the resulting edifice is complex and evolves. Yet in all instances, QM involves applying the core theory and making hypotheses regarding the underlying physical system. If the resulting application of the theory works, we accept the hypotheses as representing, in some sense, physical reality. For a pictorial representation of this point, see Bennett 1999: 177–80.

AM is a general theory of predicting classification and is not restricted to linguistic problems per se. For instance, one can use AM to predict various kinds of nonlinguistic outcomes, such as determining whether different mushrooms are poisonous or not, providing medical diagnoses based on symptoms and lab tests, and predicting party affiliation on the basis of voting patterns (for various examples, see Lonsdale 2002).

8.2 Basic structural types

The current AM computer program treats the *n* variables defined by a given context as *n* independent variables, which means that any linguistic dependencies between the variables must be built into the variable specifications. Very seldom can we construct cases where there are no linguistic dependencies in the variable specification (although there will always be behavioral dependencies between the variables). One possible example of linguistic independence of variables involves the social features for specifying terms of address in Arabic (see Skousen 1989: 97–100), which has social variables like age of speaker, gender of speaker, and social class relationship. Very often the linguistic task involves strings (in phonology) or trees (in morphology and syntax). The general approach in Skousen 1989 was to treat strings of characters as variables for which the position was specified. For instance, in predicting the spelling of the initial /h/ sound in English words (as either *h*, *wh*, or *j*), positional aspects were included in the definition of each variable, such as "the *first* vowel phoneme" and "the phoneme that *immediately precedes* the *third* vowel." This kind of variable specification allows the AM computer program to make the analysis, but it is not realistic since it requires that everything be lined up in advance so that the strings can be compared. Cases of metathesis or identical syllables in different positions are ignored, nor can they be readily handled in such a restricted version of AM.

These kind of specifications have led to the use of zeros for variables. For instance, if a word has only one syllable, then the nonexistent second and third syllables are marked with zeros. But then there is the question of how to specify such nonexistent syllables. If we mark the nuclear vowel for such a syllable with a zero, do we also mark the syllable's onset and coda with zeros, even though those zeros are redundant? One possibility is to refer to such predictable zeros as redundant variables and to ignore them when making analogical predictions (the general way of proceeding in Skousen 1989). If all zeros (both essential and redundant) are counted, then there is the possibility that the analogical prediction will be overwhelmed by excessively specified zeros. But there is also the possibility that we may want to count all the zeros (for some discussion of this issue, see Skousen, Lonsdale, and Parkinson 2002: 40–2). The important point here is that the problem of the zeros results from trying to account for strings as if they were composed of unordered symbols. One major issue that linguistic applications of AM must deal with then is how to treat strings and trees as they actually are rather than trying to define them as sets of independent variables. In the remainder of this section, I outline several different approaches to structures that one would want to use in linguistic analyses. It should be pointed out, however, that the current AM computer program has not yet been revised to handle these structures directly.

8.2.1 *Strings of characters*

A more reasonable approach for a string of characters would be to allow any possible sequence of substrings of a given string to count as a supracontext.

For instance, if the given string is *abc*, the supracontexts would include examples like **abc, a*b*c, *ab*c*, a*b,* and **c,* where the asterisk stands for any string, including the null string. Thus the supracontext **abc* would include any string ending in *abc* while **ab*c** would include any string containing *ab* followed by *c.* The most general supracontext would be simply * (that is, this supracontext would contain all possible strings, including the null string). For *n* characters in a given string, there will be a total of $2 \cdot 3^n$ supracontexts for which we will need to determine the heterogeneity, but (as already noted) this can be done independently for each supracontext by determining its heterogeneity with respect to the outcomes and the subcontexts for the data items assigned to that supracontext. The total number of supracontexts for this kind of string analysis is also exponential (like the 2^n for when the *n* characters are all independent variables), but that number $(2 \cdot 3^n)$ increases at a greater exponential rate.

8.2.2 *Scalar variables*

The AM computer program assumes that the variables specified by the given context are categorical and discrete. The question then arises of how to deal with scalar variables, ones that represent degrees of a property. Scalars can be mathematically treated as real numbers, but this leads to extraordinary problems with the number of possible supracontexts since theoretically every possible real number interval could count as a supracontext, which ends up defining a nondenumerably infinite set of supracontexts. I would propose, instead, that continuous scalars be analyzed as a sequence of finite intervals (that is, we will quantize the scalar). Having made that decision, we can then decide how to determine the supracontexts for a given sequence of finite intervals.

As an example, consider how we might apply this quantization to the problem of voicing onset time and the ability of speakers to predict whether a given stop is voiced or voiceless. Our task is to model how speakers interpret artificial stops with varying lengths of nonvoicing after the release of the stop. In this case, the data comes from experiments testing the ability to distinguish between /b/ and /p/ in English. The variables center around the problem of dealing with a time continuum. In applying AM to this problem, I assume that time should not be treated as a real number line. Instead, time will be broken up into a sequence of finite intervals of time, all equal in length, as described in Skousen 1989: 71–6. Given an overall length of about 50 msec between instances of /b/ and /p/, let us break up this overall length into five intervals of 10 msec each, so that instances of voiced stops are represented as *xxxxx* and voiceless stops as *ooooo* (where *x* stands for voicing and *o* for nonvoicing). For simplicity of calculation, I will assume that there is in the dataset but one occurrence of each stop, /b/ and /p/. The question then becomes: What are the supracontexts for the intermediate but nonoccurring given contexts (namely, *oxxxx, ooxxx, oooxx, oooox*)? I will here consider three possibilities for the supracontexts defined by the particular given context *ooxxx*:

(1) We treat each single continuous sequence of intervals as a possible supracontext. The number of homogeneous supracontexts, in this case, will be quadratic – namely, $n(n+1)/2$:

given context	/b/ outcome	/p/ outcome	probability
xxxxx	15	0	1.000
oxxxx	10	1	0.909
ooxxx	6	3	0.667
oooxx	3	6	0.333
oooox	1	10	0.091
ooooo	0	15	0.000

(2) We treat each *o* and *x* and its position as an independent variable (this is how the problem is treated in Skousen 1989: 71–6). This means that any subset of the five variables will define the possible supracontexts. The number of homogeneous supracontexts will be exponential (to the scale of 2^n-1), which means that in comparison with the previous case, the shift in predictability will be sharper. We get the following predicted chances for /p/ and /b/:

given context	/b/ outcome	/p/ outcome	probability
xxxxx	31	0	1.000
oxxxx	15	1	0.938
ooxxx	7	3	0.700
oooxx	3	7	0.300
oooox	1	15	0.063
ooooo	0	31	0.000

(3) Finally, we treat the sequence of intervals as a string and permit any set of nonoverlapping substrings to serve as a distinct supracontext. In this case, the shift in predictability will be sharper than in the second case (but also exponential) since the number of homogeneous supracontexts will have the exponential factor $2(3^n-1)$ rather than the 2^n-1 of the second case:

given context	/b/ outcome	/p/ outcome	probability
XXXXX	484	0	1.000
OXXXX	160	4	0.976
OOXXX	52	16	0.765
OOOXX	16	52	0.333
OOOOX	4	160	0.024
OOOOO	0	484	0.000

For each of these three cases, we can determine which interval length allows for the best fit for the actual experimental results for predicting /b/ versus /p/ (see Lisker and Abramson 1970, cited in Skousen 1989). For an overall interval of 50 msec, we get the following:

type of analysis	number of homogenous supracontexts	number of intervals	length of interval
(1) a single continuous substring	$n(n+1)/2$	10	5 msec
(2) n independent variables	$2^n - 1$	7	7 msec
(3) any nonoverlapping sequence of substrings	$2(3^n - 1)$	5	10 msec

Lehiste 1970 (cited in Skousen 1989) provides evidence that speakers can distinguish between sound durations differing as little as 10 milliseconds, which means that the last case (which defines the supracontexts as any nonoverlapping sequence of finite intervals) is the one that best corresponds with experimental results for humans trying to distinguish between artificial versions of /b/ and /p/ in terms of voicing onset time.

8.2.3 *Unordered hierarchical structures (branching hierarchical sets)*

Unordered hierarchical structures are found in semantics. The supracontexts for a given hierarchical set are subsets that generalize by moving up the hierarchy, thus accounting for hyponymy. Semantic variables (or features) defined for lower, more specific subsets may be ignored in higher, more general subsets.

The need for localized restrictions on the use of semantic features is well exemplified in an attempt to analyze and predict the behavior of Chinese classifiers, found in some unpublished work by my colleague Dana Bourgerie, presented at the 2000 Analogical Modeling conference at Brigham Young University ("An Analysis of Chinese Classifiers: Issues in Dealing with Semantic Variables in the AML Framework"). Some of the classifiers examined by Bourgerie were:

gè   general classifier for people, round things, and things of
        indeterminate form
zhāng for open flat things (maps, tables, tickets, etc.)
tiáo   for long, thin things (fish, leg, boat, cucumber, a long bench, etc.)
zhī   for long, branch-like things (e.g. pen, gun, candle, etc.)
bǎ   things with handles (e.g. umbrellas, swords, etc.)
jiān   mostly for rooms
běn   for bound things such as books

The need for an analogical model results from a great deal of variability in actual usage between speakers in selecting the appropriate classifier as well as the extension of classifiers to new objects.

Bourgerie's variables were as follows: relative size (*s, m, l*), flat (+, −), long (+, −), narrow (+, −), three-dimensional (+, −), handle (+, −); every instance of usage involving a classifier in his dataset was defined in terms of these specific variables. Given what we know now, the size variable should have been converted to a discrete scalar (something like −−, − +, and + + to stand for small, medium, and long, respectively); I will make that conversion here to simplify the description. In other words, the semantic description of every noun in the dataset can be analyzed as a sequence of pluses and minuses. In Bourgerie's preliminary work, pluses and minuses were assigned in all cases. For example, *bǎ* is expected for objects with a handle, even though other items with handles, such as a gun, take *zhī*. On the other hand, some objects, such as a boat or long bench (which take the classifier *tiáo*), do not ordinarily have handles, yet ' −handle' was assigned to this classifier. And finally for some nouns referring to people (which take the classifier *gè*), handles would seem implausible, although one could imagine it! Implausible or not, '−handle' was assigned to words taking the most general classifier. And similar overloading of minus-valued variables occurred for other specific classifiers. The overall result was that the classifier *gè*, being the most general classifier, had more minuses for the words assigned to it – and especially more minuses than words assigned to the other (more specific) classifiers.

The problem with assigning ' −handle' (and similarly for other specific variables) to all the nouns in the dataset is that when predicting the classifier for any given word, the minuses dominate, with the result that the general classifier *gè* consistently swamps the prediction, even when we are predicating an item close to words that take one of the more specific classifiers. To get the right results, we need to restrict ' +/− handle' to smaller groups of words where they characteristically are found. So we may mark kitchen utensils as to whether or not they have a handle, but not the refrigerator, oven, sink, dishwasher, counters, tables (although they could have them). Where the handle helps to distinguish between closely associated objects that are named differently, the variable should be assigned, but otherwise not. A table could have a handle, but such a table doesn't have a different name, so we do not specify it as a variable in such cases. The vast majority of words could always be marked as '−handle' (such as a cloud, a tree, a lake, a newspaper, philosophy, war, etc.), but AM shows that we cannot semantically analyze every word as plus or minus for every possible semantic variable. This may seem obvious: Would we really want to mark virtually every object in the world as '−human'? Semantic variables are defined within only certain restricted domains. In applying AM to Chinese classifiers, Bourgerie marked every word in the dataset as either ' + handle' or '−handle' and soon discovered that such a decision clearly made the wrong predictions.

8.2.4 *Ordered hierarchical structures (trees)*

Ordered hierarchical structures obviously have both order and hierarchy and are commonly referred to as trees. Given a particular tree as a given context, the supracontexts are defined as subtrees of the given tree. For instance, our given contexts and the data items may best be represented as trees and we may wish to predict some behavior given such a tree. The following simple right-branching structure is of interest in many different situations:

We find uses of it in specifying syntax, morphology, and syllable structure:

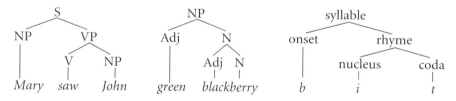

In attempting to predict some outcome based on the pronunciation for the last item, *beet* /bit/, we could restrict the supracontexts for the given context (namely, the tree itself) to combinations of categories that occur only at the same level in the tree; for instance, we could examine all syllables with the same onset, or with the same rhyme (nucleus and coda), or with the same nucleus, or with the same coda – but not with the same onset and the same nucleus or with the same onset and the same coda since those categorical combinations do not occur at the same level in the tree. Of course, we would only want to do this if there was evidence that such a restriction on supra-contextual construction would predict language behavior. In other words, the decision is more an empirical one than one that impinges on the question of whether AM is a correct theory.

We get similar hierarchical problems in specifying distinctive features. As discussed in Skousen 1989: 53–4, we cannot treat distinctive features as if they are independent variables. Suppose we compare *beet* /bit/ with two possible words, each of which differs from /bit/ in three distinctive features. If we treat this problem as a set of twelve variables, the distance between *beet* and *bought* is the same as between *beet* and *mid*:

(a)   *three-feature difference restricted to one phoneme:*

	consonant	vowel	consonant
/bit/	oral stop labial voiced	**spread high front** tense	oral stop alveolar voiceless
/bɔt/	oral stop labial voiced	**round low back** tense	oral stop alveolar voiceless

(b)   *three-feature difference spread across three phonemes:*

	consonant	vowel	consonant
/bit/	**oral** stop labial voiced	spread high front **tense**	oral stop alveolar **voiceless**
/mɪd/	**nasal** stop labial voiced	spread high front **lax**	oral stop alveolar **voiced**

Yet experimental evidence from perceptual studies show that speakers perceive *beet* and *bought* as phonetically close, while *beet* and *mid* are not especially close (see Derwing and Nearey 1986, cited in Skousen 1989). If we treat distinctive features as independent variables, we incorrectly predict an equality of phonetic similarity for this example. One way to correct this would be to define the given contexts in terms of phonemes and basic syllable structure, which would mean that there is only one difference between *beet* and *bought*, but three between *beet* and *mid* (this is how it is done in Skousen 1989). But another possibility would be to define distinctive features for only phonemic nodes within syllable tree structures, thus restricting feature similarity to apply only at isolated places in the tree.

8.3 Control over the analogical set

The general theory of analogical modeling (AM) allows for various ways of using the analogical set to predict outcomes (although the quantum version of it, QAM, does not). Here I review this aspect of AM.

8.3.1 *Reacting to a previous prediction*

One important point is to recognize that analogical modeling allows for the ability to reexamine a given analogical set or to redetermine it under various conditions. A speaker may, for instance, produce a particular outcome, but then not like the results and so produce a different outcome. The speaker does not get caught in an infinite loop, continually producing, say, the most favored outcome or randomly producing outcomes, thus leading to the repetition of the more frequent outcomes. Consider, for instance, the following two examples from my own children's speech (cited in Skousen 1989: 85–6):

Nathaniel (5 years, 10 months)

> Looking at a picture of the Grand Canyon, Nathaniel keeps trying to produce the plural *cliffs*: /klɪˈftəz/, /klɪfs/, /klɪvz/, /klɪfs/
>
> Note that Nathaniel's sequence of productions is not constantly repetitive (as if it were /klɪfs/, /klɪfs/, /klɪfs/, /klɪfs/, ...).

Angela (6 years, 10 months)

> The possessive form *Beth's* is pronounced first as /bɛs/ and then immediately followed by /bɛˈθəz/.
>
> Angela: How do you add the *s* to *Beth*? It's hard to say. How do you say it?
> Royal: I say /bɛs/ [bɛs:].
> Angela: I say /bɛθ/ like *Beth house* /bɛθ haus/.
>
> Note that Angela produced a sequence of three different possibilities: /bɛs/, /bɛˈθəz/, /bɛθ/.

Angela (7 years, 11 months)

> The plural form *ghosts* is pronounced initially as /gousts/, then as /gous/, and is finally followed by the question "How do you pronounce that?"

Similarly, suppose we have a nonce word (written out) and ask someone to pronounce it; then no matter what they say, we say that it's wrong and ask for an alternative pronunciation. Our subjects do not go into an infinite loop; instead they will typically produce a sequence of different responses. An example is the nonce word YEAD, which might be pronounced alternatively as /yid/, /yɛd/, /yeid/.

For each new prediction, we could let the analogical set be redetermined from scratch but with all data items having the forbidden outcome eliminated so that those exemplars will not play a role in constructing the analogical set, especially since the original analogical set may provide only one possible outcome. Or maybe one has a choice: Try the original analogical set first; if that fails, then revert to redetermining it by omitting the forbidden outcome.

8.3.2 *Random selection versus selection by plurality*

Another aspect dealing with control over the analogical set is the choice between random selection of an outcome and selection by plurality (discussed in Skousen 1989: 82–5). Psycholinguistic experiments show that speakers of all ages can reproduce probabilistic behavior by applying random selection to the analogical set. But as speakers grow older, by about age 8, they are also able to select the most frequent outcome, especially when they expect or want to make some gain from the choice of outcome. It can also be shown that if the choice involves some loss, then the most advantageous decision is to choose the least frequent outcome (discussed in Skousen 1992: 357–8). The ability to select by plurality would apparently require some kind of sampling or analysis of the analogical set, perhaps as it is being determined.

8.3.3 *Restricting morphological extension*

Another issue involving restrictions on the use of the analogical set asks whether there are any limits besides heterogeneity in preventing the overuse of analogy. Consider, for instance, the analogical prediction of the past tense in English for the verb *be*. The question here is whether the verb *see* (with its exceptional past-tense form *saw*) can be used as an exemplar in predicting the past-tense form for *be*:

/si/ : /sɔ/ :: /bi/ : /bɔ/   (that is, *see* : *saw* :: *be* : *baw*)

This analogical extension seems highly unlikely. One might argue that such an analogy is difficult simply because the chances of forgetting the past-tense *was/were* for the very frequent verb *be* are virtually negligible. But the question still remains: Is *baw* even possible? And if so, is there any way besides appealing to heterogeneity to restrict the applicability of *saw*? Here heterogeneity may not work since *see* is such a close neighbor to *be*, at least close enough to allow it to analogically apply to *be*.

Since we know the analogical set can be examined prior to using it, perhaps the speaker can reject an unrecognizable past-tense form. One could argue that the analogical set provides only results, not how those exemplars are derived. The analogical *baw* could therefore be possible, but at the same time unrecognizable, thus one could simply avoid using it. A similar case involves verbs of the form CX-Cɔt:

alternation	*example*	*extension*
ing-ɔt	bring-brought	sting-stought
ink-ɔt	think-thought	drink-drought
ach-ɔt	catch-caught	latch-lought
ai-ɔt	buy-bought	try-trought
ich-ɔt	teach-taught	reach-rought
ik-ɔt	seek-sought	tweak-twought

Is heterogeneity sufficient to prevent any of these analogies from applying? Probably not. But these analogies could nonetheless be rejected by speakers since the resulting past-tense forms are unrecoverable – that is, speakers are unable to determine what verb the past-tense form stands for. A past-tense prediction like *stought* would imply only that the analogical present-tense verb form began with *st*.

One could propose that unique alternations can never be extended analogically, but this is definitely false. We have, for instance, analogical extensions based on the noun *ox* and its uniquely exceptional plural form *oxen* (thus *axen* for the plural of *ax* and *uxen* for the nonce *ux*). But note that in these cases the singular forms *ax* and *ux* are recoverable from *axen* and *uxen*. The question may not be one of uniqueness, but rather recoverability.

8.4 Specifying the variables

One important aspect of AM is that we not restrict our analysis to just the important or crucial variables. We need to include "unimportant" variables in order to make our predictions robust. Consider, for example, the indefinite article *a/an* in English. Knowing that the following segment, whether consonant or vowel, "determines" the article (*a* for consonants, *an* for vowels), one could specify only the syllabicity of the following segment and thus predict *a/an* without error. Basically, we would be specifying a single rule analysis for the indefinite article. Yet in modeling the behavior of the indefinite article, AM specifies in addition the phonemic representation for that first segment in the following word as well as the phonemes and syllabicity for other segments in that word, supposedly unimportant variables. But by adding these other variables, AM is able to predict several behavioral properties of the indefinite article: (1) the one-way error tendency of adult speakers to replace *an* with *a* (but not *a* with *an*); (2) children's errors favoring the extension of *a*, but not *an*, such as 'a upper', 'a alligator', 'a end', 'a engine', 'a egg', and 'a other one'; (3) dialects for which *an* has been replaced by *a*, but not the other way around. In other words, the "unimportant" variables are crucial for predicting the fuzziness of actual language usage (for some discussion of these properties, see Skousen 2003). Finally, another important property is that AM can predict the indefinite article even when the first segment is obscured (that is, when one cannot tell whether that segment is a consonant or a vowel). In such cases, the other variables are used to guess the syllabicity of the obscured segment, thus allowing for the prediction. In other words, AM allows for robustness of prediction. If we assume a symbolic rule system with only one rule (one based on the syllabicity of the first segment), then no prediction is possible when that segment is obscured. For additional discussion of the robustness of AM with respect to the indefinite article, see Skousen 1989: 58–9.

Specifying "unimportant" variables also allows for cases where the preferred analogy is not a nearest neighbor to the given context, but is found in a gang of homogeneous behavior at some distance from the given context. An important example of this occurs in predicting the past tense for the Finnish verb *sortaa* 'to oppress'. Standard rule analyses of Finnish as well as nearest neighbor approaches to language prediction argue that the past tense for this verb should be *sorsi*, whereas in fact it is *sorti*. Yet when AM is applied to predicting the past tense in Finnish, it is able to predict the correct *sorti*, mainly because AM indirectly discovers that the *o* vowel is the "crucial" variable in predicting the past tense for this verb. In previous analyses (typically based on the historically determined "crucial" variables), the *o* vowel was ignored. But AM, by specifying variables (both "important" and "unimportant") across the whole word, was able to make the correct prediction for this "exceptionally behaving" verb. For a complete discussion of how AM solves the problem of *sortaa*, see Skousen, Lonsdale, and Parkinson 2002: 27–36.

8.4.1 *Varying the granularity of prediction*

Computationally, there is a need to limit the number of variables. The current AM program can handle up to sixty variables, although the processing times can become quite long whenever there are more than forty variables. The problem here is that the actual computer program is sequential and does not simultaneously run an exponential number of cases (as the proposed quantum computer would). Even the parallel processing provided by standard supercomputers does not appear to be capable of eliminating the fundamental exponential explosion inherent in AM. Presumably there are also empirical limitations on the number of variables that are processed. In other words, there will be a degree and type of granularity that results from how many and which variables are selected. Ultimately, we have to select the variables, but we want to judiciously select variables in a principled way that will, at the same time, allow for general applicability. In Skousen 1989: 51–4, I suggest that enough variables be selected so that each exemplar in the dataset is distinguishable or recognizable. It is this property that argues for specifying more than the first segment of the following word in predicting the indefinite article *a/an*. Or in the case of *sortaa*, we specify variables across the entire word (thus including the *o* vowel). Another suggestion is that proximity to the outcome should be accounted for. For instance, in trying to predict the ending for a word, if we want to provide variables for the antepenultimate syllable, we should also provide variables for the penultimate and ultimate syllables.

8.4.2 *Avoiding inappropriate variables*

There are undoubtedly some variables that are inappropriate, either conceptually or empirically. For instance, in predicting the negative prefix for adjectives in English, we could consider specifying the etymological source of adjectives since there is some correlation (although imperfect) between selecting the Latin negative prefixes *in-*, *il-*, *ir-*, and *im-* for words of Latin origin and the invariant Germanic negative prefix *un-* for words of Germanic origin. It turns out that such an etymological variable will have some influence in helping to predict the correct prefix (but not as much as one might suppose since historically these prefixes have been extended to words of different etymological background). From a conceptual point of view, in modern English, we cannot claim that speakers know the etymologies of the adjectives (although this may have been true for some educated speakers earlier in English when the influx of Latin vocabulary was in its beginning). For further discussion of this issue, see Chapman and Skousen 2005: 341–2.

   As an example of an empirical restriction on variables, consider whether multisyllable words should be specified in terms of stress pattern or number of syllables. For instance, in predicting the past tense for Finnish verbs, Skousen 1989: 101–4 used a restricted dataset: two-syllable verbs ending in a nonhigh, unrounded vowel (*e*, *ä*, or *a*). The results were very accurate in predicting speakers' intuitions as well as historical and dialect development. But extending the dataset to the entire verb system was much more difficult until it was realized that the variables should be specified in terms of stress pattern rather than by number of syllables. This difference may seem surprising since stress is supposed to be fully predictable in Finnish (primary stress on the first syllable, secondary stress on alternating syllables according to syllable weight). Yet there is empirical evidence that Finnish speakers rely on stress rather than number of syllables. Consider the following two analyses of the Finnish illative ending (meaning 'into'), where the first analysis is based on counting the number of syllables, the second on the kind of stress placed on the last syllable:

number of syllables

one syllable, long vowel or diphthong	-hV$_i$ n
two or more syllables	
long vowel	-seen
diphthong	-hV$_i$ n
short vowel	-V$_i$ n

stress

stressed, long vowel or diphthong	-hV$_i$ n
unstressed	
long vowel	-seen
diphthong	-hV$_i$ n
short vowel	-V$_i$ n

(Here V$_i$ means that the stem-final vowel is copied.) There is basically no difference between these two analyses since primary stress is virtually always on the first syllable. The crucial distinction between the two analyses is brought out when we consider how Finnish speakers predict the illative for two-syllable loan words where the original primary stress on the final syllable has been maintained. And the answer is that they follow the stress-based analysis:

Rousseau	rusó:	rusó:hon
Bordeaux	bordó:	bordó:hon
Calais	kalé:	kalé:hen

But if these words were nativized, with stress on the first syllable, then speakers would produce illative forms like /kále:se:n/. This means that in specifying the variables for Finnish words, we need to provide information regarding the stress pattern, not the number of syllables.

8.4.3 *Weighting of variables*

Now if we decide that we must specify the stress pattern, an important question arises: What is the strength of the stress in predicting the outcome? Is it the same as the individual phoneme? Consider, for instance, variables that might be specified for the syllable in Finnish (the nine variables listed here are much like the ones used in Skousen 1989):

 1 syllable-initial consonant (include 0 as a possibility)
   * a syllable-structure alternative:
      (1a) is there an initial consonant or not?
      (1b) if so, what is it?
 2 the nuclear vowel: specify its phoneme
 3 is there a second vowel or not?
 4 if so, what is it?
 5 is there a sonorant in the coda?
 6 if so, what is it?
 7 is there a obstruent in the coda?
 8 if so, what is it?
 9 what is the stress on the syllable? primary, secondary, none
   * a scalar alternative (10, 00, 01):
      (9a) is the stress primary?
      (9b) is there no stress?

If we follow the two alternatives (each marked with an asterisk), we have eleven variables, of which four deal with syllable structure, five specify the sounds (here the phonemes), and two the stress. If we analyze the phonemes into distinctive features, the number of variables specifying sounds would at least triple and probably overwhelm the analysis. Perhaps even as it is, the two variables dealing with stress may not be enough. Even worse would be specifying a single stress variable for the intonational contour of the entire word.

This problem becomes more acute when one specifies variables from completely different types of linguistic classification, say phonetic and semantic. Suppose we are trying to predict an outcome, say a grammatical gender, that is affected by the phonetics of the word as well as whether the word refers, say, to animates or nonanimates. We set up say ten or so variables for the phonetics of the last syllable (as a minimum). But then the question is: Do we assign just one variable to tell us whether the word refers to an animate or nonanimate object? It is very doubtful that a single variable assigned to animacy will be strong enough to show the influence of that semantic class. Just doubling or tripling that semantic variable seems awfully arbitrary, although from a pragmatic point of view one could increase the strength of such a variable until one gets the right results! David Eddington did precisely that when he considered the relative strength of phonemic variables versus morphological variables in predicting Spanish stress assignment (Eddington 2002: 148):

Therefore, in addition to the phonemic information, morphological variables were included. For verbal forms, one variable indicated the person, and three identical variables indicated the tense form of the verb. Repeating a variable more than once is the only way to manipulate the weight of one variable or another prior to running the

AM program. In essence, what this implies is that the tense form of the verb is considered three times more important that any single onset, nucleus or coda. In the AM simulation, the only significant difference that weighting this variable made was in the number of errors that occurred on preterit verbs with final stress. Fifty errors occurred without the weighting, in comparison to 27 when it was included three times.

And it should be remembered that this approach will not work if the variable being considered has no effect on the outcome. Dirk Elzinga 2006: 766 reports that, in using AM to predict the comparative for English adjectives, he used a morphological variable that specified whether the adjective was morphologically simple or complex, and he discovered that doubling, tripling, and quadrupling that morphological variable had no effect on the predictability of the outcome.

Obviously, we need a principled method of constructing variables so that the empirically determined relative strength between classificatory types is naturally achieved.

8.5 Specifying the outcomes

8.5.1 *Combining outcomes*

In making predictions, one has to specify what the outcomes are. The issue is whether we should consider two or more outcomes as different or as variants of the same outcome. Sometimes this issue involves cases of abstractness. For instance, in the Latin negative prefix *in-*, used in English, there are several variants that show up: *il-* for words beginning with *l* (such as *illegal*), *ir-* for words beginning with *r* (such as *irregular*), and *im-* for words beginning with labials (such as *impossible*). When trying to predict the negative adjectival prefix in English, do we consider these four variants as a single morphological outcome (say, the abstract *IN-*) or as four different ones (*in-*, *il-*, *ir-*, or *im-*)? In general, our decision will affect our predictions of the negative adjectival prefix, and from those results we can perhaps discover which treatment (one or four outcomes) best accounts for speakers' actual predictions. For further discussion, see Chapman and Skousen 2005: 12.

Another example of this problem of outcome specification arises in the case of the Finnish illative ending -hV_in (discussed in Section 8.4.2). There we considered this ending as a single outcome, but theoretically one could consider it as a multitude of distinct outcomes, each different with respect to the copied vowel V_i:

voi 'butter'	voihin	-hin
syy 'reason'	syyhyn	-hyn
kuu 'moon'	kuuhun	-hun
tie 'road'	tiehen	-hen
työ 'work'	työhön	-hön
suo 'swamp'	suohon	-hon

pää 'head'	päähän	-hän
maa 'land'	maahan	-han

Again, the issue is empirical; and the best predictions occur if we treat all of these forms as the same outcome, not as eight distinct outcomes (the latter leads to a substantial increase in the heterogeneity of the contextual space and subsequent loss in predictability). Such an analysis argues that speakers are therefore aware of the basic identity of all these variant forms.

8.5.2 *Separating or combining the outcomes*

Another issue deals with whether we have a single outcome or separate outcomes that apply in some order with respect to each other (or perhaps independently of each other). As an example of this, consider plural formation in German. The plural form can be viewed as two processes, adding an ending and mutating the stressed stem vowel (umlauting):

singular	*plural*	*ending*	*umlauting*
Berater 'advisor'	Berater	Ø	no
Vater 'father'	Väter	Ø	yes
Bauer 'farmer'	Bauern	n	no
Motor 'motor'	Motoren	en	no
Tag 'day'	Tage	e	no
Band 'volume'	Bände	e	yes
Band 'ribbon'	Bänder	er	yes
Band 'bond'	Bande	e	no
Band 'band'	Bands	s	no

One issue here is whether -*n* and -*en* should be considered syllabic variants of the same ending. Another issue involves the case when the stressed stem vowel is already a front vowel; in that case, we may ask whether one should consider umlauting as vacuously applying or not at all:

singular	*plural*	*ending*	*umlauting*
Rücken 'back'	Rücken	Ø	yes or no?
Bild 'picture'	Bilder	er	yes or no?
Bär 'bear'	Bären	en	yes or no?
Brief 'letter'	Briefe	e	yes or no?

Ultimately, the issue is how tightly linked are the endings with the umlauting. For some endings (such as -*er*), we expect umlauting (whenever it can apply). For other endings (such as -*en* or -*s*), we do not expect umlauting (whenever it can apply). And for some endings (such as -*e*) we can have umlauting or not, depending on the word (and again, whenever it can apply). These links between the ending and umlauting suggest that we should consider the cases of plural formation as single outcomes. But ultimately, the issue is empirical. For instance, when the stressed stem vowel is not already a front vowel, do speakers (in the historical or dialectal development of the language or as children learning the language) remove the umlauting for the -*er* ending (which expects umlauting whenever it can apply)? If so, then we may wish to predict the ending and the umlauting separately from one another – or perhaps sequentially, with one being predicted first, then the other being predicted on the basis on the first prediction.

This example brings up the more paramount question of sequential versus simultaneous prediction in dealing with syntactic prediction and, we should add, virtually every other kind of linguistic prediction. Language processing involves sequencing through time, with one prediction following another and typically depending on previous decisions.

8.6 Repetition in the dataset

The final issue that I would like to bring up here is the question of how exemplars should be represented in the dataset. In Skousen 1989, I almost always listed the exemplars for morphological problems as types rather than as tokens. And in most instances, types have worked much better than tokens in predicting morphological behavior. When tokens are specified, the highly frequently occurring types typically overwhelm the analysis. In Skousen 1989: 54, I discuss the issue of types versus tokens and observe that "ultimately, the difference between type and token can be eliminated by specifying enough variables. By increasing the number of variables every token occurrence will also represent a single type". But whether this proposal is feasible is questionable since there is undoubtedly some empirical limitation on the number of variables that can be handled.

The need to distinguish between types and tokens in phonetic and morphological problems has been emphasized in Bybee 2001: 96–136. Baayen and his colleagues (see de Jong, Schreuder, and Baayen 2000) have been arguing that a more accurate exemplar basis would be family types, where datasets would list all the morphologically related types, both inflectional and derivational, in datasets. Again, decisions of this sort regarding what to put in the dataset is an empirical issue.

8.7 Acknowledgments

I wish to thank members of the Analogical Modeling Research Group at Brigham Young University for their helpful criticisms and suggestions for improvement: Deryle Lonsdale, David Eddington, Dirk Elzinga, Dana Bourgerie, and Don Chapman. I also wish to thank Benjamin Skousen for his comments on the Chinese classifiers.

9

Modeling analogy as probabilistic grammar[*]

Adam Albright

9.1 Introduction

Formal implemented models of analogy face two opposing challenges. On the one hand, they must be powerful and flexible enough to handle gradient and probabilistic data. This requires an ability to notice statistical regularities at many different levels of generality, and in many cases, to adjudicate between multiple conflicting patterns by assessing the relative strength of each, and to generalize them to novel items based on their relative strength. At the same time, when we examine evidence from language change, child errors, and psycholinguistic experiments, we find that only a small fraction of the logically possible analogical inferences are actually attested. Therefore, an adequate model of analogy must also be restrictive enough to explain why speakers generalize certain statistical properties of the data and not others. Moreover, in the ideal case, restrictions on possible analogies should follow from intrinsic properties of the architecture of the model, and not need to be stipulated post hoc.

Current computational models of analogical inference in language are still rather rudimentary, and we are certainly nowhere near possessing a model that captures not only the statistical abilities of speakers, but also their preferences and limitations.[1] Nonetheless, the past two decades have seen some key advances. Work in frameworks such as neural networks (Rumelhart and McClelland 1987; MacWhinney and Leinbach 1991; Daugherty and Seidenberg 1994, and much subsequent work) and Analogical Modeling of

[*] Thanks to Jim Blevins, Bruce Hayes, Donca Steriade, participants of the Analogy in Grammar Workshop (Leipzig, September 22–3, 2006), and especially to two anonymous reviewers, for helpful comments and suggestions; all remaining errors are, of course, my own.

[1] Recent decades have seen a wealth of frameworks for modeling analogical inference and decision making more generally; see especially Gentner, Holyoak, and Kokinov (2001) and Chater, Tenenbaum, and Yuille (2006).

Language (AML; Skousen 1989) have focused primarily on the first challenge, tackling the gradience of the data. This work has had several positive influences on the study of analogy, particularly as a synchronic phenomenon. First, it has fostered a culture of developing computationally implemented models. These allow for objective tests of the extent to which a particular pattern can be extracted from the training data, given an explicitly formalized set of assumptions. In a few cases, such work has even led to implemented models of analogical change over time (e.g., Hare and Elman 1995). More generally, it has inspired a good deal of empirical work probing the detailed statistical knowledge that native speakers have about regularities and subregularities surrounding processes in their language. The overall picture that has emerged from such work is one of speakers as powerful statistical learners, able to encode a wide variety of gradient patterns.

In this chapter, I will take on the latter side of the problem, which has so far received far less attention in the literature: why do speakers generalize some regularities and not others? I discuss three general restrictions on analogical inference in morphophonology. The first is a restriction on how patterns are defined, which distinguishes between patterns that can be noticed and extended, and those that are evidently ignored. The second is a restriction on how patterns are evaluated, and concerns what it means for a pattern to be "well attested" or strong enough to generalize to novel items. The last is a restriction on which forms in a morphological paradigm are open to analogical change, and what determines the direction of influence. I argue that in all three cases, the observed restrictions correspond to limitations imposed by formulating processes as SPE-style rewrite rules (A → B / C__D). This observation is not a trivial one, since this rule notation is a very particular hypothesis about how linguistic knowledge is structured, and how it makes reference to positions, variables, and so on. I demonstrate ways in which statistical models that lack this type of structure suffer in their ability to model empirical data, by overestimating the goodness of various possible but unattested types of analogical inference. Based on this observation, I argue that the best formal model of analogy is one that adds a probabilistic component to a grammar of context-sensitive statements.

The outline of the chapter is as follows: for each of the three proposed restrictions, I first present empirical data illustrating how it distinguishes attested from unattested analogies. Then, I compare two representative models, one with and one without the restriction imposed by rule-like structure. Finally, I discuss the broader implications of these observations for formal models of analogy.

9.2 What is a linguistically significant pattern?

9.2.1 *Structured vs unstructured inference*

To illustrate the role that a formalism can play in restricting possible analogies, it is instructive to start by considering the most traditional of all formalisms: four-part analogy. In four-part notation, analogies are expressed in the form in (1):

(1)   Four-part notation: $A{:}B :: X{:}Y$
        "Whatever the relationship is between A and B, it should also hold between X and Y"

Discussions of four-part analogy frequently point out that the relation between words *A* and *B* is in many cases part of a much more general pattern, and that the examples *A* and *B* should be construed as representative members of a larger analogical set, consisting of more words ($A_1{:}B_1 :: A_2{:}B_2 :: A_3{:}B_3 :: \ldots$) and perhaps also more paradigmatically related forms ($A_1{:}B_1{:}C_1 :: A_2{:}B_2{:}C_2 \ldots$). The notation itself does not provide any way to indicate this fact, however, and thus has no formal means of excluding or disfavoring analogies supported by just one or a few pairs. Furthermore, the notation does not impose any restrictions on what properties particular $A_i{:}B_i$ pairs can have in common with one another. In fact the pattern itself—i.e., the relation between *A* and *B*, and the equation for *Y*—is left entirely implicit. This means that there are many possible ways to construct analogical sets, and few concrete ways to compare competing analogical inferences.

As an example, consider mid vowel alternations in Spanish present-tense indicative verb paradigms. In some verbs, when the mid vowels /e/ and /o/ are stressed, they irregularly diphthongize to [jé] and [wé], respectively. This occurs in the 1sg, 2sg, 3sg, and 3pl (as well as the entire present subjunctive). In other verbs, the alternation does not occur, and invariant mid vowels or diphthongs are found throughout the paradigm.

(2)   Spanish present tense diphthongization
        a. Diphthongizing verbs

Verb stem	Infin.	3sg pres. indic.	Gloss
sent-	sent-ár	sjént-a	'seat'
kont-	kont-ár	kwént-a	'count'

b. Nonalternating verbs

Verb stem	Infin.	3sg pres. indic.	Gloss
rent-	rent-ár	rént-a	'rent'
mont-	mont-ár	mónt-a	'ride/mount'
orjent-	orjent-ár	orjént-a	'orient'
frekwent-	frekwent-ár	frekwént-a	'frequent'

Since diphthongization is lexically idiosyncratic, Spanish speakers must decide whether or not to apply it to novel or unknown words. For example, if a speaker was faced with a novel verb [lerrár], they might attempt to construct analogical sets that would support a diphthongized 3sg form [ljérra]. Using the four-part notation, there are numerous ways this could be done, including:

(3)   Analogical set 1:

$$
\left.
\begin{cases}
errar & : & yerra \\
enterrar & : & entierra \\
aserrar & : & asierra \\
aferrar & : & afierra \\
cerrar & : & cierra \\
\ldots &
\end{cases}
\right\} \quad :: \quad lerrar : \textbf{lierra}
$$

(4)   Analogical set 2:

$$
\left.
\begin{cases}
serrar & : & sierra \\
alentar & : & alienta \\
helar & : & hiela \\
querer & : & quiere \\
\ldots &
\end{cases}
\right\} \quad :: \quad lerrar : \textbf{lierra}
$$

The first set looks more convincing, since all of its members rhyme with [lerr-] and belong to the -*ar* inflectional class. Intuitively, this provides better support for the outcome [ljérra] than set 2 does; however, such a high degree of similarity is neither required nor rewarded by the formalism. In addition, nothing formally rewards a larger set (a point we will return to below). In sum, while the generality and flexibility of four-part notation have made it a convenient tool for describing analogical changes, as is often noted in the literature, an explanatory theory of analogy depends on being able to impose restrictions on possible proportions (Morpurgo Davies 1978).

Let us start by addressing the first shortcoming of four-part notation, namely, its inability to capture the relative similarity of different analogical pairs to the target word. A common intuition about analogical sets is that they are not chosen randomly from the lexicon at large, but rather should represent the words that are expected to have the greatest influence because they are phonologically most similar to the target word—i.e., the closest analogs. For example, the existing Spanish verbs that are most similar to the novel verb [lerrar] are shown in (5) (similarity values are in arbitrary units, higher = more similar):

(5)   Existing Spanish verbs similar to [lerrar]

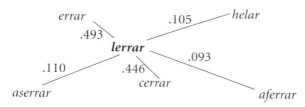

The restriction that we want the model to obey, then, is that generalization of a pattern to novel items must be supported by sufficiently many close analogs. One obvious way to do this is to adopt a similarity-based classification model, which decides on the treatment of novel items by considering its aggregate similarity to the set of known items. In such a model, the advantage of being similar to many existing words is anything but accidental; it is built in as a core principle of the architecture of the model.

There are many ways to be similar, however, and it is an empirical question what types of similarity matter most to humans in deciding how to treat novel words. For instance, the existing Spanish verbs *errar* 'err' and *cerrar* 'close' are similar to novel *lerrar* by ending in root-final [err]. The verb *helar* 'freeze' is also (at least somewhat) similar to *lerrar*, but this is due to the shared [l] (or perhaps the similarity of [l] and [r]), a similar syllabic structure, and so on. Hypothetical verbs like *lerdar*, *lenar*, and *lorrar* also share commonalities with *lerrar*, but each in its own unique way. Looking back at analogical set 1 in (3), there are intuitively two factors that make this group of analogs seem particularly compelling. First, all of these verbs share a set of common properties with each other and with the target word: they all end in [err] and all belong to the *-ar* inflectional class. In addition, those shared properties are perceptually salient (involving rhymes of stressed syllables), and are local to the change in question (being either in the same syllable as the stressed mid vowel, or in the adjacent syllable). Albright and Hayes (2003) refer to this situation, in which the comparison set can be defined by their shared properties, as STRUCTURED SIMILARITY. If we compare analogical set 2 in (4), we see that *serrar, alentar, helar,* and *querer* share no such properties.[2] Albright and Hayes refer to this as VARIEGATED SIMILARITY.

Not all similarity-based models care about the exact source or nature of similarity. In principle, the similarity of the novel word to each existing word could be calculated independently. (An example will be given in the next section.) In order to give preference to structured similarity, a model must be able to align words with one another, determine what they have in common, and ignore what is unique to individual comparisons. This requires that the model have the capacity to encode the fact that a number of words all have the same type of element in the same location—that is, the model must be able to impose structure on the data, and encode its knowledge in terms of these structures (features, prosodic positions, etc.). This sounds like a simple requirement, but in fact it represents a fundamental divide between two classes of models: those that generalize using "raw" (unstructured) similarity to known words, and those that generalize by imposing structure on novel items and parsing them for elements in common with known words.

The goal of the rest of this section is to show that structured similarity is an important component in modeling how speakers generalize morphophonological patterns. The strategy will be as follows: first, in Sections 9.2.2–9.2.3, I will present two computationally implemented models, one lacking structured representations, and one that encodes its knowledge in structural terms. Then in Section 9.2.4, the performance of the two models will be compared against experimentally obtained data concerning the relative likelihood of different novel Spanish verbs to undergo diphthongization. To preview the results, it will emerge that the ability to make use of variegated (unstructured) similarity turns out to be not only unnecessary, but even harmful in modeling human intuitions.

9.2.2 *Analogy without structure: "pure" similarity-based classification*

To assess the contribution of structured similarity to the performance of a model, we first need a baseline model that does not require structured comparisons. One commonly used model of similarity-based classification that has been widely applied in many domains is the GENERALIZED CONTEXT

---

[2] Or, more precisely, they share only very general properties which do not distinguish them from other verbs in the language, such as having a liquid, a stressable mid vowel, and so on.

MODEL (GCM; Nosofsky 1986, 1990). For some applications in linguistics, see Johnson (1997), Nakisa, Plunkett, and Hahn (2000), and Albright and Hayes (2003). In this model, the treatment of a novel item is determined by calculating its similarity to classes of known items (exemplars). In deciding whether to assign a novel item *i* to a particular class *c*, the model compares item *i* to each existing member *j* of class *c*. The similarity of *i* to the entire class is a function of the summed similarities of each individual class member:

(6)   Similarity of novel item *i* to class *c* (with members *j*) $= \sum e^{(-d_{i,j}/s)}$, where
   - $d_{i,j} =$ the psychological distance between *i* and *j*
   - $s =$ sensitivity (a free parameter of the model)

The probability of actually treating *i* as a member of class *c* is simply proportional to its similarity to the individual members:

(7) Probability of assigning item *i* to class $c = \dfrac{\text{Similarity of } i \text{ to } c}{\text{Total similarity of } i \text{ to all classes}}$

This model is based on the premise that analogical sets are more compelling when they contain more members, and when those members are more similar to the novel item. In this way, the model satisfies the restriction that analogical generalization must be sufficiently supported by known items. The model does not place any inherent restrictions on the nature of the similarity relations, however, specifying only that it reflect some generic notion of the *psychological distance* between two words. At its simplest and most neutral, this would simply be their *perceptual distance*, or some holistic measure of how similar the words sound. Intuitively, words sound similar to one another if their component segments are similar—that is, if the sounds of one word are well-matched to those of the other. In order to calculate this, we need perceptual similarity values for arbitrary pairs of sounds, and also a method of determining the optimal alignment of sounds, given their similarities.

One technique for estimating the similarity of pairs of segments is to consider how many natural classes they both belong to. Frisch, Pierrehumbert, and Broe (2004), following Broe (1993) and Frisch (1996), propose the following ratio:

(8) Similarity of sounds $s_1, s_2 = \dfrac{\text{Number of shared natural classes}}{\text{Number of shared} + \text{unshared natural classes}}$

Given these similarity values, an optimal alignment of the sounds in two words is one in which they can be transformed into one another in as few steps as possible (Bailey and Hahn 2001; Hahn, Chater, and Richardson 2003). This can be calculated by finding the minimum string edit (Levenshtein) distance (Kruskal 1983); see Bailey and Hahn (2001) and Albright and Hayes (2003) for details of how this is implemented based on segmental similarity. The result is a score for each pair of words, reflecting the degree of similarity between corresponding segments and the extent of mismatches (noncorresponding material). For example, the similarity of the novel verb *lerrar* to the existing Spanish verb *error* is calculated to be 0.493 (in arbitrary units), while the similarity of *lerrar* to *reglar* is 0.268, and to *lograr* is 0.203.

We can use this model to calculate the likelihood of diphthongizing a novel Spanish verb, by simply comparing the aggregate similarity of that verb against the set of existing diphthongizing and nondiphthongizing verbs. For example, the summed similarity of the novel verb *lerrar* to diphthongizing verbs is 4.936 (again, in arbitrary units), with the top contributors including verbs like *error* (0.493), *cerrar* (0.446), *aserrar* (0.110), *helar* (0.105), and *aferrar* (0.093). The summed similarity of *lerrar* to nondiphthongizing verbs is 15.551, with top contributors including *reglar* (0.268), *orlar* (0.240), *ahorrar* (0.213), *forrar* (0.211), and *lograr* (0.203). We see that the higher score for the nondiphthongizing comes not from greater similarity of any individual member—in fact, *error* and *cerrar* in the diphthongizing class are much more similar than any nondiphthongizing verb. Rather, this advantage is due to the fact that there are many more nondiphthongizing verbs, so small amounts of moderate similarity sum up to outweigh a small numer of very similar verbs. Using the equation in (7), the overall probability of applying diphthongization to *lerrar* is predicted to be 4.936 / (4.936 + 15.551), or 24.09%.

There are a couple points to note about the workings of this model. First, the model has the ability to make use of variegated similarity, since similarity is based on the optimal alignments of individual pairs of items. However, the examples in the preceding paragraph show that not all inferences make equal use of it; in fact, the closest analogs supporting diphthongization almost all contain -*error*. This turns out to be quite typical, and analogical sets are frequently dominated by words that all happen to share the same feature(s) in common with the target word—i.e., a structured similarity. This aspect of the model will be important to keep in mind when evaluating the performance of the GCM, since we are interested not only in how well the model does, but also in the question of whether it benefits from its ability to use variegated similarity.

9.2.3 *Analogy with structure: Probabilistic context-sensitive rules*

As noted above, an ability to refer to particular properties of words (having a certain type of sound in a certain location, having particular prosodic properties, etc.) is crucial in requiring that analogical sets share structural similarities. In fact, many modeling frameworks use structural properties to decide how to treat novel items. Feature-based classification models (Tversky 1977), such as TiMBL (Daelemans, Zavrel, Van der Sloot, and Van den Bosch 2000) and AML (Skousen 1989) directly incorporate the idea that in order for a group of items to be similar, they must share certain properties (feature values). Linguistic rules impose an even more specific structure. For example, context-sensitive readjustment rules (e → je / X __ rro]$_{1sg}$) specify a change location, immediately adjacent left and right contexts, precedence relations, and so on. Although rule application is often thought of as fundamentally different from (and incompatible with) analogical inference, in fact, it is possible to think of rules as a very specific theory of how analogical sets are constructed—namely, by picking out groups of words that can be captured using the rule notation format.

The MINIMAL GENERALIZATION LEARNER (MGL; Albright and Hayes 2002) is a computationally implemented model that finds rules covering sets of words that behave consistently (belong to the same inflectional class, share the same morphophonemic change, etc.). It employs a bottom-up inductive procedure to compare pairs of words in the input data, find what they have in common, and encode these commonalities using a grammar of stochastic rules. For details of the model, the reader is referred to Albright and Hayes (2002) and Albright and Hayes (2003); in this section I provide a brief overview.

The model takes as its input pairs of forms that stand in a particular morphological relation, such as present/past, or infinitive/1sg, as in (9). In the present case, the relation between diphthongized and nondiphthongized stem variants is conditioned by stress placement, rather than any particular morphological category. Therefore, in the simulations reported here, input data are represented as pairs of stressed and stressless stem allomorphs, abstracting away from the suffixal material of the particular inflected forms that require one or the other, but retaining an indication of inflection class information (-*ar*, -*er*, -*ir*).

(9)   Input to the minimal generalization learner: Some sample -*ar* verbs

Stressless	Stressed	Gloss	Orthography (infinitive)
jeg	jég	'arrive'	(*llegar*)
dex	déx	'leave'	(*dejar*)
jeb	jéb	'bring'	(*llevar*)
ked	kéd	'stay'	(*quedar*)
enkontr	enkwéntr	'find'	(*encontrar*)

(*continued*)

(9) (*cont.*)

Stressless	Stressed	Gloss	Orthography (infinitive)
pens	pjéns	'think'	(*pensar*)
kont	kwént	'tell, count'	(*contar*)
entr	éntr	'enter'	(*entrar*)
tom	tóm	'take'	(*tomar*)
kre	kré	'create'	(*crear*)
empes	empjés	'start'	(*empezar*)
esper	espér	'wait, hope'	(*esperar*)
rekord	rekwérd	'remember'	(*recordar*)
tembl	tjémbl	'tremble'	(*temblar*)

The first step in learning is to analyze individual (stressless, stressed) pairs, by factoring them into changing and unchanging portions. This allows each pair to be expressed as a rule, encoding both the change (A → B) and the non-changing portion (C __ D). For example, the pair (tembl, tjémbl) has a vowel change surrounded by unchanging consonants: e → jé / t __ mbl ("stressless [e] corresponds to stressed [je] when preceded by [t] and followed by [mbl]"). The pair (jeg, jég) on the other hand differs only in stress: e → é / j __ g.

Once the input pairs have been recast as word-specific rules, they are compared to find what they have in common, according to the rule scheme in (10):

(10)   Comparing *tembl-/tiembl-* 'tremble', *desmembr-/desmiembr-* 'dismember':

Residue	Shared feats	Shared segs	Change loc.	Shared segs	Shared feats
	t		—	mb	l
des	m		—	mb	r
X	$\begin{bmatrix} -\text{syllabic} \\ -\text{continuant} \end{bmatrix}$		—	mb	$\begin{bmatrix} -\text{syllabic} \\ +\text{sonorant} \\ +\text{continuant} \\ +\text{voice} \\ +\text{coronal} \\ +\text{anterior} \end{bmatrix}$

The comparison in (10) yields a very specific rule that retains all of the properties shared by *tembl-* and *desmembr-*, subject to the restriction that they can be encoded in the structural components of the rule. Shared material is expressed in terms of phonological features, while unshared material is expressed as variables. By convention, unmatched material on the left side is collapsed into a variable called 'X', and material on the right into a variable 'Y'. When such comparisons are carried out iteratively across the entire dataset, however, much broader rules can emerge through comparison of diverse forms, while further comparison of similar forms will yield additional narrow rules. A small sample of the many possible rules that could be learned from a set of Spanish verbs is given in (11).

(11)   Representative rules for Spanish verbs[3]

    i. o → wé / [+consonantal] ___ rs

    ii. o → wé / $\begin{bmatrix} -\text{continuant} \\ -\text{voice} \end{bmatrix}$ r ___ $\begin{bmatrix} -\text{continuant} \\ -\text{syllabic} \end{bmatrix}$

    iii. o → wé / $\begin{bmatrix} -\text{syllabic} \\ +\text{consonantal} \end{bmatrix}$ ___ [−syllabic]

    iv. o → ó / $\begin{bmatrix} -\text{syllabic} \\ -\text{sonorant} \\ +\text{consonantal} \end{bmatrix}$ ___ $\begin{bmatrix} -\text{syllabic} \\ +\text{consonantal} \\ -\text{continuant} \end{bmatrix}$

    v. o → ó / $\begin{bmatrix} -\text{syllabic} \\ +\text{voice} \end{bmatrix}$ ___ [−syllabic]

    vi. o → ó / ___ [−syllabic]

These rewrite rules incorporate many types of structure that limit possible comparisons. Rules specify linear relations such as precedence and adjacency. This notation rules out many logically possible sets of words, such as those that all have a certain sound, but its location is variably either to the right or the left of the change. This particular procedure also compares words by starting immediately adjacent to the change and working outwards, meaning that the descriptions of the left and right-side contexts are limited to the local contexts.[4] Rule notation also embodies a form of strict feature matching: rules apply if their structural description is met, and not otherwise. Finally, although SPE-style rewrite rules are written in a way that could theoretically make use of the full power of context-sensitive grammars, the rules employed by this model obey commonly observed conventions for phonological rewrite rules by referring to a fixed number of positions and applying noncyclically,

---

[3] Since the implemented model uses linear (flat) phonological representations, stress is encoded here as a feature of the stressed vowel, rather than as a property of the syllabic context.

[4] Ultimately, this is too strong an assumption, since contexts are sometimes nonlocal. For an attempt to extend this system to find nonlocal contexts, and discussion of some of the issues involved, see Albright and Hayes (2006).

and thus are restricted to expressing regular relations which can be captured with a finite state transducer (Johnson 1972; Kaplan and Kay 1994; Gildea and Jurafsky 1996). The system thus embodies a very strong form of structured similarity: all that matters is that words are the same in the relevant respect, and there are no penalties or rewards for additional similarities or differences.

Once all of the possible rules have been discovered, it remains to decide which dimensions of similarity the speaker should actually pay attention to. In order to do this, the rules are evaluated according to their accuracy in the training data. The RELIABILITY of a rule is defined as the number of cases that it successfully covers (its HITS), divided by the number of cases that meet its structural description (its SCOPE). Raw reliability scores are then adjusted slightly downward using lower confidence limit statistics, to yield a score called CONFIDENCE. This has the effect of penalizing rules that are based on just a small amount of data (a small scope). The confidence scores for the rules in (11) are shown in (12):

(12) Representative rules for Spanish, evaluated (hits/scope ⇒ confidence)

  i. o → wé /[+cons] __ rs   4/4   ⇒   .786

  ii. o → wé / $\begin{bmatrix} -\text{contin} \\ -\text{voice} \end{bmatrix}$ r __ $\begin{bmatrix} -\text{contin} \\ -\text{syll} \end{bmatrix}$ 6/8   ⇒   .610

  iii. o → wé / $\begin{bmatrix} -\text{syll} \\ +\text{cons} \end{bmatrix}$ __ [− syll]   68/545   ⇒   .116

  iv. o → ó / $\begin{bmatrix} -\text{syll} \\ -\text{sonor} \\ +\text{cons} \end{bmatrix}$ __ $\begin{bmatrix} -\text{syll} \\ +\text{cons} \\ -\text{contin} \end{bmatrix}$ 101/106   ⇒   .934

  v. o → ó / $\begin{bmatrix} -\text{syll} \\ +\text{voice} \end{bmatrix}$ __ [−syll]   19/22   ⇒   .795

  vi. o → ó / __ [−syll]   588/668   ⇒   .871

Finally, the grammar of rules can be used to generalize patterns to novel items. The probability of generalizing a process is defined as in (13). Since this calculation is intended to mimic the probability with which a particular pattern will be employed to produce a target output, it is referred to as the PRODUCTION PROBABILITY of that pattern:

(13) Production probability

$$= \frac{\text{Confidence of the best rule applying the pattern to the input}}{\text{Summed confidence of best rules applicable to the input, each pattern}}$$

For example, in calculating the likelihood to diphthongize the novel verb *lerrar*, the best (= most confident) applicable diphthongization and non-diphthongization rules are:

(14)   Likelihood to diphthongize *lerrar*
  - Best applicable diphthongization rule:

$$e \rightarrow j\acute{e} \; / \; \begin{bmatrix} +\text{consonantal} \\ +\text{coronal} \end{bmatrix} - \begin{bmatrix} +\text{consonantal} \\ +\text{voice} \end{bmatrix}$$

Reliability = 10/29; Confidence = .290

  - Best applicable nondiphthongization rule:

$$e \rightarrow \acute{e} \; / \; \begin{bmatrix} -\text{syllabic} \\ +\text{voice} \end{bmatrix} - [\,+\text{sonorant}\,]$$

Reliability = 86/86; Confidence = .989

  - Production probability (*lierro*) $= \frac{.290}{.290+.989} = 23\%$

For both the Minimal Generalization Learner and the Generalized Context Model, support for generalizations comes from large numbers of words that are similar to the target word and behave consistently. In the MGL, however, similarity is defined (in boolean fashion) as presence of certain structural features. This prevents the model from using variegated similarity, since such diverse sets of relations cannot be captured in the rule notation. We can contrast this with the GCM, in which the supporting words need not be similar to one another in any particular way. This leads to the possibility that analogical inference may be based on variegated support. In the next section, we attempt to test whether this additional ability is helpful or harmful to the GCM.

Finally, it is worth noting that proportional analogy is most often used in a way that conforms to the structural restrictions imposed by the rule-based model, since the antecedent in four-part notation requires that there is a well-defined relation, and ideally also a group of words that all share the same relation. Although individual analysts may disagree about what constitutes a valid relation (see Morpurgo Davies 1978 for a review of some prominent points of view), in practice, relations are most naturally thought of as a single rewrite relation, much as in SPE-style rules. This is not to say that the formalisms are equivalent, however, since proportional analogy is certainly flexible enough to encompass relations that cannot be expressed in rule-based terms. For example, nothing formally precludes setting up proportions showing relations that involve multiple changes (prefixation of [s] and nasalization of final consonant: *tick:sting* :: *crab:scram* :: *cat::scan?*), or changes that depend on the presence of an element somewhere in the word regardless of linear order (change of [ɪ] → [ʌ] adjacent to a [p]: *pinch::punch* :: *sip::sup* :: *pig:pug?*). A hypothesis of the rule-based model is that in order for a relation to be linguistically active—i.e., extended systematically to new forms—it must involve a change defined in terms of phonological features, applied to a set of words that share a common structure (again, defined over linearly arranged combinations of natural phonological classes).

9.2.4 *An empirical test: Modeling diphthongization in novel words*

In order to test whether humans are restricted to inferences based on structured similarity, we can compare the performance of the two models against experimentally obtained data in which Spanish speakers were likewise tested on how they would produce stressed forms of novel verbs. Albright, Andrade, and Hayes (2001) asked 96 native speakers to inflect novel verbs containing mid vowels, to measure the relative likelihood of diphthongized responses in different contexts. Participants were given novel verbs in an unstressed form (e.g., [lerrámos] 'we *lerr*') and were asked to produce a stressed form (e.g., [lerro]/[ljérro] 'I *lerr*'). For each verb, the production probability of diphthongization was calculated by dividing the number of diphthongized responses by the total number of diphthongized + undiphthongized responses. For example, for the verb *lerrar*, 19 participants volunteered [ljérro] and 76 volunteered [lérro],[5] yielding a 20% production probability of diphthongization. (For additional details of the experimental design and results, see Albright, Andrade, and Hayes 2001.)

In order to test the models, predictions were obtained by training each model on a lexicon of Spanish. Two different datasets were tested: one that included all of the verbs in the LEXESP corpus containing stressable mid vowels (1,881 verbs total), and another that included just the subset of verbs that fall in the -*ar* inflectional class (1,669 of the total set). The choice of dataset turns out to matter slightly for the results, with the GCM performing slightly better on the full set and the MGL performing slightly better on the smaller set. The differences were relatively small, however, and I simply report here the better result for each model (i.e., treating the choice of dataset as a parameter that can vary independently across models).

Figure 9.1 shows the overall ability of the two models to predict the probability of diphthongization on a verb-by-verb basis. We see that both models do reasonably well, though the MGL does somewhat better ($r = .77$) than the GCM ($r = .56$). Most of this difference comes from the exceptionally poor performance of the GCM on a single outlier, however (*entar*); if this one item is excluded, the performance of the GCM is approximately as good as the MGL (r increases to .74).

---

[5] One additional subject volunteered an unexpected and idiosyncratic change for this verb; this response was excluded.

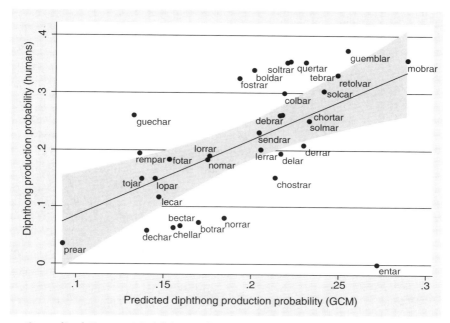

a. Generalized Context Model ($r = .56$)

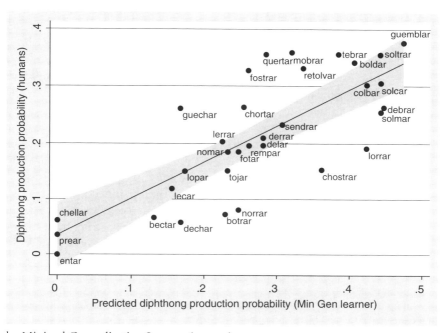

b. Minimal Generalization Learner ($r = .77$)

FIGURE 9.1 Predicted vs observed production probability of diphthongization

So what do we conclude from this result? Clearly, neither model can be rejected outright based on raw performance. In fact, the predictions of the two models are also significantly correlated with one another ($r = .53$). This means that the models are not merely making equivalently good predictions—in fact, to a large extent they are making the very same predictons.[6] When the outputs of the two models are inspected, the reason is not hard to find: in very many cases, the two models pick out overlapping analogical sets. For example for the novel word *solmar*, the MGL found that the most confident applicable diphthongization rule was o → wé / s__ℓ Y]$_{-ar}$ class (including such words as *solar* 'pave', *soltar* 'release', and *soldar* 'solder'). These same words figure prominently in the analogical set that the GCM employs; the five top contributors are *solar* (similarity .493), *soldar* (.417), *soltar* (.338), *cerrar* (.214), and *dormir* (.164). Similarly for the verb *lorrar*, the MGL used a rule o → wé / $\begin{bmatrix} +\text{coronal} \\ +\text{continuant} \end{bmatrix}$ — $\begin{bmatrix} +\text{coronal} \\ +\text{voice} \end{bmatrix}$ Y]$_{-ar}$ class supported by positive examples like *solar, sonar, soldar, rodar,* and *soltar.* Here too, the rule includes three of the GCM's five closest analogs: *errar* (.278), *cerrar* (.252), *solar* (.095), *rodar* (.094), and *soldar* (.085). The upshot is that although the GCM has access to variegated similarity—seen, for example, in the presence of analogs like *cerrar*—there is no guarantee that it is actually using it to a significant extent in any particular case. Thus, overall comparisons like the one in Figure 1 are unlikely to be illuminating about what mechanism speakers actually use to make analogical inferences.[7]

The examples in the preceding paragraph show that although in practice the role of variegated similarity is less than what is theoretically possible, the GCM does use it at least to a certain extent. What we need, then, is a way to focus specifically on the contribution of the variegated analogs, which the MGL cannot include as support for inferences. This requires a means of separating analogs that share a structured relation from those that do not. For a set like {*solar, soldar, soltar, cerrar, dormir*}, the intuitive division is between the first three, which share #*sol* (and the -*ar* inflectional class), as opposed to *cerrar* and *dormir*, which look like odd men out. Strictly speaking, however, it is not the case that these verbs completely lack structural properties with the remaining forms. In fact, all five verbs share the set of properties in (15):

---

[6] This was confirmed by a stepwise multiple regression analysis, in which the MGL predictions were entered first with a high degree of significance ($p < .0001$), and the GCM predictions were unable to make any additional significant contribution.

[7] The reason that the GCM tends to stick to such structurally interpretable analogical sets appears to be the fact that diphthongizing verbs in Spanish themselves happen to fall into such clusters. The

(15)   Structural commonality: *solar, soldar, soltar, cerrar,* and *dormir*

$$\#[\;-\text{sonorant}] \begin{bmatrix} +\text{syllabic} \\ -\text{high} \\ -\text{low} \end{bmatrix} \begin{bmatrix} +\text{consonantal} \\ +\text{sonorant} \\ -\text{nasal} \end{bmatrix} Y$$

The description in (15) expresses a structured similarity, but expanding the context to include *cerrar* and *dormir* comes at a price. The description is now so general that it includes not just these five verbs, but also many others— including, importantly, some that do not diphthongize. In other words, although the description in (15) unifies all of the members of the GCM's analogical set, it does not accurately or uniquely describe what sets them apart from the rest of the verbs in the language. A rule-based model like the MGL could state a rule that applies diphthongization in this context, but it would not be a useful rule since it has too many exceptions.

This suggests a refinement to how we isolate sets of structured analogs: they must not only have in common a set of shared properties, but those proper-ties must also be reliably associated with class membership. For example, it is not enough to be able to state what *cerrar* has in common with *soldar* and *soltar*; the properties that they share must also distinguish these verbs from nondiphthongizing verbs. In order to separate structured from unstructured analogs, then, we need a hypothesis about what those distinguishing proper-ties are. Not coincidentally, this is precisely what the MGL model is designed to identify. For example, as noted above, the MGL determines that the properties of *solmar* that are most reliably associated with diphthongization are the preceding /s/ and the following /l/, making *solar, soldar, soltar* the analogs that share the set of most relevant structural properties. It should be possible, therefore, to use the structural descriptions that the MGL selects to help identify when the GCM is making use of unstructured, or variegated similarity.

---

explanation for this may be partly phonological, since phonotactic restrictions on stem-final conson-ant combinations would restrict the set of possibilities in this position, and make it easier for commonalities to emerge. There may also be a historical component: suppose the structured model of analogy is the correct one, and structure-guided inferences have been shaping Spanish over the centuries. In this case, we would expect verbs to retain diphthongization most readily if they fall into structurally definable gangs, creating structure in the lexicon of Spanish. If this were true, then the GCM could do good job of capturing the modern language, but would be unable to explain how the language came to be this way. If, on the other hand, the GCM model were correct, we would expect diphthongizing verbs to be retained on the strength of variegated similarity, and the set of existing diphthongizing verbs could consist of variegated analogical sets which the structured model would be unable to locate. A full diachronic analysis of verb-by-verb changes in diphthongization is left as a matter for future research.

In order to quantify the contribution of nonstructured analogs in the predictions of the GCM, I first ran the MGL, finding for each nonce form the set of properties that were found to be most reliably associated with diphthongization (i.e., the structural description of the best applicable rule that could derive a diphthongized output). I then ran the GCM, collecting the set of diphthongizing analogs. For each nonce verb, the analogical set was then separated into two groups: the structured analogs, which contained the best context identified by the MGL, and the variegated analogs, which fell outside this context. Examples for the novel verbs *solmar* and *lorrar* are given in (16).

(16)   Separating structured vs variegated analogs
       a. *solmar*: best context = $[\text{sol} \dots]_{\text{-ar class}}$)

Structured analogs		Unstructured analogs	
solar	.493	*serrar*	.214
soldar	.417	*dormir*	.164
soltar	.338	*sonar*	.157
		serner	.139
		socar	.126
		(and 235 others)	

       b. *lorrar*: best context = $[\begin{bmatrix} +\text{coronal} \\ -\text{continuant} \end{bmatrix} \text{o} \begin{bmatrix} +\text{coronal} \\ +\text{voice} \end{bmatrix}]_{\text{-ar class}}$

Structured analogs		Unstructured analogs	
solar	.095	*errar*	.278
rodar	.094	*serrar*	.252
		soldar	.085
		forsar	.084
		(and 236 others)	

The contribution of variegated analogy was then defined as the summed similarity of the unstructured analogs divided by the summed similarity of all analogs (structured and unstructured). This ratio is taken as a measure of the extent to which the GCM is relying on variegated similarity for any particular nonce word.

We are now in a position to evaluate the usefulness of variegated similarity. If speakers make analogical inferences in a way that is blind to structure, then the MGL model should suffer in cases where variegated similarity is needed, since it is unable to make use of a crucial source of support. Conversely, if structure is critical to how speakers generalize, then the GCM should do

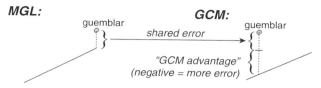

FIGURE 9.2 Calculation of "GCM advantage" score based on residuals

worse the more it relies more on variegated similarity. The word-by-word performance of each model was tested by fitting the predictions of each model against the experimentally obtained human responses using a linear regression. For each word, it was then determined how far off the model was, by subtracting the observed from the predicted values (i.e., calculating the residuals). The performance of the two models was collapsed into a single "GCM advantage" score by subtracting the GCM error from the MGL error for each word; this score is positive for a particular word if the MGL's prediction is less accurate than the GCM's, and negative if the GCM is farther off. This comparison is illustrated in Figure 9.2. Finally, the GCM advantage scores were correlated against the contribution of variegated analogy, as defined in the preceding paragraph. If variegated analogs are important to speakers, we expect a positive correlation, since in cases where variegated similarity plays a larger role, the MGL should suffer more (positive GCM advantage). If speakers do not use variegated similarity, we expect a negative correlation, since the GCM's reliance on variegated analogs would encourage generalizations that humans do not make. In fact, when the correlation is calculated as described above, the result is weakly negative ($r = -.195$). Thus, we fail to find any support for the idea that variegated similarity is needed— and in fact, there is an indication that it may even be harmful.

The same result can also be seen another way, by calculating for each novel item the degree to which the GCM overestimated the goodness of each output. This amount will be positive if the GCM assigned too high a score (overpredicting the goodness of the output), and zero if the GCM is right on or under. The rational for restricting the analysis to *overpredictions* is the following: suppose that speakers do not notice variegated similarity, and that the GCM is incorrect to use it. If this is true, then access to variegated analogs should let the GCM (incorrectly) gather extra support for some outputs, leading to overestimation of their goodness. Therefore, the negative effects of variegated similarity should be seen most clearly in the GCM's overprediction errors. To test this, the GCM's overestimation scores were correlated against the relative contribution of variegated similarity, as defined above. The result here was a positive correlation between variegated similarity and overestimation ($r = .33$). This shows that the extra sources of support that the GCM has access to are not helpful in modeling speakers more accurately—in fact, they are deleterious, causing the model to overestimate the probability of diphthongization. Albright and Hayes (2003) also make a similar point about the GCM, using data from English past-tense formation.

There is finally one last way in which structure can be seen to matter. If we examine the GCM predictions in Figure 9.1a, we see that the most blatant gaffe by far that the GCM makes is in overpredicting the probability of diphthongization in *entar*. This prediction is based on the support of diphthongizing analogs like *sentar* 'seat', *mentar* 'mention', *tentar* 'touch', *dentar* 'teethe', *ventar* 'sniff', and so on. All of these analogs have a preceding consonant, and in fact diphthongization of initial vowels is overall quite rare in Spanish (particularly in the *-ar* class). The MGL is able to encode this fact by requiring that a consonant is a crucial part of the context when formulating rules. The GCM, on the other hand, has no way to encode this beyond the standard penalty for inserting or deleting a single segment in the process of calculating the optimal string alignment; therefore, it cannot categorically block analogy to similar consonant-initial words. This is yet another indication that speakers encode knowledge of patterns in terms of properties of elements that appear in particular positions—that is, in terms of linguistic structure.

9.2.5 *Local summary*

In this section, I have discussed a major restriction on what type of pattern can be generalized through analogy: it must be supported by sets of words that share a particular combination of properties in common, both with each other and with the target word. This may seem like an obvious or trivial restriction, and in fact many models simply assume it without argument. However, it is certainly not a logically necessary part of how analogy is formalized. Many examplar-based models, such as the GCM, do not obey this restriction. This allows them to capture a wider range of patterns, and thereby makes them less constrained models. I have shown that the extra power afforded by unstructured comparisons does not help—and indeed, it seems to hurt by inflating the predicted goodness of certain generalizations. This confirms similar results shown previously for English by Albright and Hayes (2003).

Importantly, the restriction to structured comparisons is exactly what we would expect if speakers encode patterns using something like probabilistic context-sensitive rules, of the sort employed by the MGL. Of course, this is not the only model that imposes structure on its representations; similar restrictions are also found in feature-based models, such as TiMBL (Daelemans, Zavrel, Van der Sloot, and Van den Bosch 2000) and AML (Skousen 1989).

9.3 Type vs token frequency

Another possible restriction on analogical models concerns the way in which the support for competing patterns is evaluated. In principle, a pattern could be strengthened in at least two different ways: by occurring in a large number of different words (high type frequency), or by occurring in a smaller number of words that are used very commonly (high token frequency). In fact, it appears that the propensity to generalize morphophonological patterns to new forms depends primarily on type frequency, and not on token frequency. This restriction has been noted numerous times in the literature; see Baayen and Lieber (1991) for English derivational suffixes, Bybee (1995) for French conjugation classes, German past participles, and others, Albright (2002b) for Italian conjugation classes, Albright and Hayes (2003: 133) for English past tenses, Ernestus and Baayen (2003: 29) for stem-final voicing in Dutch, Hay, Pierrehumbert, and Beckman (2004) for medial consonant clusters in English, and additional references in Bybee (1995). In this section, I provide further evidence for this conclusion, and suggest that it favors a model in which patterns are abstracted from individual words and encoded in some form that is separate from the lexicon (such as a grammar).

The formal definition of similarity in the Generalized Context Model ((6) above) is compatible with counting based either on type or token frequency, since "members of a class" could be taken to mean either types or individual tokens. In practice, however, the most natural interpretations of the model would lead us to expect a role for token frequency. If we assume, as is often done, that the GCM operates over exemplar representations (Johnson 1997; Pierrehumbert 2001), then every single token should contribute a measure of support to the strength of the pattern. Furthermore, even if we assume that the GCM operates over a more schematic lexicon that abstracts away from individual exemplars, there is ample evidence from online recognition and processing tasks that words with higher token frequency are accessed more readily than low-frequency words. Therefore, even if the GCM counts over a lexicon distinct word types, it seems likely that token frequency effects would emerge simply because of the way the lexicon is accessed. Stated more generally, the premise of the GCM is that generalization is carried out by consulting the lexicon directly, and token frequency effects are characteristic—perhaps even diagnostic—of lexical access. It is important to note that the GCM is also very sensitive to type frequency, since each type contributes at least one token to the summed support for a particular class.

In principle, the Minimal Generalization Learner could also evaluate rules using types or tokens, but the rules it discovers are most naturally interpreted in terms of types. The comparisons that it carries out to abstract away from individual lexical items ((10) above) require just a single instance of each word, and nothing more can be learned from further tokens of previously seen data. In a system in which additional tokens are gratuitous, it would perhaps be a surprising design feature if token frequency played a crucial role in how rules are evaluated. In fact, calculating the confidence of rules according to their token frequency would require extra work in this model, since repeated tokens of the same lexical item could otherwise be disregarded as uninformative. This also relates to the more general hypothesis that grammars are intrinsically about kinds of words, rather than about particular instances of their use. Therefore, even if it is not strictly speaking required by the formalism, a rule-based account of analogy is most naturally limited to the influence of type frequency.

Spanish diphthongization provides a direct test of the relative importance of type vs token frequency, since although diphthongization is a minority pattern in the Spanish lexicon, affecting only a relatively small number of mid-vowel verbs (lowish type frequency), the verbs that undergo it tend to be among the most frequent verbs in the language (high token frequency). There is abundant prima facie evidence that the high token frequency of diphthongization does not make it a strong pattern: synchronically it is relatively unproductive in experimental settings (Bybee and Pardo 1981; Albright, Andrade, and Hayes 2001), and diachronically verbs tend to lose diphthongization alternations (Penny 2002; Morris 2005). Furthermore, overregularization errors among children acquiring Spanish consistently result in omitting diphthongization (Clahsen, Aveledo, and Roca 2002), even though diphthongizing tokens constitute a large portion—perhaps even the majority—of children's experience.

In order to test the influence of token frequency more systematically, I ran both the GCM and the MGL with and without taking token frequency into account. Specifically, a weighting term was introduced in the GCM, so the contribution of each analog was defined not only in proportion to its similarity, but also in proportion to its (log) token frequency. A weighting term was also introduced into the MGL, such that the contribution of each word to the hits and/or scope of a rule was weighted according to its log token frequency. The result was that both models did slightly worse when token frequency was taken into account, as shown in (17).

(17)   A negative effect of token frequency (Pearson's *r*)

	Type frequency alone	Weighted by (log) token frequency
GCM	.743	.730
MGL	.767	.742

We see that the overall effect of token frequency weighting is quite small. The reason for this is that most words in the average corpus (and presumably also the average lexicon) have very low frequency ("Zipf's Law"). As a result, weighting by token frequency influences just a small number of high-frequency words. Therefore, weighting by token frequency has relatively little effect, unless the target word happens to be very similar to an existing high-frequency word. It should be noted that these particular experimental items were not constructed for the purpose of dissociating type and token frequency, and ultimately the fairest test would be based on items that diverge more in their predictions. Nonetheless, the trend is clear across both models: to the extent that token frequency makes a difference, it is harmful in modeling speaker intuitions about the strength of the diphthongization pattern.

Like variegated similarity, high token frequency is a type of information that speakers could logically make use of in deciding whether or not to generalize a pattern to novel items. The fact that they apparently do not do so requires a formal model that is similarly restricted. As noted above, it is certainly possible to construct exemplar models that ignore token frequency; the amount and nature of frequency weighting is an independent parameter in the GCM that can be turned off completely, and Bybee (1995) explicitly defines schema strength in terms of type frequency. Conceptually, however, part of the appeal of exemplar models is that they rely on no special mechanisms except activating memory traces—a mechanism that intrinsically leads to token frequency effects (Bybee 2006). Insensitivity to token frequency follows quite naturally from a grammar of rules, however, since rules encode information that has been abstracted away from the particular exemplars that led to their creation. A rule-based account of analogy therefore involves no particular expectation that token frequency should play a role, and indeed is naturally restricted not to have access to information about token frequency.

9.4 The directionality of analogical inference

In the preceding sections, we have seen that an adequate model of analogical inference must be able to identify properties that are consistently associated with membership in a particular class, and must ensure that the association holds for sufficiently many different word types. Models that can find support for inferences in other ways, such as unstructured similarity or high token frequency, end up overestimating the goodness of many outcomes. A model without these abilities is more constrained, and has the advantage that it can more narrowly predict which analogical inferences speakers actually make. In this section I discuss one final restriction, concerning the direction of analogical inference.

Logically, statements about the relation between one form and another could be made in either direction. For example, statements about the correspondence of stressed and unstressed root allomorphs could relate either form to the other, symmetrically or asymmetrically, as in (18). This means that in principle, analogical inferences could proceed in multiple directions, both from stressless to stressed (e.g., *rentár:rénta* :: *sentár:*sénta*) and stressed to stressless (e.g., *siénta:sentár* :: *oriénta:*orentár*).

(18)   Some logically possible directions of influence (solid and doubled lines represent progressively greater pattern strength)

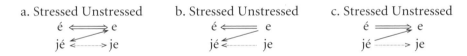

a. Stressed Unstressed   b. Stressed Unstressed   c. Stressed Unstressed

What we observe, however, is a striking restriction: both in historical change (Penny 2002; Morris 2005) and child errors (Clahsen, Aveledo, and Roca 2002), there is an overwhelming (or even exclusive) tendency for analogical rebuilding of stressed forms (i.e., *rentár:rénta* :: *sentár:*sénta*), consistent with (18b).[8] A typical example from the Spanish portion of CHILDES is given in (19).

(19)   Overgeneralization of stressed mid vowels (Jorge, age 6; 1)

    y   estonces   **volo*   a   la   pastelería
    and then (=*entonces*) fly-1sg (=*vuelo*) to   the   pastry shop
    '. . . and then I fly to the pastry shop'

---

[8] Rebuilding stressless forms to include diphthongs has been reported in some dialects of Spanish (Judeo-Spanish, New Mexico Spanish). This data should be treated with care, however, since the morphology of these dialects also differs in more radical ways from literary Spanish. A similar effect is also reported in the experimental results of Bybee and Pardo (1981), but my preliminary attempts to replicate this finding have so far been unsuccessful.

Remarkably, the converse error (e.g., infinitive **vuelar* instead of *volar*) never occurs, and children also apparently never substitute mid vowels for nonalternating diphthongs (e.g., *él *frecónta* 'he frequents' instead of *frecuénta*). Similarly asymmetric error patterns have also been observed for Greek (Kazazis 1969), German (Clahsen, Aveledo, and Roca 2002) and Korean (Kang 2006), and appear to be the norm among children acquiring languages with morphophonological alternations. An explanatory model of analogy must be able to capture and ideally even predict such asymmetries.

Characterizing the direction of analogy has been a longstanding preoccupation in the historical linguistics literature, and numerous tendencies have been observed (Kuryłowicz 1947; Mańczak 1980; Bybee 1985, and many others). The Spanish case seems atypical in several respects. It has sometimes been claimed that more frequent paradigm members are more influential (Mańczak 1980; Bybee 1985). In Spanish, the most frequent paradigm members (3sg, 1sg, 2sg) are all stressed, which should favor a stressed → stressless direction of influence. What we observe, however, is that the more frequent stressed forms are rebuilt on the basis of the less frequent stressless forms, counter to the more usual trend. Furthermore, it is often the case that the most influential forms are also less marked (in some intuitive sense of morphosyntactic markedness). What we see in Spanish, however, is that the 3sg, which is almost universally agreed to be the least marked combination of person and number features, is rebuilt on the basis of non-singular, non-third-person forms. Furthermore, diphthongs appear in the majority of present-tense indicative forms (the 1sg, 2sg, 3sg, and 3pl = 4 out of 6), yet reanalysis is done on the basis of the minority stressless forms. In short, the direction of influence that prevails in Spanish does not appear to follow from any general principle of frequency or markedness.

Albright (2002*a, b*) proposes that speakers generalize in some directions and not others because of a restriction on how paradigm structure is encoded. In particular, it is proposed that paradigms have an intrinsically asymmetrical organization in which certain forms are designated as "basic" and the remaining forms are derived from them by grammatical rules. For example, the error data suggests that in Spanish, a stressless form of the root (as found in the infinitive, 1pl, or 2pl) is taken as basic, and stressed forms are predicted—sometimes incorrectly—on the basis of a stressless form. The challenge is to understand why Spanish speakers choose this particular direction, and why paradigm organization may differ from language to language.

One principle of paradigm organization, explored also by Finkel and Stump (this volume), is PREDICTABILITY: a form is basic (≈ a PRINCIPAL PART) if it contains enough information to predict other forms in the paradigm. As Finkel and Stump point out, there are many ways in which paradigms could be organized around predictive forms, depending on how many basic forms we are allowed to refer to, whether paradigm structure may differ from class to class, and so on. Many paradigm-based theories of morphology designate specific forms as "reference forms" in one way or another, and use these forms as the basis of computation for the remaining forms in the paradigm (Wurzel 1989; Stump 2001; J. P. Blevins 2006). Albright (2002*a*) adopts a particularly restrictive hypothesis: paradigm structure is the same (static) across all lexical items, and each form in the paradigm is based on just one other base form. The task of the learner is to find the base forms that permit the most accurate mappings, while still obeying this restriction.

The base identification algorithm, in brief, works as follows: the learner starts with a small batch of initial input data, consisting of paradigmatically related forms (1sg, 2sg, 3sg, etc.). Each one of these forms is considered as a potential base form, and the minimal generalization learner is used to find sets of rules that derive the remaining forms in the grammar. The result is a set of competing organizations, shown in Figure 9.3. In the usual case, at least some parts of the paradigm suffer from phonological or morphological neutralizations, with the result that not every form is equally successful at predicting the remainder of the paradigm. In these cases, some of the competing grammars will be less certain or accurate than others. The learner compares the candidate organizations to determine which form is associated with the most accurate rules, and this is chosen as the base for the remainder of the paradigm. This process may also be run recursively among the derived forms, to establish additional intermediate bases. (See Albright 2002*a, b* for details.)

When this procedure is run on an input of Spanish present-tense verb paradigms, the organization in Figure 9.4 results. Crucially, due to the restriction that each form be based on exactly one other base form, the model allows only five possible directions of inference (out of $5 \times 6 = 30$ logical possible pairwise relations). Some of these relations, such as infinitive

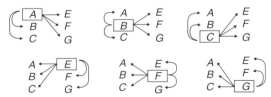

FIGURE 9.3 Candidate grammars, using asymmetrical mappings from a single base

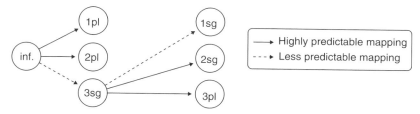

FIGURE 9.4 Predicted organization of Spanish present-tense paradigms

→ 1pl or 3sg →2sg, are virtually 100% predictable, and leave no room for error. The greatest opportunities for analogical errors involve the mapping from stressless to stressed forms (here, infinitive → 3sg), and to the 1sg in particular. In fact, both of these mappings correspond to attested child errors:

(20) Stem errors among children acquiring Spanish (Clahsen, Aveledo, and Roca 2002)
  a. Stressed stem replaced by stressless stem:
      *volo for vuelo 'fly-1sg', *juga for juega 'play-3sg', *tene for tiene 'have-3sg', *teno for tengo 'have-1sg'
  b. Irregular 1sg replaced by stem from 3sg:
      *tieno for tengo 'have-1sg'; *sabo for sé 'I know'; *conozo for conozco 'I know'; *parezo for parezco 'I appear'; *salo for salgo 'I leave'; *oyo for oigo 'I hear'

Although this analysis is somewhat skeletal and leaves many broader questions about paradigm structure unanswered,[9] it highlights some of the virtues of a rule-based model of analogy. In particular, grammatical formalisms place strong restrictions on possible analogical inferences by dictating which forms may be effected, which patterns can be extended, and so on. Naturally, the strength and nature of these restrictions may vary considerably depending on the formalism; I have argued here in favor of a grammar of probabilistic context-sensitive rules that asymmetrically relate forms in the

---

[9] In particular, it is natural to wonder how such a restrictive model could cope with systems that involve significantly more ambiguity—i.e., systems that motivate multiple principal parts in Finkel and Stump's terms. It is important to keep in mind that nothing in the current model precludes the possibility that at a given point in time, languages may exhibit patterns that may be characterized as symmetrical predictability relations. A prediction of the asymmetrical model, however, is that learners will learn implications in just one direction, and that analogical generalizations should therefore go primarily in one direction. One type of data that is often telling in this regard is the relative size and frequency of the inflectional classes involved. Frequently classes that can be distinguished only in derived (nonbasic) forms are small and consist of words with high token frequency, which may be correlated with their status as memorized exceptions rather than as grammatically principled forms.

paradigm, but other formalisms are possible. The advantage of such a restrictive model is that it makes very specific and testable predictions about possible errors, and presumably also eventual historical changes. In the cases examined, these predictions appear to be substantially correct.

9.5 Conclusion

The results in the preceding sections have a common theme: in each case, the data of Spanish contains patterns that might logically lead to analogical inferences, yet speakers appear not to generalize them to novel or unknown items. I have argued that this reveals fundamental restrictions on how speakers learn to encode linguistic knowledge, which make these patterns either inaccessible or unimpressive. Furthermore, I have shown that a model based on probabilistic context-sensitive rules is well suited to capturing these restrictions. First, it limits the type of similarity relations that are relevant in supporting analogy: they must be "structured" in the sense that supporting analogs must all share a set of properties that are reliably correlated with class membership. As shown in Section 9.2, speakers, too, appear to obey this restriction, and models that lack such structure overpredict the goodness of many logically possible inferences. In addition, attributing analogy to a grammar of rules leads us to expect that generalizations should be based on high type frequency of similar words, and that token frequency should be irrelevant; in Section 9.3, we saw that this, too, appears to be correct. Finally, rewrite rules are an intrinsically directional formalism (A → B), corresponding to the idea that inference proceeds in some directions but not others. In Section 9.4, I argued that a model of paradigm structure based on predictability relations between related forms can predict which directions speakers actually choose, in a way that appears to line up well with data from child errors and historical change. In each case, the payoff of the more restrictive formalism is clear: it provides an account for why some errors occur and some do not, providing a more explanatory model of how speakers carry out analogy in morphophonological systems.

The examples discussed here are also intended to highlight some virtues of computationally implemented models of analogy. At the most basic level, the models facilitate a quantitative assessment of the relative contribution of different types of analogical reasoning, by allowing us to compare directly the predictions of models with and without a particular capacity. Such comparisons are potentially quite important in an area where it is easy to posit many potentially relevant factors (high token frequency, semantic effects, phonetic factors, etc.), but difficult to establish their explanatory value. Equally important, though, is the role that modeling may play in shaping and refining theoretical distinctions. An example of this was seen in Section 9.2.4, in which comparison of the two models required a more careful definition of the concept of structured similarity, and testing the distinction was only possible by interpreting one model with respect to the other. We are only beginning to develop the analytical tools needed to construct theoretical arguments from such modeling results. I hope to have shown, however, that computational modeling can play a role not only in testing, but also in developing theories of what constitutes a possible analogy.

10

Words and paradigms bit by bit: An information-theoretic approach to the processing of inflection and derivation

Petar Milin, Victor Kuperman, Aleksandar Kostić, and R. Harald Baayen

10.1 Introduction

Syntagmatically oriented theories of word structure have inspired most of the experimental work on morphological processing. The way inflection is modeled by Levelt *et al.* (1999), for instance, comes close to the theory of distributed morphology proposed by Halle and Marantz (1993). In Levelt's model of speech production, nodes at the lemma stratum (what would be the lexeme stratum in the terminology of Aronoff (1994)) are marked for features such as tense, aspect, number, and person. For a given set of feature values, a node at the form stratum will be activated, e.g., *-ed* for the past tense in English. Paradigmatic relations do not have a place in this model; in fact, it is a design feature of the model that paradigmatic relations at the level of word forms are predicted to be irrelevant.

A syntagmatic bias is also visible in the comprehension model proposed by Schreuder and Baayen (1995). In this model, there is no principled difference between stems or words on the one hand, and affixes (whether inflectional or derivational) on the other hand. In their three-layered network, with access units, lemma units, and semantic and syntactic feature units, the organization of nodes within a layer is arbitrary. Paradigmatic relations do not play a role, they are simply deemed to be irrelevant. The same holds for the dual mechanism model of Pinker (1991, 1999).

In this chapter, we present a line of research that departs from the syntagmatic orientation of mainstream experimental psycholinguistics, and that is close in spirit to word and paradigm morphology (WPM, Hockett 1954; Matthews 1974; Anderson 1992; Aronoff 1994; Beard 1995; J. P. Blevins 2003, 2006*b*). WPM questions the morphemic status of lexical formatives, and assumes that words (both simple and complex) are the basic units in the lexicon. Furthermore, in WPM, inflected words are organized into paradigms, which are further organized into inflectional classes.[1]

From a processing perspective, the central tenets of WPM imply, first, that complex words, including regular inflected words, leave traces in long-term lexical memory, and second, that the processing of a given word is codetermined by paradigmatically related words.

A central diagnostic for the presence of memory traces in long-term memory has been the word frequency effect. A higher frequency of use allows for shorter processing latencies in both visual and auditory comprehension (cf. Baayen *et al.* 2003*a*; New *et al.* 2004; Baayen *et al.* 2006, etc.), and lower rates of speech errors in production (Stemberger and MacWhinney 1986). The effect of word frequency tends to be stronger for irregular complex words than for regular complex words, and stronger for derived words than for inflected words. But even for regular inflected words, the effect of prior experience clearly emerges (Baayen *et al.* 2008*c*), contrary to the claims of the dual mechanism model. The ubiquitous effect of word frequency shows that large numbers of complex words are indeed available in the (mental) lexicon, as claimed by WPM.

The focus of this chapter is on the second central processing consequence of WPM, namely, that paradigmatic organization should codetermine lexical processing. For derivational morphology, work on the morphological family size effect (see, e.g., Moscoso del Prado Martín *et al.* 2004) has clarified that processing of a given word is codetermined by other morphologically related words. This constitutes evidence for paradigmatic organization in the mental lexicon. However, morphological families are very heterogeneous, and do not readily allow words to be grouped into higher-order sets similar to inflectional classes. Therefore, the morphological family size effect provides at best circumstantial evidence for the central ideas of WPM.

In the remainder of this chapter, we first review a series of recent experimental studies which explore the role of paradigmatic structure specifically

---

[1] In what follows, we will use the term *inflectional paradigm* to refer to the set of inflected variants of a given lexeme, and the term *inflectional class* to refer to a set of lexemes that use the same set of exponents in their inflectional paradigms.

for inflected words. We then present new experimental results showing how the principles that structure inflectional paradigms can be generalized to subsets of derived words.

The approach to morphological organization and morphological processing that we describe in this chapter departs significantly from both theoretical morphology and mainstream of experimental psycholinguistics in that it applies central concepts from information theory to lexical processing. The greater the amount of information carried by an event (e.g., a word's inflected variant, an exponent, or an inflectional class), the smaller the probability of that event, and the greater the corresponding processing costs (see, for a similar approach to syntax, Levy 2008). We believe that information theory offers exactly the right tools for studying the processing consequences of paradigmatic relations. Furthermore, we do believe that the concepts of information science provide us with excellent tools to probe the *functional organization of the mental lexicon*, but we shall remain agnostic about how paradigmatic structures are implemented in the brain.

We begin this chapter with an introduction to a number of central concepts from information theory and illustrate how these concepts can be applied to the different levels of paradigmatic organization in the mental lexicon. We then focus on three key issues: (i) the processing cost of an exponent given its inflectional class, (ii) the processing cost associated with inflectional paradigms and inflectional classes, and (iii) the processing cost that arises when the probabilistic distributional properties of paradigms and classes diverge.

In what follows, we first provide a comprehensive review of previous experimental findings that use information-theoretic measures of lexical connectivity. We then present some new results that provide further empirical support for the relevance of paradigmatic organization for lexical processing, and for the importance of information-theoretic measures for gauging the processing consequences of paradigmatic structure. As we proceed through our discussion of the empirical evidence, it will become increasingly clear that there is a remarkable convergence between the psycholinguistic evidence and WPM.

Some of the key findings of the general approach to the (mental) lexicon outlined in this chapter can be summarized as follows:

1. Lexemes and their inflected variants are organized hierarchically. One can envision this organization as a higher layer of lexemes grouped into morphological families, and a lower level of inflected variants, which enter into paradigmatic relations within a given lexeme.

2. Inflected variants of any given lexeme are organized into paradigms, and all lexemes that form their paradigms in the same way define an inflectional class. Empirical evidence suggests that the degree to which the inflectional paradigm of a given lexeme diverges from its inflectional class affects cognitive processing over and above other relevant factors: the greater the divergence, the more costly the processing.

3. Results which will be presented here for the first time show that the processing of English derivatives can be seen as analogical. During lexical processing, a given derivative is compared with its base word, and pitted against the generalized knowledge about the relationship between all derivatives of the same type and their corresponding base words.

4. The *family size effect*, which is known to be a semantic effect, probably represents the joint effect of both semantic similarity and morphological paradigmatic structure.

10.2 Central concepts from information theory

A fundamental insight of information theory is that the amount of information I carried by (linguistic) unit u can be defined as the negative binary logarithm of its probability:

$$I_u = -\log_2 \Pr(u). \tag{1}$$

Consider someone in the tip-of-the tongue state saying *the eh eh eh eh eh eh key*. The word *eh* has the greatest probability, 6/8, and is least informative. Its amount of information is $-\log_2(6/8) = 0.415$ bits. The words *the* and *key* have a probability of 1/8 and the amount of information they carry is 3 bits. In what follows, we assume that lexical units that have a higher information load are more costly to access in long-term memory. Hence, we expect processing costs to be proportional to the amount of information. This is exactly what the word frequency effect tells us: higher-frequency words, which have lower information loads, are processed faster than low-frequency, high-information words.

We estimate probabilities from relative frequencies. By way of illustration, consider the inflected variants of the Serbian feminine noun *planina* ('mountain'). Serbian nouns have six cases and two numbers. Due to syncretism, the twelve combinations of case and number are represented by only six distinct inflected variants. These inflected variants are listed in column 1 of the upper part of Table 10.1. The second column lists the frequencies of these inflected variants in a two-million word corpus of written Serbian.

TABLE 10.1 Inflected nouns in Serbian. The upper part of the table shows inflected variants for the feminine noun *planina* ('mountain'), the lower part shows the inflected variants of the masculine noun *prostor* ('space'). Columns present frequencies and relative frequencies of the respective inflectional paradigm and the class to which it belongs.

feminine nouns						
Inflected variant	Inflected variant frequency	Inflected variant relative frequency	Information of inflected variant	Exponent frequency	Exponent relative frequency	Information of exponent
	$F(w_e)$	$\Pr_\pi(w_e)$	I_{w_e}	$F(e)$	$\Pr_\pi(e)$	I_e
planin-*a*	169	0.31	1.69	18715	0.26	1.94
planin-*u*	48	0.09	3.47	9918	0.14	2.84
planin-*e*	191	0.35	1.51	27803	0.39	1.36
planin-*i*	88	0.16	2.64	7072	0.1	3.32
planin-*om*	30	0.05	4.32	4265	0.06	4.06
planin-*ama*	26	0.05	4.32	4409	0.06	4.06

masculine nouns						
Inflected variant	Inflected variant frequency	Inflected variant relative frequency	Information of inflected variant	Exponent frequency	Exponent relative frequency	Information of exponent
	$F(w_e)$	$\Pr_\pi(w_e)$	I_{w_e}	$F(e)$	$\Pr_\pi(e)$	I_e
prostor-*ϕ*	153	0.38	1.40	25399	0.35	1.51
prostor-*a*	69	0.17	2.56	18523	0.26	1.94
prostor-*u*	67	0.17	2.56	8409	0.12	3.06
prostor-*om*	15	0.04	4.64	3688	0.05	4.32
prostor-*e*	48	0.12	3.06	5634	0.08	3.64
prostor-*i*	23	0.06	4.06	6772	0.09	3.47
prostor-*ima*	23	0.06	4.06	3169	0.04	4.64

We consider two complementary ways of estimating probabilities from frequencies. The probabilities listed in the third column of Table 10.1 are obtained by normalizing the frequency counts with respect to a lexeme's inflectional paradigm (column three). More specifically, the probability $\Pr_\pi(w_e)$[2] of an inflected variant w_e of lexeme w is estimated in this table as

---

[2] Here and in what follows we use $\Pr_\pi$ to denote probabilities defined with respect to paradigmatic sets.

its form-specific frequency F (hence-forth *word frequency*) of occurrence, normalized for the sum of the frequencies of all the distinct inflected variants of its lexeme, henceforth *stem frequency*:

$$\Pr_{\pi}(w_e) = \frac{F(w_e)}{\Sigma_e F(w_e)}.$$ (2)

The corresponding amounts of information, obtained by applying (1), are listed in column four. Table 10.1 also lists the frequencies of the six exponents (column 5), calculated by summing the word frequencies of all forms in the corpus with these exponents. The probabilities listed for these exponents (column six) are obtained by normalizing with respect to the summed frequencies of these exponents:

$$\Pr_{\pi}(e) = \frac{F(e)}{\Sigma_e F(w_e)}.$$ (3)

The corresponding amount of information is listed in column seven.

The second way in which we can estimate probabilities is by normalizing with respect to the number of tokens N in the corpus. The probability of a lexeme w is then estimated as the sum of the frequencies of its inflected variants, divided by N:

$$\Pr_N(w) = \frac{F(w)}{N} = \frac{\Sigma_e F(w_e)}{N}.$$ (4)

In this approach, the probability of an inflected variant can be construed as the joint probability of its lexeme w and its exponent:

$$\Pr_N(w_e) = \Pr(w, e)$$
$$= \Pr(e, w)$$
$$= \frac{F(w_e)}{N}.$$ (5)

Likewise, the probability $\Pr(e)$ of an exponent (e.g., *-a* for nominative singular and genitive plural in Serbian feminine nouns) can be quantified as the relative frequency of occurrence of e in the corpus:

$$\Pr_N(e) = \frac{F(e)}{N}.$$ (6)

The probabilities considered thus far are unconditional, a priori, decontextualized probabilities. As exponents appear in the context of stems, we need to consider the conditional probability of an exponent given its lexeme, $Pr(e|w)$. Using Bayes' theorem, we rewrite this probability as:

$$\begin{aligned}
\text{Pr}_N(e|w) &= \frac{\text{Pr}_N(e,w)}{\text{Pr}_N(w)} \\
&= \frac{F(w_e)}{N} \frac{N}{F(w)} \\
&= \frac{F(w_e)}{F(w)} \\
&= \text{Pr}_\pi(w_e).
\end{aligned} \tag{7}$$

Likewise, the conditional probability of the lemma given the exponent is defined as:

$$\begin{aligned}
\text{Pr}_N(w|e) &= \frac{\text{Pr}_N(w,e)}{\text{Pr}_N(e)} \\
&= \frac{F(w_e)}{N} \frac{N}{F(e)} \\
&= \frac{F(w_e)}{F(e)}.
\end{aligned} \tag{8}$$

For each lexical probability we can compute the corresponding amount of information. We allow for the possibility that each source of information may have its own distinct effect on lexical processing by means of positive weights ω_{1-5}:

$$\begin{aligned}
\text{I}_{w_e} &= -\omega_1 \log_2 F(w_e) + \omega_1 \log_2 N \\
\text{I}_w &= -\omega_2 \log_2 F(w) + \omega_2 \log_2 N \\
\text{I}_e &= -\omega_3 \log_2 F(e) + \omega_3 \log_2 N \\
\text{I}_{e|w} &= -\omega_4 \log_2 F(w_e) + \omega_4 \log_2 F(w) \\
\text{I}_{w|e} &= -\omega_5 \log_2 F(w_e) + \omega_5 \log_2 F(e).
\end{aligned} \tag{9}$$

We assume that the cost of retrieving lexical information from long-term memory is proportional to the amount of information retrieved. Hence the cost of processing an inflected word w_e is proportional to at least the amounts of information in (9). More formally, we can express this processing cost (measured experimentally as a reaction time RT) as a linear function:

$$RT \propto I_{w_e} + I_w + I_e + I_{e|w} + I_{w|e}$$
$$= (\omega_1 + \omega_2 + \omega_3) \log_2 N - (\omega_1 + \omega_4 + \omega_5) \log_2 F(w_e)$$
$$- (\omega_2 - \omega_4) \log_2 F(w) - (\omega_3 - \omega_5) \log_2 F(e). \tag{10}$$

There are several predictions for the effects of lexical probabilities on lexical processing that follow directly from (10). First, word frequency $F(w_e)$ will always elicit a facilitatory effect, as all its coefficients have a negative sign in (10). Second, stem frequency $F(w)$ may either facilitate or inhibit processing, depending on the relative strengths of the coefficients ω_2 and ω_4. These two coefficients balance the importance of a word's probability as such (see the second equation in (9)), and its importance as the domain on which the probabilities of its inflectional variants are conditioned (see the fourth equation in (9)). Third, the frequency of the exponent can also either speed up or hinder processing depending on the values of ω_3 and ω_5. These two weights balance the importance of an exponent's probability as such (see the first equation in (9)) and the exponent as the domain on which the probability of inflected forms with that exponent are conditioned (see the fifth equation in (9)). The first two predictions are supported by the large-scale regression studies reported by Baayen *et al.* (2008c) and Kuperman *et al.* (2008).

We now proceed from basic lexical probabilities that operate at the level of individual inflected words to the quantification of the information carried by inflectional paradigms and inflectional classes. The paradigm of a given lexeme can be associated with a distribution of probabilities $\{Pr_\pi(w_e)\}$. For *planina* in Table 10.1, this probability distribution is given in column three. The amount of information carried by its paradigm as a whole is given by the *entropy* of the paradigm's probability distribution:

$$H = - \sum_e Pr_\pi(w_e) \log_2 (Pr_\pi(w_e)). \tag{11}$$

Formally, H is the expected (weighted average) amount of information in a paradigm. The entropy increases with the number of members of the paradigm. It also increases when the probabilities of the members are more similar. For a given number of members, the entropy is maximal when all probabilities are the same. H also represents the average number of binary decisions required to identify a member of the paradigm, i.e., to reduce all uncertainty about which member of the paradigm is at issue, provided that the paradigm is represented by an optimal binary coding. We illustrate the concept of optimal coding in Figure 10.1 using as an example the inflectional class of regular feminine nouns in Serbian.

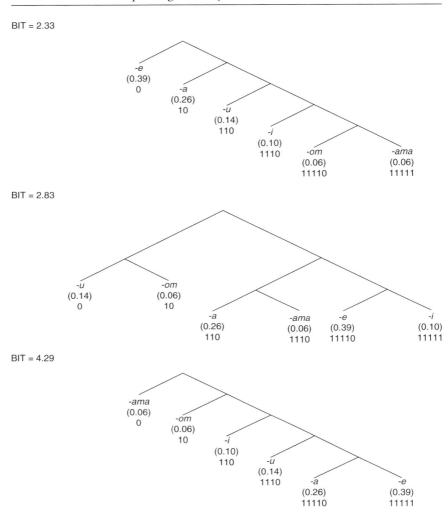

FIGURE 10.1 Optimal and nonoptimal binary coding schemes for the inflectional class of regular feminine nouns in Serbian.

The upper panel of Figure 10.1 shows an optimal binary coding scheme, in which the most probable exponent (-*e*, Pr$_\pi$ = 0.39) occupies the highest leaf node in the tree. The lower the probability of the other exponents, the lower in the tree they are located. Thus, the exponents with the lowest probabilities in the inflectional class, -*om* (Pr$_\pi$ = 0.06) and -*ama* (Pr$_\pi$ = 0.06) are found at the lowest leaf nodes. The second panel of Figure 10.1 represents another possible coding, which is suboptimal in that some exponents with relatively high probabilities are located below lower-probability exponents in the tree. Finally, the third panel shows the least optimal coding, in which the less probable the exponent is, the *higher* it is positioned in the tree. The average number of binary decisions (the number of bits) required to identify a given paradigm member, i.e., to reach the paradigm member's leaf node when starting at the root node of the tree, is the sum of the products of the number of steps and the members' probabilities. This average is never greater than the entropy of the paradigm $H + 1$ (Ross 1988). For the upper panel of Figure 10.1, the average number of binary decisions is 2.33 bits, for the coding in the second panel, it is 2.83, and for the worst coding in the third panel, it is 4.29. In Section 10.4 we will review experimental studies showing that paradigmatic entropies codetermine lexical processing.

Thus far, we have considered probabilities and the corresponding entropy at the level of the inflectional class of regular feminine nouns in Serbian. However, the probability distribution of the inflected variants of a given lexeme may differ substantially from the probability distribution of the exponents at the level of the inflectional class. As a consequence, the corresponding entropies may differ substantially from each other as well. The extent to which these probability distributions differ is quantified by the relative entropy, also known as Kullback-Leibler divergence. Consider again the Serbian feminine noun *planina* 'mountain' and its inflectional class as shown in Table 10.1. The third column lists the estimated probabilities for the paradigm, and the sixth column lists the probability distribution of the class. Let P denote the probability distribution of the paradigm, and Q the probability distribution of the inflectional class. The relative entropy can now be introduced as:

$$D(P \parallel Q) = \sum_e \Pr_\pi(w_e) \log_2 \frac{\Pr_\pi(w_e)}{\Pr_\pi(e)}. \tag{12}$$

Relative entropy is also known as *information gain,*

$$\begin{aligned}
D(P \parallel Q) &= IG(\Pr_\pi(e|w) \parallel \Pr_\pi(e|c)) \\
&= \sum_e \Pr_\pi(e|w) \log_2 \frac{\Pr_\pi(e|w)}{\Pr_\pi(e|c)} \\
&= \sum_e \Pr_\pi(w_e) \log_2 \frac{\Pr_\pi(w_e)}{\Pr_\pi(e)}, \tag{13}
\end{aligned}$$

as it measures the reduction in our uncertainty about the exponent (e) when going from the situation in which we only know its inflectional class (c) to the situation in which we also know the lexeme (w). For *planina*, $H = 2.22$, and $D(P \| Q) = 0.05$. For the masculine noun *prostor* listed in the lower half of Table 10.1, $H = 2.42$ and $D(P \| Q) = 0.07$. In both cases, the two distributions are fairly similar, so the relative entropies (RE) are small. There is little that the knowledge of *planina* adds to what we already new about regular feminine nouns. If we approximate the probability distribution of *planina* with the probability distribution of its class, we are doing quite well. In Section 10.4.2 we review a recent study demonstrating that RE is yet another information-theoretic predictor of lexical processing costs.

We will now review a series of studies that illustrate how these information theoretic concepts help us to understand paradigmatic organization in the mental lexicon. Section 10.3 addresses the question of how the probability of an exponent given its inflectional class is reflected in measures of lexical processing costs. Section 10.4 reviews studies that make use of entropy and relative entropy to gauge lexical processing and paradigmatic organization. Finally, in Section 10.5 we present new experimental results showing how concepts from information theory that proved useful for understanding inflection can help understanding derivation.

10.3 The structure of inflectional classes

The consequence of the amount of information carried by an exponent for lexical processing has been explored in a series of experimental studies on Serbian (Kostić 1991, 1995; Kostić *et al.* 2003). A starting point for this line of research is the amount of information carried by an exponent,

$$I_e = -\log_2 \text{Pr}_\pi(e),$$

where Pr_π is estimated over all exponents within a class π. Kostić and colleagues noted that exponents are not equal with respect to their functional load. Some exponents (given their inflectional class) express only a few functions and meanings, others express many. Table 10.2 lists the functions and meanings for the exponents of the masculine and regular feminine inflectional class of Serbian. The count of numbers of functions and meanings for a given exponent were taken from an independent comprehensive lexicological survey of Serbian (see also the appendix of Kostić *et al.* 2003, for a shortlist of functions and meanings). Instead of using just the flat corpus-based relative frequencies, Kostić and colleagues propose to weight these probabilities for their functions and meanings. Let R_e denote the number of functions and meanings carried by exponent e. Then the weighted amount of information I'_e can be expressed as follows:

TABLE 10.2 Exponents, case and number, frequency of the exponent, number of functions and meanings of the exponents, and amount of information carried by the exponents, for masculine nouns (upper table) and regular feminine nouns (lower table).

	masculine nouns			
Exponent	Case and Number	Frequency	Functions and Meanings	Information
ϕ	nom sg	12.83	3	0.434
a	gen sg/acc sg /gen pl	18.01	109	5.128
u	dat sg /loc sg	4.64	43	5.744
om	ins sg	1.90	32	6.608
e	acc pl	2.21	58	7.243
i	nom pl	3.33	3	2.381
ima	dat pl/loc pl/ins pl	1.49	75	8.186

	feminine nouns			
Exponent	Case and Number	Frequency	Functions and Meanings	Information
a	nom sg/gen pl	12.06	54	1.464
u	acc sg	5.48	58	2.705
e	gen sg /nom pl/acc pl	14.20	112	2.280
i	dat sg /loc sg	3.80	43	2.803
om	ins sg	1.94	32	3.346
ama	dat pl/loc pl/ins pl	1.69	75	4.773

$$I'_e = -\log_2 \left(\frac{\mathrm{Pr}_\pi(e)/R_e}{\Sigma_e \mathrm{Pr}_\pi(e)/R_e} \right) \tag{14}$$

The ratio $(\mathrm{Pr}_\pi(e)/R_e)$ gives us the average probability per syntactic function/ meaning for a given exponent. In order to take the other exponents within the inflectional class into account, this ratio is weighted by the sum of the ratios for each of the exponents (see, e.g., Luce 1959). The resulting proportion is log-transformed to obtain the corresponding amount of information in bits. The partial effects of probability on the one hand, and the number of functions and meanings on the other, are shown in Figure 10.2. The weighted information is predicted to decrease with probability, and to increase with the number of functions and meanings. Table 10.2 lists I'_e for each of the exponents of the masculine and regular feminine inflectional classes.

To assess the predictivity of I'_e, Kostić *et al.* (2003) and Kostić (2008) calculated the mean lexical decision latency for each exponent in a given inflectional class, and investigated whether these mean latencies can be

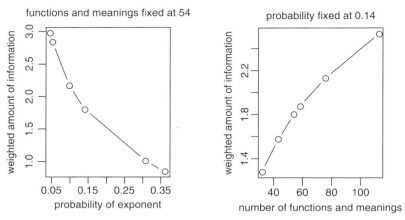

FIGURE 10.2 Partial effects of the probability of an exponent and its number of syntactic functions and meanings on the weighted amount of information I'_e.

predicted from the weighted amounts of information such as those listed in Table 10.2. The Pearson correlation between the mean latencies and the weighted information scores was highly significant for both masculine and feminine nouns ($R^2 = 0.88$ for masculine nouns, $R^2 = 0.98$ for regular feminine nouns and $R^2 = 0.99$ for irregular feminine nouns). Furthermore, when mean reaction time is regressed on the weighted information load, the slopes of the regression lines are positive. Exponents carrying a greater average amount of information are more difficult to process. In other words, these data show that the average processing cost of an exponent in its inflectional class is very well predicted from its frequency and its functional load as given by (14) and illustrated above in Figure 10.2.

The probabilities that we considered in these analyses were estimated by summing across all words with a given exponent in a given inflectional class. In this way, the information about the probabilities of the different exponents in the inflectional paradigms of specific words is lost. In order to address the possibility that word-specific probabilities of exponents also codetermine lexical processing, Kostić *et al.* (2003) first applied the same weighting scheme underlying (14) at the level of individual lexemes, giving a lexeme-specific weighted information I'_{w_e}:

$$I'_{w_e} = -\log_2\left(\frac{\Pr_\pi(w_e)/R_e}{\Sigma_e \Pr_\pi(w_e)/R_e}\right). \tag{15}$$

Kostić *et al.* (2003) then constructed two sets of lexemes (henceforth Inflectional Groups) which contrasted maximally with respect to I'_{w_e}. For each of the two inflectional groups, the average value of I'_{w_e} for each of the exponents was calculated. Regression analysis showed that these group-averaged amounts of information contributed independently to the model, over and above the general class-based information values I'_e. As before, larger values for the group-averaged amounts of information I'_{w_e} corresponded to longer mean lexical decision latencies.

It is useful to probe the lexeme-specific weighted information (15) with respect to how it relates to the frequency properties of the lexeme and its inflected variants, as well as to the functional ambiguities existing in inflectional paradigms and classes. First, consider a simple lower bound for (15):

$$
\begin{aligned}
I'_{w_e} &= -\log_2 \left(\frac{\mathrm{Pr}_\pi(w_e)/R_e}{\sum_e \mathrm{Pr}_\pi(w_e)/R_{w_e}} \right) \\
&= -\log_2 \frac{\mathrm{Pr}_\pi(w_e)}{R_e} + \log_2 \sum_e \frac{\mathrm{Pr}_\pi(w_e)}{R_e} \\
&\geq -\log_2 \mathrm{Pr}_\pi(w_e) + \log_2 R_e + \log_2 \prod_e \frac{\mathrm{Pr}_\pi(w_e)}{R_e} \\
&\geq -\log_2 \mathrm{Pr}_\pi(w_e) + \log_2 R_e + \sum_e \log_2 \frac{\mathrm{Pr}_\pi(w_e)}{R_e} \\
&\geq \log_2 R_e - \sum_e \log_2 R_e - \log_2 \mathrm{Pr}_\pi(w_e) + \sum_e \log_2 \mathrm{Pr}_\pi w_e. \quad (16)
\end{aligned}
$$

The third term is the amount of information carried by the inflected variant, I_{w_e}, see (2), and $\sum_j \log_2 \mathrm{Pr}_\pi w_j$ is a measure of the lexeme's stem frequency, evaluated by summing the log frequencies of its inflected variants rather than by summing the bare frequencies of its inflected variants. Consequently, at the level of the inflected variant, the amount of information (16) incorporates two well-known frequency effects that have been studied extensively in the processing literature. The word frequency effect ($-\log_2 \mathrm{Pr}_\pi(w_e)$) is facilitatory, as expected. Surprisingly, the stem frequency effect ($\sum_e \log_2 \mathrm{Pr}_\pi w_e$) is predicted to be inhibitory. However, both frequency effects are complemented by measures gauging ambiguity. Ambiguity of the given exponent is harmful, whereas ambiguity in the rest of the paradigm is facilitatory. Thus, the stem frequency effect emerges from this model as a composite effect with both an inhibitory and a facilitatory component. This may help explain why stem frequency effects are often much less robustly attested in experimental data (see, e.g., Baayen *et al.* 2008c) compared to word frequency effects.

In order to evaluate how well the lower bound given in (16) approximates the original measure given in (15), we examined the exponent frequency, the

TABLE 10.3 Mean reaction times in visual lexical decision (RT), exponent frequency, number of functions and meanings of the exponent (R), weighted amount of information (I′), and Inflectional Group (high versus low by-word amount of information) for the Exponents of the regular feminine declension class.

Exponent	Exponent frequency	R	I′	Inflectional Group	RT
a	12.06	3.99	1.46	high	674
e	14.20	4.72	2.28	high	687
i	3.80	3.76	2.80	high	685
u	5.48	4.06	2.71	high	693
om	1.94	3.47	3.35	high	718
ama	1.69	4.32	4.77	high	744
a	12.06	3.99	1.46	low	687
e	14.20	4.72	2.28	low	685
i	3.80	3.76	2.80	low	730
u	5.48	4.06	2.71	low	712
om	1.94	3.47	3.35	low	722
ama	1.69	4.32	4.77	low	746

group averages of the functions and meanings, the information values, and the mean reaction times for the two inflectional groups for regular feminine nouns, as listed in Table 10.3 (data from Kostić *et al.* 2003). Note that the terms in (16) represent the ambiguity of the exponent, the joint ambiguity of all exponents, the word frequency effect of the inflected variant, and the stem frequency effect of its lexeme.

For the data in Table 10.3, we first carried out a linear regression analysis with RT as dependent variable and I′ and Inflectional Group as predictors. The R^2 for this model was 0.863. We then carried out a linear regression analysis, but now with the two measures that figure in the lower bound of the amount of information (16) as predictors: exponent frequency and the number of functions and meanings of the exponent R. The R^2 of this model was 0.830. Furthermore, the effect of the number of functions and meanings was inhibitory ($\hat{\beta} = 27.5, t(8) = 2.512, p = 0.0362$) and the effect of exponent frequency was facilitatory ($\hat{\beta} = -5.2, t(8) = -5.813, p = 0.0004$) as expected given (16). In other words, the two variables that according to (16) should capture a substantial proportion of the variance explained by the amount of information I′, indeed succeed in doing so: 0.830 is 96 percent of 0.863.

The lower bound estimate in (16) is a simplification of the full model I'_{w_e} defined by (15). Because the simplification allows us to separate the word and stem frequency effects, it clarifies that these two frequency effects are given the same overall weight. There is evidence, however, that stem frequency has a much more modest weight than word frequency (Baayen *et al.* 2008c), and may even have a different functional form. This suggests that it may be preferable to rewrite (15) as:

$$I'_{w_e} = -\log_2 \left(\frac{\omega_1 \Pr_\pi(w_e)/R_e}{\omega_2 \Sigma_e \Pr_\pi(w_e)/R_e} \right), \tag{17}$$

with separate weights ω for numerator and denominator. On the other hand, at the level of a given class the lower bound estimate in (17) reduces to the exponent frequency and the overall class frequency. Some preliminary experimental evidence for the relevance of exponent frequency (in the simplified form of inflectional formative frequency) for English is available in Baayen *et al.* (2008c), along with evidence for frequency effects for derivational affixes. However, it is presently unclear how class frequency could be generalized and gauged with derivations. Inflectional classes are well contained and it is easy to count out their overall frequencies. Contrariwise, within and between derivational classes there are no clear partitions of the lexical space. While inflected words, in general, belong to only one inflectional class, any given base word may participate in several derivations. We shall address the issue of relations between base words and their derivatives in codetermining lexical processing in further detail in Section 10.5.

It is also useful to rewrite (14) along similar lines to what we did for (15). In this case, the lower bound for the amount of information can be written as the sum of two conditional probabilities. First, consider the probability of exponent *e* given its inflectional class *c*:

$$\Pr(e|c) = \frac{\Pr(e,c)}{\Pr(c)}$$
$$= \frac{\Pr(e)}{\Pr(c)}.$$

(Note that the probability of an exponent is defined strictly with respect to its inflectional class. We never sum frequencies of exponents across inflectional classes.) The information corresponding to this conditional probability is

$$I_{e|c} = -\log_2 \frac{\Pr(e)}{\Pr(c)}$$
$$= -\log_2 \Pr(e) + \log_2 \Pr(c)$$
$$= -\log_2 \Pr(e) + \log_2 \sum_j \Pr(e_j)$$

$$\geq - \log_2 \Pr(e) + \log_2 \prod_j \Pr\left(e_j\right)$$

$$\geq - \log_2 \Pr(e) + \sum_j \log_2 \Pr\left(e_j\right)$$

$$= I'_{e|c} \tag{18}$$

Note that $I'_{e|c}$ is a lower bound of $I_{e|c}$.

Next, let R_e denote the number of functions and meanings of exponent e in class c, and let R_c denote the total count of functions and meanings within the class. The conditional probability of the functions and meanings of exponent e given its class c is

$$\Pr(R_e|R_c) = \frac{\Pr(R_e, R_c)}{\Pr(R_c)}$$

$$= \frac{\Pr(R_e)}{\Pr(R_c)}$$

$$= \frac{R_e}{R_c}$$

and the corresponding information is therefore

$$I_{R_e|R_c} = - \log_2 \frac{R_e}{R_c}$$

$$= - \log_2 R_e + \log_2 R_c$$

$$= - \log_2 R_e + \log_2 \sum_j R_j$$

$$\leq - \log_2 R_e + \log_2 \prod_j R_j$$

$$\leq - \log_2 R_e + \sum_j \log_2 R_j$$

$$= I'_{R_e|R_c} \tag{19}$$

Here, $I'_{R_e|R_c}$ is an upper bound of $I_{R_e|R_c}$.

Taking into account that $I'_{e|c}$ is a lower bound of $I_{e|c}$, and that $I'_{R_i|R_c}$ is an upper bound of $I_{R_i|R_c}$, we can now approximate (14) as follows:

$$I_{w_e} \approx \log_2 R_e - \sum_j \log_2 R_j - \log_2 \Pr_\pi w_e + \sum_j \log_2 \Pr_\pi w_j$$

$$\approx -I'_{R_e|R_c} + I'_{e|c}. \tag{20}$$

In other words, the amount of information as defined in (14) is related to the sum of two conditional probabilities: (i) the probability of the exponent given its class, and (ii) the probability of the ambiguity of the exponent given the ambiguity in its class. The partial effects of these two conditional probabilities are shown in Figure 10.3. As expected, the partial effects are very similar to those shown in Figure 10.2.

At this point, the question arises why $I'_{R_e|R_c}$ appears with a negative sign in (20). To answer this question, we need to consider exponents within their classes, and differentiate between the functions and meanings that an inflected form can have in the discourse. Consider the case in which $R_e \rightarrow R_c$. The more the functions expressed by exponent e become similar to the universe of functions and meanings carried by the inflectional class, the less distinctive the exponent becomes. In other words, an exponent is more successful as a distinctive functional unit of the language when $R_c - R_e$ is large. If so, the amount of information $I'_{R_e|R_c}$ is large, and hence I_{w_e} in (20) is small, and as a consequence processing latencies are reduced. By contrast, an exponent for which $I'_{R_e}|R_c$ is small is dysfunctional, and therefore harder to process, leading to longer processing latencies.

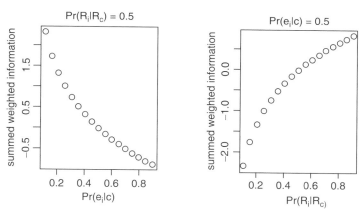

FIGURE 10.3 The left panel shows the partial effect of the information carried by the probability of the exponent given its class $I'_{e|c}$. The right panel shows the partial effect of the information carried by the proportion of the number of functions and meanings conditioned on the total number of functions and meanings for the class $I'_{R_e|R_c}$. Both partial effects are calibrated for the other effect evaluated at 0.5, and are calculated straightforwardly from (20).

10.4 The information structure of paradigms

10.4.1 *Entropy*

Thus far, we have considered the processing load of an inflected form given its paradigm, or an exponent, given its inflectional class. Moscoso del Prado Martín *et al.* (2004*b*) added a new dimension to the experimental study of morphological connectivity by considering the cost of the complexity of a paradigm as such, gauged by means of the entropy measure *H*. Figure 10.1 is helpful for discussing the difference between Kostić's approach and the one developed by Moscoso del Prado Martín and his colleagues. Ignoring the weighting for numbers of functions and meanings, Kostić's measure simplifies to $-\log_2 (\mathrm{Pr}_\pi(e))$, which reflects the number of steps from the root node to the leaf node of the exponent *e* in an optimal binary coding scheme (see the upper panel; for numbers of nodes that are integer powers of two, the $-\log_2(\mathrm{Pr}_\pi(e))$ is exactly equal to the number of steps). However, this measure is insensitive to the size and configuration of the tree. To capture these aspects of the tree, we can make use of the entropy measure. The entropy, which is the same for each and every member of the paradigm, quantifies the expected number of steps from the root to a leaf node.

Moscoso del Prado Martín *et al.* (2004*b*) applied the entropy measure to paradigms in Dutch, but used a much broader definition of paradigms that extended the concept of the morphological family. Table 10.4 shows the words listed in CELEX that contain *neighbour* as a constituent. The left two columns list the morphological family as defined by Schreuder and Baayen (1997), the middle columns list the inflected variants that were found for two of the

TABLE 10.4 Morphological family and inflectional paradigms for *neighbour*.

morphological family		inflectional paradigms		merged paradigms	
word	F	word	F	word	F
neighbour	901	*neighbour*	343	*neighbour*	343
neighbourhood	407	*neighbours*	558	*neighbours*	558
neighbouring	203			*neighbourhood*	386
neighbourliness	3	*neighbourhood*	386	*neighbourhoods*	21
neighbourly	14	*neighbourhoods*	21	*neighbouring*	203
				neighbourliness	3
				neighbourly	14

members of the family, and the rightmost columns list the set that merges the family members with the inflected variants. Moscoso del Prado Martín and colleagues calculated the entropy over this merged set, and proposed this entropy as an enhanced measure for capturing the morphological family size effect. They pointed out that, when all family members are equiprobable, the entropy of the family reduces to the log of the number of family members. Since it is exactly this log-transformed count that emerged as predictive for processing latencies, the entropy of the family can be viewed as a principled way of weighting family members for their token frequency.

Moscoso del Prado Martín and colleagues combined this generalized entropy measure with the amount of information carried by a word (inflected or uninflected) as estimated from its relative frequency to obtain what they called the information residual:

$$I_R = I_w - H = \log N - \log_2 F_w - H. \tag{21}$$

This information residual performed well in a series of post-hoc analyses of processing of Dutch complex words.

By bringing several measures together in a single predictor, I_R, stem frequency and entropy receive exactly the same regression weight:

$$\begin{aligned} RT &\propto \beta_0 + \beta_1 I_R \\ &= \beta_0 + \beta_1 (I_w - H) \\ &\quad \beta_0 - \beta_1 \log_2 F_w - \beta_1 H. \end{aligned} \tag{22}$$

However, subsequent work (Baayen *et al.* 2006) suggests that frequency, the entropy calculated over the morphological family while excluding inflected variants, and the entropy of the paradigms of individual lexemes should be allowed to have different importance (i.e, different β weights). Their study examined a wide range of lexical predictors for simple English nouns and verbs, and observed independent effects of inflectional entropy (henceforth H_i) across both the visual lexical decision and word-naming tasks. An effect of derivational entropy (henceforth H_d) was present only in the visual lexical decision task. Here, it emerged with a U-shaped curve, indicating the presence of some inhibition for words with very information-rich families. In their study of the lexical processing of 8486 complex words in English, Baayen *et al.* (2008c) also observed an independent facilitatory effect of inflectional entropy, side by side with a facilitatory effect of the family size of the lexeme.

These results suggest that, when considered in terms of optimal binary coding schemes, inflected words and lexemes should not be brought together in one encompassing binary tree. Instead, lexemes form one tree, and each lexeme then comes with its own separate disjoint tree for its inflected variants.

Inflectional paradigms in languages such as Dutch and English are trivially simple compared to the paradigms one finds in morphologically rich languages. This raises the question to what extent entropy measures inform us about the processing complexity of more substantive paradigmatic structure. We address this issue for nominal paradigms in Serbian.

10.4.2 *Relative entropy*

When the inflectional entropy is computed for a given lexeme, it provides an estimate for the complexity of this lexeme's inflectional paradigm. This measure, however, does not take into account the complexity of the inflectional class, and the extent to which the probability distribution of a lexeme's paradigm diverges from the probability distribution of its inflectional class. We could consider bringing the entropy of the inflectional class into our model, but this class entropy would be the same for all lexemes in the class. Hence, it would not be much more informative than a plain name for that class (for example, Latin declension I, or Serbian declension III). Therefore, Milin *et al.* (2009) considered the simultaneous influence of paradigms and classes on the processing of inflected nouns in Serbian by means of relative entropy, *RE*.

Milin *et al.* (2009) investigated whether relative entropy is predictive for lexical processing in visual lexical decision using masculine and feminine nouns with the case endings -*om*, -*u*, and -*e*. A mixed-effects analysis with word frequency and stem frequency, bigram frequency, number of orthographic neighbors and entropy as covariates revealed an independent inhibitory effect of *RE*, as shown in the lower right panel of Figure 10.4. Comparison with the other significant partial effects in the model shows that the magnitude of the effect of *RE* is comparable to that of stem frequency and orthographic neighborhood size. However, the effect of the entropy did not reach significance ($p > 0.15$).

What this experiment shows is that it is neither the probability distribution of the inflected variants in a word's paradigm, nor the probability distribution in its inflectional class considered separately that are at issue, but rather the divergence between the two distributions. The greater this divergence, the longer the response latencies. A similar pattern was observed for the accuracy measure as well: the greater the divergence of the probability distribution of the paradigm from the probability distribution of the class, the more errors were made.

From the perspective of cognitive psychology, these results are interesting in that they provide further evidence for the importance of structured

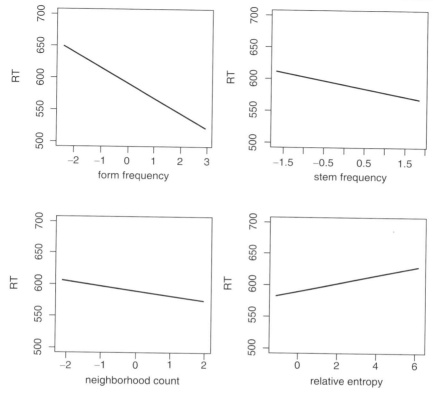

FIGURE 10.4 Partial effects of distributional predictors for the response latencies in visual lexical decision to Serbian nouns (Milin *et al.* 2008)

lexical connectivity. From the perspective of linguistic morphology, they support the theoretical concepts of paradigms and inflectional classes. Combined with the presence of a strong effect of the word frequency, an effect that is much stronger than the effect of the word's stem (compare the upper panels in Figure 10.4), these results provide strong support for word and paradigm morphology (Matthews 1974; J. P. Blevins 2003, 2006*b*) and for exemplar-based approaches to lexical processing in general (see, e.g., Baayen 2003).

10.5 Paradigmatic structure in derivation

In languages such as Dutch or English, morphological families consist predominantly of compounds. As a consequence, the family size effect (cf., Schreuder and Baayen 1997) is driven almost exclusively by lexical

TABLE 10.5 The number of monomorphemic base words that can attach the given number of affixes (prefixes or suffixes) when forming bi-morphemic derived words.

Number of affixes	Count of base words
1	3449
2	1391
3	516
4	202
5	105
6	31
7	13
8	11
9	2
10	3
11	2

connectivity between compounds. Little is known about the role of derived words. The problem here is that a given base word combines with only a handful of derivational affixes at best. Counts of the number of different prefixes and suffixes that English monomorphemic base words combine with, based on the English section of the CELEX lexical database (Baayen *et al.* 1995), illustrate that 60 percent of English monomorphemic base words combine with only one affix. Table 10.5 shows a steep decrease (a Zipfian distribution) in the number of derivational affixes that are attested for a given base word. The verbs *act* and *play* are exceptional in combining with 11 different affixes. The maximum family size in English, 187, observed for *man*, is an order of magnitude larger. With such small numbers of derived family members, it becomes very difficult to gauge the role of a strictly derivational family size count in lexical processing.

Derived words, however, enter into more systematic relations than most compounds, even when we take into account that the meaning of a compound is predictable from its constituents to a much greater extent than has traditionally been assumed (Gagné and Shoben 1997; Gagné 2001). For instance, derived adjectives with the prefix *un-* systematically express negation. Taking this fact into account, we asked ourselves whether such systematic relations between base words and their derivatives codetermine lexical processing. As a first step towards an answer, we introduce two simple concepts: the mini-paradigm and the mini-class. Here, the term mini-paradigm refers to pairs of base words and their derivatives. Thus, *kind* and *unkind* form a mini-paradigm, and so do *clear* and *clearly*. In the same line, the term mini-class refers to the set of mini-paradigms sharing the same derivational affix. All pairs of base words and the corresponding *un-* derivatives constitute the mini-class of: *kind - unkind, true - untrue, pleasant - unpleasant,* etc. Mini-paradigms and mini-classes approximate inflectional paradigms and inflectional classes in the sense that the semantic relations within the pairs tend to be more consistent and transparent than in general morphological families or in families of derived words with different prefixes and suffixes.

In what follows, we therefore investigate whether the measures of entropy and relative entropy are significant predictors for lexical processing when applied to mini-paradigms and mini-classes.

10.5.1 *Materials*

We selected six suffixes and one prefix, for which we extracted all formations listed in the CELEX lexical database and for which latencies were also available in the English Lexicon Project (Balota et al. 2007) for both the derived word and its base. The resulting counts of formations are available in Table 10.6, cross-classified by whether the base word is simple or complex. For all words, we extracted from CELEX their frequency of occurrence, their length in letters, the number of synsets for the base as listed in WordNet (Miller 1990; Beckwith *et al.* 1991, and studied by Baayen *et al.* 2006), the family size of the base (calculated from the morphological parses in CELEX), and their frequency in the demographic subcorpus of conversational English in the British National Corpus (Burnard 1995). We included these variables in order to make sure that potential paradigmatic effects are not confounded with other lexical distributional properties. From the English Lexicon Project, we added the by-item mean naming latencies and the by-item mean lexical decision latencies.

TABLE 10.6 Affixes in the study based on latencies extracted from the English Lexicon Project, cross-classified by the complexity of their base words.

	simple base	complex base
-able	70	0
-er (comparative)	98	0
-er (deverbal)	240	24
-ly (adverbial)	21	355
-ness (complex base)	0	65
-ness (simple base)	152	0
-est (superlative)	95	0
un-	18	111

For each pair of base and derivative, we calculated its entropy and its relative entropy. For the derived words, the entropy of the mini-paradigm was calculated on the basis of the relative frequencies of the derivative and its base word (e.g., for *kind* and *unkind*, the relative frequencies are $72/(72 + 390)$ and $390/(72 + 390)$). For the base words, we distinguished between base words with only one derivative, and base words with two or more derivatives. For base words with a single derivative, the procedure for estimating the entropy was the same as for derived words. For base words with more than one derivative, the problem arises how to calculate entropies. Selection of a single derivative seems arbitrary. Taking all derivations linked with a given base word into account is possible, but then the mini-class distribution would contain the maximum number of eleven relative frequencies (see Table 10.5), most of which would be zero for almost all words. We therefore opted for taking only two relative frequencies into account when calculating the entropy: the frequency of the base itself, and the summed frequency of all its derivatives.

The probability distribution for a given mini-class was obtained by summing the frequencies of all base words in the class on the one hand, and all derivatives in the class on the other hand. The resulting frequencies were then transformed into relative frequencies. These relative frequencies then served as the Q distribution (also known as the reference distribution) for the calculation of the relative entropy.

In the following analyses, frequency measures, family size, number of synsets, and response latencies were log-transformed to eliminate the adverse effect of outliers on the model fit.

10.5.2 *Derived words*

We investigated the predictivity of the entropy and relative entropy measures for word naming and lexical decision latencies to the derived words. For that, we applied linear mixed-effects modeling (Baayen *et al.* 2008*a*; Bates 2005, 2006; Baayen 2008), with Task (lexical decision versus naming) as a fixed-effect factor, and with the set of relevant covariates including length, (written) base frequency, (written) word frequency, spoken word frequency, number of synsets in WordNet, morphological family size, entropy and relative entropy. Word and affix were considered as random effects.

For the covariates, we investigated whether nonlinearity was present. This turned out to be the case only for word length. We also observed interactions of Task with word frequency and spoken word frequency, with length (only the quadratic term), and with entropy and relative entropy. Finally, we considered whether by-word or by-affix random slopes were required. It turned out that by-affix random slopes were necessary only for the two entropy measures.

Inspection of the coefficients for the entropy measures in the resulting model revealed that entropy and relative entropy had positive coefficients of similar magnitude ($H : 0.034$, $\hat{\sigma} = 0.025$; RE : 0.058, $\hat{\sigma} = 0.016$), with small differences across the two tasks. In word naming, the effect of entropy was slightly larger, while the effect of relative entropy was fractionally smaller (H in naming: $0.034 + 0.041$; RE in naming: $0.058 - 0.014$).

These observations invite a simplification of the regression model. Let β_0 denote the coefficient for the intercept, and let β_1 and β_2 denote the coefficients for entropy and relative entropy respectively. Given that β_1 and β_2 are very similar, we can proceed as follows:

$$\beta_0 + \beta_1 H + \beta_2 RE \approx \beta_0 + \beta_1 H + \beta_1 RE$$
$$= \beta_0 + \beta_1(H + RE). \tag{23}$$

Interestingly, the sum of entropy and relative entropy is equal to another information-theoretic measure, the *cross entropy* (*CE*) (Manning and Schütze 1999; Cover and Thomas 1991). Applied to the present data, we have

$$CE = H + RE =$$
$$= -\sum_L \Pr_\pi(w_L) \log_2 (\Pr_\pi(w_L)) + RE$$
$$= -\sum_L \Pr_\pi(w_L) \log_2 (\Pr_\pi(w_L)) + \sum_L \Pr_\pi(w_L) \log_2 \frac{\Pr_\pi(w_L)}{\Pr_\pi(c_L)}$$
$$= -\sum_L \Pr_\pi(w_L) \log_2 (\Pr_\pi(c_L)). \tag{24}$$

In (24), L indexes the base and derived lexemes for mini-paradigms, and the sets of base words and derived words for the mini-class. Thus, $\Pr_\pi (w_L)$ denotes the probability of a base or derived lexeme in its mini-paradigm, and $\Pr_\pi(c_L)$ denotes the corresponding probability in the mini-class. Technically, the cross entropy between the probability distribution of the mini-paradigm and the probability distribution of the mini-class measures the average number of bits needed to identify a form from the set of possible forms in the mini-paradigm, if a coding scheme is used based on the reference probability distribution $\Pr_\pi c_e$ of the mini-class, rather than the "true" distribution $\Pr_\pi w_e$ of the mini-paradigm. More informally, we can interpret the cross entropy as gauging the average amount of information in the

TABLE 10.7 Partial effects of the predictors for the visual lexical decision and naming latencies to derived words. The reference level for Task is lexical decision. Lower, Upper: 95% highest posterior density interval; P: Markov chain Monte Carlo p-value.

	Estimate	Lower	Upper	P
Intercept	6.6679	6.5830	6.7607	0.0001
Task=naming	−0.1419	−0.2158	−0.0688	0.0001
length (linear)	0.0056	−0.0109	0.0228	0.5162
length (quadratic)	0.0012	0.0004	0.0020	0.0034
written frequency	−0.0382	−0.0428	−0.0333	0.0001
spoken frequency	−0.0183	−0.0245	−0.0117	0.0001
synset count	−0.0277	−0.0339	−0.0212	0.0001
cross entropy	0.0565	0.0164	0.0937	0.0076
Task=naming: written frequency	0.0067	0.0022	0.0112	0.0036
Task=naming: length (linear)	0.0132	−0.0025	0.0283	0.0914
Task=naming: length (quadratic)	−0.0011	−0.0019	−0.0003	0.0026
Task=naming: spoken frequency	0.0124	0.0062	0.0186	0.0001

mini-paradigm, corrected for the departure from the prior reference distribution of the corresponding mini-class.

We therefore replaced entropy H and relative entropy RE as predictors in our regression model by a single predictor, the cross entropy CE, and refitted the model to the data. After removal of outliers and refitting, we obtained the model summarized in Table 10.7 and visualized in Figure 10.5. The standard deviation of the by-word random intercepts was 0.0637, the standard deviation for the by-affix random intercepts was 0.0399, the standard deviation for the by-affix random slopes for cross entropy was 0.0277, and the standard deviation for the residual error was 0.0663. All random slopes and random intercepts were supported by likelihood ratio tests (all p-values < 0.0001).

With respect to the control variables, we note that word length was a strongly nonlinear (positively accelerated) predictor for especially lexical decision, with longer lengths eliciting elongated response latencies. The word frequency effect was similar for both tasks, albeit slightly stronger for lexical decision. Similarly, the spoken word frequency added facilitation specifically for lexical decision. The effect of number of synonyms, as gauged with the help of the synset count, was facilitatory and the same across the two tasks. The effect of cross entropy was inhibitory, and also did not differ across tasks. Its effect size (roughly 100 ms) exceeds that of the spoken frequency effect and that of the number of meanings. Interestingly, the model with cross entropy as predictor provides an equally tight fit to the data as the model with entropy and relative entropy as predictors, even though the latter model had

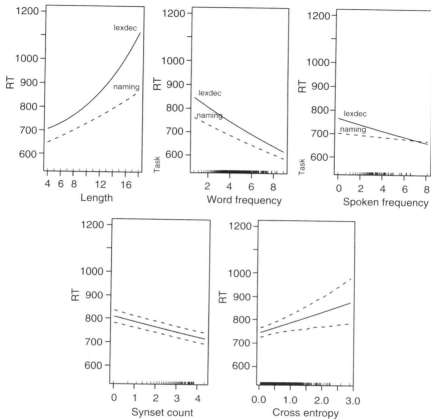

FIGURE 10.5 Partial effects of the predictors for word naming and visual lexical decision latencies for derived words. The lower panels are calibrated for visual lexical decision, and come with 95% highest posterior density confidence intervals.

two additional parameters (a beta coefficient for a second entropy measure, and a random-effects standard deviation for by-item slopes for the second entropy measure): the log likelihood of the simpler model with cross entropy was 2364, while for the more complex model with entropy and relative entropy it was 2362.[3] From this, we conclude that the relevant entropy measure for understanding the role of paradigmatic complexity during lexical processing of derived words is the cross-entropy measure.

---

[3] A greater log likelihood implies a better fit (for technical details consult Crawley 2002).

TABLE 10.8 Estimated slopes for derived words for the different mini-classes, positioned in decreasing order.

	slope
-*est* (superlative)	0.097
-*ly* (adverbial)	0.090
-*ness* (complex base)	0.086
-*able*	0.068
-*er* (comparative)	0.054
-*er* (deverbal)	0.031
un-	0.021
-*ness* (simple base)	0.004

The synset measure in our data estimates the number of meanings that a base word has (e.g., *bank* as a part of the river and a financial institution). Generally, the meaning of a derivative builds on only one of the meanings of its base word (e.g., *embank*). The lower the number of synsets, the tighter we may expect the relationship between the base and its derivatives to be. The synset measure does not interact with cross entropy, nor does it substantially affect the estimate of its slope. To further rule out potential semantic confounds, we also considered a semantic measure that specifically gauges the semantic similarity between a given derived word and its base. The measure that we used in the LSA score for the distance between the derived word and its base in co-occurrence space (Landauer and Dumais 1997), using the software available at <http://lsa.colorado.edu>. For the subset of our mini-paradigms, the LSA scores elicited a significant facilitatory effect on lexical decision latencies ($\hat{\beta} = -0.1196$, $p = 0.0001$). As for the synset measure, there was no significant effect for word naming. Crucially, the measure of cross entropy retained significance also when the pairwise semantic similarity between base and derived word in mini-paradigms was taken into account.

The presence of random slopes for cross entropy in this model indicates that the effect of cross entropy varied with mini-class. Table 10.8 lists the individual slopes for the different mini-classes that we considered. Slopes range from 0.097 for superlative -*est* to 0.004 for -*ness* formations derived from simple base words.

10.5.3 *Base words*

Because complex base words (e.g., *surprising*) come with predictors such as the frequency of the stem (*surprise*) that do not apply to the simple base words, we analyzed the simple and complex base words separately. We

TABLE 10.9 Partial effects of the predictors for word naming and visual lexical decision latencies for complex base words. Lower, Upper: 95% highest posterior density interval; P: Markov chain Monte Carlo p-value.

	Estimate	Lower	Upper	P
Intercept	6.6006	6.5428	6.6596	0.0001
experiment=naming	− 0.0397	− 0.0750	− 0.0031	0.0326
length	0.0357	0.0325	0.0387	0.0001
word frequency	− 0.0305	− 0.0363	− 0.0250	0.0001
spoken frequency	− 0.0143	− 0.0195	− 0.0090	0.0001
base frequency	− 0.0061	− 0.0086	− 0.0035	0.0001
synset count	− 0.0230	− 0.0311	− 0.0147	0.0001
cross entropy	− 0.1038	− 0.1605	− 0.0483	0.0002
Experiment=naming: length	− 0.0082	− 0.0115	− 0.0052	0.0001
Experiment=naming: word frequency	0.0100	0.0057	0.0141	0.0001

proceeded in the same way as for the derived words. We fitted a mixed-effects model to the data, observed that again the coefficients for entropy and relative entropy were very similar and statistically indistinguishable in magnitude and had the same sign, replaced the two measures by the cross-entropy measure, refitted the model, and removed overly influential outliers.

The coefficients of a mixed-effects model fitted to the lexical decision and naming latencies to the complex base words are listed in Table 10.9. The corresponding partial effects are graphed in Figure 10.6.

As for the preceding datasets, we find effects of word length (longer words elicit longer latencies, upper left panel) and word frequency (more frequent words elicit shorter latencies, uppercenter panel). Adding frequency of use in spoken English as a predictor again contributes significantly to the model over and above the written frequency measures (upper right panel). The frequency of the base word (lower left panel of Figure 10.6) also emerged as a significant predictor, but with a slope that is substantially shallower than that of the word frequency effect. The synset count of the embedded base word is predictive as well. It is facilitatory, just as observed for the derived words (lower center panel). Finally, the lower right panel shows that there is a small effect of cross entropy. But while for the derived words the effect of cross entropy was inhibitory, it is facilitatory for the base words.

Before discussing this unexpected change in sign, we first inquire whether facilitation for cross entropy also characterizes the set of simple base words. Table 10.10 lists the partial effects of the predictors that were retained after

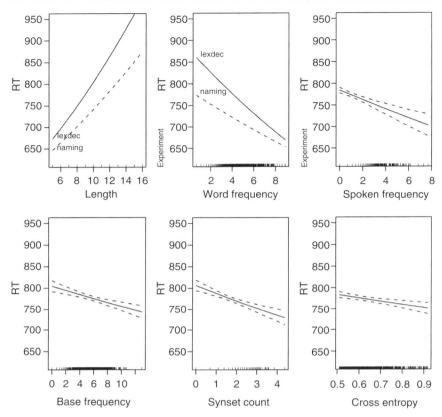

FIGURE 10.6 Partial effects of the predictors for word naming and visual lexical decision latencies for complex base words. Markov chain Monte Carlo based 95% confidence intervals are shown for those predictors that do not enter into interactions.

stepwise variable elimination. Figure 10.7 visualizes these partial effects. The upper left panel shows the effect of orthographic length, which shows a clear minimum near the median length (five letters) for visual lexical decision but not for word naming. For the latter task, the shorter the word, the easier it is to articulate. For the former task, five-letter words emerge as most easily read. The upper right panel shows that, as for the derived words, spoken frequency allows greater facilitation for visual lexical decision than for word naming.

The lower left panel presents the expected facilitatory effect of the synset count, and illustrates that words with more meanings elicit shorter latencies, for both word naming and lexical decision. Surprisingly, the lower central panel shows that the partial effect of family size is inhibitory, instead of facilitatory, as reported for previous experiments. We return to this finding

TABLE 10.10 Partial effects of the predictors for word naming and visual lexical decision latencies for simple base words. Lower, Upper: 95% highest posterior density interval; P: Markov chain Monte Carlo p-value.

	Estimate	Lower	Upper	P
Intercept	6.8433	6.7756	6.9097	0.0001
experiment=naming	−0.2520	−0.3213	−0.1885	0.0001
length (linear)	−0.0613	−0.0797	−0.0430	0.0001
length (quadratic)	0.0067	0.0052	0.0080	0.0001
spoken frequency	−0.0251	−0.0286	−0.0216	0.0001
family size	0.0107	0.0021	0.0193	0.0158
word frequency	−0.0090	−0.0125	−0.0054	0.0001
cross entropy	−0.1316	−0.1823	−0.0869	0.0001
synset count	−0.0235	−0.0321	−0.0154	0.0001
Experiment=naming: length (linear)	0.0507	0.0305	0.0722	0.0001
Experiment=naming: length (quadratic)	−0.0034	−0.0050	−0.0018	0.0002
Experiment=naming: spoken frequency	0.0173	0.0141	0.0202	0.0001

below. The partial effect of cross entropy is presented in the lower right panel of Figure 10.7. As for the complex base words, the effect of cross entropy for simple base words is again facilitatory.

The analyses of the two sets of base words leave us with two questions. First, how should we understand the change in sign of the cross-entropy effect between derived words and base words? Second, why do we have inhibition from the morphological family size for simple base words, and no effect of family size for complex base words?

With respect to the first question, we note that there is bottom-up support for only the base word, and no such support for their derivatives. By contrast, in the case of the derived words, there is bottom-up support for the derived word itself, its base word, and its affix. In sum, for derived words, three of the four elements in a proportional analogy such as

$$\underbrace{great \; : \; greatest}_{\text{mini-paradigm}} = \underbrace{A: \text{-}est}_{\text{mini-class}} \tag{25}$$

are actually present in the signal. For derived words, we can therefore understand the effect of cross entropy as reflecting the cost of resolving the proportional analogy between mini-paradigm and mini-class. More specifically, the cross entropy reflects the average complexity of identifying the derived word in its mini-paradigm on the basis of the generalized probability distribution of the

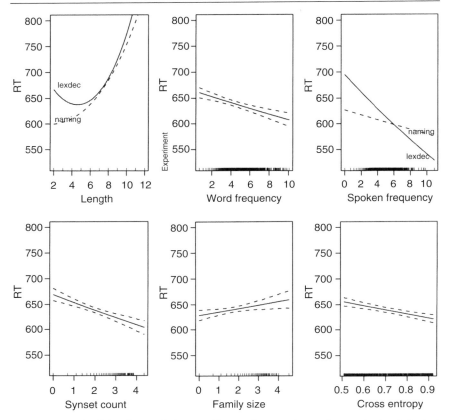

FIGURE 10.7 Partial effects of the predictors for word naming and visual lexical decision latencies for simple base words. Markov chain Monte Carlo based 95% confidence intervals are shown for those predictors that do not enter into interactions.

mini-class. Thus, the cross entropy can be understood as reflecting the cost of resolving the ambiguity in the visual input with the help of generalized knowledge in long-term memory about the corresponding mini-class. From this perspective, the inhibitory effect of cross entropy for derived words makes perfect sense: The higher the cross entropy, the more information has to be retrieved from memory to resolve the proportional analogy.

Let us now consider the facilitatory effect of cross entropy for simple base words. For simple base words, the visual input is unambiguous, with bottom-up support only for the word itself. There is no cost of a call on proportional analogy to resolve morphological ambiguity. In the absence of a

TABLE 10.11 Pairwise correlations between key predictors and lexical decision (lexdec) and naming latencies for the set of simple base words.

	Frequency	Family size	Synset count	Cross entropy	RT lexdec	RT naming
frequency	1.000	0.320	0.345	−0.527	−0.379	−0.266
family size	0.320	1.000	0.643	0.245	−0.473	−0.392
synset count	0.345	0.643	1.000	0.092	−0.552	−0.434
cross entropy	−0.527	0.245	0.092	1.000	−0.085	−0.101
RT lexical decision	−0.379	−0.473	−0.552	−0.085	1.000	0.648
RT naming	−0.266	−0.392	−0.434	−0.101	0.648	1.000

morphological parsing problem, the cross-entropy effect apparently reverses and emerges as a measure of the amount of support the base receives from related derived words co-activated by the base. Crucially, it is not simply the count of related derived words (we checked that this count is not predictive for the present data) but rather the analogical support for the base given its derivative (defined in the mini-paradigm) and the general likelihood of a base word having derivatives (defined in the miniclass).

The second question to be considered is why we observe inhibition from the morphological family size for simple base words, and no effect of family size for complex base words. The unexpected inhibitory effect of family size is probably due to what is known in the statistical literature as suppression (see, e.g., Friedman and Wall 2005): When predictor variables are correlated, and both are correlated with the dependent variable, then, depending on the strength of the former correlation, the beta coefficient of one of the predictors can become nonsignificant or even change sign. Table 10.11 presents the correlation matrix for key predictors, and reveals a large positive coefficient for the correlation of family size and the synset count, and the expected negative correlations for family size and response latencies in lexical decision and naming. This by itself is a warning that suppression might be at issue here.

We therefore inspected whether family size was significant in a model for the simple base words, excluding the synset count as predictor. It was not ($p > 0.8$). When cross entropy was also removed as predictor, the family size measure emerged as significant ($p < 0.01$), now with a negative slope, as expected given previous studies. For the complex base words, excluding only the synset measure was sufficient to allow a facilitatory effect of family size to emerge. What this suggests is that the family size effect, which has always been understood as a semantic effect (see, e.g., Schreuder and Baayen 1997; Moscoso del Prado Martín *et al.* 2004*a*), is a composite effect that bundles effects of semantic similarity and effects of paradigmatic structure. Effects of similarity would then be better captured by means of the synset count, and effects of derivational paradigmatic structure would then be better captured by means of the cross-entropy measure.

The question that arises at this point is whether the semantic aspect of the family size effect has any specific morphological component. To answer this question, we first partitioned the synset count into two disjunct counts, a count for morphologically related synsets, and a count for morphologically unrelated synsets. A morphologically related synset is a synset in which at least one of the synset members is morphologically related to the target word (not counting the target word itself). A morphologically related synset, therefore, is a family size count that only includes semantically highly related family members.

In the model for the simple base words, we then replaced the family size measure and the synset count by the counts of morphologically related and unrelated synset counts. A mixed-effects analysis revealed that, for visual lexical decision, both counts were significant predictors with very similar coefficients (-0.018 and -0.015 respectively). For the naming latencies, however, only the synset count of morphologically unrelated synsets was significant. This interaction ($p = 0.0049$) shows that in a task such as word naming, which does not require deep semantic processing, semantic ambiguity that arises through morphological connectivity does not play a role. By contrast, the lexical decision task, which invites deeper semantic processing, allows the effect of morphologically related words that are also very similar in meaning to become visible. We therefore conclude that morphologically related words that are also semantically very similar have a special status compared to semantically similar but morphologically unrelated words (see also Moscoso del Prado Martín *et al.* 2004*a*).

10.6 Concluding remarks

In the preceding sections we reviewed and presented a range of studies addressing specific aspects of the complexities of paradigmatic structure in lexical processing. In order to obtain a model for the full complexity for an inflected variant w_e, we combine equations (10), (14), and (15) and add the effects of the entropy and relative entropy measures, leading to the following equation:

$$I \propto \beta_0 + \beta_1 \log_2 \Pr_N(w_e) + \beta_2 \log_2 \Pr_N(w) +$$
$$+ \beta_3 \log_2 \left(\frac{\Pr_\pi(e)/R_e}{\Sigma_e \Pr_\pi(e)/R_e} \right) +$$
$$+ \beta_4 \log_2 \left(\frac{\Pr_\pi(w_e)/R_e}{\Sigma_e \Pr_\pi(w_e)/R_e} \right) +$$
$$+ \beta_5 H_d +$$
$$+ \beta_6 H_i + \beta_7 RE. \tag{26}$$

Large regression studies are called for to bring all these variables into play simultaneously. However, even though (26) is far from simple, it is only a first step towards quantifying the complexities of inflectional processing. We mention here only a few of the issues that should be considered for a more comprehensive model.

First, Kostić *et al.* (2003) calculated the number of functions and meanings R_e of exponent e conditionally on a lexeme's inflectional class. For instance, the number of functions and meanings listed for the exponent a for masculine nouns in Table 2, 109, is the sum of the numbers of functions and meanings for masculine genitive and the masculine accusative singular. This provides a lower bound for the actual ambiguity of the exponent, as the same exponent is found for nominative singulars and genitive plurals for regular feminine nouns. The justification for conditioning on inflectional class is that the stem to which an exponent attaches arguably provides information about its inflectional class. This reduces the uncertainty about the functions and meanings of an exponent to the uncertainty in its own class. Nevertheless, it seems likely that an exponent that is unique to one inflectional class (e.g., Serbian *ama* for regular feminine nouns) is easier to process than an exponent that occurs across all inflectional classes (e.g., *a, u*), especially when experimental items are not blocked by inflectional class. (Further complications that should be considered are the consequences of, for instance, masculine nouns (e.g., *sudija* ('judge'), *sluga* ('servant')) taking the same inflectional exponents as regular feminine nouns do, and of animate masculine nouns being associated with a pattern of exponents that differs from that associated with inanimate masculine nouns.)

Second, the standard organization of exponents by number and case has not played a role in the studies that we discussed. Thus far, preliminary analyses of the experimental data available to us have not revealed an independent predictive role for case, over and above the attested role of ambiguity with respect to numbers of functions and meanings. This is certainly an issue that requires further empirical investigation, as organization by case provides insight into the way that functions and meanings are bundled across inflectional classes.

Third, we have not considered generalizations across, for instance, irregular and regular feminine nouns in Serbian, along the lines of Clahsen *et al.* (2001). The extent to which inflected forms inherit higher-order generalizations about their phonological form provides further constraints on lexical processing.

Fourth, the size of inflectional paradigms has not been investigated systematically. Although the nominal inflectional classes of Serbian are an enormous step forward compared to the nominal paradigms of English or Dutch, the complexities of verbal paradigms can be much larger. From an information-theoretic perspective, the entropy of the complex verbal paradigms of Serbian must be much larger than the entropy of nominal paradigms, and one would expect this difference to be reflected in elongated processing latencies for inflected verbs. The study by Traficante and Burani (2003) provides evidence supporting this prediction. They observed that inflected verbs in Italian elicited longer processing latencies than inflected adjectives.

Nevertheless, it should be noted that the question of what constitutes a verbal paradigm is still open. In one, traditional, sense each verb may have not one, but several paradigms defined over various tenses and aspects. In the other sense, verbs have one exhaustive paradigm that encompasses all verbal inflected variants. Baayen *et al.* (2008c) have addressed a similar question for the paradigms of English nouns and they concluded that lexemes and their inflected variants should not be considered together as a single paradigm. In a similar way, we can tackle the question of verbal paradigmatic organization in the mental lexicon – using information theory and large-scale regression modeling. Two alternatives can be tested empirically and the result should be straightforwardly in favor of either (a) a single entropy measure calculated over all verbal inflected variants or (b) entropies within each tense and aspect, and one computed over all tenses and aspects.

Fifth, all results reported here are based on visual comprehension tasks (lexical decision, word naming). Some of the present results are bound to change as this line of research is extended to other tasks and across modalities. For instance, the effect of inflectional entropy reported by Baayen *et al.* (2006) for visual lexical decision and word naming was facilitatory in nature. However, in a production study by Bien (2007), inflectional entropy was inhibitory (see also Baayen *et al.* 2008b). In lexical decision, a complex paradigm is an index of higher lexicality, and may therefore elicit shorter response latencies. In production, however, the paradigm has to be accessed, and a specific word form has to be extracted from the paradigm. This may explain why, in production, a greater paradigm complexity appears to go hand in hand with increasing processing costs. Generally, it will be important to establish paradigmatic effects for lexical processing in natural discourse using tasks that do not, or only minimally, impose their own constraints on processing.

Sixth, it will be equally important to obtain distributional lexical measures that are more sensitive to contextual variation than the abstract frequency counts and theoretical concepts of functions and meanings that have been used thus far. Interestingly, Moscoso del Prado Martín *et al.* (2008) and Filipović Đurđević (2007) report excellent predictivity for lexical processing of more complex information-theoretic measures of morphological and semantic connectivity derived bottom-up from a corpus of Serbian.

It is clear that the information-theoretic measures that we have proposed and illustrated in this chapter capture only part of the multidimensional complexity of lexical processing. Hence, each measure can be undersood as a plane cross-cutting this multidimensional space. In spite of these limitations, the extent to which the present information-theoretic approach converges with wpm is striking. Across our experimental datasets we find evidence for exemplars, irrespective of whether the language under investigation is Dutch, English, or Serbian. At the same time, we observe the predictivity of entropy measures, which generalize across probability distributions tied to subsets of these exemplars, and evaluate the complexity of paradigms and the divergence between different levels of morphological organization. However, all the results discussed here pertain to the processing of familiar words. In order to properly gauge the processing complexity of new inflected and derived words, it will be necessary to combine wpm and the present information-theoretic approach with computational models of language processing.

Such an integration is especially challenging because across computational models of linguistic generalization, whether abstractionist and implementing greedy learning (Albright and Hayes 2003), or memory-based and implementing lazy learning (Daelemans and Van den Bosch 2005; Keuleers *et al.* 2007; Keuleers 2008), a common finding is that it is type frequencies and not token frequencies on which generalization is based. In fact, type-based generalization has been found to be reflected in processing measures as well (see, e.g., Ernestus and Baayen 2004; Krott *et al.* 2004). Typically, current computational models (cf. Albright this volume) make use of much more sophisticated analogies than the traditional four-part analogy that we have referred to as a possible explanation for the effect of cross entropy.

To resolve this paradox, we note, first of all, that our hypothesis is not a hypothesis about the choice of a linguistic form, but rather a measure of the cost of selecting a given complex word from its mini-paradigm given its mini-class.

Furthermore, note that for most of the derivational suffixes we have considered, there are no rival suffixes comparable to the rivaling options that characterize the past tense in English (Albright and Hayes 2003), or plural selection in Dutch (Keuleers *et al.* 2007). There is only one way in English to express the comparative, the superlative, or adverbs through suffixation. Hence, the probability of the selection of *-er*, *-est*, or *-ly* is equal to one. For this "degenerate" case, four-part analogy provides a reasonable model. In fact, we think it is precisely this uniformity in the analogical support for a given suffix that allows us to see the effect of cross entropy. Because there are no competing sets of exemplars supporting different outcomes, there are no overriding type frequency effects. As a consequence, the more subtle relevance of the token counts becomes visible only for the basic, type-uniform four-part analogy. The real challenge for future research, therefore, is to clarify whether subtle effects of token frequencies also codetermine the fine details of lexical processing when more complex, type-frequency-driven analogies come into play.

References

Ackerman, Farrell, Blevins, James P., and Malouf, Robert (2008). Inflectional morphology as a complex adaptive system. Paper presented at the First Workshop on Complex Systems and Language, University of Arizona.

Akhtar, Nameera (1999). Acquiring basic word order: Evidence for data-driven learning of syntactic structure. *Journal of Child Language*, **26**: 339–56.

Albright, Adam (2002*a*). *The Identification of Bases in Morphological Paradigms*. Ph.D. thesis, UCLA.

—— (2002*b*). Islands of reliability for regular morphology: Evidence from Italian. *Language*, **78**: 684–709.

—— (2008). Explaining universal tendencies and language particulars in analogical change. See Good (2008), 144–81.

—— Andrade, Argelia Edith, and Hayes, Bruce (2001). Segmental environments of Spanish diphthongization. In *UCLA Working Papers in Linguistics, Number 7: Papers in Phonology 5*, A. Albright and T. Cho (eds.). UCLA, Los Angeles, 117–51.

—— and Hayes, Bruce (2002). Modeling English past tense intuitions with minimal generalization. In *SIGPHON 6: Proceedings of the Sixth Meeting of the ACL Special Interest Group in Computational Phonology*, M. Maxwell (ed.). ACL, 58–69.

—— —— (2003). Rules vs. analogy in English past tenses: A computational/experimental study. *Cognition*, **90**: 119–61.

—— —— (2006). Modeling productivity with the Gradual Learning Algorithm: The problem of accidentally exceptionless generalizations. In *Gradience in Grammar: Generative Perspectives*, F. Gisbert, F. Caroline, V. Ralf, and S. Matthias (eds.). Oxford: Oxford University Press, 185–204.

Alegre, Maria and Gordon, Peter (1999). Frequency effects and the representational status of regular inflections. *Journal of Memory and Language*, **40**: 41–61.

Alverson, Hoyt (1994). *Semantics and Experience: Universal Metaphors of Time in English, Mandarin, Hindi and Sesotho*. Baltimore: Johns Hopkins University Press.

Anderson, Judi Lynn, Martínez, Isaac H., and Pace, Wanda J. (1990). Comaltepec Chinantec tone. See Merrifield and Rensch (1990), 3–20.

Anderson, Stephen R. (1992). *A-Morphous Morphology*. Cambridge: Cambridge University Press.

—— (2004). Morphological universals and diachrony. In *Yearbook of Morphology 2004*, G. Booij and J. van Marle (eds.). Dordrecht: Springer, 1–17.

Anttila, Raimo (1977). *Analogy*. The Hague: Mouton.

—— and Brewer, Warren A. (1977). *Analogy: A Basic Bibliography*. Amsterdam: John Benjamins.

Aronoff, Mark (1994). *Morphology by Itself: Stems and Inflectional Classes*. Cambridge, MA: MIT Press.

Baayen, R. Harald (1992). Quantitative aspects of morphological productivity. In *Yearbook of Morphology 1992*, G. Booij and J. van Marle (eds.). Dordrecht: Kluwer, 181–208.

—— (2003). Probabilistic approaches to morphology. In *Probabilistic Linguistics*, R. Bod, J. Hay, and S. Jannedy (eds.). Cambridge: Cambridge University Press, 229–87.

—— (2008). *Analyzing Linguistic Data: A Practical Introduction to Statistics using R*. Cambridge: Cambridge University Press.

—— Davidson, Doug J., and Bates, Douglas M. (2008a). Mixed-effects modeling with crossed random effects for subjects and items. *Journal of Memory and Language*.

—— Feldman, Laurie, and Schreuder, Robert (2006). Morphological influences on the recognition of monosyllabic monomorphemic words. *Journal of Memory and Language*, **53**: 496–512.

—— Levelt, Willem M. J., Schreuder, Robert, and Ernestus, Mirjam (2008b). Paradigmatic structure in speech production. *Chicago Linguistics Society*, **43**, to appear.

—— and Lieber, Rochelle (1991). Productivity and English derivation: A corpus-based study. *Linguistics*, **29**: 801–43.

—— —— and Schreuder, Robert (1997). The morphological complexity of simple nouns. *Linguistics*, **35**: 861–77.

—— McQueen, James M., Dijkstra, Ton, and Schreuder, Robert (2003a). Dutch inflectional morphology in spoken- and written-word recognition. In *Morphological Structure in Language Processing*, R. H. Baayen and R. Schreuder (eds.). Berlin: Mouton de Gruyter.

—— —— —— —— (2003b). Frequency effects in regular inflectional morphology: Revisiting Dutch plurals. In *Morphological Structure in Language Processing*, R. H. Baayen and R. Schreuder (eds.). Berlin: Mouton de Gruyter, 355–90.

—— and Moscoso del Prado Martín, Fermín (2005). Semantic density and past tense formation in three Germanic languages. *Language*, **81**: 666–98.

—— Piepenbrock, Richard, and Gullikers, Léon (1995). *The CELEX Lexical Database (CD-ROM)*. Philadelphia: University of Pennsylvania.

—— Wurm, Lee H., and Aycock, Joanna (2008c). Lexical dynamics for low-frequency complex words: A regression study across tasks and modalities. *The Mental Lexicon*, **2**: 419–63.

Bailey, Todd M. and Hahn, Ulrike (2001). Determinants of wordlikeness: Phonotactics or lexical neighborhoods? *Journal of Memory and Language*, **44**: 568–91.

Balota, David A., Yap, Melvin J., Cortese, Michael J., Hutchison, Keith I., Kessler, Brett, Loftis, Bjorn, Neely, James H., Nelson, Douglas L., Simpson, Greg, B., and Treiman, Rebecca (2007). The English lexicon project. *Behavior Research Methods*, **39**: 445–59.

Barnes, Jonathan and Kavitskaya, Darya (2002). Phonetic analogy and schwa deletion in French. In *Proceedings of the 27th Berkeley Linguistic Society*, 39–50.

Bartens, Hans-Hermann (1989). *Lehrbuch der saamischen (lappischen) Sprache*. Hamburg: Helmut Buske Verlag.

Bates, Douglas M. (2005). Fitting linear mixed models in R. *R News*, **5**: 27–30.

—— (2006). Linear mixed model implementation in lme4, Ms., Department of Statistics, University of Wisconsin, Madison.

Bauer, Laurie (1998). When is a sequence of two nouns a compound in English? *English Language & Linguistics*, **2**: 65–86.

Beard, Robert (1995). *Lexeme-Morpheme Base Morphology: A General Theory of Inflection and Word Formation*. Albany, NY: SUNY Press.

Becker, Judith A. (1994). 'sneak-shoes', 'sworders' and 'nose-beards': A case study of lexical innovation. *First Language*, **14**: 195–211.

Beckwith, Richard, Fellbaum, Christiane, Gross, Derek, and Miller, George A. (1991). WordNet: A lexical database organized on psycholinguistic principles. In *Lexical Acquisition. Exploiting On-Line Resources to Build a Lexicon*, U. Zernik (ed.). Hillsdale, NJ: Lawrence Erlbaum Associates, 211–32.

Bennett, Charles H. (1999). Quantum Information Theory. In *Feynman and Computation: Exploring the Limits of Computers*, Anthiny J. G. Hey (ed.). Reading, MA: Perseus Books.

Bergen, Benjamin K. (2004). The psychological reality of phonaesthemes. *Language*, **80**: 290–311.

Berko, Jean (1958). The child's learning of English morphology. *Word*, **14**: 150–77.

Berman, Ruth A. and Clark, Eve V. (1989). Learning to use compounds for contrast: data from Hebrew. *First Language*, **9**: 247–70.

Bertram, Raymond, Schreuder, Robert, and Baayen, R. Harald (2000). The balance of storage and computation in morphological processing. The role of word formation type, affixal homonymy, and productivity. *Journal of Experimental Psychology-Learning Memory and Cognition*, **26**: 489–511.

Bien, Heidrun (2007). *On the Production of Morphologically Complex Words with Special Attention to Effects of Frequency*. Nijmegen: Max Planck Institute for Psycholinguistics.

Blevins, James P. (2003). Stems and paradigms. *Language*, **79**: 737–67.

—— (2005). Word-based declensions in Estonian. In *Yearbook of Morphology 2005*, G. Booij and J. van Marle (eds.). Dordrecht: Springer, 1–25.

—— (2006a). English inflection and derivation. In *Handbook of English Linguistics*, B. Aarts and A. M. S. McMahon (eds.). Oxford: Blackwell, 507–36.

—— (2006b). Word-based morphology. *Journal of Linguistics*, **42**: 531–73.

—— (2007). Conjugation classes in Estonian. *Linguistica Uralica*, **43**: 250–67.

—— (2008). The post-transformational enterprise. *Journal of Linguistics*, **44**: 723–42.

Blevins, Juliette (2004). *Evolutionary Phonology: The Emergence of Sound Patterns*. Cambridge: Cambridge University Press.

—— (2006a). New perspectives on English sound patterns: 'Natural' and 'unnatural' in Evolutionary Phonology. *Journal of English Linguistics*, **34**: 6–25.

—— (2006b). A theoretical synopsis of Evolutionary Phonology. *Theoretical Linguistics*, **32**: 117–66.

—— (2008). Structure-preserving sound change: A look at unstressed vowel syncope in Austronesian. In *TBA*, A. Adelaar and A. Pawley (eds.). (to appear) Canberra: Pacific Linguistics.

—— and Garrett, Andrew (1998). 'The origins of consonant-vowel metathesis.' *Language*, **74**: 508–56.

Bloomfield, Leonard (1895). On assimilation and adaptation in congeneric classes of words. *American Journal of Philology*, **16**: 409–34.

—— (1933). *Language*. Chicago: University of Chicago Press.

Bochner, Harry (1993). *Simplicity in Generative Morphology*. Berlin: Mouton de Gruyter.

Bod, Rens, Hay, Jennifer, and Jannedy, Stefanie (eds.) (2003). *Probabilistic Linguistics*. Cambridge: Cambridge University Press.

Bohas, Georges, Guillaume, Jean-Patrick, and Kouloughli, Djamel Eddine (1990). *The Arabic Linguistic Tradition*. Arabic Thought and Culture. London: Routledge.

Bonami, Olivier and Boyé, Gilles (2007). Remarques sur les bases de la conjugaison. In *Des sons et des sens*, E. Delais-Roussarie and L. Labrune (eds.). Paris: Hermès Sciences, 77–90.

Braine, Martin D. S. (1966). Learning the positions of words relative to a marker element. *Journal of Experimental Psychology*, **72**: 532–40.

—— (1987). What is learned in acquiring word classes – a step toward an acquisition theory. In *Mechanisms of Language Acquisition*, B. MacWhinney (ed.). Hillsdale, NJ: Lawrence Erlbaum, 65–87.

Brent, Michael R. (1999). An efficient, probabilistically sound algorithm for segmentation and word discovery. *Machine Learning*, **34**: 71–105.

Broe, Michael (1993). *Specification Theory: The Treatment of Redundancy in Generative Phonology*. Ph.D. thesis, University of Edinburgh.

Brooks, Patricia J., Braine, Martin D. S., Catalano, Lisa, Brody, Ruth E., and Sudhalter, Vicki (1993). Acquisition of gender-like noun subclasses in an artificial language: The contribution of phonological markers to learning. *Journal of Memory and Language*, **32**: 76–95.

Buchholz, Eva (2004). *Grammatik der finnischen Sprache*. Bremen: Hempen Verlag.

Burnard, Lou (1995). *Users Guide for the British National Corpus*. British National Corpus Consortium, Oxford: Oxford University Computing Service.

Bybee, Joan L. (1985). *Morphology: A Study of the Relation between Meaning and Form*. Amsterdam: John Benjamins.

—— (1995). Regular morphology and the lexicon. *Language and Cognitive Processes*, **10**: 425–55.

—— (2001). *Phonology and Language Use*. Cambridge: Cambridge University Press.

—— (2002). Word frequency and context of use in the lexical diffusion of phonetically conditioned sound change. *Language Variation and Change*, **14**: 261–90.

—— (2006). From usage to grammar: The mind's response to repetition. *Language*, **82**: 711–33.

—— and Moder, Carol L. (1983). Morphological classes as natural categories. *Language*, **59**: 251–70.

—— and Pardo, Elly (1981). On lexical and morphological conditioning of alternations: A nonce-probe experiment with Spanish verbs. *Linguistics*, **19**: 937–68.

Cameron-Faulkner, Thea and Carstairs-McCarthy, Andrew (2000). Stem alternants as morphological signata: Evidence from blur avoidance in Polish nouns. *Natural Language and Linguistic Theory*, **18**: 813–35.

Campbell, Lyle (1998). *Historical Linguistics: An Introduction*. Edinburgh: Edinburgh University Press.

—— and Poser, William J. (2008). *Language Classification: History and Method*. Cambridge: Cambridge University Press.

Caramazza, Alfonso (1997). How many levels of processing are there in lexical access? *Cognitive Neuropsychology*, **14**: 177–208.

Carstairs, Andrew (1983). Paradigm economy. *Journal of Linguistics*, **19**: 115–25.

—— (1987). *Allomorphy in Inflection*. London: Croom Helm.

Carstairs-McCarthy, Andrew (1991). 'Inflection classes: Two questions with one answer'. In *Paradigms: The Economy of Inflection*, ed. F. Plank. Berlin: Mouton de Gruyter, 213–53.

Casanto, Daniel and Boroditsky, Lera (2007). Time in the mind: Using space to think about time. *Cognition*, **102**: 118–28.

Chapman, Don and Royal Skousen (2005). Analogical modeling and morphological change: The case of the adjectival negative prefix in English. *English Language and Linguistics* **9**(2): 1–25.

Chater, Nick, Tenenbaum, Joshua B., and Yuille, Alan (eds.). (2006). Special issue: Probabilistic models of cognition. *Trends in Cognitive Sciences*, **10**.7.

Chitoran, Ioana and Hualde, José I. (2007). On the origin and evolution of the contrast between diphthongs and hiatus sequences in Romance. *Phonology*, **24**: 37–75.

Chomsky, Noam (1975). *The Logical Structure of Linguistic Theory*. Chicago: University of Chicago Press.

—— (1986). *Knowledge of Language: Its Nature, Origin and Use*. New York: Praeger.

—— and Halle, Morris (1968). *The Sound Pattern of English*. New York: Harper and Row.

—— and Lasnik, Howard (1977). Filters and control. *Linguistic Inquiry*, **8**: 425–504.

Clahsen, Harald, Aveledo, Fraibet, and Roca, Iggy (2002). The development of regular and irregular verb inflection in Spanish child language. *Journal of Child Language*, **29**: 591–622.

—— Sonnenstuhl, Ingrid, Hadler, Meike, and Eisenbeiss, Sonja (2001). Morphological paradigms in language processing and language disorders. *Transactions of the Philological Society*, **99**: 247–77.

Clark, Eve V. (1981). Lexical innovations: How children learn to create new words. In *The Child's Construction of Language*, W. Deutsch (ed.). London: Academic Press, 299–328.

—— (1983). Meaning and concepts. In *Handbook of Child Psychology: Vol. 3 Cognitive Development*, P. Mussen, L. Flavell, and E. Markman (eds.). New York: Wiley, 787–840.

—— and Berman, Ruth A. (1987). Types of linguistic knowledge: Interpreting and producing compound nouns. *Journal of Child Language*, **14**: 547–67.

—— Gelman, Susan A., and Lane, Nancy M. (1985). Compound nouns and category structure in young children. *Child Development*, **56**: 84–94.

Costello, Fintan. J. and Keane, Mark T. (2001). Testing two theories of conceptual combination: Alignment versus diagnosticity in the comprehension and production of combined concepts. *Journal of Experimental Psychology: Learning Memory and Cognition*, **27**.1: 255–71.

Cover, Thomas M. and Thomas, Joy A. (1991). *Elements of Information Theory*. New York: John Wiley & Sons.

Crawley, Michael J. (2002). *Statistical Computing. An Introduction to Data Analysis using S-plus*. Chichester: Wiley.

Croft, William (2001). *Radical Construction Grammar: Syntactic Theory in Typological Perspective*. Oxford: Oxford University Press.

—— (2008). Evolutionary linguistics. *Annual Review of Anthropology*, **37**: 219–34.

Dabrowska, Ewa and Lieven, Elena (2005). Towards a lexically specific grammar of children's question constructions. *Cognitive Linguistics*, **16**: 437–74.

Daelemans, Walter and van den Bosch, Antal (2005). *Memory-based Language Processing*. Cambridge: Cambridge University Press.

—— Zavrel, Jakob, van der Sloot, Ko, and van den Bosch, Antal (2000). TiMBL: Tilburg memory based learner reference guide 3.0. Technical report, Computational Linguistics Tilburg University.

—— —— —— —— (2005). TiMBL: Tilburg memory-based learner, version 5.1, reference guide. Technical report, ILK Technical Report Series 04–02.

Daugherty, Kim and Seidenberg, Mark (1994). Beyond rules and exceptions: A connectionist approach to inflectional morphology. In *The Reality of Linguistic Rules*, S. D. Lima, R. L. Corrigan, and G. K. Iverson (eds.). Amsterdam: John Benjamins, 353–88.

Deacon, Terrence W. (1997). *The Symbolic Species: The Co-Evolution of Language and the Human Brain*. London: Penguin Press.

Deutscher, Guy (2001). On the mechanisms of morphological change. *Folia Linguistica Historica*, **22**: 41–8.

—— (2005). *The Unfolding of Language: The Evolution of Mankind's Greatest Invention*. London: Arrow.

Di Sciullo, Anne-Marie and Williams, Edwin (1987). *On the Definition of Word*. Cambridge: MIT Press.

Dinnsen, Daniel (1979). Maybe atomic phonology. In *Current Issues in Phonological Theory*, D. Dinnsen (ed.). Bloomington, IN: Indiana University Press, 31–49.

Downing, Pamela A. (1977). On the creation and use of English compound nouns. *Language*, **53**. 4: 810–42.

Dressler, Wolfgang U., Libben, Gary, Stark, Jacqueline, Pons, Christiane, and Jarema, Gonia (2001). The processing of interfixed German compounds. In *Yearbook of Morphology 1999*, G. Booij and J. van Marle (eds.). Dordrecht: Kluwer, 185–220.

Eddington, David (2002). A comparison of two analogical models: Tilburg memory-based learner versus analogical modeling. In *Analogical modeling: An Exemplar-based Approach to Language*, R. Skousen, D. Lonsdale, and D. B. Parkinson (eds.). Amsterdam: John Benjamins, 141–55.

Eisner, Frank and McQueen, James M. (2005). The specificity of perceptual learning in speech processing. *Perception and Psychophysics*, **67**: 224–38.

Elzinga, Dirk (2006). English adjective comparison and analogy. *Lingua*, **116**: 757–70.

Erelt, Mati, Kasik, Reet, Metslang, Helle, Rajandi, Henno, Ross, Kristiina, Henn, Saari, Kaja, Tael, and Silvi, Vare (1995). *Eesti keele grammatika*. Volume I: Morfoloogia. Tallin: Eesti Teaduste Akadeemia Eesti Keele Instituut.

Ernestus, Mirjam and Baayen, R. Harald (2003). Predicting the unpredictable: Interpreting neutralized segments in Dutch. *Language*, **79**: 5–38.

—— —— (2004). Analogical effects in regular past tense production in Dutch. *Linguistics*, **42**: 873–903.

Estes, Zachary (2003). Attributive and relational processes in nominal combination. *Journal of Memory and Language*, **48**: 304–19.

Fabb, Nigel (1998). Compounding. In *The Handbook of Morphology*, A. Spencer and A. M. Zwicky (eds.). Oxford: Blackwell Publishers, 66–83.

Filipović Đurđević, Dušica (2007). *The Polysemy Effect in the Processing of Serbian Nouns*. Ph.D. thesis, University of Belgrade, Serbia.

Finkel, Rafael and Stump, Gregory (2007). Principal parts and linguistic typology. *Morphology*, **17**: 39–75.

Firth, J. R. (1930). *Speech*. London: Ernest Benn.

Friedman, Lynn and Wall, Melanie (2005). Graphical views of suppression and multicollinearity in multiple regression. *The American Statistician*, **59**: 127–36.

Frigo, Lenore and McDonald, Janet L. (1998). Properties of phonological markers that affect the acquisition of gender-like subclasses. *Journal of Memory and Language*, **39**: 218–45.

Frisch, Stefan A. (1996). *Similarity and Frequency in Phonology*. Ph.D. thesis, Northwestern University.

—— Pierrehumbert, Janet B., and Broe, Michael B. (2004). Similarity avoidance and the OCP. *Natural Language and Linguistic Theory*, **22**: 179–228.

Gagné, Christina L. (2001). Relation and lexical priming during the interpretation of noun-noun combinations. *Journal of Experimental Psychology: Learning Memory and Cognition*, **27**: 236–54.

—— and Shoben, Edward J. (1997). Influence of thematic relations on the comprehension of modifier-noun combinations. *Journal of Experimental Psychology: Learning Memory and Cognition*, **23**: 71–87.

—— —— (2002). Priming relations in ambiguous noun-noun combinations. *Memory and Cognition*, **30**: 637–46.

—— and Spalding, Thomas L. (2004). Effect of relation availability on the interpretation and access of familiar noun-noun compounds. *Brain and Language*, **90**: 478–86.

—— —— (2006). Conceptual combinations: Implications for the mental lexicon. In *The Representation and Processing of Compound Words*, G. Libben and G. Jarema (eds.). Oxford: Oxford University Press, 145–68.

Gahl, Susanne and Yu, Alan C. L. (eds.). (2006). Special issue on exemplar-based models in linguistics. *The Linguistic Review*, **23**.

Garrett, Andrew (2008). Paradigmatic uniformity and markedness. See Good (2008), 125–43.

Gentner, Dedre (1983). Structure mapping: a theoretical framework for analogy. *Cognitive Science*, **7**: 155–70.

—— Bowdle, Brian F., Wolff, Phillip, and Boronat, Consuelo (2001*a*). Metaphor is like analogy. See Gentner, Holyoak, and Kokinov (2001*b*), 199–253.

Gentner, Dedre, Holyoak, Keith J., and Kokinov, Boicho N. (eds) (2001*b*). *The Analogical Mind: Perspectives from Cognitive Science*. Cambridge, MA: MIT Press.

—— and Kurtz, Kenneth J. (2005). Relational categories. In *Categorization Inside and Outside the Lab*, W. K. Ahn, R. L. Goldstone, B. C. Love, A. B. Markman, and P. W. Wolff (eds.). Washington, DC: APA, 151–75.

—— and Markman, Arthur B. (1997). Structure mapping in analogy and similarity. *American Psychologist*, **52**: 45–56.

Gerken, LouAnn, Wilson, Rachel, and Lewis, W. (2005). 17-month-olds can use distributional cues to form syntactic categories. *Journal of Child Language*, **32**: 249–68.

Gerken, LouAnn., Gómez, Rebecca L., and Nurmsoo, Erika (1999). The role of meaning and form in the formation of syntactic categories. Paper presented at the *Society for Research in Child Development*. Albuquerque, NM.

Giegerich, Heinz J. (2004). Compound or phrase? English noun-plus-noun constructions and the stress criterion. *English Language and Linguistics*, **8**: 1–24.

Gildea, Daniel and Jurafsky, Daniel (1996). Learning bias and phonological-rule induction. *Computational Linguistics*, **22**: 497–530.

Gleitman, Lila R. and Gleitman, Henry (1970). *Phrase and Paraphrase: Some Innovative Uses of Language*. New York: W. W. Norton.

Goldberg, Adele E. (2006). *Constructions at Work: The Nature of Generalization in Language*. Oxford: Oxford University Press.

—— and Jackendoff, Ray (2005). The end result(ative). *Language*, **81**: 474–7.

Goldinger, Stephen D. (2000). The role of perceptual episodes in lexical processing. In *Proceedings of SWAP, Workshop on Spoken Word Access Processes*, A. Cutler, J. M. McQueen, and R. Zondervan (eds.). Nijmegen: Max Planck Insititute for Psycholinguistics, 155–8.

Goldsmith, John A. (2000). Linguistica: An automatic morphological analyzer. In *Papers from the 36th Annual Meeting of the Chicago Linguistic Society, Main Session*, A. Okrent and J. Boyle (eds.). Chicago: Chicago Linguistics Society, 125–39.

—— (2001). The unsupervised learning of natural language morphology. *Computational Linguistics*, **27**: 153–98.

—— (2005). Review of Nevins. *Language*, **81**: 719–36.

—— (2006). An algorithm for the unsupervised learning of morphology. *Natural Language Engineering*, **12**: 353–71.

—— (2007). Towards a new empiricism. In *Recherches Linguistiques à Vincennes 36*, J. Brandao de Carvalho (ed.), 9–36.

—— (2009). Segmentation and morphology. In *The Handbook of Computational Linguistics*, A. Clark, C. Fox, and S. Lappin (eds.). Oxford: Blackwell.

—— and Hu, Yu (2004). From signatures to finite state automata. Technical Report TR-2005–05, Department of Computer Science, University of Chicago.

Gómez, Rebecca L. and LaKusta, Laura (2004). A first step in form-based category abstraction by 12-month-old infants. *Developmental Science*, 7: 567–80.

Good, Jeff (ed.) (2008). *Linguistic Universals and Language Change*. Oxford: Oxford University Press.

Goswami, Usha (2001). Analogical reasoning in children. See Gentner, Holyoak, and Kokinov (2001), 437–70.

—— and Brown, Ann L. (1989). Melting chocolate and melting snowmen: Analogical reasoning and causal relations. *Cognition*, 35: 69–95.

—— —— (1990). Higher-order structure and relational reasoning: Contrasting analogical and thematic relations. *Cognition*, 36: 207–26.

Grimshaw, Jane (1981). Form, function, and the language acquisition device. In *The Logical Problem of Language Acquisition*, C. L. Baker and J. J. McCarthy (eds.). Cambridge, MA: MIT Press, 165–82.

Guenther, Frank H., Nieto-Castanon, Alfonso, Ghosh Satrajit, S., and Tourville, Jason A. (2004). Representation of sound categories in auditory cortical maps. *Journal of Speech, Language, and Hearing Research*, 47: 46–57.

Gurevich, Olga (2006). *Construction Morphology: the Georgian Case*. Ph.D. thesis, University of California, Berkeley.

Hafer, Margaret A. and Weiss, Stephen F. (1974). Word segmentation by letter successor varieties. *Information Storage and Retrieval*, 10: 371–85.

Hahn, Ulricke and Chater, Nick (1998). Similarity and rules: Distinct? Exhaustive? Empirically distinguishable? *Cognition*, 65: 197–230.

—— —— and Richardson, Lucy B. (2003). Similarity as transformation. *Cognition*, 87: 1–32.

Halford, Graeme S. and Andrews, Glenda (2007). Domain general processes in higher cognition: Analogical reasoning, schema induction and capacity limitations. In *Integrating the Mind: Domain General versus Domain Specific Processes in Higher Cognition*, M. J. Roberts (ed.). New York: Psychology Press, 213–32.

Halle, Morris (1962). Phonology in generative grammar. *Word*, 18: 54–72.

—— and Marantz, Alec (1993). Distributed Morphology and the pieces of inflection. In *The View from Building 20*, K. Hale and S. J. Keyser (eds.). Cambridge, MA: MIT Press, 111–76.

Hamp, Eric, Householder, Fred W., and Austerlitz, Robert (eds.)(1966). *Readings in Linguistics II*. Chicago: University of Chicago Press.

Hare, Mary and Elman, Jeffrey L. (1995). Learning and morphological change. *Cognition*, 56: 61–98.

Harrington, Jonathan, Palethorpe, Sallyanne, and Watson, Catherine I. (2000). Does the Queen speak the Queen's English? *Nature*, 408: 927–8.

Harris, Alice C. and Campbell, Lyle (1995). *Historical Syntax in Cross-Linguistic Perspective*. Cambridge Studies in Linguistics, vol. 74. Cambridge: Cambridge University Press.

Harris, Zellig S. (1942). Morpheme alternants in linguistic analysis. *Language*, 18: 169–180. Reprinted in Joos (1957), 109–15.

—— (1955). From phoneme to morpheme. *Language*, 31: 190–222.

Harris, Zellig S. (1967). Morpheme boundaries within words: Report on a computer test. In *Papers in Structural and Transformational Linguistics (1970)*, 68–77. Dordrecht: D. Reidel.

Hay, Jennifer (2001). Lexical frequency in morphology: Is everything relative? *Linguistics*, 39: 1041–70.

Hay, Jennifer B. and Baayen, R. Harald (2002). Parsing and productivity. In *Yearbook of Morphology 2001*, Geert E. Booij and Jaapvan Marle (eds.). Dordrecht: Kluwer, 203–35.

—— and —— (2005). Shifting paradigms: Gradient structure in morphology. *Trends in Cognitive Sciences*, 9: 342–8.

—— Pierrehumbert, Janet B., and Beckman, Mary (2004). Speech perception, well-formedness and the statistics of the lexicon. In *Phonetic Interpretation: Papers in Laboratory Phonology VI*, J. Local, R. Ogden, and R. Temple (eds.). Cambridge: Cambridge University Press, 58–74.

Heine, Bernd (1993). *Auxiliaries: Cognitive Forces and Grammaticalization*. Oxford: Oxford University Press.

Hinton, Leanne, Nichols, Johanna, and Ohala, John J. (eds.). (1995). *Sound Symbolism*. Cambridge: Cambridge University Press.

Hock, Hans Henrich (1991). *Principles of Historical Linguistics*. Berlin: Mouton de Gruyter.

—— (2003). Analogical change. In *The Handbook of Historical Linguistics*, B. Josephs and R. Janda (eds.). Oxford: Oxford University Press, 441–80.

Hockett, Charles F. (1947). Problems of morphemic analysis. *Language*, 23: 321–43. Reprinted in Joos (1957), 229–42.

—— (1954). Two models of grammatical description. *Word*, 10: 210–31. Reprinted in Joos (1957), 386–99.

—— (1960). The origin of speech. *Scientific American*, 203: 88–9.

—— (1966). *Language, mathematics and linguistics. In T. Seberk (ed.) Current trends in linguistics, vol 3: Theoretical Foundations*. The Hague: Mouton. 155–304.

—— (1968). *The State of the Art*. The Hague: Mouton.

—— (1987). *Refurbishing our Foundations: Elementary Linguistics from an Advanced Point of View*. Current Issues in Linguistic Theory, vol. 56. Amsterdam: John Benjamins.

Holyoak, Keith J. and Thagard, Paul (1977). The analogical mind. *American Psychologist*, 52: 35–44.

—— and —— (1989). Analogical mapping by constraint satisfaction. *Cognitive Science* 13: 295–355.

—— and —— (1997). The analogical mind. *American Psychologist*, 52(1): 35–44.

Hopper, Paul and Traugott, Elizabeth C. (2003). *Grammaticalization*. Cambridge: Cambridge University Press.

Hu, Yu, Matveeva, Irina, Goldsmith, John A., and Sprague, Colin (2005). Using morphology and syntax together in unsupervised learning. In *Proceedings of the*

Workshop on Psychocomputational Models of Human Language Acquisition, Ann Arbor, MI: Association for Computational Linguistics, 20–7.

Huang, Hsu-Wen, Lee, Chia-Ying, Tsai, Jie-Li, Lee, Chia-Lin, Hung, Daisy L., and Tzeng, Ovid J.-L. (2006). Orthographic neighborhood effects in reading Chinese two-character words. *Neuroreport*, 17: 1061–5.

Hughes, Michael and Ackerman, Farrell (2002). Words and paradigms: Estonian nominal declension. In *Papers from the 37th Annual Meeting of the Chicago Linguistics Society*, M. Andronis, C. Ball, H. Elston, and S. Neuvel (eds.).

Hunt, Gavin R. and Gray, Russell D. (2004). The crafting of hook tools by wild New Caledonian crows. *Proceedings of the Royal Society of London, B. Biol. Sci.*, 271: S88–S90.

Itkonen, Esa (2005). *Analogy as Structure and Process:* Amsterdam: John Benjamins.

Jackendoff, Ray (2002). *Foundations of Language: Brain, Meaning, Grammar, Evolution*. Oxford: Oxford University Press.

Jakobi, Angelika (1990). *A Fur Grammar*. Hamburg: Helmut Buske Verlag.

Johnson, C. Douglas (1972). *Formal Aspects of Phonological Description*. The Hague: Mouton.

Johnson, Keith (1997). Speech perception without speaker normalization: An exemplar model. In *Talker Variability in Speech Processing*, K. Johnson and J. W. Mullennix (eds.). San Diego: Academic Press, 145–65.

de Jong, Nivja H. (2002). *Morphological Families in the Mental Lexicon*. Ph.D. thesis, University of Nijmegen.

—— Feldman, Laurie B., Schreuder, Robert, Pastizzo, Matthew J., and Baayen, R. Harald (2002). The processing and representation of Dutch and English compounds: Peripheral morphological and central orthographic effects. *Brain and Language*, 81: 555–67.

—— Schreuder, Robert, and Baayen, R. Harald (2000). The morphological family size effect and morphology. *Language and Cognitive Processes*, 15: 329–65.

Joos, Martin (ed.) (1957). *Readings in Linguistics I*. Chicago: University of Chicago Press.

Joseph, Brian and Janda, Richard (1988). The how and why of diachronic morphologization and demorphologization. In *Theoretical Morphology: Approaches in Modern Linguistics*, M. Hammond and M. Noonan (eds.). San Diego: Academic Press, 193–210.

Kang, Yoonjung (2006). Neutralization and variations in Korean verbal paradigms. In *Harvard Studies in Korean Linguistics XI*. Hanshin Publishing Company, 183–96.

Kaplan, Ronald M. and Kay, Martin (1994). Regular models of phonological rule systems. *Computational Linguistics*, 20: 331–78.

Karlsson, Fred (1999). *Finnish: An Essential Grammar*. London: Routledge.

Katz, Jeffrey S. and Wright, Anthony A. (2006). Same/different abstract-concept learning by pigeons. *Journal of Experimental Psychology: Animal Behavior Proceedings*, 32: 80–6.

Kay, Paul and Fillmore, Charles J. (1999). Grammatical constructions and linguistic generalizations: The *What's X doing Y?* construction. *Language*, 75: 1–33.

—— and Zimmer, Karl (1976). On the semantics of compounds and genitives in English. In *Sixth California Linguistics Association Proceedings*, San Diego, CA: Campile Press, 29–35.

Kazazis, Kostas (1969). Possible evidence for (near-)underlying forms in the speech of a child. *Chicago Linguistics Society*, 5: 382–6.

Kemler Nelson, Deborah, Jusczyk, Peter W., Mandel, Denise R., Myers, James, Turk, Alice E., and Gerken, LouAnn (1995). The headturn preference procedure for testing auditory perception. *Infant Behavior and Development*, 18: 111–16.

Kempe, Vera and Brooks, Patricia J. (2001). The role of diminutives in the acquisition of Russian gender: Can elements of child-directed speech aid in learning morphology? *Language Learning*, 51: 221–56.

Keuleers, Emmanuel (2008). *Memory-based Learning of Inflectional Morphology*. Antwerp: University of Antwerp.

—— Sandra, Dorniniek, Daelemans, Walter, Gillis, Steven, Durieux, Gert, and Martens, Evelyn (2007). Dutch plural inflection: The exception that proves the analogy. *Cognitive Psychology*, 54: 283–318.

Kibrik, Aleksandr E. (1998). Archi. In *Handbook of Morphology*, A. Spencer and A. M. Zwicky (eds.). Oxford: Blackwell, 455–76.

Kirby, Simon (2001). Spontaneous evolution of linguistic structure: An iterated learning model of the emergence of regularity and irregularity. *IEEE Transactions on Evolutionary Computation*, 5: 102–10.

—— (2007). The evolution of language. In *Oxford Handbook of Evolutionary Psychology*, R. Dunbar and L. Barrett (eds.). Oxford: Oxford University Press, 669–81.

Kostić, Aleksandar (1991). Informational approach to processing inflected morphology: Standard data reconsidered. *Psychological Research*, 53: 62–70.

—— (1995). Informational load constraints on processing inflected morphology. In *Morphological Aspects of Language Processing*, L. B. Feldman (eds.). Hillsdale, NJ: Lawrence Erlbaum, 317–44.

—— (2008). The effect of the amount of information on language processing. In submission.

—— Marković, Tanja, and Baucal, Aleksandar (2003). Inflectional morphology and word meaning: Orthogonal or co-implicative domains? In *Morphological Structure in Language Processing*, R. H. Baayen and R. Schreuder (eds.). Berlin: Mouton de Gruyter, 1–44.

Kraska-Szlenk, Iwona (2007). *Analogy: The Relation between Lexicon and Grammar*. Munich: Lincom Europa.

Krott, Andrea, Gagné, Christina L., and Nicoladis, Elena (2009). How the parts relate to the whole: Frequency effects on childrens's interpretation of novel compounds. *Journal of Child Language*, 36: 85–112.

—— Hagoort, Peter, and Baayen, R. Harald (2004). Sublexical units and supralexical combinatorics in the processing of interfixed Dutch compounds. *Language and Cognitive Processes*, 19: 453–71.

—— Krebbers, Loes, Schreuder, Robert, and Baayen, R. Harald (2002a). Semantic influence on linkers in Dutch noun-noun compounds. *Folia Linguistica*, 36: 7–22.

—— and Nicoladis, Elena (2005). Large constituent families help children parse compounds. *Journal of Child Language*, **32**: 139–58.

—— Schreuder, Robert, and Baayen, R. Harald (2001). Analogy in morphology: Modeling the choice of linking morphemes in Dutch. *Linguistics*, **1**: 51–93.

—— —— —— (2002*b*). Analogical hierarchy: Exemplar-based modeling of linkers in Dutch noun-noun compounds. In *Analogical Modeling: An Examplar-Based Approach to Language*, R. Skousen, D. Londsdale, and D. B. Parkinson (eds.). Amsterdam: John Benjamins, 181–206.

—— —— —— (2002*c*). Linking elements in Dutch noun-noun compounds: Constituent families as analogical predictors for response latencies. *Brain and Language*, **81**: 708–22.

—— —— —— and Dressler, Wolfgang U. (2007). Analogical effects on linking elements in German compounds. *Language and Cognitive Processes*, **22**: 25–57.

Kruskal, Joseph B. (1983). An overview of sequence comparison. In *Time Warps, String Edits, and Macromolecules: The Theory and Practice of Sequence Comparison*, D. Sankoff and J. B. Kruskal (eds.). Reading, MA: Addison-Wesley, 1–44.

Kuehne, Sven E., Forbus, Kenneth D., Gentner, Dedre, and Quinn, Bryan (2000). SEQL: Category learning as progressive abstraction using structure mapping. In *Proceedings of the Twenty-Second Annual Conference of the Cognitive Science Society*, 770–5.

Kuhl, Patricia K. (1991). Human adults and human infants show a perceptual magnet effect for the prototypes of speech categories, monkeys do not. *Perception and Psychophysics*, **50**: 93–107.

—— (1995). Mechanisms of developmental change in speech and language. In *Proceedings of the XIIIth International Congress of Phonetic Sciences, Vol. 2*, K. Elenius and P. Branderud (eds.). Stockholm: Stockholm University, 132–9.

Kuperman, Victor, Bertram, Raymond, and Baayen, R. Harald (2008). Morphological dynamics in compound processing. In submission.

Kupryanova, Z. N. (1985). *Nenetskij jazyk [Nenets Language]*. Moscow: Nauk.

Kuryłowicz, Jerzy (1947). La nature des procès dits "analogiques". *Acta Linguistica*, **5**: 121–38. Reprinted in Hamp, Householder, and Austerlitz (1966), 158–74. English translation with introduction by Margaret Winters (1995), The nature of the so-called analogical processes. *Diachronica* **12**: 113–45.

Lahiri, Aditi (ed.) (2000). *Analogy, Levelling, Markedness: Principles of Change in Phonology and Morphology*. Berlin: Mouton de Gruyter.

Lakoff, George and Johnson, Mark (1980). *Metaphors We Live By*. Chicago: University of Chicago Press.

Landauer, Thomas K. and Dumais, Susan T. (1997). A solution to Plato's problem: The latent semantic analysis theory of acquisition, induction and representation of knowledge. *Psychological Review*, **104**: 211–40.

Law, Vivien (2003). *The History of Linguistics in Europe: From Plato to 1600*. Cambridge: Cambridge University Press.

Lees, Robert B. (1960). *The Grammar of English Nominalizations*. The Hague: Mouton de Gruyter.

Levelt, Willem J. M., Roelofs, Ardi, and Meyer, Antje S. (1999). A theory of lexical access in speech production. *Behavioral and Brain Sciences*, **22**: 1–37.

Levi, Judith N. (1978). *The Syntax and Semantics of Complex Nominals*. New York: Academic Press.

Levy, Roger (2008). Expectation-based syntactic comprehension. *Cognition*, **106**: 1126–77.

Libben, Gary, Jarema, Gonia, Dressler, Wolfgang, Stark, Jacqueline, and Pons, Christiane (2002). Triangulating the effects of interfixation in the processing of German compounds. *Folia Linguistica*, **36**: 23–43.

Lieber, Rochelle (1992). *Deconstructing Morphology*. Chicago: University of Chicago Press.

Lieven, Elena, Behrens, Heike, Speares, Jennifer, and Tomasello, Michael (2003). Early syntactic creativity: a usage-based approach'. *Journal of Child Language*, **30**: 333–70.

Locke, John (1690/1975). *An Essay Concerning Human Understanding*. History of Economic Thought Books. McMaster University Archive for the History of Economic Thought, Canada: Hamilton.

Long, Christopher J. and Almor, Amit (2000). Irregularization: The interaction of item frequency and phonological interference in regular past tense production. In *Proceedings of the Twenty-Second Annual Conference of the Cognitive Science Society*. Hillsdale, NJ: Lawrence Erlbaum, 310–15.

Lonsdale, Deryle (2002). Data files for analogical modeling. In *Analogical Modeling: An Exemplar-Based Approach to Language*, Royal Skousen, Deryle Lonsdale, and Dilworth B. Parkinson (eds.). 349–63. Amsterdam: John Benjamins.

Luce, R. Duncan (1959). *Individual Choice Behavior*. New York: Wiley.

MacWhinney, Brain. (2000). *The Childes Project: Tool for Analyzing Talk, Vol. 1: Transcription Format and Programs. Vol. 2: The Database*. Mahwah, NJ: Lawrence Erlbaum.

MacWhinney, Brian and Leinbach, Jared (1991). Implementations are not conceptualizations: Revising the verb learning model. *Cognition*, **40**: 121–57.

Magnus, Margaret (2000). *What's in a Word? Evidence for Phonosemantics*. Ph.D. thesis, University of Trondheim.

Mańczak, Witold (1958). Tendances générales des changements analogiques. *Lingua*, **7**: 298–325, 387–420.

—— (1980). Laws of analogy. In *Historical Morphology* J. Fisiak (ed.). The Hague: Mouton, 283–8.

Manning, Christopher D. and Schütze, Hinrich (1999). *Foundations of Statistical Natural Language Processing*. Cambridge, MA: MIT Press.

Maratsos, Michael (1982). The child's construction of grammatical categories. In *Language Acquisition: The State of the Art*, E. Wanner and L. Gleitman (eds.). Cambridge: Cambridge University Press.

de Marcken, Carl (1996). *Unsupervised Language Acquisition*. Ph.D. thesis, MIT, Cambridge MA.

Marcus, Gary F., Brinkmann, Ursula, Clahsen, Harald, Wiese, Richard, and Pinker, Steven (1995). German inflection: The exception that proves the rule. *Cognitive Psychology*, **29**: 189–256.

Mattens, W. H. M. (1984). De voorspelbaarheid van tussenklanken in nominale samenstellingen. *De Nieuwe Taalgids*, **7**: 333–43.

Matthews, Peter H. (1972). *Inflectional Morphology: A Theoretical Study Based on Aspects of Latin Verb Conjugation*. Cambridge: Cambridge University Press.

—— (1974). *Morphology. An Introduction to the Theory of Word Structure*. Cambridge: Cambridge University Press.

—— (1991). *Morphology*. Cambridge: Cambridge University Press.

—— (2007). *Syntactic Relations: A Critical Survey*. Vol. 114, Cambridge Studies in Linguistics. Cambridge: Cambridge University Press.

Mayr, Ernst (1997). The objects of selection. *Proceedings of the National Academy of Sciences*, **94**: 2091–4.

McClelland, James L. and Patterson, Karalyn (2002). Rules or connections in past-tense inflections: What does the evidence rule out? *Trends in Cognitive Sciences*, **6**: 465–72.

Meillet, Antoine (1915). *Étude comparative des langues indo-européennes*. Paris: Hachette et Cie.

Mellenius, Ingmarie (1997). *The Acquisition of Nominal Compounding in Swedish*. Lund: Lund University Press.

Merlo, Lauren M. F., Pepper, John W., Reid, Brian J., and Maley, Carlo C. (2006). Cancer as an evolutionary and ecological process. *Nature Reviews Cancer*, **6**: 924–35.

Merrifield, William R. and Rensch, Calvin R. (eds.) (1990). *Syllables, Tone, and Verb Paradigms*. Studies in Chinantec Languages, Vol. 4. Summer Institute of Linguistics and The University of Texas at Arlington, Dallas.

Mielke, Jeff (2004). *The Emergence of Distinctive Features*. Ph.D. thesis, Ohio State University.

—— (2008). *The Emergence of Distinctive Features*. Oxford Studies in Typology and Linguistic Theory. Oxford: Oxford University Press.

Milin, Petar, Filipović Đurđević, Dušica, and Moscoso del Prado Martín, Fermín (2009). The simultaneous effects of inflectional paradigms and classes on lexical recognition: Evidence from Serbian. *Journal of Memory and Language*, **60**: 50–64.

Miller, George A. (1990). Wordnet: An on-line lexical database. *International Journal of Lexicography*, **3**: 235–312.

Mintz, Tobin (2002). Category induction from distributional cues in an artifical language. *Memory and Cognition*, **30**: 678–86.

—— (2006). Frequent frames: Simple co-occurrence constructions and their links to linguistic structure. In *Constructions in Acquisition*, B. Kelly and E. V. Clark (eds.). Stanford: CSLI, 59–82.

Miozzo, Michele and Caramazza, Alfonso (2005). The representation of homophones: Evidence from the distractor-frequency effect. *Journal of Experimental Psychology: Learning, Memory and Cognition*, **31**: 1360–71.

Morpurgo Davies, Anna (1978). Analogy, segmentation and the early Neogrammarians. *Transactions of the Philological Society*, 36–60.

Morris, Richard E (2005). Attraction to the unmarked in Old Spanish leveling. In *Selected Proceedings of the 7th Hispanic Linguistics Symposium*, D. Eddington (ed.). Somerville, MA: Cascadilla Proceedings Project, 180–91.

Moscoso del Prado Martín, Fermín (2003). *Paradigmatic Structures in Morphological Processing: Computational and Cross-Linguistic Studies*. Ph.D. thesis, University of Nijmegen.

—— Bertram, Raymond, Haikio, Tuomo, Schreuder, Robert, and Baayen, R. Harald (2004*a*). Morphological family size in a morphologically rich language: The case of Finnish compared to Dutch and Hebrew. *Journal of Experimental Psychology: Learning, Memory and Cognition*, **30**: 1271–8.

—— Kostić, Aleksandar, and Filipović Đurđević, Dušica (2008). The missing link between morphemic assemblies and behavioral responses: A Bayesian information-theoretical model of lexical processing. Manuscript submitted for publication.

—— —— and Baayen, R. Harald (2004*b*). Putting the bits together: An information-theoretical perspective on morphological processing. *Cognition*, **94**: 1–18.

Murphy, Gregory L. (1990). Noun phrase interpretation and conceptual combination. *Journal of Memory and Language*, **29**: 259–88.

Nakisa, Ramin Charles, Plunkett, Kim, and Hahn, Ulrike (2000). A cross-linguistic comparison of single and dual-route models of inflectional morphology. In *Cognitive Models of Language Acquisition*, P. Broeder and J. Murre (eds.). Cambridge, MA: MIT Press, 201–22.

Neuvel, Sylvain and Fulop, Sean A. (2002). Unsupervised learning of morphology without morphemes. In *Proceedings of the ACL-02 Workshop on Morphological and Phonological Learning*, Morristown, NJ: Association for Computational Linguistics, 31–40.

—— and Singh, Rajendra (2001). Vive la différence! What morphology is about. *Folia Linguistica*, **35**: 313–20.

New, Boris, Brysbaert, Marc, Segui, Juan, Ferrand, Ludovic, and Rastle, Kathleen (2004). The processing of singular and plural nouns in French and English. *Journal of Memory and Language*, **51**: 568–85.

Nickel, Klaus Peter (1990). *Samisk grammatikk*. Oslo: Universitetsforlaget.

Nicoladis, Elena (2003). What compound nouns mean to preschool children. *Brain and Language*, **84**: 38–49.

—— and Krott, Andrea (2007). Family size and French-speaking children's segmentation of existing compounds. *Language Learning*, **57**: 201–228.

Nosofsky, Robert M. (1986). Attention, similarity, and the identification-categorization relationship. *Journal of Experimental Psychology: General*, **115**: 39–57.

—— (1990). Relations between exemplar similarity and likelihood models of classification. *Journal of Mathematical Psychology*, **34**: 393–418.

Oinas, Zsuzsanna (2008). *Guide to Finnish Declension*. Espoo: Finnlibri.

Pace, Wanda J. (1990). Comaltepec Chinantec verb inflection. See Merrifield and Rensch (1990), 21–62.

Parault, Susan J., Schwanenflugel, Paula J., and Haverback, Heather R. (2005). The development of interpretations for novel noun-noun conceptual combinations during the early school years. *Journal of Experimental Child Psychology*, **91**: 67–87.

Paul, Hermann (1920). *Prinzipien der Sprachgeschichte*. Tübingen: Max Niemayer Verlag.

Penn, Derek C., Holyoak, Keith J., and Povinelli, Daniel J. (2008). Darwin's mistake: Explaining the discontinuity between human and nonhuman minds. *Behavioral and Brain Sciences*, **31**: 109–78.

Penny, Ralph (2002). *A History of the Spanish Language*. Cambridge: Cambridge University Press.

Pepperberg, Irene M. (1987). Acquisition of the same/different concept by an African Grey parrot (Psittacus erithacus): Learning with respect to categories of color, shape and material. *Animal Learning and Behavior*, **15**: 423–32.

Pierrehumbert, Janet B. (2001). Exemplar dynamics: Word frequency, lenition and contrast. In *Frequency and the Emergence of Linguistic Structure*, J. Bybee and P. Hopper (eds.). Amsterdam: John Benjamins, 137–58.

—— (2003). Phonetic diversity, statistical learning, and acquisition of phonology. *Language and Speech*, **46**: 115–54.

—— (2006). The new toolkit. *Journal of Phonetics*, **34**: 516–30.

Pihel, Kalju and Pikamäe, Arno (eds.) (1999). *Soome-eesti sõnaraamat*. Tallinn: Valgus.

Pinker, Steven (1982). A theory of the acquisition of lexical interpretive grammars. In *The Mental Representation of Grammatical Relations*, J. Bresnan (ed.). Cambridge, MA: MIT Press, 655–726.

—— (1991). Rules of language. *Science*, **153**: 530–35.

—— (1999). *Words and Rules: The Ingredients of Language*. London: Weidenfeld and Nicolson.

—— and Ullman, Michael T. (2002). The past and future of the past tense. *Trends in Cognitive Sciences*, **6**: 456–63.

Plag, Ingo (2006). The variability of compound stress in English: Structural, semantic, and analogical factors. Part 1. *English Language & Linguistics*, **10**: 143–72.

Premack, David (1983). Animal cognition. *Annual Review of Psychology*, **34**: 351–62.

Rissanen, Jorma (1989). *Stochastic Complexity in Statistical Inquiry*. Riner Edge, NJ: World Scientific Publishing Company.

Roark, Brian and Sproat, Richard (2007). *Computational Approaches to Morphology and Syntax*. Oxford: Oxford University Press.

Robins, Robert H. (1959). In defense of WP. *Transactions of the Philological Society*, 116–44. Reprinted in *Transactions of the Philological Society* **99**: 1–36.

Robinson, A. H. (1979). Observations on some deficiencies in the transformational model as applied to particular compound types in French. *Cahiers de Lexicologie*, **35**: 107–15.

Ross, Sheldon M. (1988). *A First Course in Probability*. New York: Macmillan Publishing Company.

Rubach, Jerzy and Booij, Geert (1985). A grid theory of Polish stress. *Lingua*, **66**: 281–319.

Rumelhart, David E. and McClelland, James L. (1987). Learning the past tenses of English verbs. In *Mechanisms of Language Acquisition*, B. MacWhinney (ed.). Hillsdale, NJ: Lawrence Erlbaum, 194–248.

Ryder, Mary Ellen (1994). *Ordered Chaos: An Investigation of the Interpretation of English Noun-Noun Compounds*. Berkeley and Los Angeles: University of California Press.

Salminen, Tapani (1993). On identifying basic vowel distinctions in Tundra Nenets. *Finno-Ugrische Forschungen*, **51**: 177–87.

—— (1997). *Tundra Nenets Inflection*. Mémoires de la Société Finno-Ougrienne 227, Helsinki.

—— (1998). *A Morphological Dictionary of Tundra Nenets*. Lexica Societatis Fenno-Ugricae 26, Helsinki.

Sankoff, Gillian and Blondeau, Hélène (2007). Language change across the lifespan: /r/ in Montreal French. *Language*, **83**: 560–88.

Sapir, Edward (1921). *Language*. New York: Harcourt Brace.

Saussure, Ferdinand de (1916). *Cours de linguistique générale*. Paris: Payot.

Schreuder, Robert and Baayen, R. Harald (1995). Modeling morphological processing. In *Morphological Aspects of Language Processing*, L. B. Feldman (ed.). Hillsdale, NJ: Lawrence Erlbaum, 131–54.

—— —— (1997). How complex simplex words can be. *Journal of Memory and Language*, **37**: 118–39.

Seiler, Hansjakob (1965). On paradigmatic and syntagmatic similarity. *Lingua*, **18**: 35–97.

Shannon, Claude (1948). A mathematical theory of communication. *The Bell System Technical Journal*, **27**: 379–423, 623–56.

Sharkey, William S. (1982). *The Theory of Natural Monopoly*. Cambridge: Cambridge University Press.

Skousen, Royal (1989). *Analogical Modeling of Language*. Dordrecht: Kluwer.

—— (1992). *Analogy and Structure*. Dordrecht: Kluwer.

—— (2002). Analogical modeling and quantum computing. In *Analogical Modeling*, Skousen, Royal, Deryle Lonsdale, and Dilworth B. Parkinson (eds.), 319–46.

—— (2003) Analogical Modeling: Exemplars, Rules, and Quantum Computing. *Proceedings of the Twenty-Ninth Annual Meeting of the Berkeley Linguistics Society*, Pawel Nowak, Corey Yoquelet, and David Mortensen (eds.), 425–39 [also available at <http://humanities.byu.edu/am/>].

—— (2005). Quantum Analogical Modeling: A General Quantum Computing Algorithm for Predicting Language Behavior. Preprint, posted under Quantum Physics on <arXiv.org>, quant-ph/0510146, October 18, 2005.

Skousen, Royal, Lonsdale, Deryle, and Parkinson, Dilworth B. (eds.) (2002). *Analogical Modeling: An Exemplar-Based Approach to Language*. Amsterdam: John Benjamins.

Smith, Kirk H. (1966). Grammatical intrusions in the recall of structured letter pairs: Mediated transfer or position learning? *Journal of Experimental Psychology*, **72**: 580–8.

Sproat, Richard (2008). Experiments in morphological evolution. Keynote address. 3rd Workshop on Quantitative Investigations in Theoretical Linguistics, Helsinki.

Stampe, David (1980). *How I Spent My Summer Vacation*. New York: Garland Press.

Stemberger, Joseph P. and MacWhinney, Brian (1986). Frequency and the lexical storage of regularly inflected forms. *Memory and Cognition*, **14**: 17–26.

Steriade, Donca (2000). Paradigm uniformity and the phonetics-phonology boundary. In *Papers in Laboratory Phonology V: Acquisition and the Lexicon*, M. B. Broe and J. B. Pierrehumbert (eds.). Cambridge: Cambridge University Press, 313–34.

Storms, Gert and Wisniewski, Edward J. (2005). Does the order of head noun and modifier explain response times in conceptual combination? *Memory and Cognition*, **33**: 852–61.

Stump, Gregory T. (2001). *Inflectional Morphology: A Theory of Paradigm Structure*. Cambridge: Cambridge University Press.

Sturtevant, Edgar H. (1947). *An Introduction to Linguistic Science*. New Haven: Yale University Press.

Taylor, Alex H., Hunt, Gavin R., and Holzhaider, Jennifer C. Gray, Russell D. (2007). Spontaneous metatool use by New Caledonian crows. *Current Biology*, **17**: 1504–7.

Taylor, Douglas R, Zeyl, Clifford, and Cooke, Erin (2002). Conflicting levels of selection in the accumulation of mitochondrial defects in Saccharomyces cerevisiae. *Proceedings of the National Academy of Sciences*, **99**: 3690–4.

Tenenbaum, Joshua B. and Griffiths, Thomas L. (2001). Generalization, similarity, and Bayesian inference. *Behavioral and Brain Sciences*, **24**: 629–40.

Tenpenny, P. L. (1995). Abstractionist versus episodic theories of repetition priming and word identification. *Psychonomic Bulletin and Review*, **2**: 339–63.

Tereshchenko, Natal'ya Mitrofanovna (1965). *Nenetsko-russkij slovar' [Nenets-Russian dictionary]*. St. Petersburg: Sovetskaja Entsiklopedija.

Thymé, Anne E. (1993). *A Connectionist Approach to Nominal Inflection: Paradigm Patterning and Analogy in Finnish*. Ph.D. thesis, University of California, San Diego.

—— Ackerman, Farrell, and Elman, Jeffrey L. (1994). Finnish nominal inflections: Paradigmatic patterns and token analogy. In *The Reality of Linguistic Rules*, S. D. Lima, R. L. Corrigan, and G. K. Iverson (eds.). Amsterdam: John Benjamins, 445–66.

Tomasello, Michael (2000). First steps toward a usage-based theory of language acquisition. *Cognitive Linguistics*, **11**: 61–82.

—— (2003). *Constructing a Language: A Usage-Based Theory of Language Acquisition*. Cambridge, MA: Harvard University Press.

Traficante, Daniela and Burani, Cristina (2003). Visual processing of Italian verbs and adjectives: The role of inflectional family size. In *Morphological Structure in Language Processing*, R. H. Baayen and R. Schreuder (eds.). Berlin: Mouton de Gruyter, 45–64.

Traugott, Elizabeth C. and Heine, Bernd (1991). *Approaches to Grammaticalization*. Vol. 19, Typological Studies in Language. Amsterdam: John Benjamins.

Tsai, Jie-Li, Lee, Chia-Ying, Lin, Ying-Chun, Tzeng, Ovid J.-L., and Hung, Daisy L. (2006). Neighborhood size effects of Chinese words in lexical decision and reading. *Language and Linguistics*, 7. 3: 659–75.

Tschenkéli, Kita (1958). *Einführung in die georgische Sprache*. Zurich: Amirani Verlag.

Tversky, Amos (1977). Features of similarity. *Psychological Review*, **84**: 327–52.

Vance, Timothy J. (1980). The psychological status of a contraint on Japanese consonant alternation. *Linguistics*, **18**: 145–67.

van den Toorn, M. C. (1982*a*). Tendenzen bij de beregeling van de verbindingsklank in nominale samenstellingen I. *De Nieuwe Taalgids*, **75**: 24–33.

—— (1982*b*). Tendenzen bij de beregeling van de verbindingsklank in nominale samenstellingen II. *De Nieuwe Taalgids*, **75**: 153–60.

van Jaarsveld, Henk J., Coolen, Riet, and Schreuder, Robert (1994). The role of analogy in the interpretation of novel compounds. *Journal of Psycholinguistic Research*, 23: 111–37.

Vennemann, Theo H. (1972). Phonetic analogy and conceptual analogy. In *Schuchardt, the Neogrammarians, and the Transformational Theory of Phonological Change: Four Essays*, T. Vennemann and T. H. Wilbur (eds.). Frankfurt: Athenaeum, 181–204.

—— (1993). Language change as language improvement. In *Historical Linguistics: Problems and Perspectives*, C. Jones (ed.). London: Longman, 319–44.

Viks, Ülle (1992). *Väike vormi-sõnastik: Sissejuhatus & grammatika*. Tallinn: Eesti Teaduste Akadeemia Keele ja Kirjanduse Instituut.

Wedel, Andrew (2004). *Self-Organization and Categorical Behavior in Phonology*. Ph.D. thesis, University of California, Santa Cruz.

—— (2006). Exemplar models, evolution and language change. *The Linguistic Review*, 23: 247–74.

—— (2007). Feedback and regularity in the lexicon. *Phonology*, 24: 147–85.

Wheeler, Max W. (2005). *The Phonology of Catalán*. Oxford: Oxford University Press.

Whitney, William D. (1875). *The Life and Growth of Language*. London: H. S. King.

Wilson, Rachel (2002). *Syntactic Category Learning in a Second Language*. Ph.D. thesis, University of Arizona, Tucson.

Wisniewski, Edward J. (1996). Construal and similarity in conceptual combination. *Journal of Memory and Language*, 35: 434–53.

Wurzel, Wolfgang U. (1970). *Studien zur deutschen Lautstruktur*. Berlin: Akademie-Verlag.

—— (1989). *Natural Morphology and Naturalness*. Dordrecht: Kluwer.

Yu, Alan C. L. (2007). Tonal phonetic analogy. Paper presented at ICPHS, Saarbrücken.

Zanone, P. G. and Kelso, J. A. S. (1997). The coordination dynamics of learning and transfer: Collective and component levels. *Journal of Experimental Psychology, Human Perception and Performance*, 23: 1454–80.

Zwicky, Arnold M. (1985). How to describe inflection. In *Proceedings of the Eleventh Annual Meeting of the Berkeley Linguistics Society*, M. Niepokuj, M. Van Clay, V. Nikiforidou, and D. Feder (eds.). Berkeley: Berkeley Linguistics Society, 372–86.

Index

LANGUAGES

THE CREATORS OF BATMAN

Dedicated to all my co-creators, co-conspirators, collaborators, co-workers, covens, congregations, cohorts, comrades, and companions past and present. It wouldn't be as fun to do this alone.

With special love for Beth, who gave me the courage to leap and the support to fly.

THE CREATORS OF BATMAN

BOB, BILL AND THE DARK KNIGHT

RIK WORTH

WHITE OWL

AN IMPRINT OF PEN & SWORD BOOKS LTD.
YORKSHIRE - PHILADELPHIA

First published in Great Britain in 2021 by
PEN AND SWORD WHITE OWL
An imprint of
Pen & Sword Books Ltd
Yorkshire - Philadelphia

ISBN 978 1 52677 761 4

A CIP catalogue record for this book is available from the British Library.

Typeset in Times New Roman 11.5/14 by
SJmagic DESIGN SERVICES, India.
Printed and bound by CPI Group (UK) Ltd, Croydon CR0 4YY

Pen & Sword Books Ltd incorporates the Imprints of Pen & Sword Books
Archaeology, Atlas, Aviation, Battleground, Discovery, Family History, History,
Maritime, Military, Naval, Politics, Railways, Select, Transport, True Crime,
Fiction, Frontline Books, Leo Cooper, Praetorian Press, Seaforth Publishing,
Wharncliffe and White Owl.

For a complete list of Pen & Sword titles please contact
PEN & SWORD BOOKS LIMITED
47 Church Street, Barnsley, South Yorkshire, S70 2AS, England
E-mail: enquiries@pen-and-sword.co.uk
Website: www.pen-and-sword.co.uk

Or
PEN AND SWORD BOOKS
1950 Lawrence Rd, Havertown, PA 19083, USA
E-mail: Uspen-and-sword@casematepublishers.com
Website: www.penandswordbooks.com

Contents

Introduction

Comic book history is unusual. As a field, it is a mixture of cultural analysis, business studies, biography, and art criticism. And the term 'history' is extensive. It ranges from the primordial and ancient to just moments ago. Essentially, it describes something that is not anymore. But more than that, History (with a capital 'H' that is) to your average Joe is about important things, like politics and war and moon landings.

Comics, for the most part, have not been considered important for most of their existence. Outside their once small yet dedicated fandom they were disposable trash; important only to the deeply nostalgic and the, let's face it, slightly odd. Even within comics, though the creations were important in that they made important men money, the same wasn't assumed of the creators.

The last few decades have seen that change substantially. Comic books, like novels and talking pictures before them, once seen as a distraction from important art, have stopped being a subculture and become culture itself. They're starting to be taken seriously. Society, for better or worse, is finally catching up with those of us who have been engrossed with comics since we first cast our wide eyes across their Technicolor splendour. They are becoming important.

Though it has existed for almost as long as the medium itself, comic book history is no longer just obscure lore about colourful and wild characters (and the comics they make – n'yuk, n'yuk).

It is the history of modern culture.

On the vast scale of human cultural expression and achievement, we are still incredibly close to the genesis of what we would come to recognise as comic books. We're still basking in the intense light generated by a big bang occurring in the early twentieth century.

And it's fair to say this is thanks to superheroes.

Introduction

The idea of the superhero as we recognise it is somehow distinct but similar to the folkloric legends – and yet, they are not even 100 years old.

At the same time, we're entering the period when although the light of the comic book boom still shines, the distant stars which started it all are already fading away. The men and women at the birth of the comics industry are all but gone.

It is now impossible for us to collect first-hand accounts from all those who were there at the beginning. All we have left are anecdotes from the second generation (who are themselves now reaching a venerable age), and whatever documents we're able to scrounge to give us some clue as to what was happening behind the scenes in those formative days. There is also, of course, the body of work the great creators left behind.

What makes comic book history so interesting, focusing on the individuals who worked in and built the industry rather than the progression of their characters, are exactly the same things making the four-colour capers in the pages of the books so exciting. New York in the early twentieth century was a bustling metropolis of shining avenues and shadowed alleyways. Cultures and ideas were blending (and clashing) on the island city. A romanticised but realistically tough tenement life, which housed many the industry's earliest creators, was home to heroes and villains alike, each with their own agenda, schemes and dreams.

As they built this new world of comics the creators became characters themselves, identifiable by their unique abilities, as their individual adventures weaved together towards some common goal. Idealistic underdogs faced Machiavellian machinations of the rich and powerful. Teams of creators formed and reformed with ever-changing rosters as characters dropped in and out of one another's storylines, creating a pocket universe at once both real and fantastic. Like their caped characters, they frequently participated in crossovers, team-ups, and long-standing feuds. The only difference is that in reality, the good guys didn't always win.

No one knew what they were up against or what they were creating. For most, it was something fun to do while they waiting for a real job to come along. For others, the motivation was to make a bit of cash. When the comic book boom happened, only a few were savvy enough to see just how much money could be made from the funny books. Everyone else was just holding on and hoping they made it out in one piece.

The goings-on of an American fringe industry emerging in the New York borough of the Bronx during the 1930s is even more remote still if you're trying to document them from England's dreary West Yorkshire in 2020.

To make matters worse, the creators of Batman, Bob Kane and Bill Finger are, to be polite, difficult subjects for two entirely contradictory reasons.

Kane, while confident and full of braggadocio is a deeply unreliable source, especially in details of his own life. Though he managed to make his way into the spotlight, what he presented to the world was an act; a performance in which, sometimes unintentionally and occasionally intentionally, the truth was bent, broken and twisted to make a good story. What makes a good story? Well, one with Kane at the centre, of course.

Finger, for his part, was the opposite. Easy-going to the point of retiring. He was just grateful to be in the room. He was talented and likeable, and yet he was easy to forget, and subsequently, forgotten. It is only recently, thanks to the dedicated work of comics historians in America, that he has been brought back onto the stage.

What we know about these two men is incomplete, inconsistent and scattered among multiple sources. The goal of this book is to collate what we do know so that we can better understand the relationships, motives and lives of these two men.

While they are at the heart of this book, it will also explore the larger events that affected their lives. Some space will also be given to the characters and bigger issues defining Kane and Finger's industry.

The reasons for doing this are twofold. Firstly, it gives us some context as to how their work was received, how their peers viewed them, and some idea of the external pressures both men faced as well as the impact of their actions and attitudes.

The second reason is to create some sense of fairness or at least impartiality. It is easy to find one of the anecdotes about either Kane or Finger and build an entire opinion of them from simply a few lines. As you will read, Kane is particularly easy to characterise as an egocentric villain. And all villains, by their nature, need a victim. In this case, Bill Finger. You will most certainly have some lasting opinions of both these men by the time you're finished – I certainly do. But it seems reasonable to give them a fair shake of the stick and to try to present the evidence with as even a hand as possible.

What's more, the greatest heroes, most tragic victims, and most enduring villains of any story, fact or fiction, ultimately have a human side. The events of a life are merely its plot points; the motivations and developments of the characters are the real stories.

As the creators of one of pop culture's most enduring characters, the stories of Kane and Finger ask questions about the nature of collaboration, creation, credits, and potential, both failed and fulfilled. One of the essential themes throughout the book is influence. Not only how they influenced one another and a generation of artists that followed them, but also how they were influenced.

It is fair to say this book has been deeply informed by the authors and historians whose own work precedes this one. Each successive age of comics has built on the foundations laid down by the generations working so hard before it. Comic book history is the same. Each author hopes they can add something new to the shared reservoir of knowledge, and this one is no different. This book is only possible thanks to the hard work of those closer to the events (both in time and space) and their good sense in recording these events for posterity. A full list of these writers and their respective books can be found in the acknowledgements. And as you will see, a little acknowledgement goes a long way.

A note on quotations

Direct quotes are used throughout the book. Because there is so little material available in terms of the first-hand accounts, particularly from Bill Finger, some of these quotes have appeared in multiple publications. Where vitally linked to historical events, the sources appear in the body of the text. If not, the sources will be found in one of the items listed in the Bibliography.

Chapter One

Starting Out

The American Dream

'I was born with a pencil in my hand. I'd doodle on the sidewalks in New York, I'd scribble on walls. On the subway, I'd see an advertisement with the Colgate girl smiling with that beautiful set of ivory teeth, and I'd start blacking the teeth out. I must have been one of the all-time doodle-holics in the early days. I just used to scribble on anything I could get my hands on.'

–Bob Kane, *People*, July 1989

Superheroes were born at the start of the twentieth in New York City, specifically, the Bronx. Whether it goes by its own name, Metropolis, Central City or Gotham, the shining skyscrapers of the Big Apple have always been home to the colourful caped and costumed characters who fly, swing and clobber through the avenues of our cultural consciousness.

It is often said that jazz is America's only original art form, though that statement dismisses not only the creative endeavours of the Native Americans, it misses the fact that jazz was in fact formed from a blend of cultures. It is a mixing of African and European cultures through traditional music seeping into one another in the Louisiana heat.

It's fitting then, that the New York of the Jazz Age, the most densely populated city on the planet at the time which was then alive with music at once foreign and uniquely American, would too become a crucible of cultures. It was home to millions of European immigrants who had been arriving since the before the turn of the century. Each brought with them their own languages, religions and traditions, as they fought and fell in love.

Arriving as strangers in an alien world these men and women from the Old Country would do what people around the world do best – they would go forth and multiply. Their kids, the second generation, would be caught between the traditions and stigma of the Old World whilst also being new Americans. And it was these new Americans who would create America's other original art form; the comic books.

Life was not easy for those in the immigrant communities arriving in New York. During the late nineteenth century there was already a sizable community of German Jews who were subsequently joined throughout the start of the twentieth century by Yiddish-speaking Jews from across Eastern Europe and Russia as they fled the murderous pogroms. Similarly, around 13 million Italians, who had suffered economically under Italy's unification, had chosen to emigrate to America over this time in what would become history's largest-ever voluntary migration.

America's hereditary rivalry with Britain, stemming first from the American War of Independence and later British support of Confederate forces during the American Civil War meant American leaders were sympathetic, at least in theory, to Irish settlers. The Irish had long been subject to a punishing British rule which had exacerbated the Great Famine, leading to the deaths of a million Irish nationals. America would make a new home for many Irish families seeking to escape the British yoke and it is reckoned by 1910 more people of Irish descent lived in New York City than in Dublin.

All these immigrant communities passed through Ellis Island, adopting new names to get by or to pretend they shared some relation to migrants already settled in New York. A huge number of these newly minted Americans would end up in the densely populated and poor Lower East Side. After the First World War, the Bronx would see a huge rejuvenation, as well as more industry and housing, as the subway system expanded, allowing those seeking work to travel to and from Manhattan. The new Bronx saw elevated trains rumble past tenement buildings packed with families.

Immigrants from all walks of life would move into the neighbourhoods here but many of the new industries were controlled by individual communities. There were Jewish jobs, Irish jobs, and Italian jobs. Everyone was looking out for their own. Cultural lines were hard to cross and resentments still created problems in finding work, and poverty was still a real issue.

To make matter worse, gangs based on ethnic backgrounds would control different blocks and buildings. Being caught in the wrong district would result in a beating while massive fights between gangs were not uncommon. And that was just the youths with nothing better to do. During America's ill-fated flirtation with Prohibition between 1920 and 1933, Irish, Jewish, Italian and Polish organised crime rings took to bootlegging liquor. Prohibition did not make America or its new, less prudish citizens want to drink any less, and lawmakers massively underestimated the ingenuity of people and the downright obscene lengths they would go to get booze.

Many of the immigrants in New York had been middle-class in the Old World. They suddenly found themselves at the bottom of the social ladder with unsteady incomes and menial jobs but with a middle-class sensibility to the arts. For the second generation, it was a world of toughs and chancers, crime and noir adventures in real life layered with an expectation and a responsibility to support yourself and your family. If you were not fast or smart enough to grab the few opportunities that came along, you had better make your own. It was here, in the winter of 1915, Robert Kahn was born, and it was here he would grow up. But things weren't much better for his future partner Milton Finger, nearly 1,800 miles away in Denver, Colorado.

Denver had been reeling from successive droughts and difficult winters which had damaged crops and created economic instability as the Panic of 1893 (a serious economic depression lasting four years) rolled across America. Though it created a nationwide downturn, Denver was able to survive and eventually to prosper thanks to its strong agricultural heritage. At the start of the next century, the city began to grow, with an influx of workers joining its food production industry. By annexing nearby towns, over the course of fifteen years, Denver changed from a frontier town of the Wild West to a prospering city.

Milton Finger was the firstborn child to Jewish parents, Louis Finger and his New Yorker wife Tessie, and he was born on 8 February 1914. At this time, the city was hot with union activity in response to its growing industries. The political climate was volatile, and it is possible that Louis, as a tailor, may have been swept up in union discord.

Denver also bought into the temperance movement, which would later lead to the enactment of the Volstead Act, the legal lynchpin of Prohibition. Colorado already had a state-wide ban on alcohol, believing it to be un-American but when the First World War broke out in Europe, with America joining the conflict in 1916, previously welcomed German communities and brewing industries suddenly became quite unpalatable. Anti-German sentiment quickly turned to anti-immigrant prejudice as not only were these new communities less likely to support Prohibition, there were also stories from the East Coast of foreign gangs working as bootleggers. It is unclear if Louis Finger was Polish or Austrian. If it was the latter, then he would have almost certainly spoken German and potentially, he would have identified himself as a target.

All this culminated in a dramatic rise in members of racist organisation the Ku Klux Klan across Colorado and Denver. The KKK began to routinely target Jewish and Catholic communities.

We can't be certain that this was why the Finger family returned to New York, though it probably contributed to the move. At four years old, Milton was joined by a little sister named Emily. The record isn't clear if she was born in Colorado or New York, but it seems more likely it was the latter.

Boyhood

Not much is known about young Milton's childhood save for a few scant details. His father opened a tailor shop on the family's arrival in the Bronx and Bill grew up in a household which struggled for money but was still able to indulge his creative passions. He loved the cinema and would spend whatever free time he had in the dark of the matinee enjoying the latest films from Europe; expressionist pieces like Fritz Lang's sci-fi masterpiece *Metropolis* and F. W. Murnau's copyright infringing *Nosferatu*. This was a time when feature films were still preceded by serials – short episodic tales of adventure with cliff hanger endings featuring adventure characters like Zorro, Tarzan and Flash Gordon. These mini-movies kept cinemagoers returning to the theatre even when the feature presentation was no good. In many ways, they were the precursor to cinematic televisions series we enjoy today. In fact, it was the serials that popularised the term 'cliff hanger' with one episode of 1915's *The Perils of Pauline* ending with the lead actress literally hanging from the cliffs across New York's Hudson River where many of the serials were filmed. Young Milton paid for these tickets in exchange for allowing theatre owners to advertise in the window of his father's shop.

Milton had large, dark, bushy eyebrows and a friendly face but he was nervous about smiling in front of others because of a large gap in his front teeth which were also rather crooked. At some point during his childhood, Milton was bedridden with a severe illness, most probably Scarlet fever. Unable to work in his father's store or go to the theatre to catch the latest instalments of his favourite serials, Milton turned to books to pass the time, devouring as much of the written word as he could and developing a life-long passion for reading. It was from these stories he would later take his inspiration in the building of the world of Bruce Wayne. Milton read broadly and even as a child, developed an extensive mental database of plots, characters and stories he could later use. He also demonstrated an aptitude for science and under the influence of his parents, who wanted him to become a doctor, he pursued those subjects at DeWitt Clinton High School. Within Milton's first year at high school, during the 1929 semester, his mother gave birth to his second sister, Gilda. One more mouth to feed undoubtedly put more pressure on the family and the importance of Milton succeeding at school. To make matters worse, that was the year the Great Depression hit the United States.

In the class below the studious Milton Finger was Robert Kahn. Unlike Finger, Kahn was a born and bred New Yorker. He was born on 24 October 1915, to Augusta and Herman Kahn. He, like Finger, was the American child of Eastern European Jews. Robert's childhood was better documented than Milton's. His contemporaries would remember him as a mama's boy. Even as he grew older and the other boys began to pal together, Augusta would still walk her boy to and from school. Robert was also the apple of his father's eye and he was greatly admired by his son. Young Robert would later be joined by a sister, Dorothy.

Herman worked for New York *Daily News* – not to be confused with the unrelated *New York Daily News* which preceded it – as a printer and engraver. Herman would tirelessly carve out the recesses in the metal plates used for mass printing. Around a year after its launch in 1919, *Daily News,* under the slogan 'New York's Picture Newspaper', would have a circulation of nearly 100,000. By the time of Robert's tenth birthday, it would reach over a million New Yorkers with its gossip columns, city life features, photographs of the bustling metropolis and, to Robert's joy, comic strips.

The pairing of words and images had existed in some form or another for centuries but the newspaper comic strip is where the format really came into its own at the end of the nineteenth century with the appearance of *The Yellow Kid* in Joseph Pulitzer's *New York World*. While Pulitzer would go on to give his name to the most prestigious prize in journalism, the Yellow Kid, a slum child with bad diction, a broad smile, bald head and jug ears would give his moniker to the term 'yellow journalism' – the type of journalism associated with ethically dubious sensationalism and catchy, albeit misleading, headlines. These exaggerated reports lived side by side in the tabloids with comic strips.

These strips were longer than they were tall to fit several on the newspaper page and were comprised of a few panels usually ending in a gag. The strips would have regularly occurring characters and it was common among fans to cut out and collect the strips. As the serials came to prominence in the theatres, so too did the strips. The papers diversified their cartoons to meet demands outside of comedy, adding adventures and sci-fi strips to their regular features. As they did, franchises were created, using the same characters across newspapers, cinema, and radio. So popular were these strips, newspapers would run several pages worth of them and they would frequently appear on the front page of Sunday editions. For artists, having a strip syndicated meant their work could be found in publications across the country and, while they lost ownership of the title to the corporation, they could still make a pretty penny.

Herman Kahn, working at *Daily News*, had heard rumours of the impressive paycheques being handed out to syndicated illustrators and was incredibly supportive of his son's early addiction to drawing. Robert claimed he was so focused on art his childhood nickname was 'The Doodler'. For most families living in the Bronx, professional artist was not an acceptable career goal, but this was not the case for Robert.

Herman regularly brought home the funny pages and other books on how to draw for Robert, encouraging him to copy and trace the illustrations within. Like any other artist, he discovered the first step on the road to developing his own style was to mimic the styles of those he looked up to. Robert became adept at copying the simplistic, elegant and humorous styles of the likes of Rudolph Dirks' *The Katzenjammer Kids*, which ran for 106 years from 1897 to 2003, or Frank King's *Gasoline Alley* and Elzie Crisler Segar's *Popeye,* both of which are still syndicated to this day.

Robert was further encouraged in his artistic pursuits by two victories achieved in his early years. At 14, after prompting from his father,

Robert took to drawing posters for local merchants. One such poster featured a cartoonish baker with a wide, frog-like smile holding a dripping, steaming pie, with the slogan, 'Don't go by, til you buy a pie!' It is not clear if the pie in question is a pizza pie or a filled pie. In fact, because of the crude attempt in replicating steam rising from the mystery dish, it looks somewhat like mashed potatoes with the whisk stuck in it. Still, Robert's journeyman illustration was his first commercial success. He was able to use a Photostat machine, an early precursor to a photocopier like Xerox, to make multiple copies of his poster and sold them to various bakeries across town for 50 cents each. It was his first taste of financial success.

A year later *New York American*, yet another New York title in the newspaper boom of the early twentieth century, held an art competition. Entrants had to reproduce an image of the characters from Ad Carte's syndicated comic strip *Just Kids*. After months of deliberation, the judges decided that Robert Kahn of the Bronx deserved second place for his entry depicting the *Just Kids* characters Fatso and Mush. His prize was a piece of original art from the strip, signed by its creator, and a letter of encouragement wishing Master Kahn all the best in his future cartooning career.

Robert was a handsome, charming, and outgoing kid, but not academically inclined. When he entered DeWitt Clinton High School, he began to work infrequently as a cartoonist for the school newspaper, *The Clinton Newspaper*, where he produced gag strips but was routinely beaten to the punch for recognition by his more talented classmate Will Eisner. Their relationship was amicable, however, and would come to benefit them both a few years later.

Robert and Milton attended high school during the Great Depression and they would have been all too aware of the effects it was having on families just like their own. Multiple factors lead to the American economy crashing in October of 1929, and the results were devastating. Nearly 13 million Americans lost their jobs as businesses went under and banks folded. Savings were lost as poverty saw a dramatic rise. All of this was worsened by an epidemic of tuberculosis. The disease was able to spread thanks to the inability of families to afford treatment. Cramped living conditions only made matters worse as more people moved into crowded tenement buildings where large families would live in tiny apartments, often with lodgers just needing a cheap place to stay.

In New York, in Central Park and Riverside Park, 'Hoovervilles' were erected; huge shantytowns housing hundreds of homeless families in constructs made from scrap. They were named after Herbert Hoover, the President who presided over the depression, and the man who many believed was to blame for the country's plight.

After a great influx of immigration throughout the previous century, the Great Depression saw a swell in migration. Americans, those who still had some money anyway, headed to Canada, Australia, Europe and even the Soviet Union. For those Jewish immigrants who had worked so hard to escape persecution and had little to nothing, they had no choice but to stay and tough it out.

Sometime after graduating DeWitt Clinton in 1933, with its large Jewish student body, Milton started to go by the name of Bill. It was quite common for Jewish Americans of this time to go by anglicised names for several reasons. Robert Kahn, Bill's future partner, changed his name to Bob Kane and sometimes Bob Kaye or Robert Kane for work reasons. His new alter ego allowed him to produce more work (and make more money) for publishers by working under different pseudonyms.

Fellow comics legend Jacob Kurtzman, better known as Jack 'The King' Kirby, grew up at the same time as Kane and Finger. Among the various youth gangs and rivalries, he adopted what he thought sounded like a more Irish name in the style of Hollywood tough guy James Cagney. Stanley Lieber became Stan Lee – a snappier, friendlier name which better suited the face of the comics industry. Stan 'The Man' held onto his birth name as back-up for the great American novel he always wished he had written. In all of these cases, these leading creatives tried to downplay their Jewish heritage to avoid persecution and prejudice. Milton isn't exactly a Jewish sounding name to modern ears, but back then it was. Much like how Jacob, coming from Yacov, became Jack, Milton, coming from Moishe, became William and then, Bill.

The Great Depression continued throughout most of the 1930s and although the economy started to stabilise in later years, America was still blighted by huge unemployment and low income. Both the Kahns and the Fingers were affected by this economic downturn. The tailor shop Louis Finger had opened on his arrival in New York had been hit hard and subsequently closed. For Bill, who dreamed of becoming a writer, this was a mixed blessing. It meant the parental pressure of becoming a doctor vanished as his family could no longer afford to send him off to college, but in its place he took on some of the financial burdens of contributing to the family income – a sure-fire way of hindering his literary dreams. He took on a series of menial jobs to support his parents and sisters as best he could and before hitting the big time, he would make his living as a part-time shoe salesman.

While at school, Bob had earned money in the afternoons selling newspapers and was lucky enough to obtain a $2,000 scholarship to the prestigious Cooper Union Art League, attending a two-year art course with lessons held in the iconic Flat Iron building. He had moved from tracing newspaper cartoons on a makeshift drawing board made from his mother's old breadboard to life drawing classes. At the same time, he was pitching his artwork around town to various publishers, sending out hundreds of images to magazines and studios with varying luck. He was able to make a few big sales but his output to income ratio could not sustain his life as an art student. After a year, Bob dropped out of art school and his progress in improving as an artist hit a quagmire. He had to take up a job at the garment factory managed by his uncle Sam. Though it paid $10 a week, Bob loathed factory work which provided him neither the creative output nor fame he so desired. He promptly quit after being offered a higher position (and an extra two dollars) nine months into the job. It was a huge risk financially but seeing a comfortable but unrewarding future in the garment trade was not what Bob had in mind for himself.

With little income from infrequent sales, Kane found he had to get some steady work and was taken on by the Fleischer Studio, an animation house. Founded by brothers Dave and Max Fleischer in 1921 as Inkwell Studios, and renamed in 1929, the animators made New York their home until 1939. As animation was starting to take off, the Fleischer Studio rivalled that of Walt Disney and in its time would produce features for legendary characters such a Popeye, Betty Boop and later, the Man of Steel himself, Superman. Bob most likely worked as a 'cel washer' whose responsibilities consisted of washing the paint from the transparent vinyl cels the animated art would be painted on so the expensive cels could be reused for other features. It is also possible, as he claimed, that he provided some of the fill-in art and inks, given his ability to copy the styles of other artists. But if that is the case he was never credited for his work. Despite being paid $25 a week and working there for seven to eight months, Bob did not care for his time at Fleischer. Like anything else, it became an automated chore that was uninspiring and tiresome.

It is interesting to note that when Kane worked at Fleischer, the studio was facing a massive labour strike and subsequent boycott. Due to the huge popularity of the spinach guzzling sailor Popeye, the studio was operating in overcrowded and over-demanding conditions, with artists working under impossible deadlines similar to the modern and contemptible practice in the gaming industry of 'the crunch'. It is possible the high demand for artists meant one of America's leading animation studios gave a unproven, unqualified artist like Bob a chance, or perhaps sensing an opportunity to make a quick buck, he crossed the union picket line. It would be in keeping with Kane's opportunist and survivalist approach to work.

Either way, sensing he wouldn't be given a creative position anytime soon, he jumped ship back into the exciting and unreliable world of freelancing. Bob may have been luckier, or at least ahead of the curve, than some of the other Fleischer employees. Less than a year after Bob quit, Fleischer Studios left New York for sunny Miami, both for its better corporate tax rates and to avoid further strike issues.

All this experience allowed Kane to develop his artistic skill a little, but more importantly, it gave him a good sense for business and the drive to earn more. Compared to Bill Finger's family, the Kahns were relatively well-off, but Bob himself thought of his family as struggling, if not poor. His family's difficulties, particularly the financial troubles his father had faced – having been laid off from *Daily News* in Bob's teen years – instilled in him a desire to become wealthy. It was less of a good work ethic and more of a profitable mission statement. But what would really work in Bob's favour was simply being in the right place at the right time.

Chapter Two

Comic Book Boom

The Studios

Syndicated comic strips had proven to be a huge success for the newspapers and soon after collected editions of popular strips would be available, although this still wasn't the comic book as we would recognise it today. But it was around this time, in the early 1930s, publishers began experimenting with the form. Eastern Colour Printers produced *The Funnies*, a tabloid-style paper featuring strips which weren't published anywhere else. It had the idea of original content right, but not the format, and it did not last long. Reprints seemed to be the way to go. Publishers could make an easy buck selling cheap collected reprints in bulk to newspapers. The newspapers would offer them as a bonus for readers willing to buy a subscription. Or publishers would sell them to corporate brands who knew a good thing when they saw it and who would send out these collections in return for loyal customers sending in label clippings obtained through purchases. Comics were so loved that these reprints would make kids and parents choose Canada Dry, as just one example, over a less generous or fun-loving rival.

New Yorker Maxwell Charles Gaines, a one-time teacher turned salesman, would be the accidental pioneer who first converted comic strips into comic books. While working for Eastern Colour Printing, he put together a 32-page reprint of syndicated strips called *Funnies on Parade*. He managed to sell it as a promotional giveaway item to several companies, including Proctor & Gamble which sent out all 10,000 copies they had ordered to customers. Realising they had a hit on their hands, a second edition, *Famous Funnies: A Carnival of Comics*, was put together.

Famous Funnies was eventually proposed as a series and featured top-tier syndicated strips. It was an experiment to see exactly how interested the public would be in comic books. The book was reformatted to 64 pages and distributed to department stores where it was sold for 10 cents. It was a comic for comic's sake in this sense and the first real American comic book.

It hit the stores in February of 1934 and sold out in a matter of weeks. Though Kane and Finger were in their late teens at this point, Kane at least, as a jobbing artist, would have had some familiarity with the latest fad. An ongoing series of *Famous Funnies* was quickly agreed on and the comic book industry was born.

Repackaged daily stripes proved to be a huge success with kids and adults alike. Pretty soon however, it became clear to everyone that profit was be made in bespoke, new strips written and illustrated from scratch. More than that, with so many reprints being produced, publishers were running out of pages to republish and strips to syndicate.

There wasn't yet a dedicated job title of comic book writer or artist. Lone creators worked in respectable newspapers, not this new, bizarre and slap-dash format. Instead, these new, original magazines were put together by art studios, often called shops.

One such shop which began operating in 1936 was Eisner & Iger, ran by Will Eisner and Jerry Iger. Eisner, a young illustrator, met Iger, the more senior artist, during a brief but impressive stint on a comics based publication called *Wow, What a Magazine!* Though they share the same names and work in related industries, Eisner and Iger are not to be confused with current Disney CEO Michael Eisner and former Disney CEO Bob Iger (though Bob is actually Jerry's great-nephew). Will bears no relation to Michael, but Will's signature, with its looped 'W' and a ringed dot above the 'I' bears an uncanny similarity to the Walt Disney's. However, Eisner's came first, featuring on the cover of *Wow*. The Walt Disney signature we recognise today is a stylised version of Walt's real signature which first appeared several years later.

Eisner was given the heads up on the *Wow* gig by his fellow artist and former DeWitt Clinton High School classmate, Bob Kane. Kane had worked for *Wow* on a fish-out-of-water humour strip about a hillbilly cowboy called Hiram Hick.

Kane and Eisner had an unusual relationship. Gerald Jones, author of the extensive comic book history title *Men of Tomorrow*, records that Eisner said of his relationship with Kane back then, 'We were supposedly friends because we were both artists. But really, it was so we could double date and he set me up with the most beautiful girls. Then it started to dawn on me that I wasn't getting anywhere with these girls – and neither was Bob.'

The two would frequently bump into one another as they tried to sell their wares to anyone who would take them. This was around the time Bob was still in art school and later, working at his uncle's factory. After one chance encounter and a chat about Bob's idea of unionising freelance illustrators, another thing Eisner knew wouldn't go anywhere and was likely just an opportunity for Kane to network with editors and potentially raise his day rates, Eisner made his way to the *Wow* offices and pressured the senior Iger for work.

Wow was run out of a shirt-makers factory and was soon closed, but Eisner had demonstrated his artistic skill and drive to his soon to be business partner, Iger, whose real name was Samuel Maxwell. Iger had been a cartoonist on the daily newspaper strips and worked as the news cartoonist for *New York American*. Some of his work was in the collected reprints that made up what would become the first comic book, *Famous Funnies*. Iger was fourteen years older than Kane and Eisner. He was flat broke from his first divorce as he was heading into his second. Just outside the *Daily News*, where Kane's father worked, Eisner proposed that he and Iger should set up a studio using $15 the young artist had recently received from a commercial job. The agreement was reached that Eisner would deal with all the art and editorial aspects of the company, and as chief financier his name would come first, while Iger would deal with the commercial side, meeting with clients, publishers and newspapermen.

Eisner recognised the newspaper reprints which were cut up, glued back together and sold as a comic book were limited, and the demand for more original content like *Wow* was only going to increase.

This is one of the key instances of business acumen (or perhaps sheer luck) at the genesis of the comic book industry. It was a strategy which recognised audience demand for new fictional worlds and succeeded, in part, thanks to the fiction the entrepreneurs told about themselves. It was a strategy Kane would employ later in life. Eisner had lied about his age to get the more confident, seasoned and business orientated Iger onside, telling his senior partner he was 25 rather than 19.

Iger, for his part, began to work under the name S.M. Iger, in imitation of William Randal Hearst, the newspaper tycoon who would serve as Orson Welles' inspiration for Charles Forster Kane.

The pair lied about the size of the studio, claiming several artists already worked there when in fact every artist was just Eisner working under a pseudonym, at least to begin with. This means of faking it to make it plays over and over again and it's something Bob would quickly pick up.

The Eisner & Iger studio, sometimes known as the Syndicated Features Corporation was an immediate success and Eisner quickly needed to hire additional artists to complete the commissions coming in. Perhaps returning the favour to his old pal, Kane picked up several humour pages and created the funny animal strip in the Disney tradition called *Peter Pupp*. Funny animal strips were a popular part of the cartoon and comics genre which usually, but not always, followed the light-hearted adventures of an anthropomorphic animal.

Peter Pupp was published in the Eisner & Iger title *Jumbo Comics* in 1937. It followed the adventures of a puppy, and somehow, an even smaller canine sidekick named Tinymite.

The style of the strip would often vary which suggests Kane did not draw every single page but that was not uncommon given the nature of studio work. Artists would often be pulled in to finish other artists' work or be asked to ghost or copy their style. Either way, Kane made sure his signature, which would later become iconic, was always in the strip.

But Kane, true to form, was once again became restless at Eisner & Iger. He was unsatisfied with his page rate. He was stuck at $5 a page but would frequently find he had to pay for his own Ben Day to achieve the correct grey-tones on his pages, meaning he might lose money on some of his work. Ben Day was a printing process popularised by and named after illustrator Benjamin Henry Day Jr. It was most famously used in the unaccredited and unpaid appropriation of works by illustrators like Russ Heath by the pop-artist Roy Lichtenstein. 'Whaam!' a blow-up of Heath's work by Lichtenstein sold for $4 million. Heath received nothing and spent his final days living on donations from the comic creator charity The Hero Initiative.

Iger kept tight control of the purse strings, which caused some resentment among his freelancers, including Bob. One of Iger's later employees, Lee Ames, described his boss as, 'a swarthy little asshole of a guy who had no interest in anything other than the bottom line.' But it may just have been the case Bob was not good enough to earn the higher rates.

14

The studio was partly a collaborative process, partly an art factory. Pages were passed from one artist to another, each adding to the work; first the outlines, then the pencils, then the ink, then the lettering, so on and so forth. It was creation via an industrial process, requiring multiple artists working with different skills to build the pages of one book. Eisner himself would refer to the studio as a sweatshop, only as a half-joke, while pushing the artists working under him to hit deadlines and improve their work.

Bob's ambition did not work well in that kind of environment. Perhaps he associated it with the dull garment factory he had worked in previously or the process-driven workday of the Fleischer Studios. He needed to stand out, but even Kane had to acknowledge his former school-mate and employer's talent and drive, later writing – 'Eisner was not only a better draftsman than I was, he was also a better businessman than I could ever hope to be.'

But Bob wanted to be the headline act. His goal was to make $10 a day and Iger, frugality aside, did not think Kane had the talent to be a superstar. Kane was determined but he lacked the storytelling skill and artistic deftness that Eisner would eventually make the centre of his career.

'Bob wasn't an intellectual,' Eisner said to an interviewer. Recalling to another, he added, 'Bob was a very vapid kind of guy and his talent was quite limited. The big thing he was working on at that time was a thing called *Peter Pupp*, which was an imitation of Disney. That was the limit of his capacity.' Despite this brutal review, Eisner did give Kane some credit for his tenacity: 'But he was very aggressive, and he had immensely leathery skin, so that no matter how much humiliation he suffered, it didn't even register with him.'

Peter Pupp appeared in *Jumbo Comics,* which was made up of repackaged and decoloured original work from Eisner & Iger. *Pupp* ran for twenty-five issues, though later instalments were either reprints of the work credited to Kane or appeared with the name Goleh in the by-line, suggesting that someone else took over the run.

Kane was eager to get his own title and wanted to make more money. He wanted out of the studio system and so he started to look at National Comics Publications, which was known to pay their employees a slightly better page rate.

His bitterness towards Iger would last for years to come. In 1973, at a convention in New York, Kane claims the two crossed paths once again.

Kane was being honoured for his work on Batman and Iger had with him an original *Peter Pupp* page Kane assumed was a gift. Kane recounts Iger in fact wanted to trade the page for some original Batman art. Kane reluctantly made the deal but in retelling the story he calls Iger 'penny-wise and pound-foolish', a 'leopard [that] hadn't changed his spots' who had dealt Kane 'scores of old injustices', and he assumed Iger must have been haunted by the thought of not treating the soon to be creator of Batman more generously.

It seems unlikely. The Eisner & Iger studio was a great success even during the Depression, with Eisner describing himself as having gotten 'very rich before I was 22'. Besides, the superheroes had not yet taken their pedestal at the top of the comic book cosmos. Funnily enough, Eisner & Iger didn't just miss out on Batman. Eisner had sent a rejection letter replying 'You're not ready' to two kids named Siegel and Shuster who had sent in a strip called *Superman*. Despite his business prowess at the birth of a new medium, even Eisner could not have predicted the rise of the superhero.

Going National

Around 1937, Kane managed to get work doing fill-ins for publisher Malcolm Wheeler-Nicholson, a pulp writer and military veteran. Wheeler-Nicholson had written countless war and military history stories for the likes of *Argosy* and *Adventure*. He was something of an adventuring character himself. He was the son of a suffragette and as a boy, his home was visited by the likes of Theodore Roosevelt and Rudyard Kipling. He had a decorated military career across the world and worked as an intelligence officer in the Far East. He even claimed he was the target of an American army assassination attempt after he criticised infantry training methods.

Simply known as the Major thanks to his military record, Wheeler-Nicholson, like Eisner and Iger, quickly recognised the potential of comics, and in 1934 he launched National Comics Publications, which was also known as National Allied Publications and National Allied Newspaper Syndicate having previously operated two companies under those names. Wheeler-Nicholson published *New Fun: The Big Comic Magazine* – the first comic book to contain only previously unpublished material.

The strip Bob produced for Wheeler-Nicholson was called *Rusty and His Pals*. It was the story of a group of children, the titular Rusty along with his sidekicks Tubby and Specs – named for the most obvious of reasons – who read a book about pirates and set sail on a homemade raft in search of adventure. They would eventually bump into some phoney pirates on an entertainment cruise ship and, with the help of their new-found guardian Steve, uncover an opium smuggling plot.

The artwork matched the story in that it was an awkward blend of Disney-style cartooning and a semi-realistic, illustrative two-fisted tale of action. It is fitting too that the call to action for Rusty, along with his big-boned and myopic friends, should be their reading and enjoying of a pirate-themed book. Kane based his story on the vastly popular newspaper strip *Terry and the Pirates* by Milton Caniff.

Caniff's series had been so popular it had had a dedicated radio show and movie serials, and when the 1950s rolled around, a television show too. Caniff had been such an inspiration to the young Kane, Bob even mimicked Caniff's style in his signature, aping his oversized O.

But this strip was a stretch of Kane's artistic limits at the time. Often, the characters would be stylistically mismatched and their anatomy worryingly inconsistent.

Though his artwork improved through the series, and there are even hints of the heavy gothic atmosphere which infused in his early work on Batman, Kane was far more comfortable with the cartoonist style used in funny animal and humour strips over the dynamic and visceral look readers sought in action comics.

Kane admitted as much himself. Regarding *The Case of the Missing Heir*, an adventure tale he had sold to *Detective Picture Stories* before the creation of *Rusty and his Pals,* he said, 'although I enjoyed the chance to work on a mystery story, I still considered myself a gag cartoonist at the time and drew this story primarily because I needed the money,' adding, 'I found that I didn't like drawing adventure strips as much as humorous ones.'

Given Kane's background and the difficult economic times America was facing in the 1930s, Kane's primary concern with making a living as an artist was the living part rather than the art part. That is not to say the art wasn't important to Kane.

Rusty and his Pals was originally constructed as a Sunday newspaper strip. But after failing to sell it, Kane collected each strip together and presented them as a page to the editor of the National's *Adventure Comics,* Vin Sullivan. Sullivan bought the strips but had to cut up the originals to make them fit the format of a comic book page, a bittersweet experience for Kane who recalled, 'I wasn't happy about this, but I was thrilled about getting my first adventure series into print.'

While he worked on *Rusty and his Pals,* Kane was still chasing down other work and fulfilling his previous commitments around town. Feeling he could no longer write and draw the strip alone, he needed to draft in some help.

Kane was at a cocktail party when he met shoe-salesman Bill Finger. Kane was outgoing and opportunistic while Finger was friendly and sharp but reserved. As they chatted, they realised they had both attended DeWitt Clinton High School but had never encountered one another there.

In fact, DeWitt Clinton High School has produced many artists, journalists, writers, athletes, actors, and musicians over the years. It is probably the most influential school in terms of comic book history. As well as Kane and Finger, Will Eisner, the man who coined the phrase 'graphic novel' and dedicated his life to improving the medium, is among its notable alumni, and a few years after these three graduated, Stanley Lieber, better known as Stan 'The Man' Lee, co-creator of the Marvel Universe, would also attend DeWitt.

Finger was utterly desperate to get out of the less than rewarding world of shoe salesmanship and Kane needed help putting his stories together. And so, Bob invited Bill into the world of comic books. Finger leapt at the opportunity to finally make some money writing and took over the scripting duties on *Rusty and his Pals.* Though they doubtlessly got on – Kane was impressed with Finger's vast knowledge of literature and storytelling, Finger was wooed by Kane's certainty and self-confidence – it was a relationship founded on an uneven footing. For Kane, he had conveniently found a writer, but for Finger, this was the first step into a career he was desperate to pursue as well as a better means of supporting his new wife Ethel 'Portia' née Epstein and his parents.

Kane and Finger each had high hopes for what they could achieve but could they have known they would create one of the most recognisable characters in history together? While Bob and Bill worked away on their adventure strip another duo had set themselves to empire building.

Harry and Jack and the birth of DC Comics

The two men who had the most influence on the birth of comic books, to have gained the most financially and yet to have remained largely unremembered outside of the industry were Harry Donenfeld and Jack Liebowitz. Unfortunately, their success often came at the expense of others and they created a shark tank of the early comic book industry in which creators like Kane and Finger would sink or swim. In a sense, the dynamic between Donenfeld and Liebowitz would reflect that of Kane and Finger.

Harry Donenfeld had been born in Romania in 1893 but as anti-Semitic pogroms began to sweep through Europe, his father, Itzhak, along with millions of European Jews, had headed to America looking for safety. Like so many others, they soon realised that life would not be what they had dreamed it would be in the States. Though it was certainly safer, Jews, Italians and the Irish were all looked down upon by the white Anglo-Saxon, Protestant society that controlled America.

Harry's youth, not unlike Kane's, was spent in the lower east side of Manhattan amongst the tenement buildings, running schemes with various gangs to make a buck. Harry's talent, which helped him to survive poverty and street gangs, was his gift of the gab. Harry could charm and fast-talk his way into (and out of) any situation he wanted to and he was keen to make something of himself. Striving for independence, he refused to work alongside his older brothers, Mike and Charlie, at their printing company, Martin Press. At 25, he married Gussie Weinstein and they ran a clothing store together.

When the store failed, he was forced to work with his brothers as a salesman, a job he was perfectly suited for. Donenfeld started to do well in the role, making plenty of contacts, and it has been heavily suggested some of those connections were tied to the mob. Donenfeld himself bragged about knowing gangsters – that is until the comics industry became big enough for people would take notice of that behaviour – and his wife and son later retold stories of answering the phone or door to heavies telling them Frank Costello was looking for Harry.

Frank Costello was a member of the Luciano crime family. Married to a Jewish woman, Costello was good at making connections between the usually warring Jewish, Irish and Italian factions. The theory goes that Donenfeld, who was working at a printing company, imported paper

19

from Canada. With the paper, bootleggers also smuggled alcohol into the States during the Prohibition era on behalf of the mob. Once the booze was at the printers, it was easier to deal with how to distribute the liquor to the thirsty citizens of New York. With the right blackmail or bribe, the distributor could get the liquor around the city and to newsstands where it could be sold illegally for a hiked-up price.

In exchange for his smuggling, Donenfeld was put in touch with Moe Annenberg, a publisher who had run gambling and protection rackets in Chicago to control circulation on behalf of Hearst Communications, who was now working in New York. Controlling the publisher meant controlling circulation and Annenberg would need someone like Donenfeld who would play ball.

This theory hasn't been confirmed – if it is true none of the parties involved were stupid enough to admit it – but there do seem to be plenty of reasons to believe that Donenfeld and Costello knew each other and probably worked together. What is known is that Martin Press suddenly received the contract to produce six million subscription inserts for various Hearst titles, making it a major player and the Donenfelds, or at least Harry, pretty wealthy. At the same time, Harry forced his brothers out of the company and back to the rag trade while he consolidated control.

Potentially a bootlegger and gangster, and certainly a charming but ruthless businessman, Donenfeld then moved into the field of producing and distributing erotic action novels with titles such as *Spicy Mysteries, Spicy Adventures* and *Spicy Detective.* This was pornography thinly disguised as genre fiction and its salaciousness almost landed Donenfeld in jail.

This is the man who would later foot the bill for bringing superheroes into the world and he was described by Kane as a friend. But Donenfeld would not do this alone. He had his partner Jack to help.

While Kane and Donenfeld shared the same boundless confidence, the gift of telling a tall tale and later, friendship, what Finger and Liebowitz shared was intelligence.

Liebowitz was born Yacov Lebovitz in Ukraine in 1900 and never knew his biological father. His mother, Mindi, with her new husband Julius, fled to the United States in 1910. Quickly enough, Yacov became Jacob, which inevitably became Jack. Like a lot of immigrants who settled into Manhattan's lower east side, the Liebowitz family was poor. While Jack worked as a newspaper boy for a dollar a day, his stepfather immersed himself in the socialist movement the Russian and Eastern European Jews had brought with them to the New World and he eventually became the steward of one of the largest and most influential unions in American labour history, the International Ladies' Garment Workers' Union (ILGWU).

But whereas Donenfeld – and later Kane – would use their street smarts to lift themselves out of poverty, Liebowitz relied on his book-smarts. He quickly showed an aptitude for numbers, accountancy and book-keeping.

Jack made it out of the tenements and all the way to New York University where he earned his degree in accountancy. He set himself up as a professional accountant and took on several clients, including his stepfather's socialist cause, the ILGWU, where his skill with a ledger would really be tested.

Fifty thousand union workers went on strike in 1926, relying only on union funds and Jack Liebowitz to help them get by. Thanks to Jack's talent with numbers, not only was he able to keep the strike going and its workers fed and sheltered for six months, once the strike broke, the union, which had spent almost $4 million, was still solvent.

Jack had done his stepfather proud and was well respected amongst the socialists who led the union. But the strike attracted the attention of organised crime which bought into these businesses and put pressures on the unions while the Republican government turned a legislative blind eye. Eventually, Jack found himself working on dirty accounts, for his own sake and the sake of the union, covering up payments made to gangster protection rackets.

In 1929 the stock market crash happened. All of Jack's hard work and deft manoeuvring was for nought. At the same time, he began drifting away from the socialist dream and toward capitalism, perhaps as a result of the dissolution sweeping the American socialists at the time and the need to support his wife and child. He left or was dismissed from the ILGWU and began looking for other work. Luckily, his stepfather was able to lend a hand.

Julius got in touch with a former business acquaintance, Harry Donenfeld, to see if he had any work going that his son might be able to do. Besides Liebowitz's clear skill with money and his willingness to keep shtum regarding the source of lucrative but likely illegal incomes, Harry had a loyalty to the old neighbourhood. He was more than happy to hand out jobs to family, friends and former business partners. Not only could he help those who came from the same difficult background as he did, it meant they probably owed him a favour down the line.

Liebowitz became Donenfeld's accountant and managed to bring some order, risk assessment and damage control to Donenfeld's confident but careless business strategy.

By 1931, one of Donenfeld's distributors, Eastern News, was $30,000 in debt to Donenfeld. With Liebowitz's guidance and savvy, Donenfeld was persuaded to buy up Eastern's debts and become a distributor as well as a publisher. The venture was called the Independent News Company.

Liebowitz spotted how this would allow the pair to increase their revenue streams and through Liebowitz's diligence in dealing with publishers and suppliers – as well as trying to iron out Donenfeld's bad habits of talking his way out of debts rather than paying them – the pair were able to build a bigger, more respected, and ultimately, more profitable business.

One such revenue stream was the distribution of Wheeler-Nicholson's National Allied Publications. Already broke, The Major needed to create a subsidiary company to launch his latest book *Detective Comics*. That company, part-owned by Jack Liebowitz, was called Detective Comics Incorporated, which would later be shortened to DC. Together with the purchasing and ownership of All-American Publications run by Charles Gaines, this business strategising would make Liebowitz co-owner of an extensive comic book empire alongside Donenfeld. It was this which placed the two at the centre of the comics industry and tied their fates to that of Bob Kane, Bill Finger and Batman.

While Kane and Finger as a partnership shared some similarities with Donenfeld and Liebowitz it is where they differed that is interesting. Liebowitz and Donenfeld understood the value of one another. They realised the talents the other had was what they individually lacked, and how ultimately, they benefitted from their relationship. They were also extremely focused on their goals and ruthless in business. That was an attribute that had served them well in the 1920s and 1930s and perhaps something Kane admired and would emulate. But it also created the kind of brutal business environment that would eventually exploit so many young artists and writers in the fledgeling industry, including Bill Finger.

Chapter Three

The Superheroes

The boys who changed everything

As Finger laboured in his father's shoe shop to finance his infatuation with foreign film and while Kane was schlepping up and down Manhattan, showing off his work to any publisher that would let him through the door, 470 miles away, in Cleveland, Ohio, two teenagers had caught lightning in a bottle. The spark which would change pop culture and the lives of hundreds of writers and artists for the rest of the twentieth century, including those of Finger and Kane.

Siegel and Shuster's Superman had been gestating for half a decade before he leapt from the pages of *Action Comics #1* in May 1938. Hardcore comics aficionados will know the actual date of release on the cover of the comic that started it all was June, not May. But comic book publishers are a crafty sort. In the early days, it was common practice to list the cover date as a few months after the actual release in order to keep the book appearing new and on newsstands for as long as possible

Still in their teenage years, writer Jerome 'Jerry' Siegel and artist Joseph 'Joe' Shuster had worked on a story in 1932 entitled *The Reign of the Super-man*. Though immensely different from the character we recognise today – the 'Super-man' rather than 'Superman' looked much more like the bald bad-guy, Lex Luther – it contained the earliest threads of what would grow into the Man of Steel with Siegel describing that nine-page story as 'a giant step forward on: The Road to Superman'.

One day, Superman and Batman would become the world's finest; super friends brought together in the quest for justice, and later still, with Wonder Woman, they would form the DC Comics Trinity, the pillars around which their whole universe would be built.

The relationship between Superman and Batman is reflected in the relationships between their respective creators. There is a warped symmetry existing between the characters and yet there is also an inescapable connection and pull between the two.

Batman's development may have begun as a way of emulating Superman's incredible success, but the result was quite different. The first adventures of Superman, the immigrant raised as a farmer, has him taking on wife-beaters, unjust governors, government lobbyists and corrupt landlords. He is a figure for justice and fairness even if he acts outside of the law.

Batman on the other hand, at least in his earlier stories, is a billionaire who shoots anyone threatening or jeopardising the sanctity of property ownership. Whether their creators knew it or not, between them they covered a huge swathe of the political spectrum.

This reductive dichotomy of doing what is morally valuable against doing what is profitable unfortunately played a central role at the core of the Golden Age of Comics. The term 'Golden Age' roughly covers the time between Superman's first publication in 1939 to the 1954 formation of the Comics Code Authority. It refers not only to the creativity and legacy of the era but also to the explosion of the superhero genre and the millions of sales that the embryonic industry generated in those days, and which has rarely ever been replicated. Jerry Siegel and Joe Shuster were the first in the industry to fall victim to the profit versus people problem which continues to this day; and Kane and Finger would soon follow, albeit in different capacities.

Joe and Jerry met in 1924 at Cleveland's Glenville High School after Joe's family moved to Ohio from Toronto. Both their parents were, like those of Finger and Kane, Jewish immigrants. Joe's father had made the move south after his tailor shop in the Great White North had failed, and the Shuster family was constantly in need of cash. Joe worked as a paperboy and ice cream man to help them get by.

The Siegel family was not any better off, though they lived in a two-story home rather than a cramped apartment the Shusters occupied. Jerry was the youngest of six children with three older sisters and two brothers. His father, Michael, ran a second-hand clothes' shop in Cedar-Central, a run-down ghetto in Cleveland's African American neighbourhood. Only a few months before Jerry met Joe, Michael, who was then almost 60, confronted three thieves in his store. He was assaulted and, due to the stress of the event, died of a heart attack. It's doubtful that Siegel ever shared this story with Kane or Finger despite the clear echoing of the tragedy in the killing of Bruce Wayne's parents but it seems possible this event would contribute to Superman's invulnerability in the face of evil.

Jerry was an avid reader of the pulps, particularly science fiction. Successors to the penny dreadful, the pulps were made from cheap wood-pulp paper as opposed to the high-quality paper used on 'glossies'. Pulp titles such as *Astounding Science Fiction, Weird Tales* and *Detective Story Magazine* featured genre stories usually paid for by the word count. Though it gave rise to the term 'pulp fiction' meaning trashy or disposable work, influential genre writers like Arthur C. Clarke, Raymond Chandler and H.P. Lovecraft all regularly wrote for the pulps.

As a teenager, Jerry had tried to get his short stories published wherever he could but after numerous rejection letters, and often no reply at all, he decided to become the master of his own fate and he launched America's first-ever underground fan magazine, *Cosmic Stories*. This was quickly followed by *Guests of The Earth* and later *Science Fiction: The Advanced Guard of Future Civilizations*. It was for this last publication, with Siegel as the owner, editor and treasurer, that he brought in Joe Shuster. Within just a few days of meeting him, Siegel had the good sense to draft in the young artist, eventually, giving him the lofty position of art director too.

The boys continued to work together throughout their teen years with a few impassioned arguments here and there. Their styles, simplistic yet daringly bold, complimented each other, and the two were happier exploring the fantastic new worlds they were creating than having to face the dread of talking to pretty girls.

Superman was continually developed and pitched to various publishers and syndications with no luck for a couple of years but the boys persisted and recycled unused elements from what they now regarded as their masterpiece in the creation of other heroes and stories.

Eventually, they came to the attention of the Major at National Comics Publications. Unlike *Famous Funnies*, which rejected Superman without even opening Siegel and Shuster's package, the Major used new strips which hadn't previously appeared in newspapers and sold advertising space to make up the money.

The Major took on Siegel and Shuster and bought several strips from them over an eight-month period including Superman. But correctly sensing that National Comics Publications might be running low on funds, they asked for their Superman work to be returned rather than it be squandered or lost. The boys were right, and their prudence meant the Man of Tomorrow actually lived to see another day.

Nicholson-Wheeler had racked up debts not only to his artists and writers but also to his printers and distributors, Harry Donenfeld and Jack Liebowitz. The Major's company was limping by on thousands of dollars' worth of loans which Donenfeld and Liebowitz bought up, allowing them to take control of his business. The pair, who would later deal with Kane and Finger, already published adult titles, but they wanted to expand their empire to include the minds of kids, and National was a way to do that.

The Major was bought off, leaving his company to Donenfeld and Liebowitz, who had no real interest in comics beyond what money they could make them. They retained editor Vin Sullivan who worked on *Detective Comics* and asked him to fill up a new book, for which they only had the pre-existing title, *Action Comics*.

Liebowitz asked other publishers if they had anything lying around that they didn't want to work on. The McClure Newspaper Syndicate sent over a package they had never had the chance to explore featuring the work of Siegel and Shuster. Sullivan snapped it up. He sent word to the boys he was interested but asked them to re-cut the strip from its newspaper format to fit a comics page. For good measure, the boys were paid the outstanding fee for their work with the Major. They were also paid the coveted $10 page rate Bob Kane had previously demanded, which they split between them for the 13 pages that would make up the first Superman story.

The original pages were never given back to Siegel and Shuster but were destroyed by Donenfeld and Liebowitz after the publication of *Action Comics #1*. What the boys hadn't realised was the cheque for $130 wasn't just their page rate, it was the cost of the copyright to the multi-billion-dollar industry Superman would eventually become. That very cheque, for such a measly sum, would sell at auction in 2012 for $160,000.

In no way could Siegel and Shuster have predicted that, when the day came that they needed help to right this wrong, they would have to rely on Bob Kane.

A Brave New World

During Kane and Finger's youth, comics had rapidly transformed. They went from newspaper strips to syndication to newspaper reprints to original content to corporation-owned icons in just a few years. *Action Comics* #1, featuring Superman's first appearance, had an initial print run of 200,000 and had rapidly sold out, while the series itself would go on to sell over a million copies monthly. It was a cultural phenomenon on a scale matching Star Wars or Harry Potter, but realistically its success has never been replicated. It was a pre-television, pre-internet phenomenon with an astounding reach that made some people very rich.

What needs to be taken away from the last few chapters is Kane and Finger were not yet central, and certainly not vital, to the industry they would find themselves in. There was no plan, blueprint, or expectation about how people at the core of the industry would succeed. Success relied on the mimicry, replication and recycling of the efforts of others who had stumbled into success with the help of lady luck. Most of the major players may not have even enjoyed their product but what they cared about was how the content could be converted into cash. That is what comics were at the time – just content. They were not yet an art form or a means of expression – they were just another thing that publishers did to sell advertising. Nobody then, not even Will Eisner, was pursuing this format out of purely artistic need. All that would come later. It may well be that the early purpose of comics is what ultimately restricted the medium from being considered 'real art' for so many decades.

The successes of the early industry can tell us a false story. It may seem as if history could not have played out any other way. But focusing purely on the successes obscures the countless failures and miscalculations of those the industry chewed up and spat out. Those who made it to success did not always get there unscathed by their own mistakes or the opportunist nature of those at the top. While we can be distracted by the anecdotes and the creative and wonderful nature of comic books, it is important to remember it was and is an industry. And as Kane and Finger were entering that world, it was an industry where the rules had not been laid down. Future generations of creators might have the benefit of legal protections and media scrutiny as well as room to explore their creativity but that was not always the case. Talent alone wasn't enough to promise success if it wasn't tempered by street smarts, a desire to earn some money and the ruthlessness to strike when you had the chance.

Comic books are a collaborative medium with multiple people working together, creating something together. But a Wild West industry with no regulations and an environment that favours business over art means those collaborations can be strained, stretched and broken.

Kane and Finger were now a team of sorts. They worked together but Kane paid Finger out of his cheque. Kane was the guy dealing with publishers and editors while Finger sat at a typewriter anguishing over scripts. They were just a couple of kids, but Kane was reaching for stardom while Finger was just looking to get by. In the industry as it was, they were two very different fish who found themselves in strange and dangerous waters.

Chapter Four

The Bat is Born

Enter: 'The Bat-man'

Bob Kane and Bill Finger would meet, as they usually did when they wanted to escape the hustle and bustle of the studio (Bob's bedroom), at Edgar Allan Poe Park in the Bronx. They would sit there, yards away from the great author's one-time home, and discuss ideas for new books and characters. In late 1938, the proximity of their regular haunt to the home of the inventor of detective fiction was particularly fitting given what was to come. Poe's great detective Le Chevalier C. Auguste Dupin had appeared in the 1841 short story *The Murders in Rue Morgue* with his unique, crime deducing skill of 'ratiocination'. He has influenced writers ever since. As 'The World's Greatest Detective', Batman's DNA is, of course, laden with detective and gothic fiction.

As the young men sat there, eating sandwiches, and talking comics, their opportunity to add to the canon of great fictional detectives was just around the corner.

One wintry Friday Kane had met with the DC comics editor Vin Sullivan. Sullivan had been the editor on the earliest Superman stories appearing in *Action Comics* and was currently working on DC's crime book *Detective Comics*, for which he had illustrated the first-ever cover.

The Last Son of Krypton had been a phenomenal success, sending kids crazy with his swift and unstoppable delivery of justice. Cowboys and crime, the staples of the comic book diet, were out: capes were in. Sullivan wanted to replicate the success of Superman in *Detective Comics* and was taking pitches from his regular staff. Kane had seen the money Superman was generating and promised Sullivan a new character by Monday morning.

So, Kane and Finger got to work. Before Batman and Robin, Bob and Bill were a dynamic duo, creatively at least. Kane was solely concerned with the visuals of a character, how it looked on and moved across the page. Finger, whose childhood was spent buried in the classics, understood character and motivation, but essentially, for any great comic writer, he also appreciated how vital the visual elements were too.

Before he met with Finger, Kane had developed some first concepts, blurting out as a mishmash of ideas only vaguely recognisable as the Batman we now know today. Kane wanted the character to have wings, perhaps like those of the Valkyrie-like Hawkmen from Alex Raymond's sci-fi opera epic, *Flash Gordon*.

He quickly moved from the easily recognisable Hawkmen to Leonardo da Vinci's ornithopter. One of the renaissance master's theoretical flying machines, the ornithopter was a canvas stretched across a wooden frame creating a wing for gliding.

Kane folded in visual elements of Douglas Fairbanks' *The Mark of Zorro* (1920) giving his new character a secret identity and black cowl through which you could see his pupils. Kane had loved Zorro as a child and said it 'left a lasting impression on me', adding 'It gave me the dual identity. You're influenced at once by another character, but then you embellish and bring your own individuality into it.'

Bob did what he knew best. He grabbed the latest newspaper strip of *Flash Gordon* he had lying around, traced the mid-action pose of Flash swinging on a rope, and super-imposed his ideas onto the page. It was a great visual and was very useful with the deadline fast approaching and a $10 page rate on the line.

Sketch in hand, he rushed across town to Finger's apartment. The character, with its then red costume and rigid wings, was presented to Bill as 'Bird-man'.

Bill had some notes.

Perhaps inspired by the gothic works of Poe, the namesake of the park they would regularly haunt, Finger suggested something darker and more fitting for a masked detective – a bat.

'I didn't like the wings,' said Finger, referring to the mechanical structures protruding from the shoulders of Kane's concept. 'So, I suggested he make a cape and scallop the edges so it would flow out behind him when he ran and would look like bird wings.'

Kane ran with the redesign, reminiscent of the villain from another of his favourite films, the comedy-thriller, *The Bat Whispers* (1930). The killer of the movie – adapted from the stage play *The Bat*, itself very loosely adapted from Mary Robert Rinehart's mystery novel *The Circular Staircase* – hides beneath a bat costume complete with scalloped patagia beneath his arms, a squashed snout and long, pointy ears. Finger suggested the long ears to give the image the profile of a bat but left out the nose. But he was not done quite yet. In 1936, *The Phantom*, created by Lee Falk and Ray Moore, hit the newspapers. The Phantom wore a skin-tight, dark purple costume and when he wore his domino mask, his pupils disappeared, becoming like the eyes of an ancient statue.

Finger convinced Kane to get rid of the new character's pupils, giving him an unearthly quality (while making him consistently easier to draw) and to change the costume from red to grey. The pointed cowl and brand-new cape remained black, though by the time the character appeared in print, the method of highlighting black with blues in comic strips would essentially make them blue.

Through this chimerical chemistry of creative influences, the image of The Dark Knight was born. But despite Finger's clear contributions to the design of the character, Kane would later limit his involvement to just story development, leaving out the additions that made the visuals of the character so iconic.

'Almost every famous character ever created had a simplistic, definitive design that was easily recognisable. And that is what I was striving for with Batman,' said Kane. 'When I created Batman, I wasn't thinking of the story. I was thinking, I have to come up with a character who is different.'

Not acknowledging his co-creator while self-aggrandising would, for a long time, loom like great darkness over the creative origins of Batman. But Finger contributed more than just character design. A well-respected writer amongst artists, Finger gave Batman a story and a character. He was inspired by detectives like Conan Doyle's Sherlock Holmes and Poe's Auguste Dupin, swashbuckling heroes such as Orczy's Scarlet Pimpernel and Dumas' D'Artagnan, and of course Zorro, to create a smart, formidable, but ultimately human fight against injustice. He realised that Batman, unlike his cousin from Metropolis, must not be a science-fiction hero, but instead a crime hero of the pulp tradition.

The pulps were packed to the gills with bat-related criminals and crimefighters. There is just something eternal and primordial about that little winged mammal which writers seem to be drawn to. The Black Bat was a detective who appeared in some of the 1933 issues of *Black Bat*

Detective Mysteries with the titular character having nothing to do with bats aside from the occasional appearance of one on the cover.

In 1939, *Popular Detective* featured a character who not only resembled a bat, he resembled Batman and, unbelievably, was also named the Black Bat. *Black Bat Detective Mysteries* publishers may not have had an issue with this, but *Popular Detective* publishers, Better Publications, would when Batman later crashed onto the scene. 'They were ready to sue us, and we were ready to sue them,' Finger would later say about the character. 'It was just one of those wild coincidences.'

Ultimately, no one would sue, probably because Better Publications owner, Ned Pines, was friends with DC/National own Harry Donenfeld and the pair would later form *See Magazine*.

This was not the first or most peculiar bat-themed vigilante *Popular Detective* would feature. Its very first issue, back in 1934, featured a character created by C. K. M. Scanlon. Dawson Clade was a reporter caught in a set-up by the very gangster he had set out to expose. When he ruminated on how best to clear his name and take his revenge on the gangsters, a bat flew through his window and inspired him to become the Bat – the black hooded hero who took on his foes with a gas gun, and who left his mark to terrify those who would dare to become a vessel for criminality.

Aside from the origin story which would soon come to resemble that of Bruce Wayne, there is an interesting theory behind the identity of C. K. M. Scanlon. Pulp writers were used to writing under pseudonyms, both to protect their reputation should they ever want to make a name in respectable literature and to give the publications they wrote for some veneer of continuity; to convince the readers to keep coming back to the favourite author, despite that author possibly being several different people.

Scanlon was a house name that the writers of *Popular Detective* would work under. One such writer was Johnston McCulley, who had created Don Diego de le Vega, the wealthy Californian landowner who fought against the injustices wrought upon the common man; hidden by the night, by his mask and by his soubriquet the Fox, or in Spanish, Zorro. Pulp historians have hypothesised that it may have been McCulley, with his hallmark of characters leaving behind a symbol to warn off criminals, and his distinct writing style, who created the Bat. Meaning there might be much more of Zorro's DNA in Batman than even Kane and Finger ever realised. But Finger certainly admitted to the undeniable influence of one of the other premier pulp protagonists, the Shadow.

To begin with, the Shadow was simply the name of the host of the *Detective Story Hour* radio show, a promotional segment for the crime pulp *Detective Story Magazine*. The Shadow had no real characteristics save for his ability to narrate crime stories, his immense popularity, a manic laugh, and the catchphrase – 'Who knows what evil lurks in the hearts of men? The Shadow knows!' Getting word back from newsstands that readers would be asking for *The Shadow Magazine* rather than *Detective Story* magazine, publishers Street & Smith decided to give the people what they wanted.

They drafted in Walter Brown Gibson to flesh out the character for his own magazine. Gibson got the gig having pitched a few stories to *Detective,* but his previous jobs made him more than qualified. He had been a reporter, a crossword puzzle setter, the editor of the pulp title *True Crime Stories*, a professional magician, the inventor of the 'Nickels to Dime' illusion, debunker, and ghostwriter for a collection of famous conjurors, including his friend Harry Houdini. After Houdini, well known for his debunking of false mediums, died, his wife Bess held a series of séances to contact the great escapist. When she was no longer able to perform this duty, she passed it on to Gibson. The tradition continues in the magic community to this day.

To protect his non-fiction work, Gibson adopted the pen-name Maxwell Grant, a combination of the names of two magic dealers he associated with, and he got to work on *The Shadow Magazine*. It was a hit and the Shadow returned to radio in his own, self-titled radio drama, this time voiced by none other than RKO wunderkind, Orson Welles. Welles' movie work and avant-garde cinematography would later provide inspiration for Finger and the artists he worked with in creating the atmosphere of Batman's universe.

The Shadow's original story, identity and abilities would vary from radio to magazine but what was always consistent was his long, dark cloak and hidden face. One of his many alter egos was Lamont Cranston, the millionaire playboy identity the Shadow would adopt to move undetected in high society.

While Kane traced over Alex Raymond's athletic Flash Gordon to give the Batman his dynamism, Finger scribbled over the Shadow to create a similar, gothic, crime-ridden, noir world. In fact, Batman's first appearance was essentially a Shadow reboot.

'My first script was a take-off on a Shadow,' Finger would later admit about Batman's initial adventure, *The Case of The Chemical Syndicate*. In reference to his overall approach to the character, he adds, 'I patterned my writing style after The Shadow... I liked that kind of dramatic point of view. It was completely pulp style. Sometimes I overdid it, writing phrases like "Night mantles the City". But, somehow, it all seemed to work.'

The purple prose of the pulps aside, *The Case of the Chemical Syndicate* finds the newly night-born Batman take on the world of corporate intrigue, with the son of the recently deceased Apex Chemicals owner framed for his father's murder as a shadowy figure tries to take control of the company. It is an undiluted pulp crime adventure.

It also is practically identical to the Shadow novel *Partners in Peril*. So much so that when the Shadow arrives in the story, around the same point that Batman makes his appearance in the Kane/Finger adaptation, he is repeatedly referred to as Bat-like.

Although *Partners in Peril* isn't actual a Gibson story – it was the first Shadow adventure written by one of the most prolific adopters of the Maxwell Grant mask, Theodore Tinsley – the magician and writer would later describe Batman as little more than a 'clowned-up' version of the Shadow. But history is rife with irony.

Hot on the heels of Tim Burton's *Batman* and *Batman Returns,* 1994's *The Shadow,* starring Alec Baldwin, Ian McKellen and Tim Curry, faced a wave of critics referring to it as 'a limp jump onto the Batman band-wagon' and a 'lavish Batman wanna-be.' Little did they know it was the other way around.

To top it off, despite his comments on Batman, Gibson's last published work before his death was a prose story starring Batman appearing in 1981's special anniversary issue of *Detective Comics #500* alongside a strip featuring Edgar Allan Poe.

The eight-page story entitled 'The Batman Encounters – Grey Face' sees the caped crusader take on the ashen international crime boss in Gotham's China Town. In *The Shadow in Review*, author John Olsen makes the case for this story originally being made as a vehicle for the Shadow, with the similarities between the two characters essentially making them interchangeable, and the tantalising mention of Gibson leaving notes stating his intentions to give this story to his shadowy Knight of Darkness over Kane and Finger's Dark Knight.

Sadly we may never know if this is true, but if it is, it would mean that not only is the first-ever Batman story really a Shadow story, the last ever Shadow story, written by his most famous creator, ended up a Batman tale too.

Like the Shadow, Batman needed an alter ego. Bob Kane said that the millionaire playboy and bachelor was named, and even visually modelled, after him. Perhaps Wayne is Kane's idolised version of himself, his ego on the page, but there is an alternative account of how Bruce was christened. Finger, with his broad knowledge-base and love of trivia, plucked two names from history and combined them. The first, Bruce, came from Robert the Bruce, the rebellious King of Scotland. This added the air of hereditary nobility to their character and went some way to explain his incredible wealth. He was old money. Wayne is said to have been inspired by 'Mad' Anthony Wayne. The historical Wayne was a soldier in the American Revolution and quickly made his way through the ranks to become Brigadier General. He became 'mad' after personally leading a daring and dangerous night-time assault on a British camp at close quarters. Perhaps it wasn't just Wayne's name Batman inherited but his tactics too.

What Kane and Finger were left with was a character of a good stock; assimilated from a pantheon of adventurers and crimefighters that had come before him. All they could do now is hope that Vin Sullivan would accept it and wait to see if the public would buy it.

Detective Comics #27

Vin Sullivan, who had worked under pulp writer Major Malcolm Nicholson-Wheeler and survived the transition to Donenfeld and Liebowitz, had originally envisioned the *Detective Comics* line as a visual version of the pulps. Whether he told Kane as much on that fateful Friday is unknown, but without a shadow of a doubt the DNA of The Shadow was familiar to him. He thought this 'Bat-man' was great but Harry Donenfeld was concerned he might be too creepy for the public. Given Donenfeld had been distributing erotica just a few years earlier, it was easy for Sullivan to convince him scary was less of a concern for the public than sexy. And at $60 for that first story, it wasn't a huge risk given the thousands Superman was generating.

Newsstands were hit with *Detective Comics #27* in March 1939. The series had so far featured covers fitting for the two-fisted crime tales inside, but this issue had a remarkably new and striking cover. The horned figure of Batman swooped through the skies on a thread-thin rope, as he grappled with what we must assume was a thug. Two other no-goodniks watched from the foreground, their guns pointed at this dark figure with a sweeping cape. National/DC had another hit on their hands.

Superman had been such a huge success and Vin Sullivan wasn't the only editor looking for a character just like him. Dozens of proxy Supermen started popping up, each a pale imitation of Kal-El. A former DC editor, Victor Fox, commissioned Will Eisner to create a superhero character to match the Man of Steel's success. The resulting Wonder Man resulted in National subpoenaing Fox, who lost the case when Eisner, who had been uncomfortable with the character brief from the start, openly testified that he had been instructed to rip off Superman.

Batman, though arguably a rip-off of The Shadow, was at least different to Superman. Visually, Kane's lines were not as clean as Shuster's and the strip was much darker and more claustrophobic. The characters had a cape and bodysuit in common, but Batman frowned and hid his face as he went about his serious duty of wreaking vengeance on the underworld. Superman smiled and pranked criminals as he brought justice to them. Whereas Superman was invulnerable and powerful, Batman was mortal and had only his wits and utility belt to rely on. Superman was born of a kind of optimistic science fiction while Batman had crept from the shadows of crime fiction.

That first issue, with its six-page homage to the Shadow, *The Case of the Chemical Syndicate*, was pure pulp spun into a visual medium. Even though Finger claimed it was overdone in parts, it was less excessively worded than the pulps. After all, Finger wasn't being paid by the word like the pulp authors were. And besides, they needed the room for Kane's art. Many of the pages were crammed and displayed Kane's lack of confidence in drawing action comics, but this limitation and even Kane's occasional struggle with anatomy gave the comic a darker and creepier tone than his shining and clean Metropolis counterpart. Batman complemented and contrasted with Superman, providing a balance to the superhero diet.

The strip was initially run as Bat-Man, with the hyphen being dropped pretty early in the character's publication history, but something that would remain was Bob Kane's credit on the title page. Just Bob Kane. Bill Finger's name was nowhere to be found. Not getting credit for his work on Batman would become a running issue between Kane and Finger. The later was technically employed by Kane and paid cash in hand. And despite being there from the beginning, he never really pushed hard enough to get the recognition he so deserved.

The Third Man

Even as Batman was debuting across America, Kane and Finger were putting together another feature commissioned by Vin Sullivan. This time for Action Comics, in the form of *Clip Carson – Soldier of Fortune;* a smiling Doc Savage meets Indiana Jones-type adventurer. Once again, Finger's love of literature would influence the creation, with Carson being a homage to Great White Hunter archetypes such as Allen Quartermain from Rider Haggard's *King Solomon's Mines.* It was a serviceable back-up to the Superman-dominated *Action Comics* but who really wants to follow that act?

At the time, comics were more like anthologies featuring a handful of separate characters linked only by theme. Crossovers between the characters wouldn't come until a little later. This allowed publishers to spread their bets. If one feature didn't grab your attention, not to worry, another one would be along in just a few pages. Plus, it theoretically allowed for a quicker turn around in production as multiple creative teams would be working on the book rather than one artist-writer duo or studio.

Whether it was a case of being overworked, or perhaps a lingering (and uncharacteristic) lack of confidence in his art, seven months after Batman's first appearance, Bob was starting to need some help. In September of 1939, Bob took a short break to a resort in the Poconos mountains in Pennsylvania. Bob was not much of a sportsman, so he spent much of his time lounging around the resort and talking to girls. One day he noticed a skinny rake of a teenager making his way to the tennis courts, racket in hand. He was wearing a white painter's jacket with various pockets and compartments on it, which was the style amongst college kids at the time. The jacket was covered in doodles and hand-drawn insignia like illustrated combs sticking out of pockets or silly slogans. Bob stopped the thin youngster and asked who had done the cartoons. The kid replied those were his doodles and introduced himself as Jerry Robinson. Bob told his new friend that he was one of the artists behind Batman. Robinson, who was only 17 at the time, did not know what the heck a Batman was. The two had been getting on well but Jerry's confession irked Bob somewhat so, at Kane's suggestion, they took a stroll into town to pick up the latest issue of *Detective*.

Jerry was underwhelmed. He was a fan of the Sunday strips and he particularly enjoyed Milton's *Terry and The Pirates* and Hal Foster's *Prince Valiant*. He even owned a few newspaper reprints, but this was his first encounter with a comic book and he was not won over by the draftsmanship. Regardless, Bob and Jerry became friends despite their eight-year age difference.

Jerry had been born on the stroke of midnight on 1 January 1922 in Trenton, New Jersey, not all that far away from the Bronx which was the stomping ground of so many young comic creators. He was the youngest of five kids born to Ben and Mae Robinson. His father was a Russian immigrant and potter while his mother was a New Yorker who had had the foresight to open Trenton's first cinema, the Garden Theatre. They would have been comfortable at any other time, but the Great Depression resulted in the family losing the theatre and moving into a tenement in the centre of Trenton. Though Ben was able to turn things around and move his family back to the suburbs within a few years, Jerry's early years really weren't all that dissimilar to Kane's, complete with childhood violence and gangs.

Jerry was artistically gifted from a young age. Though it was never his intention to become an artist he nevertheless showed great skill and dedication. Robinson learned naturally, by drawing the world around him rather than taking formal lessons. By the time he was 10, he was regularly sketching out accurate portraits of his relatives. His parents were extremely supportive and nurtured the cultural and intellectual pursuits of their children. There would be regular discussions of the arts, culture, and politics around the evening dinner table. All of Jerry's much older siblings had gone to college, with a few becoming doctors or dentists. One of his brothers, Harold, even foreshadowed Jerry by illustrating for Penn State's college magazine.

At high school, Jerry had loved sports, despite always being very slight, but even more than sports, reading and writing were what he enjoyed most. He became the editor, writer and cartoonist of his high school newspaper, *The Spectator*. In his afterschool job, he sold magazine subscriptions which he delivered by bike. When he picked up the magazines for drop-off, he would inevitably encounter the newsstand pulp novels, which he devoured alongside the classics. He wrote short stories and was set on becoming a journalist. Art was just something he happened to be good at it was not necessarily what he was going to do for a living.

By the time he had graduated from High School he had been accepted by three universities; Columbia, Penn, and Syracuse, but he hadn't committed to any of them. He spent that summer selling ice creams by bike, slowly getting skinnier and skinnier while trying to save for his college fund – his family was, after all, still feeling the effects of the Depression. Despite this, Robinson had been sent to the Poconos at his mother's request to fatten him up a bit before college. They would find a way to get by financially, but Robinson's mother was worried her son might disappear altogether if he lost much more weight.

Eventually, while not putting on weight and just playing tennis instead, Bob mentioned that he needed an art assistant back in New York to help with the pile of Batman work he had to chew through. Robinson knew he was probably just cheap labour but the promise of $25 a week seemed like too much to pass up on. So, he accepted the offer and was determined to make it work.

During Kane and Finger's tenure on Batman, several artists and writing assistants would work on the book, sometimes referred to as ghosts, but Robinson was one of the first and perhaps more than any other contributed the most to the foundations of the world of Batman. If Kane had the initial idea and Finger refined it to be recognisable to modern audiences as Batman, Robinson helped to build the world; contributing to the atmosphere of the books and surrounding the Dark Knight with unique and compelling characters.

After accepting Kane's offer to work as an art assistant, Jerry called up Columbia to accept his university placement. Columbia is in New York and Robinson reckoned he could juggle his academic and artistic responsibilities. He headed straight from the Poconos to New York where he lodged with his aunt Virginia in the Bronx, which was within walking distance of Bob's studio, better known as his parents' apartment. At Colombia, Jerry majored in journalism but took an elective in creative writing. He still dreamed of becoming a writer but he took his Batman work seriously all the same.

Realising that he had no formal training in art, he began to take art classes on top of his studying and comic work. When he wasn't working or studying, most of his time was spent travelling between The Bronx, Manhattan, and campus. After realising the classes focused on life drawing and the classics, rather than the cartooning Robinson felt he needed to know, he dropped the class and decided to learn on his own.

Perhaps this commitment to self-education was something the young Robinson recognised in Bill Finger. Finger had already immersed himself in the world of literature and the arts, so he took the young Robinson under his wing. Bill was a writer with a visual mind but no artistic skills while Jerry was an artist with the mind of a writer. It is just natural that the two would get on and work extremely well together. Robinson was still a kid and new to the Big Apple with its vast cultural offerings. By this point, Finger was a part of that scene and brought Jerry along for the ride. They would play golf together – one of Bill's sportier passions – and Bill's wife Portia would have Jerry over to the Finger household, where Bill, an excellent chef by all accounts, would serve up his speciality pasta. Then they would head out to the city's famous cultural hubs like the Museum of Modern Art or the Metropolitan and later schlep over to the theatre to watch expressionist films while discussing Dreiser or the pulps. It gave the pair a shared visual language with which they could both discuss their individual ideas of what the world of Batman should be like.

Even though Jerry was hired as an assistant whose primary job was to ink background, the increasing workload of the Batman books meant he quickly had to take on more and more work. Within a short amount of time, he moved from being Bob's assistant to becoming Bob's ghost. Kane, who had trained himself through tracing and copying art, thought that the role of a ghost was to mimic the style of the original artist as closely as possible and he would become uncomfortable when he saw that his character was being tweaked and changed. However, the sheer amount of work Kane's studio had to get through meant Jerry was developing his own style and approach to Batman. And it was those foreign expressionist movies that influenced him, inspiring him to play with shadows, lighting, exaggerating acting in the characters and adding steep, dramatic angles to increase the tension of the strip. Come 1941, Jerry would be taking his artistic directions from Orson Welles' *Citizen Kane* over Bob Kane.

The Bat-family of creators had a process. They would meet up, usually at Bob's apartment, and throw around ideas. Finger would then go away, work on the script and bring it back to the team, at which point they would start to develop the art. If the team was not discussing their romantic conquests or pop culture, they were discussing Batman. Finger was not satisfied with this masked vigilante existing apropos of nothing. It made no sense to him that a millionaire would risk life and limb taking on the seedy underbelly of the crime world without a real motive. And so, Finger started to ask himself what must happen to a man that would force him to dress like a bat and fight crime? What was Batman's back story?

Bob Kane wasn't the only one to get snowed under with work, though he, of course, had the advantage of being able to hire extra artists to make up when he fell behind. Finger was a perfectionist who would labour for hours at his typewriter trying to make stories work. That is when he could force himself to sit at the typewriter, as he seemed to prefer seeking out new art shows and cinemas with his theatre-loving partner Portia. He was a procrastinator of the highest order and the act of writing was not easy for Finger. He infamously took far too much time to finish and hand in scripts, a bad habit he would have for his entire career and one which would infuriate various editors.

In mid-1939, before the arrival of Jerry and after a couple of months producing Batman scripts, Finger was temporarily replaced by Gardner Fox. Fox had been a lifelong friend of *Detective* editor Vin Sullivan and Sullivan knew he loved to write. He had been brought in to write several strips across Sullivan's books before he was drafted to write for Batman. It's not clear whether he was brought in as a necessity, to make sure enough stories were produced and not perpetually postponed, or if he was always meant to replace Finger. Sullivan was still unsure of Kane's arrangements with his impromptu studio and with Bob as his only point of contact he must have worried about the level of control he could exert, as well as the legal standing of the work.

Finger never expressed any ill will about his temporary replacement by Fox. Besides, Fox would later become a genuine pulp writer, something which would have automatically put him in Finger's good books. Fox worked on the third, fifth and sixth Batman stories, introducing the gadgetry that would become one of the characters hallmarks as well as the 'bat-' prefix tradition. He also set Batman's adventures in New York, something Finger wasn't a fan of as he wanted Batman's home to be somewhere generic and undefined. But, that was something he would eventually fix following his return in *Detective Comics #33*.

Building Gotham

Batman's origin story is universally known. A young Bruce Wayne is taken to the theatre to by his parents, Thomas and Martha Wayne, to see a movie – with later writers winking to the audience by making this move *The Mark of Zorro*. Thomas Wayne, being a man of high intelligence and savvy, takes his family down an avenue which would later be revealed to be known as 'Crime Alley'. A mugging takes places and the boy Bruce witnesses the murder of his parents. In tears, the young orphan makes a vow to wreak vengeance on the criminal underworld and dedicates his life to the pursuits of physical and mental perfection.

Once ready for his crusade, Bruce ruminates over what symbol he can adopt to strike fear into the hearts of his foes. Like *Popular Detective's* Dawson Clade, the answer comes in the form of a bat flying through the window. The final panel of those thirteen panels (if you included make-shift cover-panel) on that two-page origin tale ends with Master Wayne's new alter-ego, Batman, ready to leap from the city rooftops – commemorated with the caption, 'AND THUS IS BORN THIS WEIRD FIGURE OF THE DARK. THIS AVENGER OF EVIL – THE BATMAN.'

Like every other Batman story, Bob Kane received a solo credit for this crucial piece of bat-lore. Finger had certainly scripted the short story, but it is possible the two had discussed the Caped Crusader's origins. But by this point, not only had Finger contributed to the image of the character and the tone of the book, he had fundamentally added significant input as a creative driving force while developing the psychological origins of the character. He had expanded Batman beyond his image and actions, and given him a personality and motives. These are the elements future creators would turn over and over again, deepening and expanding on exactly who Batman/Bruce Wayne is and why he does what he does.

What is and isn't essential to Batman is a woolly question. Does he always need a Bat-Cave? What about Robin? Is he still the Caped Crusader if he isn't wearing a cape? Do any of these things guarantee the success and resilience of the character over the years? These are tough questions to answer, but the murder of Bruce Wayne's parents seems to be immutable and inseparable from the core of the character.

That said, he wasn't the first protagonist to have his parents killed and then seek justice. Hamlet, as just one example of many, has the same story. So perhaps it's a combination of all these elements that makes Batman. One thing is certain though. These components were not created by Bob Kane alone.

There are a few interesting theories for why Finger may have chosen the death of a family member as the impetus to create a superhero alter-ego. By the time of *Detective Comics #33,* Kane and Finger had likely met their super heroic Cleveland cousins Siegel and Shuster. As already mentioned, Siegel's father had died from a heart attack brought on by an armed robbery. Could that tragic event have inspired Finger? It makes for a compelling explanation and suggests more than the similarities being a simple coincidence but it's unlikely.

Another dark theory is based on Finger's relationship with his own family. His parents, Louis and Tessie, were known to take his paycheques before Bill had a chance to spend them, sometimes waiting outside the DC offices on payday to collect the payments immediately from their son. It seems to be around this time that Bill stopped communicating with his eldest sister Emily too. There is no record of what exactly drove the wedge between the siblings but the distance between them is illustrated by a lack of involvement in one another's lives, when they'd previously been much closer. It has been suggested Finger was resentful of the pressure his family was putting on him and their pilfering of his wages. And although this creeps into the realms of pop-psychology, there is a theory the murder of Wayne's parents was some cathartic expression of Finger's frustration with his own mother and father. But again, this may be a case of chasing shadows in the darkness when the most obvious answer is the death of Bruce's parents is simply convenient way of explaining why a grown man dresses as a rodent to fight crime.

The Supporting Cast

In addition to Gardner Fox picking up the stories Bill Finger couldn't finish in time and Jerry Robinson literally filling in panels for Bob Kane, George Roussos was also brought in as Robinson's assistant to provide more art support by inking and lettering the comic. By construction or coincidence, Bob Kane had affectively built his own comic shop, albeit one entirely dedicated to the production of Batman comics.

Kane was the face of the whole operation. As far as readers were concerned, he was solely responsible for Batman's adventures. As for DC/National, at least to begin with, they either didn't know or didn't care how the books were coming together just so long as they sold well and were handed in on time.

In *Detective Comics #38*, Batman was joined by Robin, the Boy Wonder, whose parents, both acrobats, had been killed by the mob.

Kane claimed it was his idea to add the boy hero to the strip as a means of capturing the imagination of children and increasing the appeal (and profits) of the Batman comics. Finger, on the other hand, grew frustrated with having Batman brood and talk to himself endlessly. In the tradition of Sherlock Holmes, Batman needed an indispensable assistant he could impress, rely on, and rescue. For Finger and the other writers, Batman simply worked better with a sidekick with whom he could plot and plan.

Finger had been reading the Frank Merriwell novels and short stories, which followed the adventures of Frank, a sporty do-gooder at Yale University. Frank was frequently paired up with his younger half-brother, Dick. The name Grayson, been taken almost at random by Finger from the name of a book editor, Charles Grayson, Jr. Dick Grayson (Robin's official moniker) was a great name and the brother/boy-ward angle was appealing. Grayson was given a similar story to Wayne's in that his parents had also died – this narrative thematically connected the two characters and provided a justifiable reason for a millionaire bachelor to spend most of his time with a young boy.

To Kane, it offered a sense of adventure to young readers he thought would identify with Dick and through him, would be able to vicariously join Batman in his crime-fighting capers, as Kane himself had wished to join Douglas Fairbanks' Zorro when he was a boy.

Finger came up with the core concepts of Batman's sidekick and maybe a list of a dozen names for Kane and Robinson to look at. They were all rejected out of hand as the two had already landed on Robin. Bob said it had come from his love of the Robin Hood stories, but Bill suspected Bob had been convinced to use a shortened version of Jerry's own surname.

Jerry, for his part, later recalled that it was Bill Finger who came up with the idea of the Boy Wonder. Perhaps he meant in terms of fleshing the concept out or maybe he simply wasn't around for Bob and Bill's joint conversations about adding a boy character. Further, Robinson claimed he suggested the name Robin first, as it was in-keeping with Batman's tradition of the very mortal and human heroes whom Batman represented as opposed to the otherworldly gods that Superman stood for.

But Jerry and Bob had come up with slightly conflicting stories. Kane later claimed that the design for Robin came from the stories of Robin Hood, from what he called 'King Arthur's day'. Robinson makes a similar but much more specific claim, saying the character design was inspired by paintings of Robin Hood by the realist painter Andrew Wyeth, whose work featured in the immensely popular children's book *Scribner's Illustrated Classics* series. Robinson claimed those paintings gave Robin his design and name. The competing stories of the origin of Robin, 'The Sensational Comic Find of 1940' as he was originally billed, continued the trend of Bob Kane placing himself at the centre of the Bat-universe. He doubtlessly had something to do with the creation of Robin, likely through discussions regarding the adding a boy side-kick with Finger. But unlike the creation of Batman, Robinson differed from Finger in that he would always be more vocal about his involvement and version of events.

Kane took the idea to Vin Sullivan who initially wasn't keen on it. He feared that rather than children seeing Robin as a way of joining the adventure, parents would view him as a worrying example of child endangerment. After all, the world of Gotham was dark, dangerous and full of mindless, orphan-creating murders. A small boy in pea-green pants equipped with nothing but enthusiasm, quips and a slingshot wouldn't last long there. Still, Kane managed to convince Sullivan to take a chance on Robin for a single issue.

Luckily, Robin was a hit and sales instantly soared. Kane returned to the DC office where Sullivan weighed up his concern against Robin's profits and decided the Boy Wonder was to stay. Kane was vindicated, but he would become the victim of his own success. Though he was pleased with how much more popular and profitable Robin had made Batman, the inclusion of a child dressed in primary colours inevitably changed the tone of the book. The blend of pulp crime, high gothic and occasional horror had to bend to accommodate Dick Grayson's boyish persona. The books became more fun, light-heart and occasionally, quite ridiculous. This change, combined with greater influences from his ghost artists, meant Bob enjoyed the adventures of what he claimed was his sole creation less and less.

In 1939, The World's Fair, an exhibition of humanity's greatest achievements, produced *New York World's Fair Comics*. A promotional comic featuring Superman put together by editor Vin Sullivan. Though it was not a huge success, DC agreed to co-produce an edition for the 1940 fair, again with Sullivan at the helm. The cover featured not only Superman but Batman and Robin too. Despite the two pop culture heavyweights hanging out on the cover, they had separate stories in the comic. The book was far from a commercial success, but it would inspire the 1940s *World's Best Comics* series, which followed the same segregated format. *World's Best* quickly transformed into *World's Finest Comics* and it would later become the home of Batman and Superman's joint adventures.

Unfortunately, the lack of interest in the World's Fair comics floored Sullivan, who was held responsible for the poor sales of the book by Donenfeld and Liebowitz. This was not an enviable position for Sullivan to occupy, so he left DC/National, and his position was quickly filled by Whitney Ellsworth.

Ellsworth was a cartoonist and writer who had written for pulps such as *Black Bat* and who had first-hand experience with syndicated strips. In an unusual twist of fate, he would also provide the name of a gold prospector played by Jim Beaver in the HBO western *Deadwood*. (Beaver, in between roles, was researching George Reeves, the man who played Superman before Christopher Reeve, and plucked the name Whitney Ellsworth out of his research. It is a small world.)

The hiring of Ellsworth, the editor not the fictional prospector, was indicative of the fact the combination of comic books and superheroes was, by this point, solidifying into a rather lucrative industry. Combined with his experience in writing for the pulps and syndications, Ellsworth took a much more hands-on role with the boys creating the world of superheroes and he would ensure more financially safe choices were made. It was a change of management style after Sullivan's give-it-go approach.

The very first Batman stories in *Detective Comics* had the Dark Knight emulating The Shadow in more than just his ownership of an alter-ego. Batman liked to use firearms. In one adventure, he even gunned down his opponents with the hood-mounted machine gun of a plane. Though Finger bristled at too much editorial control, he admitted gunplay was not his best idea, saying, 'I goofed. I had Batman use a gun to shoot a villain, and I was called onto the carpet by Whit Ellsworth. He said, "never let us have Batman carry a gun again." He was right.'

'No guns' was far from Ellsworth's only suggestion. The new editor introduced a slew of rules to make comics more palatable to parents and less likely to fall under scrutiny. Writers and letterers were told to avoid words like 'FLICK' lest the low-quality printing ran the 'L' and 'I' together and created a 'U'. References to sex were strictly forbidden, though ironically, the fact Wonder Woman was constantly getting tied up to appease her creators' genuine bondage fetish flew under most people's radar, at least for now. Violence was to be downplayed all around; whipping, knife violence and hangings were all abolished. Pick up a modern-day Bat-book and much of this has returned, so perhaps ultimately Ellsworth's most important and lasting restriction was to stop the murder of the Joker.

Like Robin, the creation of Batman's arch-nemesis was a battleground between Kane and Robinson, with Finger playing a supporting role to each of them. The stories they recalled in the later years were like a sprint to get to the earliest possible iteration of the character.

Batman #1 was all set for release but the Kane/Finger/Robinson trio was swamped with work. They were still creating Batman stories for *Detective Comics* and they needed four new stories for the latest book. On top of which, Jerry was now helping Bob out with art duties on *Clip Carson* and *Rusty and His Pals*. It was getting to the point where the team was robbing Peter to pay Paul and they had started to take work already finished for *Detective* to use for *Batman*. Specifically, the story they used in *Batman #1* was *Dr Hugo Strange and the Monsters* featuring one of Batman's earliest recurring foes in Hugo Strange, a character who would later be central to the themes of psychiatry and insanity in the Bat-verse.

Meanwhile, Robinson was taking a creative writing class at college and he needed to hand in a story to pass. Knowing Finger struggled with getting his scripts in on time and thinking he might be able to kill two birds with one stone, Jerry offered to write a story the team could use. This meant he could pass his class, get paid and the team would scratch back some time in their tight schedule. Robinson recalled the villains of comic books at the time being no different than the villains of real life; they were crooks, gangsters and fifth columnists. He didn't think there was such a thing as a supervillain yet. Taking his cue from Finger and following in the Conan Doyle tradition, Jerry figured Batman needed a worthy opponent, his own Moriarty; a nemesis. Jerry thought the way to make this character memorable would be to explore the juxtaposition between the dark, gothic, crime-ridden world of Gotham and comedy. He needed a dangerous comedian or a clownish villain and just like that, the name of the Joker jumped to his mind.

From there, he naturally made the leap to playing cards. After fanning through a deck, he put together a sketch of his Joker in the form of a card. The powder white face, scarlet lips and wicked smile are all there, although his shock of green hair is covered by a harlequin hat. Robinson says he took the story and art to Bob and Bill who loved it but sensing the character's potential, thought he would be safer in the hands of Finger, the more seasoned writer. Robinson, who was only 18 at the time, had tears in his eyes as he reluctantly handed over the character to Finger. It was a blow, but Robinson was close to Finger and trusted him to do the character justice. And that is that, at least as far as Robinson was concerned.

Bob recalled the story a little differently and would later claim that the Joker came from his own playing card-based sketches of a harlequin character but unlike Robinson's claim, no visual evidence has ever surfaced to back this up. Kane insisted that his inspiration for the character, like so much else of Batman's world, came from his own life and his love of playing practical jokes. Kane thought a pathological practical joker could really put Batman through his paces and he recalled how he took some sketches to Finger, who liked the idea but not the art which he thought was too clownish for Batman.

In this version of events, Finger had been reading a photo-play edition of Victor Hugo's *The Man Who Laughs*. This edition used stills from the 1928 silent drama based on the book, directed by the German expressionist Paul Leni. It's certainly something Finger would have been captivated by. While reading the book he came across a photo of actor Conrad Veidt in full character dress and makeup as Gwynplaine, the romantic lead with a disfigured face and rictus grin. This is the image he took to Bob. This wasn't clownish, it was carnival horror. It was the face that makes the character come to life and lets him exist in the same world as the Batman.

The similarity between Veidt and the Joker is undeniable, and Kane would later point out that DC editor Edward Nelson Bridwell supported this version of events in the introduction to *Batman: From the 30s to the 70s*. But again, Robinson would claim the image of Veidt was simply attached to the script as a reference to flesh out the character rather than given directly to Bob as the design the new character must take.

Meanwhile, Bill Finger's son Fred would later claim it was the distorted smiling face advertising the Coney Island Steeplechase attraction which inspired the character.

The Joker's exact origins fall somewhere between all three stories. Like Batman, the character was derived from multiple sources and was filtered through a couple of creators. Unlike Batman, no creator was willing to roll over and let someone else take sole credit. The chances are, in the confusion of the creative process, warped by history and various egos, we will never know for sure how the Joker came about. But we do know that Bill Finger killed off the Clown Prince of Crime in his first appearance. And he would have probably got away with it if it had not been for that meddling editor, Whitney Ellsworth.

Ellsworth instantly saw the appeal of the Joker and the value of reusing characters rather than having to endlessly create new, faceless, disposable bad guys. At the last minute, Ellsworth had the team redraw and re-letter the final panel to reveal that after accidentally stabbing himself the Joker had not died but was instead in a critical condition. This last-minute reprieve created a new precedent for comics and made the Joker the first supervillain to thwart death and return to terrorise Batman, something he has been doing for eighty years now.

Alongside the Joker *Batman #1* featured the first appearance of Batman/Bruce Wayne's on-again-off-again regular beau Catwoman aka Selina Kyle, who was then simply known as 'The Cat'. Kane admitted that Catwoman was a collaboration between him and Finger. Using the up and coming bombshell Jean Harlow as his inspiration, albeit as a brunette. Kane discussed with Finger the possibility of introducing a new, sensual, feline character – Bob's feeling that cats were girls and dogs were boys would almost be considered childlike if it wasn't for the semi-sexual undertones. Kane was known to pursue women and so, Batman would pursue the elusive, seductive but ultimately benign Catwoman. She represented more of Kane building parts of himself into the Batman mythos, even if it was figurative. Her introduction served two purposes; it brought a female character to the mix which might appeal more to girls, and it further cemented young boys' interest in the book. Sex sells, after all, even if Ellsworth had banned it.

Despite this, the character spent most of her first issue disguised as an old woman, and her costume is a knee-length purple dress and skirt combo complete with kitten heels (obviously), a short green cape and cowl. It was hardly the stuff of *Spicy Detective*. On top of which, despite his desire to inject some sex appeal into the Batman books, Kane's limited skill as a draughtsman meant the other artists in the Batman stable considered his women to be unappealing. His cartooning heritage and 'bigfoot' style, as it was referred to, hampered the delicacy required to draw traditionally attractive dames.

What is telling about Kane's relationship with women is how he viewed Batman and Catwoman's dynamic. The idea of women as felines, and felines as distant, unreliable animals is something Kane admitted to feeling himself. He once described his relationship with women as a 'love-resentment thing' and claimed that he never remained friends with women once the romance was done with. In a jaw-dropping display of self-awareness, ego, or perhaps just the prevailing attitudes of the time, he also admitted with no sense of irony or self-recrimination that his attitude was chauvinistic, or at least he was aware that's what the women he dated then ghosted might have felt.

Kane's bigfoot, cartooning style is most visible in the Penguin. Finger had an idea for a villain who used a plethora of gimmicked umbrellas to dispatch his foes. His idea for the character; a stuffy, monocle-wearing, English toff in coat and tails was inspired by emperor penguins. Kane, however, said the character was inspired by the smoking penguin used to sell Kool menthol cigarettes. The two characters do look remarkably similar in that they are both, squat, rounded creatures with simple, comedic designs. When you look at the early recurring characters, the Penguin stands out exactly because his design is so cartoonish. The visual design of the Penguin certainly could not have been done by anyone other than Kane; it's too inconsistent with the rest of the strip.

Where and when Kane would admit to collaboration or to solo effort is oddly inconsistent. In his autobiography, he specifically wrote that he created Two-Face, who was originally named Harvey Kent but had to be immediately changed to Dent because of the obvious connection to Clark Kent. The film version of *The Strange Case of Dr Jekyll and Mr Hyde* – he hadn't read the book – would serve as Kane's inspiration for Two-Face, a man literally half good and half bad. But then Kane goes on to say it was with Finger that they created the gimmick of his moral compass being decided via a coin flip, and further, that Finger came up with the original story. Although, he admits to Finger creating the story only in reference to its similarity to the origin story of the Black Bat, Batman's one-time copyright rival. Like Harvey Dent, the Black Bat aka Tony Quinn, was a district attorney scarred by an acid attack from a criminal in the docks.

Kane would cite various films as the inspiration for his creation of a number of other smaller Bat-villains; Scarecrow came from *The Cabinet of Dr Caligari* while the morphing mass of horror that is Clay Face was a nod to the master of movie make-up Lon Chaney, who would dramatically alter his appearance for various roles in Hollywood's horror hits. This era of cinema clearly made a huge impact on Batman but Kane underplays the roles of Finger and Robinson, who were known for their passion of new, experimental films with dramatic lighting, Dutch angles, and the tinge of horror. It was Finger and Robinson who mined these movies for more than character ideas. They wanted to replicate the sensation and experience these movies though reconstructing their visual language.

At the worst, these stories of the origin of characters display a need for these creators, usually Bob Kane and hardly ever Bill Finger, to make themselves central to the story and to cast themselves as the smartest, most innovative, most talented guy in the room. But realistically, these were stories told decades later by creators who are sadly no longer with us about a time in their early twenties. These guys, Kane, Finger, and Robinson, were working as a group, watching films together and constantly talking over their work. It is hard to create collectively while monitoring discrete and distinct contributions, and to really be sure which words or images transform a cartoon character into something ageless and iconic. It is likely there was a lot more collaboration and shared inspiration between the creators than is easy to admit to or document. But just as important, for the purposes of this book, are the attitudes and personalities that emerge in the retelling of these stories rather than just the credits themselves.

Chapter Five

The Golden Years

While they were building the Batman's universe, the Bob Kane comic studio, which at any given point comprised of Bill Finger, Jerry Robinson, George Roussos, Gardner Fox and Kane's sometime ghosts, Sheldon Moldoff, Win Mortimer, Charles Paris and Jack Burnley, underwent some change.

Jerry was making a name for himself inside the industry with his dramatic *Detective* and *Batman* covers. Robinson's covers featured intense, dynamic, expressionist scenes and contributed to the idea that comics were art rather than disposable entertainment. Because Robinson preserved so much of the original art, rather than allowing DC to engage in its standard practice of destroying originals, he inadvertently became a much relied upon creator for future comic art historians. In 1940, however, it was enough to get him out of Bob Kane's apartment and away from the prying eyes of Kane's father who would check in on Bob's ghosts to make sure they were working and would then ferry their finished pages to the DC office.

That year, Finger and Robinson were hired directly by the DC editors so their talents could be used on other comics. With Kane in control of Batman and his collaborators picking up extra work in the DC bullpen, things were looking good for Bob and Bill professionally. For Bill, it led to so many more opportunities he might never have sought out had he remained working in Bob's bedroom.

Bill was well-liked amongst the other artists and writers. Though he worked slowly, he was known for putting together great stories and he had a clear understanding of the visuals he wanted to create with an artist. He was known to take clippings from magazines and newspapers to provide a visual reference for what he wanted on the page. The most notable instance of this was when he took a clipping of an underground plane hangar from *Popular Science* to give to Kane. The cross-section showed how planes stored underground would be winched to the surface ready for take-off. With the addition of a colossal coin and a robotic tyrannosaurus this clipping served the basis for the Bat Cave.

Finger quickly became known throughout the DC bullpen for his fabled gimmick book. Here he collected titbits of trivia and scientific information he could use to build his stories around – such as facts about Chinese symbols or technical aspects of railway maintenance. Bill was generally thought of as sweet, generous and creative, if not slightly conflicted about his position as the co-creator of Batman. The readers had zero idea who he was, but in the industry it was becoming fairly well known how much he had contributed to the creation of Batman and that in fact, he was the driving creative force behind the stories while Kane got all the credit. Still, Finger didn't seem all that interested in getting a by-line on the back of DC's second most popular character. But by 1940, Finger was writing stories for the World's Fastest Man, the Flash, as well as for Batman, providing fill-in stories for none other than his own some-time replacement Gardner Fox.

Meanwhile, Philadelphia-born artist Martin Nodell, who was also a writer for DC, had put together a character inspired by the colourful combination of Wagnerian opera alongside Greek and Chinese mythology. The result was Alan Scott, the original Green Lantern. Less recognisable than his many modern successors who sport jade leotards as they policed the darkness of space, Scott wore green trousers and a billowy red shirt – which clashed beautifully – with a dark cape and domino mask. This golden-haired hero drew his powers from a magical lantern rather than an extraterrestrial one. Max Gaines of *All-American Comics,* now part of the growing National Publications comics family, bought the strip but enlisted Bill Finger to tighten up the concept and work on the scripts. It was Finger who gave the character his true name of Alan Scott. Working on the idea of a magic lamp, Finger's mind went to Middle Eastern folklore and was inspired by the tale of Aladdin from *A Thousand and One Nights* (or as it is better known in English speaking countries as *The Arabian Nights*) and came up with the name Alan Ladd. The actor Alan Ladd wasn't a famous figure at the time, but when he showed it to Batman ghost Sheldon Moldoff, the artist thought the name was terrible. Reacting on the fly and noticing a book about Sir Walter Scott, Finger spat out Alan Scott, which Moldoff conceded was much better. Together Finger and Nodell worked on the character for seven years and Bill's name actually appeared alongside Nodell's in the credits.

By 1941, The Green Lantern was successful enough to be promoted from *All-American Comics* to its own self-titled book. The back of the first issue had a page titled 'Introducing Bill Finger and Marty Nodell, creators of Green Lantern' in which Bill was given a half-page biography. Bill may have been happy to be given some visible credit at long last, although his bio might have left a sour taste in his mouth. It described his early life, his attendance at DeWitt Clinton, his love of science – even describing a home laboratory he set up in his father's store – and the jobs he took on before becoming a writer (he was listed as a former taxi driver but that seems unlikely given he never had a driver's licence). But the real insult came in how his role in the creation of Batman came about.

Kane is described as the single creator of Batman and Robin, the creative supremo who gave Finger an opportunity and introduced him to *All-American* editors, allowing Bill to finally 'dig his fingers into the juiciest assignment of his career – THE GREEN LANTERN'. Though parts of that story are true, it is framed in such a way as to suggest that Kane had already created Batman in his entirety, only later plucking Finger from obscurity. It completely downplayed Bill's impact on the Batman franchise. Perhaps the suggestion that Finger's success had come at the grace and generosity of Kane, who had opened the door for the writer, was something Bill had internalised, and although the detail wasn't accurate, perhaps the sentiment was. Or perhaps the credits for a kid's character, even one as profitable as Batman, was beneath Finger.

Sensation Comics would be remembered in comics history as the vehicle that propelled William Moulton Marston's Amazonian princess Wonder Woman into the constellation of comic book superstars in 1942. It was also where Finger received his second recurring credit for co-creating a costumed character. Bill worked with yet another DeWitt Clinton graduate Irwin Hasen, to create Wildcat. The man in the sleek, black cat onesie, complete with whiskers (which looked suspiciously like Catwoman's later costumes), was actually Theodore 'Ted' Grant. Like C. K. M. Scanlon's *Popular Detective* Batman prototype, The Bat, Grant had been framed for murder. Unlike Scanlon's character, he dressed like a cat and was a boxer rather than a reporter.

Kane continued to work on Batman, or at the very least, have his ghosts work on Batman. Though Jerry Robinson and the other artists working for Bob had started to modify his style, it was a young new artist by the name of Dick Sprang that would visually revitalise the Batman book in the coming years, albeit under Kane's name. Sprang had been a calculated hire by editor Whitney Ellsworth who was busy building up a back catalogue of Batman stories in anticipation of losing his creative stable to the draft and the Second World War.

Creators at war

The birth of the superhero comic book coincided with the dawning of war in Europe. The over the top, unfathomable heroes of fiction were matched by over the top, unfathomable villains of reality. Just four months after *Detective Comics #27* was released, Hitler and the Third Reich invaded Poland and started the Second World War. Even though the United States subtly helped its British and French allies, there was a general reluctance on the behalf of the Americans to commit to another mass conflict in Europe after 'The Great War'. On top of which, influential industry leaders like Henry Ford, a noted anti-Semite who circulated the conspiratorial forgery *The Protocols of the Elders of Zion*, strongly contested America's involvement and continued to do business with Nazi Germany. Incidentally, Bob Kane's classmate Will Eisner would later make a comic book account of the true history of *The Protocols of the Elders of Zion*, called *The Plot*, to help combat anti-Semitism.

The comics industry, being principally made up of the second generation, Eastern-European Jewish sons, whose parents had fled the growing turmoil which had led to the Great War, were quick to react to the rise of Fascism while the rest of America dragged its feet. Comic characters began taking on Nazi and Fascist forces in the funny books. Across town from DC Comics, competitor Timely, which would one day become Marvel Comics, solidified the resistance as early as December 1940. *Captain America #1* was put together by Jewish creators Joe Simon and Jack Kirby. The cover to that first issue has the Star-Spangled Avenger socking Hitler squarely in the jaw. It was wish fulfilment on behalf of the young creators. But even these defiant young Jews underestimated the scale of the war. Kirby and Simon worried that Hitler would be taken down by European forces before their book was released. The book was a huge success and spawned dozens, if not hundreds of copy-cat patriotic superheroes. The uniform (or maybe, in-uniform) message across comics was that it was the right, good, and American thing to fight the Nazis.

Some comic creators volunteered for service in foreign militaries despite America's official stance of neutrality. Then, on 7 December 1941, almost a year after Cap's debut, the unthinkable happened. A Japanese *kamikaze* attack at Pearl Harbour Naval base in Honolulu, Hawaii killed 2,403 people and brought the war to America in a way impossible to ignore.

Americans were called up to fight. Will Eisner, Stan Lee, Mort Weisinger and Jack Kirby all served in various capacities, either in communications, propaganda, or the frontline. Superman creator Joe Shuster was rated 4-F, unfit for service, thanks to his poor vision while his co-creator Jerry Siegel was repeatedly passed up for the draft. A myth began to spread that the government was trying to protect Siegel as, so he claimed, Hitler was angry with the Jewish creator of Superman, banning the last son of Krypton from Germany and demanding Siegel dead. This is most likely a Siegel family story, but it is true the SS newspaper *Das Schwarze Korps* mocked Siegel and his creation, calling him 'intellectually and physically circumcised'.

Though Siegel was eventually drafted there are various conflicting stories that he was reluctant to go to war, both for his own safety and the safety of his beloved Superman. At the same time there were rumours that Harry Donenfeld was keeping his cash cow out of the war with help from his political allies.

The Batman creators had to sit out the war too. Kane, Finger and Robinson were all classified 4-F for different and mysterious reasons.

Robinson was drafted twice but failed the physical on both counts for being too skinny. Finger's records changed throughout his drafting history. First, he was excluded on grounds of having a dependant – presumably his wife. He was later drafted on the grounds of military need, then finally rejected on medical grounds. There is no clear indication of what those medical grounds were but they were most likely related to his extended childhood illnesses. His contemporaries described it intriguingly, or just politely, as being a personal matter. This wasn't particularly unusual as the military worked from a basis that every man can fight and made its way back to justifying conscription from that position. What is interesting about Bill's file is that 'Bob Kane All American Comics' rather than National or Harry Donenfeld was listed as his employer when he was rejected from service in 1943. Perhaps he had not updated his details after America joined the war, or perhaps he still felt that Bob was his boss. No physical contract has ever been discovered to have existed between Kane and Finger, and by as early as 1940, Bill was picking up work directly from All American and National so it's odd that Finger would still list Kane as his boss.

As for Bob, he was listed as 4-F because of a group of injuries sustained as a teenager. As he told it, he had convinced his father he wanted to take up the violin and one day he was walking through an enemy gang's territory with his instrument. His own gang was apparently called the Zorros, though this could just have been further myth-building for Kane. The toughs of this gang took umbrage at Bob's audacity and chased him. After sneaking through a worksite and some high-flying acrobatics worthy of the Caped Crusader himself, Kane was eventually caught and violently pummelled, his violin irreparably destroyed and worse, his drawing arm broken. Eventually, after physical therapy, Kane was able to use his drawing arm again though he did have to give up the violin. However, his injuries meant that he was unable to turn his right palm all the way around to face skyward. Combined with a punctured eardrum and being underweight, this kept Bob out of the war.

Though the Batman studio couldn't participate directly in the war effort, Batman and the Boy Wonder Robin, along with their super-pal Superman were drafted into the propaganda campaign. Despite paper rations, comics were still a huge part of American life and 15 million issues were being bought every month. Harry Donenfeld was keeping the publications running either though his less legitimate channels or because the funny books were an essential part of the American propaganda machine.

Though the comics were primarily aimed at kids, the covers prompted patriotic parents to buy war bonds. In military training camps, two-thirds of men read comics while a quarter of every printed periodical shipped from the United States was a comic book. The Navy even listed comics as an essential supply for sailors in the Pacific Theatre.

Batman got light duties in the Second World War. Just under a dozen covers from the Bat-family of comics featured him participating in the conflict, and even then, it was as a war bonds salesman. In the pages of the books, few stories took place in or even referenced the war. It may have been that the struggle for editorial control over these years played some part; with editors trying to avoid the ire of parents who didn't want their children, or Robin, at risk of death in some foreign field. Or, perhaps, the Bat-creators, unable to take part in the fight themselves, felt guilty writing fiction about the reality so many of their contemporaries would soon be facing, instead preferring escapism with tales of action where nothing valuable could be lost except time.

Jerry Robinson, for his part, was more active in depicting the war in comics than Kane and Finger. Robinson's contribution came through a rush job for publisher Lev Gleason. Gleason had paper stock left over that he had to use, otherwise it would be taken by the government for the war effort. On Friday, 7 March 1941, Robinson, and a crew of other artists, including one of his closest friends, Bernie Klein, rented a shabby room to put together an entire comic in one weekend. Unexpectedly, they became snowed in. What happened next has become a romantic vision of how comics were made in that time, with a bunch of guys passing cigarettes, liquor, pencilled pages and scripts back and forth while one of them ventured out into the snow for supplies which are inevitably thrown together in a fire. Even Kane, who wasn't there, would repeat this story of his team getting snowed in and him having the genius idea of baking potatoes over a fire. It's here, in the Robinson version, that Jerry created his first solo character.

Marc Holmes was London, the mysterious radio broadcaster who fought for Britain in a blue tux, rouge cape and cowl adorned with a calligraphed 'L'. Robinson was very politically-minded and supported the British war effort, even giving his character the catchphrase 'London can take it!' in reference to the Blitz. London was a personal triumph for the young artist but hardly a commercial one, in comparison to Batman anyway.

Robinson's friend, Bernie Klein, got to join the fight first-hand the next year and was sadly killed. The reality of war, and losing a close friend, had a devastating and lasting effect on Robinson.

The World's Finest

By the mid-1940s, Kane and Finger were facing yet more shifts in their careers. Finger was picking up more work across the DC lines, and over the years, he had written scripts for other publishers long since forgotten; the notable exception being Timely Comics, later known as Marvel Comics, where Finger picked up a few post-war gigs writing the likes of Captain America, the Sub-Mariner and the Human Torch (a pre-Fantastic Four flammable android) while their regular creative teams were serving abroad. Over the decade Bill made more friends, including the creators for Superman, Joe Shuster and Jerry Siegel. But he constantly suffered from money troubles, borrowing here and there from pals in the bullpen or asking for advances from editors who were reluctant to help such a tardy employee. It is claimed Jack Liebowitz once offered to buy Finger a car if he could get his script in on time. Needless to say, Finger took the subway to the DC offices for most of his career, when he could afford the fare at least. The fact that he was always so broke and so obviously bad with money was a great source of shame to Bill and by the end of the decade, he would have to support a son, Fred, as well as his wife Portia.

Bob meanwhile got married in the 40s to a woman named Beverly and the couple would have a daughter, who they named Deborah. Unlike Finger, in 1943, Kane was doing alright and believed that he had just hit the big time. Batman was to become a syndicated comic strip featuring in newspapers across America. The *Superman* syndicated strip had been a huge success and the hope was that the Caped Crusader's *Batman and Robin* would continue that trend. For Kane, this was the meaning of success in the comics industry. He had gone from tracing newspaper strips in as a boy and aping his heroes in the earliest Batman stories to at last having his own syndicated comic. It would not be exactly fair to say that he had faked it until he made it, but ironically, it's a close enough approximation. Kane stopped working on the Batman comic books to focus on newspaper strips but quickly came unstuck.

The intense, daily workload meant he handed over pencilling duties for the Sunday strip to one of his regular ghosts, Jack Burnley. Kane was frustrated at the lack of space available in the newspaper strip and would often pass his weekday work onto Dick Sprang while Charles Paris consistently inked the entire series. Bill Finger worked on the strip every now and again, but the high rate of work needed and immovable deadlines, Finger's folly, meant other writers were brought in to work the stories out on schedule. The series did not live up to the same level of success as the Superman strip, however, and was cancelled after three years – a generation of story telling by today's industry standards.

Though Kane still received solo credit for the entire Batman stories, by stepping back from the main comic, its whole dynamic shifted and it was Dick Sprang who came to dominate the visual world of Batman. Kane may have been happily collecting the cheques for Batman drawn by other artists, but he still thought his design of the character as the definitive version. He disliked another artist reinterpreting what he saw as his work and Sprang was reinterpreting Batman in a major way. He made Gotham a much brighter and more colourful place while Batman hit the gym, his barrel chest becoming as impressive as his strong, square jaw. As Sprang injected colour into the post-war Batman, Finger was allowed to try out more elaborate and preposterous stories. He became known for his love of ludicrously oversized props which included giant typewriters as big as vans or bowling pins the size of a man. The Sprang-Finger era was the first tentative step from the shadows of Batman's noir-pulp, expressionist origins to the high camp and colourful, holy-Bat-tootsie dancing world of Adam West and Burt Ward.

Despite this clear shift in the creative influences on the Batman lines, DC doubled down on the myth of Bob Kane as a lone, innovative genius. His solo credit only told readers that he was the man who had created Batman, but they did not yet know how. All that would change in 1946 with the release of *Real Facts Comics #5.*

Real Fact Comics was DC's only contribution to the slew of educational books produced across the comic book industry which were part of a counterattack to the growing concern of the prominence of funny books in children's lives. In 1940, Sterling North, children's author and literary editor of the *Chicago Daily News,* had written a piece condemning comic books as a growing fungus among children's literature and he accused comic book publishers of a cultural slaughter. He became one of the first public figures to criticise comics for their fanciful and dangerous content, which terrified parents and brought the comics industry under pious public scrutiny. Worried comic book publishers were determined to disprove these insane, but on occasion justified, claims. *Real Fact Comics* told the true stories of figures and events around the world (as if there is nothing in history which might expose children to violence and the dark cruelty of humanity) and in issue 6, it told the true story of the creation of Batman.

Only it didn't. The five-page strip, delivered in a slightly saccharine style, ignored the work of Bill Finger, Gardner Fox and Jerry Robinson, and credited everything to Bob Kane. The young Kane of the story, the central character (obviously), is depicted as a lucky go-getter, making illustrations for charity events, and endlessly frequenting the library. Bizarrely, the story has Kane dress up a fellow named Larry in a complete Bat-suit, which he then uses as a real-life reference, before approaching DC with the character as opposed to taking on the task of creating the character to make money the way Superman did. Here Kane comes up with the gadget and gimmicks Fox and Finger were responsible for, and the strip has him flippantly finding inspiration for the Joker and the Penguin from ridiculous encounters.

Real Fact Comics #5 was edited by Whitney Ellsworth rather than Vin Sullivan, the editor who commissioned the creation of Batman in the first place. Ellsworth was more concerned with appeasing parents than providing an honest account, and he may not have even known the true version of events himself. This was yet another enshrining of Bob Kane at the centre of the Batman myth and another slight to the creators he had worked with. Perhaps it was just a way of keeping panicking parents happy and the truth was less important than reassuring them that comics were just kids' stuff. But it was all kids' stuff, and what's more, it was kids' stuff people had worked hard on and were receiving no public credit for, except, of course, for Bob Kane. Though it's only a metaphorical footnote in comics history now, this was the first glimpse behind the curtain the public got into the creation of Batman, and Bill Finger was nowhere to be found.

After the war, Sprang moved out to Arizona but continued to work on Batman. On many occasions, he would find himself sending off incomplete pages of artwork to the DC office, unsure of how the story was going to end thanks to Finger's slow work rate. But the tension Finger created in Sprang with his tardiness, he was also able to inject into the script with his writing. He would toil all night over a script to get it right and Sprang thought they were well worth the wait, saying of his friend that he was 'the best comic writer I ever encountered'. He was certainly good enough for DC to let him work on their number one property, Superman.

Superman's origin story is iconic. It's so simple, yet it has become a part of our shared cultural language; a tale that comics writer Grant Morrison was able to reduce to eight words: 'Doomed planet. Desperate scientists. Last hope. Kindly couple.' Readers knew that Superman had crash-landed onto Kent farm from a distant planet, they had even heard about it on the radio, but they had yet to read about it in the comic books.

'Who is Superman? Where did he come from? How did he obtain his miraculous powers?' – this was the opening gambit of the story Bill Finger penned for Superman which explored the Man of Tomorrow's extraterrestrial background. Eventually, Finger would even take Kal-el back to his homeworld to learn more about his Kryptonian heritage. Never one to pass up a good idea when he heard it, Finger permanently changed the name of Siegel's K-metal, the mysterious mineral which weakened the Man of Steel, to match its radio serial counterpart, kryptonite.

As the creators of two of the biggest characters and properties on the planet, Kane and Finger, and Siegel and Shuster, ended up becoming friends. They even vacationed together. Kane recounted a story of a holiday in Miami where he was left waiting at dinner for Joe Shuster, the Superman artist. Shuster had awful eyesight and by the end of his life, he was practically blind, but even in the 1940s, it was failing. Before meeting with Kane, he had been admiring an expensive car he had seen in the street, leaning in a close as he could to offset his poor vision while holding onto the side-door handle for balance. Kane would be left waiting as local cops had thought Shuster was trying to steal the car and had thrown him in prison, refusing to believe his story of bad vision or that he was the creator of Superman. Somehow word got back to Harry Donenfeld who was also vacationing in Miami at the time. Donenfeld promptly rescued his artist and Shuster signed Superman sketches for the slightly embarrassed but star-struck police officers. Kane thought the whole thing was a hoot. But business has a way of bringing out the worst in people and Kane wouldn't save Shuster when it was Donenfeld who became his tormenter.

Of all the DC stable of creators, Jerry Siegel was the most influential to end up fighting in the Second World War while his creative partner's sight prevented him from joining the military. At the start of their careers, Kane and Finger (or at least Kane on Finger's behalf) had signed a similar contract to Siegel and Shuster which stated that the creators were to offer DC the right to refusal for any new property they come up with and DC, in exchange, would reply within six weeks, with a failure to do so allowing the creators to do what they liked with the new characters. Superman had made Harry Donenfeld and Jack Liebowitz very wealthy men and the character was practically responsible for launch padding the entire success of DC. Though between them, over the years Siegel and Shuster had received around $400,000 in payments from DC, they didn't control the copyright to Superman. Besides which, this was a fraction of what the character had made for the company.

Before he left for the war, Siegel had pitched the character Superboy to DC with the intention of following the childhood adventures of Clark Kent. It had been rejected in 1938 and the editors failed to respond to a second submission in 1940. By rights, Siegel had followed their agreement and the failure to reply meant he controlled the character.

But while Siegel was stationed in Hawaii between 1943 and 1946, Superboy appeared in *More Fun Comics*. Parts of Siegel's script had been used and Shuster had done the art, the problem was that no one at DC had bothered to tell Siegel. After a brief falling out and reunion between the creators, these slights ultimately resulted in Siegel and Shuster starting a legal campaign against National to get what they felt they deserved for creating one of the most lucrative characters on the planet. It is a legal battle they would fight for most of their lives.

Though justified, Jerry wrote frustrated letters to Donenfeld and Liebowitz filled with hyperbole and melodrama fit for a comic book. He also became indiscriminate in his rage; he even claimed that his pal Bob Kane had been in cahoots with DC in creating one of the many Superman rip-offs that flooded the newsstands, Batman. The argument didn't hold water (the difference 'make a new character similar to this old character' and 'make a new character that will make money like this old character' is an important distinction) and it is probably a perturbed expression of how influential Jerry knew Superman to be and his anger with his employers.

Still, according to Gerard Jones' comprehensive work, *Men of Tomorrow: Geeks, Gangsters and the Birth of the Comic Book*, this didn't stop Siegel and Shuster approaching Bob Kane for support as they geared up for their day in court. A coalition between the creators of Superman and Batman would be unstoppable. But it didn't work out that way. Jones claimed that Kane told Donenfeld and Liebowitz about Siegel and Shuster's plan, and used it to renegotiate his own contract. It was known that Kane's father, having worked in publishing, and his uncle, who may have known Liebowitz from his time in the garment industry, would come into the National offices to argue contracts on Bob's behalf (many creators recalled Kane's father working as a lawyer though that may just be that he acted on Bob's behalf legally. Kane himself never mentioned his father working as a professional lawyer). Depending on who is telling the story, Bob takes on Liebowitz alone or his uncle is present in the negotiations.

Liebowitz, as hard-nosed as ever, wasn't threatened or worried by the lawsuit. It was clear to him that National owned the rights to Superman and Batman and the work Kane had created (or for that matter, sub-contracted) fell under work-for-hire. The labour and intellectual properties were paid for in full. That much was as clear as day in the contract Kane had first signed in 1939. Only the Kane family now claimed that the contract was invalid. They said Bob had been a minor when he signed the contract.

This wasn't the case. He had been at least 23. He had possibly lied about his age previously though. His given date of birth was October 1915, but he had been in the same school year as Will Eisner who was born in March 1917. This suggests that Bob was held back a year (or Eisner was put forward one). Several comic creators over the years have mentioned that Kane was not intelligent. Batman writer Alvin Schwartz, born in 1916, claimed to be a classmate of Kane's at school – again creating a discrepancy in dates – and recalled Kane having to sit in the corner of the room while wearing a dunce cap as punishment for falling behind. Schwartz suggested that Kane may even have had some learning difficulties. Although Schwartz did also later claim to have met Superman in real life on the form of a *tulpa,* a Buddhist thought-being, so who knows?

Bob's picture had appeared in *Batman #1* released in 1940 with his age listed as 24, again confirming that the character was created and the contract signed in Bob's adulthood. Everyone in the office and bullpen knew Kane's claim was a lie. But his parents had been immigrants and it was not unknown for documents like birth certificates to go unissued or to conveniently go missing in order to secure work throughout the Depression years. It worked. Whether Harry still had a soft spot for kids from the old neighbourhood or Liebowitz made a calculated expenditure, it was cheaper to renegotiate Kane's contract than to face a legal battle with this kind of complication.

Kane would often be cited as creating Batman at the tender age of 18, to maintain the facade of him having been a particularly youthful yet perfectly legal employee of National. It created a permanent inconsistency in Kane's life with *The New York Times* even repeating this claim in his obituary. At the same time, the obituary stated he died aged 83, which would give Kane a birth year of either 1915 (counting 83 years back from 1998) or 1921 (counting 18 years back from 1939) – a pretty large margin of error.

The resulting contract between Bob Kane and DC has become somewhat legendary in comics history. Signed at DC's then offices at 666 Fifth Avenue, it was shrouded in mystery, intrigue, and corporate manoeuvring. It has never been made publicly available but some of its details seem to have leaked out through industry channels. In it, Kane is reported to have gained back some ownership over Batman, as well as some subsidiary rights – meaning he could earn money from Batman merchandise as well as Batman serials. On top of which, it would give him the ability to stop the selling of the character by DC to another company. Kane also received an inflated page rate, far beyond the meagre $10 a page he had dreamed of a decade earlier, which would be enough to keep him financially stable while supporting the various artists whose work was then signed under his name. There were two catches: Bob would have to provide DC with an incredible number of pages in a year and he had to keep schtum about the deal. One of Kane's regular ghosts, Sheldon Moldoff, later claimed that Kane was required to provide DC with 365 pages of Batman art a year. Of course, drawing 365 pages a year is quite a different task to providing 365 pages, which could easily be obtained through a team of ghosts, particularly with an inflated page rate and merchandising money to pay for them. Bob Kane had gone from accidentally creating a studio to accidentally become an entire subdivision of DC comics.

Similarly, Kane could not reveal the exact details of the contract. This meant that nobody could use the same tactic to get more out of DC while nobody would be able to challenge Bob lying about his age. Jerry Shuster and Joe Siegel were out on their own. It is uncertain whether Kane's support would have helped the two of them. It is possible he may have ended up in his own legal battle with Finger over who really created Batman, but the result was National Publications, not Sigel and Shuster, were found to be the owners of Superman. The boys retained the rights to Superboy and received some of the payments for outstanding merchandising of Superman. But an out of court settlement resulted in Jerry and Joe handing Superboy over to Donenfeld and Liebowitz too. The boys walked away with only a fraction of what they were owed and worse still, they had lost their creations.

Kane continued to receive the sole credit for the Batman books and legally consolidated his position as the single creator of the Dark Knight. Now the contract was signed, it would be impossible to for him to go back on this position. Some comics fans have, maybe fairly, vilified Kane because of this contract. Firstly, there is the sticky matter of him lying about his age and secondly, he did not help his friends Siegel and Shuster when he had the chance, which condemned them to a lifetime of struggling. Finally, we need to ask this question: where was Bill Finger in all of this?

Well, some dynamic between to the two meant that Finger still felt that Kane was his boss, at least when it came to Batman. On top of which, the world had no idea about the extent Finger's contribution to the creation of Batman and it's likely he had no legal footing to ask for a better contract or to join in with Siegel and Shuster's campaign. We will never get an answer for why Kane, at this point, failed to bring Finger in on the deal. Kane, knowing Finger's contribution to Batman, had the chance to give his writer the respect and recognition he deserved. This is when he could have made a difference, before it was too late. But he did not, and we will not know why. Was it something legal, some restriction jeopardising the deal, or just simply Bob's chance for fame and fortune? Or was it in Bob's nature; was he uncaring and selfish or savvy yet inconsiderate?

Jerry Robinson later recalled an event between Kane, Kane's mother and Sheldon Moldoff which may give us some insight. In the early days, when Batman's adventures were imagined into existence in Bob's bedroom, Bob's mother would occasionally bring the boys meals. One evening, after Shelly and Bob finished working, Bob's mother brought them dinner; for Shelly, the guest, a small hamburger, and a potato; for her baby boy, a thick, juicy steak. When Shelly asked to trade, or for the boys to share the steak and hamburger, Bob just laughed and his mother left the boys to their nonsense. Bob would never share his superior meal or ask his mother to split the dinners equally. It never even occurred to him to ask. After all, everyone was getting fed, Bob was just getting the lion's share.

When Bob was renegotiating his contract, Bill was doing fine. Sure, he had a few money worries, but he was working. In fact, it was thanks to Bob that he was no longer working as a shoe salesman. He opened the door of an entire industry to Bill and had given him hamburger and potatoes. Bob's number one concern was, as ever, himself. It was fine for him to treat himself to the steak.

Moldoff later said Finger did not even consider asking for rights or royalties and was simply happy to be a writer. In an interview in *Alter Ego* magazine, Moldoff said, 'Bob Kane never was a nice guy. He had a tremendous ego. If I came up with an idea, he had no problem stealing it and claiming it as his own. Was Bob generous to Bill Finger? No. Was he nice with him? No. Bob wasn't nice to anybody.'

Unlike Jerry Robinson and Shelly Moldoff, Finger did not know how to stand up to Bob. He may not have been happy with his lot, but he lacked the courage to do anything about it. Finger's partner in creating the Green Lantern, Martin Nodell, witnessed the heart-breaking dynamic between the fathers of Batman during a visit to Kane's apartment. 'When Bill entered the room, it was if he was greeting the king. Bill was bowing down, his hands out, just to say hello. That was the way it was. Bill felt as if he had to condescend before Kane.'

Chapter Six

Knight Fall

The 1950s and the decline of Batman

After his savvy renegotiations, Bob Kane entered the 1950s on a high. He was making good money and as far as the world was concerned, he was the creator of DC's second most lucrative character. Batman was Bob's career and life. He was known to tell fans and co-workers (and anyone who would listen) 'I am Batman.' Batman had not swooped into Bill Finger's life and rescued him like he did Kane, but the hit character had at least provided Finger with a start in the comics industry.

The reality was that Kane was further away from the comics than ever while Finger and Sprang, along with other fill-in writers and ghosts, became the principle directors behind Batman. Sprang's new visual approach to the comics was starting to give dedicated readers a hint that perhaps the art wasn't all the work of one man while Finger's trivia-laden stories and outlandish plots began to hit on a regular but successful three-part formula. Upon meeting a villain, for example, the Finger-Sprang created Riddler (the culmination of each of their individual talents), Batman would lose in the first encounter, draw in the second and finally, be victorious, in the third and final tryst.

But things were not great for Bill. His $12 page rate and terminally slow pace meant that he had constant money worries and borrowed from everyone.

Illustrator William Woolfolk even recalled his wife Dorothy giving money to Finger while at the funeral for DC editor Bernie Breslauer.

Rumours began to spread about a Bill having a problem with alcohol. Later in life, his close friends would say Bill, like many writers they knew, enjoyed a drink but was not an alcoholic. It is hard to say if this was the case or whether his closest friends were defending his honour. It is important to remember too that attitudes to alcoholism were different to what they are today. On the other hand, alcohol dependency fits in nicely with the story of a down on his luck, struggling writer and Bill would not be the first artist to turn to the bottle in hard times. Whatever the case, the rumours circulated.

Though his stories were still popular, Finger bristled under the yoke of the editors at DC. He felt they took away the freedom for writers to do what they wanted and the ability to creatively explore new ideas. In the case of Whitney Ellsworth, this resulted in probably quite prudent decisions like not having Batman carry a gun, or bringing back popular villains, but the infamous DC editor Mort Weisinger took this editorial control to a new level.

Weisinger was another kid from the Bronx and a huge fan of science-fiction, even setting up one of the first sci-fi fan clubs in his parents' house as a boy. His sci-fi posse set up an underground fanzine call *The Time Travellers* and called themselves the Scienceers. He had a domineering presence and had made his way up through the DC ranks with his lifelong friend Julius Schwartz. Weisinger, like Donenfeld and Kane, knew how the game was played. He worked the industry to his own ends. Even more so than Ellsworth, he was known to impose his control the stories of the publications he worked on. He had a very tight set of rules he demanded his writers follow, and he would practically tell them what to write, on the grounds that it would save time for them to do as they were told now, rather than them having to rewrite copy later anyway. One of the lighter results of Weisinger's later tenure as an editor on the Superman and Batman lines was the frequency with which giant gorillas and apes appeared on comic covers. Weisinger would keep track of which issues sold best and found stories featuring gorillas outperformed non-gorilla narratives.

He would also frequently strip Superman of his alien powers so Kal-El would have to rely on his smarts to beat the enemy. Weisinger felt this vulnerability allowed readers to identify with the character more, as they did with his favourite character, Batman. And although Weisinger was a fan of Batman and his mortality, he was not a fan of Bill Finger, the very man who gave Batman that quality. Weisinger was known to be a terror to the creative staff at DC, so much so that artist Curtis Swan would feel physically sick at the thought of dealing him.

There are stories he would shout abuse at them and laugh in their faces while ripping their pitches to shreds. He would reject story ideas from one writer only to give it to another and claim he had come up with the story. Writers Alvin Schwartz and Don Cameron left DC because of Weisinger's treatment of them, but not before the latter would become so frustrated he held Weisinger out of an open window. Weisinger liked Jerry Siegel and thought he produced the right kind of melodrama Superman needed to sell books, but that didn't stop him bullying the writer, pushing him to get the best possible (and usually most tragic) story out of Jerry.

In Finger's case, Weisinger's pre-emptive punishment fit the presumed crime. Bill would be forced to sit outside Weisinger's office for hours while he brought in other writers ahead of the tardy Finger. If Bill popped in for a quick meeting, Weisinger would make sure to keep him waiting just to humiliate him. Weisinger, like Finger, had been a huge fan of the pulps but one of the essential elements the editor took from that tradition was the idea that writers should be able to churn out pages on demand, something Finger simply wasn't capable of. Weisinger thought Finger was lazy, and would openly mock the writer's financial predicament, laughing about it to the other writers and artists, and admonishing those who would spot Finger a few dollars to get by. As far as Weisinger was concerned, if Finger needed more money, all he had to do was hand in more pages on time.

But the start of the 1950s would kick-off Bill's exploration into other fields in a very literal sense when he attended a 1949 New Year's Eve party with his wife Portia, Jerry Robinson and Jerry Shuster. Coral Nieland, a part-time actress, supporting player in the *Superman* radio serial and a secretary at the DC offices, was also at the party with her then-husband, Charles Sinclair, a writer for radio and a magazine editor (not to be confused with the murderer Charles Sinclair, the Coin Shop Killer). Sinclair was living in New York after returning from the Second World War. He had studied at Columbia University like Jerry Robinson, and at the party, Nieland introduced Charles to her friend Bill. Sinclair and Finger began to bump into each other more and more through their friendship group. They had similar interests and without the pressure of the DC offices, Bill was an easy-going, engaging and funny guy. Sinclair was impressed by Bill's self-taught literary education and a near-encyclopaedic knowledge of film.

Around this time, Bill was living in New York's Greenwich Village, a cultural and liberal hub built from cafes, cabarets, restaurants and jazz clubs which in the 1950s would become the playground for the growing

Bohemian Generation. The term 'Off-off-Broadway', meaning either a rejection of commercial theatre or an incredibly cheap performance, is said to have originated there because of its developing theatre scene. A scene which Portia, and therefore probably Bill, would have patronised.

Bill and Portia had their son, Fred, in 1948 and would take him to New York's various museums, galleries and zoos. Portia was a heavy set woman with curly dark hair that matched Bill's. She came from a more middle-class family than Bill had and was better educated, having graduated from Bernard. She was very liberal and had even campaigned on behalf of the Progressive Party candidate Henry Wallace in the 1949 Presidential Election. By all accounts, Portia was a smart, confident but domineering woman. Someone Bill did not want to get on the wrong side of, but people liked her.

Bill and Portia would dine with her friends or double date with Jerry Robinson or Charles Sinclair and whoever they were dating at the time – Sinclair and Nieland were going through a tough time. Sinclair only met a few of Bill's comics colleagues, including Mort Weisinger, which we can imagine was awkward for everyone involved. But otherwise, it seems Bill kept his work and personal lives as separate as he could. By this point, he had fallen out with his parents, possibly thanks to their habit of waiting outside the DC office to claim his pay cheques. Also, his sister Emily had disowned him entirely (later in life she had no idea Bill had anything to do with Batman). Similarly, though Sinclair knew Finger was the writer and creator of Batman, he had no idea to what extent he had been involved. Though Bill would sometimes express frustration with his situation, he never went into the details with his friends, and didn't have the ego to demand his name get its place in the credits.

Sinclair and Finger found themselves in one another's company more and more, eventually reaching the conclusion that a pair of freelance writers like themselves could make a buck working together. So, around 1950 the duo got to work on a script for the radio series *Nick Carter, Master Detective.*

Though largely unfamiliar to a modern audience, Nick Carter was a prominent, early franchise character. Carter was a detective who first appeared in an 1886 short crime series published in *New York Weekly*. The character proved so popular he was promoted (or demoted depending on who you asked) to the pulps with his own magazine,

Nick Carter Weekly, which eventually went out of print in 1915. There was a brief attempt to revise the character for *Detective Story Magazine* in the mid-1920s, however the character fell away again. But bad sales cannot keep a good man down for long. The pulp explosion in the 1930s which had contributed so much to the recreation of Batman resurrected Carter for his second self-titled magazine, *Nick Carter, Detective Magazine* and a few years later, his own line of novels. In 1943, the character was given a radio series which was successful enough to run for twelve years. Proof that the world of the pulps was a small and self-devouring place, Carter would also star in his own strip featured in *The Shadow Comic,* itself a reaction to the kid-friendly comic book fad created by Superman and The Shadow's cousin Batman. The Shadow's principal writer Walter Gibson wrote for the *Nick Carter, Master Detective* radio show, but was kicked off the team for asking for more money, only for Batman's principal writer Bill Finger, as part of his own quest to make more money, to later get a gig on the very same radio show starring the character.

Sinclair had previously worked on the show as a freelancer and knew that he and Finger stood a good chance of getting a script on the show. What they put together played to both their strengths. Finger's gimmick book, which he used for his Batman stories, had notes on the precious stone jade – notably, that it wasn't just mined in China and a huge vein of the mineral was found in the Wyoming mountains. The villain of the piece was a smuggler by the almost comical name of 'Rocks' Melvern. In the story, Carter finds the truck used in the smuggling operation and notices it has three pre-set radio stations all labelled with Wyoming based stations. Sinclair's knowledge of the radio meant he picked out three real stations in Wyoming and had Carter use their locations to pinpoint where the illegal jade mining operation was. It was a textbook crime story and the stations mentioned in the story, who aired *Nick Carter, Master Detective* as part of their syndicated programming, loved that they had become part of the adventure.

More importantly, Finger and Sinclair enjoyed working together and getting paid for their efforts. The pair split a cheque for either $300 or $600 (Sinclair could never quite recall exactly how much it was) and they celebrated by going for dinner after listening to the show. It was commissioned work and neither writer could claim ownership of Nick Carter but that did not matter. They had worked together on the script, each contributing their talents, complementing each other's skills and splitting the profits down the middle. It was the start of a strong friendship and creative partnership. Over the next few years, while they each worked on their individual projects, Finger and Sinclair would often write and pitch stories together for various radio shows. But they had their sights on bigger fish. The exciting new medium of television was beginning to make waves and though Finger didn't yet know it, Batman was in for a tough few years.

Seduction of the innocent

In the mid-1950s Batman and his boy ward were at the centre of a scandal that shocked society and made its way to the Senate of the United States of America. The dynamic duo had recently made an enemy in the guise of a liberal, psychiatrist of German descent, Dr Fredric Wertham.

Wertham grew up in Nuremberg, Germany and studied at the universities of Erlangen, Munich, and King's College London. He was a correspondent of the father of psychoanalysis Sigmund Freud, who had inspired Wertham to specialise in psychiatry after he had obtained his MD from the University of Wurzburg. In 1922 Wertham moved to the United States at the invitation of another pre-eminent psychiatrist, Adolf Meyer.

Wertham, progressive and intelligent, quickly became highly respected in his field. He was an expert witness for the defence in the trial of the Vampire of Brooklyn – rapist, serial killer and cannibal, Albert Fish. Wertham had detailed Fish's obsession with religion and young boys, summarising the nature of Fish's crimes with the laconic and obvious, 'He is insane.'

In 1946, recognising the mistreatment, racism and economic disadvantage faced by African American communities, Wertham set up the Lafargue Mental Health Clinic at St. Phillips's Episcopal Church in Harlem, New York. Then the chief psychiatrist at Queens General Hospital, the doctor realised black patients were either unable to afford mental health care or faced racism from doctors who refused to care for them. His work there would later be cited in the case of Brown versus the Board of Education, which ruled that segregating classrooms based on skin colour was unconstitutional and illegal.

Later in his career, he would publish a work called *A Sign of Cain: An Exploration of Human Violence* wherein he attempted to look at the root causes of violence in society and posited an economic driver to events like the Holocaust. But, despite his compassion and attempt to improve society, he is best remembered for attacking the humble comic book.

Seduction of the Innocent, Wertham's 1954 provocatively entitled treatise on the cause of juvenile delinquency, took aim at the world of comics. Wertham claimed, and at least tried to demonstrate that comic books, particularly those dominating the crime and horror genres, turned the angelic children who read them into demonic thugs. Superhero comics were also responsible for a swathe of sins. Wertham, perhaps unaware of the Last Son of Krypton's Jewish originators, considered Superman, literally interpreted as Freud's 'Ubermensch' (literally 'over man'), a symbol of Nazi fascism. Perhaps aware of William Moulton Marston's predilection for bondage or just the first academic to notice subtext in comics, Wertham took Wonder Woman's repeated capturing and binding as the youth of America being exposed to sadomasochistic sex. Marston, the creator of Wonder Woman and the lie detector, had based the character on one of his students with whom he and his wife lived and were in a relationship with. His enjoyment of healthy sadomasochism has been widely documented now but Marston moved in academic circles and it is easy to imagine that Wertham had heard rumours of Marston's kink on the grapevine.

Batman's great sin was Bruce Wayne's love of Dick Grayson, or at least, his assumed love. Wertham called into question the sexual alignments of the billionaire vigilante and his boy ward, who were often depicted in bed together, and wrote: 'Only someone ignorant of the fundamentals of psychiatry and of the psychopathology of sex can fail to realize a subtle atmosphere of homoeroticism which pervades the adventures of the mature "Batman" and his young friend Robin.'

At the time, homosexuality was still considered a mental illness and the American government was in the process of a mass firing and persecution of gay, or suspected gay, employees in what would become known as the 'lavender scare'.

Comic book historian and academic Aaron David Lewis makes the case that Wertham was less interested in homosexuality as an illness, even avoiding phrases such as 'sickness' or 'disease' and was instead more concerned by the lack of a traditional family structure in Batman's world; something Wertham had already identified as a contributor to bad behaviour among kids. Although, even this interpretation is homophobia by proxy.

Regardless, Wertham had already set in motion a chain of events that would include mass book burnings and eventually, Wertham giving testimony against comic book publishers at the Senate Subcommittee on Juvenile Delinquency in the summer of 1954.

Picture Book Burnings

Only one comic creator would give testimony at the Senate hearing and his performance was so bad it resulted in the self-governing body of the Comics Code Authority being formed. That man was William 'Bill' Gaines who was the son of the Charles Gaines, the man who published all American Comics, who had brought in Finger to work on the Green Lantern and had created those early promotional proto comics. His son Bill was the head of EC comics. Originally, EC had produced educational and biblical comics, but it quickly turned to the much more fun yet lurid horror and crime genre to make money. Bill, suffering from a fever, was asked by Tennessee senator Este Kefauver whether he thought a comic depicting the severed head of a woman was in good taste. Bill replied 'Yes sir, I do, for the cover of a horror comic. A cover in bad taste, for example, might be defined as holding the head a little higher so that the neck could be seen dripping blood from it, and moving the body over a little further so that the neck of the body could be seen to be bloody.'

It didn't go down well. Gaines would weather the storm and go on to create the infamous satirical comic *MAD Magazine*, but his miscalculated response didn't paint a pretty picture of the comic book creators.

The men of the comics industry tried their best to keep their heads down. Regardless of what they personally thought about Wertham, they had become social pariahs who must be ashamed of what they were doing to the youth of America. It was embarrassing to admit you worked on comics before, when then they were just regarded as picture books for children, but now you were evil incarnate. Kane and Finger were likely no different. What is a shame is these pilloried creators did not realise at the time that Wertham's methods of reaching these conclusions were deeply flawed. For instance, much of his research was based on anecdotes from a relatively small sample size and the subjects chosen had already been attending Lafargue Mental Health Clinic for anti-social behaviour.

Not to mention the fact comics were so hugely read among children that almost any behaviour seen in kids could have been ascribed to them.

It may be the fact publishers were at the centre of this debate or, even if Bob's sole signature did grace the front of Bat-books across newsstands, the creators were still largely unknown to a wider world but Kane and Finger only let their opinions be known years later.

In a 1972 interview with Robert Porfirio, Finger described Wertham as, 'a first-rate psychiatrist and a good man in his field. However, he was like the old maid always looking for somebody under the bed. He saw sex and violence in everything.'

Finger gave an example of how his own work had been taken out of context in a Superboy script he had written; 'Superboy is jumping up a tree to get an apple for somebody and Wertham saw this as a sexual symbol. The tree was a phallus and the apple, balls.'

Again, Finger's love of literature was the seed from which the Bat-family had begun to grow but had Batman and Robin become more than just friends?

'I knew many homosexuals, but I certainly didn't think of Batman in those terms. I thought of it in terms of Frank Wharton, and Frank Merriwell and Dick Merriwell, his half-brother, who was the kid he was taking care of. Wertham got his views on the homosexuality of male heroes in popular culture from Gershon Legman's book, *Love and Death,* and he extended this analysis to literary characters like Ishmael and Queequeg in *Moby Dick.*'

He then added, 'There was no homosexual relationship. It was just that the author realized [sic] that you've gotta [sic] have somebody to talk to. Sherlock Holmes had Watson – were they homosexuals? Baloney. You can't just have your hero walking around thinking aloud all the time. He'd be ready for the men in white coats after a time. So, we created a junior Watson and that's all he was.'

Finger may have been unfamiliar with gay interpretations of classic literature (including the consulting detective) but his answer to the question of Batman's sexuality was much more concerned with the function of storytelling rather than condemning homosexuality.

A decade after Wertham's study, Batman was on the television and being very camp indeed. Kane took a slightly different view than Finger. Journalist Paul Sann, the king of tabloid journalism, interviewed Kane for his book *Fads, Follies and Delusions of the American People* in

1967 as Adam West donned the cape and cowl for TV sets across the world at the same Bat-time, on the same Bat-channel.

Kane first addressed the impact Wertham had on the comic books:

'Batman is the epitome of virility and manliness – just the opposite image of the fag. Wertham read homosexuality into this thing because I had a man and a boy living in a big house together – in the same bedroom – with just a butler and no female around. The doctor read homosexuality into it, through his eyes, but for that matter he also put down the Wonder Woman comic as a lesbian invention.

'It was all hogwash, but I had to do something about it anyway. So, I changed their bedrooms and I added Aunt Harriet – sort of a mother to both of them.'

Presumably, by Aunt Harriet, Kane means Aunt Agatha, a creation for the comics later adapted for television. His claim he added the aunt is probably a mistake too. It was much more likely a prompt from DC editor Jack Schiff to his writers to avoid some of the scrutiny parents put on the books after Wertham's gay panic.

Kane, in one statement, managed to distance himself from the campy undertones of *Batman* all the while benefitting from a homophobic imagining of its audience.

'Even so, I suppose the homosexuals like the TV show because of those tight outfits Adam West and Burt Ward wear. I imagine they sit around watching them on the screen and slap each other on the knees with the sheer joy of it all, but what can you do about that? I can't change the characters because they weren't homos in the first place and because you have to be crazy to fight success.'

Whitney Ellsworth had been sent to Hollywood in the 1940s to work on DC's various superhero properties, including the Batman serials which would directly inspire the creation of the 1960s television series. Jack Schiff had taken over the editorial responsibilities on the Batman and Superman books while Mort Weisinger served in the Second World War, but he continued to work on the books when Weisinger returned. Like Weisinger, Schiff gave Bill Finger a tough time, although to nowhere near the same degree, and like Ellsworth before him, he knew he had to change the Batman line to keep the parents happy and sales up. It being the 1950s, criticisms Batman books promoted a homosexual lifestyle simply would not do, regardless of them being true or not. So, Schiff instructed writer Edmond Hamilton and Kane ghost Shelly Moldoff to give Batman a super heroic girlfriend. And thus, Kathy Kane – named for Bob – became Batwoman. Later she would be joined by her niece, the original Batgirl, Bette Kane, so that Robin would not feel left out.

Finger on the television

The addition of female characters may have gone some way to easing the worry of overzealous parents, but Finger and Kane were having woman troubles of their own. In 1957, Kane was divorced from his wife Beverly, with whom he shared a daughter, Deborah. Kane was known to be a womaniser and constant flirt. There are rumours infidelity was the cause of the separation. Kane was kicked out of the house, and later his former housekeeper found a treasure trove of original Batman comics, scripts and original art in the trash, some of which is believed to have been returned to Kane as part of his new, secret contract. Presumably, they were thrown away by his ex-wife, which for Kane, would have been the equivalent of cutting up all his favourite suits. Kane had become a collector of comic art and he would frequently mention the value of his work to other collectors. It is almost unbelievable he would allow this work to be so easily destroyed. If we are being cynical, we might ask what the contents of those pages contained and how they might contradict Bob's claim to the Batman throne. On the other hand, perhaps Batman is just a supporting character in this drama and when people get divorced things get lost.

Finger was also divorced or, at least, separated and working on divorce, by the late 1950s or early 1960s. Given much of Bill's private life has never been recorded it is impossible to say exactly when the split happened, but it was certainly no later than 1963. We know this because it was around then Charles Sinclair, apparently following the trend of the time, divorced his wife Coral and moved into an apartment Bill had been letting on his own. We do know one of the contributing factors to Finger's divorce though. Bill had met another woman in 1954, Edith 'Lyn' Simmons, and had been seeing her while he was still married. Their first date was to see one of the foreign films Bill loved so much.

Bill's divorce only increased his money troubles as now he had to pay Portia, already a dominating woman and now rightfully frustrated with Bill, alimony. More than once, Bill ended up in jail at Portia's hand for failing to pay up, relying on tall tales of perpetually sick grandparents to secure advances from editors to keep his head above water. Bill's health was also failing. He suffered a heart attack in 1963 and was ordered to take medication and take it easy, a task more easily said than done when you need money. The rumours of Bill's alcoholism may have been exacerbated by his poor health, though if the rumours were true, this could easily be the other way around.

Bill and Charles continued to work together after their success on *Nick Carter, Master Detective* and had more scripts purchased for radio, including for the anthology show *Murder by Experts*. The show was a collection of mystery stories with a special guest expert who would comment on the story, including the likes of mystery genre luminary, Alfred Hitchcock. Finger's training with Batman (and his trusty gimmick book) meant he and Sinclair were beginning to carve out some small reputation as reliable and smart crime writers. Television, with all its charm, glamour, and large pay cheques beckoned the pair. Luckily, like Kane before him, Sinclair had some contacts in the industry and wanted to bring Finger along for the ride.

Sinclair had worked for several television trade magazines including *Sponsor* and *Billboard*, which is now famous for its music coverage, and later he became the bureau chief for *Television Digest*. Through his contacts, he was able to get an opportunity to pitch for a show called *Foreign Intrigue*. Sometimes referred to as *Foreign Assignment* and rather confusingly, *Dateline Europe, Oversea Adventure* or *Cross Current* when it was re-run, the show followed the adventures of American foreign correspondents in Europe as they uncovered various stories and schemes. The show was produced and shot by New York producer Sheldon Reynolds but was filmed across Europe giving it an authentic and rich production value. Reynolds would later become famous for bringing Finger's favourites, Sherlock Holmes and Dr Watson, to American audiences.

Sinclair was able to secure a commission for the show, so he and Finger got to work. Reynolds wanted a story about a hitman travelling around Europe undetected while assassinating defectors from an unnamed, but clearly Soviet, organisation. It was a standard brief for this genre and not much to go on, but that scant direction allowed Finger to explore his more eccentric storytelling impulses. Taking his cue from Cecil B DeMille's *The Greatest Show on Earth* starring Jimmy Stewart, Finger suggested the villain of the piece could move around Europe with anonymity as part of the circus, disguised as a clown of all things. While Sinclair remembered it was the Stewart flick which inspired the plot, you must wonder whether the Joker had crept into the script through Finger's subconscious.

At some point around this time, Sinclair and Finger must have become signed up members of Mystery Writers of America (MWA) in New York as they began to develop stories for *The Web*, a show entirely dedicated to MWA produced scripts.

This entire time Finger and Sinclair worked as freelancers, meaning they were never on staff; their jobs were never guaranteed or secure. Writing for TV was their side hustle and not their main source of income. The two worked well together, despite Finger occasionally being dismayed at having borrowed and spent his share of the cheques before Sinclair had received them from the production companies. It wasn't just elaborate stories and crazy gimmicks which made Finger a good writer for television crime dramas. The limit of space on a comic book page meant he was efficient with dialogue. It might have been slightly melodramatic, but it wasn't indulgent, and it did the job of expressing plot and character succinctly and with a low word count, which kept the pace quick and the dialogue punchy. The downside is the production budget for Sinclair and Finger's script could become laughably high. Drawing a complicated fight scene with multiple vehicles, bystanders, and explosions in just a few small panels isn't easy for an illustrator, but it's a damn sight less expensive than filming it. Finger's comic-based imagination could sometimes create scenes simply too expensive to put on film.

It was Sinclair's effort with another writer that would give the duo a continued boost later in the decade. With writer David Osborn, Sinclair worked on the first spec script from Associated Dragons productions, a venture by none other Douglas Fairbanks Junior, the son of the man who played the Batman prototype, Zorro. The film is a crime mystery called *Chase A Crooked Shadow* and was a relatively minor success, but it did open the door for Finger and Sinclair at Warner Brothers, which had been the film's US distributors.

Sinclair was always the business end of the partnership, so it was often him who would prompt Finger into working on a project. And when he got word of Warner's new detective series *77 Sunset Strip*, he knew they had to give it a shot. The series revolved around the adventures of a secret agent turned private investigator and was a huge hit.

Its Hollywood setting gave it an illusion of the exotic and one of the supporting characters, Kookie, played by Edd Byrnes, became a teen sensation. Kookie was a hipster, slang-slinging, apprentice to the lead PI character and was so popular Warner released a novelty single of the character singing. It got to number four in the US charts. Over its six-year run the show would play with the format and take real storytelling risks, like episodes with absolutely no dialogue.

Finger and Sinclair played with this experimental style after hearing producer Howie Horwitz nearly had a heart attack upon reading and estimating the shooting costs of one of their scripts. To bring the balance sheet back to black and reign in some of the production costs, Sinclair suggested an episode with only one character on screen for the full hour. Warner was happy to let the duo give it a go and they were more than happy with the results. Not only did Finger and Sinclair turn the script around within a week, but the sheer courage and creativity of the episode also made the studio and the show a critical success.

The heart-attack-inducing script that put the pair in the position to write that innovative episode in the first place was a more run of the mill (if not expensive) affair but it almost propelled Finger and his partner to the big time. The episode was called 'The Positive Negative' and again relied on Finger's gimmick book. He had made notes about an infrared light which, when passed over human skins would reveal any tattoos that had been chemically removed. Inspired by the recent trial of Adolph Eichmann, a Nazi war criminal who had been hiding under a false identity in Argentina, the writers put together a story about a photographer who uses the new, futuristic, technology and ends up sleeping with the fishes. He is killed after taking a picture at a pool party when one of the party-goer's hidden SS tattoo is captured on film. The detective is brought in to solve the murder of the photographer and inevitably, is caught up in hunting the hidden Nazi, who is also fleeing Israeli special forces.

When Finger and Sinclair submitted the script Warner Brothers considered taking it from the show and turning it into a movie. Bill and Charles waited with anticipation, imaging how their Nazi crime mystery would look on the big screen. But, after being held in a story committee for some time, Warner kept the script for the show. It was a near-hit for Finger and Sinclair and surely a little disappointing but they could take solace in the fact 'The Positive Negative' went on to be one of the best received, most syndicated and most repeated episodes of the show's entire run.

The 'New Look'

It wasn't just Finger who had made the leap to television, however. *Courageous Cat and Minute Mouse* was an animal funnies cartoon developed for television by Kane with Tran-Artists productions. Trans-Artist's other productions were a number of Sinbad feature cartoons starring the son of the adventuring pirate and a series called *Bucky and Pepito*, which, although most of its episodes have joined the ranks of television shows genuinely lost to time, the few unlucky people which have seen it hated it, and it made the list of the worst cartoons of all time.

Kane claimed the inspiration for the *Courageous Cat* came to him after a meeting with Walt Disney during a post-divorce excursion to California. Kane always prided himself on the simplicity of Batman's design and he attributed the character's explosive success to his visual readability and ease of reproduction. Like Mickey Mouse, the cartooning of the character stuck with readers, and the two doodlers, Walt and Bob, expressed this thought about their respective characters to one another. In his autobiography, Kane also recalled asking Disney how he had come up with the character of Mickey Mouse to which Disney replied the truth and the myth of the matter had become so conflated he wasn't quite sure anymore. But Kane was well aware Disney had worked with fellow cartoonist Ub Iwerks in the development of Mickey Mouse. Like Kane and Finger, Disney had brought a rough idea of the character to Iwerks and Iwerks redefined it to the character we now recognise as the early Mickey Mouse. Likewise, outside of the industry, it was the business savvy Disney who would get most of the credit. Kane, of course, reiterated Disney's centrality to the success of the House of Mouse in his book, but it seems at once like a subtle admission of Kane's reliance on other creators and a declaration of his own authority in the creation of Batman.

Once again Kane employed his most regular and reliable ghost, Sheldon Moldoff, in the creation of *Courageous Cat and Minute Mouse*, by employing the work-horse artist to both draw storyboards and write scripts for the animated adventures. The cartoon was fairly successful. Its five-minute running time meant it could be easily slotted into gaps in children's programming and the show had 130 episodes made over three years. The result was a decent and flexible product which was syndicated across America and the rest of the world for years. It was also clearly recognisable as a homage to Batman. Courageous Cat relied on a bevy of gadgets stored in his belt as well as an all-purpose gimmick gun which fired any ammo the story needed while Minute Mouse was his Robin-esque clumsy, youthful sidekick. The duo protected Empire City from various villains. Summoned by the Cat-Signal, they would fire up the Cat-Mobile and explode from the Cat-cave to fight crime. Though it may have been new money for old rope, the show was quite well received.

Batman was not doing quite so well at the start of the 1960s. Superman was dramatically outselling the Caped Crusader, and by Mort Weisinger's reasoning, that meant changes were needed. In addition to Robin, Alfred, Batwoman and Commissioner Gordon, additional crime fighters joined Batman in his quest to clean up the streets of Gotham in the forms of Ace the Bat-Hound and Bat-mite. Created in the 1950s by Bill Finger and Sheldon Moldoff, Ace and Bat-mite were meant to recreate the success of the Superman characters, Krypto the Super Hound and the 5th dimension imp who tormented Superman, Mr Mxyzptlk (pronounced Mr miks-yez-pit-el-ik, though, this is debated) respectively. For the Man of Steel, these characters played into obscene science-fiction fun which no one can claim made sense, but at the very least did not destroy the heart of the character. For Batman, however, this command to follow the speculative sensations of the Superman family had a detrimental effect on the character. Sales dropped as the Batman's shadow of the night, detective persona was eroding and what replaced it was beginning to look ridiculous. This represented the first turn of the now-familiar cycle which is Batman's existence. He starts out as a dark, brooding, gritty and violent noir-ish vigilante then slowly he becomes more light-hearted and colourful, before eventually reaching an almost mocking, mirror version of his original self. Finally, a new creative team (and demanding audiences) force Batman back to his origins and begin the cycle again.

By the mid-1960s Mort Weisinger's childhood friend Julius Schwartz was brought in as the editor on the Batman books. Schwartz was the opposite of Weisinger in many ways. He was friendly and engaging and actively sought to connect with the readership on a personal level. While Weisinger tried to keep sales up by searching for the formula that would always work, Schwartz liked to try out new things. He would later be considered one of the greatest and most influential comics editors of all time.

By this point, Harry Donenfeld's son, Irwin had become the executive vice president of DC. Irwin was not a creative type but had been raised well by his father and 'Uncle Jack'. Batman's ridiculous storylines may not have concerned him, but the plummeting sales did. So, he tasked the new editor Schwartz with turning the book around. If he could not, Batman would be cancelled. It was a high stakes situation so Schwartz began the process of reinventing Batman.

At the time he was given this weighty task, he was apparently completely unaware that the artist Bob Kane was actually the ghost artist Sheldon Moldoff. But most of the DC creative stable knew Kane had some arrangement going on. Other artists would sit in the offices and work while Kane always took his work home. Schwartz later recalled in his autobiography asking Kane to make some edits on a page he had submitted to the editor, including fixing a poorly drawn arm. When Kane brought the page back, the corrections were all there save for the arm. Bob had forgotten to mention this when he had given the work to Moldoff, but the pages were needed imminently, so Kane had to redraw the arm there and then. When the page came back it was terrible, but Schwartz gave him another shot. The second attempt was perfect but Schwartz could not understand why there had been such a dramatic improvement between attempts. When he asked Kane what had happened, Kane admitted he had artist Murphy Anderson, who was working in the bullpen at the time, fix it for him. When Schwartz enquired why, Kane apparently replied, 'Three little words: Lack of talent.'

None of that mattered, however. Schwartz wanted to replace Kane and Moldoff with Carmine Infantino. Infantino was part of the next generation of comic creators, those who had read comic books in their recognisable form in their youth and had been too young to be drafted during the Second World War. They were the first comic book fans to become comic book creators.

Infantino was a talented artist with a distinctive style who started at a young age. In the 1950s, Schwartz had brought Infantino into the DC freelance pool along with writer Robert Kanigher as part of his scheme to revitalise golden age characters who had fallen out of favour after the war. At the time, at DC, only Superman, Batman and Wonder Woman had their own self-titled series, but with a dynamic new costume design and kinetic lines, Infantino resurrected the Flash. Gone were the blue trousers and winged hat of his previous incarnation. This new Flash wore a skin-tight leotard of scarlet and a streak of electrifying energy followed the character as he flew across the pages of DC's *Showcase #4*. This would mark the beginning of the Silver Age of Comics which spanned from 1956 until 1975. It was a time of reinvention of characters, redesigning of costumes and re-addressing what stories cape-comics could tell. At DC, this took the form of supporting, second-tier characters returning to become fan favourites in new guises. A few years later, the Silver Age would be solidified as the second most important era in comic book history since their birth when a bored Stan Lee would write a comic for himself rather than the bosses under the assumption it would get him fired from Timely/Marvel. A comic about the human side of heroes being as, if not more, important than their super side. That comic was *Fantastic Four #1* and it would lead to the creation of the Marvel Universe as we know it.

What became known as the 'New Look' Batman, helmed by Infantino, meant changes for Finger and Kane. For Kane, it would be the first time another creator would have cover credits for illustrating Batman. Kane could not deny Infantino's style was so different from his own and the one his ghosts had loosely followed. Readers would know immediately it wasn't Kane or his stand-ins who had illustrated these new issues. Infantino's heroes were much sleeker and athletic than the barrel-chested strong men who had come before. Perhaps his most influential re-design for Batman was the inclusion of the now-famous yellow chest emblem. *Detective Comics #327* was the first outing for the Infantino – Kanigher New Look Batman. Schwartz was still getting to grips with the character and accidentally allowed him to use a gun again, clearly unfamiliar with the long-standing rules. In the editorial pages at the back of the issue, Schwartz broke another rule by referencing previous writers and artists other than Bob Kane who over the years had worked on Batman, including Bill Finger.

But it wasn't all smooth sailing. Despite his new, nicer boss, Finger had the same old problems. Schwartz once recounted having to force Finger to sign a note forbidding the writer to ask for his cheque until he had completed his assignment. Regardless of his continued tardiness under the new regime, Schwartz's new approach meant Finger would get some recognition for his work and his name would appear in collected reprints of his early Batman work

One thing Schwartz did know about was the previous decades' accusations of what Bruce, Alfred and Dick might be getting up to all alone in Wayne Manor and what that could do to sales. So, he had Finger kill off Alfred and replaced him with Aunt Harriet, a new and improved version of Aunt Agatha and means of deterring claims of so-called sexual deviancy. Although Pennyworth wouldn't remain dead for long. He was resurrected by the Outsider, a villain named for an old, weird science story by H.P. Lovecraft, a former colleague of Schwartz, so that the Butler might appear alongside his upcoming TV counterpart.

Kane's contract caused some sticking issues, however. He was still entitled to so many pages worth of work a year. So, a compromise of sorts was achieved. Infantino would take the lead on *Detective Comics* while Kane would retain dominion over *Batman*. Of course, this meant *Batman* would often actually be pencilled by Moldoff after Kane. And when the time would come for Moldoff to provide occasional fill-in work on *Detective*, Kane's longest-serving ghost was more than capable of imitating Infantino's new, illustrative style. Even as late as 1965, Kane claimed he produced ninety per cent of the artwork for Batman in comics when the truth was his input had been minimal since the mid-1940s.

'A Finger in Every Plot'

Alongside the Flash, Bill Finger and Martin Nodell's Green Lantern was reborn as Silver- Age hero Hal Jordan, the pilot turned intergalactic cop with a tighter, figure-hugging costume than his cape-wearing predecessor Alan Scott. Silver Age creators, writer John Broome and artist Gil Kane (no relation to Bob), paid homage to Finger with a new Green Lantern villain, Black Hand. A pretty lazy alter-ego, Black Hand's real name was William Hand, with the black part of his sobriquet coming in from the fact William was the black sheep of his family. The on the nose naming of the character and perhaps the subtle reference to Finger being distanced from his family (both Bat and real) aren't the only 'Fingerisms' that made it into the character. Julius Schwartz later admitted Black Hand was initially based on Finger's personality. His comic counterpart was known to be a genius in his youth but too reliant on old clichés and purple prose. He knew the world of crime and detection inside out, keeping a ledger filled with esoteric criminal and scientific knowledge to keep one step ahead of the police. It seems Black Hand as a nod to Bill Finger was a tongue-in-cheek but fun homage to the writer. It would not be Bill's only appearance by another name in a DC comic, though sadly, a later appearance would not be quite so kind.

The Silver Age did not just bring in fans turned creators to the comics industry. It introduced the fan turned curator. People who had lived their entire lives in the shadows of the superhero had prudently begun to document what was going on behind the scenes. The 1960s saw new artists taking over and being credited for their fresh work on old creations. Marvel introduced a bull-pen column to their books wherein editor/artistic director/owner/publisher Stan Lee would reply to readers directly and offer a human, albeit embellished, look at life working on the funny books. Though credits had appeared on comics since their creation, the 1960s saw a shift from comic books just being thought of as something appearing on newsstands created by slightly embarrassed adults who really ought to know better, to vessels, the content of which changed depending on who was working on each title. They now had popular creators who could be followed from property to property, whose talent transcended the character they worked on. As comics' fandom grew, the human side of the industry was getting more attention than it ever had previously.

One such fan intrigued by the goings-on behind the curtain was Jerry Bails. Bails was born in Kansas City in 1933 and had grown up with comic books. In his early 20s, he began a correspondence with various comic creators, including Batman writer Gardner Fox and editor Julius Schwartz. In the late 1950s and early 1960s fanzines, fan-made magazines dedicated to a single piece of pop culture, started to pop up and Bails, who would later be known as 'The Father of Comic Book Fandom', would write and edit several of them. Through letters sent back and forth between Bails and comic creators, he would be put in touch with Roy Thomas, and in 1961 they set up *Alter Ego*, a magazine dedicated to the workings of comic book history. Thomas would later go on to be a major editor at Marvel comics.

Bails' good relationships with Fox and Schwartz meant he was able to make great headway into digging up stories about the origins and inspirations for the ever-growing roster of comic characters. He also helped to set up the industry's first awards, the Alleys. Despite his friendship with Schwartz, in 1962, he gave *Batman* the award for 'Comic Most in Need of Improvement', likely contributing to Schwartz's desire and understanding that the 'New Look' Batman was direly needed.

Bob Kane's signature. *(Public Domain)*

Milton Caniff's signature. *(Public Domain)*

Douglas Fairbanks in *The Mark of Zorro. (Public Domain)*

A painting of The Shadow by Charles Joseph Coll. *(Public Domain/Creative Commons)*

Photograph of a vintage copy of *Detective Comics #27* by Jim The Photographer. *(Use allowed with credit under creative commons)*

Scan of *Batman #1* by The National Archives and Records Administration. *(Public Domain/Creative Commons)*

Kane with a painting of Catwoman used with permission of the estate of Paul Sann, Howard V. Sann executor.

Bill Finger at the 1965 Comic Con.

Examples of Kane's Batman pop-art paintings from the William Dozier Collection, American Heritage Centre, University of Wyoming.

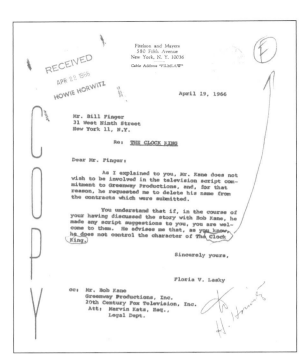

The letter from Bob Kane's lawyer, giving Finger the permission to go ahead on *The Clock King* script. William Dozier Collection, American Heritage Centre, University of Wyoming.

The rejection letter for Kane's Scribbler pitch 2. William Dozier Collection, American Heritage Centre, University of Wyoming.

Above left: Bob Kane's grave. Photo by Gary Wayne.

Above right: Jerry Robinson at the 2008 San Diego Comic Con. Photo by Dan Chusid. *(Creative Commons)*

Cover to *Bill The Boy Wonder* by Marc Tyler Nobleman and Ty Templeton. *(Permission from MNT)*

Bill Finger Way. Photo by Marc Tyler Nobleman. *(Permission from MNT)*

Above left: A comic book burning in the 1950s.

Above right: Bob Kane in 1966.

Though there had been comic fan gatherings before, usually small affairs in basements and spare function rooms (and sometimes in Bails' spare room at his Detroit home) where traders and fans could mingle with each other, the year 1964 gave birth to the first comic convention, the New York Comic Con, which was put together by Bails's organisation, the Academy of Comic-Book Fans and Collectors. The difference was this time comic creators would be there alongside fans as part of the event. In its second year, the New York Comic Con was held on 31 July – 1 August in the Broadway Central Hotel. One of its panel was hosted by Bails himself and featured Otto Binder, Gardner Fox, Mort Weisinger and Bill Finger.

Fans may have known Finger through his work across the DC lines and hardcore collectors might have even known he was the creator of the original Green Lantern, but only the obsessives, who had the Green Lantern's first appearance in 1940's *All American Comic's #16* published twenty years earlier, would have had an inkling about his early involvement in Batman. Even then, they would have had no idea of the scope of his contribution to the Dark Knight.

There were around 200 attendees at the convention, which wasn't half bad for the fledgeling event. Many of those in attendance would go on to be famous names in the industry in later life including Len Wein, Jim Steranko and Marv Wolfman (who, comic legends falsely claim, wasn't allowed to have his name on books he wrote because it alluded to lycanthropy, which was banned under the Comics Code Authority).

At 11.00 am on Saturday 31 July, the attendees crammed into the hotel's ballroom to attend the panel on Golden Age comics. Mort Weisinger was not originally intended to be on the panel but he was spotted in the audience and asked to be a stand-in for Finger, who was running characteristically late and as a result had to join in midway through the discussion. When he did eventually show up, Bill was introduced as a 'Batman writer from the very first'.

The discussion was recorded and later transcribed and published in *Alter Ego*. It is one of the few substantial interviews Finger gave. Far from being the dejected and wounded figure you might imagine him to be, Bill was cheery, friendly and funny on the panel. Even with Weisinger present, Bill seemed to enjoy his time talking to a room of fans. He joked that the recent 2 cents price hike for comics is what the writers got paid and he agreed with Binder when his fellow writer made the self-deprecating comment that the Golden Age writers and ghosts who worked without credit were just 'the invisible horde'.

Finger talked about his process of writing comics and how much he related it to his writing for television. He made the case that in a sense comics writer needed to be like cameramen and directors, ensuring they have a strong enough grasp of the visual aspects of comics to work with and guide artists. He also told an amusing anecdote about working with Kane. The duo had been put to work on a Weisinger story for Batman. The caped crusader was celebrating a birthday or anniversary, Finger recalled, and the rest of the Bat-cast had bought him bat-related items. One character gave Batman a stuffed bat and Kane, somehow missing the point, had drawn a scene where the Dark Knight received a stuffed baseball bat rather than a cuddly toy.

Bill alluded to the fact that one of the drawbacks of his trivia stuffed gimmick book was every slightly inaccurate factoid or spurious urban myth appearing in the comics resulted in annoyed letters from better informed fans. He also subtly mentioned his editors surreptitiously plucked more than one story idea from fan letters. Weisinger and Finger politely disagreed on Stan Lee's new approach to comics, Finger believing Lee's dialogue and storytelling was shaking up an industry in danger of becoming stodgy and stagnant whereas Weisinger was less impressed by the new, alter-ego focused approach to the superheroes. Weisinger even complimented Finger at one point, saying it was the writer who had taught him how to improve dialogue in comic fight scenes, and had helped him to incorporate the characters' surroundings into the story. The panel ended with Binder and Finger stumbling over each other to say how thankful they were that so many fans had attended the event and had wanted to listen to what they had to say.

Maybe Bill was just having a good day. Weisinger had dropped a hint at the panel that one of their characters would be making their way to television and Finger knew it was Batman. He could have been excited about that, or maybe he just enjoyed the recognition he got from fans. But how Bill acted on that panel – jocular, engaged, and thankful – also tells us something important that we should keep in mind. When looking at history, we reduce people to the events in their lives. It is easy for us to see Finger as an uncredited and unfairly treated creative who struggled to make ends meet. From this, it is easy to assume he was a perpetually unhappy man. But the truth is anecdotes and historical events only ever offer us a small glimpse of how people really felt. We can extract parts of their personality from this evidence, but we can't fully understand what it is to know them. Likewise, we may be tempted to define Bill Finger by the actions of Bob Kane, but this reduces them both; boiling them down and diminishing the complexity of their relationship and identities to characters neatly fitting into a narrative with an over-arching theme. We want to define a life though some recurring pattern we spot, but a tragic life doesn't mean the person who lived it spent their days in tragedy. People aren't all good and they aren't all bad, neither are they all exuberance or misery or indifference. They're all these things through the course of their time on earth.

Jerry Bails mentioned during the panel he had spoken to Finger beforehand, and it was either then or shortly afterwards Bails decided to write a small feature about Finger which would reveal the true extent to which the writer had been involved in the creation of Batman.

Bails produced a two-page article for *CAPA-alpha,* a high quality, comics fanzine distributed through a distributions manager also known as an Amateur Press Association. The article was entitled 'If The Truth Be Known, or "A Finger In Every Plot"' and many years later, it would be reprinted in *Alter Ego.* In it, Bails gave a quick outline of Finger's involvement in the creation of Batman as inspired by Zorro and The Shadow, as well as his contributions to Robin, the Joker, various Bat-trappings such as Batman's iconic cowl and utility belt, and Gotham City itself. It painted Finger as a genius who didn't realise the value and quality of his own talent only for Kane to be quicker on the uptake.

It was a rapid and rousing shout of support for Finger which wraps up by saluting his work on other properties, including his short post-war run on Captain America and Bucky, and claims that the Batman who readers were currently missing is the classic Batman the comics had drifted away from – the Batman of Bill Finger. And, for the first time in print, the words 'Batman, as created by Bill Finger' appear.

Going beyond the 200 or so comic convention attendees in the ballroom of the Broadway Central, this article introduced Bill Finger to the comics' world proper. Released in September of 1965, it would have reached hundreds of committed comics fans and changed their understanding of Batman, Kane, and Finger. Bill was no longer just a credit on a second-tier title in the form of the golden age Green Lantern. He was suddenly a real person and a central part of comics history and DC's massive success. What's more, whether it was just a poor choice of words or a deliberately unsubtle and pointed remark, Finger was referred to as the creator of Batman, not the co-creator. Not only would this make Bails the first champion in the quest to get Bill Finger credit for Batman, it would also imply that without Finger, there would have been no such thing as Batman. Inevitably, this article would thoroughly annoy Bob Kane. A couple of days after reading it, he wrote an angry retort to Bails which he sent in into the Julius Schwartz-approved Batman Fanzine *Batmania,* edited by Biljo White. The general gist of the three-page document was that Finger was horribly mistaken and even delusional if he thought anyone other than Bob Kane was the creator of Batman.

White held onto the article at the prompting of Tom Fagan, a fellow Batmaniac. Fagan was a reporter and a long-time contributor to the fanzine circuit. He informed White he had been in touch with Finger and he knew the writer and Kane were discussing what had been said at the convention, and that it would be best to let them talk and sort it out before they published anything that might fan the flames. Fagan had even forwarded a copy of Kane's letter to Finger just so they could be clear about what was being claimed.

In his reply to Fagan, Finger thanked him for Bob's 'fantastic letter' while admitting to angrily speaking his mind and having jogged 'Bob's failing memory'. The result was the duo agreed to meet for dinner to discuss it like old friends and Kane offered to revise the letter. Finger implied there was no real animosity between the two and it was, in fact, a separate reference in *Batmania* to the superiority of Carmine Infantino's 'New Look' that had irked Kane so much. Finger wrote that he doubted the letter would ever need to be published and thanked Fagan and White for the right to reply and their discretion in keeping this entire affair private.

White obliged for a while, but the letter would surface a year and a half later after Batmania ceased to be the name of a niche fanzine but instead became the banner of an international, television phenomenon.

Art Heist

While Schwartz was on his crusade to save Batman from cancellation and to re-capture the imaginations of readers across the country, Gotham's guardian had started to build a new following outside the four-colour limitations of the comic books.

The drop in sales of the Batman comics and being side-lined as the driving force in Batman's world was worrying Bob Kane. He wrote in his biography that at the time he was becoming more interested in spirituality and it was through mediation he had realised he should not tie his life to the success of just the Batman comics. He needed to diversify his portfolio creatively and financially. There is little information on how committed to his new metaphysical calling Kane was save for his scant mentions of it in his biography and the biography's dedication, which includes the name Dr Michael Zuekal. The 1960s were awash with New Age movements and it appears Kane was swept up in the flood. Dr Zuekal was a bit of a mysterious figure. He was a psychoanalyst and founder of the World Brotherhood Foundation or The Federation for Universal Brotherhood, which seems to have been a charitable organisation which supported children and promoted new age beliefs. Kane was photographed with Zuekal at a gallery opening for the former's new artistic venture. Knowing he needed to expand his horizons beyond drawing Batman – Kane started creating paintings of Batman.

Rather than work on the comics page, Kane was inspired by the growing pop art movement, which re-appropriated (if you're being nice, 'stole' if you're not) so much from comics. Kane's reproductions of Batman, Robin, Batwoman, Catwoman and the Joker were sold in up-market galleries across New York City and on the West Coast, in many ways, pre-empting the modern-day practice of selling reprints of classic comic book covers. Kane, the pop artist, felt he was unique among his new peers as he was the only one not repackaging the work of others; he was repackaging his own work. Of course, Kane was blowing his own trumpet yet again, forgetting the hordes of illustrators he had traced over and swiped from during his years establishing Batman, as well as his dependence on others to do his work.

Kane, of course, made a pretty penny from selling his original paintings but there were still rumours of him using a ghost. Comic books writer Arnold Drake rejoiced in telling the story of how he was invited to Kane's home after finding out his brother lived next door to Batman's creator. Kane introduced Drake to the editors at DC who would give the young writer a chance. One evening at Kane's home, Arnold and Bob were discussing a new newspaper strip they could work on, which Kane would sign but hire a ghost to illustrate. Drake lamented the shame of Kane no longer being an artist to which Kane showed Drake his new pop art painting enterprise.

A little while later, Drake was talking to his fellow writer Ed Herron in the DC offices. Herron mentioned Kane was being sued by his ghost artist to which the room was in shock. Sheldon Moldoff had worked under Kane for years, this was a shock. Herron laughed at his colleague's confusion and informed the collected artists and writers that it wasn't Moldoff who was taking Kane to court, but instead the artist behind his new Batman paintings.

The story has been repeated over the years with the mystery artist sometimes being a woman, but there doesn't seem to be a record of a legal case against Kane and sadly, Herron died in 1966 meaning the tale couldn't be verified. What we do know is that Bob had limited skill as an artist and happily relied on ghosts for his other work. Kane would often produce simple Batman sketches drawn from rote that he would give to admirers, while the lithographs themselves are relatively uncomplex, so, the evidence against Kane is compelling but circumstantial.

Pop-art pioneer Andy Warhol had paid homage to Batman in 1964 with his film *Batman Dracula*. It was an early fan film of sorts but most of it has been lost to time, but it was Batman of the 1940s silver screen rather than the 1960s art house that would bring the Dark Knight swinging into the public consciousness once more.

'NA NA NA NA NA NA NA NA BATMAN'

DC had struck a deal with The American Broadcasting Company (ABC) on the rights to a new Batman TV show. ABC, in turn, worked with 20th Century Fox to produce the show, who then hired Greenway Productions' William Dozier to make the show. ABC had gone after the rights, following an unusual trend sweeping the nation which was kicked off by none other than *Playboy* publisher, Hugh Hefner. Kane and Hefner could have been cut from the same cloth, and certainly, Kane always dreamed of the bachelor lifestyle Hefner became known for (among other things). But the connection was deeper than that. Hefner had grown up reading comics books and, like Kane, as a child he had wanted to be a cartoonist. Some of his earliest published work was as an illustrator in his high school newspaper. While he later became a champion for the *MAD* magazine-style editorial cartoons, he was also a fan of Batman. Hefner would throw sexy costume parties and have people show up in Batman and Robin outfits, which, if anything seems timid for one of America's most prolific pornographers.

Like Bill Finger, Hefner had a passion for obscure cinema. The original Playboy mansion was based in Chicago, as was Hefner's Playboy Theatre where he would show art-house and foreign-language movies, and even host the early Chicago International Film Festival. In between features, the theatre would run instalments of the 1943 Batman serial.

At the time it was made, *The Batman* consisted of a fifteen part, black and white adventure serial starring Lewis Wilson and Douglas Croft as Batman and Robin. It follows Batman trying to foil the plot of Japanese forces infiltrating Gotham city, and reinvents Alfred as a thin moustachioed man rather than the portly figure he originally cut in the comics. It is also obscenely racist. Once again, it was meant to follow in the successful steps of the Superman serials but even Batman's creators didn't like it. Jerry Robinson visited the set during filming and attended a story conference, where he quickly concluded the team responsible for the picture were hacks who could greatly benefit from the help of Bill Finger – which they never sought. Meanwhile, Bob Kane felt the producers were ruining his vision with a chubby lead actor and too few bat-accoutrements such as the Batmobile or Batman's utility belt. He did, however, enjoy the Hollywood after-party where he got to show off as Batman's creator and flirt with Hollywood starlets, including, in his account, Norma Jeane Mortenson, the woman who would one day become Marilyn Monroe.

Now though, repeated at the Playboy Theatre, the mini-movies were a huge success and kids in Chicago lapped up the serials, laughing with ironic cynicism at the low production quality and sheer obscenity of it all. College kids and movie-buffs attended every viewing they could, selling out the theatre, resulting in a special midnight showing with all fifteen parts edited together into the first of Batman's feature-length presentation.

News of the special event made it back to Columbia Pictures which still owned the serials. If it worked in Chicago, it might work across the rest of America. Billed as *An Evening with Batman and Robin,* Columbia turned the serial into a four hour and eight-minute special. Kicking off in the city Superman was born in, Cleveland, they took it to twenty different cities where it played to packed audiences. It was through seeing this audience reaction, ABC knew Batman was ready for television and Dozier knew he could make it a hit.

Dozier started reading old Batman comics as research and decided to adapt the comics as literally as possible. This meant the bright colours, ridiculous scenarios, and the deadpan acceptance everything happening was completely regular and should be treated seriously. Somewhere in the magical transition from comics to the screen, this turned into the high camp fun the series would be known for. The show is sometimes described as a homage to or parody of Batman, but it is actually a fair representation of what was happening in the comics at the time. The universe constructed in comics, which were targeted mainly at children, had some internal logic that frayed and lampooned itself when it had to exist in the 'real world' of television. Fans would, and still do, point to the Caped Crusader dancing the Bat-tusi as evidence the show wasn't taking the character seriously, at the same time blissfully ignoring that just a few years previously DC had The Dark Knight transformed into Bat-Baby, a crime-fighting toddler.

Bob Kane, who at this point was receiving some of the rights for franchised Batman properties, went on the press trail. He sent letters to *Batmania* singing the praises of the forthcoming show and appeared at department stores and on talk shows for launch events. Kane wasn't a consultant on the show but met with Dozier and would later claim he had suggested the show follow the same format of the serials by having cliff hanger endings with each episode but Dozier never corroborated Kane's story.

By this point, Bill Finger and Charles Sinclair were no longer living together. Bill tended to get angry at Charles for leaving the dishes unwashed, so Sinclair made himself scarce. By 1964, Sinclair had a new woman in his life and was ready to marry her. Bill wouldn't be Sinclair's roommate and perpetual third wheel anymore, so he'd have to settle with being Sinclair's best man.

The newly-weds didn't get far, however. Sinclair moved out of the apartment but, in a few years' time, the writers ended up in the same building again on the Eastside, with Finger living just two floors beneath the Sinclairs.

When Finger and Sinclair had worked for Warner Brothers, they regularly ran into the ire of Lorenzo Semple Jn, the chief story editor. Semple was quite dictatorial and according to Sinclair, generally quite unpleasant to be deal with, often commissioning scripts from himself to edge out other writers. On the upside, they had made a great contact in Howie Horwitz, the producer of *77 Sunset Strip*, after their impressive and innovative scripting. Some internal politicking resulted in Horwitz leaving Warner and moving over to 20th Century Fox. Eventually, Semple and Horwitz joined Dozier on the new Batman show.

Part of that camp charm of directly mistranslating a comic to the silver screen came from Semple. Semple was not a fan of the Batman comics, and for his first episode, he simply adapted Gardner Fox's story 'Remarkable Ruse of The Riddler', published only a year before, into the two-part adventures 'Hi Diddle Riddle' and 'Smack in the Middle'. Semple was likely unaware the toys he was playing with, Batman, Robin and Riddler, had been co-created by his very own freelancer Bill Finger. And the chances are even if he had known, he simply wouldn't have cared anyway. Horwitz, however, was a different matter.

Once Sinclair and Finger found out their old pal Howie was working on the series they sent him a telegraph with the gentle reminder that Bill knew Batman better than anyone, along with a simple question, 'Can we write for your show?' The answer was of course yes. So, in the second season of *Batman*, Finger and Sinclair scripted two episodes aired in October of 1966, 'The Clock King's Crazy Crimes' and 'The Clock King Gets Crowned'.

The plot revolved around Temple Fugate aka Clock King and a series of convoluted clock-based robberies and gadgetry. A previous Clock King had appeared in comics in 1960, created by France Herron and Lee Elias, though that chrono-criminal was the enemy of the Green Arrow and named William Tockman. The two share some similarities but it is unclear whether Finger based his character on Tockman. The consensus seems to be that the two characters are distinct entities although that doesn't mean Finger wasn't inspired by the Clock King in the same way he was inspired by The Shadow. But the Clock King was far from Finger's first clock-based Batman villain. In 1947, a villain simply named the Clock, with a round face and pencil moustache took on Robin in a solo adventure for *Star Spangled Comics* and he would make two later appearances taking on the Boy Wonder. Finger rewrote Batman's history in a story in 1959 billed as 'Batman's First Case'. The opening panel featured Batman fighting a new (or possibly old) iteration of The Clock on a huge clock face. Aside from Finger's trademark giant prop, this villain was different from his previous incarnation, in that he wore an elaborate costume. In 1961, shortly after the appearance of Heron and Lee's Clock King, Finger introduced the Clock Master to Gotham, with this character looking more like the original villain who had taken on Robin four years earlier.

The chronology of clock-based comic characters aside, Finger and Sinclair's script received good feedback from their supervisor and their notes were generally positive. The biggest issue, though, was production costs. This was a constant issue for the *Batman* series. An episode later in the series (not penned by Finger and Sinclair) would have the Dynamic Duo become invisible to fight a mob of invisible villains, allowing the producers to simply film empty sets and save money.

The usual arrangement between the writing duo was for Sinclair to take the lead credit. This made sense not only because Finger was generally less concerned with credits, but also because it was Sinclair who had actually secured the work. But this time was different. Whether Bill asked, or Sinclair felt it was the right thing to do, they arranged for the credits to read 'Bill Finger and Charles Sinclair', much to Bill's joy. This was the first time he had received an actual by-line for writing Batman, and bizarrely, it was his friend Charles and their connection in the world of television, not Kane and the comics industry, that gave it to him. Throughout the series, Lorenzo Sempler would lift storylines from comics written by the likes of Garnder Fox, John Broome, Lee Herron and, of course, Bill Finger. Sometimes Semple would make minor changes, such as substituting the Riddler for the Joker, but for the large part, he adapted directly, and the Bat-writers didn't receive royalties or credits. Finger was the only Batman writer to make the jump from the page to the screen.

Although Kane and Finger seemed to be on good terms with one another following Jerry Bails' revelations about Bill being the actual creator of Batman, there were still some frustrations behind the scenes. Letters from the William Dozier Collection at the University of Wyoming reveal the two were facing a breakdown of communication. A letter dated 9 April (1966) but evidently posted some date later, from Finger to Horwitz, hints at several issues. Firstly, as Finger and Sinclair were the only writers working on the show from the East Coast, their outlines were extensive so as not to confuse the production team working primarily in Hollywood. Secondly, the treatment for the episode was late. This may have been standard for Finger's comic work, but the letter points out scripts for *77 Sunset Strip* were always on time, perhaps thanks to Sinclair. The delay, in this case, appears to have been created by Bob Kane.

For some reason, Finger had been trying to contact Kane, who was in Florida at the time, for some permission approval to use in the planning stages of the episode. Finger's tone was jocular, but he expresses frustration with Kane's lawyer, whom he needed permission from. It appears Finger had filed contracts for his work on the show and had included Kane as one of the signatories. Throughout the letter, Finger refers to Bob as 'Bog'. It was simple enough typo, but it is notable that elsewhere in the letter, Finger had corrected other spelling mistakes. It could be Finger was making a subtle and ineffectual dig at Kane or he was in a rush to send the letter off so as not to lose the opportunity to write Batman for TV. As frustrated as he may have been with Kane for the delay, it would have been out of character for Finger to behave with such pettiness.

Also, a letter from Kane's legal office at around the same time explained why he did not want to be involved in Finger's TV contract. It stated: 'in the course of your having discussed the story with Bob Kane, if he made any script suggestions to you, you are welcome to them. He advises me that, as you know, he does not control the character of The Clock King.'

This suggests Finger thought either he should include Kane in his work out of some loyalty, or he believed he had to ask permission to use the character of the Clock King, perhaps assuming the various incarnations of clock-based criminals Finger had written over the years, like Batman, were owned in part by Kane.

Kane's dealings with the production company didn't do much to clear the situation up, but they revealed Kane had designs of his own. Aside from the regular rogues' gallery of the Joker, the Riddler, the Penguin and Catwoman, new villains provided an opportunity for the show to feature guest stars and that presented a chance for those in the know to get new properties on the show. A letter from Kane to Horwitz reveals the former had started working on a new character called The Scribbler – perhaps a play on Kane's childhood nickname 'The Doodler'. Kane suggests his 'Mad Artist' could be used as a vehicle for Walter Slezak or Robert Morley. Morley had been lined up for a role in the show but had pulled out and was replaced by Slezak, who ultimately took the role of The Clock King. These letters were sent after the Finger and Sinclair treatment and it is unclear if Kane got the information about the upcoming role from Horwitz or Finger. Kane also wrote that he was now free to work on new characters, but there didn't seem to be any indication whether this was freedom from a legal bind or whether he was just saying that as he had returned from his trip to Florida, which had delayed his response to Finger, and now had more free time. Regardless, the outcome was the same. Horwitz thanked Kane for his submission but gently let him down by informing him all roles had been cast and all the scripts needed for the show had already been commissioned.

Most of Kane's other correspondence regarded meeting producers at the Hollywood and New York premieres of the shows, but there were two others of note. One provides a little glimpse into Kane's softer side. Addressed to producer William Dozier, it is a request to set up a studio visit on behalf of Julius Schwartz and his family. The second letter, unfortunately, reinforces the idea of Kane as egomaniacal. It is a reply from Dozier to Kane, congratulating him on the recent success of the Batman comics at home and abroad (though Dozier makes sure to imply it is a result of the television show's success) but unfortunately the producers didn't see any merchandising money from increased circulation. He also added that as much as he'd like to, because the network had strict rules for how long individual credits could be shown on the screen, Bob's name could not appear in the screen for a longer amount of time than it did already.

'Hey Biljo...'

After Bill Finger finally received a writing credit for Batman, albeit the Adam West incarnation, he was riding high. His buddy and co-writer Sinclair recalled happily that Finger was delighted and almost moved to tears at seeing his name on the screen in glorious Technicolor. With Sinclair, he had created a career as a reliable and creative television writer with acclaim for his work on *77 Sunset Strip* and now, he had become the first comic book writer to make a successful shift to television and was working on the story he had helped to create. With this growing success came a little bit of money and Bill was able to visit a dentist. The crooked teeth which had made him anxious to smile were finally capped in brilliant white veneers. Not only did this give him a brilliant flash of a smile, it also made him more confident. As he revealed in his letter to Tom Fagan, other than golfing, working, and listening to records, he was dating a lot more. Sinclair recalled Finger being extremely courteous towards women and Sinclair's wife remarked that with his dark, bushy eyebrows and dazzling new smile, he had the appearance of a friendly wolf.

A lot of things were happening around this time in Finger's life. He was working with Sinclair on film and TV and was beginning to achieve some success in this field, and he was finally starting to be recognised for his work on the Batman comics too. The growing convention circuit, as well as the fanzines, had allowed Finger to step into the spotlight much more than he ever had before. Although he was not one for boasting, he would happily answer fans' questions and openly share his version of how Batman had come into being when he was asked. Finger and several other Batman writers, artists and editors (including Julius Schwartz) appeared at the fist Batman focused convention, Con-Cave, held in New York in August 1966, just months before the second season of *Batman* and Finger's 'The Clock King's Crazy Crimes' aired. Tom Fagan was there yet again and reported in *Batmania #14,* published in February of the following year, after Finger's episode had hit screens, a reiteration of Finger's involvement in the building of Batman and his universe. Finger didn't neglect Kane or imply instead that he and Jerry Robinson had done all the work. His account was consistently far more collaborative, though he did rebuke the idea of Kane's Penguin character as being inspired by a cigarette-selling mascot.

Once again, select New Yorkers at the convention as well as the dedicated Batmanians signed up to *Batmania's* mailing list, were given an account of their favourite character's history differing from the previously accepted reality. Among the community, 'Batman by Bob Kane' was a hot topic and one which needed answers. From Finger's perspective, these comments were just conversational anecdotes given to excited and admiring fans, they weren't an effort to set things straight. He may have been excited by the prospect of the Batman on the television bearing his name, but it is doubtful he would have felt he was overstepping a mark or deliberately causing trouble. After all, he had written to Fagan and explained he and Kane understood one another and there was no ill-will between them.

Batmania's editor, Biljo White, felt the discussion among the Batmanians and creators warranted a retort from Bob Kane (as if eighteen years of a solo credit printed in hundreds of Batman stories was not enough). Nearly two years after he had first received it, he decided to publish the letter he had been sent by Kane refuting Jerry Bail's (and therefore, Finger's) claims. Perhaps it was an innocent enough attempt to calm down Batmaniac discussion and present both sides of the story, but its lasting effect was that it placed Kane and Finger at loggerheads.

The letter itself opened with 'Hey Biljo' and set out to make three cases: Bob Kane was the sole creator of Batman and history would remember him that way, the 'New Look' Batman still involved Kane (but perhaps wasn't as good), and Bat-fans should be excited for the Batman television production (which had already aired by the time of publication). In reference to the 'A Finger In Every Plot' article, Kane wrote ferociously, but his frustration could have been directed at Jerry Bails, with Finger being part of the fallout. What is important to remember is this letter, written nearly two years earlier, may not have represented Kane's opinions on the matter at that time. As a matter of fact, at one point Kane remarked he would like to see Finger make the claims about the creation of Batman to his face, but we know from Finger's letter to Fagan written at the time of 'A Finger in Every Plot', the writer and artist had already talked this over to some extent. Nevertheless, Kane, in his temper, made contradictory and untrue claims. Annoyed as he was at Bails for failing to contact him, he still painted Finger as a boastful character who claimed far too much credit. And at one point, with a complete lack of self-awareness or lack of irony, he even accused Finger of delusions of grandeur.

Kane stressed *he* created Batman, the format, the costume, the name, and the masthead in 1939. He also stated many of the stories were his ideas and Finger simply typed them up. The problem was Kane would also later admit he originally had a character called Bird Man with a much different, Da Vinci-inspired costume, which Finger helped him to refine before they took the work to Vin Sullivan. Further, given Finger's direct use of *The Case of the Chemical Syndicate* in that first Batman adventure, even if the pair discussed story ideas, Finger clearly took the lead on putting the stories together.

Kane did concede, however, that Bill Finger was influential in the earliest Batman stories and was the creator of other characters who appeared in the books. He also stated that in the 25 years since Batman's inception, the truth and the myth of his creation had blended together – offered as a suggestion that he forgave Finger for his transgressions rather than a confession Kane himself might have got the facts wrong too. His attitude toward Finger in the letter switches from indignant to almost even-tempered. What irritated Bob doesn't seem to have been Finger's claims of involvement (which he continued to make at conventions after their discussion) but the framing of Bill as the true, side-lined and singular genius behind the Batman.

Unfortunately for Kane, he didn't explain his view of how Batman was created, which doesn't disprove his case but does somewhat weaken it. And the evidence he did provide was circular. Kane argued that if Finger was really the co-creator of Batman, then he would have been credited in the by-line, but as he wasn't, this was proof he wasn't the creator. He cites Siegel and Shuster's joint by-line on Superman as an example of co-creation but of course, it missed the entire issue. We might be quick to say that Kane actively reduced Finger's contributions, or was perhaps attempting to secure his position in history while protecting his contract with DC, but it's interesting that while he recognised collaboration in Siegel and Shuster's work and admitted how much support he had received in his creative work, he didn't accept how that support had contributed to his career.

In those early days, it had been Kane with the contacts, the experience and the entrepreneurial spirit while Finger had been his employee of sorts. But over the years, as Kane believed his own hype and the distance between the two grew, the dynamic had changed. In the same way Harry Donenfeld had created an environment for Superman to become a success, and later dismissed Siegel and Shuster's contributions, was this what Kane was doing to Finger?

In the section of the letter about the 'New Look' Batman, Kane reduced anonymous creators and ghost artists to followers and remarked they need to get credited in order to become leaders, although he of course knew that Finger was a major contributor to Batman. Once again Kane put the by-line credit for work ahead of the creation of the work. In Kane's mind, ownership ultimately came down to whoever had the first impulse to create the character and had the gumption to attain the matching legal status. Creator was a legal term, not a creative one as far as he was concerned.

As Finger pointed out in his letter to Fagan, much of Kane's annoyance with *Batmania* and Biljo White's editorial stance arose from the repeated claims that Kane was no longer top-dog in the Batman stable and not only was Carmine Infantino now the chief Batman artist, he was also better than Kane. Infantino and Kane did not get on, with the former thinking the latter a bully and 'a pain in the ass'. In the letter, Kane states, truthfully, that Infantino was only working on *Detective Comics* and was really a supporting player in the saga, but by publication, fans would have been aware of Infantino quickly catching up with the Golden Age copyist. As he had done with classmate Will Eisner, Kane freely admitted that Infantino was a better artist, but he did so with a proviso. Though Infantino was more illustrative and realistic, Kane claimed his style was mundane, mainstream and lacked individuality; and perhaps, most importantly, didn't adhere to Kane's more cartoonish and warped style.

It's an honest statement, especially when you recall the odd, drawn-out and dark style that Kane and his ghosts had followed in the early days, which was both iconic and fundamental to the tone of Batman. Despite the 'New Look' and the campy TV show, whenever an artist or film-maker talked about taking Batman back to his roots, it was always the Kane studio version (or an imitation of that version) they were aiming for.

Kane's letter makes two points which while irrelevant to his work in comics and his opinion of his co-workers tells us a couple of things worth considering. The first is that he claimed at the time he did not talk about his personal life much. This was true. Most interviews with Kane focused on his relationship to Batman, and even in this respect, he contradicted himself and knowingly or unknowingly lied. At the same time as he forced himself into the centre of the Batman myths, he ceased to be Bob Kane the person and created the image of Bob Kane the icon. Not only did this make Kane important and help him achieve the fame and success he desired, but it also protected him in sense. In the letter, he lamented the fact newspapers and journalists were becoming too obsessed with the private lives of movie stars.

He claimed fans were becoming too concerned with who lettered, pencilled, inked or coloured each issue. It is unclear why this would have been a problem, but when Kane had started out, things had certainly been different. But as the child fans of Batman aged, it is inevitable they became more interest in how their beloved comics were made, rather than focussing purely on the adventures in their pages. In the modern world, our relationship with celebrity has changed too. The rise of tabloid sensationalism and reality TV blurs the line between the public and private lives of the rich and famous. Kane was more old school in his approach and thought of his fame as a kind of status separate from his life. He wanted to be recognised without people knowing everything about him. Of course, once a persona is built up, it is difficult to ever take it down again.

The second point is Kane's involvement with charity. He mentioned in the letter his upcoming pop-art show in the Paul Stooshnoff Gallery at New York's Carlton House and briefly alluded to it being part of a Cancer Fund charity event. This could be read as Kane promoting his own generosity, but the event was only mentioned in passing and the rest of the section was much more concerned with the art itself rather than Kane's virtuous side. After his work on the Batman comics, Kane worked with several charities, particularly children's organisations, but he barely mentioned this fact in interviews or his biography. In some cases, he was selling his autographed paintings to the charities for a percentage of what they would have then sold at auction. There are certainly some ethical quandaries to consider if the work being auctioned by a charity organisation was actually the work of another artist paid by Kane with Bob simply adding his signature later, but the question we need to ask is why he would offer them up to a charity in the first place? There was certainly an existing market for the work and Kane could have made more money selling his art directly to collectors. The fact that he worked with charities and kept this largely to himself, suggests a side to Kane which doesn't really tally with his own myth of himself or the impression he made on others in the comics industry. While Bob may have always put himself first, this doesn't mean that he didn't ever consider anyone else. He had friends, family and causes he cared about, personal passions and a sense of spirituality, but none of these things were central to his identity as the creator of Batman, so he didn't talk about them.

The 'Hey Biljo' letter is significant because it appears to document a clash between Kane and Finger. It sets up a narrative of a self-aggrandising Kane angrily whitewashing the humble, unrecognised genius Bill Finger out of history. And while there was an element of truth in this, the sequence of events was sometimes misrepresented. The letter is often referred to as a direct and immediate response to Finger's statements at the 1965 New York Comic-Con, but by the time it was published, Finger and Kane had already spoken in person about the issue between them and had come to some agreement which at the very least resulted in Finger feeling it fine to publicly reiterate his point of view. What was published in the final issue of *Batmania,* was an angry excerpt from a fight which had finished a year and a half before.

There does not seem to be any record of a further falling out between the co-creators of Batman and neither seemed to hold a grudge against the other. By 1966 Kane essentially stopped drawing for comics and all his work was carried out by Moldoff for the next few years. Finger, meanwhile, was having some success on television and had finally gotten a by-line on Batman, but his comics career was about to take a turn for the worst.

The Writers' Purge

Between 1967 and1969, the writers at DC were becoming uneasy with their positions at the company. Several, including Finger, began to form an impromptu union. They had several goals; an increased page rate, company health insurance and ultimately, ownership of some of the properties they worked on. Mort Weisinger's continued abuse of writers only stoked the flames of frustration among them. Many had been working for DC for years and had seen the company grow fat on their work while they scraped by. The writers would meet at homes or in venues across New York to discuss what they could do to improve their lot. Finger wasn't known for taking a hard line with editors or concerned with making sure he got his by-lines but of all DC's entire stable of artists and writers, with the exception of Siegel and Shuster, he had missed out the most on benefitting from his creation. The group faced two major problems.

The first was artists. Comics are a visual medium. The chance of a book being bought more often relies on the skill of the artist over the writer. DC was aware of this. They valued artists, who were specialists in their field, over writers, who were considered easily replaceable. The writer's union needed to get the artists on their side if they were to make an impact. But the artists were in a much better financial position than the writers. They received a much higher page rate and did not want to unnecessarily jeopardise their positions, so while they sympathised with their colleagues they did not lend their support in large numbers.

The second obstacle was the duo of Irwin Donenfeld and Jack Liebowitz. Though Irwin's father Harry had been brutal with employees at times, he knew when to offer an olive branch. Harry had personally paid for some of Joe Shuster's eye treatment as the Superman artist started to lose his sight. Harry knew these minor gifts kept the wheels greased and stood him in good stead when it came to telling creators to get lost on issues of bigger payments and copyright. Irwin wasn't as charming or as well respected amongst the creative teams as his father had been. Whenever a representative would come forth on behalf of the writers, the younger Donenfeld, he would offer a small raise for that individual on the grounds they kept it from the others. In effect, he was trying to offer out as little as possible to break the union. It was largely ineffective in quelling unhappiness among the writers and instead increased their solidarity.

Liebowitz, who had done so much to keep the International Ladies' Garment Workers' Union alive in the 1930s, was much more calculating and knew time could kill the writers' revolt. He had fought off similar attempts to unionise in the 1950s by giving writers a $2 increase in page rates across the company, deflating the larger movement for character ownership and healthcare. After a few skirmishes with disgruntled writers, Liebowitz came to the group with the outline of how to move forward. It wasn't the case the company was simply being difficult with the writers, but in their rush for more benefits, the writers hadn't considered the legal complications of the company handing over part ownership of the properties he said. There were hundreds of characters at this point, both major and minor, as well as books built using multiple properties, and the matter of figuring out just who had contributed how much to each character was clearly extremely complicated. Furthermore, how do you account for the work of long-serving writers who had not created characters but had authored their stories for years now? It was a difficult issue which could cause the writers more trouble than they'd bargained for, so Liebowitz suggested he would let the legal department work on the matter and come up with some solutions regarding who owned what. Then, he would work out the small matter of money.

Liebowitz was stalling for time. He knew DC was going to be purchased by Kinney National, a multimedia conglomerate which would later become Warner Communications. This meant corporate restructure.

Meanwhile, artist Carmine Infantino had done a brilliant job on the 'New Look' Batman and sales were back on track. He was taking on more work across the DC lines, and because of Julies Schwartz's new approach of giving creative teams by-lines on books they had worked on, Infantino was becoming a celebrity amongst comics' fans. At this time, Stan Lee was head writer, art director and editor of Marvel, and DC's chief threat. Lee tried to poach Infantino from DC with a $20,000 pay cheque. DC could not match the offer, so instead he was promoted to art director, and he later became DC's editorial director when the company was taken over by Kinney National. This gave Infantino control over the entire DC line, and in a few years, he would return the favour by poaching comics legend Jack 'The King' Kirby from Marvel.

There was some support for the writers from a few of the artists and some of the editors, but it was waning while Liebowitz's legal decoy was being dealt with. At the same time, Infantino, who was initially sympathetic to the writers, was becoming a company man. He got on with Donenfeld and Liebowitz and was good for business. As he started his tenure as editorial director he began to draft in new editors. In turn, they drafted in new writers. These new, excited and bright-eyed writers were happy to be starting their careers and didn't know or care enough to support previous and ageing stable. The Golden Age writers were frozen out. Writer Arnold Drake claimed new editor Joe Orlando told him over dinner he would not employ any writers over 35 while Justice League of America writer Mike Friedrich strongly suspected the new editorial direction had been suggested by the corporate heads of the company to stop the writer's union from gaining better benefits. Whatever the case, it was the older writers, who had over the years made DC millions, who ultimately lost out. Bill Finger, Otto Binder, Gardner Fox and a slew of other writers were all but blacklisted in the DC offices. Bill Finger's last Batman story would be published in 1968, the same year – the television show was cancelled.

Infantino's ascension to the top of DC comics was well deserved but sadly, it came at the inadvertent expense of numerous Golden Age creators. Though Kane had stopped drawing in 1966, or at least claiming to draw, it was not until Infantino became editor that Kane would stop having oversight on the Batman comics. He and Infantino never saw eye to eye but Batman was riding a wave of popularity and Kane's contract was up for renewal. He resigned the editorial input he previously had on the character while in return retaining the continuing recognition as the sole, legal creator of Batman and a percentage of merchandising. He was also given a golden good-bye in the form of $1 million to be paid out in $50,000 instalments for the following twenty years. His first contract had not accounted for Bill Finger, his second contract may have jeopardised Siegel and Shuster's legal campaign to regain the rights to Superman, and his final contract would end with Batman's most prominent artist, Sheldon Moldoff, out in the cold.

Moldoff was no stranger to being disregarded by Kane. In the early years of Batman, Moldoff had inked, lettered, and provided backgrounds for Bob. Kane's Father took a shine to Shelly. The kid was a couple of years younger than his own son and like Bob, had grown up in the Bronx and attended the same comic-book legend generating high school. There were talks of the Kane patriarch setting up an office for Bob and Shelly where they could work together to create new comic characters. The plan never came to fruition, but they had discussed the idea of working on a new boy superhero together. Of course, that character would turn out to be the Boy

Wonder, Robin. Moldoff only found out after dropping off work in Vin Sullivan's office and seeing pages featuring the character, illustrated by Jerry Robinson, on Sullivan's desk. Moldoff, who turned 20 in the same month Robin was introduced to the public, was upset by this betrayal. Sullivan was reluctant about the inclusion of a child character anyway and told Moldoff editorial was struggling with Kane's light fingers with other creators' work. He offered to spike the story for Shelly, but with no concrete proof Robin had been his idea, Moldoff walked away. Finger and Robinson were apparently unaware of Moldoff's previous involvement with the concept of a boy sidekick. Their accounts trace back to Kane but no further, while Kane's account started and ended with himself.

Moldoff fell out with Kane and went to get work elsewhere in comics. They did not talk to one another for a decade as they were both building their reputations. Then, in the fifties, a chance encounter at a cartoonist's industry weekend retreat brought them back together. Moldoff had established himself as a reliable artist and Kane needed a ghost artist to help with his new contractual obligation of 365 pages a year. The two patched up their partnership, shook hands and worked out a gentlemen's deal; a steady flow of pages for Shelly to draw in return for Moldoff's keeping schtum about doing the work. Moldoff became Kane's chief ghost from 1953 to the day Kane left comics.

Moldoff was shocked when Kane stepped away in 1967 but didn't bear him ill will. While he was working on Batman, with editors completely unaware of his arrangement with Kane, he worked on countless other books and was thankful for the steady work. Like Finger, he seems to have valued a continuous income over recognition. While Kane paid him on the side for his ghost work, he was also regularly receiving cheques from the editors at DC who never mentioned his work on the Dark Knight. Like every other artist working for DC, Moldoff knew the work Kane did do was mostly swiped, copies of past classics, but unlike his contemporaries he respected Kane as an artist. He thought of himself as an extension to Kane, following his direction for a treasured vision Kane couldn't quite express alone. He thought Kane had great visual ideas, but he just couldn't draw them. Moldoff left comics once Kane handed over the Bat-reins to Infantino but was content with a career in animation and advertising, as well as the reprint royalties he received on the three years' worth of 'New Look' books which featured his by-line courtesy of Julius Schwartz.

Chapter Seven

Life After Comics

Batman was now bigger than the comics and so was Bob Kane. In 1966 Kane became a regular guest star on a popular kid's show called *Wonderama*. Filmed in New York, local celebrities were easy to book for the show and Kane hosted a regular feature where he would draw out Batman and his supporting cast in front of a live studio audience. Joe Giella had worked as a ghost on the Batman syndicated newspaper strip and had signed off his work with Bob Kane's signature for years. He had no problem with the fact Kane was just tracing over his lightly pencilled work the cameras couldn't pick up. Like Moldoff before him, a job was a job.

New York was the home of publishing and comics, but Hollywood was dominated by film and television. With his £50,000 a year buy-out, Kane relocated on a more permanent basis to Hollywood. He happily played the part of celebrity promoter for the Batman television series and enjoyed a movie star lifestyle. Aside from the few noted examples, he generally avoided comic conventions and fan events. But off the back of the success of the Batman TV show, Kane was able to combine his relative success in television and his celebrity for a new venture.

Kane worked with King Features Syndicated to create another cartoon television series. Producer Al Brodax must have been counting his lucky stars when he met Kane to discuss ideas. Brodax had been made head of King Features' film and television department at around the same time *Courageous Cat and Minute Mouse* aired. *Batman* had been an international phenomenon while Kane was more than familiar with King properties, having grown up on and swiping from *Flash Gordon,* plus briefly working on *Betty Boop* while at Fleischer Studios. Now Kane was pitching a cartoon series lampooning the 1965 smash hit *Get Smart* from Mel Brooks and Buck Henry. *Cool McCool* only ran for a single series but was well received. Each episode featured two segments. The first starring Cool McCool, a trench coat-wearing, gadget spy with an asterisk shaped moustache taking on supervillains in a contemporary setting. The second feature followed Harry McCool, the beat cop father of Cool, whose adventures took place decades earlier and who would act as the inspiration for Cool to improve his police work and surpass his comedy limitations. The show might seem hammy to modern audiences, but it had a few moments of genuine humour as it pastiched shows and films like James Bond, *Get Smart* and *The Prisoner.* Still, Kane, couldn't help but cannibalise both Batman and Courageous Cat yet again in his new project. Cool's favourite mode of transport was the Cool-Mobile while regular villains the Owl, the Rattler, Jack-In-A-Box and Dr Madcap were all thinly veiled parodies of Bat-villains The Penguin (Bob's favourite), the Riddler, the Joker and the Mad Hatter.

Though it only ran for one season, it was re-run for three years across networks. But it was small fry compared to the Brodax's other cartoon concerns, namely the animated adaption of The Beatles' *Yellow Submarine.* Even Batman and Bob Kane were nothing compared to Beatlemania.

While Kane had managed to capitalise on Batman, Finger was having to look at other creative avenues. The slow phasing out of his regular work at DC and his perpetual money troubles meant Bill had to find a regular gig to keep the wolves from the door. This is what prompted him to enter the complicated world of international science-fiction B-movies.

Science fiction was once again gaining momentum in the pop culture consciousness. *Star Trek* had aired in 1966 and *2001: A Space Odyssey* would come to theatres only a few years later. Like comics, science fiction had gone through a golden age carried by the pulps, and in the crucible of the space race, New Wave writers began to push the boundaries of what science fiction could be. Writers like Frank Herbert, Ursula K. Guin and J.G. Ballard stoked an interest in a new, more literary approach to genre fiction. Sadly, Finger's work in the genre would not be the same.

The Gamma 1 Quadrilogy

Metro Goldwyn Meyer (MGM) decided to capitalise on the speculative fiction boom of the 1950s and 1960s. New York-based producers Ivan Reiner and Walter Manley, working for MGM, invested in director Anthony M. Dawson to produce a science fiction series. Dawson was the Americanised working name of Italian genre-fiction director

Antonio Margheriti. Margheriti had been a science-fiction fanatic as a boy and had made a name for himself in Europe directing sci-fi, horror and western movies that were colourful, over the top, and most importantly, cheap. American studios loved to film in Italy as the production costs were far lower and the unions less interfering than their American cousins. Also, European directors had their own distinct style and they were far less concerned with swiping material from other directors, most notably, Japanese filmmakers; swapping out samurai and ronin for gunslingers and outlaws. The prominence of filming these inexpensive genre pieces in Italy gave rise to the term Spaghetti Western.

Over the course of three months, Margheriti produced four films for MGM, with just two weeks shooting time for each feature. Initially, they were intended to be features on *Fantascienza* (literally translated as 'science fiction'), an Italian television series, but MGM was so pleased with the results that it decided to give the films a theatrical release. The series, which would become known as the Gamma One Quadrilogy featured, *The Wild, Wild Planet*, *The War of The Planets*, *War Between the Planets* and *Snow Devils*. Because the films mostly revolved around the titular Gamma One space station, this allowed Margheriti to recycle props, special effects, footage, and actors from each feature.

As a bugbear to all science-fiction cinema historians, each film had numerous release dates and titles as well as a loose approach to sequence and continuity. They were probably all filmed in either 1964 or 1965 and released out of sequence over the following seven years.

Bill Finger's involvement in the series is equally confusing. The Internet Movie Database lists Bill (as William Finger) and Charles Sinclair as writers on the fourth film, *Snow Devils*. This is confirmed *The Batman Archives Volume 3* which mentions Finger being the writer of *Death Comes to Planet Aytin*, one of the many monikers *Snow Devils* was billed under, and it is corroborated in statements made by Sinclair. However, in the same interview, Sinclair mentioned he and Bill made five films together. One of which was *Snow Devils*, with two other non-Gamma One flicks coming later. This leaves two Finger-scripted movies unaccounted for. It is entirely possible that Sinclair forgot how many films he and Finger wrote together or, given the tight turnaround on the production of the features, the pair did work in some capacity on other films in the Gamma 1 series. But of course, the two missing credits and *Snow Devils* don't make a full Quadrilogy.

Producer Ivan Reiner is listed as a co-writer as well as a producer on the series but it may be the case that Finger and Sinclair were drafted for some uncredited rewrites on two of the three pre-*Snow Devils* movies.

Further muddying the waters is the fact *Snow Devils* seemed to have a much sillier approach to storytelling than its predecessors (the plot follows Gamma One's attempt to stop blue-faced aliens invading the Himalayas) and it is visually distinct from the rest of the series. This could have been Finger's Batman sensibilities sneaking into the script, perhaps indicating it was the only film he worked on, or it could have been a result of Margheriti leaving the production early to start work on his next batch of films and his assistant taking over the final filming.

In yet another plot twist, the relative success to the cost of the series meant Reiner and Manley wanted a fifth film in the four-part series, but this time, they would go to Japan. MGM took the Gamma One property and, working with Toei, made *The Green Slime* based on a script from Finger and Sinclair. This gives us two of the five potential movies Sinclair alluded to (the third film they definitively worked on coming later). All things considered, it seems more likely the duo worked in some capacity on more than one film in the Gamma One series, which was very quickly made. They were probably then regularly credited when the property changed production methods once Margheriti left, and later when it involved Toei. Even if Finger only ever worked on *Snow Devils* and Sinclair was mistaken about their output, at least Bill had the opportunity to work in the foreign cinema he loved so much, even if it was a rapidly churned out sci-fi romp.

Directed by Kinja Fukasaku, who would become renowned for directing *Tora! Tora!* and *Battle Royale, The Green Slime* has been largely forgotten by anyone outside sci-fi/Japanese cinema fandoms. In the story, astronauts from the Gamma Three space station accidentally traipsed through intergalactic sludge on an away mission and brought it back to base where it promptly mutated and caused general mayhem on the ship. It was a disaster and was panned by the critics. Finger and Sinclair's writing was considered passable for this kind of pulp science fiction outing, but the special effects completely undermined their work. To make matters worse, it was released at the same time as Stanley Kubrick's *2001: A Space Odyssey*, instantly making it look dated and childish by comparison. But *The Green Slime* did have some other cinematic significance. It was one of the first joint US/Japan productions, with MGM supplying Finger and Sinclair's script as well as the cash for the Japanese unit to work on. Previously, Japanese films had been dubbed and reshot in order for them to be resold to the American market, but this film was designed with the potential audience in mind from the beginning. Like Batman, it was cashing in on a successful genre already established; only this time, despite Finger's work, it didn't pay out.

Hard times

As the 1960s started to close, Bill was finding less and less work. He had been frozen out of the DC talent pool, *The Green Slime* had been a massive flop, and his TV work was drying up. But in 1968, Finger was in love. After 13 years of dating Lyn Simmons, who he had met while he was still married, the couple decided to tie the knot. Finger had by then been separated from Portia for five years but Lyn later recalled that Bill's divorce wasn't finalised until only a few years before they got married. The two lived together intermittently before their wedding and Simmons had children from her previous marriage. She lived out in Great Neck, Long Island, where Bill would join her and her three kids. Bill's comic life was all but behind him and Simmons rarely met any of his old DC pals. And as the years passed, Bill's relationship with his own son Fred, who was 15 when his father remarried, became increasingly distant.

While they were together Bill was offered the chance to head out to Hollywood to work on the Superman animated series, but he had turned it down to stay in New York. He was a re-married man by then with a wife, an ex-wife, a son and stepchildren to look after. Turning down work was not a sustainable option, so Bill found a new job. He started working at the Army Pictorial Centre on Long Island. The Pictorial Centre was a movie studio owned by the army and was operated by the Signals Corps. It was here they produced training material for new recruits. Before the military bought it, it was where New York acts like the Marx Brothers had filmed their features.

There is a tradition of comic creators working with the Signals. Stan Lee had served in the Second World War as one of the nine soldiers whose job description had been 'playwright'. Lee's unit also included Dr Seuss himself, Theodore Geisel, and Charles Addams, the cartoonist who created the New Yorker strip 'The Addams Family'.

Famously (or infamously) Lee helped to create the 'VD? Not Me!' campaign designed to protect promiscuous G.I.s stationed in Europe.

Bob Kane's old pal and sometime rival Will Eisner also worked with the military. It was during this time he created the comic character Joe Dope; an oafish character used to humorously demonstrate the importance of proper equipment maintenance, use, and repair.

Lee had been known as the writer of Captain America and Eisner was the creator of the Spirit when they worked in the army. If the Pictorial Centre had known that Finger was the co-creator of Batman, he might have been given a better role and enjoyed his time there more. Finger worked on the scripts for training films, receiving neither the recognition nor creative freedom of those who came before him. Both Simmons and Sinclair recalled him hating his work there. Travelling was a slog and the work was dull. Luckily, he was only there for a few years. Unluckily, his marriage lasted the same amount of time.

Sinclair said the two had been much happier before their marriage but at least they seem to have split-up on relatively good terms. Sadly, Simmons' eldest son lived across the country in California and was in a tragic traffic accident. Lyn moved out west to look after her boy, but Finger did not follow, and they were divorced by 1971. Finger had been terrified of flying but there are a few additional factors beyond Bill's travel anxiety which may have contributed to the break-up. Finger's health was declining and he suffered another heart attack in 1970. Portia, perhaps justifiably, had not been easy for Lyn to deal with and Finger's first ex-wife still harassed him for alimony money, which he was struggling to get as his career was stagnating. While he and Lyn had been courting, he'd still been married to Portia so hadn't had to pay her any maintenance. Back then he'd also been having some measurable success. As all that started to slip away, it must have caused frustration between him and Lyn. Other creators who visited Finger implied Lyn had been overly flirtatious with Bill's friends which likely exacerbated the turmoil between them. Despite all this, Lyn still called Bill regularly to chat on the phone and they maintained a decent relationship from their respective coasts.

Bill moved back into the city. He still had his friendship with Sinclair, but Charles had his own family and work issues to deal with. Sinclair would later say it was around this time that Finger started to withdraw from socialising. With Sinclair following his own career and the editors at DC favouring new writers, Bill did not seem able to get much work of his own. Although he did give some of few known interviews to comics historians at this time, again staking his claim to be co-creator of Batman.

The Steranko Incident

In 1970, quotes from Finger appeared in *The Steranko History of Comics Vol. 1* by Jim Steranko and Finger was referred to as the creator of Batman in equal terms to Bob Kane. The story presented in Steranko's book seemed even-handed regarding the claims made by Finger, Kane, and Jerry Robinson. Once again, this demonstrates that Finger and Kane may have come to some comfortable truce about Batman's origins. Bob could have the fame and money, but he could not stop Finger (or Robinson) from telling their sides of the story.

At the time his book was published, Steranko was a writer and artist superstar at Marvel and a part of the Silver Age revolution taking over comics. His success at wrestling a writing by-line from Stan Lee would contribute in part to Jack Kirby's defection to DC comics under Carmine Infantino. Being in the position of writer/artist and understanding the importance of those two skill sets interacting effectively probably contributed to Steranko's respect for Finger, who was recognised for his visual approach to writing. Conversely, Steranko's business savvy, superstardom and celebrity wasn't too far from Kane's. Years later, at the 2014 San Diego Comic-Con, Steranko would become entwined with the legend of Bob Kane. At a panel, Steranko reiterated his admiration for Bill Finger and mentioned he would occasionally hang out with the writer while he was working at DC, spotting him $20 here and there, or taking him out for dinner and covering the bill. He also mentioned he wanted *The Steranko History of Comics* to be a positive look at comics, so left out a lot of the negative stories he had heard about Bob Kane, saying that among the comics community, Steranko hadn't met anyone who really knew him or had anything positive to say about him. On this panel, Steranko was prompted to recall an encounter with Kane after the publication of his books on comics' history.

Steranko was introduced to Kane and his hangers-on in the morning, and after a brief chat, Kane said farewell to Steranko then stepped into an elevator. As the doors were closing, Kane slapped Steranko on the face and said, 'See you later, Jim baby.' This huge personal slight and the stories Steranko had heard about Kane played on Steranko's mind all night and he could not let the slap go. So, he allegedly set off into the evening to find Kane and upon finding him slapped him in the face saying, 'See you later, Bob baby.'

That story has become a humorous anecdote in comic circles. The idea of Kane getting his comeuppance is inherently entertaining. Steranko claimed Kane was unwilling to get into a fight despite Kane having a clear height advantage – though Steranko didn't mention it, he was nearly twenty-five years Kane's junior and at the very earliest this could have happened Kane would have been 58 (Steranko's second history of comics was published in 1972) and besides, he might not have had any idea he had offended Steranko.

But Steranko may have been correct in a broader sense about Kane's fear of conflict. What we see in Kane's reactions to Finger's statements and the constant propping up of his ego is based on the fear he could have lost it all. He would cease to be the most important man in the room, which bear in mind, was usually filled with people with much more talent than he had. Once we consider that Kane was probably scared, it is much harder to see him as just a villain.

Bill alone

Finger had all but become a recluse by the early 1970s. His career was diminished, his cash was dwindling, and his health was deteriorating. In 1972 he gave a brief interview to Robert Porfirio about his involvement in the creation of Batman, his reaction to the Comics Code Authority, and Fredric Wertham's critique of Batman and Robin as a homosexual couple. It was here Finger dismissed that idea and referred to having known gay people (see *Seduction of The Innocent*, Chapter Six). Certainly, his ex-wife had been involved with the LGBT community while they lived in the Village and chances are Finger at least socialised with gay people. His own son, Fred, now in his mid-twenties, was also bisexual. Though it seems Finger was accepting of homosexuality in general, Bill's second wife Lyn, in an interview with Marc Tyler Nobleman, suggested Fred's sexuality caused some friction between the father and son. Though Finger had been an attentive father in Fred's youth, at least when he had been around, a distance was growing between them, figuratively and literary, as Fred was living in San Francisco. Bill's time at the Army Pictorial Centre caused some tension between the two also. Both Bill and his son were pacifists and as much as it pained Bill to be working for the military, for Fred it was a betrayal of everything his father claimed to have stood for. America had been at war with Vietnam for several years; Bill's involvement with the military and Fred's liberal upbringing by his mother were clashing – not as a matter of differing opinions, but as a matter of morality.

Separated from two ex-wives, his parents and siblings, and now with a rocky relationship with his son, while living in a small, one-bedroom apartment, Bill was becoming increasingly isolated. As talented a writer as Bill Finger was, his work had largely been facilitated by the connections of others; first Bob Kane, then pals at the DC offices and then Charles Sinclair. Outside the cottage industry of comics historians, Bill Finger was starting to disappear entirely. No one was asking him for his work, and he was not putting anything out there.

It's also worth noting the same Porfirio interview features one of the very few times Finger seems to have publicly spoken out against Kane, saying the artist used him as a tool to bolster his own pay cheques. It is an assessment of their relationship that is brutal in its honesty. But this seems to refer to the earliest days of Batman, when everything was run through Kane, including Bill's pay, and the writer hadn't yet started working directly under contract for National. It was a passing statement which without context seemingly expressed an ongoing frustration with Kane rather than something which was resolved.

Eventually, Charles Sinclair came to Bill with a job offer. Sinclair had got the tip-off film production companies were looking to cash in on New Mexico's new state subsidies for filmmakers. Essentially, the state was offering benefits and tax reductions to film production companies in return for the boost they could bring to local economies. Sinclair did some quick research into New Mexico with its rich myths and folklore and got in touch with Finger. They had a tight deadline and a few ideas to play with, so they bashed out the script over a weekend. Sinclair described their resulting film as, 'a literary one-night stand, honest to God. It came, it went, and I kind of forgot about it. Mercifully perhaps.'

They met with the producers over coffee, debated the fee (Sinclair could not recall if it was $20,000 or $12,000, which he and Finger of course split) and sold the script. Initially entitled *The Lunar Analog*, the film was released as *Track of the Moonbeast*. The Moonbeast in question was a mineralogist struck by lunar debris which caused him to transform into a reptile every full moon. By a phenomenal chance of fate, this same event had happened in the past and was documented in Native American legend. *Track of the Moonbeast* was another budget science fiction feature released to poor reception. Sinclair suggested he and Finger had been quite mercenary about the work, looking to make a quick buck. Sinclair had forgotten (or suppressed the memory) he had even worked on the movie until years later. His son called him up one evening to tell him it was being shown on *Mystery Science Theatre 3000,* a comedy show featuring terrible old movies the host is forced to watch as a form of torture; retaining his sanity only by mocking the film with his robot companions. Interestingly, the unaired pilot of *Mystery Science Theatre 3000,* created to sell the unusual concept of characters talking over the showing of a bad movie had used Finger and Sinclair's *The Green Slime* as the featured B-movie. This prompts the question, was Batman co-creator Bill Finger also a passive co-creator of the cult, sci-fi satire show, *Mystery Science Theatre 3000?*

Track of the Moonbeast* was the last project Finger and Sinclair worked on together. It is a disappointing final outing for the writing duo and a far cry from the excellent genre work they had done for television. They had been great crime and detective fiction writers with a deft grasp of the tropes and trappings of the genre but when it came to science fiction, limited budgets brought out the worst in rush-job scripts. Finger would not get to see *Track of the Moonbeast* or even enjoy it being lampooned. Though it was finished in 1972, it wasn't released until 1976, two years after Finger's death.

The late Bill Finger

In July 1973, at the New York Comic art convention, strange amendments to comic history were being made. Not only had Bob Kane travelled from sunny LA to speak to comic fans, Fredric Wertham, the psychologist who had painted comics-reading as the deviant practice of juvenile delinquents also appeared. The scales had fallen from Wertham's eyes. Not only did he express regret at limiting children's access to stories, but he had also reached the new conclusion that comic book fandom and fanzines promoted literacy and creativity and helped young fans build communities together. In the same year, he published a book detailing his new theory, entitled *The World of Fanzines: A Special Form of Communication*. Alas, it was too little too late. Batman had already and repeatedly undergone changes (some for the better) while the comics industry had set the regulations which all but choked the life out of horror and crime comics. Wertham would be remembered as the witch hunter of comics and his new approach would be forgotten, ignored, and overshadowed by his more sinister legacy. Kane would suffer a similar fate.

Bob appeared at a luncheon panel alongside fellow cartoonists C.C. Beck and Sol Harrison. He mentioned he was still on the National payroll and that he was working on a new television project he called *The Bob Kane Show*. The brief outline he gave for the show was a half-hour children's programme with 'how-to-draw' segments and educational features about comic book history and, maybe as an off-colour joke, about what happened when young men discovered young girls. Perhaps thankfully, there is no evidence the show was developed beyond these comments.

Like Wertham, Kane also made several statements suggesting a change in the narrative of comic's history. He made a public complaint that creators receive less per television episode in royalties than whoever wrote the episode and he made the case for a creators' guild which would help to protect the livelihood of creators of popular characters. He proposed a creators' union which could help creators retain a percentage of the rights to properties. It was an unusual stance for Kane to have taken, given that he was one of the few comic creators who retained some ownership of his character and needn't have advocated for something he already had. By the time of the Writers' Purge, he had also effectively retired and, lest we forget, Gerald Jones claimed that Kane used Siegel and Shuster's lobbying for control of Superman to his own ends. But even back when he was schlepping the streets on Manhattan in his *WOW! What a Magazine* days he had mentioned to Will Eisner the idea of an artist's union. It may be Kane was speaking for his own interests, but he must have been quite conflicted about his position in the world of comics. As with his charity work, just because Kane thought about himself before anyone else doesn't mean he never thought about others. What was good for all artists, would be good for Bob too.

On the same panel, Kane admitted that he didn't write a lot of the Batman stories and relied on ghosts. Writing, in this sense, seems to be more general as Kane never wrote any scripts for Batman but he did contribute to

118

the discussions about stories. Not only does Kane soften his hold over the Batman creation myth here, but he also doled out an unofficial credit to Bill Finger, describing him both as the unsung hero of Batman and instrumental in the creation of the denizens and stories of Gotham. Here Kane all but admitted to Finger's contribution without saying he was the co-creator. It's was line Kane wouldn't or couldn't cross, and he said the only reason Finger never received a by-line on the Batman comics, unfortunately, was because Finger joined the process after Kane had created the Batman figure. Still, Kane referred to Finger as the best example of a Batman writer and he also mentioned that he hadn't seen him in a while.

Finger suffered a third heart attack in 1973. Both his ex-wives were aware of the situation but their literal distance and Bill's seclusion meant there was little they could do to help him. Comics colourist Sol Harrison, on the panel with Kane, mentioned he had bumped into Bill at National, where Finger had managed to get some freelance work, writing suspense tales for DC's mystery anthology series *House of Mystery* under artist and editor Joe Orlando. Finger had handed in one of the two scripts he'd been commissioned to write. The second script, true to form, was going to be late.

In California on the 17th of January 1974, Lyn Simmons waited for her ex-husband in New York to pick up the phone. She would often call in the evenings when she knew Bill would be home to chat with him; she knew Bill was a night owl who liked to work on scripts under the cover of darkness. When she didn't get an answer she was worried and called Charles Sinclair to get to the bottom of it.

Sinclair had a key to Bill's apartment and when he entered on that Friday afternoon, he found Bill dead, face down on his couch. He had died as a result of atherosclerosis, a condition of the heart. He was only 59 years old. As comic's historian Marc Tyler Nobleman notes, Finger's death certificate summarised his life in a tragic way – 'No history. No family'.

Of course, that wasn't true and Bill's son Fred gave his father a send-off that stood as a testament to both his history and his family. After his father was cremated, Fred took the ashes to a beach in Oregon. He poured them onto the beach in the shape of a bat for the drifting tide to take away. Despite a fractured father-son relationship, and Bill all but unremembered in the public eye, this touching goodbye was an elegant expression of Bill Finger's life and legacy by his family.

Though Finger was still unknown outside of the comics industry and his death, like his life, may have gone unnoticed by the general public, his contribution to comics was well known and respected amongst his peers. He was not the first Golden Age creator to have died, but his relatively young age and the massive impact he had on comics could not go uncommented on.

The Amazing World of DC was a mail-order exclusive fanzine produced by fans turned artists on behalf of DC. It was a behind the scenes look at life in the DC offices for dedicated enthusiasts. It's very first issue was released in the summer following Finger's death and featured a memorial written by Edward Nelson Bridwell. Bridwell had written for *MAD magazine* and the Batman syndicated newspaper strip and he had the unofficial post of 'continuity cop' at DC, where he tried to keep a track of stories to make sure they didn't contradict one another. It is fitting that he should be the one to record Finger's contribution. The page features Batman stood mournfully next to a cenotaph remembering the late writer. Again, with a certain sense of poetic circularity, the image was actually a swipe of a Neil Adams Superman cover modified by Carl Gafford. Bridwell's testimony is short but presents Finger's design contribution to Batman and his extensive comics work beyond the Caped Crusader. It ends with the statement, 'Few men have contributed as much to comics as Bill Finger.'

In the same year, the New York Comic Art Convention had a full-page tribute to Finger in their programme. It featured a Dark Knight, looming over a headstone engraved with the poet John Masefield's quote, 'His imagination has made life an intense practice of all the lovelier energies'.

Batman #259 published in the autumn following Finger's death featured a small dedication to the writer too. It appeared in front of a cross over story between Batman and the Shadow, only the second time this had happened. In this story, a young Bruce Wayne is traumatised after he witnessed the Shadow using a gun to save his parents from a mugging. Not only does this imply Wayne's parents had a knack for attracting criminals, it retrospectively explained why Batman didn't use guns. Like Finger had done almost thirty-five years early, it placed the Shadow at the centre of Batman's identity and in a way, for those in the know, it placed Finger there too.

Carmine Infantino, who had now reached the top of DC and had taken on the role of publisher, went a step further with his tribute to Bill in the 1975 *Famous First Editions Vol.1 #5*. The series featured reprints of Golden Age comics and Infantino dedicated this reprint of

Batman #1 to Finger in his editorial. Not only did Infantino include a similar biography to Bridgwell's from the year before, but he also leaned further into Finger's efforts to take Kane's earliest sketches of Batman and turn them into the recognisable icon he became. Almost in passing, Infantino suggested that Kane's Batman was broken until Finger offered his thoughts.

Sadly, Infantino's editorial gaze would not stretch over the entire DC catalogue. Issue 10 of *The Amazing World of DC*, also released in 1976, around a year and a half after Finger's death, featured a six-page story mocking the writer. It was penned by Batman ghost writer David Vern Reed, who had worked on the Gotham Guardian throughout the 1950s alongside Finger while the story was illustrated by Ramona Fradon, who was best known her work on Aquaman. Reed and Fradon put together a story about Phil Binger (clearly a spoonerism of Bill Finger) called *Through the Wringer*. It starred a talented DC writer who was perpetually late with scripts and constantly asking The Editor, a character bearing some semblance to Julius Schwartz, for advances. Binger's excuses for late scripts became increasingly dramatic and convoluted and the plot ends up with the character literally dying as part of his research process. The Editor could only escape being haunted by the spirit of the late writer when he handed over yet another advance.

If you had just stumbled across the comic with no context it was genuinely quite a funny story in the vein of *Tales of The Unexpected* or *The Twilight Zone*. But given it was published so quickly after Finger's death, and it was so obviously meant to be Finger, its publication was perhaps in poor taste. The story was also presented by the character Cain from *The House of Mystery*, the series Finger had been working on when he died, so the whole thing had the air of a bad taste joke. Fradon later claimed she had no idea the character was based on a real person as she mostly worked away from the DC offices. The editor had been Carl Gafford, who had worked on the image for Bridwell's tribute in *The Amazing World of DC* the year before and Reed had worked as a writer with Finger in the 1950s, so it's hard to imagine the story was created out of spite or some unmentioned rivalry with Finger. The story was complimentary to the late writer's talent, and in part, it may have been written in jest, but it certainly seems like no one stopped to ask if it was a good idea to reduce Finger's impact on the comics industry to a punch line, told by a character named Cain no less.

Chapter Eight

What Bob Did Next

It would be hard to claim Bob's life after Batman was a failure given his enormous payout and his percentage of merchandising rights plus the fact that he could always claim to be the creator of Batman. He was living his life as a semi-retired semi-celebrity, cashing in where he could on the Dynamic Duo's success. But at the same time, he never really broke free from the success of his earlier achievements either. Throughout the 1970s, he continued with his one-man art shows and contributed paintings to charity organisations. Many of the paintings attributed to him are still in circulation amongst collectors today and provide small glimpses into the organisations that Kane worked with. But for the large part, Batman had moved on without Kane. Without help from the Caped Crusader, or the editors, artists and writers who had worked for and with him, Kane creatively floundered. Batman had moved on, but Kane did not.

Kane Enterprises

Kane was living on the West Coast and trying to continue his limited television success. But without recycling Batman or parodying other television trends, he did not have much luck. He claimed to have written film and television scripts but evidence of any of these making it to the screen is meagre. Kane claimed to put together a treatment for a Western show featuring a sheriff who could not shoot his gun. He described this series to comics historian Mark Evanier as being bigger than Batman. Paramount bought the script but did not do anything with it for a year. Gun violence on television had been under scrutiny since Robert Kennedy's assassination, but at the same time, a cowboy series without any gunplay was never going to be a hit. Kane's treatment was eventually converted into a script by Clyde Ware called *A Silent Gun.*

It hit television screens as part of the network anthology series *ABC Movie of The Week* and starred Lloyd Bridges as the Sheriff. Far from using his wits rather than his firearm to defeat the black hats, he used up all of his ammo in the opening scene where he violently destroyed his enemies and was forced to carry an empty revolver around for the rest of the film. The series was popular, and *A Silent Gun* was a decent entry, but Kane did not receive any credit nor did this lead to any extra work on the series. Though Kane referenced the TV movie in his autobiography as part of his work, one has to wonder if the distance between his treatment and Clyde's final script was as far as the distance between his idea of Batman and the character he and Finger ended up with.

A little later in the decade, Kane was credited with writing a song for Hank Leids and Courage called 'Have Faith In Me'. It was the title of the album and the opening track. The record also featured a 1950s style rearrangement of Bob's ballad Kane had donated a painted cover for the album featuring Batman, the Batmobile and Hank himself but it was later repainted to include children of the nations of the world as profits from the track were donated to UNICEF. Despite its good intentions the record failed to perform in the charts.

In 1975, Kane set out on his boldest adventure not to pay off. He decided to set up a movie and television studio in Las Vegas with a man called Russ Gerstein, who was most probably a TV producer. Concept drawings for a proposed production indicate the studio may have been named Bob Kane Productions. The one property they almost secured was a Marx Brothers animated series. Harpo, Groucho, and Chico nearly had a previous animated series in the 1960s. They had even advertised 156 forthcoming shorts in trade magazines. The series fell through but the pilot episode, *A Day at the Horse Opera*, the only cartoon to make it to production, became a treasure for lost film seekers. The series seems to have failed due to some issue over rights.

Kane met with the last remaining Marx brother, the 85-year-old Groucho, in the run-up to the new production. The two got on well enough and Kane's company produced some concept art for the series, but the plug was pulled when Groucho's business manager asked for a $100,000 upfront payment for the series. That was the end of the show and potentially the end of Bob Kane Productions. Las Vegas talent broker Jaki Baskow offered some insight into Kane's would-be studio. In recounting her own tale of success in interviews and the self-help/inspirational book series *Chicken Soup for the Soul,* she tells of how she met Kane in her early twenties while vacationing in the Catskills. Like Jerry Robinson, though perhaps with even less honest intention, Kane spotted Baskow at the resort and asked her to work with him in Vegas. The aspiring young actress took a chance and headed out to Vegas where she worked for Kane for a few months. She was excited to be getting her big break in movies but was disappointed when Kane's studio turned out to be nothing more than a small office. Shortly after her arrival, Kane left for LA. Baskow mentioned in her *Chicken Soup* entry that Bob's departure was in order to work with Bill Finger. But as she wrote this in 2014, and with Kane not producing any further work in Hollywood, (and Finger by then being dead) this is probably an assumption made by Baskow as she put her memories together.

Time passed for Kane (as is often the case for wealthy men of leisure) with him doing lots but achieving little. Despite the success of The 'New Look' and the excellent work from the likes of Denny O'Neil and Neil Adam on Batman in the 1970s (ironically by returning him to the shadowy, gothic realm Kane had envisioned), the Adam West television series had made Batman into a public joke. The character was popular amongst the ne'er-do-well who read comics but, for the large part, he had fallen out of the pop-culture foreground and his descent had taken Bob Kane with him.

In 1980 Kane would be a judge on Miss America. Even in his mid-sixties, he would continue to keep up his Bruce Wayne, playboy persona. But in that same year, his relationship with the women in his life would change drastically.

He lost his beloved mother and met his next wife all in the same week. Kane had lost his father decades earlier and was incredibly close to his mother. Her death affected him deeply and he described himself feeling a 'terrible void' when she died aged 92. The woman he had begun courting just days earlier was Elizabeth Sanders, a 30-year-old actress and acting coach who lived in the area and who Kane compared to Goldie Hawn. Unbeknownst to Kane, they had lived in the same neighbourhood for a decade, but after bumping into her several times in just a few weeks, Kane sensed it was serendipity. He introduced himself as Batman and took Elizabeth for coffee. Afterwards, he wondered if their meeting was fate, a thought perhaps prompted by his exploration into spirituality. Though he was mostly private about his personal life, he credited Sanders with helping him through his mother's death and with coming into his life at exactly the right moment, the time he needed her most. They would get married in 1987.

Stan Lee also moved out to Hollywood in 1980. Kane and Lee were arguably the two most famous comic creators on the planet at the time. Their personalities had stretched well beyond the four-colour pages of the characters they had co-created. While Kane appeared on TV in the 1960s promoting himself, and if he had time, the Batman television show, Lee toured college campuses, giving lectures to counterculture students who loved the realism, philosophy and psychedelia of characters like Spider-Man, the Silver Surfer and Dr Strange. The pair had plenty in common. They grew up in the same area, went to the same school, worked with the same people, and had been the public face of comics; although, whereas Kane was Batman's earthly representative, Lee was the face of an entire universe of characters. The two men both endured similar criticism within the industry. At best, they were considered creative geniuses, but at the worst, they were seen as egotists who stole the rightful credits of hardworking collaborators. Certainly, Lee had a tendency to place himself in the spotlight as he moved from the office boy who fetched the coffee to a writer, editor and eventually publisher of Marvel Comics. But the work he did always featured the by-line of whoever he worked with. Moreover, Lee didn't own any part of the characters he created and always understood his creations to be work-for-hire, he was paid to create something the company would then own, something he didn't share with, but admired in Kane.

The two had known each other for years. But out in California, where they both sought to translate their experience into film and TV work, the two became good friends. Bob and Elizabeth would invite Stan and his wife Joan out for dinner, inevitably showing up late. The Lees once purposely showed up thirty minutes late to teach the Kanes a lesson, only for the Kanes to appear fifteen minutes after that. Stan, famed for his self-promotion, would be uncharacteristically speechless as Bob shamelessly handed out sketches of his creation to waiters, or more likely waitresses, as he introduced himself as the creator of Batman completely unprompted. Even Stan Lee thought Bob Kane was a bit much. Kane and Lee would compare their accomplishments in jest, playing on the old DC-Marvel battle, rivalling the fame and success of Batman and Spider-man. The Dark Knight had a three-decade head start over the wall-crawling web-head, and the fact National had been Marvel's distributor, meant for a long time that DC financially profited from the sale of Marvel comics. But Stan Lee was a superstar. He was 'The Man' – 'nuff said. But as the 1980s rolled on, Batman would undergo yet another transformation and retake his spot at the top of the pop-culture pantheon, and Kane would once again take the top-billing.

Batmania reborn

In 1986, Frank Miller wrote, and with Klaus Janson, illustrated *The Dark Knight Returns,* a new Batman mini-series. It was darker than anything even Kane had envisioned and explored the psychology of a man who dresses up like a rodent to fight crime. The story followed a retired and bored Bruce Wayne, now in his 50s, returning to his cape and cowl for one last adventure. Bob Kane thought it was weird.

Regardless, it was advertised in *Rolling Stone* magazine, made the *New York Time* best sellers list and became one of the finer examples of what would become known as the Dark Age of Comics; a period defined by a gritty realism and moral bleakness applied to superhero stories. Its massive success reignited the public passion for Batman and two years later, The Dark Knight was making his way back to the big screen.

The development of 1989's *Batman* is a fascinating and complex story. A Batman movie had been announced as early as 1980 at the New York Comic Convention but it had spent eight years in development hell and the script had been re-written nine times by nine different writers. At one point, Bill Murray and Eddie Murphy were attached to play Batman and Robin but calmer heads eventually prevailed. A script by Tom Mankiewicz, who had worked on Richard Donner and Christopher Reeve's *Superman: The Movie*, was eventually settled on but when director Tim Burton, the doyenne of gothic Americana, was brought in, he quickly dumped it. Burton found Mankiewicz's story to be too camp and close to the Adam West series. Though he was not a comic book fan before he started pre-production, it was Frank Miller's *The Dark Knight Returns* and Alan Moore/Brian Bolland's *The Killing Joke* that Burton would eventually draw his inspiration from. But the resurgence of Batman gave his fans a new sense of ownership.

Burton's major successes up to then had been *Pee-Wee's Big Adventure,* a comedy-adventure starring the child-like persona of stand-up comic Paul Ruebens, and *Beetlejuice,* a comedy horror about a poltergeist starring Michael Keaton, who was then mostly recognised as a comedy actor. The Batman fans did not like this one bit. In fact, they hated it. Burton's admission of not being a fan of the comics and his casting of Keaton as Bruce Wayne incensed the fan base who were worried they were going to turn their reborn Batman into another campy joke. Kane agreed quite publicly. The creator of Batman was bad-mouthing the new Bat-flick before filming had even begun.

Though he had approved of the new Sam Hamm script, he openly criticised the casting of Keaton. The actor did not match the artist's vision for the character. Instead of the 6ft 2ins square-jawed he-man Kane envisioned, Keaton was a 5ft 10ins, neurotic, every-man. Tens of thousands of letters, as well as petitions to have Keaton removed from the project – some signed by comic book creators – were sent into Warner Brothers. Eventually the studio felt it had to battle the backlash, and that started by getting Kane on side. They paid him to be a special consultant on the film, in theory helping the development of the project while in practice providing cover from angry fans. Burton showed Kane *Clean and Sober,* a drama starring Keaton about a recovering drug addict. While it proved to Kane that Keaton had the acting chops, he still wasn't convinced. Bob was particularly obsessed with Keaton's small chin, to which Burton had to reply that he wasn't casting for a chin, he was casting for a character. Burton had to repeat his justification for casting Keaton countless times, always pointing to the psychology of Batman rather than his chin, as a defining aspect of the character. Eventually, Kane was persuaded of Burton's vision. In 1988 Kane appeared at the San Diego Comic Convention to defend Keaton's casting but was cynically dismissed by the gathered fans and critics. His change of opinion was immediately attributed to Warner employing him as a consultant, and he was considered a sell-out.

Of course, Bill Finger wasn't around to comment on Burton's vision of Batman or the acting ability of Michael Keaton's chin but when Lyn Simmons, Finger's second ex-wife, heard the film was in production, she set out to get Bill the credit he had long been missing. With her son Steve, who for a little while had been Finger's stepson, she started writing to Warner Brothers executives and journalists to get Finger some sort of credit on the upcoming movie. In her letters to the studio, she explained

Finger's significance to the creation of Batman, citing Bill's entry in *The World Encyclopaedia of Comic Books*, and she almost made some headway. It appears Warner Brothers were willing to give Finger a credit in exchange for Simmons waiving her claim to any royalties or rights to the movie. Simmons was happy to sign the waiver. It wasn't money she wanted, only acknowledgement for her ex-husband. She made the modest suggestion that the film might feature the line, 'In memoriam of William Finger, who helped to create Batman'. Even after the waiver was signed, cutting off any legal challenge at the pass, Simmons' request was denied, apparently on the grounds of her being his ex-wife rather than his widow. A rather callous reason to deny such a humble request.

Frustrated, Simmons turned to the press, sending the details of her struggle to the *San Francisco Chronicle*, the *Palo Alto Weekly* and the *LA Times*. Lyn's story appeared courtesy of Steve Weinstein beneath a feature on Danny Elfman's score for the Bat-flick in the *LA Times* with a reply from Bob Kane. Kane once again reiterated that Finger came in on the creation after he had already drawn a Batman character and states Finger was a 'writer for hire'. He did stress though that Finger was the first and best Batman writer and he would be happy for the film to credit him that way. But he mentioned Warner Brothers was against this option as it opened up the door to any number of writers and artists who worked on the early comic who might also want to claim recognition. Though it continued an injustice perpetrated half a century earlier, this does seem to be a reasonable (legal) stance. Although it is questionable whether the other creators who knew of Finger's contribution to Batman would have sought out a similar level of recognition in this case.

Simmons had assumed it would be a simple and fair addition to the film but was left disappointed. She may not have been able to get Finger a credit on the movie but the story was covered in several major publications and it at least brought any discussion of Finger's contribution to Batman out of the niche world of comics and onto a larger, blockbuster stage.

The Mark of Kane

As the promotion machine picked up speed, Kane was presented with more opportunities to enjoy his re-established fame. He produced art tied to the Burton movie which seemed to fall between the worlds of concept art and promotional materials. Kane hired Greg Theakston to help with the work. Theakston had started out working for Jim Steranko's Supergraphic publishing house. He was a skilled illustrator and comics historian who later became highly regarded for his process of restoring old pages of original comic book art to make them suitable for reprinting. The method was even named 'Theakstonising'. Theakston was brought in as the last of the Kane ghosts; inking, colouring and occasionally signing pieces with Kane's name. Theakston said Kane provided complete, if rudimentary, pencils for him to work from, and was asked to be discreet about his role.

But old habits die hard. The cover of magazine *Comic Scene #6* featured a lean, vampire-like Batman, wrapped in an exaggerated flowing and angular cape. There were several pieces in this style attributed to Kane doing the rounds at the time as part of the film promotion. Even to the untrained eye, this new, baroque style was strikingly different from Kane's usual smiling and simple Batman. That is because they were swipes from Todd McFarlane who briefly worked on Batman between 1987 and 1988 before moving to Marvel and eventually starting Image Comics. McFarlane was able to exact minor revenge of sorts for the swipe. In 1990, as McFarlane's run on Spider-Man was becoming a hit, the upstart artist drew a cover for *Amazing Heroes,* yet another magazine about the world of comics. It featured two kids looking at a poster of the Wall-crawler, with the first commenting, 'HEY!! WHO DID THIS DRAWING? LOOKS AN **AWFUL** LOT LIKE **ERIK LARSON**... AND **BOB KANE!**' To which the second child replies, '**YEAH!** THE NERVE OF SOME GUYS! IT'S BY SOME NEW PUNK NAMED **TOM McFARTHING** OR SOMETHING!'

Kane appeared in behind the scenes videos, talk shows, and mini-documentaries detailing the creation of the new movies, repeating how Batman came into being in countless interviews. By this point, he could repeat his account almost as rote.

In October 1988, Kane and his wife were invited out to Pinewood Studios in the UK to see Gotham brought to life. Kane was scheduled to make a cameo in the film but sadly, saw his chance at becoming a real-life movie star, even a minor one, come and go. Because Joker actor Jack Nicholson wanted to get his scenes finished early in the shooting schedule, the sets for the scene Bob was to cameo in were not yet constructed. Kane became sick and flew home before the set was built and so missed the opportunity to film his scene.

Likewise, his wife Elizabeth had been hired to appear in a scene early in the movie, a role Kane described as 'small but juicy'. But British Equity, the actors union in the UK, had denied her a work permit meaning Mr and Mrs Kane didn't get their chance to appear on the screen. Aside from the opening credits stating the film was based on characters created by Bob Kane, the film did feature one nod to the would-be star. In a scene where reporters are joking about who or what the Batman could be, a character is handed a sketch of bat-headed man in a pinstripe suit. The sketch is signed Bob Kane, though the jury is out on whether the sketch itself was a prop or a Kane original.

Now 74 and back in the limelight, Kane released a biography with lots of help from pop culture historian Thomas Andrae. Andrae contacted Kane to see if he would be interested in the idea and he said yes – Kane had already been working on an autobiography which was by then at the 800-pages mark. In an interview with Bill Finger historian Marc Tyler Nobleman, Andrae gave a fascinating insight into what it was like to work on *Batman & Me*. Kane's original manuscript, unsurprisingly, was hugely self-centred and littered with wandering nostalgic asides. Andrae recalled Kane as being forgetful, egotistic, and prone to exaggerating his own history while downplaying the role of others. At the same time, he was also friendly, open, honest, and occasionally insecure. Andrae challenged Kane on Finger's involvement in the creation of Batman and told Nobleman that Kane seemed to be genuinely remorseful. Kane felt guilty his old friend had died poor and unknown, and he admitted it had been his own ego that had prevented him from including Finger in that original by-line. As much as he wished he could, he insisted he couldn't change his story because it would have opened him up to legal challenges over the ownership of Batman. Even then, in his old age and with his friend gone, Bob's retrospection and empathy had a legal limit. The creation of Batman started and ended when Bob had the vague idea of a character with that name, everything else was minor adjustments. Andrae felt Kane never did enough to make amends.

After heavy editing, Andrae estimated he had written or re-written around half of *Batman & Me,* using his own research to fill in the blanks where Bob's memory had failed. Like Kane, the book itself seems to have a dual persona, which can probably be attributed to Andrae's attempt to get Bob's work into shape. The book swings wildly from documenting Kane's life and work to overly indulgent anecdotes about celebrities. Kane, even in his childhood, is painted as a sort of dashing rogue, who may face obstacles but always comes out on top. It is occasionally petty, borderline obsessed with wealth, and full of bravado masculinity. At one point, Kane recalled his romantic encounter with Marilyn Monroe, which apparently had a much more explicit conclusion in private tellings than in the book. But then occasionally, the manuscript is sincere and heartfelt, almost to the point of being saccharine.

Kane dedicated the book to the memory of Bill Finger, and he went so far as to say that if it had been possible, he's have put Finger's name on Batman before the writer had died. He even lamented the fact Finger had spent his comics career in anonymity and that he never achieved the status of a great film and TV writer. In the final analysis though, Kane attributed his friend's failure to a wasted talent rather than taking any personal responsibility for Bill's fate.

But Kane wasn't just a contradiction in terms of his nature and the fact that his ego and his empathy were permanently at war with one another; in *Batman & Me* Kane even contradicted himself over the details of Batman's creation. On one page, there is a character design sheet featuring a recognisable Batman with a flowing, scalloped cape, alongside sketches of the Leonardo Di Vinci flying device, the ornithopter. The image is dated 1939 and signed 'Robert Kane' – an earlier version of Kane's signature. The accompanying caption identified the image as being drawn months before Batman's first appearance. There are also images dated from 1934 which feature a crude Batman but complete with pointy ears and a bat symbol on his chest. Only pages later does Kane recall showing Finger his first images of the character, and Bill suggesting that he make the ridged wings into a cape, the costume grey and black rather than a red boiler suit, and turn the black domino mask into a hooded cowl with bat ears. It can't be true that Kane both had these complete sketches of Batman five years before the first Batman story and that Bill Finger provided the character notes Kane himself admits to.

What this suggests is that Kane forged these images to place the creation of Batman at an earlier time than history records, but then forgot to get his story straight before publishing. It is a shame Kane had over the years become more accepting of Finger's influence, despite the fact that he was still bound legally to keep quiet, only to make a bizarre mistake like this. Of all the times Kane purposely acted on his own behalf, self-aggrandising or self-promoting or acting selfishly at a cost to others, this slip up was the cruellest because it was so blatantly deceptive. Kane's ghosts didn't get credit, but they did get paid and there was an element of a business transaction between them. But it seems the intention of presenting this image with those dates, whether or not they were meant to go to press or not, was to create a forgery which allowed Kane to tighten his stranglehold on the Batman myth. It seems unlikely Kane would have forged those dates specifically for this book only to contradict himself, and the chances are they are from several years earlier (though not as early as he claimed), but it's revealing Kane would stoop to such dishonesty at any time.

Batman was a blockbuster success and kicked off a thirty-year trend of Batman on the big screen which continues to this day. A sequel went into the works almost immediately and Kane continued his press tour. In 1991, he appeared on *Stan Lee's Comic Book Greats,* a straight to video series featuring a host of comic book legends new and old who were interviewed by Lee. The format started with an conversation between Lee and his guest, covering their history and work in the industry, followed by the guests illustrating characters for Lee and then discussing their approach to the medium. The Kane episode makes for difficult viewing. Bob is sometimes funny and self-deprecating, admitting to his limitations as an artist and referring to himself as 'a legend in his own mind' but he is also extremely bullish and occasionally mean. He repeats his usual version of events and points to his autobiography as proof. Mostly it was used as an excuse to sell his book, but he did briefly dip into the controversy surrounding the creation of his characters. Bill Finger was mentioned in passing, but Kane vehemently attacked Jerry Robinson and his claim to have invented The Joker. Andrae, in his interview with Nobleman, claimed Kane bore a grudge against his former assistant, implying that Kane was jealous of Robinson's success.

Not only was Jerry a better Batman illustrator than Kane, but he was also a better cartoonist who far surpassed Kane in his first love, the world of comedy strips. Robinson gained respect in the world of comic books but was able to move onto political editorials and advertising. He met with President Carter, became the head of the National Cartoonist Society, and in the seventies, when Superman creators Siegel and Shuster were ageing, sick and broke, Robinson spearheaded the campaign to get them at least a fraction more of what they deserved. In the industry, this kid who Bob Kane had stumbled across on holiday, who drew for fun and wanted to be a journalist, had become one of the most respected, admired and honoured people in comics. In many ways, he was the exact opposite of Kane. He was talented and loved in the community, and he cared about the treatment of the creators the brutal Golden Age business had chewed up and spat out.

Kane lambasted Robinson throughout the show as Lee awkwardly tried to get the conversation back on track. Lee was also close to Robinson and desperately tried to calm Kane down to which Kane replied, 'No friend of yours is a friend of mine, and that goes automatically for Jerry Robinson'. He became further aggravated when Lee tried to move the conversation on by taking a neutral stance as to who created the Joker. Kane's one-time quip 'Without my ghosts and assistant Jerry Robinson, I might not be able to draw the Batman' is a funny, flippant remark but sadly there was possibly a deeper truth to that statement than Kane intended. One of the great ironies of the entire situation is that the cover to *Batman & Me* featured a smiling Kane next to an illustrated and equally cheery Batman – a Batman illustrated by Jerry Robinson.

Arguably, it was the film series of the 1990s which most strongly bolstered the myth of Kane as the sole creator of Batman to the non-comic book reading public. The 1960s campy television show was somehow seen as not being the real Batman in the way nineties movies were deemed to be. The films, with Bob Kane's credit in massive letters on screens across the planet, reached a far larger audience than ever before. Even though comic books are the origins of so many recognisable and lucrative franchised characters, the truth is these days the medium itself plays second fiddle to the movies, even more so in the 1990s, when comic books were still seen as an outsider medium. Batman had broken through into the mainstream as a character regular people could enjoy while the comics were still generally considered to be kids' stuff. Kane's name was recognisable to the world, and outside pockets of resistance within the comic book subculture, he was the sole creator for Batman.

Kane spent the nineties enjoying and occasionally criticising the Tim Burton/Joel Schumacher Batman Movies. He returned as a creative consultant for *Batman Returns* and later praised the chins of Val Kilmer and George Clooney, even celebrating Kilmer as the best possible choice for the role. Though, like everyone else on the planet, he was not best pleased with nipples on the Bat Suit. His wife Elizabeth even managed to get a cameo in the sequel as Gothamite #4, but for *Batman Forever* and *Batman & Robin,* she was upgraded to the speaking role of Gossip Gerty, the celebrity columnist who simply must know who Bruce Wayne has brought to the big party.

Kane and Finger were introduced into the Jack Kirby Hall of Fame in 1994, the year after Siegel and Shuster, and in 1996, Kane entered the Will Eisner Hall of Fame, named for his old school chum. Kane would appear at premieres for the Batman movies and was always swamped with fans; *The LA Times* even commenting that Kane was a bigger draw for autograph seekers than the stars of the film. He was regularly inundated with fan mail at his Hollywood home and would pour over the letters of admiration. But Bob was growing old. A year after the release of *Batman & Robin,* aged 83, Bob died peacefully at the Cedar-Sinai Medical Centre.

Obituaries flooded the newspapers. Kane's widow, his daughter and his sister asked for any memorial donations to be sent to children's charities, presumably continuing Kane's commitment to those causes. Kane was buried at Forest Lawn Memorial park. Comic book historian Mark Evanier recalled how Kane's family were under the assumption DC and the comics community at large had sent representatives to honour Kane's memory in the form of Evanier, Stan Lee, artist Paul Smith and writer Mike W. Barr. The truth is their appearance at his funeral was a coincidence and no such arrangement had been made. Lee was asked to give an impromptu eulogy that he had not been prepared for but, with help from Evanier, he gave a dedication to his late pal and sparring partner. Unusually, Barr, who was a freelance editor on *The Outsiders,* a book about a team of superhero-misfits brought together by Batman, had lost his job in the late eighties after he wrote to the *Comics Journal* to suggest Bill Finger should have been receiving credits on Batman titles. He was fired by then DC editor Dick Giordano for speaking out against the company.

Kane's gravestone is in the form of a book falling open. It lists his real date of birth as well as the publication date of Batman's first appearance and features the Bat-signal shining down on Kane's name. Part of it reads:

> Bob Kane, Bruce Wayne, Batman—they are one and the same. Bob gave his dual identity character with his own attributes; goodness, kindness, compassion, sensitivity, generosity, intelligence, integrity, courage, purity of spirit, a love of all mankind.

With regards to his relationship to Finger, it is easy to read these words as hypocritical, but that also misses the point that these words weren't written by Kane. They were written by those closest to him; it's what the people who knew him best and loved him most thought about him. To that point, Evanier wrote that of the dozen or so times he met and socialised with Kane, he had encountered one of two personas. The first was affable and friendly; he remembered the contributions of his colleagues and loved to reminisce, even if it was with rose-tinted but highly reflective glasses. The other was Bob Kane, the sole creator of Batman; a creature of pure ego who was hungry for celebrity and recognition and would not countenance challenges to his myth.

Kane spent so long constructing and enforcing this myth in the public, that it became all people needed to know about him. His self-mythology had become his truth. The problem is that when what is thought of as true begins to change, the mythology changes along with it. And, when Kane was no longer around to play the hero, he would inevitably be cast as the villain.

Chapter Nine

A Noble Quest

Back to the beginning

In 1999, shortly after Bob Kane's death, Batman had his sixtieth anniversary. To commemorate it, *Alter Ego* ran a commemorative issue dedicated to the Caped Crusader. Its cover featured a collage of inspirations for the character arranged around the man himself swinging dramatically from a thin wire. Only it wasn't the Batman we would recognise today. It was a Batman without Bill Finger's input, illustrated by Arlen Schumer and complete with red spandex, flowing blonde hair and wooden wings. Schumer also wrote an article entitled *The 'Bat-Man' Cover Story* detailing the true history of Batman's earliest origins (see, *The Bat is Born*, Chapter Four) and *Real Facts & True Lies*, which presented *Real Facts Comic #5*, with its story of how Bob Kane created Batman on his own, as a false account of history. The details of those arguments have already been covered here, but for clarity, it is worth mentioning this publication for several reasons.

The first point Schumer made was that without Finger's contributions to the design of Batman, the character would not have been anything special. The Kane 'Bat-man' was generic and indistinct from the swathes of heroes who took to the skies in Superman's wake which ultimately failed because of a lack of originality and poor sales. Schumer introduced the reader to the idea that a Batman without Finger would have been no Batman at all, and that the cultural phenomenon giving Kane a life as a minor but wealthy celebrity would never have happened.

The book also alluded to Kane swiping art from *Flash Gordon* creator Hal Foster for the character layout on the cover of *Detective Comics #27*. *Alter Ego* editor Roy Thomas stated in his editorial that no-one really wanted to deny Kane credit for Batman, only that perhaps sixty years on, Finger did deserve a co-credit while Schumer himself has elsewhere said Kane can't entirely be removed from the by-line. Both Finger's contributions and Kane's limitations were already known within the industry and to fans who were interested in that sort of thing, but along with the feature on *Real Fact Comics,* this issue, perhaps unintentionally, started to change the tone of that discussion. It moved away from the usual professional opinions on the two given by contemporaries suggesting Kane took too much credit while Finger did not get enough. As Finger's contributions became further understood and appreciated, Kane started to look more sinister – stealing from those around him and giving little back in return.

In fairness, Finger did not get away scot-free. The issue also featured an old interview with his son, Fred, detailing what he could remember about his father's work. But it was hardly complimentary. Fred referred to his father as weak and spineless. Bill was presented as a poor parent, who was often absent and unable to pay child support, who Fred remembered as either idly daydreaming or arguing with the various women in his life. He said that his father enjoyed writing but had a weird, 'negative pride' about comics and claimed that Bill hated them. Although Fred said he had loved his father, the fact he referred to him as 'Bill' throughout the interview reiterates the distance between the two.

Perhaps because Finger lived outside of the limelight, the truth of his personal life was less important than the lies of Kane's public life. Either way, that issue of *Alter Ego,* started the ball rolling on a much bigger movement. Though a few people had made individual attempts to get Finger credits in the past, the start of the new millennium would bring an explosion of interest in superheroes and with it, renewed interest in their history. At the same time, accessibility to the internet was rapidly increasing, meaning finding out the truth was becoming a lot easier.

Bill the unsung hero, Bob the silent crook

Since his Green Lantern writer's biography, Finger's legacy was always available to those who were looking for it. Dedicated fans of comic book history could dig up the truth if they committed the time and effort, but the average comics fan was still unlikely to stumble across his name. In 2005, Mark Evanier and Jerry Robinson started to change that. San Diego's

Comic-Con had been growing as the industry's leading event and was increasingly becoming a visible platform for promotion beyond the comic book pages. Hollywood, and therefore the world, was taking an interest. Marvel and Sony's X-Men and Spider-man films started to undo the damage done by the Joel Schumacher Batman films, and eight years after Bob Kane had strolled around the sets of Gotham mocking the Dark Knight's nipples, Hollywood was ready to take another chance on the Gotham Guardian with Christopher Nolan's *Batman Begins* – yet another return to the characters dark origins. It was at that year's event, in 2006, that Evanier and Robinson launched the Bill Finger Award for Excellence in Comic Book Writing.

Robinson had long worked on getting creators the credits they deserved. Just a year after Finger's death, he and Batman artist Neil Adams had been instrumental campaigning for Jerry Siegel and Joe Shuster to gain recognition. DC agreed to pay each of the creators $20,000 each a year (although this was later increased) for the rest of their lives. Finger had taken Jerry under his wing when the artist had first moved to New York and had introduced him to the city's rich cultural and artistic attractions, and as a result, Robinson had always held Finger in high regard. Presented under the auspices of the Will Eisner Comics Industry Awards, the Bill Finger Award is presented to two writers each year, one living and one deceased, whose work has gone without the proper recognition. Robinson viewed the awards as a way of righting the wrong of Finger's name being known only to his colleagues and comic historians.

Over 100,000 people attended that year's convention, which was a far cry from the 200 or so who turned up forty years earlier in New York to see 'the Batman writer from the very first' show up late to a panel. There is no doubt that in its fifteen years, this award exposed more people to Finger's comics contribution (or even just his name) than his entire 30-year career at DC. Finger had become the patron saint of the unremembered while he was starting to gain a reputation as the unrecognised co-creator of Batman beyond a niche community.

Henry E. Vallely was a largely forgotten illustrator who worked in the 1930s on the Big Little Books series from Western Publishing. These books could have upwards of 400 pages but were incredibly compact, at around 4 inches tall and 3 wide. The reason they were so long was every right-hand page featured an illustration to go along with stories, which were usually based on popular characters from movies, radio, comic strips and children's books. They fell into the space between pulp novels and comics, featuring a lot of the same characters, including The Shadow.

In 2006, DSK, the mysterious writer of the Vallely Archive blogs, dedicated to celebrating the works of the artist, started the first of six posts. The post compared images from Vallely's Big Little Book work, in particular, *Gang Busters in Action* and *Junior G-Men and the Counterfeiters*, with Kane's work on *Detective Comics #27* and *#33* – Batman's first appearance and later, origin. It is undeniable that Kane traced Vallely's work (and the work of Tarzan strip artist Hal Forster) in those comics. As previously mentioned, it was known that Kane swiped from other artists, but the Vallely Archive blogs visibly demonstrated just how shockingly common his practice of doing this was. Of the thirteen panels which made up the two-page story of how Batman came to be, the blog documented that four came from Big Little Books. And those were just the ones that DSK found.

Around the same time, 'Robby Reed' aka Kirk Kimball of the excellent comics history site Dial B for Blog, did a three-chapter exposé on the work of Kane, referencing both the Vallely Archive Blog and Arlen Schumer's work for *Alter Ego* on what Batman would be like without Finger. This series was the first in-depth look at trying to figure out just exactly who was responsible for the creation of Batman and it analysed the various claims of inspiration that Kane made – much of which has informed this book.

As with Schumer, Kimball presented his case with fantastic visual aids and more than a fair share of melodrama. Kimball also investigated how much Finger swiped the works of Walter Gibson in his plotting of *The Case of The Chemical Syndicate,* – something Finger had freely admitted to. He also discovered more Kane 'swipes', including some apparently from Tom Lovell, the illustrator of The Shadow based inspiration for Finger's plot, *Partners in Peril*. Some of those swipes are debatable, though. For the most part, swipes replicated an image very tightly, with identical poses, postures, blocking etc. It is easy to see that one image is almost identical to the other save for a few embellishments. Some of the evidence Kimball presented was not that clear cut though as the comparative images featured similar forms without having the same key details. That isn't to say that one didn't inspire the other, only that it's unfair to say one artist appropriated another's work, after all, there are only so many ways you can depict someone picking up a phone or slouching in a chair.

It is worth pointing out that in the earliest days of comics, swiping was a lot more prevalent than it is now. Lots of young artists swiped when trying to learn their trade and the sheer amount of work carried out by the shops meant an excellent character pose became convenient shorthand. Even Jack 'The King' Kirby swiped on occasion when he was working with Joe Simon. To a degree, it was an accepted practice in an age when comics were still figuring out what they were. Kane probably got much more criticism for it because unlike other well-known artists who copied from the greats, he never grew as an artist. He so quickly relied on other artists to help make up his workload and gaps in his talent that the accumulated effect, when it was uncovered, presented Kane as being like a thief or a con artist.

Finger did the same in a sense; lifting plot ideas and characters from literature. But with comics being a primarily visual medium, as well as Finger growing as a writer and the kind of sympathy his story and lack of credit started to provoke, he hasn't been held to the same standards as Kane in this regard. More generally, it seems for writers, recycling plots is almost acceptable. After all, plot devices are hardly unique; they're just events which move characters from point A to point B. They are not the same as the story. Plenty of stories feature the plot of an orphan raised in humble conditions meeting a wiser, older figure who propels them into a new world (Luke Skywalker, Don Draper, Oliver Twist, so on and so forth), but that does not mean those stories are the same. Writers can put their style onto the plot and rearrange the parts to make it their own. With art swipes in comics, it is a unique style, technique and hard work that is being stolen, rather than a plot function.

Kimball's investigation ended with a judgement delivered in character by the Shadow – the vigilante who 'Knows what evil lurks in the heart of men' and has less self-control than Batman and an even greater love of violent retribution. It's a comically over the top monologue in which Kane is labelled a 'duplicitous glory hound', presenting his success as far surpassing Finger's and his unwillingness to help his former colleague as his ultimate sin.

The power, depth and brilliant presentation of Kimball's argument went a long way to changing the narrative of how Kane is now recognised. And the fact this information is on the internet means it is now more widely accepted. It may not have been anyone's direct intention, but it was soon the consensus that Bob Kane would have been nothing without Bill Finger and Finger was the hapless victim of Kane's success. The reality was, of course, slightly more nuanced, but it is an understandable conclusion. Yet with both creators deceased, how else can we hold people accountable? Or better yet, how can we give them what they really deserve?

The Great Detective

Something must have been in the air during 2006 because while DSK and Robby Reed were blogging about Bob Kane, Marc Tyler Nobleman was thinking about Bill Finger. Nobleman is a writer of fiction and non-fiction books for younger readers, covering everything from historical figures and important inventions to cowboys and werewolf infested high schools. He also happens to be a Batman fan.

At this point, Bill Finger was gaining recognition as the co-creator (or key-creator) of Batman, but he was still essentially a mystery. There were only three known photographs of the creator, one of which wasn't Finger at all but Robert Kanigher, a fellow DC writer who was best-known for his work on Wonder Woman. Outside of a few scattered interviews, Finger's existence was locked away in the memories of old men who had worked with him in their youth. He was a mysterious figure hidden in the shadow of Bob Kane, but Nobleman wanted to find out more about him, with an eye to writing a picture book about the writer. This was not to be his first book about comic creators. While he was still researching Bill, in 2008, Nobleman published *Boys of Steel: The Creators of Superman* with illustrator Ross MacDonald, retelling the tale of Siegel and Shuster's youth and their creation of Superman. Finger, another Golden Age creator who helped to shape the pop culture landscape seemed like a great candidate for a book in the same vein.

Nobleman is a dedicated researcher who trawled through countless names and databases whilst spending hours calling strangers who might have been linked to the case. History is better for it because a lot of what we now know about Bill Finger is a direct result of Nobleman's insane commitment to the cause. Charles Sinclair came to Nobleman's attention though his listing with Finger on IMDB. Searching across America, he eventually came across a Sinclair in the Writers' Guild East website, where he was listed as being owed subsidiaries for his work alongside one William Finger. Nobleman was able to get in touch with Sinclair who was happy to get some money he did not know he was owed and to chat about Finger. Incidentally, Sinclair suggested Finger's uncollected subsidiaries should go towards funding the Bill Finger Award, a nice suggestion which doesn't appear to have been taken up.

Sinclair revealed the existence of Bill's second wife, Lyn Simmons, to Nobleman. Because of her previous marriage and maiden name, finding Simmons was tough but Nobleman had an ingenious solution. He searched the high school yearbooks of Long Neck, where Simmons had lived, for the name of her daughter. Upon getting a hit, he was able to track down her phone number, and eventually make contact with Lyn. Along the way, Nobleman also interviewed old comic book creators and historians, constantly building a bigger picture of what Finger was like. He also started to uncover more images of the camera-shy writer.

In terms of relatives, leads were thin on the ground. Fred Finger, the heir apparent, had contracted AIDS in the eighties and had died at just 43 in 1992. After the death of his father in 1974, Fred had tried to get in touch with DC to offer them Bill's collection of comics and his fabled gimmick book. Had DC said yes, we would have an even greater insight into Bill's approach to writing and the inspirations for his stories but, sadly, the company declined and the collection was thrown away. Bill's son tried several times to seek legal justice for his father, but most lawyers didn't have the time, funds or ability to take on the massive corporate conglomerate Warner Communications, which DC was now owned by. Fred did, however, receive the money his father was due for reprinted editions of his work. Before his death, Fred had signed the royalties over to his roommate, Charles Shaheen, who died in 2002.

With no direct blood relative still alive, Nobleman turned his attention to Bill's first wife Portia. If she was still alive, he knew she would be incredibly old, but perhaps her family would have some recollection of Finger and his work. There was still the strong possibility that Portia was also owed Finger's posthumous pay cheques.

Portia had died in 1990 but by searching through hundreds of obituaries and cross-referencing them with ancestry websites, Nobleman was able to find Portia's twin sister Irene Flam. Irene had died just three years after her sister but her children, Eric and Judy, the nephew and niece by marriage of Bill Finger, were still alive. Nobleman was able to get in touch with them, and more interviews and family photos of Uncle Bill were obtained. But much better than that, Nobleman was given a fresh lead, the name of Bill Finger's previously unknown granddaughter.

In the later seventies, after his father's death, Fred (who was bisexual and not gay as Nobleman and other comics historians had previously been thought) had been married to a woman named Bonnie Burrell and they had a daughter together. Athena was born two years after Bill's death. In 1980, the Fingers moved to Portland so Fred could open a restaurant, as he had been making a name for himself as a chef, but the relationship fell apart soon after. Athena lived with her mother but maintained irregular contact with Fred. It would seem that the curse of the Finger line struck again as Bill, Fred and Athena all struggled in the relationships with their parents. Fred dying when she was only 15 had a deep impact on her while Charles Shaheen becoming the inheritor of the Finger estate only confused and worsened those emotions. Comparable to the difficulty of a teenage girl trying to make sense of her father's life and her place in it, is the struggle Fred had been going through at the same time.

The AIDS epidemic hit in the eighties and men like Fred were demonised by a conservative culture that neither understood the disease or the gay community. Many of those who were diagnosed with HIV were treated like pariahs and treatment could be difficult to access and afford. A friend of Fred's revealed to Nobleman that, in 1988, Fred was living in social housing with his partner Ritchie along with Charles Shaheen and a man named Alvin. All of them had AIDS and Shaheen was getting treatment through the black market. As Tim Burton's *Batman* was hitting cinemas and Bob Kane was visiting sets and shaking hands with the press, Fred did make a few attempts to get his father credited by contacting DC, unaware that across the country, Lyn Simmons had attempted to do the same thing. Ritchie died in 1991 and Fred began to falsely claim social security checks under Richie's name. When Fred died, Charles then forged Fred's signature to get the Finger royalty cheques. Charles became involved with a man named John Maloney, potentially with a brother named Jesse. Certainly, Bill Finger's royalty checks were being sent from DC comics to a Jesse Maloney before Athena came to their attention.

It is a complicated, nearly farcical and dishonest game of pass the parcel for the royalties to Batman. But like his dad before him, Fred was poor and ill, but for a short time, his life and the lives of his friends were made slightly better because of Bill's work. They were all trying to look after one another when nobody else would.

Nobleman couldn't believe he had found Bill Finger's legal heir. He searched for Athena Finger on MySpace. One of the hits featured a picture of a dog named Bruce Wayne. Athena turned out to be a maths instructor and a single parent living in South Florida. Nobleman introduced himself.

Putting things right

Not only did the discovery of Athena Finger help Nobleman's research, it meant there was now someone who could viably make a legal case for crediting Bill. It also meant Athena could collect Bill's outstanding royalties which by rights should have been going to her in the first place. With a little bit of help from Nobleman, Athena got in touch with DC, who handed her back her claim to Finger's royalties once she had proved she was his granddaughter. However, Finger's legal status remained unchanged – Bob Kane was still the creator of Batman in the eyes of corporate law.

The people who make up the comics industry and the corporate entities they are employed by are not entirely the same thing. The people who work at DC, for the most part, are comic fans. They were excited that Bill Finger was visible again, manifest in his granddaughter, and they wanted to treat her like family. Whether or not they could say so, they knew what had happened behind the scenes and in all likelihood, sympathised with Finger's position. Athena was given a small but generous payout as a form of compensation for what had happened and was invited into the fold. Marc Tyler Nobleman continued his research into Finger's life and posted regular updates of his discoveries on his website, Noblemania. At the same time, Christopher Nolan's *Batman Begins* had surpassed what anyone thought Batman could be – the world was on the edge of its seat waiting for *The Dark Knight*.

As part of the family, Athena was invited to special DC events. The company flew her out to parties for *The Dark Knight* where she mingled with Christian Bale and Aaron Eckhart. She even met with her grandfather's protégé Jerry Robinson; a moment Robinson described as 'incredibly special' in a memoir published after his death in 2011. In that same year, she would be brought to the premiere of her grandfather's lesser-known creation, *The Green Lantern*. In 2012, the final part of Nolan's trilogy was released, *The Dark Knight Rises*. It is also at this point, Athena claims, DC had offered her a substantial amount of money to give up any future claims to the rights to Batman.

When Siegel and Shuster had complained to Harry Donenfeld that a joint fee of $130 was not enough for their work on Superman, he'd occasionally throw then a small bonus to keep them quiet for a while without ever handing over a percentage of the rights. When the Golden Age writers had demanded better rates and healthcare, Jack Liebowitz had feigned trying to resolve the issue while letting it exhaust itself. Now Athena Finger was in a similar situation.

The word was out on who she was, so she started to appear at comic conventions and events telling the story of Bill Finger, the Father of Batman. So did Nobleman. In 2012, his book, illustrated by Ty Templeton, *Bill the Boy Wonder: The Secret Co-Creator of Batman* was released. Whereas other creators had spoken up for Finger in the past individually, this started a campaign. Finger had never made a claim for the credits to Batman in his lifetime and after his death he was forgotten. But now public voices were calling for the Bill Finger name to be put in its rightful place; in the Batman by-line.

A groundswell was being created. Fansites and communities started to reassess the accepted history of comic books and wanted to know who really created Batman. And what they were starting to agree on was that Bill Finger was the victim of a great injustice. More and more people took up the cause of Bill Finger. Come 2014, the seventy-fifth anniversary of Batman's first appearance was going to be a big celebration of all things Bat in the comic world, and as it edged closer and closer, the pressure for DC to do something was mounting and getting more intense. Nobleman even appeared on the podcast *Fat Man on the Batman*, hosted by celebrity comic book-fan, filmmaker, and occasional Silent Bob, Kevin Smith. He was also in the process of turning his book on Bill Finger into a documentary. Nobleman had started out as biographer of a hidden creator and ended up becoming an integral part of bringing him into the spotlight and getting him justice.

The intensity of the need for justice would burst in April 2014 on 'The Men Who Made Batman' panel at WonderCon in Anaheim, when one Bat-fan innocuously asked DC executives why Finger was not given a credit for his work on Batman.

The panel went awkwardly silent and made a few remarks suggesting they could not or didn't want to answer the question. The panel's moderator was Larry Ganem, DC Entertainment's vice-president of talent relations. He jumped in and replied, 'We cherish what Bill Finger did and his contribution to creating Batman, and we're all good with Finger and his family.'

Athena Finger, however, begged to disagree and the following month, she released a statement through the Comics Art Council, a charity organisation promoting the scholarly appreciation of comics and comics' history. It read:

> 75 years of Batman! No one could have predicted the longevity and the continued relevance of this comic book hero that has become a cultural icon when my grandfather, Bill Finger, collaborated with Bob Kane back in 1939. My grandfather has never been properly credited as the co-creator of Batman although was an open secret in the comic book industry and is widely known now. It is now my time to come out of the shadows and speak up and end 75 years of exploitation of my grandfather, whose biggest flaw was his inability to defend his extraordinary talent. Due to what I feel is continued mistreatment of a true artist, I am currently exploring our rights and considering how best to establish the recognition that my grandfather deserves.

With the *Gotham* television show due for release in the fall, the 'all good' statement, innocent though it may have been, and Athena's reply shared across comic fandom, once again, the DC execs failed to paint themselves in the best light. The perception was that the company was trying to whitewash its past mistakes. In a year where Batman was to be celebrated, it was the last thing they needed and so, DC once again invited Athena to meet with them, this time, coming to an agreement on how, if at all, Bill Finger should be credited. In addition to the fandom mostly being on the side of the Finger family, there was a boost of momentum from another comic's credit case over at Marvel. The family of Jack Kirby, the artist who had undoubtedly contributed to the characters, stories and visual designs which gave Marvel its edge over the Distinguish Competition (the Marvel bullpen's joke name for DC), had recently settled a suit with Marvel granting them some financial compensation for Kirby's work.

It was a shift in the right direction, but it did not mean it would be plain sailing for the Fingers. Firstly, it was a different company with an entirely different lawsuit and there was a huge difference in relative contribution and public recognition between Kirby and Finger. On top of that, copyright law in relation to intellectual property and work-for-hire, particularly in the world of comics, is immensely complicated and the Kirby case didn't necessarily set a clear precedent for other sidelined creators and their families.

And for Athena Finger, there was a substantial financial risk in the legal challenge to DC. She was a single parent on a relatively low income versus a billion-dollar company. The cost of sustained litigation could turn the situation into a war of attrition. The cases of Siegel and Shuster, and Kirby, took decades to resolve. But it was a risk she had to take.

Final Credits

A conclusion was reached. The details of the agreement and how it was agreed upon were not made fully available to the public but on Friday, 19 September 2015, DC's lawyers released the following statement to the press:

> 'DC Entertainment and the family of Bill Finger are pleased to announce that they have reached an agreement that recognizes Mr. Finger's significant contributions to the Batman family of characters. Bill Finger was instrumental in developing many of the key creative elements that enrich the Batman universe, and we look forward to building on our acknowledgement of his significant role in DC Comics' history,' stated Diane Nelson, President of DC Entertainment. 'As part of our acknowledgement of those contributions, we are pleased to confirm today that Bill Finger will be receiving credit in the Warner Bros. television series Gotham beginning later this season, and in the forthcoming motion picture Batman v Superman: Dawn of Justice.'

Athena Finger, Marc Tyler Nobleman and a legion of comic book fans had finally convinced DC to give Bill Finger a by-line for his work on Batman. His first official credit didn't appear on *Gotham* as everyone presumed it would, however. Only a few weeks later, on 10th October, *The Dark Knight Universe Presents: The Atom #1* came out. It was a short, miniature-sized comic that fleshed out the universe of Frank Miller's version of Batman – the one which had resurrected the Dark Knight in the eighties and left Bob Kane confused. No doubt if he had been alive to see the comic he would have been confused again as his co-creator was resurrected in the by-line, 'Batman created by Bob Kane with Bill Finger.' It was the first in a deluge of Finger by-lines that came thick and fast.

Finger's first official television credit as Batman's creator was a week or so later on Adult Swim's stop motion, comedy show *Robot Chicken DC Special II: Magical Friendship*. The use of franchised characters on the show had to be signed-off on by DC officials so it may have just been scheduling which resulted in this, but as a show made by and for fans, it is fitting that *Robot Chicken* should be the first show to credit Bill officially, given the campaign to give him recognition was built on the back of comics fandom. The following evening, he was credited as creating Batman with Bob Kane on *Gotham* and the following week, freshly released Bat-family comics all featured his name.

On the same day that those books were released, in Hollywood, Bob Kane was posthumously awarded a Walk of Fame Star for his contributions to motion pictures. A few months later in March 2016, despite its mixed reviews, *Batman V Superman: Dawn of Justice* opened and made over $170 million, reaching audiences far and wide. As promised, in the opening scenes, Bill was credited alongside Bob, in huge shining letters in front of a global audience. Press around the world covered the story as Batman's co-creator finally got his credit. There doesn't seem to be any legal prompting for this change, or outside pressure demanding a more equal footing, but later that same year, DC changed the 'created by Bob Kane with Bill Finger' by-line to 'created by Bob Kane **and** Bill Finger'. It was a change unasked for but certainly welcomed.

The campaign was not quite finished. Over the following years, two small historical fiction plays would be based on the relationship between Kane and Finger. Nobleman's research into Finger and the quest to get the late writer a credit would be the subject of 2017's *Batman and Bill*, the first Hulu original documentary. Not only would Bill finally get his credit, but the world would also start to know his story. Charles Sinclair featured in the documentary but, sadly, Bill's long-time friend and champion died just a few short months before its release.

At the time of writing, yet another Batman reboot is on the horizon and *Joker* is winning countless awards (it is also credited to Bob Kane, Bill Finger and Jerry Robinson). Finger may not have become a Hollywood star (yet) but New York has honoured the creator who spent almost all his life in the state. Kane may have a few square feet in Hollywood with his name on, but Finger was given an entire street in New York. On 12th August 2017, Nobleman, Athena Finger, Jens Robinson – the son of Jerry Robinson, Batman voice actor Kevin Conroy and a host of fans attended the unveiling of Bill Finger Way on the corner of East 192nd Street and Grand Concourse in the Bronx. The very streets Finger and Kane had grown up in. Bill Finger Way runs along the southern edge of Poe Park.

It is here, back in 1939, that the pair would sit and eat sandwiches, watching girls stroll by and discussing what to do with this Batman character they suddenly found themselves with. It is a remarkable place for Finger to be honoured. After decades of shadows and secrecy in just a few short years, family, friends, and fans had changed the story of Bob and Bill, the creators of Batman.

Epilogue

It is hard to read about Bob Kane and not see him as the bad guy, particularly when he is held next to Finger. There is no doubt that he was self-centred, egotistical, and hypocritical. But there is a desire to see these traits as the make-up of a two-dimensional villain rather than the flaws of a human. Headlines from mainstream news about Kane's legacy have, by necessity, cut out any analysis of his behaviour. But what we are left with is an easy to understand but simplified story. There is no doubt, Kane could have done more – or in the case of misdating documents, done less – for his fellow creators. Kane could have been a better man. But there are circumstances which explain his actions in a human way, without exonerating or mitigating, his flaws.

We might be inclined to think in the very earliest instance that he should have credited Finger with the co-creation of Batman and that his own contribution was a lot less substantial than Finger's. This is a case built on the privilege of decades of campaigning for creator's rights. In the nineties, superstar creators whose books were selling millions, such as Todd McFarlane, Jim Lee, Rob Liefield, Erik Larsen and several other artists, left Marvel and DC to form Image Comics. They knew their creations were valuable, so they wanted ownership of what they had created. But in the history of comics that was a pretty new idea. It is an idea only comprehendible because those individuals had seen how the Golden Age creators had been treated. In 1939, not only was there no mechanism to do that kind of thing, it was literally unthinkable. Kane was not alone in the belief that the person who had the idea first was the de facto creator. It was accepted knowledge that the guy who signed the strip was the creator regardless of how poor the idea might have been to start with.

Finger may have believed this too. He was a huge fan of the pulps which were often written under pseudonyms; it was an accepted part of the gig. In the then new medium of comics, which people were rushing to understand and using the pulp industry as a framework, it is reasonable to think people thought the same rules about authorship versus ownership applied. Putting your name on something was not as important as having your name on the cheque for the work at the end of the day. Because we know of the disparity between how Kane and Finger's lives turned out, the initial agreement between Bill and Bob may have seemed like a cruel manipulation on Kane's behalf when in fact it would probably have been the standard approach to this kind of work. Finger definitely contributed to the look of Batman, but he had simply recycled a pulp story for money. Perhaps he could have asserted himself more but it's possible that Finger simply saw Batman as a way of making a quick buck, rather than a future business empire.

Ironically, Kane was somewhat a pioneer in term of creators' rights. He was the first comic book creator to part own one of his characters. It would be decades before any other creators would come close to pulling this off. In retrospect, it is unfair that this privilege didn't include Finger but at the time it was still a bold move on Kane's behalf. This industry was run by Jack Liebowitz and Harry Donenfeld; it was new and it was ruthless. During the Great Depression, with rampant poverty and little employment, selfishness could be considered an admirable survival trait because it could lead to success. Kane, or at least his father and uncle, knew his value and they were able to play the game, act in their own interests and to come out on top. This isn't a nice or comfortable idea to accept, and it's not one the industry should promote today, but it does give us a more three-dimensional character and justifiable motive for Kane's actions.

Whatever gentleman's agreement Kane and Finger might have had did not come into consideration when Kane was securing his creative legacy and his financial position. Unfortunately, once he had ensured his own security, he couldn't legally back down without jeopardizing himself. And while it is easy to say that including Finger in this credit would have been the right thing to do, Liebowitz and Donenfeld weren't known to play fair. They bankrupted Malcolm Wheeler-Nicholson to get control of his company and rumour had it they were connected to the mob. Kane admired Donenfeld but once he had made it, and Batman had secured his fame and fortune, how might Donenfeld, and more importantly, Liebowitz have reacted if Kane had suddenly become a problem? So, the further into success Kane travelled, the more trapped he became by his own position.

Sheldon Moldoff worked as Kane's uncredited ghost for fifteen years. And like Finger, you would have thought that he would have a point of contention to pick with Bob. But not only did Moldoff insist that Bob could be charming and likeable, he also reiterated that Kane's personality and his desire to be a celebrity were driving forces behind Batman. It is hard to quantify the value who wrote or drew what, but Bob's promotion of the character and himself certainly bolstered Batman's success. In an interview with Marc Tyler Nobleman before his death in 2012, Moldoff even suggested that the credits for Batman should go unchanged. Not only does this demonstrate the Golden Age mindset of the guy with the initial idea is the creator, but it also shows the legal mess that could follow was a consideration for others beyond Kane. Perhaps as he was not a part of the creation of Batman, Moldoff could more easily separate the work-for-hire mindset from the ownership but at the least this shows Kane wasn't a singular anomaly in this approach to the work.

We might feel Kane's fame is undeserved because of his swiping of art and his use of ghosts. The nature of swiping has been discussed previously. In short, Kane relied on it too much, but it was a much more common practice than we might think. As for the ghosts, it's odd that we should feel frustrated about this. For the large part, Kane's ghosts knew what they were getting themselves into; they made an agreement with Kane that they would illustrate his work for him and he would sign it. Many of them got more work in the industry because they were known to be doing this. It seems unsavoury then that Kane would then claim he illustrated most of Batman, but at the same time, it's bizarre to think he'd do anything different – what would be the point in hiring ghosts and admitting to it? It's still a deception, but it's important to remember that every single one of those artists was in on it.

All of this is to say that the negative side of Kane, which is often portrayed, is sometimes more palatable when viewed within a fairer context. This doesn't mean Kane was always a nice or likeable person, but that his behaviour wasn't as extreme as it might at first seem.

Sympathy is not the first word that springs to mind when considering your reaction to Bob Kane. He made lots of money and for the large part, he lived a comfortable life. But, in terms of his creative talent, Kane was limited and surpassed by every single one of his peers. Batman was Kane's only successful idea (which he had a lot of help with) and he spent most of his life recycling it. *Courageous Cat and Minute Mouse* was simply Batman by another name. His formative work, like any artist, were imitations of more successful strips and even *Cool McCool,* Kane's only work to eschew the Bat-format, was a homage to the then-popular spy-comedy fad.

Kane was fond of saying 'I am Batman' and the truth is Batman was all he ever had. He was a creative one-hit-wonder. Granted that hit has been playing for a while now but Kane was never better than when he was in his twenties and there is something quite sad about that. His peers built an entire industry, defined and redefined a medium, and had countless successes. They were true creatives. Bob had one lucky idea and worked at the right time with the right people. When judged by his talent and creativity, Kane falls well below Finger.

Bob's public persona was entirely constructed on the concept that he was the sole creator of Batman. Not his talent or his creative mind but one idea. As we better understand that idea, Kane is becoming increasingly disliked and disregarded. His legacy is becoming tarnished and he can't do anything about it. Bob Kane has been and will continue to be on trial by the comic book community. His reputation being pulled apart is a fitting punishment for someone who wanted nothing more than to be admired.

Ask the average man in the street to name a famous comic creator and the chances are they will mention Bob's buddy Stan Lee. His classmate Will Eisner gave his name to the most prestigious awards in the comic industry and invented the modern graphic novel. Bill Finger's name is on the award for excellence in writing while Jerry Robinson was known as the ambassador of comics. Bob had few friends in the comics industry and fewer people who could think of anything nice to say about him. For someone who clearly loved cartooning and illustration, spending most of his life in that industry, the fact that most people in that industry were glad to see the back of him seems tragic.

Unlike Kane, it is easy to sympathise with Bill Finger. Just the fact he died poor, alone and unknown is enough for us to appreciate the justice of him finally getting a credit on Batman, even if it's a somewhat bittersweet victory

Kane is villainised because it is always satisfying to knock an egomaniac down a peg or two and also because there is an impetus to claim in Finger's defence that without Bill Finger, Batman would not have been a success. Therefore, some of Kane's success belongs to

Finger. But equally, we can make the claim that the little success Finger did have was all thanks to Kane. That is not to say that Finger should have been thankful for his lot in life or that he doesn't deserve credit. Without Bill Finger, there would have been no Batman, but we must also accept that without Bob Kane, comics would not have had Bill Finger.

Kane, for his faults, knew about the emerging comics industry. He had the connections, the commercial drive and disposition to make a career from being a doodler. Had he never met Finger, he would have drafted in some other schmuck to help him write. And although he might never have had a mega-hit like Batman, there's no reason to think he wouldn't have found success from another project through his shameless self-promotion. Without Kane, Finger could have lived out his life as a shoe salesman, attracting little, I'd even wager zero, acclaim from fans and co-workers. He could have also written a great American novel, but from what we know of Finger's nature, he probably wouldn't have made this happen on his own. Batman was Kane's project and undoubtedly, Finger was a huge collaborator but it's also true that Kane opened doors for him that might otherwise have remained closed forever. No Batman, no National New Year's party, no chance encounter with Charles Sinclair, no film and TV work. Something about Finger suggests he was always waiting for something to come along rather than going out there to find it.

Finger was like a well of good ideas; some were his own, some were deposited by other artists, writers, and filmmakers, but without his collaborators, ideas never seemed to surface. Even when he met Charles Sinclair and had the promise of a great or at least profitable screenwriting career, Finger floundered. He constantly relied on others to make the pitch or to meet the right people. Others brought work to him, he never seemed to seek it out for himself. Yes, he was the co-creator of Batman, but 'co-creator' might be the more central part of the idea of who Finger was than Batman. All the great work he achieved was with or at the behest of others.

It's easy to imagine that Finger's destiny would have been much brighter if he'd had credits on *Detective Comics #27*, that this issue is a flashpoint which ruined his life forever. Certainly, he might have been able to afford better healthcare or maybe found more work. But the truth is, he had opportunities both in comics and outside, which for some reason he just was not able to capitalise on. He was unable to build momentum in the comics industry and he let whatever goodwill he had created with *77 Sunset Strip* and his other television and radio work peter out.

When you try to sum up Kane and Finger you often end up with something like 'they co-created Batman and one took all the credit and became rich while the other died young and poor' which implies some causality. But Kane wasn't the only reason Finger's life turned out the way it did. Finger was responsible for that too.

Unlike Kane, Finger was free from Batman, and in terms of creative output and talent, vastly beat out his partner. We want to believe in a meritocracy where the most talented people rise to the top and we feel there a great injustice has been done when that doesn't occur. If we can hold Kane responsible for Finger's situation, it's only in terms of the success of Batman. At what point do we ask why Finger didn't stand up for himself?

The story of Finger and Kane is so compelling because they stand in such great opposition to one another. Kane had reached his creative potential by the time they met, but he unleashed Finger's potential. Finger was talented, liked by colleagues; slow but prolific while obscured. Kane bought his talent and basked in the perpetual glow of a single achievement. Between them, they represent a conflict at the heart of creative industries – art versus profit and creator versus corporation.

On one side, we see the worth of art and its ability to connect and entertain people. On the other is the value of that connection, and the need for creators to make money. It's a delicate balancing act. Right now, creators are entering a much fairer and more established industry than the one cobbled together by Donenfeld and Liebowitz. But the scales are still heavily in favour of the corporation and, we assume, the unartistic businessmen for whom the bottom line is the best indicator of success. As mentioned repeatedly, although he is the best example of a creator treated unfairly by his artistic partner, Finger was not the only creator to go unfairly rewarded by the industry. Golden Age creators like Siegel and Shuster, Jack Kirby and Steve Ditko all faced litigation to claim rights for their work. Alan Moore and Dave Gibbons were told they would retain the rights to *Watchmen* once the book went out of print, but unfortunately, this has not yet happened; a prospect unheard of when they signed their contracts.

No one knew Superman was going to be a success, no one knew *Watchmen* would change the face of the industry. The family of Rocket

Racoon creator Bill Mantlo had to crowd-fund money to pay for Mantlo's healthcare after a tragic accident. While the family had $100,000 in debt, *Guardians of the Galaxy Vol.2* made $863 million worldwide in 2017. Corporations take low-level risks on these creators and pay them for their time but that doesn't mean these examples are fair, only legal. When these things happen, the companies (and some fans) look back and say, 'Well, you knew what you were getting into.' And that's simply not true; no one knows what they are getting into. What is important is how the people at the beginning are treated when their work surpasses all expectation and people who were never in the room when those characters came to life are left counting their millions.

With Finger finally getting credit for Batman and his family receiving compensation for his hard work, can we say justice has been served? Perhaps, but not if the concept of justice relies on Kane's legacy being dismantled. Kane was one man benefitting from a larger system. The closest we can get to justice is if we learn from Finger and Kane; if fans across the world who consume and spend money on these characters understand that at their genesis there are people we should be thankful to. More importantly, the massive franchise character industry needs to learn how to respect the creative talents behind their huge commercial successes, without whom their massive fortunes would be impossible. All of the campaigning to set things right time and time again for different creators is all for nought if we do not learn any lessons and make continuous changes. Like Batman, to make the world a better place the story of Kane and Finger need to become a symbol of justice.

Acknowledgements

This book would not be possible without the hard work of journalists and comics historians, living and passed, who came before me. I would particularly like to thank Marc Tyler Nobleman who is the leading authority on all things Bill Finger and a very nice chap to boot. My thanks also go out to Jim Steranko, Roy Thomas, Arlen Schumer, Tom Fagan, Gerald Jones, Howard Sann and his father Paul, Darren Turco, Jerry Bails, Christopher Couch, Michael Eury and Michael Kronenburg, Fred Van Lente and Ryan Dunlavey, Will Brooker, Kirk Kimball, Schima Weinstein, Robert Porfirio, Mark Fertig, Les Daniels, Piper Marie Thompson, John R. Wegener and everyone at the American Heritage Centre at the University of Wyoming.

For help with the book I'd like to give thanks to Jordan Collver, Ben Sledge and Robyn Vinter, Eileen Pringle, Kate Bodhanowicz, Laura Hirst and Lucy Benyon. And finally, I would like to give thanks to my wife, Bethany Mather-Worth for putting up with me while I stressed out about my two old comic creators day and night – RW.

Material from *The Steranko History of Comics Volume One* used with permission of the author. All Rights Reserved.

Material from *Fads, Follies and Delusions of The American People* used with permission of the Paul Sann estate. All Rights Reserved.

Bibliography

Books and Magazines

Alter Ego, no 20 (Raleigh, NC: TwoMorrows, January 2003).

Alter Ego, no 84 (Raleigh, NC: TwoMorrows, March 2009).

Alter Ego: The Comic Book Artist Collection (Raleigh, NC: TwoMorrows, August 2001).

Amazing Heroes #179 (Fantagraphics Books, May 1990).

Andrae, Thomas and Porifino, Robert. *Creators of the Superheroes* (Neshannock, PA: Hermes Press, 2011).

Bails, Jerry. "If the truth be known" or "A Finger in Every Plot!", *CAPA-alpha,* no 12 (September 1965).

Batman Archives Volume 3. (DC Comics, November 1997)

Brooker, Will. *Batman Unmasked* (London: Continuum, 2000).

Bridwell, Nelson E. "In Memoriam of Bill Finger", *The Amazing World of DC #1* (DC Comics, July 1974).

Couch, N.C. Christopher. *Jerry Robinson Ambassador of Comics* (New York, NY: Abrams Comic Arts, 2010).

Daniels, Les. *Batman: The Complete History* (London: Titan Publishing, 1999).

Eury, Michael and Kronenburg, Michael. *The Batcave Companion* (Raleigh, NC: TwoMorrows, April 2009).

Fagan, Tom. "Bill Finger – Man Behind The Legend." An unpublished article appearing on Noblemania.com (1965)

Fertig, Mark. *Take That Adolf! The Fighting Comic Books of The Second World War* (Seattle, WA: Fantagraphics Books, April 2017).

Finger, Bill and Kane, Bob. "The Case of the Chemical Syndicate." *Detective Comics #27* (May 1939)

Fradon, Ramona and Reed, David Vern. "Through The Wringer". *The Amazing World of DC #10* (DC Comics, January 1976).

158

Green Lantern #1. "Introducing Bill Finger and Marty Nodell Creators of Green Lantern!" (National Publications: Fall, 1941).

Hajdu, David. *The Ten-Cent Plague: The Great Comic-Book Scare and How it Changed America* (New York, NY: Picador, February 2009).

Jones, Gerard. *Men of Tomorrow: Geeks, Gangster and the Birth of the Comic Book* (New York, NY: Basic Books, 2004).

Kane, Bob. "An Open Letter to all 'Batmanias' Everywhere." *Batmania #17* (1967)

Kane, Bob and Andrae, Thomas. *Batman & Me* (Forestville, C: Ecplise books, 1989).

Newmark, Amy and Slocum Lahav, Loren, *Chicken Soup for the Soul: Time to Thrive: 101 Inspiring Stories About Growth, Wisdom and Dreams* (Chicken Soup for the Soul Publishing, May 2015)

Nobleman, Marc Tyler with Templeton, Ty. *Bill the Boy Wonder, The Secret Co-Creator of Batman* (Watertown, MA: Charlesbridge, 2012).

Olsen, John. *The Shadow in Review.* (Pulplandia, September 2016).

Real Fact Comics #5. "The True Story of Batman and Robin" (National Publications: November 1946).

Robinson, Jerry. *Jerry and The Joker: Adventures and Comic Art* (Milwaukee, OR: Dark Horse Comics, April 20170.

Sann, Paul. *Fads, Follies and Delusion of The American People* (New York, NY: Bonanza: 1967).

Schwartz, Julius with Thomsen, Brian M. *Man of Two Worlds: My Life in Science Fiction and Comics* (New York: Harper Entertainment, 2000).

Steranko, Jim. *The Steranko History of Comics Volume One* (Reading, PA: Supergraphics, 1970).

Dark Knight Universe Presents: The Atom #1 in The *Dark Knight III: The Master Race #1* (DC Comics, November 2015).

Tye, Larry. *Superman: The High Flying History of America's Most Enduring Hero* (New York, NY: Random House, 2012).

Van Lente, Fred and Dunlavey, Ryan. *The Comic Book History of Comics* (San Diego, CA: IDW Publishing, 2012).

Weldon, Glen. *The Caped Crusader: Batman and The Rise of Nerd Culture* (New York, NY: Simon and Shuster, 2017).

Weinstein, Simcha. *Up, Up, and Oy Vey! How Jewish History, Culture, and Values Shaped the Comic Book Superhero* (Fort Lee, NJ: Baracade Books, 2006).

Wertham, Fredric. *Seduction of The Innocent* (Rhinehart 7 Company, April 1954).

Websites

http://www.bailsprojects.com/whoswho.aspx
https://www.bleedingcool.com
https://www.cbr.com
http://henryvallely.blogspot.com/
https://www.noblemania.com/
http://regionalhorrorfilms.blogspot.com/
https://thepulp.net/thatspulp/

Index